John Lord

COMPETITION IN ELECTRICITY: NEW MARKETS AND NEW STRUCTURES

Edited by

James Plummer, QED Research, Inc.

Susan Troppmann, QED Research, Inc.

Published by

PUBLIC UTILITIES REPORTS, INC.
Arlington, Virginia

and

QED RESEARCH, INC.
Palo Alto, California

This publication is designed to provide accurate and authoritative information in regard to the subject matter covered. It is sold with the understanding that the publisher is not engaged in rendering legal, accounting, or other professional service. If legal advice or other expert assistance is required, the services of a competent professional person should be sought. *(From a Declaration of Principles jointly adopted by a Committee of the American Bar Association and a Committee of Publishers.)*

First Printing, March 1990

ISBN: 0-910325-26-X

Printed in the United States of America

TABLE OF CONTENTS

EDITORS' PREFACE

The origin of this book was a telephone call from Public Utilities Reports asking if it would be a good idea to do a book similar to the one published by QED Research, Inc. and Public Utilities Reports in 1983 entitled *Electric Power Strategic Issues*. We all agreed that it should not be described as a second edition because the issues and the players had changed completely from what was anticipated in that book. Looking at the content of that book and this book is a very humbling experience. In 1981 and 1982, when the contributions to the earlier book were written, the issue was potential "deregulation" of the electric utility industry, with analogies to the deregulations that had already occurred in airlines, trucking, telephone, and railroads. Those were "top down" deregulations, with much of the initiative coming from the courts, federal regulators, and Congress.

Whatever else we may have learned or not learned in the last few years, it is clear that the process of moving toward a more competitive structure in the electric utility industry is more of a "bottom up" process, with many diverse forms of competition springing up and many different new players in both the private sector and the public sector. State regulators, industrial electricity customers and independent electricity producers are playing a more important role than was anticipated in the debates of the early 1980s. In 1990, there are three broad forms of increased competition that are progressing steadily: 1) increased bulk power market competition and wheeling, continuing a trend that has been going on for decades, 2) competition to serve the needs of the "non-core" industrial and commercial customers by Qualifying Facilities, self-generators and independent producers, and 3) regulator-initiated state-level wholesale bidding systems. This book attempts to present a broad range of informed analysis on all three of these forms of increased competition.

We would like to thank our families for their tolerance, our QED colleagues for their ideas and encouragement, and Public Utilities Reports for being an extremely patient and understanding co-publisher. Mr. Lars Johnsen, a senior Research Associate at QED, did a splendid job in completing the editing process.

James Plummer, President
Susan Troppmann, Principal
QED Research, Inc.
Palo Alto, California

FOREWORD

The evolution of electricity competition, in all its forms, will include many stages of change. As we recall the unpredictable twists and turns that electricity competition has taken in the last few years, we can only be humble about our ability to anticipate the future stages in the process of change. We should not expect to protect ourselves completely against surprises. The best early warning system any of us can have is to keep abreast of the articulation of positions and ideas by the best advocates of all the parties and the best analysts.

In Competition in Electricity: New Markets and New Structures, co-editors James Plummer and Susan Troppmann have brought together many diverse viewpoints on electricity competition issues. They have tried to fairly represent the positions of the various market players and also many of the ideas that have been contributed from the academic and consulting communities. Readers of these contributions can greatly reduce the likelihood of unpleasant surprises. Such a benefit improves the chances that future debates will be constructive.

Charles Stalon
Former Commissioner
Federal Energy Regulatory Commission

SECTION A

OVERVIEW

CHAPTER 1: OVERVIEW OF EMERGING COMPETITION*

James L. Plummer
President, QED Research, Inc.

There are three general kinds of electricity competition going on right now, as depicted in Figure 1-1. One has been going on for a long time, and that is simply increased competition within the bulk power market, within power pools, and between power pools. This is competition primarily among regulated utilities and municipal utilities, and it's a continuation of trends that have been going on for several decades. The regulatory arena of this kind of competition is primarily at FERC, the Federal Energy Regulatory Commission.

Figure 1-1

THREE KINDS OF ELECTRICITY COMPETITION:

- Increased bulk power market competition among regulated utilities. This is a continuation of trends that have been going on for decades.

- Competition among QFs, IPPs, purchased bulk power, and regulated GENCOs to satisfy the needs of the regulated TRANSCO/DISCO. Variations of this have been called "FERC–style competition" or "bidding systems." This is usually a "top down" regulator-initiated form of competition.

- Competition relative to large industrial and commercial customers. These non-core customers can be self-generators, QFs, suppliers to other non-core customers, or merely buyers from suppliers other than the regulated utility. This is usually a "bottom up" private sector-initiated form of competition.

The second type of competition is more recent. It is among qualifying facilities, independent power producers, purchase power, and regulated GENCOs, or generating companies that are related to regulated utilities. This is a competition to

---

*Adapted from the opening address given at the California Energy Commission "Symposium on Electricity Competition," June 30 and July 1, 1988.

satisfy the needs of the distribution companies, the part of the regulated electric utilities that is a natural monopoly. Chairman Imbrecht referred to the Diablo Canyon settlement. I agree with him that this is a very strong piece of evidence that the generating portion of an electric utility will have to compete with other sources of generation. This type of competition can be formalized, and it has been in the initiatives that were started by Chairman Martha Hesse of the Federal Energy Regulatory Commission about a year ago, and which have continued through technical conferences at FERC, and then in April with the issuance of notices of proposed rulemaking. This type of competition has come to be called "FERC-style competition." At the state level it's sometimes referred to as "bidding systems" or "bidding scams". Sometimes it's formal bidding and sometimes it's not as formal. The primary characteristic of this type of competition is that it is a "top-down", or a government- or regulator-initiated form of competition. It will go through iterations, but it is, you might say, social engineering of the regulatory side.

The third kind of competition probably precedes the bidding type of competition. It has been going on for roughly ten years. This is competition relative to serving the needs of large industrial commercial and agricultural customers. These are non-core customers. Core customers refer to smaller customers, residential customers, customers who don't have another option, either to produce or to buy from somebody other than the regulated utilities. In the electricity area, non-core customers might be self-generators, they might be qualifying facilities, they might be suppliers to other non-core customers. Or they might just be buyers, but buyers who wish to have the option, at least, of buying from suppliers other than the regulated utilities. They will increasingly have options of those kinds. It's important to realize that this is not something that awaits too much in the way of regulatory decision, although regulatory decisions can speed the process along or permit it to move faster or slower. However, this process has been going on for roughly a decade and will continue. It's not the sort of thing that is designed in an across-the-board system planning or social engineering sense, it's something that occurs in very small chunks — one battle, one change, at a time. And thus, it

4   COMPETITION IN ELECTRICITY

Figure 1-2

INDUSTRIAL ELECTRICITY BYPASS

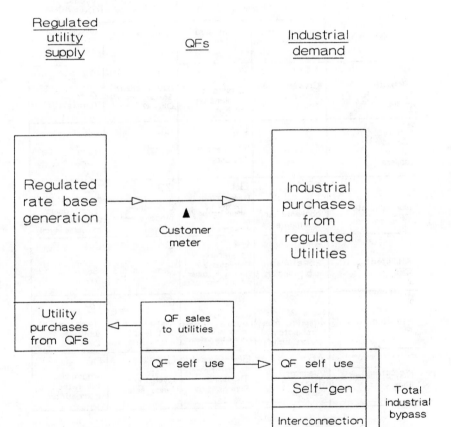

Figure 1-3

ELECTRICITY COMPETITION MARKET SEGMENT MATRIX

Demand / Supply	Regulated utility buyers		Potential industrial bypass retail buyers	
	Interconnected power **A**	Wheeled power **B**	Interconnected power **C**	Wheeled power **D**
1 Regulated utility sellers	**A1** Conventional power pools	**B1** Expanded wholesale market	**C1** Lukens case? Grumann case? Others?	**D1** GM? Others?
2 Canadian utility sellers	**A2**	**B2** Conventional imports	**C2** ?	**D2** GM? Others?
3 Non–affiliated QFs	**A3** Present conventional QF market	**B3** Presently only weird "wheel instead of buy" situations	**C3** Over–the– fence sales	**D3** Presently only "quiet" deals (e.g. two sites of some firm)
4 Affiliated QFs	**A4** 25 affiliates (e.g. Mission)	**B4** 25 affiliates (Protected by PURPA in other service territories	**C4** Same as C3	**D4** Same as D3
5 Affiliated IPPs	**A5** Same 25 affiliates, plus many potential "export arms"	**B5** Same as A5 (Maybe discriminated against in other service territories)	**C5** Same as C6 (but less?)	**D5** Same as D6 (but less?)
6 Non–affiliated IPPs	**A6** Alamito Thousand Springs	**B6** Thousand Springs	**C6** Over–the– fence sales	**D6** Aggressive full retail competition

can't be stopped by any one decision. So I refer to this as a "bottom-up" or private-sector-initiated form of competition. In a strategic sense, either from the side of government or from the side of private entities, it's perhaps more important than either of the other two forms of competition. This form of competition involves the concept of bypass. It refers to methods whereby customers can satisfy their needs by other than buying from the regulated utilities.

In the electricity area, one needs to be clear about what the definitions are and one also needs to avoid double counting. Figure 1-2 illustrates the definition applicable to industrial QFs. A qualifying facility sells part of its output to regulated utilities — you see that block of power moving from the center to the left in this diagram as utility purchases from QFs. Part of the electricity output of a qualifying facility also moves from the QF to industrial uses within that industrial firm, so I call that QF self-use. Added to the QF's own use is self-generation by other parties, and retail purchases, some of which now occur even though we don't have retail wheeling in California. We do have some over-the-fence or retail interconnection purchases. All three of these categories fall under the general title of industrial bypass, because all of them involve satisfying electricity needs without purchasing from the regulated utilities.

The market segment matrix shown in Figure 1-3 is intended to identify the various players in this new game of electricity competition. All three forms of electricity competition are represented here. The bulk power market competition is represented in the upper left-hand cells. The regulated utility buyers, to satisfy part of their needs, buy from other regulated utility sellers and Canadian importers.

The second form of electricity competition, among smaller producers to sell to regulated utilities, is represented in the lower left-hand corner of this matrix. By affiliated and non-affiliated QFs, I mean affiliated or non-affiliated with a regulated utility. Most of the QFs, for instance, that the California Energy Commission has dealt with in permitting are non-affiliated QFs; they are not affiliated with a regulated utility. Mission Energy would be an example of an affiliated QF that is affiliated with Southern California Edison.

Likewise, IPP stands for independent power producers. These are power producers that are not regulated themselves, and which have chosen for one reason or another not to come under the regulatory requirements and benefits of PURPA, and thus they're not QFs. Now, it might seem to be a contradiction in terms to say that there would be affiliated IPPs or independent power producers. If they're affiliated with a regulated company, how can they be independent? What is meant is that they are affiliated with a regulated company, through a holding company probably, in the same manner that Mission is with SCE, but they are not themselves regulated. They may have a significant role to play down the road.

The third type of competition, industrial bypass, is represented by the two columns on the right of this matrix. We see examples of this where industrial firms want to interconnect with someone other than their own utility. We've seen that in the Lukens Steele v. Philadelphia Electric case, and in the Grummond Aircraft v. Long Island Lighting Company case. There are about a dozen other cases like that across the country. We've seen cases where industrial firms such as General Motors go out of their own service territory for a particular plant and buy from somebody else, perhaps even buy from Canadian sources. The lower right-hand portion of this matrix is probably the most dynamic portion of all, and that's where the key institutional movement and changes are likely to take place. There are currently retail over-the-fence sales in California. A QF in California is allowed to interconnect with other parties and sell to them. There are instances of wheeled power from non-affiliated QFs to other industrial customers, but their presence is rare. It is the evolution here in these lower right-hand boxes of institutions' regulations that will be very strategically important over the next few years.

Within the rubric of FERC-style competition, the states would be permitted under the notices of proposed rulemaking to adopt a very broad concept of wholesale competition for sale to regulated utilities. The broad box shown in Figure 1-4 illustrates what is sometimes called an "all source" competition. The narrowest concept would be one confined to simply the sales by qualified facilities to regulated utilities, and that's the narrower box illustrated in Figure 1-4.

Bidding systems, and other types of competition FERC is talking about, can be very important in the long run. How-

　　　　　　　　　　　　　COMPETITION IN ELECTRICITY

Figure 1-4

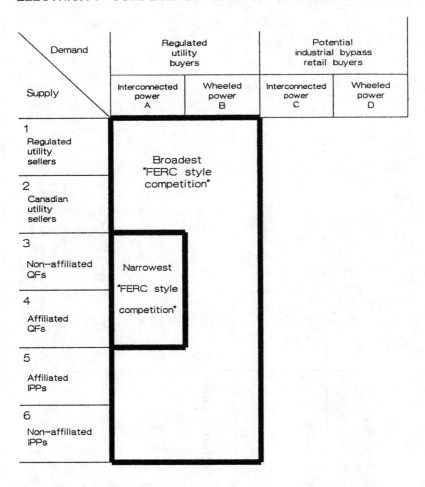

ELECTRICITY COMPETITION MARKET SEGMENT MATRIX

Figure 1-5

DIFFERENT BEHAVIOR OF PLAYERS DEPENDING ON RELATIONSHIPS AMONG COSTS AND RATES

Independent Power Producers (IPPs)	Regulated utility	
	Rates < costs $R_R < C_R$	Rates > costs $R_R > C_R$
$C_I > R_R , C_R$	$C_I > C_R > R_R$ Customers will buy from the utility. Utility/regulators will attempt to minimize sales and load.	$C_I > R_R > C_R$ Customers will buy from the utility, but ask for rates at cost. Utility/regulators will try to keep customers on line.
Intermediate C_I	$C_R > C_I > R_R$ Sames as above, except that potential QFs will sell to utility, sizing at thermal load.	$R_R > C_I > C_R$ Utility/regulator tries to maintain load. Customers use self-generation to negotiate lower rate with utility; self-generation is last resort. Independent generators push for transmission access, to sell under utility price umbrella.
$C_I < R_R , C_R$	$C_I < R_R < C_R$ Same as above, except that customers who could generate but can't get QF status will self-generate on-site, push for transmission line access to sell to other customers.	$C_I < C_R < R_R$ Utility/regulator tries to maintain load. Customers will self-generate if possible, may sell excess to utility. All IPPs will push for transmission access.

COMPETITION IN ELECTRICITY

ever, I think one needs to be clear that although industrial bypass competition can benefit directly from bidding or FERC-style competition, industrial bypass competition will move on step by step, battle by battle, regardless of what happens to the FERC initiatives and regardless of what happens to bidding at the state level. As important as the FERC initiatives are, I think from an institutional change point of view, the ball is really in the industrial, commercial, and agricultural competition arena much more than it is in those debates in Washington. Only five states have introduced bidding so far: Maine, Massachusetts, Connecticut, New York, and Virginia. Those bidding schemes have been rather limited in their scope.

The behavior of the various players varies all over the board, depending upon the cost and rate relationships within a given state and within a given service territory. This is very important because people less knowledgeable on this subject can look at the behavior of players in one service territory and extrapolate from that to another service territory, and then be quite surprised that something very different is happening in that second service territory. You get very different behavior of the players, as shown in Figure 1-5, depending upon whether the rates of the utility are greater or less than their marginal costs of producing electricity. Likewise, you get very different behavior, depending upon the relationship of the costs of the various parties and those of the utility. In a given state, there can be ten independent power producers that have costs higher than the utility, and there could be others that have costs lower.

Figures 1-6 through 1-11 depict what may be a likely scenario of the evolution of electricity competition. In this first stage, which I call the present status quo, there are affiliated QFs, indicated by QFs that have superscripts, selling to the distribution companies they are related to, and there are unaffiliated QFs, also selling to those regulated entities. Those regulated entities have their affiliated GENCOs which I'm assuming are regulated here. I make a distinction between core and non-core customers. It isn't an operational distinction, because although there are latent demand-only non-core customers, they're still buying from the regulated affiliate.

The next stage is when other independent power produc-

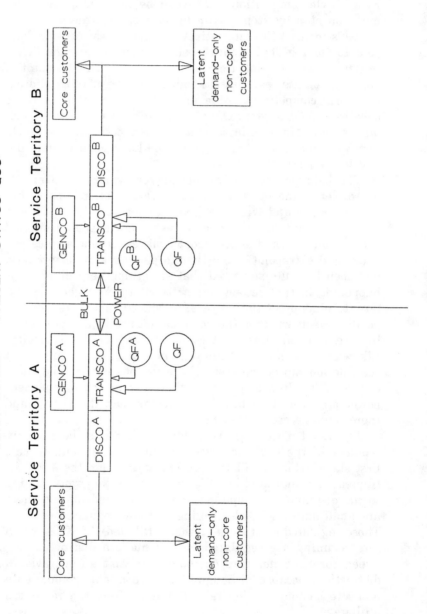

Figure 1-6

FIRST STAGE -- PRESENT STATUS QUO

COMPETITION IN ELECTRICITY

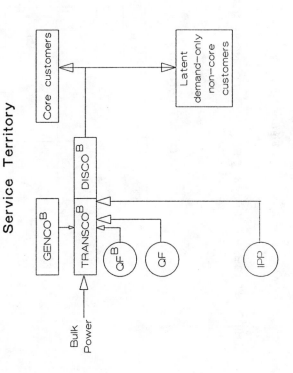

Figure 1-7

SECOND STAGE -- IPPs ENTER

Service Territory

Figure 1-8

THIRD STAGE -- IPPs & QFs SELL TO NON-CORE CUSTOMERS

Service Territory

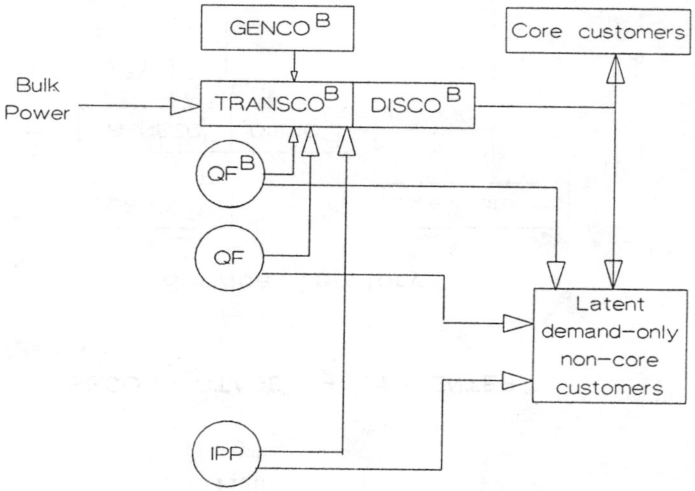

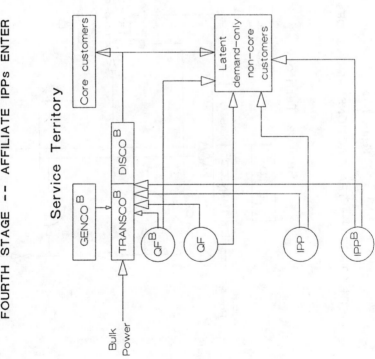

Figure 1-9

FOURTH STAGE -- AFFILIATE IPPs ENTER

Service Territory

Figure 1-10

FIFTH STAGE -- TRANSACTIONS AMONG QFs AND IPPs

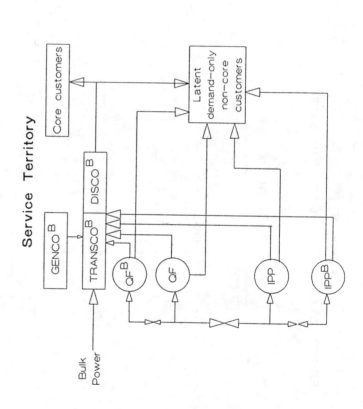

COMPETITION IN ELECTRICITY

Figure 1-11

SIXTH STAGE -- CROSS SERVICE TERRITORY TRANSACTIONS

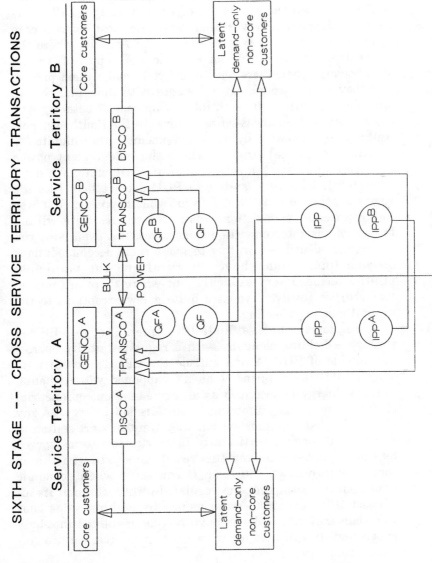

CHAPTER ONE

17

ers enter. They might at first be self-generators who use all the electricity strictly for their own needs. But of course, any self-generator is a potential independent power producer; it is an independent power producer producing for self-use. Also, there are independent power producers, not just as self-generators, that have power in excess of their own needs. We occasionally see the beginning of what we might call "merchant" independent power producers. The most colorful case so far is probably the case of Alamito, in Arizona, where the generating assets of Tucson Electric were spun off to the stockholders. Then there was an effort to make them private and they went through several stages with that, and they're still playing with it. It is an interesting case of both regulatory history and business-sense history. In the Southwest now we have the famous rallying cry, "Remember the Alamito."

The next logical stage is where the independent power producers and the QFs sell to non-core customers. We don't have retail wheeling, and the CPUC doesn't look like it's very receptive to that idea. I think what happened first was interconnection transactions where the parties were willing to pay for the interconnection themselves. But even now, you see regulated utilities willing to make some accommodations on wheeling. I don't have the rural and the municipal utilities included very explicitly, but where there are municipal utilities involved, you see quite a few exceptions to the general rule on wheeling.

In the fourth stage, affiliate IPPs enter. They're affiliated through a holding company with a regulated utility operating outside of PURPA and outside the CPUC's jurisdiction. Why would this happen? It hasn't happened yet. Although Mission Energy is described as an aggressive entrepreneurial entity, I don't hear rumblings from Mission Energy or any other affiliated subsidiaries that they want to start selling to non-core customers, particularly in service territories served by the regulated company they're affiliated with. So this is some distance down the road. It can occur when economic conditions are such that the regulated utility, through its affiliated IPP, can make more money by making sales that way than they can make through regular regulated rate-base generation. It will also occur in relation to cross-service territory transactions.

The fifth stage would be where the QFs and the IPPs bor-

COMPETITION IN ELECTRICITY

row a page out of the regulated utilities' book. The regulated utilities have always said, "Well, we can be much more efficient because we can handle diversity of loads, through having diversity of sources, and thus we can be more efficient overall than any one customer or any one supplier. So we have quite an advantage." Well, I think the users, the self-generators, the non-core customers and the independent power producers who are wired up together by this time, either through interconnection or wheeling, will make those same arguments. That's apparently what has happened with other industries in telecommunications and natural gas.

The last figure is the sixth stage, and this is where the importance of service territory boundaries starts to break down. A regulated utility that is a low-cost producer may decide to poach on the customers, or participate in bidding systems outside their own service territory. It would be a real breakdown in the clubbish mentality of regulated utilities, but of course that happened in other industries, and it is happening already to a small extent in the electric power industry. You see some CEOs openly and a few others more privately who say, "You know, I think I'd be the low cost producer there, too. Why shouldn't I have an opportunity to serve customers outside my service territory at lower cost if I'm a lower cost producer?" Sounds logical. The last figure here is depicting cross-service territory competition of all three types from QFs, from IPPs that sell to their affiliated utilities and to utilities in other service territories, and also to the non-core customers.

The evolution of electricity competition will no doubt follow very different paths in different states. These figures are pedagogical tools for conceptualizing how the process might evolve. Of course, policymakers at both the federal and state level are in a position to mold and change how the process evolves and where it ultimately winds up. I do not mean to imply that there is anything immutable or deterministic about the scenario I have described.

CHAPTER 2: NEW EVIDENCE ON BENEFITS AND COSTS OF PUBLIC UTILITY RATE REGULATION*

Mike A. Denning
Exxon Company, USA

and

Walter J. Mead
Professor of Economics, UC Santa Barbara

INTRODUCTION

In the late 1870's, a U.S. Supreme Court decision (Munn vs. Illinois, 1876) gave states the authority to regulate the prices charged by firms whose economic power enabled them to exploit their customers. The Court stated that when " ... private property becomes affected with a public interest the owner must submit to such controls as might be established for the common good". The formation of Wisconsin's Public Utility Commission in 1907 and the Public Utility Holding Act of 1935 marked the beginnings of formal state and federal electric utility rate regulation in the United States. Between 1907 and 1914, twenty-seven states passed legislation authorizing state Public Utility Commissions (PUCs) to control electricity rates (Jarrell, 1978). By 1976, all states having investor owned electric power companies provided for state regulation of rates. Thus, rate control was shifted from many municipalities where regulatory (as opposed to market) control was relatively weak, to stronger state control.

Initially, the justification for such regulation was a belief that apparent scale economies in electric power generation, transmission, and distribution would lead to natural monopoly. Due to the (possibly large) adverse effects of an inefficient allocation of scarce resources resulting from a monopolist setting prices substantially above costs, some type

*This study has been financed by the University of California, Universitywide Energy Research Group. The editors and authors wish to thank The Energy Journal for permission to reprint this paper which appeared first in that journal.

of public control over the prices charged in the industry was deemed to be in the interest of society. It has been proposed, however, that the type of regulation instituted to protect ratepayers may be a double edged sword. That is, while regulation seeks to establish prices near those that would prevail in a competitive industry, it also promotes inefficiency by eliminating the incentives for firms to reduce costs. Further, it adds new social costs of administering and complying with state PUC regulations. An interesting question then is whether the expected benefits of regulation, in terms of reduced rates, outweigh the associated efficiency losses and administrative compliance costs it causes.

In recent years the effectiveness of regulatory bodies in promoting the public interest through their decisions and procedures has been debated. Many industries previously subjected to state and/or federal regulation (including the airline, cable television, and natural gas industries) have been partially or completely deregulated, and proposals to deregulate the electric power industry have recently been receiving attention. In response to these proposals, a considerable literature has emerged dealing with the extent and form of deregulation, and to a lesser degree the issue of whether deregulation should be undertaken.

Since the early 1960's, several studies have examined the costs and benefits of rate regulation. The techniques employed as well as the results obtained have been mixed. Contrasting with the large body of literature which strongly advocates the imposition of regulation in natural monopoly markets, Stigler and Friedland (1962), Moore (1970), Posner (1969), Primeaux (1986), Demsetz (1968) and Crew and Kleindorfer (1985) have produced theoretical arguments and empirical results indicating that the benefits of regulation may very well be quite small if indeed they exist at all. While this disagreement among theoreticians will likely persist, the aim of this study is to extend the existing body of empirical results.

We will examine several economic issues relevant to state PUC electric power rate regulation as follows: (1) Does state regulation cause electric power rates to be lower than without such regulation? (2) Do the important subsidies received by government owned utilities (compared to investor owned utilities) translate into lower rates? (3) Does regulation lead to increased plant and equipment investments when rates of return allowed by regulation exceed the cost of capital (the Averch-Johnson thesis)? (4) Does regulation lead to X-inefficiency in the form of higher operating and Maintenance (O&M) costs as well as higher wage and salary payments? (5) Are electric utility profits constrained by regulation? (6) What are the costs of administering PUC rate regulation, and what are the utility company costs of complying with such regulations?

Figure 2-1

Conventional Monopoly Model with Economies of Scale

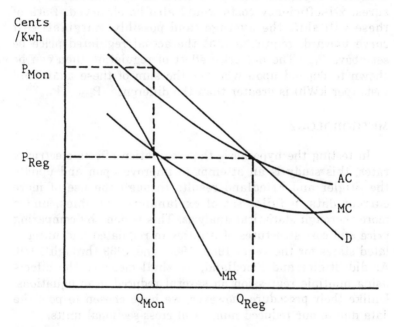

Even if there are positive benefits of rate regulation in the form of lower electricity rates, these benefits may be lost if the cost of administering regulation plus the cost of utility company compliance with regulation exceeds any such rate reductions. Using Figure 2-1 it is possible to explore the relationship between rates and regulation in a straightforward manner. A profit maximizing monopolist will charge P_{mon}

cents / kwh, selling Q_{mon} kWh of electricity. Rate of return regulation, which allows a firm to recover all of its operating costs and a "fair rate of return" on its investment, is identical to setting average revenue equal to average cost. Under regulation, the firm depicted in Figure 211 would be allowed to charge P_{reg} cents / kwh, at which price it could sell Q_{reg} kWh of electricity.

Implicit in this analysis is the assumption that average costs remain unchanged with the imposition of regulation. This supposition, however, is unlikely to be true. At the very least, the costs of complying with regulation must be added to the firm's existing costs. In addition, it is expected that because a regulated firm faces little or no competitive pressures, x-inefficiency costs would also be observed. Both of these will shift the average (and possibly marginal) cost curve upward, requiring that the actual regulated price be set above P_{reg}. The net price effect of regulation then can be shown to depend upon whether the sum of these additional costs (per kWh) is greater than the difference (P_{mon} - P_{reg}).

METHODOLOGY

In testing the hypothesis that regulation affects electricity rates, this study is an attempt to improve upon and update the Stigler and Friedland results through the use of more current data, a fuller set of explanatory variables, and a more thorough statistical analysis. This is done by comparing price and cost structures of utilities in regulated and unregulated states for the years 1960, 1965, and 1969 through 1979. As did Stigler and Friedland, we shall measure the effects using multiple regression on several reduced form equations. Unlike their procedure, however, we have chosen to pool the data due to our reduced number of cross-sectional units.

The data for each state (with all values expressed in 1985 dollars) include the following:

> p = average price (in cents) per kWh, based on typical bills, from sales to residential customers with monthly consumption of 250 and 550 kWh, commercial customers with monthly consumption of 6,000 kWh, and industrial customers with

COMPETITION IN ELECTRICITY

monthly consumption of 200,000 kWh;

hyd = percentage of total capacity accounted for by hydroelectric sources;

iou = percentage of investor-owned utilities;

reg = dummy variable for regulation, equalling 1 if regulated by a state commission with jurisdiction over rates, 0 if otherwise;

inc = personal income per-capita;

den = population density in terms of population per square mile of land area;

fuel = weighted average cost of fuels per kWh of electricity produced.

Following Stigler and Friedland, the **reg** variable defines states as being regulated beginning three years after the establishment of a state regulatory commission with jurisdiction over rates. Variation in the reg dummy variable is due to the states included in the sample that were regulated or came under regulation during the period 1960-1981. These states and the years in which state public utility commissions were established are Alaska (1960), Iowa (1963), Minnesota (1975), South Dakota (1976), and Texas (1976). In addition, Nebraska electric utilities, which are all publicly-owned, remain unregulated. Typically, only privately-owned utilities are regulated at the state level.

Stigler and Friedland cautioned in 1962 that after 1937, the comparison of regulated and unregulated states "would be ambiguous" because beyond 1937 every unregulated state had at least two adjoining states with regulatory commissions and a showing of no difference would fail to acknowledge the threat of regulation. However, they also acknowledged that this argument did not seem "wholly convincing". (1962, p. 4) We further note that the five states still having no state regulation as of 1960 were not totally free of regulation. Where regulation existed, it was by municipalities and covered only that municipality's political jurisdiction. Such regulation was generally felt to be ineffective and this was the political force leading to state regulation. Finally, the research problem is further complicated by the fact that some electric utilities are owned by public agencies, usually municipalities or public utility district (PUDs), and in many cases are subject to the same rate regulation as the privately owned utilities. Regulation of municipal utilities by state commissions has been found to be ineffective (Michaels, 1987).

Based on economic theory we can form expectations concerning the direction of the relationship between electricity rates and each of the above variables. A high share of hydroelectric generation is expected to associated with low costs (and rates), especially after 1972 when fossil fuel prices increased.

Population density would seem to be negatively correlated with electricity rates. The greater the population density in an area, the greater the economies of scale in electricity distribution and the lower the rates.

Increases in the cost of fuels used in the generation process should shift the cost curves upward, resulting in higher rates.

States with a large share of publicly-owned (federal and municipal) utilities should have lower electricity rates. It has been shown in several studies (Moore, for example) that the rates of investor-owned utilities are higher than those of publicly-owned utilities. This is due to the subsidies granted publicly-owned utilities in the form of lower capital costs (by issuing tax free bonds), reduced corporate income and property tax burdens, and priority in purchasing low cost power from government owned (mostly hydroelectric) projects.

Per-capita income and rates are expected to be negatively correlated. Since electricity demand is an increasing function of income, and the cost curves of utilities are assumed to be downward sloping over the relevant range of output, increased income should lead to greater consumption and lower rates. Finally, we wish to ascertain the relationship between electricity rates and regulation. As mentioned earlier in reference to Figure 2-1, the sign of this coefficient depends on whether the increase in average costs due to regulation is larger (or smaller) than the difference between the initial regulated price (where average revenue equals average cost for the *unregulated monopolist*) and the unregulated monopoly price.

RESULTS : THE EFFECTS OF STATE REGULATION ON RATES

The results of the estimation are contained in Table 2-2.

COMPETITION IN ELECTRICITY

Estimates were obtained by using both the Error Components and Covariance models for analyzing pooled time series and cross section data. Because the estimates obtained by two methods were nearly identical, only the Error Components model's results are presented. We find that the coefficients' signs mainly conformed with expectations.

Table 2-2
Results of Pooled Regressions of
Real Electricity Rates by Customer
Class and Combined, on 6 Independent Variables

Residential (250 kWh)

fuel price	0.031	2.10
income	-0.239	-3.68
% hydro	-0.007	-1.11
% iou	-0.007	-1.26
regulation	-0.072	-2.15
pop density	-0.073	-2.00

$R2 = 0.20$, $F(7, 656) = 23.4$

Residential (500 kWh)

fuel price	0.042	2.39
income	-0.251	-3.28
% hydro	0.010	1.46
% iou	0.003	-0.50
regulation	0.017	0.42
pop density	-0.034	-1.01

$R2 = 0.21$, $F(7, 656) = 24.7$

Commercial

fuel price	0.053	2.97
income	-0.331	-4.27
% hydro	-0.007	-0.93
% iou	0.002	0.29

regulation	-0.114	-2.86
pop density	-0.071	-1.58

$$R^2 = 0.19,\ F_{(7,656)} = 22.1$$

Industrial

fuel price	0.122	5.66
income	-0.258	-2.77
% hydro	0.005	0.58
% iou	0.002	0.23
regulation	-0.059	-1.23
pop density	-0.019	-0.46

$$R^2 = 0.16,\ F_{(7,656)} = 18.45$$

Combined

fuel price	0.070	4.54
income	-0.274	-4.05
% hydro	0.004	0.61
% iou	0.001	0.02
regulation	-0.053	-1.51
pop density	-0.061	-1.65

$$R^2 = 0.19,\ F_{(7,656)} = 21.4$$

Despite the fact that the iou and *hyd* variables were found to be insignificant, they were included in the model in view of the fact that inclusion of irrelevant variables is preferred to the exclusion of relevant variables.

Regarding the combined effects, the most interesting conclusion is that state regulation has no significant effect on electricity rates. The negative sign suggests the possibility that regulation is associated with lower rates, but the relationship is not statistically significant. Also of interest is the finding that investor-owned utilities do not have significantly higher rates than publicly-owned systems, in spite of the three important subsidies received by the latter. Apparently, these subsidies are offset through inefficiencies associated with government ownership and management.

Contrary to our hypothesis, the percent hydro variable is not significant and has a positive sign. This might be explained by the fact that hydroelectric systems commonly produce surplus energy. Much of this surplus is exported, often at very low prices, to utilities in neighboring states. This will tend to understate the cost advantages associated with hydroelectric generation. It is interesting to note that six of the ten states with the largest proportions of hydroelectric capacity have electricity rates that are above the national average.

Regarding the customer class models, we find that state regulation causes some shifting of wealth between customer classes. Small residential customers (250 kwh/month) were favored with a 6 percent reduction in rates due to regulation. The medium size residential class (500 kWh/month) possibly pays higher rates, but the relationship is not statistically significant. Further, commercial customers paid approximately 9.3% lower rates under state regulation, thus receiving subsidies from other customers, or from the regulated utility in the form of lower profits. Returns on total assets for unregulated utilities were found to be about 17% higher than for regulated ones, making the latter proposition feasible.

Further analysis of our results revealed that the effects of regulation in reducing small residential (250 kWh) rates only appeared beginning in 1975. This result is consistent with the hypothesis that the establishment of baseline rates for low income customers in some states was largely responsible for the decrease in small residential rates. In addition, we found that regulation served to lower commercial rates only in the period prior to 1974. Larger residential and industrial customers were unaffected by rate regulation. This seems to indicate a restructuring of regulatory policy consequent to the energy crisis of the 1970's causing favorable rates to be shifted from commercial to small residential customers.

Notwithstanding the differences in the time periods studied and the statistical techniques employed, we have obtained results for small (250 kWh) residential customers similar in terms of sign and magnitude to those Moore and Stigler & Friedland found for all residential consumers. Because commercial and industrial customers were grouped into a single class in the previous studies, we are unable to precisely compare our other results with theirs.

THE EFFECTS OF REGULATION ON CAPITAL STOCK, COMPENSATION AND OPERATING COSTS

We also tested hypotheses related to cost structures and levels of capital employed by affected utilities. The data used were for 31 utilities during the period 1962-1979. That either became regulated during the period or were regulated during the entire period. The independent variables used were regulation (as defined above), average heat rate of generating units, average fuel cost, percent residential customers, load factor, the amount of power purchased/imported, and system peak load. These variables characterize, in a very general way, the operating environment, supply system size and efficiency, and demand volatility of electric utilities.

Three dependent variables were regressed on the above explanatory variables using the Error Components model (see Table 2-3). As a test of the A-J hypothesis that regulation induces firms to increase the value of their capital stock when allowed rates of return exceed the cost of capital, we regressed electric plant per kWh of sales on the explanatory variables. Electric plant was used as a proxy for the value of a firm's physical capital stock. We found the regulated firms' capital stocks to be approximately 6.2% higher (significant at the 1% level) than those of unregulated firms. This finding further validates the hypothesis of Averch and Johnson and is in agreement with the majority of previous empirical tests (see Israilevich and Kowalewski, 1978).

We hypothesized that because the revenue of state regulated utilities is governed by regulatory commissions, the incentives for these companies to economize is greatly reduced. In order to test the hypothesis that regulation has this effect on utility expenditures, average employee compensation and operating and maintenance expenditures per kWh of sales were separately regressed on the exogenous variables above. It was found that the average salaries and wages paid employees were approximately 20.6% higher (significant at 1%) in state regulated companies. This result, however, is suspect because several seemingly relevant variables were excluded due to lack of data. We found that operating and maintenance (O&M) expenditures were about 4.4% higher per kWh of sales in regulated states (significant at 1%). Compliance costs are included in operating and maintenance charges in utility accounting.

Consequently, higher O&M costs would be expected under regulation in addition to any X-inefficiency costs.

TABLE 2-3

Results of Several Tests for the Effects of Rate of Return Regulation on the Operating Characteristics of Electric Utilities*

	Electric Plant Per kWh of Sales		Avg. Employee Compensation**		O&M Expense Per kWh of Sales	
	coef	t	coef	t	coef	t
Regulation	0.29	6.91	0.22	3.86	0.45	5.41
heat rate	1.28	4.89	1.47	3.48	0.57	1.09
fuel cost	0.04	1.36	0.02	0.87	-0.04	-0.92
% res. cus	. 0.28	0.91	1.31	1.95	1.64	2.24
sys. peak	-0.08	-4.15	-0.11	-4.87	-0.14	-3.53
pur. & int.	0.01	1.02	0.01	1.22	-	-
load factor	-0.21	-1.68	-0.99	-5.15	-0.91	-2.92

$$R^2 = 0.49 \qquad R^2 = 0.86 \qquad R^2 = 0.48$$

$$F_{(8,209)} = 25.5 \qquad F_{(8,209)} = 154.7 \qquad F_{(7,126)} = 16.7$$

*With the exception of regulation and imported power, all variables are in logarithmic form.
**Includes wages and salaries.

COSTS OF ADMINISTERING AND COMPLYING WITH RATE REGULATION

Rate regulation responsibilities are found primarily in two government agencies, the Federal Energy Regulatory Commission (FERC) at the federal level, and the California Public Utility Commission (CPUC) at the state level. The

California Energy Commission has no rate regulation authority. The costs of FERC rate regulation administration are borne by taxpayers. In contrast, CPUC administration costs are passed on to the regulated utilities who add their own costs of complying with CPUC regulations and pass all such costs on to ratepayers. The CPUC has always approved this dollar-for-dollar pass-through. Therefore, part, but not all, of the administration and compliance cost is reflected in rates, while part is taxpayer burden.

Our analysis will concentrate on the money costs of regulation. While these money costs generally correspond with resource (social) costs, we make no effort to estimate all resource misallocation costs due to regulation. For example, we do not consider the possibility that the cost-plus characteristic of rate regulation reduces management incentives to closely monitor costs, knowing that costs, whether wasteful or not, are normally fully recovered in higher rates. This is why we observe relatively high plant investments, employee compensation, and operating and maintenance costs. Consequently, our estimates of money costs will likely understate the social costs of rate regulation.

In estimating government administration costs, we start with government budgets using 1986 data. The FERC is responsible for rate regulation of interstate power and for all purchases from federal agencies such as the Bonneville Power Administration. The FERC budget for electric power rate regulation was $19.85 million in 1986. Given that California's share of U.S. electric power consumption is approximately 7.7%, we estimate that the FERC cost of administration in California was $1.53 million.

For the CPUC, we again start with budgeted costs for 1986. Working with CPUC budget personnel, we estimated the purely electric power rate regulation cost at $12.76 million. In addition, consultant services are normally used, adding about $2.4 million for a total of $15.16 million. Combined with FERC costs, the total government administration cost becomes $16.7 million per year.

Regulated public utility companies are required by their franchise to provide reliable electric power services to all potential customers within their service area at rates approved by the Commission. Consequently, compliance requires that regulated utilities defend themselves against complaints received by the Commissions and passed on to the utilities. Further, rate requests must be fully documented and defended before the Commission. This requires employment of well-paid lawyers, accountants, engineers, and other support personnel.

In order to estimate these compliance costs, we worked with budget and regulatory personnel within two companies (Pacific Gas and Electric and Southern California Edison) that together account for 76% of all electric power sales in California. Costs for these two utility companies were then expanded to the entire state of California by simple arithmetic extrapolation (multiplying by 100/76). This procedure probably understates compliance costs because it assumes that such costs per kWh are the same for the smaller utilities that account for the remaining 24% of sales. This assumption ignores the high probability that scale economies exist in rate regulation compliance.

We set research guidelines that would identify the incremental compliance costs relative to a regime in which no rate regulation exists. We carefully explored the need for specialized rate making personnel under conditions in which rates would be constrained only by potential competition from nearby utilities, alternative suppliers such as manufacturing companies able to generate power for their own needs directly or by cogeneration, and by competition from substitutes for electricity such as gas, solar, wind, etc. All parties understood that precise cost estimates were impossible and that "best guess" estimates were the relevant goals.

The year 1986 involved extra costs due to the entry of the Diablo Canyon and San Onofre nuclear power plants. Consequently, these special costs were estimated separately. We reasoned that these extra costs might be encountered about every fifteen years and consequently only one fifteenth of such extra costs should be included in the estimates for 1986. This analysis indicated that the incremental cost of compliance would be about $22.3 million dollars for the entire state of California.

Combining our estimates of $16.7 million government administration cost with $22.3 million compliance costs gives an estimated $39 million cost of administration and compliance for the State. If this estimate is extrapolated to the entire nation, the estimate becomes approximately $500 million per year.

Our estimates indicate that rate regulation imposes $1.34 of compliance costs for every dollar of government administration costs. We have indicated above that for several reasons, the compliance costs are probably understated. This conclusion is similar to finding by Weidenbaum and DeFina (1978, p. 2) that compliance costs exceed government administration costs by a factor of about twenty to one.

In 1986, California utilities sold approximately 180 billion kWH of electricity. The $39 million cost of rate regulation then corresponds to a total cost of 0.022 cents per kWh. For the average electric power consumer, regulation accounts for a mere 0.3 percent of his electricity bill. However, given our prior conclusion that regulation fails to lower overall electric power rates, the presence of any positive costs leads to the conclusion that the cost of regulation exceeds its benefits. We are left with the social cost of resource misallocation in the form of excessive plant investment, employee compensation, operating and maintenance expenditures, and now joined by $39 million per year costs for California rate payers and taxpayers.

CONCLUSIONS

The fact that the results of two models, which utilize the most widely accepted techniques for pooling time series and cross-section data, are very similar in sign and magnitude adds to the credibility of the results. Due to this apparent robustness, we feel a high degree of confidence in our principal conclusion that state regulation has no net effect on electricity rates.

The results presented indicate that regulation at the state level did not lead to lower overall rates being paid by consumers. While we have found that regulation benefitted small residential customers after 1975 and commercial customers before 1974, it did not significantly affect the other customer classes' rates. It is important to mention that these results are only valid insofar as average monthly consumption within each customer class corresponds to the values (250 and 500 kWh for industrial customers) used in this study.

Our evidence indicates that regulation retards the incentives of firms to control costs, leading to a misallocation of resources. State regulated utilities have 6.2% higher investments in capital stock per kWh of output, a finding that is consistent with the Averch-Johnson thesis. Wages and salaries were 20.6% higher, and O&M expenditures 4.4% higher, than in non-state regulated utilities. Also, government administration and company compliance costs in California in 1986 were estimated at $39 million. Adding these results to the finding that state regulation fails to reduce (overall) rates, it seems clear that such regulation has not only failed to accomplish the task for which it was designed — to protect consumers from high electricity rates-but it also has some negative (resource allocative) side effects.

In order for state regulated rates to equal unregulated rates in the aggregate, as we have found, it must be the case that the sum of administration and compliance costs borne directly by the regulated utilities, plus the increased operating expenses occurring due to regulation, equal the monopoly rents that would prevail without state regulation. In terms of Figure 2-1, this means that average cost must rise to the point where it intersects the demand curve at P_{mon}, The only other effect that is evident is that state commissions have, through altering rate structures, redistributed income among the customer classes. Based on the inefficient resource allocation mentioned above, it is doubtful that the resulting income distribution is superior in any sense to the one that would occur if economic agents were responding to the incentives produced without state regulation.

The results indicate that public utility rate regulation offers no net benefits to customers and results in efficiency losses given the fact that there are positive costs of regulation not internalized in electric power rates, it follows that deregulation of this industry would produce net benefits for society. A survey (Bailey, 1986) of deregulation effects in several other U.S. industries which have been deregulated within the last decade confirmed that "there have been real welfare gains through lower costs, greater varieties of services, and increased productivity." (p. 1216)

REFERENCES

Averch, Harvey and Leland L. Johnson. "Behavior of the Firm Under Regulatory Constraint", *American Economic Review*, 1962, pp. 1052-1069.

Bailey, Elizabeth E. "Deregulation: Causes and Consequences", Science, 2t4, Dec. 5, 1986, pp. 1211— 1216.

Crew, Michael A. and Paul R Kleindorfer. "Governance Costs of Rate-of-Return Regulation", *Zeitschrift fur die gesamte Staatswissenschaft* (ZgS) 141, 1985, pp. 104-123.

————. *The Economics of Public Utility Regulation*, MIT Press, Cambridge, MA 1986.

Demsetz, Harold. "Why Regulate Utilities?", *Journal of Law and Economics*, 11, 1968, pp. 55-65.

Israilevich, Philip and K.J. Kowalewski. "The Effects of Regulation on Ohio Electric Utilities", *Economics Review*, Federal Reserve Bank of Cleveland, 1st Quarter, 1987, pp. 10-19.

Jarrell, Gregg A. "The Demand for State Regulation of the Electric Utility Industry", *Journal of Law* and Economics, Vol. 21, October 1978, pp. 269-295.

Maddala, G.S. "The Use of Variance Components Models In Pooling Cross Section and Time series Data, *Econometrica*, Vol. 39, No. 2, March, 1971, pp. 341-358.

Michaels, Robert J. "What Can Regulators Regulate? The Case of Municipal Electric Utilities", unpublished paper given at the 1987 annual meeting of the Western Economic Association, Vancouver, B.C.

Moore, Thomas Gale. "The Effectiveness of Regulation of Electric Utility Prices", *Southern Economic Journal*, Vol. 36, No. 4, April 1970, pp. 365-375.

Mundlak, Yair. "On the Pooling of Time Series and Cross Section Data", *Econometrica*, Vol. 46, No. 1, January, 1978, pp. 69-85.

Posner, Richard A. "Natural Monopoly and Its Regulation", *Stanford Law Journal*, Feb. 1969, pp. 548-643.

Primeaux, Walter. *Direct Electric Utility Competition–The Natural Monopoly Myth*, Praeger, New York, 1986.

Stigler, George J. and Claire Friedland. "What Can Regulators Regulate?", *Journal of Law and Economics*, Vol. 5, October, 1962, pp. 1-16.

U.S. Department of Commerce, Bureau of the Census. *Statistical Abstract of the United States*, Washington D.C.

U.S. Department of Energy, Energy Information Administration. *Typical Electric Bills*, Washington, D.C.

————. *Electric Power Annual*, Washington D.C.

U.S. Federal Power Commission. *Typical Electric Bills*, Washington D.C.

Wallace, T.D. and Ashiq Hussain. "The Use of Error Components Models In Combining Cross Section With Time Series Data", *Econometrica*, Vol. 37, No. 1, January, 1969, pp. 55-72.

Weidenbaun, Murray and Robert DeFina. *The Cost of Federal Regulation of Economic Activity*, Washington, D.C., American Enterprise Institute Reprint No. 88, 1978.

APPENDIX

MODEL

The demand equation to be used for each customer class is of the constant elasticity form

$$P = f(inc)Q^{1/n} \tag{1}$$

where n is the elasticity of demand, and Q is electricity consumption. We further assume that the production function is homogeneous of degree $1/r$ in its arguments (Y) and of the general form

$$Q = Q(Y) \tag{2}$$

where Y represents observations on the fuel, den, iou, hyd, and reg variables. This implies a cost function that can be shown to be multiplicatively separable and written as

$$C(Y,Q) = g(Y)Q^r \tag{3}$$

From this cost function, marginal and average cost equations

$$MC = dC/dQ = rg(Y)Q^{r-1} \tag{4}$$
$$AC = C/Q = g(Y)Q^{r-1} \tag{5}$$

are easily obtained. In order for the above specification of the firm's production and cost functions to coincide with the characteristics of a natural monopoly (decreasing average costs), it is evident from equations (4) and (5) that r must be restricted to lie in the open interval (0,1). Setting MC=MR and solving for P yields he reduced form defining the unregulated monopoly price as a function of the exogenous variables in the model

$$P = [rg(Y)/a]^{n/b} f(X)^{-(n+b)/b} \tag{6}$$

where b=n-n+1 and a=(n+1)/n.

Rate of return regulation eliminates the profits of the firm by effectively setting average cost equal to average revenue. Setting (1) equal to (5) and solving for P yields

$$p = f((X)^{-(n+b)/b} g(y)^{n/b} \tag{7}$$

which is the reduced form defining regulated electricity rates as a function of the exogenous variables affecting the demand for and cost of supplying electricity. Comparison of equations (6) and (7) reveals that the regulated price differ from the unregulated monopoly price by the factor $(r/a)npb$. Define the switching variable d as equalling 0 if a state regulatory commission exists and 1 if otherwise. It is now possible to write a single reduced form equation

$$P = (r/a)^{dn/b} f(X)^{-(n+1)/b} g(y)^{n/b} \tag{8}$$

defining the rates charged by regulated and unregulated utilities as functions of the exogenous variables in the system. Taking logs of both sides of (8) and combining terms yields

$$\ln P = b_0 + b_1\ln(\text{fuel}) + b_2\ln(\text{den}) + b_3\text{hyd} \tag{9}$$
$$+ b_4\text{iou} + b_5\ln(\text{inc}) + b_6\text{reg} + u$$

where u is assumed to be distributed with zero mean and finite variance. The estimated parameters bO through b6 are nonlinear functions of the parameters in the demand and cost equations. Also note that since d = 1-reg, it does not appear in the reduced form equation. Equation (9) will be estimated in order to determine the relationship between state

COMPETITION IN ELECTRICITY

regulation and the rates charged by electric utilities.

ESTIMATION

Several techniques exist for pooling time series and cross-sectional data and the decision of which model to use is complicated for several reasons. One is that model choice requires either a knowledge of or assumptions about the error structure. In the case of pooled data, and particularly when a complete time series is not available for all variables, it is difficult to test for and/or identify nonspherical disturbances.

In addition, even if an error structure is assumed, GLS may not be possible as the covariance matrix cannot be estimated by traditional methods. Another problem with model choice is that there is no consensus in the econometrics literature as to which of the more widely used models is generally most acceptable.

The models receiving the most attention in the econometrics literature (see Wallace and Hussain (1969), Maddala (1971), and Mundlak (1978) for example) are the Covariance and Error Components (EC) models. These models are similar in that they both allow effects to vary over time and across cross-sectional units, but they differ in the way that these variations are specified. In the Covariance model, dummy variables are created for each cross-section unit and each time period. These dummies pick up the unmeasured effects that are specific to each state and time period. For instance, since no adjustment has been made for the qualitative difference between the intensity of regulation across states and over time, we might expect the resulting variations to be reflected in these dummy variables. The EC model also allows for the intercepts to differ between states and over time as explained above. The difference is that the EC model captures this feature in its error term.

Justification for using the EC model is based on the desirable properties of its estimators. In comparison with the Covariance model, the EC model has more degrees of freedom, which means that the significance of the estimates will be increased. In addition, the EC model has been shown to perform at least as well as the covariance model in many cases. A possible reason is that, as discussed by Maddala (1971), the Covariance estimator uses only the "within" group variations, whereas the EC estimator uses both the "within" group and the "between" group variations. Maddala also argues that because economic effects are more likely to be random than fixed, a random effects estimator may be more appropriate when applied to economic data. Finally, a more recent article on pooling data by Mundlak (1978) has shown that these two estimation procedures are, in most instances equivalent. Since it is not known which of these competing models is most appropriate, we derived the estimates using both. We found that the results were similar.

ENDNOTES

1. For a discussion of the origins of regulation, see Crew and Kleindorfer (1986), pp. 93-111.

SECTION B

LARGE CUSTOMER BYPASS

CHAPTER 3: BYPASS CONCEPTS AND TRANSMISSION ACCESS

James L. Plummer
President, QED Research, Inc.

WHAT IS BYPASS?

To understand utility bypass, one must go back to the origins of regulated monopolies — the laws that sanction the existence of a monopoly and set up regulatory commissions to protect the public interest. These laws authorize regulatory commissions to offer monopoly franchises in certain essential service areas that exhibit "natural monopoly" characteristics. As part of the social compact that the regulatory commission creates, the regulated monopoly is obligated to serve all customers that demand to be served.

Usually when regulatory commissions issue franchises, the boundaries or domains of the franchise are not always well defined. "Bypass" occurs when one or more customers decide not to take from the regulated monopoly a product or service it normally provides or to reduce substantially the amount of that product or service taken. They may decide to provide the product or service to themselves, or to buy it from a seller other than the regulated monopoly. If this seems like a contradiction in terms, it is. How can a regulated "monopoly" have "competitors"? And if it does have competitors in the real world, why was it considered to be a "natural monopoly" in the first place, and thus a candidate for regulated monopoly treatment? The existence of actual competitors in the real world would deem to be a very strong prima facia evidence that the regulated monopoly does not deserve its special regulated monopoly status. The answer to this puzzlement is that the market that the regulated monopoly serves is not homogeneous, but is made up of many different segments. In some or most of these market segments, the strong returns to scale characteristics that provide a natural monopoly justification may still be present. In other segments, changing technologies, changing relative prices of economic resources, changing industry structure or changing public policies may create the potential for competition by competitors who can themselves operate at a sufficient scale to undercut the regulated prices of the regulated monopoly. The potential competitors will first zero in on the segments where the uniform (and historic-cost-based) prices of the regulated monopoly are high relative to the (current marginal) cost of providing service, and thus present the juiciest targets. This process is often referred to as "cream skimming" or "cherry picking."

Theoretically, a regulatory commission could step in to prohibit the competitor from invading the exclusive franchise territory of the regulated monopoly. One way of doing this is for the regulatory commission to subject the new entrant to price regulation, in an attempt to eliminate whatever price advantage that the new entrant was offering to customers. While this is a theoretical possibility, it rarely occurs. One reason is that it is too inconsistent and embarrassing for regulatory commissions to be arguing out of both sides of their mouths — first, that a given activity has "natural monopoly" characteristics and thus deserves to be a regulated monopoly; and second, that it is necessary for the commissions to step in and protect the poor regulated monopoly from competitors. Another reason is that the new firm may actually have a lower cost structure than the existing regulated monopoly. The more usual and more correct course of action is for the commission and the regulated monopoly to accept some erosion in the domain of the regulated monopoly. So, bypass amounts to a movement in the boundaries between the regulated and unregulated portions of an industry.

That is not to say that the movement of the boundary is anticipated, or deliberate, or even welcomed by either the regulated monopoly or the regulatory commission or other ratepayers. There is frequently strong resistance to this movement by either the regulated company or the commission. Both entities may regard the bypass as an "unfair" invasion of their turf. One argument is that it is unfair for the regulated monopoly to have to maintain "standby capacity" in case the errant customer should return to the regulated system. A counterargument to this is that the new providers of service (either the customers themselves, or new direct sales to the regulated company) must also make capital commitments that are not easily reversible. So, once they leave the system, the chances of them coming back very soon are fairly remote. In addition, the rules of the game for standby capacity can be redefined to preserve fairness in bypass situations. For those bypassing customers who wish to retain their rights to return to the regulated system on demand, standby rates can be designed to compensate the regulated company for the cost of providing this "insurance" for the bypassing customers. Those customers who do not choose to pay for the standby capacity insurance can be required to give sufficient notice of intent to return to the system so that the cost impact on the regulated company is minimized. Thus, the standby capacity issue is really a pricing issue, rather than a real basis for prohibiting bypass.

BYPASS AND UNBUNDLING OF SERVICES

Bypass and unbundling are two separate things, although they are closely related. If customers are offered unbundled services, then there may be natural monopoly types of returns to scales in some of the bundles, and thus less potential for competition, and lower returns to scale and more potential competition in others.

In both gas and electricity, the overall services provided by utilities can be subdivided into market segments. The sale of the energy resource to the end user can be differentiated from the transport and delivery of that resource. The delivery of "energy" undifferentiated by time of delivery can be separated from the delivery at a specified time (e.g. at peak demand periods). High reliability service can be differentiated from interruptible service. High quality, in many technical dimensions, can be differentiated from lower technical quality. Thus, what was previously viewed as a homogeneous utility service can be segmented in many directions. The more unbundling and differentiation permitted by commissions (and technology), the more opportunities there will be for bypass.

BYPASS AND "SELF HELP"

When customers of a regulated company leave the system to do business with a competitor of the regulated company, it is recognized to be a bypass transaction. The regulated company will sometimes make reference to its previous customer

Figure 3-1

"QUALIFIED FACILITY" COGENERATORS	SELF-GENERATORS
• "Qualify" by meeting all the criteria of PURPA	• Existence not related to PURPA
• Price threshold is the level of "avoided cost" (marginal cost) of the regulated utility	• Price threshold is the level of industrial rates, which are determined by average cost levels and then modified through cross-subsidies from industrial customers to residential customers
• In California, subject to CEC "need tests"	• In California, not subject to CEC "need tests"
• Often unprofitable in excess capacity service territories	• Often most profitable in excess capacity service territories, where high cost nuclear plants have driven up industrial rates

COMPETITION IN ELECTRICITY

as though it is an errant spouse that is "playing around" and urge the customer to "return home." Thest jokes reveal much about the mentality of regulated utilities, as compared with ordinary companies that have to battle every day to keep their customers and woo new customers away from competitors.

A different situation arises when the customer decides to provide the service previously provided by the utility. This "self help" has the same effect on the regulated company, but it is harder for either the utility or its commission to reverse. A utility may argue to its commission that it is unfair for a new unregulated competitor to steal its customers and still remain free from the burdens of regulation, but what is the utility to argue when the customer decides to serve himself? The utility can hardly argue that the customer has insufficient scale to provide reliable and cost-efficient service, since nobody but the customer himself will suffer if that turns out to be true.

In electricity, "self help" is labeled "self generation." Those electricity customers who decide to self generate with cogeneration present a special challenge to utilities and regulators. They are rebels who do not need or want many of the special treatments "Qualifying Facilities" (QFs) receive under the Public Utility Regulatory Policy Act (PURPA). As an example, the California Energy Commission regulates the siting of cogeneration facilities over 50 Megawatts in size. recently, an impending surplus of QF capacity in California has led the CEC into the difficult area of prioritizing types of QFs, and making some types of QFs pass a "need test." The cogenerators who intend to satisfy mainly their own electricity needs have argued before the CEC that they are self generators and thus no subject to the need test constraints of other QFs. Figure 3-1 illustrates some of the contrasts between QFs and self-generators.

Cogenerators who are also self generators are a special problem for utilities, because the use of thermal output may replace gas purchases. Thus self generators have the potential for being "double bypassers."

INAPPLICABILITY OF THE NON-PARTICIPANT BREAKEVEN TEST

In debates over utility conservation and avoided-cost pricing for QFs, one of the regulatory tests that has been applied is the "non-participant breakeven test," also known as the "no losers test." Although some people have proposed using this test to determine whether bypass should be allowed, careful analysis shows it is inapplicable for that purpose.

As an example of this test, there are various conservation measures that can be used to save electricity, and some have higher cost per kwh of electricity saved than others. It makes economic sense to pursue (subsidize) the lower cost measures before pursuing the higher cost measures. But at what point do you stop? The criterion of the non-participant breakeven test or "no losers" test is that you stop at the point where going further would impose costs on those who do not participate in the program. In many cases, this point corresponds to where the size of the subsidy per kwh saved is equal to the difference between the marginal cost and average cost of producing a kwh. As long as one does not proceed beyond this point, there are no losers among the non-participants. The customers participating in the program gain from receiving the subsidy and from lower electricity bills. The utility and society gain from the electricity conservation. The non-participating customers are no worse off than they would have been in the absence of the conservation program.

Although the non-participant breakeven or no losers test is sometimes useful for the above types of regulatory decisions, it is not really applicable to bypass situations. If there are fixed costs involved in producing and delivering the utility service, the consequence of some customers leaving the regulated system will be that the fixed costs have to be spread over fewer remaining customers, and those customers will have higher rates. This should be no surprise to anyone. *So it is an inherent characteristic of bypass that the bypassing customers will be "winners," and the customers remaining behind on the regulated system will be "losers."* It isn't possible to have a happy outcome of a change that benefits one group, and leaves another group no worse off.

Beyond the efficiency and equity considerations just described, there is the fact that in bypass "no money changes hands." The potential bypassers are not lobbying for a subsidy, or an advantageous avoided-cost rate. All they wish, is the freedom to be left alone if they decide to leave the regulated system.

ECONOMIC BYPASS v. UNECONOMIC BYPASS

In debates over bypass issues, distinctions have sometimes been made between "economic bypass" and "uneconomic bypass," without a clear definition of what those terms mean. Usually, the implication of "uneconomic bypass" has something to do with a "mistake" by either the bypassing customer on the one hand or the utility on the other hand. Let us probe the alternative meanings of "mistake" and "uneconomic" in this context.

One meaning is that the bypassing customers are taking an uneconomic action of making a mistake, even from the viewpoint of their self-interest. This is true only if the long-run cost of getting service from the utility system (either from an alternate supplier or through "self-help") will be higher than the long run cost of paying the utility for the service. If we assume that the bypassing customers are rational (i.e. "economic" persons) and informed, this kind of "uneconomic bypass" should never arise. Nevertheless, one often hears utilities, regulators or certain customers or activists claiming that the bypassers don't understand fully the relative cost situation and that the opponents to bypass merely hope to save the bypassers from themselves. These arguments should not be taken too seriously, for there is little reason to believe public policy intervention will work better than individual choice on such decisions. In fact, experience provides great reason to believe that individual choice works better to achieve public economic goals. If public policy does anything to remedy the situation, it should focus on the disseminating information to help individual choices yield more optimal results.

A second meaning of "uneconomic bypass" is that the gains to the bypasser are less than the losses to the remaining customers on the regulated system, and so the overall interests of society are not served by the bypass in question.

Regulators and utilities would, of course, want to avoid such bypass. However, as a practical matter, it will always be very difficult for them to know or measure the gains to the bypassers, since bypass choices are based on private information concerning alternative costs which bypassers are not required to divulge to them. Even if the bypass gain was known to be less than the losses to the remaining utility customers, this fact would constitute justification only for lowering the rates charged to potential bypassers by just enough to keep them on line, as long as the rate charged covers the utility's out-of-pocket costs for providing the service. It would not be a justification for prohibiting bypass or subjecting the bypassers to rate regulation. The main point, though, is that the key to this kind of "uneconomic bypass" is that the utility and its regulators have erred in making bypass overly attractive by charging rates high enough to cause bypass. by reducing the utility's revenue base, the bypass action may damage the utility, its remaining (who face a higher share of the utility's fixed costs than they did before the bypass), or both.

In discussion of bypass, a distinction is usually made between "core" and "non-core" customers. Core customers are residential and small commercial and industrial ratepayers whose bypass opportunities are very limited to measures such as conservation from lower thermostat settings, typically because the "transactions" costs for more substantial measures are high relative to the expected benefits for them. Non-core customers are those with fuel-switching capabilities or other easy (relative to their means) and significant ways of bypassing utility service. In part because core customers are much more numerous, their interests are often given greater weights by regulators. Some commissions pursue this "political weighing" of customers further than others. It is a delicate balancing act. If the commission tries to prevent bypass by keeping rates lower for the non-core group, it may get in political trouble with the more numerous core customers. On the other hand, if the commission tries to protect its *image* with core customers and lets rates to non-core customers rise high enough to cause bypass, then the commission is doing a disservice to the long-run interests of the core customers (as well as the utility), because they will have to bear the losses due to bypass. Figure 3-2 illustrates this dilemma

Figure 3-2

THE DILEMMA THAT BYPASS POSES TO STATE RATE REGULATORS

	Charging industrial customers rates that are higher than their alternative costs	Charging industrial customers rates that are lower than their alternative costs
ADVANTAGES	• Short-term popularity with core customers • Minimizes risk of "leaving money on the table" for industrial (non-core) customers • Encourages entry of new competitive suppliers	• In the long-term interest of core customers • Simplifies life for those industrial customers who would prefer not to "get into another business"
DISADVANTAGES	• Long-term greater damage to core customers	• Risk of "leaving money on the table" for industrial customers • Requires disaggregating rates among categories of industrial customers (e.g. Ramsey pricing) • Discourages entry of new competitive suppliers

that bypass poses to state rate regulators.

So long as non-core customers are charged more than the marginal (out-of-pocket) cost to serve them and thus are making some contribution to the overhead or fixed cost of the utility, it is better for the core customers and the utility that the non-core customers stay on the system. but, typically, regulators and utilities will be reluctant to "leave money on the table." That is, they would like to charge a potential bypasser a rate just slightly lower than the alternative cost that a customer faces (either from self help or supply by a competitor to the utility). The problem is that this "optimal rate" from the viewpoint of protecting the long-run interest of the core customers varies among the individual non-core customers. This forces regulators and utilities into the complicated world of discriminatory pricing.

DISCRIMINATORY PRICING TO PREVENT BYPASS

The discussion in the previous section established two points concerning pricing of utility services to avoid uneconomic bypass:

1. Utilities must be willing and able to lower rates to potential bypassers as much as necessary to keep them from bypassing, subject only to the condition that the rates must be greater than the short-run marginal (out-of-pocket) costs of the service to those customers. As long as a rate exceeds the SRMC, the utility and its other ratepayers are better off to keep the potential bypasser using utility service and making some contributions to margin than having him bypass (because rates are too high) and thus make no contribution.
2. Since the above method of combatting bypass lowers rates to potential bypassers from what they otherwise would have been (or were), rate regulators and utilities will wish to practice price discrimination in the rates charged to potential bypassers. The "best" price discrimination system is one that allows the utility to maximize the contribution of non- core customers to utility margins, thus keeping rates for core customers from escalating more than the minimum necessary to combat bypass.

The remaining question is: "What is the best way to do this pricing and still avoid the problems inevitably raised by practices such as discriminatory pricing?" An approach favored by many economists is called "Ramsey pricing". The next few paragraphs of this section discuss Ramsey pricing, including its origins and the reason for its appeal.

Ramsey pricing is marginal cost pricing modified to satisfy a revenue constraint in an economically efficient way. It is called by economists a "second-best" solution because:

1. it departs from the purely efficient and theoretically generally preferred approach of marginal cost-pricing in order to accommodate the real world requirements of allowing utilities to collect prescribed revenue levels: and

2. it departs in a way that is least damaging to the goal of economic efficiency.

Ramsey pricing starts by estimating the marginal costs for all services for all customers. Then a test is made to determine whether rates set on this basis will produce a revenue surplus or deficit for the utility, with the results typically being a deficit. The existence of a deficit requires the rates to be set above MC levels, and the existence of a surplus allows rates below MC. In its purest form, Ramsey pricing is the apportionment of the deficit (rate increase) or surplus (rate cut) throughout the rate structure in inverse proportion to the price elasticities of demand (i.e. to the responsiveness to the change in price) for each service by each customer. A reasonable approximation to Ramsey pricing is made by aggregating customers into ratepayer classes and allocating the deficit or surplus in inverse proportion to price elasticities; this allocation may often be accomplished through simple pricing rules.

Ramsey pricing originated in taxation policy, rather than economic regulation of utilities. F.P. Ramsey proposed the idea of allocating government revenue requirements in a manner that causes the least possible distortion in the economy (or least decrease in net social benefit) in a 1927 article.[1] W.J. Baumol and D. F. Bradford first applied the same notion systematically.[2]

Ramsey's idea that revenues should be raised in the most

economically efficient or least damaging way has a clear interpretation in utility pricing: since pricing at levels other than MC will cause ratepayers to use more or less of the utility service than the efficient amount they would use under the ideal solution (pure MC pricing), this pricing should be done, if it must be done, in the manner that causes the least net departure from the most efficient use (demand) pattern. Since the price elasticity of demand is the direct measure of customers' inclination to change the quantities consumed, allocating the deficit or the surplus in inverse proportion to these elasticities assures minimum net deviations from the efficient levels of use of the utility service.

Viewed in light of its basic principle, Ramsey pricing is obviously an approach to the bypass problem that does the minimum collateral damage. Saying that customers will bypass a particularly utility service at a given price level is merely saying that the price responsiveness is great near that price. If the threshold price is greater than the marginal cost, the high price elasticity of demand dictates that rates above marginal cost (required generally because of a utility revenue deficit at MC prices) be kept clearly below that level in order to change quantities consumed as little as possible from the efficient levels. Thus, Ramsey pricing directly precludes uneconomic bypass by keeping rates to potential bypassers below the utility's MC level, and under those circumstances bypass is economic and should be encouraged.

There are other issues raised by Ramsey pricing that are outside the scope of this paper:

1. If Ramsey pricing is good for overcoming a small deficit in the revenue requirements of a regulated utility, might it be abused to collect revenues that support a wasteful utility? This is not a fault of Ramsey pricing itself, but a practical regulatory problem of discriminatory pricing.

2. If a utility is given full liberty by regulators to practice Ramsey pricing of non-core customers, will the utility or its regulators be able to discern when or if that power is being used to preempt potential competition or to punish present competitors? There is a fine line between fighting bypass in the interest of core customers, and actions that damage competition

THE RELATIONSHIP BETWEEN BYPASS AND ISSUES OF TRANSMISSION ACCESS AND PRICING

Once bypass moves beyond self-generation, the implementation of bypass competition depends on both the degree of access to transmission facilities and the degree of discrimination present in the pricing of transmission wheeling services.

Figure 3-3 shows how access proceeds gradually from wholesale/interconnection transactions (cell #1), to retail/interconnection transactions (cell #2), to wholesale/wheeling transactions (cell #3), and finally to retail/wheeling transactions (cell #4). It is retail wheeling that regulated utilities fear the most, because it could open up parts of their customer base to competition from small power producers. Taken to its ultimate state, this could effectively end the "exclusive franchise" concept, and along with it much of the justification for regulation.

There is a continuum of pricing practices for wheeling services that extends from "less open" wheeling pricing and access to "more open" wheeling pricing and access. That spectrum of practices is illustrated in Figure 3-4. The terminology (e.g. "contract carriage" and "common carrier" pricing) is being adopted in the electricity industry as a legacy from the recent and similar history of deregulation of natural gas transportation. The electric power industry is considerably behind the natural gas industry in the degree of movement down the continuum depicted in Figure 3-4.

A new world of bypass transactions might look very confusing to observers of the present vertically integrated electric utility industry. There are analytical devices for depicting the flows under a competitive system, and avoiding doublecounting. Figure 3-5 uses the formate of input-output analysis to indicate how complicated electricity trade flows might be in a completely competitive industry. "GENCO" stands for the generation stage of the industry, which even in this depiction is still assumed to be in the same corporate entity as the transmission facilities. "DISCO" refers to the still-regulated electricity distribution company. Every cell of the matrix marked with a "B" represents bypass transactions. Every cell marked by a large *empty* circle represents wholesale transactions to a DISCO. Given the diversity of

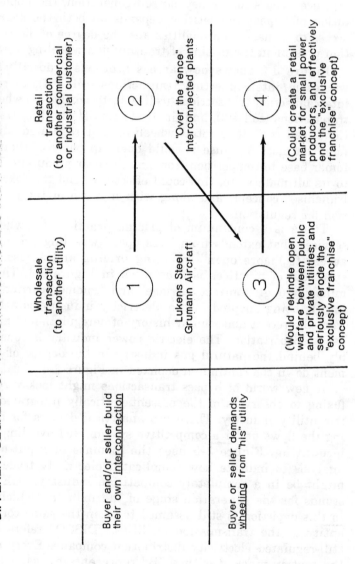

Figure 3-3

DIFFERENT DEGREES OF TRANSMISSION ACCESS IN BYPASS COMPETITION

Wholesale transaction (to another utility)

Retail transaction (to another commercial or industrial customer)

Buyer and/or seller build their own <u>interconnection</u>

① Lukens Steel Grumann Aircraft

② "Over the fence" Interconnected plants

Buyer or seller demands <u>wheeling</u> from "his" utility

③ (Would rekindle warfare between public and private utilities; and seriously erode the "exclusive franchise" concept)

④ (Could create a retail market for small power producers, and effectively end the "exclusive franchise" concept)

COMPETITION IN ELECTRICITY

Figure 3-4

DEGREES OF OPEN PRICING OF TRANSMISSION

- "Open access" in the sense of not allowing utilities to deny access to other parties if they are allowing access to any party

- Forcing "contract carriage" -- open access, but on terms that are negotiated individually with each party

- "Non-discriminatory pricing" among transmission customers

- Full "common carrier regulation" requiring posted rates and terms of access

---

- Same continuum as above, but with prices that make allowance for peak and off-peak usage

- Same continuum as above, but with capacity charges that recognize the need for selected transmission capacity additions

Figure 3-5

An Input-Output Table Representation of Competitive Electricity Trade Flows

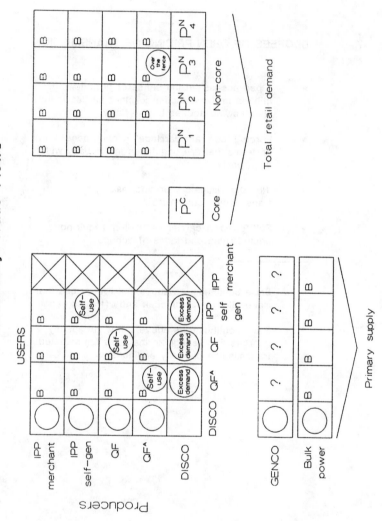

COMPETITION IN ELECTRICITY

transactions represented in Figure 3-5, input-output accounting is necessary to avoid counting the same electricity twice as it changes hands in the competitive system.

ENDNOTES

1. "A Contribution to the Theory of Taxation", *Economic Journal*, 37, 47-61.

2. "Optimal Departures From Marginal Cost Pricing", *American Economic Review*, June 1970, 60, 265-283, although such outstanding economists as Pigou, Hicks and Boiteaux had done earlier work in applying this principle to monopoly pricing.

CHAPTER 4: POLICY CHANGES AFFECTING NON-UTILITY GENERATORS

Electricity Consumers Resource Council (ELCON)

BACKGROUND

At the turn of the century, industrials were heavily self-generators. More than fifty percent of all electricity was generated by industrials. But the utility industry gave industrials two good reasons — technological and economic — to get out of the generating business. Utility economies of scale allowed utilities to lower the cost of generation — and, hence, the rates they charged for power purchases. Declining rates gave an economic signal to buy, rather than generate. The signal was very bright. By the 1970s, less than five percent of all electricity was generated by industrials.

Then, things changed. Inflation, interest rates, environmental concerns, anti-nuclear activities and, of course, skyrocketing fuel prices acted together to distort utility costs and raise rates.

The price signals sent to industrials clearly told them to reevaluate self-generation. We emphasize that the return to self-generation was not emotional — it simply was an economic reaction to rates that either were higher than cost of service or simply out of sync with economic reality. Business pressures required industrials, and others who had options, to take them. These actions have had severe impacts on many utilities; self-generation is taking load away.

Some utilities were caught in a vicious cycle that would continue to be played for years to come; having built too much capacity, they found errors compounded as existing load was forced to leave the system because of the resulting rate shock. And, as existing load left, utility excess capacity and/or rates rose even higher.

Congress saw that the events of the 1970s played havoc with the traditional regulatory structure. Under this structure, utilities have total control over generating, buying and selling electricity within their service territories. In exchange, they are regulated. The compact, which worked for decades, was disrupted.

What became apparent was that in times of strongly disruptive outside forces, the compact could not hold. Neither utility planning nor regulatory oversight was a match for the technical and economic pressures forcing change in the electricity industry in the 1970s. Congress addressed these pressures in 1978 and passed the Public Utility Regulatory Policies Act (PURPA). This bill created a new class of generators — the qualified facility (QF) — and gave this class certain benefits.

Utilities are not only monopolies, they are also monopsonies. They control their markets not only in terms of sales, but also in terms of purchases. This dual role has always given utilities great bargaining power, which they have used well.

PURPA removed the utility's authority to refuse to purchase energy from QFs. PURPA requires utilities to purchase electricity from generators that meet the characteristics spelled out carefully in FERC regulations implementing the law. PURPA also requires utilities to offer nondiscriminatory back-up, standby and maintenance power, and it relieves QFs from certain specified regulatory burdens.

PURPA has worked quite well. Many QFs have been built — more than 20 gigawatts in the United States at present. QFs have not caused reliability problems. Indeed, most QFs operate at higher capacity factors than utility generators and it is a well-accepted principle that there is higher reliability in multiplicity of sources.

WHERE ARE WE HEADED?

Technological innovation and economic forces have driven the electric utility industry to change. These forces will continue to influence the structure of the industry in the future. The status quo is not a realistic option. Change will occur.

Unfortunately, the change is happening in an unplanned or unstructured way. There are several ramifications we see in this unplanned or unstructured change.

First, utilities will be severely impacted by change. Those with excess capacity will try to sell. The "haves" will see increased competition as they search for new markets and ways to reach the markets. They may attempt to have unneeded capacity deregulated and made available on a spot market. They may test the boundaries of their service territories for new customers.

Those "haves" with natural advantages will push hard to reach bigger markets. For example, Canada, with its inexpensive hydropower, and utilities like Duke Power, which have shown that they can build generators efficiently, will want to build and sell to others in distant markets.

Utilities will be required to interconnect and integrate many new non-utility generators into their grids, whether the capacity is needed or not. Increasingly, utilities will be required to provide transmission to non-utility generators. Utilities will not be able to charge "exit" fees to departing loads and they will be expected to serve loads that return, although under better-defined terms and conditions.

Customers will not be immune to the change. They, too, will be divided into haves and have-nots; however, the division is not simply between residentials and industrials. The residentials of Geneva, Illinois, are haves. Many industrials without options are have-nots. The market is continuing to drive the installation of non-utility-owned, small-scale generation, especially in areas of excess capacity — and increasingly by non-industrial customers.

Large consumers, driven by economic forces to seek change, will be persistent and creative in their push to control electricity costs. They will do a number of things, including:

1. Push harder on regulators and legislators for changes in rules and laws to stimulate more competition.
2. Identify friends (such as municipals) who may have more immediate market flexibility and develop productive relationships with them.
3. Build power lines on their own property or perhaps even along abandoned railroad rights of way.
4. If all else fails, exercise their last resort — something they hate to do: they will move (or threaten to move) to obtain electricity at costs that will keep them in business. This is a very expensive action for an industrial to take, for obvious reasons. But it can happen and will happen if push comes to shove. Moves such as this are desperation moves; the large consumer simply has no choice.

Regulators also will be drawn into the fray. Commissions

will be forced to deal with equity issues that get stickier with each case. As an example, PUCs cannot stop customers from cogenerating, even if it means leaving so-called "stranded investments" for other customers to pay.

However, increasingly PUCs will be asked to rule that wheeling transactions, — even if they leave similar "stranded investments" — are "better" than cogeneration because they don't result in the construction of new generating capacity, especially in areas where excess capacity already exists.

Commissions will be forced to deal with equally sticky technical issues, such as whether the addition of a QF at a load center might not "free up" transmission capacity for other uses. A particular example that bears careful watching is the addition of 800 megawatts — or maybe even 1,600 MW — of Bahamian power to the Miami area. Will this reduce the north-to-south loadings sufficiently to allow substantial third-party wheeling in other areas of the state?

Commissions also may find new or newly defined federal/state jurisdiction issues. There is no doubt that FERC has jurisdiction over transactions that clearly are interstate in nature. However, we hear more and more that certain wheeling arrangements only move money, not electrons. If so, can one demonstrate that there is an interstate transaction? If not, do state PUCs have jurisdiction?

The immediate result of these changes is that the transaction costs of the confrontations, negotiations and litigation we have described will keep many lawyers happily employed for a long time.

THERE'S A BETTER WAY

Send Better Price Signals

A major effort should be made to send consumers better price signals. We should recognize, however, that this is only a start. No one can set perfect prices. Even if they could, it wouldn't produce optimum results in the electric industry unless it's done in every other market throughout the economy.

Give Competition a Chance to Work

What *will* produce better results is to give competition

more room to work within the framework of regulation. We know that increasing competition will drive us toward economic efficiency. We know that the free market brings the greatest efficiency. The question is how much efficiency should be introduced and how much regulatory protection should be retained.

Competitive bidding is a step in adjusting the balance between market freedom and regulatory protection that keeps the industry in sync with changing outside forces.

ELCON members are strong supporters of competitive bidding. As *consumers*, they think they have a lot to gain in competitive bidding. They know the process well. They ask for bids to buy their raw materials and they compete against other companies to make bids to sell their finished products. They know it drives economic efficiency.

One of the most significant forces changing the utility industry is that over the last few years there have been some very inefficient power procurement decisions — decisions that have been based on a variety of inefficient or inaccurate notions, such as a need to achieve economies of scale, a need for a preconceived fuel mix, or the questionable notion that electric utilities must get off oil and gas.

Competitive bidding won't tolerate inefficiencies, which is why consumers like it so much. We think it is very good for all consumers.

We must be careful, however, as bidding is implemented. If not fair and nondiscriminatory, bidding can be harmful to consumers and cogenerators.

Why are we concerned? PURPA created a new class of generators in QFs while continuing to recognize the monopsony power of utilities. In the delicate new balance, the cogenerators, the utility and the utility's customers all benefit from each other.

Our concern is that we are changing the delicate balance by adding competition at the *selling* end without making any offsetting change at the buying end.

There *is* room for improvement. At present, there is QF-to-QF competition in electricity sales to utilities, but it is an unstructured kind of competition. It is first-come, first-served competition. It can be like the lawyers' "race to the courthouse" to get your bid into the utility before others have had a chance to negotiate their own contract.

The present system gives utilities a chance to make QFs bid against each other unfairly. It is a time-consuming process to negotiate a sales contract with a utility. It can take years to complete, involving thousands of elements. And, sometimes, there are questions about the honesty and integrity of the negotiations. State commissioners certainly cannot scrutinize every detail of every contract to ensure fairness, nor should they.

Competitive bidding does away with many of these drawbacks and offers a number of its own advantages. As examples:

Lower prices for purchased power. Because everyone bids on a clearly defined proposal for power with clearly specified criteria, the total universe of competing cogeneration capacity and the total dollar figure to be spent on it are readily apparent.

A more efficient power supply. Any successful bidder would have to meet both cost and reliability standards. Inefficient generators — either utility or non-utility — would not be able to stand the rigors of the bidding test.

De-emphasis on political concerns. Utilities would focus on low price and reliability — on getting solid contractual guarantees from bidders that the power contracted for will be available when promised, as promised — without regard to such political or social concerns as the "appropriate" fuel mix and "desirable" environmental characteristics.

Transfer of risk, especially for fuel price changes. Utilities would contract for electricity at specified prices. Fuel price escalators and other fuel concerns would be specified.

"Better" avoided cost estimates. The avoided cost estimate should be the ceiling for both utility purchases and for a utility's own construction of generating plants. We believe that this will motivate utilities to do a better job in estimating and publishing avoided cost estimates.

Furthermore, it has been shown that competitive bidding can work in practice. We have the experiences of the states of Maine and Massachusetts as evidence. At ELCON's seminar on electricity last October, both Commissioner Keegan from Massachusetts and Commissioner Moskovitz from Maine reported that bidding works well to ration capacity and promote the development of economically efficient cogeneration.

The often-cited but little-documented fear of contract

"problems" need not materialize. Utilities will write tough, solid contracts with outside providers that stipulate how much power will be available, when it will be available, for how much and under what conditions. Utilities write complex contracts for coal; why not for electricity produced from coal? They write contracts for purchases from other IOUs across a region and from Canada; why not from IPPs?

The point is that competitive bidding can be an orderly improvement over the current way cogenerated power is sold to utilities. But what concerns the members of ELCON is that in trying to improve the process, society may lose all that it has gained.

The biggest reason for apprehension is the natural fear of large, powerful entities with carefully carved territories that say, "Trust me." Utilities want in on the bidding, and they say they'll be fair; they say they won't self-deal.

But frankly, it is difficult for customers to believe these assertions. We remember that all too often these are the same utilities that brought us $5,000-per-kilowatt plants and then emphasized over and over again that the 14-cent power coming from their plants was better for customers than the 4-cent power non-utilities were producing. They are the same utilities that brought us power plants with 60-percent capacity factors and then told us that 95-percent capacity factors on IPPs will cause a less reliable power supply.

And they are the same ones that brought us cross-class subsidies and now try to kid glove certain industrial customers with super-low rates without first trying to correct the improper price signals that are exacerbating — if not causing — the problem.

The notion of "letting the camel's nose in under the tent" via competitive bidding frightens consumers. It also raises a legal question. Legislation established the balance in PURPA. Can regulation change that balance? The answer is clearly "no." Regulators must respect the fact that PURPA gave qualified facilities bargaining power. Bidding legally can't take that bargaining power away.

Economic theory says that increasing the number of sellers in a market while maintaining the status of a monopsonist increases the ability of the monopsonist to exploit. This has been shown in single-employer company towns, where increasing the competition between sellers may actually leave the town worse off.

Fortunately, there is a way to bring change without upsetting the balance. It draws on the lessons learned in the ongoing state experiences. It implements what state regulators have been saying for some time. It takes only a small modification to FERC's proposal.

First, bidding should be limited to QFs unless all the bidders are given guaranteed access to multiple markets. Without an increase in the number of buyers, there should be no appreciable increase in the number of sellers (except, of course, those new entrants willing to compete under PURPA as it now stands).

And all bidding, whether it involves QFs or a larger universe of power providers, must be fair and nondiscriminatory. There are ways to ensure that this happens. Certainly, transmission access is one way. However, a well-structured bidding process would also do it. The process should include an advance notice of the request for bids with clearly detailed criteria, it should provide sufficient time for bids to be prepared, it should be done in a completely open, nondiscriminatory manner, and it should provide for PUC oversight.

This bidding process will not exclude IPPs. However, they will be included along with other sources of generation rather than directly in the bidding process.

The ceiling on bids should continue to be the calculated avoided cost of the utility. And that avoided cost should be the ceiling not only for QF or independently produced power, but for all sources of power — the utility's own construction projects, utility-affiliated power, Canadian-Bahamian-Mexican power, federal marketing administration power, coop power, muni power, other public power and other IOU power, to name just a few of the possible sources.

These are all sources of electrons; no one's electrons are better than any one else's. The ones that should be used are the ones that cost the least, all else equal.

What we are saying is that we believe that it would be inappropriate and legally deficient to implement all-source competitive bidding without access to transmission.

It would be inappropriate because it would upset the careful balance created by PURPA between maintaining the monopsony power granted utilities by their exclusive service territories and encouraging the development of efficient, non-utility-owned generation. It would be legally deficient because it would create a harmful, anti-competitive condition.

More specifically, the FERC is obligated by the Federal-Power Act "maintain" competition to the maximum extent possible consistent with the public interest.[1] Additionally, it is well established that FERC's regulatory power over electric utilities "clearly carries with it the responsibility to consider, in appropriate circumstances, the anti-competitive effects of regulated aspects on interstate utility operations".[2] Given the potentially discriminatory and anti-competitive consequences of a competitive bidding program, the Commission is not only fully empowered but obligated to condition the voluntary implementation of such a program on the participating utility's agreement to offer wheeling to all generators — notably, the QFs and IPPs who are unsuccessful bidders on a nondiscriminatory basis. The most relevant precedent here, of course, is the recent D.C. Circuit Court of Appeals decision regarding FERC Order No. 436.[3] Although the court ultimately vacated and remanded Order No. 436 on other grounds, it upheld the nondiscriminatory access condition as a reasonable and appropriate exercise of the Commission's authority to prevent undue discrimination.

ELCON submits that parallel findings to those underlying Order No. 436 exist with equal force here. First, electric utilities clearly have and are continuing to exert monopoly power over non-utility generators of electricity who lack transmission access. Second, the impact of this monopoly power is to deny potential sellers of electric power access to the market and thereby deprive consumers of the benefits of a competitive electric generation market. To the extent competitive bidding will perpetuate and, more likely, exacerbate this discriminatory situation, its voluntary use must be conditioned upon the utility's willingness to provide wheeling and, thereby, access to the electric power market.

A competitive bidding program, alone, utterly fails to address the monopsony market power that utilities have over transmission, and fails to recognize the studied reluctance of utilities to wheel for QFs, which has led to market distortions and resulting inefficiencies. Thus, only by conditioning bidding systems upon an agreement by participating utilities to engage in conduct truly reflective of a free market can

FERC's competitive bid guidelines pass muster.

The issue is not the goal, but the method. Where do we factor all of these non-utility generators into the process? Do we do it above or below the avoided cost calculation?

ELCON in no way criticizes all-source competitive bidding. We think it makes a lot of sense. And we think it should be pursued.

However, real life experience shows that bidding can produce widely varying results, depending on how it is implemented. Only where there is true competition can economic efficiencies be achieved. We think FERC should proceed to implement all-source bidding, but it must be conditioned on true competition. The states have shown the way.

We can see the day when utilities purchase electricity the same way they purchase fuels today. They will make potential suppliers compete. They will negotiate contracts specifying the terms and conditions under which they will receive and pay for power. But for this to work, non-utility generators must have options, as fuel suppliers now do. Otherwise, utilities will exploit their monopsony powers and deal with their affiliates.

Continue to Rely on Appropriately-Determined Avoided Cost Ceilings

Exclusive service territories give utilities unique and potent power over cogenerators. They are monopolists by refusing to wheel backup, maintenance or standby power from other sources, and they are monopsonists when they refuse to wheel the cogenerator's power to other prospective buyers.

Congress recognized the monopsony and monopoly powers granted to utilities by the governmentally guaranteed service territory. With PURPA, Congress tried to protect QFs from these monopoly and monopsony powers without upsetting the service territory.

PURPA requires utilities either to buy all the energy produced by a cogenerator or wheel the energy to a distant utility. The choice is strictly controlled by the utility. *De facto*, wheeling is not a viable option because utilities do not agree to wheel.

The cogenerator has no influence over the utility's decision. Neither does the cogenerator have any option or re-

70   COMPETITION IN ELECTRICITY

course if the utility makes a decision that is harmful to the cogenerator. PURPA thus changes neither the monopsony nor the monopoly status of the utility.

The avoided cost provisions of PURPA, and the rules implementing these provisions of the act, have worked well. Neither the rules nor the act mandate any rate for purchase. Rather, they place a *ceiling* on rates equal to the purchasing utility's avoided cost, recognizing that payments in excess of the actual costs avoided would require other customers to subsidize the cogenerator.

Actual rates paid for purchased QF power are negotiated on a case-by-case basis for large cogenerators. Utilities and cogenerators negotiate contracts at arm's length taking into consideration the length of the contract, termination procedure penalties for non-compliance, the ability to dispatch, timing of schedule outages, etc. In nearly every instance, large QFs are paid less that avoided costs.

This point was documented in a recent study prepared for the U.S. Department of Energy.[4] Specifically, this report states:

"Most large QFs must negotiate rates somewhat below full avoided cost to obtain concessions for the utility in certain contractual matters not guaranteed under Section 210 (e.g., levelized payment, long-term contracts, etc.) but which are frequently necessary to obtain project financing. For example, in 1982, the Southern California Edison Company (SEC) testified that the average purchase for rate contracts it had negotiated with 60 QFs for over 1000 MW of capacity, was 93 percent of full avoided cost. The full avoided cost rate, SEC noted, was appropriate and paid for projects involving "emerging technologies" (i.e., solar, wind, and geothermal). Similarly, Houston Lighting and Power Company has signed contracts for over 500 MW of cogeneration capacity at rates reportedly *below* its full avoided costs. As noted below, Maine utilities have negotiated over 150 MW of QF contracts under a quasi-competitive bidding scheme at rates *below* avoided costs as calculated under applicable state regulation. Similar purchase agreements at rates below avoided costs have been negotiated by a number of other utilities in other jurisdictions."

There certainly are examples of utilities purchasing QF power at rates that exceed avoided costs. These examples include purchases from "standard offers" (such as in California and Idaho), and from state-legislated rates (such as New York's 6 cents/kWh law).

However, these examples (1) often are self-correcting and (2) are not the creatures of PURPA. Regarding the former, the regulatory commissions of California and Idaho recently reconsidered earlier orders. They now require substantially lower payments for the purchase of QF power.

Specifically, several years ago the Idaho Public Utilities Commission ordered Idaho Power Company to pay more than 70 mills/kWh for purchased cogeneration and small power-production (C & SPP) power. This price signal was very attractive to prospective C & SPP developers. Idaho Power signed for approximately 55 MW — or two to three percent of its total load. Other C & SPP developers indicated that another 200 MW may be installed.

Idaho Power took several steps to have the rate adjusted downward. The Commission responded. First, the Commission issued an interim order in 1985, lowering the rate to approximately 40 mills. Second, the Commission issued a final order setting the rate at 20 -48 mills, depending upon the date signed and the duration of the contract.[5]

Of more importance, not only are above-avoided-cost rates not created by PURPA, they are in violation of PURPA. This act specifies that avoided cost is the ceiling for rates for purchase of QF power. Individual *state* regulatory commissions balance the needs and desires of their citizens and utilities in implementing the PURPA provisions in their states. PURPA has not caused above-avoided-cost rates, and changes in federal law will not remedy the situation. Proper state implementation is the key.

ELCON carefully studied the avoided cost issue. We proposed several years ago that certain principles be followed in establishing rates for purchases of cogenerated power. Specifically:[6]

- Contracts setting forth pricing structures for avoided energy and capacity purchases should allow arm's length negotiations between the utility and a cogenerator.
- All cogenerators selling non-firm energy at one point in time to a utility should receive a payment based on the same methodology for calculating avoided energy costs.

COMPETITION IN ELECTRICITY

The actual payment to individual cogenerators could be different due to differences in delivery characteristics, etc.

- Capacity payments for purchases of non-firm power are warranted if the utility avoids capacity costs. Payments for purchases of non-firm cogenerated power should be for energy only if it is demonstrated that the purchases do not allow the utility to avoid capacity costs.
- Purchases of cogenerated energy should include payments for avoided fuel, variable operating and maintenance expenses, start-up and shutdown expenses and energy losses that are avoided because of the purchase of cogenerated power.
- Capacity payment should be made for purchases of firm power.
- If a performance standard is imposed by a utility on a cogenerator, the standard should be no more stringent than the performance of the utility's units.
- The method selected to calculate avoided costs should be rigorous and must be carefully monitored to be certain that it is producing reasonable estimates.

We believe these principles are as applicable today as they were then.

CONCLUSION

The electric utility industry is changing. It is becoming more competitive. We believe strongly that relevant questions should focus not on whether it will become more competitive — but only when and how the competition will be introduced.

This does not mean that the industry will be deregulated. Indeed it won't, and it shouldn't be.

It does mean that competitive forces can and should replace certain aspects of administrative regulation where competition can and does exist.

One such area involves power procurement. There presently are many utility-owned generators providing power to the grid. Additionally, however, there are many non-utility-owned generators providing very reliable supplies of power at locations geographically dispersed throughout the grid.

Economic and technological forces convince us that new non-utility-owned generators — perhaps many of them — will be added in the future. This will increase the competitiveness of the industry. It will add capacity, often precisely where it is least needed. It will leave so-called "stranded investments." And it will force regulators, charged with balancing the needs of consumers with utilities, to review and renew policies over many aspects of the electric utility industry.

Many PUCs already have been confronted with proposals that dramatically increase the competitiveness of certain aspects of the electric industry. They have taken the challenge and carefully carried out real life experiments that prove that competition can work. Maine and Massachusetts bidding and Texas wheeling experiments come vividly to mind.

Walking down the competitive path can — and should — involve careful, reasonable and reasoned steps. Moving to a fully competitive market is not like jumping a chasm, you don't have to take it all in; one bound.

ELCON believes strongly that steps toward increased access can be taken while protecting the reliability and integrity of the system. Specifically, ELCON recommends the implementation of a procedure such as that outlined below.

Under such a proposal, customers, including cogenerators, could request a wheeling order. The appropriate regulatory commission would have to make a public interest finding in accordance with applicable laws and rules of procedure. In making such a finding, the commission could address critical issues such as obligation to serve; length of the contract term; availability, terms and conditions of back-up service; and minimum size of the transaction.

A critical component of the procedure involves the establishment of a rebuttable presumption that the capability to wheel exists. This would force utilities to place data into the record regarding power flows that now are unavailable from a practical standpoint.

Regulatory authorities would have the authority to order wheeling. Commissions would not assume that the status quo necessarily is optimal. Commissions would have the authority to order the construction of both new transmission lines and appropriate modifications to existing lines to facilitate wheeling if the net costs associated with the request are

74   COMPETITION IN ELECTRICITY

borne by the wheeling applicant and the utility is unable to demonstrate significant adverse impact on the system. Commissions would not offer wheeling unless and until it is determined that adequate capability and capacity exists or will exist with the commencement of the transaction. Published wheeling tariffs would be cost-based and nondiscriminatory. Individually negotiated arms-length contracts among the applicable parties would also be acceptable provided that they meet the specified terms.

Utilities would be required to treat all entities in a nondiscriminatory way. Customers returning to the system would be treated exactly the same as any other new customer. Wheeling services would be available for either part or all of the applicant's load.

Implementation of such a procedure would allow commissions to determine, on a case-by-case basis, where wheeling can take place without harming customers or the reliability of the system. It would not allow willy-nilly shopping around. It would authorize responsible and sensible transactions to take place and provide "test-case" data before proceeding to a system of mandatory, common carriers.

We do urge reliance on competitive bidding in power procurement. Non-utility-owned cogeneration is here, and will grow. It is not subversive. It does give consumers freedom from noncompetitive utility rates and cross-class subsidies. It should be controlled by the cost of alternative power sources.

In the larger picture, we believe that access is the ultimate question. It is a question that must be dealt with before we can have a truly efficient electricity system. We never can have a truly competitive, nondiscriminatory bidding system without access. We look forward to working with this Committee as we move toward this longer term solution.

RECOMMENDED POLICY STATEMENT ON OBTAINING TRANSMISSION WHEELING SERVICES

Wheeling Eligibility

• Users, including cogenerators, desiring wheeling services should make a request of the appropriate regulatory commission for a public interest finding in accordance with applicable laws and rules of procedures.

- In making the public interest finding, the Commission can address such issues as:

1. Minimum size of the wheeled transaction
2. Length of the contract term
3. Backup service
4. Obligation to serve

The Utility's Role

- Nondiscriminatory treatment of all entities involved.
- Rebuttable presumption that capacity to wheel exists.
- Customers returning to the system must be treated exactly the same as any other new customer.
- Wheeling services should be available for part of an applicant's load or the total load itself.

The Commission's Role

- The appropriate commission should have the authority to order wheeling.
- The public interest finding should not necessarily assume that the status quo is optimal.
- Commissions should have the authority to order the construction of both new transmission lines and appropriate modifications to existing lines to facilitate wheeling if the net costs associated with the request are borne by that wheeling applicant and the utility is unable to demonstrate significant adverse impact on the system.
- Commissions should not order wheeling unless and until it is determined that adequate capability and capacity exist or will exist with the commencement of the transaction.
- Published wheeling tariffs should be cost-based and non-discriminatory.
- Individually negotiated arms-length contracts among the applicable parties may also be acceptable provided that they meet the terms specified above.

ENDNOTES

1. *Otter Tail Power Company v. U.S.*, U.S. 366,374 (1973).
2. *Gulf States Utilities Company v. FPC*, 411 U.S. 747,758-59 (1973).
3. *Associated Gas Distributors v. FERC*, F. 2nd (D.C. Circuit No. 85-1811) (June 23, 1987).
4. Pfeffer, Lindsay and Associates, *Emerging Policy Issues in PURPA Implementation*, a report, prepared for the U.S. Department of Energy, Contract No. PEACOI-83-70404, March 1986, page 5.37.
5. Idaho Public Utilities Commission, "In the Matter of Application of Idaho Power Company for New Cogeneration/Small Power Production Rates," Case No. V-1006-248, Order No. 20402, April 18, 1986, p. 23.
6. *Issues Facing Industrial Cogenerators*, Electricity Consumers Resource Council (ELCON), Washington, DC, February 1984, pp. 12-15.

SECTION C

STATE BIDDING EXPERIMENTS FOR WHOLESALE SUPPLY

CHAPTER 5: POWER PROCUREMENT: SHOULD COMPETITIVE BIDDING BE REQUIRED?*

Robert J. Keegan
Former Commissioner, Massachusetts Department of Public Utilities

INTRODUCTION

Section 210 of the Public Utilities Regulatory Policies Act of 1978 (PURPA) was passed by Congress in an effort to remove institutional and regulatory impediments facing the developers of cogeneration and small power production facilities who desired to sell electricity to public utility companies. Under Section 210, a facility (qualifying facility, or QF) that meets the qualifying criteria established by the Federal Energy Regulatory Commission (FERC) pursuant to PURPA is exempt from classification and regulation as a utility. Public utilities, in turn, are required to purchase electricity from QFs. In addition, PURPA requires that the price applied to such purchases must be just and reasonable to the customers of the purchasing utility and may not be discriminatory against small power producers and cogenerators. Specifically, the price prescribed may not exceed "the incremental cost to the electric utility of alternate electric energy." [16 U.S.C. 825a-3]

Based on the experiences of the 1970s there was ample justification for the passage of PURPA. The United States, having just witnessed a severe energy crisis, was faced with a clear reluctance on the part of electric utilities to deal fairly with cogenerators and small power producers. Congress, noting the potential gains in efficiency available from a better integration of QF supplies with traditional utility supplies, enacted in PURPA a mandatory framework for such coordination.

A key provision of PURPA was a reliance on individual

These comments were presented by Commissioner Keegan as testimony before the United States House of Representatives at the oversight hearing on cogeneration and PURPA conducted on September 22, 1987, by Representative Philip R. Sharp presiding as Chairman over the Subcommittee on Energy and Power of the Committee on Energy and Commerce.

state public utility commissions (PUCs) to prescribe specific standards, within Federal Energy Regulatory Commission (FERC) guidelines, that would be applied to determine the prices, and terms and conditions that would hold for transactions between utilities and QFs. The early experience of state PUCs in implementing the requirements of PURPA and administratively determining avoided cost prices has provided mixed results.

Some PUCs adopted avoided-cost rules and standard contract provisions so favorable to QFs that a veritable flood of contracts swamped the utilities. As typified by California, such approaches made it virtually impossible for utilities to integrate QFs into their supply planning processes. These approaches also left the ratepayers of those states as the guarantors for clearly uneconomic QF projects.

Other PUCs adopted approaches so conservative that PURPA had virtually no impact on power planning in their states. In Massachusetts, for example, PURPA regulations adopted in 1981 basically institutionalized prior difficulties encountered by QFs in negotiations with utilities. Those rules failed to recognize the dominant bargaining power of a utility in a one-to-one negotiating session with a QF located in its service territory. As a result, ratepayers in that state failed to obtain many of the efficiency advantages that might otherwise have been offered by QFs.

Based on these early experiences, a number of states have revised their approaches to PURPA. This process has given birth to a second generation of PURPA regulations. The PUCs instituting such revisions have benefited from the experiences of the late 1970s and early 1980s. In general, the new regulations show a greater level of sophistication on the part of the PUCs in integrating QF supplies into the overall utility planning process. Equally important, such regulations tend to incorporate a more market-based approach, one that is designed to result in a greater level of benefits to ratepayers than earlier administrative approaches.

PURPA ACCOMPLISHMENTS

Despite these early implementation difficulties, PURPA has affected a number of significant accomplishments.

COMPETITION IN ELECTRICITY

PURPA has succeeded in opening the electric generation market to a variety of non-utility providers. It has in many instances overcome the monopsony power of electric utilities and given PUCs, as well as the industry, invaluable experience in attempting to integrate non-utility supplies into the overall mix of electric generation. In addition, the avoided cost standard has resulted in an increased familiarity with value of service-pricing principles and efforts to approximate the market clearing price which would be derived in a truly competitive market for electric generation.

The amount of competition which electric utilities have seen develop from QFs, however, has not resulted from PURPA alone. Competition has developed because the generation segment of the electric utility industry has undergone fundamental changes in its cost structure. Escalating costs for the construction of large central generating stations, combined with reductions in fossil fuel costs, have undermined the strategy of substituting capital for fuel and deprived many utilities of their traditional role of being the least-cost provider of electric service. The economies of scale associated with generating electricity, which the industry had succeeded in capturing for decades, appear to have been exhausted as the size of central generating stations has increased to the 1,000 megawatt range. Meanwhile, technological advances in generating electricity efficiently in smaller quantities and in smaller facilities has made electric generation from non-utility providers more attractive and competitive.

Escalating electricity prices have also made investments in conservation and load management more economically attractive than before. In addition, state PUCs have recognized the need to send price signals which more accurately communicate on a time-differentiated basis the real cost of electric service. This has resulted in the development of rate structures which rely more on marginal costs than embedded costs.

These fundamental changes in the electric industry have contributed significantly to the increased role which QFs are playing in meeting our nation's electric needs. As the proportion of electricity from these non-utility suppliers increases, it becomes more important to ensure that they are fully integrated into a coherent utility planning and procurement strategy. Therefore, state PUCs have begun to focus on regulatory changes which will promote an integrated supply and demand planning and procurement strategy by electric utilities that will result in the development of a least-cost means of meeting electric service requirements. It is within the context of the increasing array of competitively priced supply and demand options for meeting electric needs, and not just in the limited context of PURPA, that competitive bidding systems and FERC's recent initiatives in this area need to be evaluated. This analysis must also be made in the context of the potential that competitive bidding systems have for bringing the efficiencies that derive from competitive market forces to the process of choosing between these options.

THE MASSACHUSETTS BIDDING SYSTEM

On August 25, 1986, following eighteen months of hearings and investigation, the Massachusetts Department of Public Utilities ("Department") adopted final regulations implementing a competitive bidding system for establishing eligibility of small power producers and cogenerators to enter into long-term contracts for the sale of their electrical output to electric utility companies. These rules, codified in 220 C.M.R. 8.00, were promulgated by the Department pursuant to Sections 201 and 210 of Title II of PURPA.

In the Department's investigation concerning appropriate modifications to its initial regulations implementing PURPA, the following objectives for establishing an appropriate wholesale price structure were identified and explicitly set out in an interim order issued on September 12, 1985 in D.P.U. 84-276:

- optimization of the electric industry;
- consistency between utility pricing policy and non-utility pricing policy;
- matching investment risks and investment rewards;
- elimination of non-price barriers to development; and
- simplicity of wholesale price structure.

The competitive bidding system established by the De-

COMPETITION IN ELECTRICITY

partment was designed with the intent of fulfilling these objectives.

Under the new rules, each jurisdictional retail electric company is required to issue annually a request for proposals (RFP) indicating the amount of capacity and energy (supply block) it is interested in purchasing from QFs under long-term contracts. The amount of capacity and energy which a utility is required to put out for bid each year must be equal to five percent of the utility's peak demand in the previous year, or its actual need for new capacity, whichever is larger. The calculation of this supply block must be based on the utility's optimal demand and supply plan for a twenty year period.

In addition to specifying the amount of capacity and energy being solicited, each RFP must include the utility's avoided cost and indicate the degree to which specific non-price criteria will be relied on in selecting the winning proposals. The avoided-cost calculation of each utility will include, where applicable to a utility's specific situation, a long-run energy cost component, a capitalized energy cost component, and a long-run capacity cost component. These cost components are to be derived on the basis of a utility's optimal resource supply plan. The long-run energy cost component must be supported by production cost calculations for the twenty-year planning horizon. Capitalized energy cost projections are to be derived on the basis of the difference between the projected capital cost of a peaking facility and the cost estimates for potential investments in new generating facilities, conservation and load management measures, and long-run power purchases. Long-run capacity costs are to be calculated according to the levelized real revenue requirement of a utility peaking plant excluding fuel costs and variable operating and maintenance expenses.

The utility's calculation of its avoided costs will result in a ceiling price against which QFs will bid. The ceiling price will contain a peak and off-peak time-differentiated energy rate and, if the utility anticipates a need for new capacity in the near future, a capacity component. If there is no anticipated need for additional capacity during the planning horizon, the avoided cost will be based on an estimate of the time-differentiated value of displacement energy only. While QFs are competing against the ceiling price developed by the utility from its avoided-cost calculations, they are also competing against each other in the bidding process.

The RFPs issued annually by utilities are also required to specify any non-price criteria (e.g., dispatchability, location relative to load centers, level of progress in obtaining permits, etc.) which the utility will be evaluating in selecting winning proposals. The RFPs must also indicate the relative importance which will be attached to each non-price criteria. Thus, bidding QFs will be able to estimate prior to the submission of their proposals the score they will receive pursuant to the ranking formula contained in the RFP. The ranking formula proposed by a utility must recognize continuous trade-offs in net ratepayer benefits between the various measurable criteria used to score QF proposals. The ultimate goal of a utility's ranking formula must be to maximize net benefits to ratepayers. All RFPs are required to be submitted to the Department for approval based on a review and evaluation of the supply block, avoided-cost calculations, and ranking formula for both price and non-price criteria.

Under this scheme, the winning bidders in the solicitation will have the right to enter into long-term, fixed-price standard contracts with the electric utility. The selected bidders also have an obligation to make a modest "earnest money" payment of $15 per kilowatt of installed capacity at the time they sign the contract. This money is forfeited to the utility under a schedule set forth in the regulations if the QF is unable to meet its contractual obligations.

The Massachusetts regulations are designed to carry out the purposes of PURPA by creating an environment which will stimulate the development of QFs, while protecting ratepayers from paying an excessive amount for QF power. This approach undertakes to integrate the development of QF power into the utility's planning process by requiring an annual solicitation based on the utility's actual need for power. The annual review will also allow the utility to compare the amount of QF capacity contracted for in previous years with the amount actually delivered, permitting a refinement to each successive year's solicitation. It is further designed to encourage competition among QFs, bringing to ratepayers the advantages of a market-based price.

ADVANTAGES OF COMPETITIVE BIDDING SYSTEMS

The market-based approach to PURPA adopted by Massachusetts, and variants of this theme developed by other states, may have major ramifications for other aspects of public utility regulation. For example, many state PUCs are reviewing the rules under which utility-owned generation will be treated in the future. Such examinations encompass fundamental issues concerning the role of regulation in utility power planning, the rights and obligations of public utilities in serving the public, and the rights and obligations of consumers of electric power. Ultimately, what is to be decided in these reviews is the form of the social contract between the public and the serving utilities.

In such analyses, PUCs are looking at the possibility of a more market-based ratemaking standard for utility-owned generation. (See, for example, *Electric Generation*, Massachusetts DPU Docket No. 86-36, April 1987). Such an approach would place a greater share of the risks and rewards of utility generation investment on the utility managers and, ultimately, on the utility shareholders. It could thereby solve many of the problems of perverse incentives inherent in rate-base regulation.

An underlying assumption of proposals to expand the competitive bidding experiments being conducted by PUCs into all-source bidding systems is that utilities or independent power producers (IPPs) do not have the type of market power that requires the current form of pervasive economic regulation. Deregulated rates for all-source generation, based on a market-determined value or usefulness of investment, requires the demonstrated existence of a sufficiently competitive generation market to ensure an adequate supply of electricity available at a reasonable cost. Most observers would agree that, at present, the existence of a sufficiently competitive market for electric generation has not been demonstrated. Such a showing would be necessary before PUCs would be able to implement a ratemaking standard employing pure market rates determined solely by competitive bidding.

The states' experiments with more market-based approaches to PURPA, however, can be viewed as a first step in the development of a competitive electric generation market. As the states gain more experience with the implementation of the type of PURPA regulations discussed here, they will be able to conclude whether there exists a potential competitive market for electric generation. If so, the current form of regulation of electric utility investments can be expected to change dramatically and all-source competitive bidding, incorporating IPPs and conservation and load management initiatives, may become a reality. If, however, natural monopoly characteristics of scale economies and barriers to market entry reemerge in electric generation, then the expansion of competitive bidding systems beyond their current limited PURPA role may be clearly inappropriate or undesirable.

The competitive bidding experiment for QFs being conducted in Massachusetts offers the opportunity for the PUC to evaluate the nature and characteristics of the market for electric generation. It must be clearly understood, however, that this effort represents an experiment designed to elicit additional information before expansion of the system for other uses is considered appropriate. The system has therefore been designed with a number of protections which we view as critical at this point in the experiment.

It requires utilities to develop plans for how they would intend to meet their obligation to serve over an appropriate planning horizon and then requires them to test the relative economics of their solutions in the market through competitive bidding. The utility continues to bear the obligation to serve, and if the bidding system reveals that the utility's proposal represents the least-cost approach to meeting its obligation, then the utility would proceed with its plan. The ratemaking treatment applied to such utility projects could be based on cost of service principles or rely more on a market-based approach for setting prices based on the results of a competitive bidding system.

It is also important to be able to adjust competitive bidding systems to ensure that they result in a desirable generation mix for each utility. The Massachusetts system attempts to accomplish this by allowing each utility to establish specific technical criteria in its RFP so that the utility can exercise a degree of control over how it meets its obligation to serve. In the first round of RFPs submitted to the

88   COMPETITION IN ELECTRICITY

PUC in Massachusetts, there were significant differences in the weight given different technical criteria based on the system profile and needs of individual utilities. It is important that states be able to retain the flexibility to implement and adjust bidding systems which appropriately respond to the specific circumstances encountered in each state and by each utility company.

The requirement that RFPs contain the specific technical criteria being considered and the degree to which they will be weighted and relied on in the final selection process is extremely important to the success of the Massachusetts bidding system. This requirement makes the solicitation and selection process open and reviewable by all parties and minimizes the suspicions concerning utility self-dealing.

RECENT FERC INITIATIVES

FERC has recently held a number of regional hearings to help it assess the current status of PURPA implementation and to determine whether modifications to its original PURPA regulations are either necessary or appropriate. At the hearing held in Boston, the Massachusetts PUC indicated the following:

> "In general, we believe that the current PURPA regulations are adequate to carry out the purposes of PURPA in a manner that gives the state PUCs the discretion to experiment with alternative approaches that might provide greater benefits to ratepayers. Accordingly, we do not feel that any revisions to the regulations are required."

The Massachusetts PUC views its competitive bidding system as entirely compatible with the letter and intent of PURPA. It believes that the method of determining avoided costs through a bidding system has significant advantages over methods which administratively determine avoided costs. No changes in FERC's PURPA regulations, therefore, are necessary to allow state PUCs to continue to refine their PURPA implementation strategies.

From recent statements by Chairman Hesse, however, it has become clear that FERC recognizes that PURPA must be integrated more fully into utility planning processes in a manner which is consistent with the fundamental changes in the industry's cost structure. FERC's indication that it seeks to lessen the institutional and regulatory barriers currently limiting the participation of non-QF IPPs in competitive bidding systems is a positive step. We see no reason why state PUCs conducting competitive bidding experiments should not be able, if they determine it appropriate, to allow IPPs to participate equally with QFs in such systems. We agree with Chairman Hesse that there are additional economies which the competitive bidding system can capture if it is extended to IPPs as well as other supply and demand options.

We are, however, concerned that FERC may intend to go further than simply removing the regulatory barriers to IPP participation in competitive bidding systems. Any action on the part of FERC which would mandate that state bidding systems be structured in a specified way will be detrimental to the further development of competitive bidding experiments. The states are making significant progress in developing systems which are tailored to the specific circumstances and characteristics of the markets emerging in the individual states and individual utility company service territories. It is essential that the PUCs continue to have the flexibility to adjust whatever system they implement in a way which responds to the markets they see developing. Any standardization of bidding approaches required by FERC at this time would have the seriously detrimental effect of constraining further experimentation in this important area and deprive regulators of the benefits of learning from the successes and mistakes of PUCs in other states. It is largely because of the experience gained from the different approaches used by the states to implement PURPA over the past eight years, both the mistakes as well as the successes, that we have come so far today. FERC should take no action at this point in the development of bidding systems which would limit the availability of information which will result from states seeking to develop ever better approaches to these issues.

We therefore encourage FERC in its efforts to allow states to expand their bidding systems to incorporate supplies from non-QF developers. Such efforts will provide states with the opportunity to test further the degree to which a viable competitive market for electric generation can be relied upon in choosing supplies and setting prices. It is essential, however, that FERC not presume that there is a single competitive bidding framework which is appropriate to implement in all states and in all situations. It must not restrict states using competitive bidding to adhere to rigid requirements. States need to retain the flexibility to implement bidding systems which ensure that their jurisdictional electric companies obtain supplies from appropriately-sized facilities with the necessary diversity of fuel mix. States should also be left with the discretion to determine the best way to incorporate utility bids into any all-source competitive system. An essential provision of PURPA was reliance on the states to derive appropriate methods of implementing the requirements of PURPA. FERC should not at this time in the development of competitive bidding systems ignore that intent by limiting the types of bidding systems eligible for experimentation by the states.

FERC has indicated that following its consideration of competitive bidding systems it will proceed to address significant issues dealing with access to the transmission grid and the pricing of wheeling arrangements. These transmission issues as well as the need to bring a more market-based approach to the pricing of bulk power transactions within power pools are areas over which FERC has exclusive jurisdiction and which are in need of immediate attention. These are areas where, unlike competitive bidding initiatives, the states are preempted from acting and require action on the part of FERC. We are encouraged that FERC is committed to addressing these critical issues in the context of a comprehensive framework for regulating the electric power industry and we urge them to move to deliberations and resolution of these issues at their earliest opportunity.

CHAPTER 6: CUSTOMER INTERESTS AND CONCERNS IN COMPETITIVE BIDDING FOR NEW POWER SUPPLIES*

Jerry L. Pfeffer
Skadden Arps

INTRODUCTION

It has become evident over the past several months that proposals for competitive solicitations of new power supplies offer both potential advantages and substantial risks from the perspective of a utility's major industrial customers. The following are among the considerations which I believe should be addressed in any effort to analyze the pros and cons of particular competitive bidding schemes from an industrial customer perspective.

What Are Such Proposals Seeking to Achieve?

Competitive bidding has been suggested as a more economically efficient alternative to continued reliance on traditional cost-based regulation of new electric generating facilities. some have argued that the traditional "regulatory compact" which has historically governed the electric power industry has been irrevocably breached as evidenced by regulatory refusal to allow full-cost recovery for utility investment in recently completed plants. Others challenge this assertion and suggest that any problems that may have been incurred in recent years are one-time difficulties associated with absorbing large and costly new generating plants (primarily nuclear) into a demand-constrained marketplace. They also note that recovery of "imprudent" investment was never part of the regulatory compact. Thus, they argue, there is no demonstrated need to implement fundamental changes in the structure and regulation of an industry that seems to be recovering well from its recent financial difficulties and is back on track in terms of providing adequate and reliable

---

*Presented to a seminar sponsored by the Electricity Consumers Resource Council (ELCON) entitled "Electricity's Future: Is Competition the Light at the End of the Regulatory Tunnel?" on October 8, 1987.

supplies of power at reasonable costs.

From a customer perspective, the key question which must be asked at the outset is whether competition has become an end unto itself and if so, do bidding schemes seeking to promote greater competition really offer the potential for significant customer benefits or are such schemes simply "a solution in search of a problem" as some have alleged. Recent experience derived from the introduction of competition into other previously regulated industries has left some customer groups questioning the long-term benefits of greater competition. Competition clearly has the potential to enhance efficiency and reduce costs. However, industrial customers should challenge the presumption that "imperfect competition" is always preferable to "imperfect regulation." Furthermore, they should focus on the specific market segments in which they operate to determine if such markets really are workably competitive under the proposed set of rules governing market functioning.

Who Will Maintain the Ultimate Obligation to Serve in a Competitive Bidding Environment?

From the perspective of most industrial customers, adequate and reliable service is of greater concern than improving overall economic efficiency from a regional or national perspective or even than the potential for modest cost savings in their own monthly bills. Competitive bidding proposals for new generation are premised on the notion that market-based price signals will somehow assure that adequate supplies of power will be forthcoming when and where needed. Relying on the marketplace in lieu of a traditional utility service obligation, however, places considerable faith in the ability of "price signals" to attract a sufficient number of market entrants willing to construct the most cost-effective mix of new power supplies to meet future demand. This article of faith may be appropriate in certain markets, while totally inappropriate in others. In particular, three key questions should be addressed in this regard by utility customers when examining specific competitive bidding schemes.

First, will continued "downstream" regulation of the distribution segment of the industry and associated prudence reviews of bulk power purchases by state PUCs allow prices to rise to whatever level is needed to assure that adequate new supplies of power are constructed on a timely basis? Responses to both formal and informal competitive solicitations conducted by utilities thus far among QFs suggest that there is a substantial reservoir of third-party investors willing to commit funds to new generating projects under the rules adopted in various jurisdictions implementing Section 210 of PURPA. Extrapolating this experience outside the PURPA model, however, may lead to misleading results.

The second question to be asked is, even assuming (arguendo) that prices are allowed to rise to whatever level is needed to attract sufficient market entrants, will independent power suppliers be capable of both constructing and operating new generating capacity that provides a level of service reliability at least comparable to what would have otherwise been provided under the traditional scenario of a utility constructing its own generation to meet its projected power supply needs? Again, the experience thus far with the reliability of non-utility generation under PURPA has been positive, though it is risky to extrapolate these results to a future characterized by a much larger percentage of non-utility generation in the overall power supply mix.

Finally, one must ask whether utilities will be willing to function as "suppliers of last resort" (under a cost-based regulatory scheme) if a competitive solicitation fails to bring forth adequate new supplies and, if so, what are the reliability implications of such a "backstop" scenario? Recent experience suggests that unless they are guaranteed recovery of prudent investment ex ante, few utilities will expose themselves to ex post determinations of allowable cost recovery (possibly based on prevailing market prices) if they are still subject to regulated rate of return.

Can Competitive Bidding Schemes Be Integrated into Existing Bulk Power Supply Arrangements without Jeopardizing the Adequacy and Reliability of Electric Service?

While everyone in the recent debate dutifully acknowledges the importance of assuring adequate and reliable service, advocates of competitive bidding have yet to provide much insight as to how such schemes can be integrated with existing bulk power supply arrangements. In particular, they have yet to specify the details of how such schemes can be implemented without disrupting the orderly development of new power supplies or diluting the incentives which have historically encouraged extensive planning and operational coordination across utility systems to assure economic and reliable service. This criticism obviously presumes that some burden of proof should be placed on those advocating fundamental changes in the status quo.

Questions which have yet to be adequately addressed include how system expansion planning will be undertaken in an environment wherein generation and transmission development are undertaken by separate (vertically disintegrated) entities whose legal obligations and economic motivations are distinctly different. Also, will a competitive bidding process subject to extensive regulatory control provide purchasing utilities with sufficient flexibility to determine the need for new power supplies and the timing and engineering characteristics of new capacity additions?

While state commissions currently exercise considerable control over need-for-power and choice-of-technology decisions, they rarely seek to become involved in the details of such non-price factors as fuel supply, unit reliability, load-following capability, dispatchability and other technical characteristics. These are issues which presumably would continue to be within the primary discretion of the utility if it had been allowed to construct new generation under traditional regulatory arrangements but which may be subject to considerable state commission oversight under some bidding schemes. While the importance of such non-price considerations are explicitly recognized in many proposed bidding schemes, real-world political considerations in some jurisdictions may dictate that competitive bidding outcomes would ultimately favor those developers offering the lowest near-term prices at the expense of the most economical and reliable long-term supply options. Also, while bidding advocates correctly note that power sale contracts can be written that address virtually any non-price issue of concern to utilities, it is difficult to imagine how a utility would seek to enforce specific operational and performance requirements especially in tight capacity markets. While financial penalties may be extracted for nonperformance, the utility is still confronted with the immediate problem of meeting its customer's demand for energy.

Finally, some have expressed concerns that competitive bidding for new supplies has the potential to erode many of the existing incentives for inter-utility coordination that are premised on mutual perceptions of self-benefit among neighboring systems. It is true that increasing competition in some regions has already resulted in visible strains within existing power pools and coordination mechanisms. However, while these strains could be exacerbated and long-term system economy and reliability could be compromised as we evolve into a more competitive bulk power market place, it is incorrect to automatically assume that this will be the outcome of a competitive bidding process. Considerably more information is needed on the impact of competition on existing coordination arrangements.

Are the Customer Benefits of "Supply-Side" Competition that Are Achieved through Competitive Bidding Sufficient to Forego Near-Term Efforts at Achieving Equivalent "Demand-Side" Treatment?

Recent proposals for competitive bidding are strictly limited to providing greater *supplier access* to bulk power markets. They do not, however, provide for equivalent *customer* access to a wider range of electric service providers as would be the case if such bidding proposals were coupled with parallel provisions for off-system purchases by requirements end users. FERC has indicated its intention of deferring any consideration of transmission access issues until *after* it has addressed competitive bidding.

Intense utility industry and state regulatory opposition to mandatory transmission access schemes that would allow large customers to bypass their local utility and shop around for lower embedded-cost power available off systems makes it unlikely that any modified proposal providing for *both* "supply-side" and "demand-side" competition would succeed in the near term (either at FERC or in Congress). Some customer groups will inevitably be concerned as to whether the potential near-term benefits of supply-side competition alone warrant their foregoing (at least for the interim) their primary goal which is to obtain greater transmission access so as to provide themselves with the option of negotiating off-system purchases.

The issue is probably more a question of strategy than the outcome of an objective cost-benefit analysis, (i.e., will customer group support for a FERC effort to implement all-source competitive bidding *without* transmission access strengthen or weaken their longer-term efforts to obtain customer access to the grid). The final decision here is likely to depend on how customer groups respond to the FERC's vague commitment to address transmission access and pricing matters on a "comprehensive" basis at some point in the future.

Can Competitive Bidding Schemes be Reconciled with the Traditional Role of State Regulation of Retail Utility Service?

The transition to a competitive bidding scheme to govern utility purchases of bulk power supplies has the potential to profoundly affect the existing allocation of regulatory responsibility between federal and state authorities. In recent years there has been a gradual transfer of regulatory authority from the state to the federal level as utilities obtain a greater percentage of their bulk power needs through transactions that are subject to Federal Energy Regulatory Commission (FERC) jurisdiction under the Federal Power Act. This outcome reflects the growth of inter-system bulk power transactions and utility restructurings which have resulted in the isolation of generation and distribution assets in separate entities, thereby rendering inter-company transactions (i.e., from a generating company to a distribution-company affiliate) as FERC jurisdictional "sales for resale."

Competitive bidding schemes have the potential to further erode state regulatory jurisdiction as a function of the precise rules under which such solicitations are implemented. Even though proposals for competitive bidding are frequently characterized as "optional," states desiring to implement such schemes will likely have to do so under rules promulgated by the FERC. Also, while FERC rules will certainly assure that state commissions always have the option of reviewing the prudence of individual purchases made pursuant to a competitive bidding scheme, the process itself is likely to provide considerable insulation to utilities for any purchase decisions they make in strict accordance with the rules governing such

COMPETITION IN ELECTRICITY

a scheme. Thus, it is likely that any sort of competitive bidding scheme would result in some reduction in the ability of individual state commissions to control the *level* of retail rates. What is unclear however, is the question of whether competitive bidding will affect rate design decisions by state PUCs. At this point there is no reason to expect any noticeable impact on retail rate design unless one anticipates that a competitive bidding process will have dramatic near-term effects on rate levels.

What Regulatory Standard, if Any, Should Govern Utility Acquisition of Power Supplies through Competitive Solicitations?

Recent proposals for competitive bidding are premised on the notion that when a utility's power supplies are acquired through a formal competitive solicitation, the need for regulation of prices to protect against monopoly abuse is substantially reduced, if not completely eliminated. This presumes, however, that bulk power markets are workably competitive and the utility's monopsony power has been sufficiently neutralized so that the outcome of a competitive solicitation is a reasonable approximation of prices that would prevail in a competitive market situation. However, there are obvious limitations on how effectively individual markets can perform in the absence of assured transmission access to all potential suppliers; the latter (as noted above) is a politically unworkable proposition at this point in time.

Proposals by the FERC staff and others, however, suggest that rates resulting from a competitive solicitation could automatically be deemed as "just and reasonable" under the regulatory standard established by the Federal Power Act and thus the FERC could effectively forego regulatory oversight of individual purchases made pursuant to such a solicitation. The staff position is rationalized in terms of the absence of "downstream" monopoly power by independent power suppliers who are not engaged in retail sales. However, if one accepts this rationale, the same logic would presumably apply to *any* negotiated bulk power sale made by Utility A to Utility B (located at some distance from Utility A), since A lacks monopoly power in markets served by B. Serious consideration must be given to the economic logic underlying whatever regulatory standard is adopted by FERC to forego regulation of transactions undertaken in a competitive bidding context and the implications of such a standard on FERC regulation of wholesale bulk power transactions occurring outside such structured competitive solicitations.

How Will Rules Governing Eligible Participants in Competitive Bidding Schemes Affect the Interests of Utility Customers?

Rules which have the effect of limiting the number and scope of eligible participants in a competitive solicitation for new bulk power supplies may have dual implications for utility customers. In certain circumstances, rules which limit the degree to which utilities (or their affiliates) may participate in competitive solicitations conducted in their local service area may be helpful in addressing potential discrimination and self-dealing problems. At the same time, however, such rules may deny utility customers the potential benefit of lower-priced and more reliable supplies that could be developed by utility affiliates who may be among the lowest-cost and most efficient producers in a given market. Indeed, any regulatory restrictions on the type or ownership of facilities which may respond to a competitive solicitation would invariably have the effect of increasing the cost of power supplies acquired through a competitive bidding process by limiting the number of eligible participants. Likewise, any regulatory restrictions (e.g., the Public Utility Holding Company Act) which discourage participation by existing utilities, their affiliates, or non-utility market entrants would also have the effect of reducing the number of market participants and raising the overall cost of power acquired through competitive solicitations. Utility customers must weigh the advantages (if any) of such restrictions, and the protections they seek to afford, against potential abuses in relation to the effects that such restrictions will generally have in terms of increasing power supply acquisition costs.

If Properly Implemented, Can the Existing Avoided Cost Purchase Scheme Established under PURPA Effectively Simulate the Outcome of "All-Source" Competitive Bidding?

Under the existing avoided-cost purchase arrangements established under Section 210 of PURPA, a utility *should* be

COMPETITION IN ELECTRICITY

allowed to consider all potential sources of bulk power supply in establishing the rate at which it offers to purchase power supplies from qualifying facilities (QFs). Thus, a proper determination of avoided costs would provide for consideration of all potential sources of supply including the utility's own construction options as well as power purchases from both QF and non-QF sources. The demonstrated willingness of the utility to construct its own generation, or a firm commitment by another utility or an independent power producer (IPP) to supply power to the utility at a given cost, imposes a ceiling on what the utility should be required to pay for power purchases from QFs. As is evident in recent studies of PURPA implementation, however, this has not always been the case. Avoided costs in many jurisdictions frequently fail to reflect the lowest cost option available — especially where such options include purchases from other utilities and IPPs.

While failing to encourage competition among QFs, a properly structured and administered avoided-cost determination would provide for an implicit all-source "competition" between QFs and all other supply options in that the QF must "beat" the lowest price offered by the utility, or any alternative supplier, (non-QF), in any power solicitation made to the utility, (i.e., utility construction costs or IPP costs establish a "benchmark" that QFs must at least match). In this context, any competitive bidding scheme limited to QFs is strictly a means of allocating capacity credits among a subset of QFs, all of whom must be lower-cost generators than the purchasing utility, other utility suppliers, or IPPs. While failing to achieve the broader efficiency benefits of a formal all-source competition, a bidding scheme limited to QFs is clearly preferable to reliance on a first-come, first-serve rule governing utility purchases from QFs.

CHAPTER 7: COMPETITIVE BIDDING FOR ELECTRIC SUPPLIES: UTILITY RESPONSIBILITY AND THE INTERVENTION OF THE REGULATOR*

Mark Reeder
Chief of Regulatory Research, New York State Department of
Public Service

INTRODUCTION

Competitive bidding for electric generation is a very important topic in the electric industry. It is also a game. The rules of the game are only now being invented and, in most cases, by parties who have never played the game before. There are many important details that are involved in setting up the game properly. This paper describes a collection of observations — there are many more that could be discussed — from a regulator's perspective.

UTILITIES CAN, THROUGH THEIR ACTIONS, RETAIN CONTROL OF THE DESIGN OF BIDDING PROCESSES

Currently, a score of utilities in states such as Maine, Massachusetts, New Jersey, Vermont, Virginia and New York are putting forward competitive bidding proposals that their respective regulators are reviewing and, generally, approving. In many instances, regulatory approval will come only after modifications recommended by the regulators are made to the proposals. But, at this time, it is clear that the utilities themselves are the ones that are in the lead in designing the bidding request for proposals (RFPs) and ranking formulas that will determine which new electric supplies will come on line in the near future. This could easily change.

It is important that the utilities fully appreciate the control they currently have over the design of bidding systems, and maintain that control by gaining the respect, if not the trust of the regulators, by putting forward public spirited proposals. One key factor that is a gauge of a utility's sense

---

The views expressed herein are those of the author and do not represent the policies of the New York Public Service Commission.

of public duty is the way it treats the environmental impact of generating (and demand-side management) projects in its RFP. Most RFPs contain both price and non-price factors that are used to determine the winning bidders. Among the non-price factors, a factor that considers the environmental impact of competing generating proposals is essential. It should carry a relatively strong weight in the overall selection process; the equivalent of 20 or 30 percent of price is reasonable. The weight given to environmental impacts can be thought of in the following way. With a 20 percent price differential between the best possible generator and the worst possible generator, the process is revealing a willingness to pay a 20% premium for close to perfectly clean electric generation. If all electricity was currently produced in perfectly clean ways, and was accompanied by a 20% increase in wholesale electric costs (which would translate to a less than 20% increase in retail electric rates), it would appear to be a bargain.

Obviously, all projects must satisfy the requirements of the federal, state, and local permits required for construction and operation. But, one must recognize that among electric supply sources that can satisfy the permit requirements, there are large differences in environmental impacts (air, water, land use, noise, etc.). The electric ratepayers, through their use of electricity, are directly responsible for the environmental impacts of the generators that are used to satisfy their needs. A selection process that explicitly considers the environmental costs of electric generation is essential.

Regulators generally don't want to intervene in the design of bidding systems and get involved in the details of the rankings and weightings. For one thing, they don't generally have the staffs to get involved with any confidence that they'd be doing more good than harm. If a regulator sees a utility doing a comprehensive analysis with a sense of duty to society that adequately handles factors such as the environment, demand-side management, and fair play, the regulator will usually be more than happy to let the utility try it out without significant modifications. On the other hand, regulators have to intervene when they see a utility acting solely in the interest of maximizing the welfare of their stockholders or their ratepayers while ignoring other important considerations. A utility whose ranking system ignores environmental impacts (or gives them negligible weight) is, in effect, inviting the regulator into its RFP design process. In doing so, it runs the risk that the regulator will find RFP weightings fun, and tinker around with other parts of the RFP. In the extreme case, the utility could lose control of the RFP design altogether and, in effect, cede that control over to the regulator.

In some states the regulators would prefer that the utilities take the lead in designing bidding systems. The utilities should seize upon this opportunity and adopt a public spirited perspective in order to gain the confidence of their regulators so that they can retain the lead role in something so important as bidding. To fail to do so would be shortsighted and foolish.

CEILING PRICE OR CEILING RANKING?

Most bidding systems select winning bids based on both price and non-price project features. However, when describing a ceiling for determining if a utility should go ahead and build a facility itself rather than buy electric capacity from bidders, most RFPs refer only to a price ceiling (the utility's long-run avoided cost). To be consistent with the non-price emphasis contained in the RFPS, a ceiling ranking rather than a ceiling price should be developed which incorporates non-price features as well as price.

A ceiling price is generally based on the price component of the buying utility's proposed resource plan (i.e., the plant additions it would build to supply its future needs if no supplies were available from bidders).[1] A ceiling ranking is also based on the host utility's resource plan, but captures both price and non-price features. Essentially, whatever facilities the host utility proposed to construct would be ranked according to the same criteria to be used in assessing bids, (i.e., price, the extent of frontloading in that price, environmental effects, location, fuel type, etc.). The numerical ranking that results is the ceiling ranking; projects that rank worse than the ceiling ranking are deemed inferior to building a rate-based utility plant, at least in the objective ranking portion of the bid selection process.[2]

To reflect the increased risk to ratepayers of the cost-plus nature of rate-based generation, the ranking formula should assign negative points to plants proposed by the utility that would receive traditional regulatory rate base treatment. In New York, this has been referred to as the "price risk" factor. The price risk factor also applies to non-utility plants by assigning a high score to fixed priced bids, a lower score to bids indexed to inflation, and even lower still for bids indexed to oil prices. Whether an oil price indexed bid should be considered a greater risk to ratepayers than a utility built, rate-based plant, is unclear, and probably depends on the type of plant proposed by the utility.

The workings of a ceiling ranking can be illustrated by the following three examples. First, if a bidder's project was exactly the same as the utility's except that the bidder offered a fixed price contract, (whereas the utility offered rate-based treatment), the bidder's project would win because of its better ranking. (The utility project would lose due to the negative points assigned to it for the risk of rate base treatment). Second, a bid by an independent power producer could have a price level that was 5% above the expected price of the utility's rate base option, but still could win if its non-price features were superior to those of the utility plant. Third, an independent power producer with a bid whose price was 10% lower than the utility plant's could lose if it had undesirable non-price features.

With a ceiling ranking included in the RFP, the bidding process provides an overall assessment of the value — both price and non-price — to ratepayers of the utility-built option compared to bids offered by non-utility competitors. As such, the comparison of bids with each other and with utility-built options is made on a consistent basis.

TRANSLATION OF NON-PRICE WEIGHTING FACTORS INTO PRICE EQUIVALENTS

Many RFPs have points awarded for both price and non-price factors. A simple means of judging the relative importance of non-price factors compared to price, and compared to other non-price factors, is to translate the points awarded for each non-price factor into their price equivalent.

This can best be seen through the use of an example. Niagara Mohawk Power Corporation, a New York utility,

COMPETITION IN ELECTRICITY

has proposed a ranking system that contains a total of 690 points, 500 of which are for price and 190 for non-price factors. The full 500 price points are obtainable only in a theoretical sense since one would have to put forward a bid price of zero to get all 500. In fact, assuring that no bids will be submitted at less than 50% of avoided cost, only 250 price points are truly on the table to be had. A close look at the Niagara Mohawk scoring system reveals that one receives 5 points for each percent by which one's bid falls below avoided cost (and negative 5 points for each percent by which the bid exceeds avoided cost). As such, points translate into price at the rate of 5 points per 1% of avoided cost.

This translation can be easily used to evaluate the importance of non-price factors in Niagara Mohawk's ranking formula. First of all, Niagara Mohawk's total of 190 points for non-price features means that it is willing to pay a 38% premium for a generator that has a perfect score on all non-price factors over a generator that satisfied none of them. The price equivalent of some specific non-price factors can be found on Table 7-1. Niagara Mohawk will pay a 2% premium for generators that agree to be fully dispatchable, a 2% premium for fuel diversity, a 1% premium for quick start ability, a 1.2% premium for projects with superlative project team experience, and a 0.6% premium for projects with favorable environmental impacts.

This can be compared to Long Island Lighting Company (LILCO) which is willing to pay a premium of 10% for dispatchability, 8% for fuel diversity, nothing for quick start ability, 4% for project team experience, and 12% for projects with favorable environmental impacts. The differences between Niagara Mohawk and LILCO are largely because the former has excess reserves and is in the middle of an interconnected pool whereas the latter is threatened with a shortage of reserves and is connected to its pool only via relatively weak transmission interconnections; LILCO cannot afford to have generation projects go bust that it is counting on.

SECOND PRICE AUCTIONS THAT INCORPORATE NON-PRICE CHARACTERISTICS

Several states have considered the use of second price auctions and California has adopted rules requiring them. In a second price auction, all winning bidders receive a price equal to the bid price of the best losing bid. In the case of bidding for electric generation, where low prices are preferred to high prices, bids would be ranked from lowest to highest prices, with the low priced bidders selected as the winners. All winners would receive a price equal to the bid price of the lowest priced losing bid. This is in contrast to the more commonly used first price auction in which winning bidders receive a price equal to their own bid price.

One potential problem with the use of second price auctions in soliciting bids for electric generation derives from the fact that non-price features are of critical importance in determining the best choice among bids. Auctions based solely on price are rare. Most utilities use complex ranking systems that assign points to price and to numerous non-price features of proposed generators.[3] At first glance, a second price auction appears inconsistent with the use of selection processes that rely heavily on non-price features.

The concept of price equivalents offers an easy answer. As described above, in any scoring system, each and every non-price feature can be translated into its price equivalent. This means that the scores produced by the ranking system not only yield a ranking of projects from best to worst, but also reveal a relative measure of the value to the utility of each project. A second price auction can be implemented simply by paying every winning bidder by reference to the score of the highest ranked losing project. Winning bidders, all of whom, by definition, have scores that exceed the highest ranked losing project, are directed to raise their bid prices just enough to lower their scores to match the score of the highest ranked losing project. In so doing, all winning bidders receive an award — consisting of both price and non-price features — that has a value to the utility, as measured by the scoring system, that equals that of the best losing bid. This approach preserves the essence of a second price auction and adapts it to the presence of non-price considerations.

Nevertheless, there are reasons why second price auctions are inferior to first price auctions in the purchasing of generation capacity. A good explanation of the weaknesses of second price auctions for electric generation procurement has been presented elsewhere.[4]

EVALUATION OF DISPATCHABILITY BENEFITS

The one area of bidding evaluation that probably needs the most improvement is the way in which the economic benefits of dispatchability are measured when comparing bids. While several utilities have issued RFPs that handle dispatchability well, most have not. The goal is a scoring algorithm for dispatchability that can be used by bidders themselves in a self-scoring ranking system.

Most RFPs ask for bidders to split their bid prices into $ per KW and $ per components. The total bid price is then computed by (1) estimating a total energy cost by multiplying the per kWH bid times the number of hours the generator is expected to be available, (based on a projected annual availability factor), and (2) adding the annual $ per KW component of the bid. This method overstates, sometimes severely, the cost to the utility of low capital cost, high energy cost generators, such as combustion turbine peakers that are dispatchable and are expected to sit idle most of the time. This approach evaluates all generators as if they were producing electricity during every hour in which they were available, which is accurate only for baseload generators, and is far off the mark for intermediate and peaking generators. A combustion turbine that is dispatachable will, in fact, run very infrequently since the dispatcher will choose to run other lower-cost units during all hours that lower cost units are available on the margin. Scoring systems generally attempt to reflect this concern via a non-price element called "dispatchability" that awards extra points to generators that agree to be dispatchable.

The problem is that, while an offer of dispatchability by a generator with a high per kWh running cost may have a lot of value to the buying utility, the same offer from a low running cost generator may have little or no value. A dispatcher will choose to run a cheap plant as much as possible whether the plant's contract offers dispatchability or not. For high cost plants, however, dispatchability is valuable to dispatchers because it allows them to shut the plant down when lower cost power is available. Nevertheless, the dispatchability scoring algorithms proposed by most New York utilities, and others, do not differentiate between low cost and high cost plants when awarding points for dispatchability. As such, intermediate, and especially, peaking generators that offer dispatchability receive adjustments to their bid prices that are insufficient to offset the overstatement that occurs in the price scoring described above, and, therefore, have little or no chance of ever beating a baseload generator.

The economic benefits of dispatchability to the buying utility depend upon the relationship between the generator's running cost and the hour to hour marginal energy cost of the buyer's electric system (or the power pool to which the buyer belongs). Dispatchability has economic value only during hours in which the running cost of the generator exceeds the marginal energy cost of the buying utility. A small subset of utility RFPs have handled this correctly. Central Vermont Public Service Corporation, for example, provides potential bidders with a computer program that contains hourly estimates of the utility's marginal energy cost for every year of the planning period.[5] The bidder simply inputs its projected running cost into the program which then computes dispatchability benefits. The approach is more complicated than simply awarding 20 points in the scoring system for dispatchability, but its greater sophistication yields a much better selection of winning bids and corrects a potentially devastating flaw in the simpler scoring systems.

For utilities that are interested solely in baseload power, a flawed dispatchability scoring algorithm may cause little damage. However, for utilities desiring to procure a mix of capacity that includes either intermediate or peaking units, a more sophisticated approach is needed to compare different kinds of units and is critical.

DEMAND-SIDE BIDDING: THE SEARCH FOR A LEVEL PLAYING FIELD

Demand-side bidding is much more complicated and tricky than supply-side bidding. It contains many of its own dilemmas such as whether or not to grant exclusive franchises for energy service companies, how to measure the demand savings, whether or not to tailor the auction so that individual customers rather than just energy service companies can bid, how to avoid cream skimming and get a mix of short payback and long payback demand savings measures, and

110   COMPETITION IN ELECTRICITY

how to integrate the demand-side auction with a utility's own on-going demand-side management programs. Perhaps the most difficult question however, is how to compare demand-side bids with supply-side bids to form an integrated approach to the provision of new electric supply that is properly balanced.

The tricky part of this derives from the fact that demand-side measures are already, even before an auction starts, being given a standard offer — call it standard offer number 5 — that pays any demand-side measure a price per kWh and/or per KW equal to the utility's retail rate. For example, in Orange and Rockland Utilities, where the commercial rate is 5.4 cents per kWh and $8.22 per KW, a standard offer of, on average, 7.3 cents per kWh is there for any customer considering installing a commercial lighting conservation measure. The problem is that, even though the costs of installing the conservation measure are estimated to be only 3 cents per kWh, most customers have ignored the standard offer.

Utility conservation programs often take the rebate approach which says, if most customers won't install a 3-cent measure when given the standard offer of 7.3 cents, maybe if we add 4 cents to the standard offer, raising it to 11.3 cents, they will. Doing so is often defended (often validly) by noting that a societal benefit results whenever a customer spends 3 cents to reduce demand that would have cost electric producers 6 cents to generate (6 cents is the avoided cost in this example). The 8.3-cent windfall for the customer (11.3 cents minus 3 cents) is simply a transfer payment that is needed to induce the desired change in the customer's behavior.

Demand-side bidding is no different. One is facing a situation where customers are not responding to the standard offer that exists in the form of their retail rate. In many instances, the standard offer is well above avoided costs. An extra payment is needed to induce a change in customers' behavior, and in demand-side bidding, that extra payment is the bid price. But how much should that extra payment be? And how does that extra payment affect the desire for a level playing field between demand-side and supply-side bids?

Some have argued that demand-side bids be capped at avoided costs, but that is clearly erroneous. As noted above, most demand-side options are already receiving a standard offer that exceeds avoided costs. To add another avoided cost to the total will surely raise the offer, but it may raise it too much or too little, depending on the demand-side measure. In the example above where the standard offer (i.e., the retail rate) is 7.3 cents, the avoided cost is 6 cents and the cost of the measure is 3 cents, the use of avoided cost as a ceiling price on a demand-side bid is the same as saying that, since customers won't spend 3 cents on a lighting measure when offered the standard offer of 7.3 cents, then the appropriate offer should be raised by 6 cents to 13.3 cents. This is illogical. An offer of 13.3 cents may be too small and may induce little change in customer behavior if there are severe market imperfections, or it may be too much to offer if the retail rate was only slightly below the amount needed to get customers to install the conservation measures. Clearly, simply hanging one's hat on avoided costs to choose the adder misses the whole point.

So, what is the answer? I don't know, but I do have some observations on how one must go about finding it. First, market research is needed to estimate the level of total incentive (the retail rate plus an adder) that is needed to induce significant changes in customer behavior for certain demand-side management (DMS) measures. Second, since it is the total incentive that counts, DSM bidding programs should recognize the importance of the retail rate in their design. Utilities with high retail rates should expect lower bids and have lower ceiling prices than utilities with low retail rates. The magnitude of the retail rate is often reflected in the form of lost revenues that the utility realizes when a DSM measure is installed.

Third, the comparison between demand and supply measures should start at the core question of the costs to society of doing one versus the other. In DSM parlance, this comparison is often called the societal cost test or the resource cost test. The supply-side bidding program will reveal the avoided cost of supplies, and the ranking system's non-price factors will yield adders to the avoided cost that apply to the favorable features of demand-side options such as environmental impact, small size, etc. The resulting avoided cost, adjusted for non-price factors, can be compared to the true resource costs of installing and maintaining the demand-side measure to determine which one is preferable from a societal perspective.[6] A societal cost advantage, where one is found, needs to then be weighed against the fact that, as opposed to supply-side options, demand-side options need to receive a payment (the retail rate plus an adder) that far exceeds the option's true cost. The extra payment needed to induce the demand-side supplies costs electric ratepayers more, via higher rates, than supply-side options. How this tradeoff is made is a controversial issue in the industry, and is left for other papers (see, for example, Reeder, M.A. and Whittaker, R.L., "Demand-Side Management Cost Effectiveness Tests and Incentives Faced by Customers," NARUC Least Cost Planning Conference, Aspen, Colorado, April 12, 1988).

Table 7-1

Price Equivalents of Non-price Factors: Percent Premium Utility is Willing to Pay for Favorable Characteristics

	Niagara Mohawk	Long Island Lighting Co.
1. Breakeven Period	10%	36%
2. Price Risk	0%	10%
3. Likelihood of Project Completion	12%	20%
• Level of development & technical/environmental feasibility	9.4%	12.8%
• Sponsor experience	1.2%	4.0%
• Additional contract dep.	0.8%	2.0%
• Accept base contract	0%	1.2%
• Economic development	0.8%	0%
4. Operational Longevity Confidence Factor	4%	6%
• Fuel supply secured	1.4%	2.8%
• Operation & maintenance	0.4%	1.2%
• Optional operating security	1.2%	2.0%
• Debt coverage	1.2%	0%
5. System Optimization Factor	11%	46%
• Dispatchability	2.0%	10.0%
• Interruptibility	0%	10.0%
• Fuel type	2.0%	8.0%
• Size	0.6%	2.0%
• Location	0.8%	12.0%
• Unit commitment	1.4%	0%
• Automatic generation control	1.0%	0%
• Black start	0.6%	0%
• Other	2.6%	4.0%
6. Environmental Impact	1%	12%
TOTAL NON-PRICE	38%	130%

All values are from draft RFPs and should therefore be considered preliminary and subject to change.

COMPETITION IN ELECTRICITY

Table 7-2

Overall Weight Given to Non-price Factors

Factors	Total Price Equivalent Utility Non-Price
Orange & Rockland Utilities	75%
Long Island Lighting Company	130%
Niagara Mohawk Power Corporation	38%
Consolidated Edison Company of New York	30%
New York State Electric & Gas Corporation	85%
Central Hudson Gas & Electric Corporation	N/A
Rochester Gas & Electric Corporation	202%

All values are from draft RFPs and should therefore be considered preliminary and subject to change. The percentages are not always directly comparable since making a given desired characteristic an eligibility requirement, in effect, gives it infinite weight, even though it appears to have no weight in the scoring algorithm. For example, both Central Hudson and Rochester are seeking peaking capacity. Rochester emphasizes peaking capacity by giving peaking characteristics lots of non-price weight in its scoring system, whereas Central Hudson simply establishes those characteristics as eligibility requirements.

Table 7-3

Competitive Bidding in New York State: Preliminary Schedule and General Information**

Utility	Expected Date to issue Final RFP	MW Amount	Year Capacity is sought
Orange & Rockland Utilities	May 1989	100 MW	1995
Long Island Lighting	June 1989	300 MW	1998
Niagara Mohawk Power	June 1989	350 MW	1994
Consolidated Edison	July 1989	200 MW	1993
New York State Electric & Gas Corp.	July 1989	130 MW	1994
Rochester Gas & Electric	August 1989	100 MW	1998
Central Hudson Gas & Electric	August 1989	30 MW	1994

** *Based on internal PSC working schedule and each utility's draft RFB. MW amounts and dates are not final and subject to change.*

ENDNOTES

1. The rules in place in Maine, Massachusetts, and California are structured this way, for example.
2. The term "ceiling ranking" as it has been used in New York, is derived from the "ceiling price" approach that has been used previously in auctions held in other states. In reality, a better term is "floor ranking" since high rankings are preferred to low rankings (conversely, the preference for low prices rather than high prices led to the use of the word "ceiling" in "ceiling price").
3. California has adopted a price only selection method, perhaps, in part, due to a perceived inconsistency between the use of a selection process that relies on non-price features and the adoption of a second price auction.
4. See Rothkopf, M.H., T.J. Teisberg, E.P. Kahn, "Why are Vickrey Auctions Rare?," Report LBL-24277, Lawrence Berkeley Laboratory, University of California, 1987. See also, Rothkopf, M.H., T.J. Teisberg, E.P. Kahn, J. Eto, and J.M. Nataf, "Designing PURPA Power Purchase Auctions: Theory and Practice," Report LBL-23406, Lawrence Berkeley Laboratory, University of California, 1987; reprinted by the Office of Policy, Planning and Analysis, U.S. Department of Energy as Report DOE/SF/00098-Hl, November 1987.
5. Central Vermont Public Service Corporation, Request for Power Supply Proposals, issued October 3, 1988.
6. In practice, the costs of DSM devices can be difficult to estimate, depending on the device. For example, the societal costs of an air conditioner curtailment program can be dominated by the discomfort costs of the customer being curtailed which are different for each customer depending on how often he or she otherwise would have used the air conditioner and how much suffering or inconvenience is caused by a non-working air conditioner.

CHAPTER 8: PRICING A NEW GENERATION OF POWER: A REPORT ON BIDDING

Jan Hamrin
National Independent Energy Producers

THE CONTEXT

Any discussion of bidding must begin with a definition of terms. One of the reasons there is so much confusion about bidding is that conceptually bidding is an empty vessel into which all sorts of exotic liquids may be poured. In this discussion, bidding is defined primarily as price-oriented bidding on the Massachusetts model, i.e. a bidding process in which price is the dominant factor in selection. In Virginia, New Jersey, Connecticut, and other states, there are a wide variety of methodologies for selective procurement in which price competition is either non-existent or distinctly subordinate to non-price factors such as location, technology or fuel preference, reliability of fuel supply, experience of firm, security guarantees and dispatchability. While these selection processes are often highly competitive on non-price factors, they are distinguished in this discussion from price-based bidding systems.

A second key assumption in this discussion is that bidding is applicable only to states where there is a demand for incremental capacity and energy and where the potential supply from independent power producers exceeds the demand. Bidding is a system for allocating finite capacity and energy credits. If there is no need for new capacity and full avoided cost is already very low, bidding is unlikely to provide any additional economic efficiencies and may act to depress the cogeneration and small power industry.

A third key assumption in this report is that adoption of a bidding program will be optional. A state may adopt or reject a bidding program depending upon whether decisionmakers believe bidding will contribute to achievement of state energy goals.

Reasons for Bidding

Bidding has been proposed as a solution to perceived problems in the implementation of PURPA. According to comments by Chairman Hesse in her Cincinnati speech of June 10, 1987, and statements by the PUCs of Massachusetts and other states which have either adopted or proposed bidding, bidding is not conceived as an alternative to PURPA and does not presage repeal of PURPA. Instead, the justification for bidding rises or falls on the ability of its proponents to demonstrate that bidding is a more efficient instrument for carrying out the statutory goals of PURPA than are existing state procedures for allocating and pricing capacity and energy payments to QFs. Price-based bidding may be viewed as a "market determination" of avoided cost.

According to its preamble and legislative history, PURPA's primary goals may be described as the following: national security, (an electric energy supply made more secure by reduced dependence on imported fuel), and efficiency, (savings to ratepayers through adoption of a least cost strategy for meeting incremental demand).

There are several secondary objectives which are related to achieving these primary goals: Risk shifting from ratepayers to generators; diversity of generating technology and fuel mix; and diversity of ownership and size of facilities. One fundamental purpose of PURPA which ties many of these objectives together is the encouragement of cogeneration and small production.[1]

The tension between the goals of energy independence and least cost generation and between long term and short term cost of energy supply, has affected PURPA from the outset and therefore will influence the structure and content of any bidding system which is consistent with PURPA.

Judging from the commentary in the various states, competitive bidding may be described as a solution in search of a problem. Before we can discuss the solution, we must identify the problem.

What are the problems in the implementation of these goals of PURPA and national energy policy which bidding is designed to solve? A review of the bidding systems discussed by FERC or proposed by utility commissions around the country reveals several rationales for the introduction of competitive bidding:

• Economic Efficiency: To provide savings to ratepayers

COMPETITION IN ELECTRICITY

beyond avoided cost.

- Allocation: As a solution to the allocation of excess supply.

- Administrative Convenience: As a simpler way to administer PURPA.

- Competition: To increase competition as a stimulus to deregulation.

Economic Efficiency

PUC staff reports in Massachusetts and Illinois offer, as a justification for price bidding, the desire to obtain for ratepayers some of the cost savings achieved by QF developers who manage, through greater efficiency, to produce electricity at less than avoided cost. Some utilities assert that when QF developers' actual costs are less than avoided costs, ratepayers should share in the developers' profits. Price bidding, by squeezing the developers' profits, passes on to the ratepayer even more of the cost savings from the QFs' ability to produce electricity more efficiently than traditional power plants.

However, the staff of the New Jersey BPU has questioned whether this approach will provide savings to the ratepayer in the long run.[2] The New Jersey Commission Staff report states that QFs already provide major savings to ratepayers by shifting the risk of construction cost overruns or failed projects from the ratepayer to private capital, by stabilizing rates through avoidance of the capital required for large central station generation plants, and by reducing fuel risks through diversity of technology.

Price bidding, by shrinking the developers' risk premium, may have the effect of discouraging QF development. In such a bidding system, QFs may have incentives to underbid, making it more difficult to finance the winners' projects and increasing the risk of project failure. If this occurs and utilities become "builders of last resort",[3] ratepayers may be denied the benefitsof QF development inthe long run.

Allocation of Capacity and Energy

The most common justification for bidding is as a means for managing oversupply, an issue not foreseen by Congress when it enacted PURPA in 1978. By 1984, only five years after PURPA's effective date, there was already an extraordinary response by QF developers willing to build new capacity. In several states, most notably California, proposed projects exceeded the host utility's estimate of needed capacity in a given period. Most observers now agree that the "California problem" may be attributed to PURPA's growing pains during initial implementation when regulators were struggling with unfamiliar avoided cost methodologies. Now that most states have matched long-term avoided cost with a specific increment of capacity and instituted timely adjustment of avoided costs for new contracts, oversupply by itself is not a justification for the introduction of a bidding system. So our survey of QF allocation in New Jersey, Virginia and Connecticut shows there are a number of ways to deal with oversupply within existing procedures without the use of a bidding system. In fact, only a few states have cited QF oversupply as a reason for instituting bidding.

The Texas Public Utility Commission, for example, rejected Houston Lighting and Power's bidding proposal in 1984 but allowed the utility to establish a limit on the amount of capacity it would purchase from QFs in a given year. The capacity for a given time frame is to be determined by the utility's demand forecast for that period. Subsequently many states have restricted specific avoided costs offers to finite supply blocks.

Administrative Convenience

Price bidding is also proposed as the fairest and most efficient means of selecting which QF will be able to build future generation capacity. Selection on the basis of price bidding is said to be a more objective process — and therefore a less litigious one — than other methods of allocating incremental capacity and energy. It reduces the burden of a state regulatory agency in acting as a board of review to insure that all bidders are treated fairly. It makes the utility less

120   COMPETITION IN ELECTRICITY

vulnerable to challenge by disappointed bidders.

It should be noted, however, that Connecticut, Virginia, New Jersey, Texas, and other states have to date rejected price bidding and have allocated capacity among QFs using other means of selection. These states use or have proposed the use of model contracts, a variety of non-price criteria, and a capacity quota, sometimes in combination with a "first to contract" approach, to select QF developers. One state is even considering the use of a lottery for allocating capacity needs. While these systems can put a greater administrative burden on regulators and the utilities than does price bidding, the systems do allow for more flexible procurement of needed power that can take into account a greater variety of state energy goals.

Some state regulators also see bidding as a means of reducing their regulatory burdens. If proposed utility projects are subject to the bidding process, state regulators are relieved of the burden of a separate "certificate of need" process for utility projects. However, some determination of need will still be required before a block of power can be offered for bid. If the utility as builder of last resort participates, the state regulatory agency might not have to regulate the rate of return on utility projects selected through bidding, assuming that utility projects are held to the costs and completion dates specified in the bid. This would not relieve utility projects of all regulation but might limit some of the more contentious cost issues. Where bidding has been proposed without the use of a long-term avoided cost cap, regulators avoid having to make determinations of avoided cost and therefore are relieved of this regulatory burden.

Increased Competition

A bidding system in which all potential generators of new capacity participate is attractive to those advocating increased competition for electric generation. Bidding is seen by many as the fraternal twin of deregulation. The high efficiency of cogeneration technology, coupled with Wall Street's reluctance to finance large central station nuclear and coal plants, has greatly reduced traditional utility advantages from economies of scale and access to capital. The response by QF developers to the opportunities created by PURPA has demonstrated that a competitive market can exist in the generation of electricity. The collapse of traditional barriers to entry for non-utility generators has removed the "natural monopoly" premise on which rate of return regulation has been built.

Price bidding offers a means of giving all potential players entry to competition in a deregulated environment. With the abundance of independent power available, regulators nationwide have been increasingly reluctant to approve traditional utility rate of return construction with high risk exposure for ratepayers. Theoretically, price bidding offers a fair and objective mechanism for allowing utilities and non-QF independent power producers to compete with QFs in supplying new capacity. Specifically, it gives utilities a way to get back into the business of new construction from which they are being gradually excluded in many states. Finally, price bidding is viewed with favor by utilities where it eliminates after-the-fact prudency reviews.

Conclusion

These rationales have created a strong momentum for price or auction bidding in many states. Our survey of the states reveals there are six states which have either already adopted bidding or competitive procurement programs, and thirteen states which are presently reviewing the adoption of bidding and alternative competitive systems. It is, therefore, timely for FERC to take the initiative to provide some guidelines for a model bidding system which will be consistent with the objectives of PURPA.

Whatever one may feel about bidding in the abstract, most observers agree that any successful system requires close attention to the details of implementation. In our conversations with the staffs of state PUCs and with successful and unsuccessful bidders, independent power producers, and utilities, we have identified a number of problems along the path of implementing price based bidding systems.

ISSUES AND ELEMENTS OF A BIDDING SYSTEM

A bidding system similar to that outlined by Chairman Hesse in the Cincinnati speech and by the FERC staff in workshops in July and August is the model being addressed. The major elements of that model are:

- Voluntary participation by states
- Consistency with PURPA and other Federal regulations
- Major Goal   Economic efficiency through obtaining needed power at least cost
- Sub Goals:
    a)   Enhancement of the competitive market for FERC-regulated bulk power suppliers, and
    b)   Substitution of market forces for traditional state utility regulations
- Range of participants: "All-source", including utilities, QFs, non-QF independent power producers, etc.
- Defer to transmission access issues until bidding system is in place
- Prudency Review: To be eliminated in favor of explicit up-front review.

The purpose here is to list[4] the major issues expressed at hearings, workshops, and other meetings between federal and state regulators, QFs, and utility representatives regarding development and implementation of a bidding program for new capacity additions.[5] The last section synthesizes from the identified issues a list of critical elements which might appropriately be addressed in guidelines for a bidding program.

Goals

A number of concerns have been expressed about the goals of a bidding system, and their interaction with other possibly conflicting objectives of prudent energy policy.

Obtaining Least Cost Energy

Within this fairly straight-forward goal, there are conflicting elements depending upon the definition of "least cost."

Long Term vs. Short Term Costs: Technologies or fuels which may seem to be less costly in the short term may be more costly over their life cycle due to changing circumstances over time. "Least cost" must be carefully defined. An example: A gas generation system built in 1987 may appear to be least cost because natural gas costs are currently low. If gas prices go up in the future, that generation system may not be as cheap as other options which looked more expensive in 1987.

Fixed vs. Variable Costs: This issue is related to the previous one. Any generation resource has both fixed and variable costs. Some technologies include more of one than the other. Competitive bidding systems tend to favor low fixed costs, higher variable cost options unless designed to take this into consideration. An example: Some cogeneration and combined cycle gas systems have low capital (fixed) costs but high variable (fuel & maintenance) costs over time. Many renewable energy technologies have very high capital (fixed) costs but very low fuel (variable) costs.

Economic Efficiency from Bidding vs. the Cost of Bidding:

1. Theoretically, bidding can bring about lower prices through competition. On the other hand, a bidding program, unless it is a pure price system, may be more expensive to administer than capacity allocation by a "first come, first served" or "first to contract" method.

2. A bidding system can be more expensive for the participants since, (depending upon the entry requirements), it may add significant up-front expenses with no assurance of winning. If the bid is lost, these expenses must be allocated to the costs of other projects being proposed or developed by the same company. The cost of increased risk and bidding expenses must be borne by someone. Either the cost of new generation will increase over time or fewer competitors will participate which may also increase costs.

3. To the extent the expense of participating in the bidding process keeps some projects from participating, ratepayers may be systematically denied some project options which may be less costly than the winning bidders. An example: A small company can build projects for a low cost per KW but may not be able to afford the expense of entering a bidding system. The winning bidder's price may actually be higher than if there had been a broader range of participants.

Security of Electric Supply

Security of the Physical Supply of Electricity: There may be a relationship between participants in the bidding process and security of supply:

   1. To the extent the bidding process is open to technologies dependent upon imported fuels or imported supplies of electricity controlled by other governments, and these options win the bidding, the national security could be jeopardized. As a result, these options might not be least cost.
   2. If least cost bidding results in very large amounts of electricity being transferred between utility systems over a few large transmission lines, the electrical system can become more vulnerable to disruption (purposeful or accidental).[6]

Diversity of Supply and the Bidding Process: Diversity is a frequently stated energy goal because of its relationship to security, reliability and the economic efficiency of the system.

   1. Diversity of fuel: A bidding process focusing on least cost goals can result in less diversity in fuel and technology thus making the system more vulnerable to a catastrophic event, either physical or economic. Such an event can remove a large portion of the generation from service, resulting in greater rather than lesser costs to ratepayers. As outlined in the Department of Energy's March 1987 report, *Energy Security*, "The diversity of renewable resources invites the development and application of a diverse family of technologies. Because the various resources are more widely dispersed than those associated with conventional fuels, the former are less susceptible to suppliers' control, and to the sorts of supply manipulation that result in adverse economic and political consequences." (page 200) An example: Economic curtailment or weather interruptions could in the 1990's jeopardize supply if a bidding system heavily favored gas cogeneration in the 1980's.
   2. Diversity of size: Economies of scale can lead to larger plants providing all the needed capacity. Depending upon the size of the system, this can increase required reserve mar-

gins, and decrease system reliability and security, all of which would add costs not generally captured in a bidding system. An example: A 1000 MW plant requires greater back-up reserves than do 10 individual 100 MW plants.

3. Diversity of ownership: To the extent that bidding systems increase risks and the cost of participation, and therefore reduce the number of players[7], control of the generation supply can become vulnerable to manipulation due to a lack of diversity of ownership. The concept underlying PURPA was that regulation of QFs was unnecessary because no one company alone was likely to control a significant portion of the generation system. This may not be true in the future if non-QF independent producers are given the privileges of PURPA, (with no size and transmission limitations), especially where the bidding emphasis is primarily on price alone.

4. Demand reduction versus supply: Theoretically, conservation and load management programs should be allowed to participate in bidding programs. Problems such as how to prevent participants from "gaming" the system, e.g., seeking payments for energy saving technologies which they would have installed anyway, must be resolved before participation is practical.

Reliability of Supply and Bidding: To the extent a bidding system results in significant amounts of underbidding in order to win the competition to fill capacity needs, the result can be: defaults of projects, lowered reliability of the projects brought on-line due to cost cutting to build to the bid demands for renegotiation of price by the bidder, (wiping out perceived economies of competition), and reduction in long-range planning capabilities due to increased uncertainties about what capacity may come on-line. The ultimate outcome could be increased ratepayer costs and a perception that the independent power industry is unreliable — and thus justifying a return to cost plus regulation.

Transfer of Risks

It should be noted that PURPA, without bidding, transfers cost risks of electric generation construction and operation from ratepayers (or in limited cases, shareholders) to the private sector. The issues discussed here only deal with the incremental risk transfers caused by the introduction of bidding and how this transfer of risks will be altered further by bidding.

Financing: When the uncertainty of bidding increases the risks of investing in electric generation, the cost of providing that generation will increase. The financing costs of private sector (QF) projects under a bidding system versus under traditional PURPA avoided cost may go up, depending upon how Wall Street reacts to entry requirements, security provisions, and squeezed project margins.

Reopeners: Reopeners or after-the-fact prudency reviews can make the risks too big for anyone to take. This is already an issue with traditional PURPA contracts and conventional utility power plants, but can be expected to be magnified under a bidding scenario. It remains to be seen what the cumulative effect of these transfers of risks in bidding will have on the ability of developers to finance their projects. The investment banking community has been conspicuously absent from the bidding debate to date.

State and Regional Goals

States and regions frequently have additional non-energy goals which can conflict with a least cost bidding system. It is unclear how a bidding system can incorporate these other goals:

Economic Development: States frequently want to encourage economic development within the state or region which can take the form of encouraging small business or local energy development companies and construction jobs related to energy development within the area.

Resource Development: States frequently want to encourage development of indigenous resources within the state or region such as geothermal, wind, wood, or hydro resources.

Environmental Concerns: States frequently have environmental concerns involving acid rain, carbon dioxide emissions, waste disposal problems, and other environmental impacts and associated costs. These can result in some technologies or fuels being preferred over others. Environmental costs to society may not be captured in a "least cost bidding system" if not explicitly considered.

Responsibility and Accountability

Introduction of a bidding system requires an allocation of responsibilities among the various players that ensures that system will be efficient, fair and accountable. The players include federal and state regulators, the host utilities, other IOUs, public power, QFs, non-QF independent power producers and foreign sources of power. This section raises some of the issues that need to be addressed if price bidding or other competitive systems are to be successful.

Federal Energy Regulatory Commission

What are the responsibilities of FERC in recommending a bidding system and how far does their authority go in allowing them to make substantive changes in the PURPA system?

Goals and Objectives: What are the chief goals and objectives which should influence FERC's decisions and recommendations about bidding and the PURPA program?

Expertise and Oversight: If FERC suggests substantive changes to PURPA in order to advance bidding, what are their obligations in providing the states expertise, training, and oversight in the program's implementation?

Legality: Given the risks of having a bidding system result in unintended impacts contradictory to stated goals and/or contrary to law, what are FERC's responsibilities in mandating some bidding program elements crucial to the success and legality of such programs? Many state regulators have delayed decision on bidding because of uncertainty about its legality. FERC will have to describe the essential elements of a legally defensible bidding system in its recommendations to the states.

State Regulators

The appropriate responsibilities and roles of state regulators and decision makers if they choose to adopt a bidding program become a critical factor:

State Status: States are at widely differing both in the levels of development of an independent energy industry and in the implementation of PURPA. Design and implementation of an effective bidding system confronts the state with another level of complexity. Bidding because of increased risk, lower prices and complexity may have a dampening effect on the state regulatory efforts to develop a local QF industry.

Goals: State decision-makers may have a variety of goals which may or may not be compatible with a cost-based bidding system.

Expertise: State regulatory commissions may or may not have the staff or expertise required to implement and oversee a complex bidding system. If they have had difficulty implementing PURPA, they may have even more problems implementing bidding.

Performance Reviews: To the extent that risks of new generation construction are removed from ratepayers, prudency reviews and after-the-fact regulatory reviews are inappropriate.

Host utilities

As mentioned earlier, there are a variety of possible roles for the host utility ranging from non-participant to bidder. The majority of states considering or using bidding and other competitive systems are turning to the utility to administer the program. In order to avoid the real or perceived problems associated with this policy, it is critical that the role of the host utility and its subsidiaries in building electric generation is clearly defined.

Role: For competitions in their own service territory, should the host utility be a bidder, a "builder of last resort", restricted from any participation, the administrator of a bidding program or some combination of these roles? To the extent that the host utility's affiliates or subsidiaries are bidders, should the host utility administer the bidding program?

Non-Investor Owned Utility Accountability: If the utility becomes the "builder of last resort" but is not regulated, (i.e., not an investor owned utility), how can one insure against the utility submitting unrealistically low cost estimates of new capacity in order to be able to build?

Utility Accountability: If the host utility is allowed to bid and wins the bid, what protection is there against the utility requesting halfway through construction to renegotiate the contract for a higher price due to "changed circumstances"?

Conflict Between Shareholder and Ratepayer Interests: One of the major obligations of an investor-owned utility is to its shareholders. The shareholders' earnings are based upon the size of the ratebase which depends upon continued capital investments by the utility. Given that the major capital investments by any electric utility are in new electric generation units, there is an inherent incentive for the utility or its affiliates to build new generation or invest in new generation. To the extent that host investor-owned utilities are removed from construction of new generation, the basis for shareholders' dividends and earnings may have to be reconsidered.

Role of Other Utilities

Zone of Economic Influence: If utilities bid in competitions outside of their service territory, but within their "zone of economic influence", there can be a danger of "clubbiness" between a utility and the host utility if they have multiple business transactions with each other, such as existing power sales/purchases, power pool arrangements, or power exchanges. What is to prevent the non-host utility or its subsidiaries from bidding low and using cross subsidies from other transactions with the host utility in order to win the bid? This can undermine the fairness of the bid process.

Therefore, should utilities be restricted from bidding within their zone of economic influence? How should "zone of economic influence" be defined with regard to the interrelations of utility transactions? If non-host utilities are not prevented from bidding within their zone of economic influence, what protections need to be incorporated in the bidding procedure to insure fairness?

Accountability: Should another utility or governmental entity be able to tender a bid if such a bid for constructing new generation facilities is known at that time to be below the actual cost of construction and operation of the plant? An example: Utility A submits a bid for electricity at 6 cents per kWh for power from a new coal plant which will cost its ratepayers 11 cents per kWh to build. The ratepayers of Utility A would then be forced to subsidize this new plant at a rate of 5 cents per kWh.

Subsidies: Should a utility or governmental entity be al-

COMPETITION IN ELECTRICITY

lowed to submit a bid using a newly constructed generating unit which has not yet been ratebased if the bid is below the actual cost of constructing and operating the plant? Such a case would result in one set of ratepayers subsidizing another.

Independent Power Producers

Subsidies: Should a non-QF independent power producer be allowed to submit a bid which would require a subsidy from other ratepayers or a governmental entity? An example: A public entity bids below its costs to get a contract which will result in its other customers paying more to make up the difference. This is another case in which one set of ratepayers is subsidizing another.

ACCESS TO TRANSMISSION

Wholesale Wheeling

Resources are seldom distributed in the same way as the need for electric power. Therefore, the question arises: Should utilities with less need for new capacity, (as evidenced by a lower avoided cost rate and/or the lack of a long run contract offer), be required to wheel power for QFs or IPPs located within their service territory who wish to bid for capacity in a neighboring service territory.

Wheeling Rates

If a utility is required to wheel, there is a necessity that the terms, conditions, and rates be fair, equitable, and "nondiscriminatory".

Wheeling Expenses and Bidding

If entities with generation located in service areas outside the host utility are allowed to bid, what transmission, wheeling charges, and line losses should be included in the bid? If the host utility is bidding, or is "builder of last resort," incremental transmission, interconnection, and line loss charges should be included in their costs. Wheeling and transmission costs can be a major element of costs if the new plant is located in another service area or another state. Public entities or utilities should be sure to include these costs in their bid if generation options are to be compared fairly.

Balancing Competing Interests

If wheeling is required to facilitate a broad based bidding program, how should the economic efficiency of one set of ratepayers vs. another be factored into determinations of wheeling and by whom should this be done? An example: When the wheeling of power from QFs or IPPs in service area "A" to a neighboring utility service area "B" is found to provide a greater per capita benefit to ratepayers in Utility B than the per capita benefit to ratepayers in Utility A, should wheeling be required?

IMPLEMENTATION DETAILS

Length of Contract

Minimum Contract Length: In a bidding program designed to provide new capacity, there is a minimum contract length required to ensure a project actually supplies the new capacity solicited by the bid. This minimum contract commitment is necessary to insure financability of new generation.

Maximum Contract Length: Should the maximum contract length be at least as long as the average useful life of the new generation? Contract length may also determine whether high fixed, low variable cost projects can successfully compete. Renewable energy projects can more equitably compete with fossil fueled projects on a twenty-five year contract than on a ten or fifteen year contract.

Contract Terms and Conditions

It is widely recognized that contract terms and conditions can be as important as price in determining who builds new capacity. One of the main impacts of contract terms is in determining whether or not a project can be financed. Some examples: Dispatchability requirements can have a major impact on income, depending on when a project is curtailed and the number of hours it is curtailed. Open-ended requirements with no specific delimiters can render a contract non-financeable.

Pricing Terms and Conditions: Pricing terms and conditions, (i.e. levelization and front loading), can be used as tools for balancing the needs of different types of technologies or fuels or they can be used as a way of limiting participation by some technologies.

Standard Contracts: Given the importance of contract terms and conditions on the financial viability of a project, standard contracts can reduce risks and improve the precision of bids whenever a bidding system is used.

Renegotiation of Price: Material renegotiation of the contract after the awarding of bids will be counter-productive to the purpose of bidding. The use of preapproved standard contracts should eliminate the need for material renegotiation.

Entry Requirements

What are appropriate entry or qualification requirements?

Entry: Entry or qualification requirements can be used to limit bidding participation. An example: only projects with a guaranteed fuel supply at a specified price, or only companies which can provide performance security over the life of the project, will be allowed to bid. These kinds of requirements limit entry.

Criteria for Awarding Bids

Responsibilities: A "point system" implicitly imputes values for various project characteristics. Theoretically, if one can impute a value through points or other weighing systems, a monetary value can be calculated as well. Who are the appropriate parties to make these determinations, and is there a more appropriate method for encouraging specific project or operational characteristics than awarding points? Using non-price factors as an alternative to price in the awarding of bids is highly subjective. How can application of non-price factors be monitored to prevent favoritism for a particular company and special interest groups at the expense of the ratepayers and other bidders?

CHAPTER EIGHT   133

Determination of Winning Price: Winning bidders can all receive the same price (as in the California method) or each receive the price they bid. Is there a reason to prefer one method over the other?

Block Size: The size of the capacity increment offered for bid can have a significant influence on the extent of the competition generated by the bidding process and the economic efficiency of the bids. If the capacity increment is too small, and/or if there is a repeated pattern of very small capacity increments being put out to bid relative to the size of the utility system, this practice can discourage competition and result in only one winning bid or, if many, diseconomies of scale.

EXISTING CONTRACTS AND PROGRAMS

Existing Contracts

Some QFs have expressed concern that if FERC issues statements recommending bidding and guidelines for bidding, some utilities may challenge existing full-avoided price contracts as being overpaid and try to have them abrogated.

Existing Programs

Concern has been expressed that if FERC recommends bidding as a preferred method of costing new generation, states will eliminate their existing full-avoided cost programs just at the point when they have been fully implemented.

LEGAL ISSUES

Public Utility Regulatory Policies Act

There is great concern among some states, QFs, and utilities that a cost-based bidding program is in basic conflict with the goals of PURPA. All parties are looking to FERC to provide a review of the legal status of bidding vis-a-vis PURPA.

Utilities

How do FERC's legal obligations differ with regard to investor owned utilities and non-investor owned utilities? There has been little, if any, FERC oversight of PURPA implementation by non-investor owned utilities. The introduction of bidding programs may compound the difficulty of insuring PURPA is properly implemented by non-IOUs.

Enforcement

Proper implementation of PURPA has been spotty at best. The introduction of bidding raises the level of complexity even further. From past experience, expertise, oversight and enforcement will be extremely important if bidding is to be properly implemented.

Congressional Action

What, if any, are FERC's recommendations for Congressional actions necessary to allow general adoption bidding programs, especially "all source" bidding?

OTHER ISSUES

Given the multitude of FERC and state environmental reviews, permitting and licensing requirements applicable to hydroelectric projects, should hydro projects be treated in the same way by a bidding program as other types of technologies and fuels?

Conclusion

The following is a partial list of issues which NIEP believes should be addressed by any FERC recommendations on bidding:

- An explicit statement of FERC's goals and objectives in issuing guidelines or recommendations for a bidding program.
- A listing of any mandatory elements which must be included in a bidding program if it is to be in compliance with PURPA and other federal statutes under FERC authority. Include an explanation of the FERC's role in

oversight and enforcement of compliance with such statutes.

- Delineate federal and state roles in policy and program development relating to bidding.
- Include recommendations for the possible integration of multiple goals into the bidding process. This should include some discussion of least cost energy as a goal, (including relevant definitions), vis-a-vis other non-quantifiable, more subjective goals.
- What, if any, should be the role of transmission access in any bidding program and what is FERC's perception of its own jurisdictional role in this area?
- What role should both host and non-host utilities play in bidding?
- State how FERC's bidding program recommendations effect:
  a) existing contracts;
  b) existing state bidding programs;
  c) subsidies from one set of ratepayers to another.
- What, if any, recommendations does FERC have for state and/or federal legislation necessary to the successful conduct of a bidding program?
- What, if any, technologies or fuels should receive special treatment due to extraordinary circumstances (such as hydro licensing procedures)?

ENDNOTES

1. See Draft Power Keystone Foundation Report, January 27, 1987, p. 5.
2. "An assessment of Cogeneration and Small Power Production Policy in New Jersey 1981-1986." A Report by the staff of the New Jersey BPU: Steven Gabel, et al.
3. "Builder of a last resort" means the utility estimates the cost of its avoided plant and is only allowed to build it if no other bidders are able to build generation for that price.
4. This issues list is limited to what appear to be the most critical issues related to bidding. Important issues not exclusive to bidding are not included. However, some issues which are magnified in importance by bidding are discussed. No attempt was made to systematically exclude issues

important to other parties though our familiarity with QFs may cause the list to include more concerns expressed by that sector.

5. The issues and questions raised in discussions on bidding have been isolated from the conclusions in Chapter IV so they can receive proper consideration even if the reader disagrees with NIEP's recommended solutions.

6. It can be argued that if a utility purchases large amounts of power from sources outside its service territory, the need for taking part of their capacity from dispersed generating units within their service territory will be greatly increased. This will reduce the utility system's vulnerability to transmission line failure.

7. Large companies and companies doing multiple projects are best able to amortize the risks and costs of bidding.

CHAPTER 9: DESIGNING PURPA POWER PURCHASE AUCTIONS: THEORY AND PRACTICE*

Michael H. Rothkopf, Edward P. Kahn, Thomas J. Teisberg, Joseph Eto, and Jean-Michel Nataf

Energy Analysis Program, Lawrence Berkeley Laboratory, University of California

EXECUTIVE SUMMARY

The Public Utilities Regulatory Act (PURPA) requires there to be procedures for electric utilities to buy electric power from qualifying cogenerators and small power producers (QFs) at rates up to "avoided cost". This has led to price-posting procedures at prices calculated as the utility's marginal cost. Unexpectedly large sales at these prices and slow adjustment to falling energy cost are partially responsible for payments to QFs in excess of the utility's true avoided cost. Using competitive bidding instead of posted prices has been proposed as a way to avoid this outcome. This report reviews bidding theory and explores four issues that arise in designing auction systems for the purchase of power from QFs under PURPA. It does not consider broader auctions involving non-QF bidders. One of these four issues is the choice of auction format between progressive oral auctions, Dutch oral auctions, standard discriminatory or "first-price" sealed bidding (if you win, you get paid the amount of your bid), and nondiscriminatory or "second-price" sealed bidding (all winning bidders are paid the amount of the best losing bid). Another issue is the extent to which non-price factors influence the auction and the manner in which they do. A third issue is the way in which bid acceptance procedures deal with the discrete quantities of power offered by different bidders. For example, if a utility that needs 500 MW that it can supply at 10 cents per kWh, receives three all-or-nothing bids, one offering 300 MW at 7 cents, one offering 250 MW at 8 cents and one offering 200 MW at 9

*This work was supported by the Director of the Office of Policy, Planning and Analysis, the U.S. Department of Energy under Contract No. DE–ACO376SFOO098. Work performed under DOE Field Task Proposal Number ASD-4717.

cents, which bids should it accept? The fourth issue is the frequency of auctions.

With respect to auction format, the report recommends sealed procedures over oral ones. It identifies flaws in the arguments in favor of the economic efficiency of nondiscriminatory sealed bidding and recommends familiar discriminatory sealed bidding over the much less common nondiscriminatory format.

In discussing non-price features, we note the tradeoff between simplicity and economic precision. We identify some factors, such as capacity value and transmission access costs, that are relatively amenable to differentiation into components with separate payment streams and performance factors. Others, such as financial risk and dispatchability are not. We also note with approval the approach taken in Massachusetts to deal with financial risk, and we note the difficulty of dealing with dispatchability when it is important.

The discrete nature of bids can cause difficulties. There are many different ways to decide which of a given set of bids to accept. We recommend that bid acceptance rules be spelled out precisely before an auction. The minimum cost selection of bids for meeting a given power requirement may involve accepting a bid with a higher unit cost than a bid that is rejected. It is undesirable for the utility to accept rigidly the discrete nature of the bids and select the set of bids that provides the desired amount of power at the minimum cost. We recommend four measures that a utility can use to reduce the impact of the discrete nature of the bids. These are (1) encouraging multiple bids by a bidder offering incremental quantities, (2) allowing a marginal bidder to downsize the quantity offered if it is too big (given the other lower bids) to be acceptable, (3) allowing a reasonable tolerance in the definition of the required quantity, and (4) valuing excess power beyond the desired quantity at its value to the utility in deciding if a marginal bid is acceptable. With these four measures, we recommend a bid acceptance procedure that considers bids sequentially in order of increasing cost per kWh. Such a procedure will have good economic and bidder incentive properties and will be more stable and "fairer" than a procedure that rigidly minimizes utility cost given the bids.

We recommend that PURPA power purchase auctions be

COMPETITION IN ELECTRICITY

held at least every few years if utility need for capacity allows and that they not be held at much shorter intervals. Too frequent auctions can put large projects at a disadvantage and facilitate collusion. Too infrequent auctions can put at a disadvantage time sensitive potentially attractive projects.

INTRODUCTION

The PURPA Power Purchase Problem

Under the Public Utilities Regulatory Policies Act (PURPA), state regulatory commissions are required to establish procedures under which electric power, produced by Qualifying Facilities (QFs), would be purchased by electric utility companies. Typically, the procedures established have allowed QFs to obtain long-term contracts to sell power to the utilities at a fixed price or a price tied to the costs of fuels used to generate power. The contracted prices were to be set to represent the utilities' avoided costs when QF power is substituted for the power that the utilities would otherwise have generated themselves or purchased elsewhere.

Recently, the availability of PURPA contracts to sell power to utilities has created, in some areas, an oversupply of power from QFs. There were two reasons for the oversupply. First, the regulatory formulas setting prices for QF power were insufficiently responsive to decreases in fossil fuel prices. Consequently, lowered expectations concerning fuel prices created a large influx of QF power offerings starting in 1984. Second, the utilities' (marginal) avoided costs fall as more power is obtained from QFs. Consequently, the avoided cost estimates used to set PURPA contract prices have proved excessive, in light of the large amount of QF power that has been offered to the utilities. These shortcomings are discussed in a DOE report prepared by Pfeffer, Lindsay & Associates [1986].

The existing PURPA power contracting system can be characterized as a price posting" procedure -- a price for offerings of PURPA power is announced, and the utility is then obligated to take all the power it is offered at that price. An alternative system could be based on a procedure of announcing the quantity of PURPA power from new capacity that a utility expects to use in the future, and then accepting bids from QFs to supply this quantity. Under this bidding system, the quantity of power obtained from QFs would be controlled directly, while the price of the power obtained would be set by the bidding procedure.

This Report

There are many ways to conduct auctions. Different auction designs can lead to very different results. This report explores the design of auctions for the purchase power from QFs under the PURPA, making recommendations where justified and identifying relevant factors and their effects when the design choices are difficult. While it appears that a well designed auction can eliminate some abuses of the posted price system, it is not the primary purpose of this report to argue that auctions are superior to posted price systems. Nor, with the exception of the brief discussion in the following subsection, do we consider negotiations an alternative to PURPA auctions.

Negotiations and PURPA Auctions

Though there are many variants and combinations, there are basically three different ways of arriving at a selection of QF power suppliers and the price for their supply: posted prices, auctions, and negotiations. By requiring utilities to buy PURPA power at or below avoided cost, the PURPA effectively eliminates the utilities' right to say no and therefore their ability to negotiate. It is beyond the scope of this report to review the reasons that led to that decision or to review its current appropriateness. However, electricity production is so complicated that a formal selection process is unlikely to set perfect terms for it. Hence, post-selection negotiations between a successful QF bidder and the utility are likely to be desirable. In considering auction design issues, we have kept in mind that such negotiations are likely to occur and that participants in the auction process are likely to anticipate them.

Another issue that arises in discussion of bidding for the right to supply QF power is the possibility of combining bidding and negotiations. They might be combined in a number

142   COMPETITION IN ELECTRICITY

of different ways. One possibility, for example, is that bids would be used to select a "short list" of potential suppliers; the utility would then negotiate in a relatively unrestricted way with those on that short list. In our view, this approach effectively restores to the utility the right to refuse and, therefore, the ability to discriminate between potential suppliers for its own purposes (including, possibly, its ownership interest in one or more of the potential suppliers). Such a process is, however, fundamentally a negotiation of the kind that the PURPA was intended to eliminate, so we do not attempt to analyze it further or to consider other similar schemes here.

Another very different possibility is that bidders could modify their initial bids in a way that is generally understood before the bids are made. In a sense, this too is a negotiation, but it is prestructured. We consider such prestructured bid modification processes and recommend one.

Finally, it is important to mention the role of negotiations, subsequent to an auction, between successful bidders and third parties such as permitting authorities, construction firms, financial institutions, and labor unions. Such negotiations are highly likely. We have considered the effect of such subsequent third-party negotiations on the choice of auction format, and, as we describe below, we have found them to have significant implications which have apparently not been dealt with previously in auction theory.

Report Organization

The introduction to this report continues with an extensive survey of the literature relevant to the PURPA auction design issue. The following section of the report examines potential criteria for designing PURPA auctions and then examines several particular auction design issues. These include the auction format (e.g., oral progressive auction, "Dutch" oral auction, discriminatory sealed bids, and nondiscriminatory sealed bids), the factors to take account in evaluating bids, dealing with possible mismatches between the discrete quantities of power offered by low bidders and the quantity needed by the utility, and the frequency of auctions.[1] The main body of the report ends with a brief conclusion.

Bidding Theory

This section reviews of the extensive literature on competitive bidding. (Surveys of this literature have been written by Engelbrecht-Wiggans [1980] and by McAfee and McMillian [1987], and Stark and Rothkopf [1979] published a bibliography of almost 500 items).

Our literature review helps us find theories useful for analyzing the PURPA problem.

The bidding theory literature can be divided into decision theoretic and game theoretic categories. The former examine the optimal strategy of a single bidder; the latter are concerned with describing auctions in equilibrium, i.e., in which each bidder follows a strategy that is optimal with respect to his competitors' strategies. (Key theoretical papers in decision theory literature are by Friedman [1956], Capen, Clapp and Campbell [1971], and Oren and Williams [1975]. While no great difficulty is involved, apparently no theoretical paper in this literature discusses the simultaneous determination of the optimal quantity and price to offer).[2] The rest of this section reviews the game theoretic literature.

Most of the bidding literature is concerned with the situation in which the bid taker is the seller of the item ("high-bid-wins"). In many cases, however, the bidder may be a seller ("low-bid-wins"). This would be the case for the PURPA power auction, for instance.

In considering theoretical bidding model results, it is usually not important whether the auction is a high-bid-wins auction or a low-bid-wins auction, since in most respects these auctions are mirror images of each other, and any result for one of them will have an analogous result for the other. Since the PURPA power auction would be a low-bid-wins auction, our discussions of it will reflect this. On the other hand, most results from the bidding literature are expressed in terms of a high-bid-wins context, and it is convenient to present results from the literature in this form.

Bidding Model Common Assumptions

Almost all theoretical analyses of bidding equilibria share the following assumptions about the nature of bidding:

144   COMPETITION IN ELECTRICITY

- Each bidder behaves rationally and expects his competitors to also behave rationally.
- Competitors share a common view of the information available to them and of the rules of the auction.

In any real world context, of course, one or both of these assumptions may be violated, particularly if the auction situation under consideration is a new one, with which the bidders have had little experience. See Rothkopf [1983a and 1983b] for a discussion of reasons for apparent non-rational behavior by bidders.

In addition, most theoretical bidding analyses make the three assumptions discussed next. (The effect of relaxing these assumptions is examined in more detail in section 1.3.4 below).

- The number of bidders is fixed and known to the bidders.

In fact, the number of bidders participating in an auction may be influenced by the nature of the auction itself, including the auction rules (discussed below). For example, there will often be prebidding expenses borne by bidders, in order to prepare themselves for the actual auction. Since, in the long run, these costs must be recovered from bidders' profits earned in the auction, the extent of these costs will affect the number of bidders. (For an analysis of these issues, as they arise in the Federal oil and gas lease auctions, see Gaskins and Teisberg [1976]). Consequently, the number of bidders and the return to the seller may depend upon the extent to which any particular auction form creates incentives for bidders to incur bid preparation costs.

Most theoretical bidding models also assume:

- The auction is a one-time event that can be analyzed in isolation from subsequent or earlier events.

The one-time event assumption needs to be modified to take account of effects on cost and competitive behavior. The cost effects may be accounted for, in principle, by estimating in a cost calculation the opportunity value in future auctions of physical and organizational assets. For example, a bidder on a construction project has to consider that he may lose future opportunities for projects by tying up his crew and equipment on the current project. Taking account of cost effects has been discussed in the literature dealing with bid optimization by a single bidder by Kortanek, et al. [1973]. The competitive effects of sequential auctions have been dealt with by Oren and Rothkopf [1975]. Using a reaction function approach, they found that bidders would bid less aggressively as the time between auctions decreased, as the discount rate decreased, and as the assumed future reaction by competitors to aggressive bidding increased. To the extent that PURPA auctions involve repeated sales (over time) of a number of power contracts in each sale, the majority of theoretical results should be understood as suggestive only, for the PURPA bidding problem.

Finally, most theoretical analyses of bidding assume:

• There is no collusion among bidders.

While there is no particular reason to expect collusion in the PURPA power bidding context, it is nevertheless appropriate to note that there are relatively few QF suppliers, they tend to belong to a few trade associations, and the stakes are high. Thus, it is also appropriate to be aware of the no-collusion assumption in considering theoretical results from the literature, In particular, there is evidence from other auction contexts an auction system's resistance to forms of cheating (rather than optimality in a model without cheating) has determined the choice of auction system.

Bidding Model Classes

While the assumptions above are common to most bidding models, the next assumptions separate theoretical models into a variety of classes. The first of these assumptions concerns the number of items for sale in the auction:

1. Item(s) for Sale (or Purchase)
   (a) Single item,
   (b) Multiple items.

A large part of the theoretical literature on bidding deals

with the problem of selling a single item through a bidding process. Since the PURPA bidding situation involves selling a number of power sales contracts (or, perhaps more appropriately, power sales options) in a single auction, the theoretical literature on the sale of multiple items in a single auction is more directly applicable to the PURPA bidding problem.

The second assumption concerns the value of the item (or items) and the information available to the bidders about this value:

2. Values and Information

   (a) Symmetric independent private values,
   (b) Asymmetric independent private values,
   (c) Symmetric common value,
   (d) Asymmetric common value.

In an independent private values model, the expected value of the item to each bidder is exactly and certainly known to that bidder. At the same time, however, the value of the item to each other bidder is not known to any one bidder, and instead is taken to be an independent random drawing from a known probability distribution. If this probability distribution is the same for all bidders, the model is referred to as a symmetric model; while if this probability distribution is different for one or more bidders, the model is an asymmetric model. The independent private values model is presumably most appropriate for auctions of items desired by bidders for their personal use, e.g., an auction of antiques to antique collectors.

The alternative to the independent private values assumption is the common value assumption. Here, the value or the item for sale is the same for all bidders, but it is not known to any of them. Instead, each bidder typically has some information, represented as a random observation from a probability distribution which depends on the unknown true value. Again, if the probability distribution from which the bidders' information is drawn is the same for all bidders, the model is a symmetric model; while if the distribution is different for at least one bidder, the model is an asymmetric model. The common value model is most appropriate as a representation for auctions of mineral rights. Since mineral rights presumably will yield approximately the same future net revenue stream to whichever bidder wins, the value of the rights must be approximately the same to each bidder, even though it may be quite uncertain to all of them.

The PURPA power auction appears to combine some characteristics of both the independent private values model and the common value model. The PURPA auction is like the common value model to the extent that bidders intend to use tile same technology to produce their power, and there is uncertainty about the costs of this technology. On the other hand, to the extent that bidders are intending to use different technologies and there is little uncertainty for a bidder about the cost of its own technology, the PURPA situation is like the independent private values model.

To the extent that the PURPA auction is like the common value model, it may be like a symmetric version of that model. That is, all bidders are assumed to have approximately the same quality of information about the cost of the common technology to be used to supply the power. On the other hand, to the extent that the PURPA auction is like the independent private values model, it is most reasonably treated as an asymmetric version of this model, because the value of the contract to each bidder is driven by the technology which that bidder intends to use to supply power. Since these technologies differ among bidders, there is no reason to think that in the independent private values formulation of the problem, each bidder would assume all other bidders' contract values were drawn from the same probability distribution.

The third assumption concerns the risk aversion or the bidders:

3. Risk Aversion

(a) Bidders are not risk averse, or only risk averse in placing a value on the item, if they owned it,

(b) Bidders are risk averse with respect to the outcome of the auction.

The most common assumption is that bidders are risk neutral. When bidders are assumed to be risk averse with respect to the outcome of the auction, this specification of the bidding problem seems to be inconsistent with common intuition about what it means to be risk averse. When we speak of someone being risk averse, we normally mean that he or she is cautious. In this sense, a risk averse bidder will be one who bids cautiously in case the asset won is worth less than anticipated or the contract won is unexpectedly expensive to execute. However, the application of the classical risk-utility theory of von Neumann and Morgenstern to auctions — especially in an independent private values contest — focuses on the risk of losing the auction. Thus, in this context a "risk averse" bidder bids more aggressively than a "risk neutral" one. For the most part, we will not put a lot of weight here on the bidding models that incorporate bidders' risk aversion.

The last assumption concerns the rules of the auction:

4. Auction Rules

   (a) First-price sealed bid,
   (b) Dutch,
   (c) English,
   (d) Second-price sealed bid.

The first-price sealed bid auction is common sealed bidding in which all bidders submit a single bid in a sealed envelope (or some other private communication). When the bids are opened, the winning bidder is the one with the highest bid, and this bidder obtains the item by paying the seller the amount of his bid. If there are to be multiple winners, the auction is "discriminatory." With K winners, the K highest bids win, and each winner pays the amount of his own bid.

In the Dutch auction, prices are called out (or otherwise made public), starting at a very high price at which no bidder would be willing to purchase the item. Then, progressively lower prices are called out until one of the bidders indicates his willingness to pay the last price named. This bidder is the winner, and he obtains the item by paying the last named price to the seller. If there are multiple items for sale, this first bidder takes as many as he wishes at its price. If there are any items left, the auction resumes with the calling of successively lower price.

The English auction is also known as an open or progressive auction. This is the standard kind or auction in which bidders indicate to an auctioneer that they will top the current best offer by a certain (usually small) amount. Once the price reaches the point where no one is willing to top the last price bid, the bidder submitting the last bid is the winner, and he obtains the item for sale by paying the last bid price to the seller. Note that the winning bidder need pay only marginally more than any other bidder is willing to pay no matter how much he would be willing to bid.

Finally, the second-price sealed bid auction is one in which all bidders submit a single bid in a sealed envelope (or some other private communication). The bidder submitting the highest price is then the winner, and he obtains the item by paying the amount of the second highest bid to the seller. If there are multiple identical items for sale, "second-price" becomes "highest-losing-price."

Taken together, assumptions 1, 2, 3, and 4 above create the logical possibility of 64 distinct types of bidding models (or even more, if the possibility of part independent private values, and part common value is admitted). Therefore, we will not attempt to present results exhaustively for each of these bidding model types. Instead, we will concentrate on the results which are most prominent in the literature, and those which have special significance for the PURPA bidding problem.

Prominent Bidding Results Under Basic Assumptions

A number of important results in the literature have to do with the way that the four auction rules mentioned above affect the behavior of bidders and the performance of the auction. The bulk of this theory is developed around the following assumptions:

(1a) Single item,
(2a) Symmetric independent private values,
(3a) Risk neutral bidders.

(For the seminal work on this model, which contains most of the results cited below, see Vickrey [1961]). For this kind of model, the first-price sealed bid and Dutch auction rules are "strategically equivalent." This means that the optimal bidding strategy for each (non-colluding) bidder in the auction is the same under either auction rule. Consequently, the winning bidder will be the same as the revenue to the seller, under either auction rule.

In simple terms, the optimal bidding strategy in a first-price sealed bid or Dutch auction is as follows. Any given bidder determines the probability distribution of the second highest bid for the item, assuming that the given bidder himself places the highest value on the item. Then, the given bidder submits a sealed bid (or stops the auction process in the Dutch auction) at the price that represents an optimal trade-off between a lower probability of winning, on the one hand, and a higher profit if he does win, on the other hand. It turns out that in equilibrium, the bidder who wins this auction submits a bid equal to the expected value of the second highest valuation.

In addition, for the model with the above assumptions, the English and second-price sealed bid auctions are also strategically equivalent. In the English auction, each bidder stays in the competition until the bid called by the auctioneer exceeds his valuation. At that point, he drops out. The auction is over once the second highest valuation is reached. Although less intuitively obvious, the optimal strategy for bidders in the second-price sealed bid auction is to submit bids equal to their own valuations. Then, the winning bidder pays the amount of the second highest bid, which is exactly the same as what this bidder would have paid in an English auction. Consequently, the revenue to the seller is the same under the English and second-price sealed bid auction rules.

Because the optimal strategy of each bidder in the second-price sealed bid auction is to bid exactly his own valuation of the item being auctioned, this auction rule is said to lead to "truth revealing" behavior. Second-price auctions are "truth revealing," because they "disconnect" the price a winning bidder pays from the decision to award the item to that bidder. To understand this, consider the situation faced by bidders in a PURPA auction of a single power contract.

For any given bidder in the auction, consider the alternatives of bidding more or bidding less than that bidder's true cost of power production (true cost of production here is meant to include normal cost of capital, appropriately adjusted for the risk of the investment). Since the bidder does not know whether or not he will be successful bidding his true cost of power, he must consider both situations.

First, suppose the bidder would be successful, bidding his true cost of production. If he lowers his bid from this level, he will still be successful and he will still be paid the same price for power-so there is no advantage in lowering his bid. If he raises his bid, the amount he is paid (if successful) will still be same, but he starts to run a risk of becoming an unsuccessful bidder-so there is a disadvantage in raising his bid.

Second, suppose the bidder would be unsuccessful, bidding his true cost of production. If he lowers his bid from this level, he may become a successful bidder. However, if he does become a successful bidder, it will only be because his bid is less than another bid that was below his previous bid (i.e., his cost of production). If this happens, the bidder will be successful, but the price he will be paid will be less than his cost of production. Consequently, there is a disadvantage in lowering his bid in this situation. On the other hand, if the bidder would be unsuccessful bidding his true cost of production, he will still be unsuccessful if he raises his bid from this level-so there is no advantage to raising his bid.

In sum, raising or lowering the bid from true cost of production will either be disadvantageous to the bidder, or it will have no effect on the bidder. Consequently, the best strategy for the bidder to follow is to bid his true cost of production. Note also that this is true regardless of the bidding strategies being followed by other bidders.

Either the second-price sealed bid auction or the English auction is guaranteed to sell the item being auctioned to the bidder who values it most. This is an efficient outcome. It is also true that the first-price sealed bid and Dutch auctions will result in the item being sold to the bidder who values it most highly. (Note, however, that this result is true only under the symmetry assumption — see below for more on this.)

The final result for auctions that conform to the assumptions listed above is that all four auction rules return the same expected revenue to the seller of the item. While this result is quite surprising at first, it is less so in light of the result cited above concerning the optimal strategy of a bidder in the first-price and Dutch auctions. Recall that this strategy is to submit a sealed bid equal to the expected second highest valuation, on the assumption that the bidder is

COMPETITION IN ELECTRICITY

himself the highest evaluator of the item. This implies that the expected value of the winning bidder's bid will be the expected value of the second highest valuation. Since this is exactly the expected value of the winning bidder's payment in the second-price and English auctions, the revenue equivalence of all four auctions is apparent. (For a very general mathematical proof, see Myerson [1981]).

It is useful to discuss revenue equivalence further and in the context of an auction in which there are many bidders, each with one item to sell at a different cost, and a single buyer who desires many items (but fewer than there are bidders). If the auction is nondiscriminatory, the optimum strategy for each bidder is to bid at his cost. This results in a supply demand situation as shown in Figure 9-1. If, on the other hand, the auction is a discriminatory auction, then each bidder will adjust his bid (as dictated by decision theory) so as to just balance the potential extra profit from bidding higher with the potential loss of all profit from bidding above the cutoff value. If all the bidders were to estimate a high cutoff value relative to the economic equilibrium, then the actual cutoff value would, in fact, be high relative to the equilibrium although lower than the bidders estimated; bidders would tend to get higher than equilibrium profits. If all the bidders were to estimate that the cutoff value would be low relative to economic equilibrium, then the value would, in fact, be low (but higher than the bidders estimated), and bidders would tend to get lower than equilibrium profits. If, however, bidders tend to estimate a cutoff value that is approximately at the economic equilibrium value, then the bids will follow approximately the pattern shown in Figure 9-2. In this figure, the two shaded areas are equal, which implies equivalent revenues.

With consistent expectations, the top price paid in a discriminatory auction will exceed the uniform price paid in a nondiscriminatory auction, and the lowest price paid will be less. Revenue equivalence means that the average price will be the same. Relative to the nondiscriminatory auction profits, profits for bidders whose costs are low will tend to be smaller and profits for winning high cost bidders will tend to be larger. The more accurately the bidders can forecast the cutoff price, the smaller these differences will be.

Figure 9-1

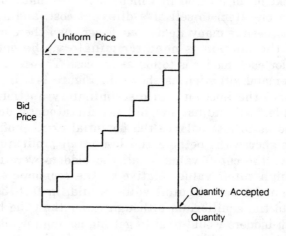

Figure 9-2

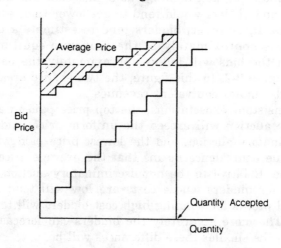

COMPETITION IN ELECTRICITY

Variation of Basic Assumptions

Next, we turn to the implications of different types of bidding models. First consider changing the symmetry assumption, i.e. the new assumption is

(2b) Asymmetric independent private values.

Under the second-price sealed bid (or English) auction rule, it remains optimal for each bidder to bid his true valuation of the item (or remain in the competition until the current bid exceeds his own evaluation). Thus, these auctions reveal truth, and they result in the item being awarded to the bidder who values it most highly, when the symmetry assumption is given up.

For the first-price sealed bid and Dutch auctions, however, the situation changes when symmetry is given up. To understand this, first suppose that there are only two bidders, and that, by chance, they happen to "draw" the same valuation of the item. Because these valuations are drawn from different distributions (and the bidders both understand this), each of the two bidders will assess a different distribution for the competitive bid, and hence, each will submit a different bid, even though their valuations are the same. Next consider increasing the valuation of the bidder who bids low. Increasing this valuation will cause this bidder to bid more, but since his bid started out as the lower bid, it will usually be possible to increase his valuation at least a little bit, without causing him to become the higher bidder. Thus, it is possible to have a situation where this bidder actually has a higher valuation, but submits a lower bid.

This kind of outcome is certainly inefficient, and gives revenue to the seller that is different from what the seller would receive under a second-price or English auction. In general, the seller's revenue could be higher or lower than it is under the second-price or English auction rules. See McAfee and McMillan [1987, pp. 713-714].

To some extent, the possibility of inefficiency in the first-price auction depends upon the ease of transferring PURPA power contracts after the auction has been concluded. If it is easy to transfer such contracts, then any misallocation of contracts in the initial auction is theoretically correctable after the auction, through privately negotiated deals between possible PURPA power' suppliers. Whether such deals would or should be allowed is a separate question. However even if they are allowed, whether they would actually take place, is uncertain. Information that a deal is mutually advantageous to the deal makers may not be available, and even if it were, transaction costs might be large enough to eliminate any potential gains from making a deal.

Next we change the perspective to consider another major class of bidding models, characterized by the values and information assumption:

(2c) Symmetric common value.

As indicated above, a PURPA power auction could have something of the character of a common value model if many or all bidders were intending to use the same technology to produce power, but each one of them has independent information about the true cost of power produced by that technology.

It is in the symmetric common value context that the idea of the "winner's curse" arises. This is the observation that if two or more bidders each independently estimate the (common) true value of an item being auctioned, then the bidder who places the highest value on the item is statistically likely to have overvalued it. This is true even though each bidder's value estimate, taken by itself, is an unbiased estimate of the value of the item. In symmetric common value models, of course, the bidders are fully aware of the "winner's curse," and they bid less than their estimates of value, in order to avoid winning the auction with a bid that is too high.

Most of the models incorporating the symmetric common value assumption also assume that the auction form is the first-price sealed bid rule. In this context, one standard result is that the expected price to the seller increases as the number of bidders increases, that the expected price converges to the true (common) value, as the number of bidders becomes arbitrarily large (Wilson [1977]). A second standard result is that the expected price to the seller increases as the uncertainty in bidders' value estimates decreases. This is clear in the limiting case w.ere bidders have no uncertainty in their estimates — the equilibrium strategy is then for each bidder to bid exactly the known true value, in which case the seller obtains the true value, regardless of the number of bidders in the auction.

Some more recent work has revealed interesting differences in the performance of the alternative auction rules (Milgrom and Weber [1982]). As in the independent private values model, the first-price sealed bid and Dutch auctions are strategically equivalent in the common value model. That is, the bidders' optimal strategies and the seller's expected revenue are the same in both auctions.

However, the second-priced sealed bid and English auctions may no longer be strategically equivalent to each other in the common value model if during the English auction process information is revealed about each bidder's estimate of the common value. Information is revealed to the extent that bidders can determine when their competitors drop out of the bidding. This information can be used by the bidder who ultimately wins the auction to improve his own estimate of the true (common) value of the item being sold. The result is that the English auction form may return, on the average, more revenue to the seller than the second-price sealed bid auction, under the common value assumption.

Moreover, the second-price sealed bid auction returns more revenue that the first-price or Dutch auction. Thus, there is a ranking of auction forms, in terms of the seller's expected revenue, in the common value model. From highest to lowest, the ranking is English, second-price sealed bid, first-price sealed bid and Dutch (tie).

There is another interesting theoretical result for the common value model. This is that information available to the seller about the true value of the item being auctioned should generally be fully and honestly reported to the bidders before the auction (Milgrom and Weber [1982]). This result occurs because with equilibrium bidding the seller's revenue goes up as bidders' uncertainty goes down. However, Kagel and Levin [1986] found persistent disequilibrium behavior in experimental common value auctions. With the behavior they observed, bidtakers would be better off not reducing bidder uncertainty.

Next, we turn to the symmetric independent private values assumption, and consider the class of models in which there is more than one item being auctioned; i.e., the new assumption is:

(1b) Multiple items.

Since two or more contracts would most likely be awarded in a PURPA power auction, this change of assumption is particularly relevant.

The major implication of selling multiple items in the same auction is that the truth revealing property of a second-price or English auction may be lost, together with the assurance that the items will be awarded to those who value them most highly. To see why the truth revealing property may be lost with multiple bids, consider a hypothetical second-price auction of PURPA power contracts. In such an auction, with the possibility of multiple contract awards, the winning bidders would receive a price equal to the amount of the lowest unsuccessful bid. Suppose, for example, that there are bids at 2.5, 3.1, and 3.3 cents. Suppose, further, that the two lower bids are large enough to satisfy the power requirement of the utility. Then, the second-price procedure applied in the multiple bid context requires that both of the successful bidders (who bid 2.5 cents and 3.1 cents) would receive contracts to sell power at 3.3 cents per kWh.

If it happens that the bidders submitting all three bids are different, then the truth revealing property of second-price auctions persists. This is because the price received is not connected to the price bid. However, if one or more of the bidders submits more than one bid, the situation changes: suppose that the same bidder has submitted the 2.5-cent bid and the 3.3-cent bid. If we again consider the incentives for this bidder to raise or lower his bid from true cost, it is apparent that such incentives now exist. Specifically, if the 3.3-cent bid is raised, the profit earned on the 2.5-cent bid will be increased. In general, any higher bid submitted by one bidder will affect the profitability of all of that bidder's lower bids.

As observed by Dubey and Shubik [1980], the disconnection between the bid and the price paid can be recovered in the multiple bid case, by employing the following procedure.

158   COMPETITION IN ELECTRICITY

For each bidder, the price paid is determined by the highest losing bid, calculated as if none of the bidder's higher bids had been submitted. Extending the example given earlier, assume that there is a fourth bid at 3.5 cents, which was submitted by an entirely different bidder. Then, the bidder bidding 2.5 and 3.3 cents would receive a price of 3.5 cents for the successful bid at 2.5 cents. The successful bidder at 3.1 cents would continue to receive a price of 3.3 cents.

By preserving the disconnection between bid(s) submitted and price paid, the above procedure preserves the truth revealing property of a second-price auction, even in the race of multiple bids by a single bidder. This approach, however, has distinct disadvantages. While it may reveal the bidders' valuations, it is clear, that the utility's average cost of power goes up, as more bids are submitted by each bidder, holding everything else constant.

Also, it is clear that bidders submitting more bids may be paid a higher average price on a successful bid than is paid to another bidder with an identical successful bid, but no other bids in the auction. This is an explicit acknowledgment of market power. It may create at least an appearance of unfairness. While one aspect of this unfairness could be corrected by paying all successful bidders the highest price determined for any one bidder under the procedure described above, doing so would further increase the utility's costs of obtaining power in the auction. It would also destroy the truth revealing incentives for bidders.

Finally, we return to the single item, symmetric, independent, private values model, but consider bidders to be risk averse in the classical sense of von Neumann and Morgenstern.

(3b) Risk Averse Bidders

If PURPA bidders are risk averse in the sense that they are concerned about the risk of losing the auction, then bidding theory indicates that with equilibrium bidding strategies the utility will do relatively better with a first-price auction (sealed bid or Dutch oral) than with a second-price auction (sealed or English). (See McAfee and McMillan [1984, p. 719] and their references, including Riley and Samuelson [1981]). In effect, bidders concerned about the risk of losing the auction will tend to bid lower, sharing more of their cost advantage with the utility in order to lessen that risk. There are no equivalent formal results for correlated value auctions, but intuition suggests that as the correlation of values increases towards a common value, the risks associated with winning the auction become important and compete with the risks of losing it, thus reducing or reversing this result.

Relaxing Common Assumptions

This section examines the implications of changing a few of the common assumptions that underlie most of theoretical bidding work. First, if the common assumption,

- The auction is a one-time event that can be analyzed in isolation from subsequent events,

is relaxed, the truth revealing property of second-price auctions may be lost because the information revealed in a second-price auction may damage the competitive position of the bidders after the auction is over. For example, if PURPA power auctions are relatively frequent and dissemination of cost information increases the number of future competitors using the best technology, the bidder who pioneered the best technology will see his profits in future auctions reduced. Alternatively, revelation of cost information could put at a disadvantage a bidder in future situations where the bidder must negotiate with potential business partners, suppliers, labor unions, the bid taker, or government regulatory agencies.

Once the above assumption is relaxed, there would also be differences in the performances of auctions relying on sealed versus oral bidding, because different amounts of information are revealed in the course of these auctions. For example, in a low-bid-wins oral auction, minimum acceptable prices of winning bidders are not revealed. In the PURPA power auction, for example, an auctioneer would call out a decreasing sequence of prices, beginning with avoided cost, until the amount of capacity offered by QF bidders at each price had been reduced to the amount of capacity required by the utility. At this point, the auction procedure would be over, and the minimum price that each winning bidder would have accepted is would not be revealed. By contrast, in a second-price sealed bid auction, the actual bids would make public the minimum acceptable prices of the winning bidders unless there was a successful effort to keep them secret.

Next we consider the assumption that

• The number of bidders is fixed.

It is clear that the auction outcome can be influenced by the decision of potential bidders to bid and that the form of the auction can influence that decision. Both theoretical arguments and observations of practice support this conclusion. Engelbrecht-Wiggans [1987], critiquing a prestigious paper on optimal reservation prices in auctions, has shown theoretically that the results depend heavily on the assumption that changing the reservation price will not affect the number of bidders. There is also empirical evidence for this from the early history of U.S. commerce.

In the years before the war of 1812, Philadelphia, New York and Boston handled roughly equal volumes of import trade. Much of the imported merchandise was sold at auctions not far from the docks. Shortly after the end of the war, the New York auctioneers, with the express intent of attracting buyers to New York, obtained legislation requiring that all goods offered at auction in New York be sold without reservation (i.e., without withdrawal from sale) to the highest bidder. It worked. Apparently, buyers came to New York to find the bargains, and the ships came to New York to find the buyers. By 1825, when the Erie Canal was ready to open, the port of New York was handling three times the volume of imports handled by either Boston or Philadelphia. All of this is documented in considerable detail in a 1961 history of that port (Albion [1961]).

There is also recent evidence that form of auction matters. The timber industry has consistently lobbied for the use of progressive oral auctions rather than sealed bids for federal timber sales. Regression studies (Weiner [1979]; Hansen [1986]) give results consistent with the government getting more revenue from sealed bids. Apparently, the cause of this deviation from classical revenue neutrality is the reluctance of bidders with distant mills to enter an oral auction for timber near another bidder's mill (see Mead [1967]). In an oral auction, unlike a sealed bid situation, a bidder can react to unexpected competition, thus depriving a bidder with a cost disadvantage of any chance of winning and of any incentive to bid.

The relevant point to PURPA here is not one about optimal reservation prices (avoided cost will be the reservation price in a PURPA auction) or about geographic proximity. Rather it is that the results of the standard "high theory" of auctions use the assumption of a fixed number of bidders and are quite sensitive to it. Any variation in auction rules that tends to attract additional bidders could be of economic importance.

Next we turn to the common assumption

• There is no collusion among bidders.

Some theoretical work indicates the degree to which the alternative auction rules might facilitate collusive agreements among bidders. This work indicates that the greater amount of information generated in an oral auction can facilitate collusion among the bidders (Robinson [1985]). If there is a collusive agreement among bidders, it may be possible in an oral auction to observe whether or not others are sticking to their parts of a prearranged bargain. To this extent, the oral auction procedure is more susceptible to collusive behavior than sealed bidding.

For example, assume (1) there are two bidders in a PURPA power auction, (2) either bidder can supply exactly the amount of capacity desired by the utility, (3) Bidder One has a minimum acceptable price of 2.5 cents, while Bidder Two has a minimum acceptable price of 2.6 cents. Suppose, further, that they have agreed to collude, with Bidder One agreeing to make a small payoff to Bidder Two, if Bidder Two will behave as if his minimum acceptable price were 4 cents.

In an oral auction, Bidder One can directly observe whether or not Bidder Two drops out of the bidding at a price of 4 cents, as they had agreed. If Bidder Two does not drop out, Bidder One can respond by remaining in the bidding until the price drops to 2.6 cents, at which Bidder Two will certainly drop out. Naturally, Bidder One would not make the agreed payment to Bidder Two in this case. Consequently, Bidder Two would end up with nothing, while BiddermOne would end up with only a 0.1 cent profit on his winning bid. Since this outcome is undesirable from the point of view of both bidders, we would expect that the bidders would in fact be adhere to their collusive agreement.

In a sealed bid auction, however, the result could be different. Suppose, for example, that Bidder Two agrees to bid 4 cents, while Bidder One plans to bid, say, 3.5 cents, in order to avoid a conspicuously large difference between the two bids submitted. Now Bidder Two may be tempted to bid, say, 3.4 cents, hoping to steal the bid from Bidder One and make a profit of 0.8 cents. Assuming this is in excess of the payoff promised by Bidder One, and assuming that Bidder Two is not worried about the long-term conse-quences of double crossing his colluding partner, Bidder Two might adopt this strategy in the sealed biding context. Consequently, collusion may be more difficult for bidders to enforce, under a sealed bidding procedure, and this in turn may increase the reluctance of bidders to collude.

ANALYSIS OF ISSUES THAT WOULD ARISE IN PURPA AUCTIONS

Criteria for Designing the Auction

Several auction characteristics are of interest in designing an auction to sell PURPA power contracts: the economic efficiency of the auction; the utility's cost of power obtained through the auction; possible tendencies, if any, of the auction to create and sustain collusive behavior on the part of the bidders; the fairness and appearance of fairness of the auction; and the general workability of the auction design.

Efficiency

A PURPA power auction is economically efficient if QFs with the lowest costs of providing power are the successful bidders. Intuitively, one might expect this outcome from any kind of auction system. However, as indicated in the preceding review of theoretical bidding models, auction inefficiency is certainly possible in some common bidding situations, such

CHAPTER NINE   163 as the situation with asymmetric independent private values. And, of course, inefficiency may also result if bidders do not understand the consequences of their bidding behavior in a complicated auction system or if they misjudge the bidding behavir of their competitors. The latter sources of inefficiencies can exist, in any bidding situation.

Although the second-price auction procedure is efficient in some theoretical situations where first-price auctions might not be efficient, the theoretical analyses fail to include two important aspects of the real world which are important in the PURPA bidding context. Specifically, the truth-revealing property of second-price auctions, which creates the theoretical efficiency of these auctions, is unlikely to be preserved in a PURPA auction. One reason is that there are frequently situations following the auction where it would be disadvantageous to the winning bidders to have fully revealed in the auction their costs or power production. The other reason is that bidders often have different amounts of power to offer at different costs. We, therefore, believe that the theoretical efficiency advantage of second-price auctions is not a compelling reason to favor this auction form over the first-price auction.

Cost of Power

If the lowest cost power producers are the successful bidders in an auction, the cost of power to the utility should be minimized. However, the relationship is not direct, since the cost of power to the utility will depend upon how the benefits (the economic rent) of low-cost power are divided between the power producer and the utility purchasing the power. From a policy perspective, this is a difficult issue. If rent is shifted to the utility purchaser, the ratepayers benefit. However, if the rent is retained by the power producers, the long-run incentive to develop PURPA power is enhanced. Both of these results are usually considered desirable policy objectives.

Most alternative auction forms theoretically provide the same cost of power to the utility. The most compelling exception to this statement is that the progressive oral auction may produce a lower cost of power, to the extent that bidding behavior during the course of the bidding generates information that reduces the uncertainty of the bidders who ultimately win the auction. This theoretical result would carry less weight, to the extent that bidders are quite certain of their costs before entering the auction, or to the extent that other bidders are using different technologies, so the bidding behavior of any one bidder provides little information to the others. If bidders are averse to the risk of losing the auction, then sealed first-price bidding should produce lower costs.

Risk of Collusion

The existence of incentives for collusion among bidders is generally considered to be undesirable. Collusion would tend to raise the costs of power to utilities, together with the profits of colluding bidders. Also, collusive bidding behavior may create inefficiencies, by setting a price umbrella that encourages entry of new higher cost producers. Finally, of course, collusion is explicitly illegal.

As discussed above, the progressive oral auction is more susceptible to collusive behavior on the part of the bidders. To the extent that collusion is a risk, the expected cost of power to the utility will be higher under an oral progressive auction procedure.

Fairness

Since PURPA auctions would be sanctioned by governmental regulatory agencies, and possibly include regulated electric utilities as sponsors, participants or both, it is important that the auction design be perceived as fair to all participants.

Although theoretical results obtainable under strong assumptions indicate that the cost of power to the utility may be the same under either a first- or second-price auction procedure, the public is likely to think that a second-price procedure is giving something away to the winning bidders. First-price auctions do not usually create such an impression. On the other hand, a case can be made for both the fairness and the appearance of fairness associated with a nondiscriminatory second-price auction which pays all winners the same price.

Workability

The costs and practical considerations of carrying out an auction can be affected by auction design. When transactions are small, ease and speed may be prime considerations, some form of oral auction is often used. With PURPA auctions, the amounts involved are large compared to the cost of the auction itself. However, the large amounts involved suggest formal procedures with written bids that can be carefully checked by several different persons in a bidding organization.

Workability can also be a factor in bid acceptance procedures as the discussion below of "lumpiness" will indicate.

Overall Auction Format Recommendation

A principal decision in the design of a PURPA auction system is the choice between sealed first-price, sealed second-price, oral progressive, and oral Dutch procedures. The California PUC, following the sophisticated analysis of Southern California Edison (Vail [1986]; Jurewitz [1986]) has decided to implement a sealed second-price procedure (California PUC [1986]). Other states are moving towards sealed first-price procedures (Massachusetts [1986]), often without explicitly considering other alternatives. We are not aware that any active consideration being given to oral procedures.

Of the four procedures, we recommend the sealed first-price format. Here is our logic.

First, the PURPA auction is a formal procedure involving large amounts of money and simultaneous decisions on multiple bids. This strongly argues for written bid procedures. In particular, the oral Dutch procedure offers no advantages over sealed first-price bidding and can be eliminated from further consideration.

Second, the theoretical arguments for the superior economic efficiency of sealed second-price auctions fail for two reasons: (1) bidders will often have different quantities of electricity to offer at different prices, and (2) bidders often must engage in subsequent negotiations with third parties whose positions may be influenced by the perceived amount of "extra" compensation received by the bidder in a the second-price auction. Each of these factors destroys the incen-

COMPETITION IN ELECTRICITY

tive of the bidders to bid in a truth revealing manner. Note that these incentive effects are in addition to any purely behavioral reluctance of bidders to engage in the "truth revealing" (i.e., cost revealing) behavior called for by the theory of second-price auctions. It is important to acknowledge, however, that the failure of the argument for the economic superiority of the second-price auction does not prove that the first-price auction is more efficient.

The choice on economic efficiency grounds would seem to require a balance between the inefficiency induced in first-price auctions due to the inability of competitors to estimate the cutoff price, and the inefficiencies induced in second-price auctions by bidders' concerns about extra rent capture by third parties and by that rent capture itself. The more regular and important PURPA auctions become, the heavier the latter factors weigh relative to the former as bidders learn to estimate cutoff price more accurately. Finally, it is not clear to us that either procedure has a relative advantage in dealing with the economic distortions induced by the monopoly power of those bidders able to supply varying amounts of power at different prices.

Having failed to find an advantage for sealed second-price auctions on economic efficiency grounds, we have other reasons for preferring sealed first-price auctions. Such auctions do not raise fairness issues of apparent "overpayment" or explicit recognition of market power. More important, sealed first-price auctions are familiar. They are unlikely to intimidate or scare off potential bidders. Sealed second-price procedures, on the other hand, are almost unknown. Although it is not likely to be a significant problem in the PURPA context, they require an additional level of trust in the bidding process (i.e., trust that the bid taker will not insert a losing bid that lowers the compensation of winning bidders after the sealed bids are opened). Finally, the appropriate strategy for bidding in sealed second-price auctions will be uncertain at least at first.

Finally, we have reconsidered an oral progressive auction format as a potential second-price alternative to sealed formats. Relative to sealed second-price, the oral progressive format has two advantages. It is familiar, and it does not require bidders to reveal how far they would be willing to go. These advantages, however, have offsets. As we have already mentioned, the amounts of money involved in PURPA auctions are very large for oral bidding. In addition, oral progressive auctions are stable under bidder collusion and, therefore, are more subject to it than sealed bids.

On balance, we find nothing superior to familiar sealed first-price bidding.

Multiple Price Bids

As the next section discusses, the commodity offered by the bidders has multiple aspects such as reliability, dispatchability and financial risk. There are auctions in which a single bid offers multiple unit prices for different commodities. This is most common in bidding for construction contracts (See Stark [1974]) but also occurs in federal timber auctions. Such an auction form is typically motivated by the desire of the bid taker to retain the quantity risk. It is notorious that such auctions can be gamed (Stark [1974], GAO [1983]) in ways that lead to undesirable results. Since the common motivation for such auctions is not important in PURPA auctions and since such auctions have difficulties even when that motivation is present, we do not recommend them.

Bid Evaluation Process

The commodity offered by bidders is complex. It may be desirable to reflect that complexity in the bid evaluation schemes that are used to rank offers. The problem posed by this complexity is that all the relevant dimensions are not easily monetized or reducible to some common measure. Further, as the evaluation scheme becomes more complex, it can become more arbitrary and more subject to gaming by the participants. The tension between simple and complex bid evaluation is illustrated by the contrasting evaluation schemes of the California PUC and the utilities in Massachusetts. In California, the price offered by bidders is the one and only measure of their relative value.[3] The auction design adopted by the California PUC reduces the price issue to a single variable. In Massachusetts, the utilities are proposing complex schemes which involve the balancing of qualitative factors against price.

168   COMPETITION IN ELECTRICITY

To elucidate the bid evaluation issue, we first summarize the schemes proposed by Boston Edison (BE) and Western Massachusetts Electric (WEMCO). With this background we then review the various non-price issues that must be dealt with in an auction either through formal evaluation schemes or other procedures. The non-price issues include dispatchability, reliability, financial risks and transmission access.

Summary of Massachusetts Proposals

The Massachusetts Department of Public Utilities (MDPU) adopted an order on August 25, 1986 defining a procedure under which private producers of electricity would submit proposals to sell power to utilities. The MDPU order outlined the general form of the competitive procedure including the factors used to rank different proposals. The utilities submitted Requests for Proposals (RFP) in October 1986. The essential element of the RFP is a scoring system for ranking projects. The two major utilities, BE and WEMCO, took somewhat different approaches. We summarize the formulas proposed by each utility.

The BE formula is the simpler of the two. The bidders' score is computed by the following expressions:

Bidder's Score = Price Component + Quality Component,
where Price Component = Ratepayer Benefit X Risk
Breakeven Factor X Risk
Mitigation Factor,
and Quality Component = (Present Value Avoided Cost)/
(Present Value Quality Adjusted Bid)

The Price Component is straightforward. Ratepayer Benefit is the ratio of present value avoided cost to present value of the bid. The two other terms address the risks associated with a bid stream that is "front-loaded." Bidders may need revenue above avoided cost in the early years of their projects. Bids of this kind are allowed, but they impose risks on ratepayers. The Breakeven Factor adjusts for time required for ratepayer benefits to become positive (i.e. present value of bid costs are less than present value of avoided cost). The Mitigation Factor adjusts for the kind of security bidders offer to the utility as insurance against the risk of front loading.

The Quality Component is designed to address less concrete issues. It has two parts. One is a "Development Score" which measures how well-developed the bidder's project is. The second part is a set of Bonus Points. Projects obtain these points if they exhibit features that BE deems desirable. The greatest value is assigned to projects which are not oil or gas-fired (this fuel diversity quality is given three points). The next most important qualities (two points) are dispatchability, maintenance scheduling by BE, favorable site in the transmission and distribution network, and previous development experience. Finally a number of other qualities are assigned a single bonus point. The project score is averaged over all qualities. Both the Development Score and the Bonus Points are used to compute a quality adjusted price. This adjusted price determines the Quality Component of the score.

WEMCO developed a scoring process that can be expressed by the following formulas:

Bidder's Score = (Expected Ratepayer Impact)/ (Confidence Factor X System Compatibility),
where Expected Rate Impact = Sum of Probability(i) X Rate(i) Scenario Impact,
Rate(i) Scenario Impact = (Price Factor (i))/ Front-Loading Factor (i);
Confidence Factor = Operating Risk Factor X Development Risk Factor;
and System Compatibility = Weighted Average of Attributes.

The Expected Rate Impact is a probability weighted average of rate impacts in a high, a medium and a low avoided cost scenario. The rate impact in a given scenario is a ratio of the Price Factor (which is the same quantity as the BE Ratepayer Benefit) and a Front Loading Factor. WEMCO's measurement of the front loading effect differs from BE's by concentrating only on the first five years of operation. The Confidence Factor consists of two components called Operating Risk Factor and Development Risk Factor. The Operating

Risk Factor is addressed to the potential default of the project. One of its components is a function of the security deposit posted by the developer against cumulative front loading. its other component depends on estimates of the project's ability to cover its costs with its own projected revenues. For this computation, the developer must supply cost and revenue data that is normally confidential. The Development Risk Factor is a more complicated version of the BE Development Score. Finally, the System Compatibility Factor is similar to the Bonus Points used by BE to weight attributes of projects such as dispatchability, fuel availability, location, project size, and voltage impacts.

This outline of the BE and WEMCO RFPs does not reflect all the details of their scoring processes. It does, however, illustrate some of the pitfalls and promises of complicated scoring systems. The pitfalls are a certain degree of arbitrariness and duplication. In complex formulas such as these, relatively firm economic relations get traded off against qualitative features. The "exchange rate" between the economics and the features is not grounded in anything explicit. WEMCO's formulas seem to involve some double counting. Front loading is treated both in the Ratepayer Impact and the Operating Risk Factor. On the positive side, the explicit treatment of various avoided cost scenarios in the WEMCO formula gives a better picture of the bid economics than using a single scenario.

The sections that follow consider several of the important non-price features which might be considered in evaluating a bid. We discuss the merits of incorporating these into an evaluation scheme and into methods for assessing their relative importance.

Dispatchability

A private producer must choose whether or not to allow the utility control over the project's output. The producer's choice is influenced by both technological constraints and economic values. On the utility's side, the ability to dispatch a project has greater or less value depending on the supply and demand balance and the degree to which system constraints are binding. Indeed, the amount of control implied by the term dispatchability differs qualitatively. At the lower limit of control is the ability to interrupt or curtail briefly during low load hours. At the opposite extreme is total utility discretion. The Massachusetts utilities do not place much value on dispatchability in their scoring systems. It is treated as one among many qualitative features, and not the most important of those. In California, however, dispatchability has much greater value, particularly in Northern California because of the large but variable amount of hydro energy available. Furthermore, existing QFs which cannot be curtailed have limited the utility's ability to purchase inexpensive power from the Pacific Northwest.

Recent regulatory decisions in California regarding the siting of large private cogeneration projects show an increasing emphasis on dispatchability. This has been a response to the perception of a potentially excessive amount of baseload capacity that would have to be purchased under the PURPA regulations. By shifting resources from the baseload to the dispatchable category, the utility is able to purchase larger quantities of low-cost energy from other sources. The terms of the resulting dispatchable purchase contracts vary substantially from project to project and across utilities. The Gilroy Cogeneration Project is a 120 MW facility which will be fully dispatchable by Pacific Gas and Electric (PG&E) during the first four months of each year and completely curtailable from midnight to 6 AM during the last eight months of the year. The utility pays a premium of approximately 15% above the energy cost it would otherwise offer for this flexibility. In addition, the utility also pays the start-up costs of the project when it has been shut down under these provisions (CEC [1985]). Recently, a similar project agreed to somewhat greater dispatchability without any energy cost premium (BAF [1987]). A 220 MW project has signed a contract with PG&E that provides for complete dispatchability in all hours for a fifteen year period (Marcus [1986]). The utility pays no premium for this right, which is offered by the project in answer to regulatory concerns about excess baseload PURPA power in Northern California. The same concerns in Southern California appear to be less severe. The typical dispatchability condition on large cogeneration projects is approximately two thousand hours of curtailment of only 25% of the project's capacity, as opposed to the total shutdowns contemplated by PG&E. A representative case is the 345 MW ARCO Watson project (CEC [1986]).

The value of dispatchability is difficult to estimate and clearly depends on particular system conditions that can change over time. It can be thought of as analogous to the operating benefits of energy storage plants or other "quick start" resources. Spinning reserve requirements are reduced, load following capability is improved, and minimum loading on other plants can be decreased. The economics of these operational benefits are now being studied systematically (Decision Focus [1986]). It is therefore difficult to imagine an easily understandable "avoided cost" characterization of dispatchability. An auction procedure could certainly allow for bidders to offer dispatchability, but there would be the problem of determining what different kinds of dispatchability were worth compared to price offers.

Incorporating dispatchability into the bidding process would require sufficient analysis to differentiate this property into a number of distinct categories. Such analysis might determine, for example, three categories: (1) limited curtailment of up to 1000 hours per year, (2) "off peak" curtailment of 4000 - 5000 hours per year, and (3) total curtailment potential in all hours of the year. Bidders proposing baseload projects would only offer type (1) dispatchability, if any. Types (2) and (3) would seem to compete against each other. Some bidders might propose to "migrate" from a type (2) or (3) status to a type (1) status over a period of years. Some kind of point scoring system would be necessary to evaluate differentiated offers of this kind. As system conditions change, the values of different types of dispatchability also change. One method to deal with this problem would be to have separate auctions for baseload and dispatchable projects. Our category (1) would apply to baseload, category (3) to dispatchable. Category (2) is ambiguous. It is a policy question whether dispatchability ought to be explicitly incorporated in bid evaluation or through separate auctions. Because of its importance, however, it is unlikely that it can be treated through post-hoc adjustment, which is more appropriate to capacity valuation, where performance standards can be used to appropriately price reliability.

Reliability and Capacity Value

The value of electric power can be separated into a capacity or reliability component and an energy component (NERA [1977]). Pricing schemes for bidding or any other purpose can bundle these components together or separate them. The Massachusetts RFPs choose the bundling approach. In California, PURPA pricing has traditionally unbundled capacity and energy. When capacity is priced separately, measurement requires careful definition. The basic questions are: when does power have capacity value, what is the basis for that value, and how do you segment that value into components? The segmentation question is fundamental to developing performance standards that can translate a producer's actual output into a payment that reflects value to the utility. The value basis question addresses issues involving the supply and demand balance, and the variation in the total value of capacity with greater or smaller reserve margins. We begin our discussion with the value basis issue. This is an avoided cost question. (The segmentation issue leads to the question of performance standards).

The value of capacity depends on the supply demand balance. If that balance is tight, then capacity has a higher value than if there is substantial excess capacity. Traditionally, utilities have relied on probability indices to define the need for capacity and to measure excesses or insufficiencies (Bhavaraju [1982]). The baseline reliability deemed acceptable has always been somewhat arbitrary. Recently, efforts have been made to tie the baseline level more closely to impacts on customers. PG&E has developed an approach based on the cost of interruptions to customers (Hall, Healy and Poland [1986]). The PG&E method has been extended to situations in which there is "excess capacity" (Poland [1986]). The purpose of this extension is to provide a rational system for discounting the equilibrium capacity value. In equilibrium, i.e., when the system is at the appropriate baseline level of reliability, the value of capacity is measured by the costs of a combustion turbine. The combustion turbine represents the cheapest way of providing reliable capacity to the system.

Once the annual value of reliability has been determined,

i.e. the combustion turbine cost has been estimated and a discount applied if appropriate, the issue of performance standards arises. Private producers contract to provide reliable capacity, but they only have value if they deliver power when the system needs it. Setting performance standards defines the match between need and the producer's output. The California PUC adopted the rule under all Standard Offers that QFs had to maintain an 80% capa-city factor during the summer on-peak period to receive the full contracted capacity payment. This simple requirement is roughly equivalent to the expected performance of a combustion turbine.

A more detailed view of reliability involves differentiating performance into components. The California PUC has begun to pursue this line of investigation at the request of the representatives of the QF industry (CPUC [1986]). The California QF industry views the various aspects of capacity performance, such as emergency availability, reactive power support and coordination of maintenance as added benefits of QF capacity. The California utilities view these qualities as either already available under current performance standards (in particular, coordinated maintenance) or implicitly valued under current methods. The theory of implicit valuation means that these performance features should be supplied by the QF and would, in principle, be supplied by equivalent utility resources. Therefore, if a QF did not supply these features, the capacity payment should be reduced (SCE [1986]). Despite the conflict about whether these features add to or potentially reduce capacity value, both parties agree that complex measurement issues are involved.

What is significant about this discussion is that the complexity of the value issue is focused on post facto measurable performance. None of these questions enter into the auction process which the California PUC is establishing. Bidders will be chosen on an essentially bundled basis, but they will be paid separately for energy and capacity. If their capacity performance meets specified standards, they will be paid their bid price for the capacity component. If not, there will be downward adjustments. None of these performance issues needs incorporation in the bid evaluation process. The advantage of performance standards is that they address concerns about bidders from the system, for example, by diverting power to their own use during peak periods.

Figure 9-3

Abandonment exposure

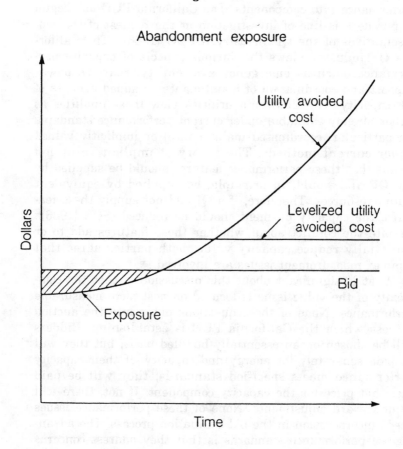

176   COMPETITION IN ELECTRICITY

Financial Risks

The Massachusetts RFPs devote considerable attention to issues associated with the financial risks imposed on ratepayers by "front loaded" bids. "Front loading" is a situation in which the bidder seeks payment in excess of avoided cost at the beginning of his project, and compensates for this by receiving less than avoided cost in the later years. The ratepayers are exposed to the project's potential default until the initial overpayments are recovered on a present value basis. If the project is abandoned before this repayment occurs, ratepayers have lost money relative to the avoided cost. Figure 9-3 illustrates this abandonment exposure.

It is important to note that the financial risks of front-loaded bids are distinct from the risk of capacity shortage resulting from project failures. Under any scheme of capacity, purchase there is always a capacity shortage risk if the supplier fails to meet his obligation. This applies to PURPA contracts as well as non-PURPA contracts. If a QF receiving front-loaded payments fails to deliver, then ratepayers are injured economically over and above the shortage costs imposed by that failure. Since the risk of shortage costs is common to all contracts, it is not a unique PURPA problem. For this reason, we ignore it and concentrate only on the financial problem of front loading.

There are a number of ways to handle the risks imposed by front loaded bids. The simplest method is to prohibit them. Such a step would reduce the number of potential bidders, but in the event of a sufficient supply this may not be harmful. Front loading may be symptomatic of a relatively undeveloped private power industry. As bidders gain experience, they may be able to structure their projects so that front loading is unnecessary. If front loading is not explicitly forbidden, it can be limited, discouraged, or compensated for in several ways. These include the use of security deposits or related instruments, or implicit or explicit discounting of front loaded bids. These various alternatives can be used separately or in combination.

Security deposits or guarantees are essentially forms of default insurance. Front loading can be thought of as a loan from ratepayers to project sponsors. If security is required from the project developer, the ratepayer's exposure is eliminated or reduced. There are a number of ways that security can be obtained, but all of them are costly to the developer. Requiring security, therefore, is a disincentive to developers. The Massachusetts RFPs discuss a weak form of security, which is a lien on the project. In the event of default, the utility would acquire the facility. Since this is not cash security, it is less burdensome to the developer. It is, however, also worth less to ratepayers than cash security, since a project that proves uneconomic to the developer would not necessarily be economic to the utility either. Still, liens can be valuable in the event of a capacity shortage. It might be desirable to combine liens with insurance if front loading is allowed.

In addition to security, the utility can insist on a discount from avoided cost as a condition of front loading. This approach has been used to some extent in California, particularly with wind turbine projects developed in the early 1980s (Kahn [1984]). It is difficult but possible to find a reasonable basis for trading off risk against price in this situation. The mechanics of the trade-off also require attention. If interest is charged on the overpayments, different methods may be used to select an appropriate rate. If the discount is deferred until after the debt to ratepayers is repaid, the benefit of discounting may never be realized in the event of default.

A final alternative, used by the Massachusetts utilities, is implicit discounting through the bid evaluation process. Massachusetts' scoring systems give lower rankings to projects that require front loading. The greater the degree of front loading, the more the scoring system penalizes a bid. In addition, these evaluation systems rank higher those projects that provide security. These indirect methods impose no revenue penalty on front loaded projects, but they require bidders to lower their prices to compete successfully. Although the qualitative effect of these scoring systems is reasonable, their precise formulation is somewhat arbitrary. WEMCO appears to penalize front loading more than BE, if only because its scoring system counts the financial risks twice rather than once. Although this may be appropriate, it will take experience to fine tune the evaluation of financial risk.

If the PURPA auction mechanism matures into a large market, then methods to accommodate financial risk will almost certainly appear. If financial risks are the limiting factor on the development of the PURPA auction market, however, then perhaps projects requiring front loading will be precluded from competing.

Transmission Access Cost Impacts

PURPA projects require access to the utility transmission network. In small amounts, this will probably not impose significant constraints on the power system. At some point, however, transmission can become a limiting factor. In Northern California, there appears to be more QF capacity than there is spare transmission capacity. To deal with this imbalance, a rationing system has evolved that is essentially a first-come, first-served procedure. The alternative to this for developers without access is to construct their own transmission line to a point in the network that can accommodate their output. Developers in the Stockton area are planning such a project to be funded at their own expense (Meek [1986]). An even more extreme example is the proposed 200-mile line from central Nevada to Southern California that is being sponsored by geothermal developers (Oxbow Geothermal [1986]).

The exclusive rationing and do-it-yourself approaches to transmission access represent polar extremes. Intermediate cases would involve costing transmission access either through a bid evaluation mechanism, an explicit charge to projects or both. In any of these intermediate cases, there is a transaction cost to estimating what the appropriate access charge should be. Clearly, the utility is in the position to determine this cost. Analysis of transmission systems is difficult; in particular, the marginal costs at a particular point may not even be well-defined.

Given the analytical difficulties, some indeterminacy may be introduced into the auction and development process. It is possible, for example, that a bidder would agree to pay whatever access charge was deemed appropriate if his project is selected. An after-the-auction determination might produce a cost that makes the project infeasible. One alternative to after-the-auction determination would be a case by case analysis for all potential bidders, which could be quite costly and time consuming if the number of potential bidders is large. Another alternative would be some simple pre-announced tariff which might approximate the true costs. This would have the virtue of reducing bidder uncertainty and providing some cost recovery to the utility. Striking the proper balance among virtues of these alternatives would depend upon circumstances.

The Massachusetts RFPs use a simple scoring approach to this problem by assigning bonus points to projects that are located in areas which impose no transmission difficulty. Their scoring systems give a very small weight to this factor, which implies that the anticipated scale of QF power coming to the utility will not be a serious problem. If capacity limits are approached, scoring systems will have to give greater weight to this factor.

It may also be desirable to create a transmission tariff for PURPA projects. This would have to be a posted price that bidders could take into account as another cost of production. It could substitute for a bid evaluation mechanism in much the same way as capacity performance standards substitute for a reliability scoring system. The closest analogy is the "wheeling" charges that utilities impose on PURPA projects that use one utility's transmission system to deliver power to another utility. These charges usually take a "postage stamp" form of a few mills per kilowatt hour. The advantage of such a variable charge is that it imposes no extra capital costs on developers yet can provide cost recovery to utilities.

Conclusions

Bid evaluation mechanisms can range from simplification through constraints to a system of weights addressing non-price factors. Simplicity encourages bidders; complexity has the potential to reflect values more accurately. Formulating complicated evaluation systems involves the inherent difficulty of evaluating non-price factors. Bid evaluation systems using weights to reflect non-price factors can be constructed with greater or less care. The Massachusetts RFPs show a good deal of thought has gone into weighing such factors. Arbitrary weighing schemes that are unrelated to economic costs can do more harm than good, however.

One method or simplifying the process is to differentiate the payment stream to PURPA projects into components that are subject to performance standards. Capacity value and transmission access seem amenable to this treatment. Financial risks and dispatchability do not. Of these two non-price features, financial risk is probably more easily incorporated into an evaluation scheme. The Massachusetts RFPs have useful approaches to this. In this case, complexity contributes constructively to evaluation of bids. Dispatchability is a more difficult problem. There are many different kinds of dispatchability, and any evaluation system must make the appropriate distinctions, which are system dependent. Of all properties of power delivery, dispatchability will be the most difficult to value either implicitly in a bid evaluation scheme or explicitly in a pricing scheme. It may be preferable to bid separately for dispatchable projects.

It is clear that the range of choices for evaluating bids is large. Much of the significance of this diversity may narrow when the process of subsequent negotiation and implementation of auction results is considered. If issues have been neglected in the evaluation phase this can be corrected in negotiations that define more precisely the obligations of producers and the payment mechanism. The anticipation of rewards in such negotiations can even lower bids.

Any bid evaluation scheme will be an approximation. If a particular quality is important in a given case, then economic efficiency requires that bidders be differentiated in that regard. The importance of local conditions suggests that no uniform or standard national practice is necessary.

The Problem with Lumpiness

A bid from a QF will offer a specified quantity of power at a price. Sometimes, the specified quantity will be large relative to the amount of power the utility still needs after accepting bids at lower prices. Furthermore, because of the economics of this technology the bidder may be unwilling to supply only a fraction of the specified quantity of power he offered at the same price. This presents the bid taker with a potential dilemma. Because of the potentially discrete nature of the quantities of power offered by the bids and of the technologies underlying the bids — we term this "lumpiness" — the following bid acceptance rules are not equivalent to each other:

1. Accept the set of bids that provides at least the desired amount of power at the lowest total cost provided that no bid is accepted that exceeds the utility's published avoided cost per kWh.
2. Accept a set of bids that provides no more than the desired amount of power and that minimizes the cost of that amount of power on the assumption that the utility will supply any unpurchased power at its published avoid cost per kWh.
3. Accept bids sequentially in increasing order of cost per kWh until either the cost of a bid would exceed the utility's avoided cost per kWh or the amount of power accepted would exceed the desired amount.
4. Same as Rule 3 except that if a bid is rejected, the sequence continues with consideration of bids with higher costs per kWh.
5. Accept bids sequentially in increasing order of cost per kWh until the cost per kWh of desired but as yet unaccepted power offered by a bid exceeds the utility's avoided cost per kWh of desired power (i.e., giving excess power no value).
6. Same as Rule 5 except that if a bid is rejected, the sequence continues with consideration of bids with higher costs per kWh.

Some examples may help clarify the differences. Consider the situation described in Table 9-4. Bid acceptance rule number 1 would accept Bid 2 and reject Bid 1, while the other five rules would accept Bid 1 and reject Bid 2.

Table 9-4

Desired Power: 100 MW
Utility Avoided Cost: 5 cents/kWh

Bid #	Amount Offered	Price
1	80 MW	3.5 cents/kWh
2	100 MW	4.0 cents/kWh

If we add a third bid, creating the situation described in

Table 9-5, then rules 3 and 5 accept Bid 1 only, while the other rules accept Bids 1 and 3.

Table 9-5

Desired Power: 100 MW
Utility Avoided Cost: 5 cents / kWh

Bid #	Amount Offered	
1	80 MW	3.5 cents / kWh
2	100 MW	4.0 cents / kWh
3	20 MW	4.5 cents / kWh

In the situation described in Table 9-6, Rules 2, 3 and 4 would accept Bid 1 and reject Bid 2, while the other three rules would accept both bids. If a third bid is added to the two in Table 9-6 to create the situation described in Table 9-7, Rules 1, 2, and 4 accept bids 1 and 3, while Rule 3 continues to accept just Bid 1 and Rules 5 and 6 continue to accept Bids 1 and 2.

Table 9-6

Desired Power: 100 MW
Utility Avoided Cost: 5 cents / kWh

Bid #	Amount Offered	Price
1	60 MW	3.5 cents kWh
2	50 MW	4.0 cents kWh

Table 9-7

Desired Power: 100 MW
Utility Avoided Cost: 5cents / kWh

Bid #	Amount Offered	Price
1	60 MW	3.5 cents kWh
2	50 MW	4.0 cents kWh
3	40 MW	4.1 cents kWh

Several factors are important in a bid acceptance procedure. First of all, the procedure should promote economic efficiency. This concern has two parts. We would like the procedure to make the best economic choice among the bids offered. In addition, we would like a procedure to send the right incentive message to the bidders so that bidders with lower costs will submit winning bids. In addition to economic efficiency, we must be concerned with fairness and the appearance of fairness. Furthermore, we want the procedure to be operational (i.e., unambiguous) and reasonably simple. Finally, it may prove to be helpful if the procedure is stable in the sense that if one or more accepted bids are withdrawn, the acceptance procedure applied de novo to the unwithdrawn bids does not, or at least is less likely to, lead to the rejection of any bid that was acceptable before the bid withdrawal occurred. These preferences are in conflict, however, and an acceptance procedure must compromise among them.

Next, we discuss various ways of dealing with lumpiness or of reducing it. After those discussions, we examine how some of the individual measures interact with each other and then assess overall approaches to the bid decision process.

The Measures

We have considered four measures that would reduce lumpiness or the difficulties it poses. Some of the measures also have advantages that extend beyond their effect on the lumpiness problem. Two of the measures are directed at reducing the lumpiness of bids and two at dealing with the lumps that remain in ways that are simple, fair and economically reasonable.

Multiple Bids

The first lumpiness reduction measure is to allow and even encourage multiple bids by a single bidder. To the extent that bidders do this, the utility receives fewer bids involving large quantities and more bids involving small quantities. However, even without the lumpiness problem, both the bidder and the utility stand to gain if, technology permitting, the bidder offers capacity incrementally beyond the amount that results in the minimum average cost per kWh.

184   COMPETITION IN ELECTRICITY

An example will illustrate this. Suppose that a small bidder can produce one MW for 4 cents per kWh and a second MW for 6 cents per kWh. Suppose the auction is a first-price auction and the bidder estimates the cutoff acceptance price to be equally likely to fall anywhere between 4 cents and an announced avoided cost maximum of 8 cents. The optimum bid is half way from the bidder's cost to the maximum price. If the bidder submits a single bid for 2 kW its average cost is 5 cents, its best bid is 6.5 cents, its probability of winning is 3/8, and its expected profit is proportional to (6.5-5) X 3/8 X 2 =1.125.

If, instead, the bidder submits two bids, each for 1 MW, the best bids will be 6 cents and 7 cents, these bids will have probabilities 1/2 and 1/4 of winning, and the bidder's expected profit will be proportional to (6-4) X 1/2 + (7 - 6) X 1/4 = 1.25. This is 11% more. The extra expected profit for the bidder is matched by an equal expected savings to the utility. If the cutoff price is between 6.5 and 7 cents the utility will end up paying 6 cents per kWh for 1 MW from this source instead of 6.5 cents for 2 MW. If the cutoff price is between 6 and 6.5 cents, the utility will get 1 MW from this source at 6 cents instead of paying the cutoff price. Each of these changes is a gain for the utility. Any other cutoff price results in no difference in either quantity or price for the utility.

Downsizing

Another measure is "downsizing." This measure would reduce lumpiness by allowing a marginal bidder whose bid is too big to reduce the quantity (without changing the price per kWh) to a level that would allow the bid to be accepted. If the reduction is unacceptable to the bidder, nothing has been lost. However, if the bidder accepts, the utility will have gotten the lowest cost power offered to it.

Again, an example may help. In the example given in Table 9-4 above, Bidder 2 is the marginal bidder. If Bidder 2 would prefer to sell 20 MW at 4 cents/kWh to selling none, then the utility has obtained its desired 100 MW at an average cost of 3.6 cents/kWh — the lowest possible cost given the bids, even ignoring the lumpiness issue completely.

The bidder may be willing to sell 20 MW at 4.0 cents/

KWh because its technology is modular so that its cost is proportional to capacity or nearly so. Alternatively, it may have moderate economies of scale but, none the less, have a sufficiently low cost that 20 MW at 4 cents/kWh is still attractive. A third possibility is that the technology of Bidder 1 is flexible and that Bidder 2's costs are low enough that Bidder 2 can afford to buy from Bidder 1 the right to supply some of the 3.5 cents/kWh electricity Bidder 1 is contracting for. For example, Bidder 2 might buy the right to 30 MW of capacity so that each supplied the utility with 50 MW — Bidder 1 at 3.5 cents and Bidder 2 at an average cost of 3.7 cents.

Tolerance

A third way to deal with lumpiness is to allow a tolerance in the desired capacity. For example, Southern California Edison proposed to the California PUC that when it sought a given amount of electricity, it would accept bids below its avoided cost in increasing order of cost until the next bid acceptance would increase the total quantity of bids accepted beyond the amount of its requirement. It proposed that the last bid be accepted anyway, if its acceptance would not raise the total quantity to more than 110% of the required power and be rejected otherwise. Thus, using this rule, Southern California Edison would accept both bids in the example shown in Table 9-6 above. A plausible rationale for this rule is that the power requirement is known only within 10% so this degree of flexibility has no significant adverse effects.

Demand Curve

More generally, it is reasonable to assume that the utility values power beyond the desired amount. It is possible for the utility to develop a demand curve for such power and use it in its bid acceptance procedure. This fourth measure would add some complexity to the bidding procedure, but it would also add some economic rationality and help in dealing with lumpiness.

For example, a utility that required 100 MW and had an avoided cost of 5 cents/kWh for that quantity might also have an incremental value of 4 cents/kWh for an incremental MW. If faced with the bids shown in Table 9-4 above, the utility would accept both bids. In general, the utility would accept or reject a marginal bid; (i.e., the bid that, if accepted, would put it over the desired quantity) based upon a comparison of its economic situation with respect to avoided cost with and without that bid.

Measure Interactions

Each of these four measures has value on its own. However, it is useful to consider how various measures interact. It is desirable to integrate measures in a way that avoids unnecessary anomalies and, in particular, unnecessary "discontinuities." By a discontinuity, we mean a large change in the cost incurred by a utility being caused by a small change in the price or quantity of a bid. (There will be discontinuities, of course, in the choice of winning bids). Discontinuities in cost suggest that, on one end or the other, the cost could be improved by a small change.

The downsizing measure can reduce discontinuity when used without the demand curve measure, which also removes discontinuities. Without the demand curve measure, a small increase in the quantity of a bid can make it unacceptable and force the utility to accept a much higher cost for the power it would have supplied. Since a bidder is likely to accede to a small downsizing requirement, this measure will normally eliminate discontinuities.

The demand curve measure has similar properties by itself or in proper combination with other measures. In particular, care must be exercised in integrating the tolerance and demand curve measures. These measures may be viewed as partial substitutes for each other or as complements. If they are both used, care must be taken in defining them so that a small increase in the quantity of the marginal bid beyond the tolerance level does not result in a large decrease in its apparent valuation. Such a decrease can be avoided by valuing power in the tolerance range at avoided cost or by, at least, not penalizing a bid's evaluation for shortfalls relative to avoided cost in this range.

Auction Design

We have considered two opposite auction design philosophies for dealing with lumpiness an well as variants and combinations or them. One philosophy is to take the bids as given and have the utmlity accept those bids whose selection will solve exactly the problem of minimizing its total cost for its quantity requirement. In this approach, the "hard" nature of the quantity limit can lead to results that are not as efficient economically as their "cost minimizing" definitions might lead one to expect. This approach completely ignores any unfairness implicit in accepting a high-priced bid while rejecting a lower-priced one. It also ignores the fact that a bid withdrawal may lead to the rejection of previously accepted bid. In addition, it ignores any willingness of a bidder to accept a partial contract. Because of the extra variability it induces in the prediction of the maximum acceptable price for a bid, it will tend to increase the variability of the bids by giving relatively high bidders an incentive to bid higher (they still might win) and relatively low bidders an incentive to bid lower (to lower the risk of losing).

The other philosophy is to rank the bids by cost per kWh, accept bids in order of increasing cost until the desired quantity is reached or it no longer pays to accept any more, and to use as many as possible of the measures discussed above for reducing lumpiness. In its pure form, this approach stops with consideration of the marginal bid, and is fair in the sense that it never accepts a higher bid than a rejected one and stable in the sense that withdrawal of a bid will never lead it to reject a bid that would have been acceptable without the withdrawal. It takes advantage of a marginal bidder's ability to cope with a partial acceptance, and it is computationally simple. However, unless the marginal bidder is willing to accept a partial award, it does not guarantee the utility the lowest possible cost set of the given bids for meeting the required quantity.

There is a potentially attractive variant of the second approach that sacrifices the stability property with respect to inframarginal bids in return for some economic improvement. In it, the utility follows the second procedure except that, if the marginal bid is not accepted even in part, it then goes on to consider other bids. Thus, for example, in the situation de-

COMPETITION IN ELECTRICITY

scribed in Table 9-8, if Bidder 2 refused to downsize sufficiently, bids 3 and 4 would be accepted and Bidder 5 would be given an opportunity to downsize. Some aspect of fairness is lost too, because Bidder 2's price is lower than Bidder 3's and Bidder 4's. On the other hand, given the existence of Bidder 1's bid, Bidder 2's bid is not as attractive to the utility, and Bidder 2's low price has obtained for Bidder 2 the right to adjust quantity to make it as attractive. Having declined this opportunity, Bidder 2's claim for having been treated unfairly is weak.

Table 9-8

Desired Power: 100 MW
Utility Avoided Cost: 5 cents/kWh
2 cents/kWh beyond 100 MW

Bid #	Amount Offered	Price
1	60 MW	3.5 cents kWh
2	100 MW	4.0 cents kWh
3	20 MW	4.1 cents kWh
4	10 MW	4.2 cents kWh
5	50 MW	4.5 cents kWh

An interesting question that must be answered in following this approach is by how much Bidder 2 would have to downsize. There are at least three possible ways of calculating the required downsizing. First, we could do so assuming that there are no other bids. Under this assumption, the first 40 MW of Bidder 2's bid saves the utility 1.0 cent/kWh and every additional MW costs the utility 2.0 cents/kWh. Therefore, if the second bid were scaled down to 60 MW (= 40 + 40 X 1.0/2.0), the utility would break even.

Second, we could calculate the required scale down taking account of other bids but not assuming any other bid will be scaled down. Under this assumption, the utility's average cost for the last 40 MW would be 4.35 cents (20 MW at 4.1 cents, 10 MW at 4.2 cents, and 10 MW at 5.0 cents). Thus, the required scale-down would be to 47 MW (= 40 + 40 X 0.35/2.00). (If there is a 10% tolerance on accepted quantity so that the utility is required to accept up to 110% of its stated requirement, then that tolerance would supersede this calculation, and the required scale-down by Bidder 2 would be only to 50 MW.)

A third possible calculation of required scale down would assume, at least tentatively, scale down by later marginal bidders. Under this assumption, the utility's average cost for the last 40 MW would be 4.225 cents/kWh (20 MW at 4.1 cents, 10 MW at 4.2 cents and 10 MW at 4.5 cents), and the required scale down would be to 44.5 MW ($= 40 + 40$ X $0.225/2.000$) unless superseded by a tolerance of more than 4.5%. presumably, under this rule a bidder's rejection would be tentative. If a subsequent marginal bidder refused to scale down, the bidder would then be offered a second, less strict scale down requirement based on the new situation. If the rejection were not tentative, both fairness and economic efficiency issues would arise.

If the "pure" second philosophy is followed in that subsequent bids are never considered after a marginal bid is rejected, then the first rule for deciding the required amount of downsizing is clearly appropriate. Under the variant procedure, we prefer the second rule. This makes more economic sense than the first given that subsequent bids will be considered. We prefer the second rule to the third because it maintains strictly the sequential nature of the bid acceptance and because it avoids the possibility of strategic decision making by a bidder faced with a downsizing decision. In the example discussed above, strategic decision making would occur under the third rule if Bidder 2 declined to downsize to 44.5 MW even though this was economically preferable to losing the auction because it doubted that Bidder 5 would in fact downsize and it preferred to downsize only to 47 MW.

Overall, we prefer the second philosophy to the first. We believe that, in combination, the measures we have suggested will reduce the lumpiness problem significantly. We believe the fairness, stability, and simplicity are worthwhile advantages. On the other hand, we do not believe that they are absolutes. Hence, we tend to prefer the economic advantages of the variant of the second philosophy to its pure form.

Finally, we note that since there are many different plausible bid acceptance procedures, a great deal of difficulty and dispute may arise if acceptance procedures are not explicitly defined in advance.

Frequency of Auctions

To some extent, the frequency with which a utility holds auctions to purchase PURPA power will be determined by perceived needs for additional capacity. As the events of recent years have demonstrated, perceived needs can develop unevenly as expectations of demand growth change and adjustments for prior misestimates are made. However, to the extent that a utility anticipates a need for new capacity, it can try to meet that need with relatively infrequent auctions to buy large amounts of power, or relatively frequent auctions to buy smaller amounts. To the extent that, everything taken into account, there are significant economies of scale remaining in utility constructed power plants, the utilities' avoided costs will be lower if the auctions are sufficiently infrequent that large plants are economic. However, PURPA power will often not have as large economies of scale. Furthermore, it may be disadvantaged by long delays between auctions. In particular, the opportunity for integrated cogeneration in a new industrial facility may be lost if there is no auction near the time when the industrial facility design decisions are being made. Hence, there is reason to hold PURPA auctions with some regularity.

While it is difficult to be quantitative, it is clear that there are disadvantages to both too frequent and too infrequent auctions. In addition to the concern about economics of scale in utility plants already mentioned, too frequent auctions may encourage collusion if they have the same or significantly overlapping participants. Each bidder has the opportunity to take into account the way that his bid in one auction will affect those of his competitors in future auctions. Oren and Rothkopf [1975] have shown that if the auctions are frequent, the effect of such behavior can be to increase bids significantly.

A secondary complication of too frequent auctions may be difficulty in calculating avoided cost. The problem arises because with frequent auctions the utility may perceive that the cheapest way to meet its capacity need is to wait until a later PURPA auction and buy the power offered then. The less frequent PURPA auctions are, the less likely this is and the more appropriate is the convenient and traditional course of avoiding any allowance for this in calculating avoided cost.

If auctions are too infrequent, three problems may arise. One problem has to do with the economics of utility capacity additions. If t.ese additions are deferred too long because of infrequent auctions, total utility costs will be higher than necessary. Another problem has to do with PURPA projects with a limited time frame. For example, a manufacturer planning a new plant may be considering including cogeneration capability. There is a limited period during which his plant design decisions are being made. If there is no PURPA auction during this period, then the opportunity for integrated cogeneration is likely to be lost. When an auction is eventually held, cogeneration from this plant would carry retrofit costs. Finally, if many utilities waited many years between cogeneration auctions, the stability of businesses capable of providing cogeneration might be undercut.

On balance, it would seem advisable for utilities to hold auctions at least every two or three years. This period is long enough to allow the utilities' demand estimates to be clarified and to allow decisions from the previous auction to be made. In addition, it would be hard to develop tacit collusion in auctions that far apart. Finally, most large new plants with cogeneration potential can be fit into such a schedule.

CONCLUSIONS AND RECOMMENDATIONS FOR PURPA AUCTIONS

This section briefly states the main conclusions and recommendations made in this report. These cover the four main concerns of the report: the general form of the auction, dealing with the discrete nature of bid quantities, dealing with non-price aspects of bids, and auction frequency.

With respect to the overall auction form, we recommend standard (i.e., first-price, discriminatory) sealed bidding. We do so because it is familiar, relatively collusion resistant, appropriate for large, complex transactions, and because the economic theory suggesting that sealed second-price (nondiscriminatory) auctions are more efficient clearly does not apply. It does not take account of the facts that in PURPA auc-

192 COMPETITION IN ELECTRICITY

tions there will be subsequent negotiations with third parties and that a single bidder or economic interest may offer several blocks of capacity.

As we have noted, the choice or the rule to use in deciding which bids to accept is not straightforward. Most generally, we recommend that in advance of the auction there be an explicit, thoughtful determination of the rule that will be used. More particularly, we recommend that a rule be adopted that accepts bids in order of increasing cost per kWh subject to several measures to reduce the impact of the discrete nature of the bids. The measures we favor include encouraging multiple bids (for incremental quantities) by a bidder, allowing a reasonable tolerance in the definition of the required quantity, valuing excess power beyond the desired quantity at avoided cost in deciding if a marginal bid is acceptable, and allowing a marginal bidder who offers too large a quantity the option of reducing that quantity.

We recommend that non-price factors be included in bid evaluation only in ways that reflect costs. We conclude that bidder incentives and post-sale negotiations will tend to narrow the difference between different schemes for dealing with non-price features of bids. We also conclude that there is probably not one best approach nationally for dealing with non-price features.

Finally, we recommend that bidders hold auctions every few years if they need capacity but not much more frequently because, if auctions are too frequent, collusion is made easier, large projects are disadvantaged and the calculation of true avoided cost may become more difficult because it will tend to depend upon the outcome of future auctions. On the other hand, if auctions are too infrequent, promising potential cogeneration projects may be missed.

ENDNOTES

1. The original report contains a case study and various technical appendices.
2. The original report contains such a discussion in an appendix
3. Might want to mention the Cal. utilities proposal.

CHAPTER 10: CONSIDERATION OF ENVIRONMENTAL AND FUEL DIVERSITY FACTORS IN COMPETITIVE BIDDING*

James Plummer, QED Research, Inc.
Susan Troppmann, QED Research, Inc.

This chapter explores the subject of whether and how to allow for fuel diversity and environmental impacts in the evaluation of competitive electricity bids. In the parlance of competitive electricity bidding, fuel diversity and environmental factors are a subset of "non-price factors." Other non-price factors, not covered in this chapter, include those that come under the label of "performance factors." These are characteristics such as dispatchability, curtailability, and location in the transmission and distribution grid.

THE EXPERIENCE WITH BIDDING SYSTEMS

Seven states have adopted bidding systems — Connecticut, Colorado, Maine, Massachusetts, New Jersey, New York, and Virginia. They are all at different stages in the evolution of their bidding systems, and there is quite a diversity in the approaches taken.

It is important to realize how limited the experience is at this stage. Even though bids have been received and awards made (in some states), no megawatts are actually on line. Representatives of larger cogenerators, as well as other observers, often point this out in order to caution against rushing into ill-conceived bidding systems, and to stress that project viability and financial stability should be important criteria in evaluating bids. Smaller QFs, on the other hand, are usually more hesitant to see project viability used as a significant weight in bid evaluations.

Another important generalization is that the regulatory commissions in these other states have chosen (with the exception of Connecticut) to allow the regulated utilities to design the bidding systems and carry out objective and subjec-

---

*Adapted and condensed from a report to the California Energy Commission, entitled "Consideration of Environmental and Fuel Diversity Factors in Competitive Bidding Systems," QED Reasearch, Inc., March 31, 1989.

tive evaluations of the bids. The degree of intervention by the regulators in the design and implementation of the bidding systems is probably less in these other states than what is now contemplated in California. Also, these commissions and utilities have been willing to proceed with less formal and quantitative bid solicitations and evaluations even though they knew that the process was very imperfect and would have to be improved substantially in future rounds of bidding.

EXPERIENCE IN TREATING NON-PRICE FACTORS

The term "auctions" is used more in academic discussions than in actual regulatory practice. Although the term "bidding" is frequently used, it is often replaced by terms such as "competitive solicitation," or "merit competition." These broader labels are deliberate signals that more factors than just price are being considered in bid evaluation. The Requests for Proposal (RFPs) sent out by utilities often did specify the weight to be given to price and other factors. Sometimes those weights were set by the commission and sometimes by the utilities. In New York and Massachusetts, there was explicit recognition that each utility would set its own weights. Regardless of who set the weights, a lot of discretion was left to the utilities to decide how to score those non-price factors. The commissions merely set the overall rules of the game, and chose not to set the specific parameters of the game. They, of course, reserved the right to conduct *ex post* reviews of the process, and the utilities certainly had those reviews in mind when they designed and implemented their bidding systems.

Of all the non-price factors, the heaviest weight was given to "performance factors" such as dispatchability, curtailability, and location within the transmission and distribution grid. Virginia Power took the most aggressive approach by simply requiring the bidders to be dispatchable and curtailable, making those resources economically and operationally very similar to resources owned by Virginia Power.

ALLOWANCE FOR FUEL DIVERSITY AND ENVIRONMENTAL FACTORS IN BIDDING SYSTEMS

From the telephone interviews conducted as part of this study, it was obvious that terminology is used a bit differently in some of the other six states than it is in California. For example, when the term "fuel diversity" is used in other states, it often refers to whether a given facility has dual fuel capability — any two fuels. So a project that has oil/gas versatility, or oil/coal versatility, or gas/coal versatility will be considered to be contributing to fuel diversity. This derives from the history of the Northeast states in encountering gas shortages in 1975, and fuel oil shortages in 1973/74 and again in 1979/80. In California, the term "fuel diversity" more often refers to broadening the resource mix away from oil and gas, and particularly away from oil. So, in California, a project that has oil/gas fuel versatility may not be considered to be any better than one that burns only oil or only gas.

To make things more confusing, the term "fuel diversity" is also used in the other states in the sense of favoring renewable resources over non-renewable resources. Although when this meaning was employed, it was usually in the context of "preferred technologies" versus "non-preferred technologies," rather than an aversion to oil and gas technologies in particular. These meanings of "fuel diversity" are somewhat different than the regulatory meaning in California, which stresses the social costs and risks of over-dependence on oil and natural gas in electricity production.

Although Maine has implemented a bidding system, the commission exercises very little oversight over the process as it is carried out by the utilities. The only consideration given to environmental factors is whether a project can get its environmental permits. The only consideration given to fuel use is whether the project has a firm long-term fuel contract.

Except for Maine, all of the states and utilities that have implemented bidding systems have made some allowance for fuel diversity and environmental factors in the bid evaluation system (albeit with different definitions than described above). It was recognized by commissions and utilities that, because of the inclusion of these factors in the bid evaluation process, it was possible for a project to win even if its price was higher than the avoided costs of the utility. For example, in Connecticut an environmentally preferred project was determined to be a winner even though its price was higher that the avoided cost of the regulated utility.

In Virginia, a 30% weight was given to non-price factors. Within this 30% weight for non-price factors, a weight of 10% was given to issues of financial stability, team experience, and project viability. Another 10% weight was given to factors such as location, steam contribution, and whether the proposer accepted the model contract. Finally, a 10% weight was given to considerations of dual fuel capability, and whether the project utilized Virginia fuels. Virginia Power was given considerable regulatory latitude in deciding how to apply these weights in bid evaluation. Winners and losers were not given detailed information on how those judgments were made.

In New York, the weights vary by utility and the combined weight given to fuel diversity and environmental factors is in the range of 5-15%. In the case of Orange and Rocklin Utilities, a 10% allowance was made for preferred versus non-preferred technologies. Solid waste, hydro, or demand-side-management projects received the full 10%. Coal projects received 7%, gas projects received 2%, and oil projects 0%. These might be called "preferred technology bonus points." Mark Reeder, Chief of Regulatory Research at the New York State Department of Public Service, has calculated the price equivalents for each non-price factor by figuring what change in price would be necessary to convert a project from a loser to a winner.[1] The diversity of weighting systems used by various New York utilities, and the debates within the staff of the New York commission, resemble more closely the approaches to these issues now being taken in California, although differences still outweigh similarities.

In Massachusetts, the weights are chosen by individual utilities. Non-price factors account for 35-50% of the total weight, but fuel diversity and environmental factors are only 10-20% of the overall weight. Northeast Utilities has experimented with the use of a microcomputer self-scoring system. It is much simpler than the one now proposed by the California regulated utilities, and is also the product of a study by the same consulting firm (Putnam, Hayes & Bartlett).

In Connecticut, the Department of Public Utilities has played a heavy role in bid evaluation, and the relative influence of different factors is more open to subjective judgments. The relative weight given to fuel diversity and environmental factors was in the range of 10-25%.

In Colorado, the process is at an early stage. No RFP has been issued. The commission has decided to allow the utility to set the weights in the RFP, if the utility will hire a third party to do the evaluation of bids. The categories of weights indicated thus far by Public Service of Colorado are as follows:

25% Cost
20% Operational characteristics
20% Facility characteristics, including a flexible start date
15% Fuel issues, including dual fuel capability, oil dependence, and fuel contract features
10-15% Features of the power sale contract
5-10% Project team experience.

To summarize, most of the other states that have tried to allow for fuel diversity or environmental factors have done so by simply assigning a relative weight within the bid evaluation process, and allowing a great deal of judgmental discretion to the utilities in deciding how to apply those weights. *Importantly, neither environmental factors or fuel diversity factors have been weighted heavily in these bidding systems.*

AVERSION TO USING SET-ASIDE APPROACHES

One way of allowing for fuel diversity factors or environmental factors in bidding systems would be to set aside a certain portion of the block of power up for bid for projects with preferred characteristics. Under this kind of system, the preferred projects compete on price with each other, but not with the non-preferred projects. Set-aside approaches have been used by the federal government to award a certain percentage of defense contracts to small business, to minority-owned businesses, or to businesses located in labor surplus areas.

There are variations of set-aside approaches that do not insulate the preferred projects completely from price competition. For example, preferred projects could be guaranteed a certain portion of the power block if they were able to match the winning price bid in the non-preferred competition, or if they were able to match that price plus a "preference differential" of X cents per kwh.

In the telephone interviews with the staffs of commissions and utilities in the six states that are implementing bidding systems, there was no support by anyone for set-aside approaches. There was concern that the first round of bidding draw as many bidders as possible so that there could be no challenge to the process on the grounds that there were not enough players to constitute "workable competition." It was felt that any set-aside approach would lessen the credibility of the bidding process, and thus threaten the public acceptability of the bidding process. Also, given the relatively low weights assigned to fuel diversity and environmental factors in the bidding rounds that have occurred, it would have been inconsistent and out of character for these commissions or utilities to have separated out projects for preference on fuel diversity or environmental considerations.

THE PROPOSAL BY CALIFORNIA REGULATED UTILITIES FOR A MULTI-ATTRIBUTE SELF—SCORING SYSTEM FOR BID EVALUATION

In November 1988, the three regulated California utilities (Pacific Gas and Electric, San Diego Gas and Electric, and Southern California Edison) proposed a methodology for modifying the currently approved biennial update methodology by including non-price factors in the bid evaluation. It would be a self-scoring system, in that the methods for including non-price factors would be provided to the bidders (in the form of Lotus 1-2-3 templates) with the RFP, so they could use the system to design their own optimized bid.

The proposed system differs from those in use in many of the seven other states that are implementing bidding systems in that it calculates all the non-price costs and benefits in dollars. Although there are many judgmentally determined parameters in the system, the intended goal of the system is the minimization of ratepayer cost. This is quite different from the percentage weight approach to non-price factors taken in other states.

Most of the emphasis in the proposed methodology is on

COMPETITION IN ELECTRICITY

attributes such as dispatchability, curtailability, location in the transmission and distribution grid, a flexible start date for a project, and project viability.

There is only a token representation of environmental factors in the current preliminary version of the proposed methodoloy. Non-fossil technologies are given "bonus benefits" of 0.1 cent per kwh (same as 1 mill per kwh). The explanation given was that this represented an allowance for the differential environmental impact of NOx emissions from fossil fuel technologies as compared with non-fossil fuel technologies. Although this is only a token representation of environmental impacts, there is nothing in the conceptual framework of the methodology that would preclude a larger representation of environmental impacts.

Fuel diversity benefits are explicitly represented in the methodology. The bidders would be given assumptions about fuel price scenarios and load growth scenarios, and ratepayer risk aversion coefficients, and then asked to use these to calculate the dollar benefits of greater fuel diversity.

FOUR GENERIC POLICY OPTIONS

Option A: **Price-only bidding.**

Option B: **Adjustment of price bids for performance factors only.** It is performance factors such as dispatchability, curtailability, and location of transmission interconnection that matter most to the regulated utilities, and they can be expected to continue pressing the case for their inclusion in the bid evaluation process.

Option C: **Allow for environmental and fuel diversity factors through use of numerous (disaggregate) functions, each representing a separate type of impact.** This would be a "bottom up" approach in which the utilities would be directed to use many "adder" or "subtractor" functions, as an attempt to achieve more precision in allowing for externalities in the bid evaluation process. This option can be thought of as a "multi-attribute" approach to considering environmental and fuel diversity factors in competitive bid evaluation. Environmental point scoring systems are one variant of this approach.

Option D: **Allow for environmental and fuel diversity factors through use of "surrogate functions."** Under this option, the regulators would provide the utilities with a surrogate function or functions, which would specify "adders" or "subtractors" from bid prices, and would be intended to represent the social cost impacts of environmental factors and fuel diversity factors.

OPTION B: NO CONSIDERATION OF ENVIRONMENTAL OR FUEL DIVERSITY FACTORS IN BID EVALUATION

It is arguable that it is unnecessary to consider environmental impacts in the bid evaluation process because these impacts are already taken into consideration by environmental regulations. Both federal and state environmental regulation rely heavily on the standards approach. Thus, for electricity and other commodities in the economy, no cost is borne by the producer for the residual "below standard" environmental damage he causes. Thus, the relative price structure does not incorporate these costs. They are social costs (externalities) rather than private costs (internalities). It will certainly be argued by the bidders in an electricity auction that it is "unfair" (inequitable) for regulators to single them out for special (and thus unfair) treatment.

Perfect social efficiency might dictate going beyond Options A or B. From an economic efficiency point of view, optimality (highest overall social output) is achieved if the social marginal cost (including both private production cost and "externality" social costs) of production is equalized among all winning bidders. However, even if it were preferable from a social efficiency point of view to go with Option C or D, the strength of that preference depends somewhat on the probable magnitude of the error involved in not doing so. For example, the shaded area in Figure 10-1 measures the dollar value magnitude of the residual environmental damages involved in using a "standards approach" to pollution regulation.[2] If the environmental damage function has a steep upward slope, like the one in Figure 10-1, the given pollutant is considered a "threshold pollutant." For these kind of pollutants, there is less economic justification for considering environmental impacts in bid evaluation. If the environmental damage function is more horizontally shaped, the pollutant is considered a "non-threshold pollutant," and there is more economic justification for considering environmental

COMPETITION IN ELECTRICITY

Figure 10-1

"Below Standard" Damage for a Threshold Pollutant

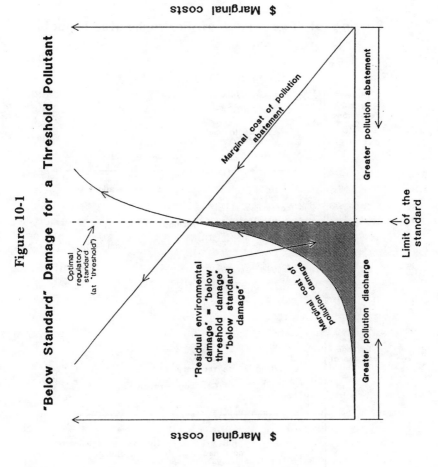

Figure 10-2

Scoring of Two Kinds of Environmental Impacts

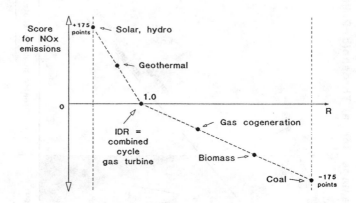

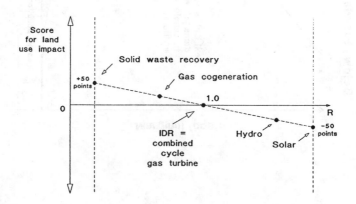

COMPETITION IN ELECTRICITY

impacts in bid evaluation.

Similar challenges can be made to consideration of fuel diversity factors in bid evaluation. In some bidding systems, the bidder is required to have a fuel contract forthe facility that locks in a price schedule for a given period of time (e.g. five or ten years). To the extent that these absolute requirements for submitting a bid reduce future risks of price increases, there is less economic justification for considering fuel diversity factors in bid evaluation. The arguments against considering fuel diversity factors in bid evaluation also relate to whether the size of fuel price risk is really significant, the complexity of the analyses required to monetize fuel price risks, and the fact that the magnitude of any "adder" or "subtractor" (defined and discussed later in this chapter) would vary with the size of the block of power put up for bid. There will be more discussion of these issues later in this chapter.

OPTION C: AGGREGATION OF ENVIRONMENTAL DAMAGES (BENEFITS) THROUGH POINT SCORE SYSTEMS

Figure 10-2 shows how environmental point score functions could be used for aggregating more than one kind of environmental impact. In Figure 10-2, the two different kinds of environmental impacts are NOx emissions and land use impacts. As can be seen, different technologies (and even different projects within the same technology) score quite differently on these two different scales. A project would receive points on each scale, and then these points would be totaled to arrive at an overall environmental score. The horizontal axis is a ratio, R, that measures the level of environmental threat of a particular kind (say, a particular air pollutant) *in relation to the level of environmental threat of the IDR* ("identified deferrable resource"). Thus, the basic reference point on the horizontal axis is where R = 1.0. At that point the environmental threat is neither better or worse than the IDR. Most regulatory commissions define the IDR (or some other similarly worded label) as the resource that would be build by the regulated utility in the absence of new capacity from competitive biddings. In the late 1980s and early 1990s, the IDR was often a combined cycle gas turbine facility.

The environmental point scoring system illustrated in Fi-

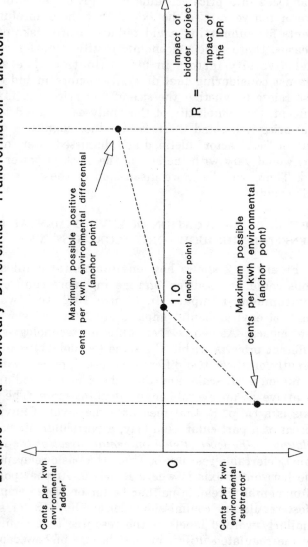

Figure 10-3

Example of a "Monetary Differential" Transformation Function

Cents per kwh environmental "adder"

Maximum possible positive cents per kwh environmental differential (anchor point)

1.0 (anchor point)

$$R = \frac{\text{Impact of bidder project}}{\text{Impact of the IDR}}$$

Maximum possible cents per kwh environmental (anchor point)

Cents per kwh environmental "subtractor"

gure 10-2 *could* be used to quantitatively implement the percentage weighting systems used in the other six states that are implementing bidding systems. For example, following the numbers on the scales in Figure 10-2, the maximum number of positive points that can be scored on these two environmental attributes combined would be 225. If the total maximum points possible (on all price and non-price factors) were 1,000, then this would correspond to an environmental weight of 22.5%. In the telephone interviews conducted as part of this study, there was no indication that any utility or commission went about doing this kind of *disaggregate* environmental scaling. It has been debated in memos within commission staffs, and perhaps utility staffs.

OPTION D: USING A MONETIZED ENVIRONMENTAL DAMAGE FUNCTION TO PROVIDE "ADDERS" OR "SUBTRACTORS" IN BID EVALUATION

The function in Figure 10-3 is different from the environmental point functions in Figure 10-2 in two respects. First, this function measures undesirable environmental damage rather than positive environmental point scores on the vertical axis. So the shape of this function is the vertical mirror image of the shape of the other function. Secondly, monetary rather than environmental point score functions are measured vertically.

The vertical axis measures the penalty or bonus that regulators wish to attach to the presence of an environmental threat that is greater or less than the reference IDR. It can be considered a "environmental cost adder" or "subtractor" to regular private sector costs. Thus, X mills per kwh would either be added or subtracted from a bidder's price as part of the bid evaluation.

Suppose we had an empirical measure of the dollar value of environmental damage per ton of NOx. Then, we could find where each project was on the horizontal axis by measuring the ratio of pounds of NOx per kwh for the given project to the pounds of NOx per kwh for the IDR. Note that this kind of environmental damage function approach is already superior to the approach taken by the California regulated utilities in their "multi-attribute" bid evaluation proposal. Under their proposal, non-fossil technologies would get a bonus of 0.1 cents per kwh. However, they would get this bonus regardless of how well or badly they did in NOx emissions themselves. Likewise, the fossil technologies would be implicitly penalized 0.1 cents per kwh regardless of how well or badly they did in NOx emissions. It is far better to reward good environmental performance and penalize bad environmental performance evenly across technologies, rather than choose identified technologies for bonus points.

Note that the environmental damage function does not necessarily have to cross the horizontal axis at the point where R = 1.0. Suppose the IDR is a combined cycle gas turbine. Regulators may decide not to take the emissions of a combined cycle gas turbine as their reference point for "neutral" environmental impact. They might decide that a technology had to do better than the IDR in order to get a "subtractor credit." Or, they might decide to create a "neutral buffer zone" around the IDR where no adder or subtractor was applied unless there was a substantial variation from the IDR.

USING ONE "SURROGATE" ENVIRONMENTAL DAMAGE FUNCTION VERSUS USING SEVERAL DISAGGREGATE ENVIRONMENTAL DAMAGE FUNCTIONS

It is up to regulators whether to use several environmental damage functions, each representing a particular kind of environmental threat, or use one "surrogate function" as a simpler, even if imperfect, representation of several types of environmental impact. The term "surrogate" simply means that one particular environmental threat variable (e.g. NOx emissions per kwh) is used as a proxy or an aggregate representation for the multiplicity of different environmental threats involved in producing electricity. If a surrogate variable is chosen, such as NOx emissions, then that variable can replace R on the horizontal axis.

FUEL DIVERSITY FACTORS IN BID EVALUATION

The energy cost of electricity production, in cents per kwh, is the product of multiplying the cents per million BTU (MMBTU) times the heat rate in production, in MMBTU per kwh. This is a fundamental identity of energy analysis. The

208   COMPETITION IN ELECTRICITY

vulnerability of ratepayers to oil or gas price increases goes up whenever *either* more MMBTUs of oil and gas are used as compared with use of other fuels, *or* when more MMBTUs of oil and gas are used than would be used if more efficient oil and gas technologies were utilized.

As the point of departure for measuring the vulnerability of ratepayers to oil and gas price increases, the methodology illustrated in this section uses the reference point of the oil and gas intensity of the IDR. This is measured by the MMBTUs of oil and gas per kwh produced. If a bidder project has a higher oil and gas intensity than the IDR, it is considered less desirable from the perspective of fuel diversity.

ESTIMATING THE RISK PREMIUMS PER KWH THAT CORRESPOND TO DIFFERENT LEVELS OF OIL AND GAS INTENSITY[3]

Once the impact of greater or lesser oil and gas intensity on rates is analyzed, the results can be arrayed in the probability distributions shown in Figure 10-4. There are several interesting features to these distributions. First, there is considerable uncertainty in the size of electricity bill for any level of oil and gas intensity. Second, the magnitude of uncertainty in the size of electricity bill is larger when oil and gas intensity is higher than when it is lower. This is indicated by the greater horizontal spread of the probability distribution at the top of the page as compared with the horizontal spread of the distribution at the bottom of the page. Third, the expected value of the size of electricity bills is higher when oil and gas intensity is higher. So electricity ratepayers have a stake in the oil and gas intensity of electricity production. This stake may justify regulatory action to hold down the risks to ratepayers that derive from the oil and gas intensity of electricity production.

For each level of oil and gas intensity (each of the three separate graphs shown in Figure 10-4), there is a certain level of electricity bill (expressed either in total size of bill, or in cents per kwh) that ratepayers would be willing to pay in order to not live with the uncertainty shown in Figure 10-3. In decision analysis, this figure is called the "certain equivalent." For each level of oil and gas intensity, the level of the "certain equivalent" will always be higher than the

Figure 10-4

The Effect of Varying Oil and Gas Intensity on the Level of Ratepayer "Certain Equivalents" (Risk Premiums)

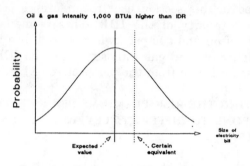

Oil & gas intensity 1,000 BTUs higher than IDR

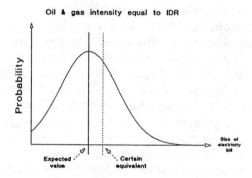

Oil & gas intensity equal to IDR

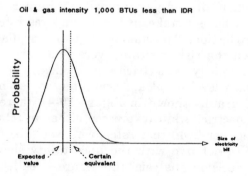

Oil & gas intensity 1,000 BTUs less than IDR

COMPETITION IN ELECTRICITY

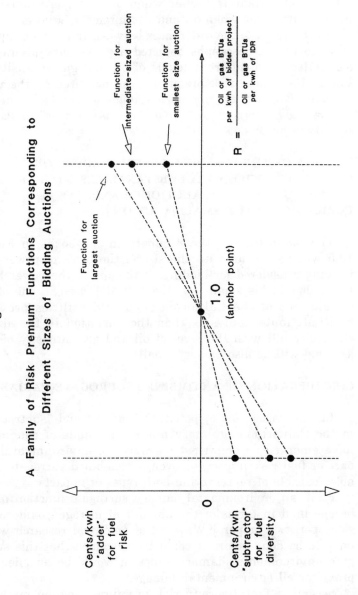

Figure 10-5

A Family of Risk Premium Functions Corresponding to Different Sizes of Bidding Auctions "expected value" electricity bill, because ratepayers are risk averse and are willing to pay a higher electricity bill in order to reduce their uncertainty. Note that the level of the certain equivalent is higher when oil and gas intensity is higher, and lower when oil and gas intensity is lower.

In Figure 10-4, the differences between the certain equivalents in the three graphs depicted are the "risk premiums" associated with different levels of oil and gas intensity. In Figure 10-5, these risk premiums are measured on the vertical axis. *They are the appropriate amounts per kwh that regulators should impose as "adders" or "subtractors" in the bid evaluation process.*

THE SIZE OF THE FUEL RISK PREMIUM ADDER OR SUBTRACTOR WILL VARY SUBSTANTIALLY WITH THE SIZE OF THE POWER BLOCK AUCTIONED AND MAY BE INSIGNIFICANT FOR SMALL AUCTIONS

The magnitude of the numbers in the boxes in Figure 10-5 will vary a lot with the size of the block of power that is being considered for bidding. If the size of the power block up for bidding is small (e.g. the 160 MW used in one of the simulations of the California regulated utilities proposed multi-attribute analysis), then the variation in the size of electricity bill with the level of oil and gas intensity of projects bid will be also be very small.

CONSIDERATION OF A COMBINED SURROGATE VARIABLE

In the discussions of potential "adders" and "subtractors" in the California regulatory process, a couple of candidates have emerged as empirical measures of environmental impact or fuel risk impact, or even a "combined surrogate variable" capable of representing both types of impacts.

First, an environmental damage surrogate function might be specified in terms of the amount of nitrogen oxide emissions per kwh or per KW. A lot of empirical research would have to be done before it could be concluded that this surrogate environmental damage function would be an adequate proxy for all environmental damages.

Second, a fuel diversity risk premium function might be specified in terms of the degree of oil and gas intensity

(MMBTUs per kwh or KW).

Since there may be a high degree of correlation between intensity of NOx and oil and gas intensity, there is also the possibility of a combined environmental/fuel diversity surrogate function. This would have enormous advantages in terms of winning earlier acceptance with the regulators and other parties. The initial use of a combined environmental/fuel diversity surrogate function would not necessarily lock the regulators into that concept permanently.

CONCLUSION: INTEGRATION BETWEEN PRICE AND NON-PRICE FACTORS IS DESIRABLE

If one desires to move beyond Option B and explicitly consider environmental or fuel diversity factors in bid evaluation, Option D (use of monetized adder and subtractor functions) is preferable to either percentage preference systems or environmental point scoring systems.

The use of monetary "adders" and "subtractors" to represent environmental and fuel diversity could achieve greater integration of price and non-price factors than has occurred thus far in state bidding systems. The practice of other states in just setting a guideline that 5% or 10% of the utility bid evaluation be based on environmental or fuel consideration does not really achieve much integration.

Likewise, a system that just awards judgmentally determined mills per kwh "subtractors" to technologies that are considered better (on environmental and fuel diversity criteria) than the IDR and also uses mills per kwh "adders" to penalize technologies that are considered worse than the IDR does not achieve much integration of price and non-price factors. There would be prolonged debates as to how to define categories of technologies. Once a project was defined to be within a particular technology category, there would be no incentive to improve the characteristics of the project in terms of meaningful environmental or fuel diversity variables. All technologies should have an equal *incentive* to reduce pollution or reduce fuel price risk.

ENDNOTES

1. See Mark Reeder, "Competitive Bidding for Electric Supplies: Utility Responsibility and the Intervention of the Regulator," presented at the 1989 winter meeting of the IEEE Power Engineering Society, January 31, 1989.
2. Figure 10-1 is obviously somewhat heroic and conceptual in that it presumes a) that the environmental damage function can be accurately measured, b) that the standard is optimally set, and c) that there is 100% compliance with the standard. The term "threshold" refers to whether there is a steeply sloped point in the environmental damage function where a standard can be set.
3. A detailed explanation of the concepts of "certain equivalents" and "risk premiums" is beyond the scope of this chapter. The reader is referred to Howard Raiffa, *Decision Analysis: Introductory Lectures on Choices Under Uncertainty* (Addison-Wesley Publishing Company, Reading, Massachusetts, 1970); and Robert Schlaifer, *Analysis of Decisions Under Uncertainty* (McGraw-Hill, New York, 1969); and David B. Hertz and Howard Thomas, *Risk Analysis and Its Application* (John Wiley and Sons, 1983).

SECTION D

CONSERVATION AND COMPETITIVE BIDDING

CHAPTER 11: THE ROLE OF CONSERVATION RESOURCES IN COMPETITIVE BIDDING SYSTEMS FOR ELECTRICITY SUPPLY*

Ralph Cavanagh
Senior Staff Attorney, Natural Resources Defense Council

I appreciate the Subcommittee's invitation to address the role of demand-side options in utilities' bidding systems for electricity supply. The Chairman is in part responsible for the recent prominence of this issue, of course; his letter of last November to the Federal Energy Regulatory Commission helped spur FERC's recent efforts to incorporate demand-side options in its guidelines for state-administered bidding procedures.[1] Some have questioned this concept, including FERC Commissioner Charles Stalon and Professor Paul Joskow, who appears with me today as a witness.[2]

In responding below to the Subcommittee's questions, I will address critiques of recent "all source bidding" proposals. I do so from the perspective of nearly a decade's work with utilities throughout North America on the acquisition of "conservation resources", by which I mean the creation of new electricity supplies through utility-financed improvements in the efficiency of energy-using buildings, appliances and industrial processes. Contrary to what some might think about the relationship between environmental groups and utilities, those efforts have been collaborative, not adversarial.[3] n addition to my work at NRDC, I also serve as a member of the National Academy of Sciences' Energy Engineering Board, and I have taught courses on electric utility regulation at the Harvard and Stanford Law Schools.

My testimony begins with an overview of the resource planning process into which bidding systems fit, and continues with some general observations on the role of conservation resources in bidding systems. The last section responds to the five questions posed in chairman Sharp's letter.

Statement before the House Energy and Commerce Committee's Subcommittee on Energy and Power: Hearing on All-source Bidding Systems for Electricity. Washington, D.C., March 31, 1988.

A GENERAL PERSPECTIVE ON UTILITIES' RESOURCE ACQUISITIONS

Electric utilities constitute the nation's most capital-intensive industry. Over the two years ending in 1987, their investments in plant and equipment exceeded the total recorded for all of America's airlines, railroads, mines, aerospace companies, and iron and steel foundries — combined.[4] These utilities are legally obliged to stand in readiness to meet any demand for service; their resource acquisitions rely on forecasts of system needs that will not appear for a decade or more.

The industry's recent years have been tumultuous, reflecting both forecasting failures and technological changes that have transformed the electricity business. From 1972 through 1984, utilities cancelled nearly 200 coal-fired and nuclear power plants, with accompanying losses in the tens of billions of dollars.[5] Many other plants were completed in anticipation of demand that did not materialize on schedule. A world of rapidly changing interest rates and energy consumption placed a premium on resource options that allowed for modular construction and flexible scheduling, as opposed to giant facilities with siting and construction periods of ten years or more.

Increasingly, legislatures and regulators have responded by insisting that future proposals for new large-scale generators must be weighed against less costly alternatives. Among those alternatives are improvements in the efficiency of electricity consuming buildings and machines, which have emerged not only as ways for consumers to save money, but also as sources of power for utility systems. For reasons that I explored at length in my last appearance before this Subcommittee, an array of market barriers has left much of this conservation potential unrealized.[6]

Given untapped savings opportunities on the order of 65 to 95 percent for many energy services, conservation programs have become an attractive substitute for new generators in providing the kilowatt-hours needed by new families and businesses.[7] Utilities in California and the Pacific Northwest were spending almost half a billion-dollars annually on such programs in the mid-1980s, and by 1986 their regulators had established savings targets exceeding the peak power production of eighteen 1000 Megawatt power plants.[8] A national survey in 1987 determined that "[b]etween one-third and one-half [of] the utilities in the country are now offering energy efficiency rebate programs", which provide ratepayer-funded cash rewards for customers' decisions to save electricity.[9]

Viewed as a resource for utilities, conservation has several distinctive advantages. As listed by the Northwest Power Planning Council, which Congress created in 1980, these include:

1. Conservation programs are flexible. They can accommodate midcourse corrections to account for changing conditions.
2. The relatively short lead time required to design and implement conservation programs avoids the need to make large capital investments far ahead of the time when a new resource is expected to be needed.
3. The small incremental size of each conservation activity permits a closer matching of supply with new demand.
4. Conservation opportunities tend to track economic cycles, ensuring that the resource is largest when the need or it is greatest.
5. Conservation savings occursimultaneously with the expenditure of the investment. This reduces the risk of investing large sums of capital in projects that may never actually produce power.[10]

California's regulators recently added another major item to this list:

6. Uncertainty in demand forecasting can be lessened through increasing energy efficiency. The uncertainty introduced by economic growth projections — such as future commercial floor space totals — can be reduced by lowering per unit consumption, by using more efficient appliances, and designing more efficient buildings.[11]

Integrating conservation in utilities' resource plans requires a practicable means of comparing the life-cycle costs of conservation and generation options. A "least-cost planning" label is frequently applied to a cluster of methods for performing these comparisons and integrating the results into resource acquisition schedules. By 1987, utilities and regulators in some 37 states were embarking on efforts to minimize the long-term costs of reliable electricity service, to credit comparative advantages of scale and lead-time when evaluating candidates for utility investment, and to defer new generators until utilities had exploited less expensive conservation opportunities.[12] The planner's challenge was no-longer to fit large generators to a forecast of inexorably growing demand, but rather to develop more flexible resource portfolios and to manage power needs instead of simply trying to predict them. The U.S. Department of Energy recently endorsed least-cost planning before this Subcommittee, and attested its "significant contribution in helping to balance energy conservation opportunities with electricity generation capabilities in the future."[13]

THE ROLE OF CONSERVATION RESOURCES IN BIDDING SYSTEMS

Historically, utilities channeled capital into supply options by building power plants and recovering the cost, plus a reasonable return, from ratepayers. The Public Utility Regulatory Policies Act of 1978 (PURPA) gave independent power producers access to these payment streams. However, as construed to date by FERC, that access is limited to entrepreneurs who build generators; no comparable right has been extended to developers of conservation resources.

FERC is now preparing guidelines for a new PURPA implementation system. Utilities would secure new power supplies through auctions open to any bidder willing to supply all or part of the utilities' predicted power needs. The question before FERC, and before this Subcommittee today, is whether conservation resources should be allowed to compete for these payments.

Power supply auctions certainly are not the only mechanism for acquiring conservation resources. Many end uses of electricity are relatively homogenous, are produced in large numbers through standardized methods, and are amenable to simple and inexpensive efficiency improvement

COMPETITION IN ELECTRICITY

strategies. Examples include residential appliances, new housing, and new commercial lighting systems. Regulatory strategies, supplemented on occasion by modest utility payments, may be the most reliable ways to deliver such savings. Recent success stories along these lines include the National Appliance Energy Conservation Act of 1987 and various states' residential and nonresidential building efficiency standards, which are attracting some direct financial support from the utility industry.

For states that have not adopted such regulations, and for end uses that are not amenable to them, the issue is whether auctions are a useful supplement to the utility-financed conservation programs that are proliferating around the country. I join regulators in California, New York, Maine and Massachusetts in believing that conservation should be able to compete in power supply auctions[14] even as I recognize that such a competition creates implementation issues that are not trivial. How are savings to be measured, and how can we be sure that initial performance will be sustained? How do we avoid paying people to do things they would have done anyway? What about impacts on other ratepayers and utilities' profits? Why do we need to pay people to conserve when electricity rates are relatively high in most parts of the country? Professor Joskow may well add to this list in his testimony.

What is most revealing to me about such questions, however, is that they have little or nothing to do with the auction mechanism *per se*; rather, these are issues that arise whenever utilities decide to invest in conservation. If these problems are insuperable, then utilities are wrong to be investing in conservation today, auctions or no auctions, and their regulators are wrong to be adopting least-cost planning approaches that treat conservation as a resource. As indicated below, I think that the implementation problems can be solved; I also think, however, that it is important for the Subcommittee to understand the full implications of the arguments against opening power supply auctions to conservation.

RESPONSES TO THE SUBCOMMITTEE'S QUESTIONS

Chairman Sharp has posed five questions to today's witnesses, with an eye to sharpening the debate over demand-side bidding.

1. *Is demand-side bidding feasible? Some have suggested that electric supply and demand are fundamentally different from one another and that the attempt to link them to one another in a unitary bidding system constitutes a fatal conceptual error.*

RESPONSE: Generators and efficiency measures are different in more ways than can be listed here, but in one fundamental respect they are interchangeable: for purposes of meeting new system needs for power, a kilowatt-hour preserved from waste is indistinguishable from a kilowatt-hour delivered to customers by a new power plant. That is not just my opinion; it was the opinion of Congress in the Pacific Northwest Electric Power Planning and Conservation Act of 1980,[15] and it is the opinion of every public utility commission and utility that has embraced the Act's least-cost planning principles. If conservation can function as a power supply resource, it ought to be possible to accommodate it in an auction for power supply resources.

2. *Is demand-side bidding practicable? Assuming that the answer to the first question is yes, what would be the necessary components of a bidding structure that would allow demand options to compete on an equal footing against supply options?*

RESPONSE: A bidding structure would need to solve problems that arise under any utility's conservation acquisition regime. Conservation bidders must demonstrate that they are providing reliable savings that do not duplicate those produced by other programs or existing regulations, and must identify ways to confirm their performance claims. The easiest cases will involve end uses covered by efficiency standards or preexisting contractual demand limits.

For example, it is straightforward to demonstrate that an industrial plant has reduced consumption 10 megawatts or 10,000 megawatt-hours below its contractual entitlement (and is willing to amend its power service contract accordingly), or that a low income housing development's refrigerators are 200 kwh/unit more efficient than the new federal standards require, or that a commercial lighting system beats state code by one watt per square foot. Examples like this will cover a multitude of end uses. Elsewhere, bidders will have a heavier burden to surmount in order to demonstrate savings; if they cannot meet it, they should be sent home empty handed.

Another implementation issue involves a pervasive institutional barrier to conservation options, which would create special problems for all-source bidding: under conventional rate regulation, utilities' near-term profits generally rise and fall in synchrony with kilowatt-hour sales. The more electricity an utility sells, the greater its net revenues, and vice versa. As I have argued at length elsewhere, other states should follow California's lead in decoupling returns to utilities' shareholders from kilowatt-hour sales.[16] Otherwise every decision to accept a conservation bid over a competing generator would be taken at the immediate expense of an utility's shareholders.

Also, like their generation counterparts, conservation bidders can anticipate requirements to provide information about timing of power deliveries, resource lifetimes, and quality controls. They presumably will bid along with power plant sponsors for part or all of the right to provide some specified number of Megawatts and megawatt-hours. Nothing that FERC proposes to require of generation bidders in its guidelines could not also be required of conservation bidders.

Indeed, in its apparent lack of familiarity with conservation resources, FERC falls victim to occasional ironies in its proposed guidelines. For example, FERC urges auction administrators not to "reject outright" "capital intensive technology, such as coal or hydroelectric plants, which involv[e] a higher risk of capital cost escalation", since the alternative (in FERC's view) is likely to be "a supply alternative offering more immediate but lesser capital cost economies and greater risk of exposure to fuel cost escalation."[17] But there is one category of supply alternatives that is insulated against both types of escalation, and it should not be denied the opportunity to press that advantage in a competitive market.

3. *Are demand-side options reliable? Some have argued that investments in efficiency or conservation are inherently less reliable than supply alternatives, and that such investments therefore undermine the reliability of the nation's electric system.*
RESPONSE: Others have argued much more persuasively that investments in efficiency or conservation are inherently

more reliable than supply alternatives, and that such investments therefore improve the reliability of the nation's electric system. One of the best illustrations is the recent and exhaustive conservation assessment commissioned by the Congress under the Pacific Northwest Electric Power Planning and Conservation Act, 16 U.S.C. Section 839b(k). Here it suffices to restate the Council's conclusion (p. 2): "[C]onservation serves as the cornerstone of the regional energy plan, not only because it was found to have a lower cost than other resources, but because it has additional desirable attributes that reduce risks and improve environmental quality relative to electricity generators."

4. *Is demand-side bidding good policy? It has been suggested variously, that utilities are ill-suited to bring demand-side options to the marketplace, and that utility conservation initiatives grant an inequitable windfall to some consumers at the expense of others.*

I have taken the liberty of breaking this into four questions, which draw on recurring themes in the current debate over demand-side options. Of course, the Chairman's question really goes to the merits of utility investment in conservation *per se*, as opposed to the use of the auction mechanism.

a) Why rely on utilities to break down market barriers to electricity efficiency improvements? After all, no one tries to make oil companies pay their customers to insulate their homes or buy cars with good gas mileage.

RESPONSE TO 4a: From a public policy perspective, there are some crucial distinctions between our regulated and unregulated fuel companies. We have created an extensive regulatory system to oversee electric utilities' investment policies and enforce a legal obligation to meet any increases in electricity demand; included in that system are publicly administered cost recovery mechanisms designed to assure utility stockholders a return on their companies' investments in new electricity supplies. Least-cost advocates are trying to ensure that demand side resources have a fair chance to compete for access to these publicly administered cost recovery mechanisms, which serviced more than half a trillion dollars in capital investment over a recent decade.[18] Also, for reasons set out earlier, conservation resources have a number of special advantages from the perspective of utilities' resource planning responsibilities. As more and more utilities are demonstrating, learning to identify and exploit conservation resources contributes vitally to success in the modern utility business.

This is not to say that market barriers to conservation do not exist, and should not be addressed, for petroleum. But the oil industry has no counterpart to utilities' resource planning obligations, cost recovery mechanisms, or the regulators that oversee them. I suspect that Professor Joskow and I concur in supporting a broad range of alternative approaches for oil conservation, including but not limited to efficiency standards for automobiles and furnaces and taxpayer-financed weatherization assistance for the indigent. We might also concur that federal subsidies for oil production were inappropriate, at least pending an assessment of whether the same public dollars could buy more oil by financing efficiency improvements.

b) As long as electricity rates approximate or exceed the cost of additional power supply, won't payments for efficiency result in excessive incentives to conserve? Conservers get paid twice; once when they pocket the incentive, and again when they receive their reduced electricity bill.

RESPONSE TO 4b: Even relatively high electricity rates do not elicit remotely commensurate conservation investments. The best available evidence indicates that efficiency does not sell unless it produces real annual returns, in reduced energy costs, on the order of 30-200 percent; this is equivalent to a payback requirement of six months to three years.[19] Such findings have been reported for all major categories of electricity consumption, including those in the commercial and industrial sectors.[20] By contrast, utilities typically earn less than 15% on invested capital, and a new large-scale coal or nuclear power plant cannot even begin generating a marketable product until the conclusion of a ten-to-sixteen year siting and construction period.

The disparity in investment criteria for conservation and generation suggests that widely differing discount rates are used in decisions about building generators and buying conservation.[21] Buyers of conservation in the residential, commercial and industrial sectors apply high discount rates to saved kilowatt-hours, while utilities evaluate future kilowatt-hours from new generators more favorably. Strong elements of rationality underpin the behavior of both groups, but the gap invites low return investments in power plants that cost-effective conservation could displace.[22] Society is the clear loser under such circumstances.

Moreover, customers who insist on rapid paybacks from long-lived efficiency measures are imposing a cost limit per conserved kilowatt-hour that falls far below applicable retail electric rates. Most conservation expenses are incurred upfront, while the savings are spread over a period of years or decades. Typical discount rates for conservation imply that costs must be amortized over the initial year or two of savings. Based on findings by the Northwest Power Planning Council, for example, it appears that the average consumer would decline or ignore appliance efficiency measures with twenty-year lifetimes costing less than one cent per kilowatt-hour saved, even if that consumer's electricity rate were as high as eight cents per kilowatt-hour.[23] Comparable conclusions apply to long-lived industrial measures.[24]

Relying on electricity rates to spur full development of cost-effective conservation resources is like expecting spot market prices to provide adequate incentives for the construction of new power plants. Given current market barriers, the last thing we need to worry about is "excessive" conservation investment. Utilities' conservation payments are the analogues to the assured revenue streams that independent power producers typically require in order to construct generators under successful PURPA acquisition regimes.

c. Why should utility customers who don't or can't conserve subsidize those who do?

RESPONSE TO 4c: Utilities' conservation payments are not "subsidies"; they are purchases of a resource for the power system. Under the approach I am describing, utilities target only conservation that is less costly than alternative sources of generation, and opportunities to participate are widely distributed throughout the system. And no ratepayers are "nonparticipants" in the resulting systemwide benefits, which were reviewed earlier.

It remains troubling, moreover, that those who challenge conservation on distributional grounds seldom apply the same criteria to power plant investment. This selective approach has been justified on the ground that all ratepayers are "participants" in the electricity demand that necessitates power plant construction, so that all should share in the resulting costs.[25]

But customers differ significantly in their ability to avoid those costs, and here the market barriers to conservation take on a new and harsh significance. Access to the capital and knowledge needed to improve building and equipment efficiencies or to switch fuels is hardly independent of wealth. For the indigent, the options for escaping new power plants' costs are dominated by curtailment and discomfort. Analogous complaints can be raised by those who depend on fixed electricity-intensive equipment for livelihoods or comfort. Such ratepayers are at a relative disadvantage in the system-wide competition to avoid higher power bills-associated with additional generators.[26]

There is no principled basis for distinguishing these issues from the distributional concerns raised by critics of utilities' conservation investments. Neither power-plant nor conservation investments are invulnerable to claims of inequity; both add to society's energy bill, and some individuals will be more successful than others at escaping the ensuing pain. Cost effective conservation programs have the advantage of inflicting less pain in aggregate, and utilities' conservation payments reach a broader cross section of society than payments for the construction and operation of power plants.[27] From 1984 to 1986, for example, California utilities financed conservation measures in more than 63,000 businesses and 1.5 million households; almost one-fifth of the households were classified as "low income."[28]

d. Won't payments for conservation reward those who are most inefficient, and encourage deceptive practices? If a storeowner offered you five dollars not to buy a fish, wouldn't you be tempted to tell him you had been planning to buy two fish, so he should pay you ten dollars instead?

The example is Professor Joskow's; the concern is one that he shares with Commissioner Stalon, who is concerned that one cannot pay for energy savings "without creating incentives for inefficient use so there are more 'savings' to sell".[29] This is a familiar issue to those involved with conservation resource acquisition. The solution, as noted earlier, lies in careful selection of indices to use in measuring "savings." Thus, for example, appliance efficiency promoters should not be permitted to claim that, but for their intervention, everyone in the neighborhood would have purchased the worst guzzler on the market. The industrial customer with a contractual entitlement to 50 Megawatts cannot be allowed to measure savings from a baseline of 75 Megawatts. Auction guidelines can and should demand rigorous justifications for savings estimates, but exclusion of conservation resources on this basis is unjustified.

5. *Would a demand-side option in the FERC all-source competitive bidding rule jeopardize the progress of the FERC initiative? It has been argued that the issue of demand-side bidding is not yet ripe for Federal administrative action, both because state experimentation is at an early state of development, and because FERC has already taken on an overly ambitious agenda.*

RESPONSE: The utility industry has had at least a decade of experience with demand-side alternatives. To omit demand-side options from the FERC initiative would be to exclude from power supply competitions the least expensive resources available to modern electricity systems. FERC need not prescribe in detail how to integrate supply and demand side options in power supply acquisitions under PURPA, but FERC should insist that this goal be achieved, based on the principle of fair competition in allocating utilities' resource payments.[30]

This recommendation is reinforced by FERC's concern that poorly designed bidding systems will result in "an inefficient use of the nation's resources: electricity [would be] produced from a high cost source when it could have been produced from a lower cost source." According to FERC, this could readily happen if "some sources of supply were ignored in the bidding process."[31]

I agree. And that is why FERC's agenda, however ambitious, will be dangerously incomplete until it accommodates the integration of conservation resources in PURPA acquisition procedures.

ENDNOTES

1. Letter from Hon. Philip R. Sharp to Hon. Martha O. Hesse, November 13, 1987 (urging that "[e]nergy efficiency should be treated equally as a potential source of power in any competitive bidding system").
2. See Charles Stalon, "The Role of "Conservation" Pro-

grams in the Bidding NOPR (RM88-5)", March 4, 1988 (memorandum to Commissioners); Letter from Paul Joskow to Hon. Philip Sharp, December 11, 1987).

3. Thus, for example, a jointly sponsored initiative of NRDC and Pacific Power & Light won the 1984 Oregon Governor's Award for Energy Conservation Achievement, while five years of NRDC work on conservation and least cost planning issues earned the Bonneville Power Administration's 1986 Award for Exceptional Public Service.

4. See *Capital Spending to Rise Sharply in 1988*, Electrical World, January 1988, at 29 ($65 billion for electric utilities versus $64 billion for the other five industrial groups combined, for 1986-1987).

5. This record is reviewed in Cavanagh, *Least-Cost Planning Imperatives for Electric Utilities and Their Regulators*, 10 Harvard Environmental Law Review 299, 302 & n. 11 (1986).

6. Statement of Ralph Cavanagh on Behalf of the Natural Resources Defense Council, November 4, 1987, at 2-3.

7. Potential savings are reviewed in, e.g., Cavanagh, note 5 above, at 312-14; Rocky Mountain Institute, Competitek: Advanced Techniques for Electric Efficiency (March 1987) (identifying potential savings for lighting,   water heat, space cooling and appliances of 82-96%, 65-85%, 80-90%, and 65-85%, respectively).

8. California's eight investor-owned utilities spent almost $1 billion on conservation programs between 1984 and 1986, according to the Energy Conservation Program Summaries published for those years by the Evaluation & Compliance Division of the California Public Utilities Division. By 2005, savings from programs already adopted in California are expected to reach 12,858 Megawatts. California Energy Commission, Conservation Report II-11. The Northwest Power Planning Council estimates that utilities in Idaho, Montana, Oregon and Washington invested between $800 and $900 million on conservation resources between 1981 and mid-1987. Northwest Power Planning Council, A Review of Conservation Costs and Benefits 2 (October 1, 1987) . The Council has identified ten programs that are expected to save 3900 average megawatts — the equivalent of 5300 peak megawatts operating at 70% capacity — if load growth is at the

high end of the range deemed plausible over the next two decades. Northwest Power Planning Council, 1986 Northwest Conservation and Electric Power Plan, at 8-3 (1986).

9. *Study Finds Increasing Use of Rebate Programs as Utilities Seek Alternatives to Generation*, Energy Conservation Digest 1, 1 (January 4, 1988) (summarizing survey published by Electric Power Research Institute).

10. See Appendix to testimony, at 5.

11. Report to the Legislature on Joint CEC/PUC Hearings on Excess Generating Capacity (SB 1970), at II-7 to II-8 (November 1987).

12. These methodologies are described in greater detail in Cavanagh, note 5 above, at 322-24 & 330-42; Northwest Power Planning Council, Pacific Northwest Conservation and Electric Power Plan, at 3-1 to 3-7 (1986); Wellinghoff & Mitchell, *A Model for Statewide Integrated Resource Planning*, Pub. Util. Fort., Aug. 8, 1985, at 19, 19-20. According to a recent Energy Conservation Coalition study, "37 states have undertaken 61 different actions — either through legislation, regulation or studies to explore and/or promote least-cost electrical planning . . . over the 18 month period from January 1986 to June 1987." Energy Conservation Coalition, A Brighter Future: State Actions in Least-Cost Electrical Planning 1 (December '1987). Within that group, "twenty-three state regulatory commissions were engaged in either examining or initiating least-cost planning", "twelve state legislatures introduced and/or passed least-cost planning bills and resolutions", and "six states released studies which recommend that utilities prepare least— cost resource plans to be submitted to the appropriate state regulatory agency." *Id.*

13. Testimony of Donna R. Fitzpatrick, Assistant Secretary, December 2, 1987, at 2.

14. Maine and Massachusetts are already experimenting with conservation auctions; authorities in New York and California have endorsed the principle. See M. Cuomo, State of the State, at 68 (1988); Joint CEC/PUC Report, note 11 above, at V-11.

15. See 16 U.S.C. Section 839a(19) & 839b(e) (Northwest Power Planning Council shall adopt least-cost plan to

COMPETITION IN ELECTRICITY

acquire resources for meeting regional power needs; "'resource' means electric power, including the actual or planned electric power capability of generating facilities, or actual or planned load reduction resulting from direct application of a renewable energy resource by a consumer, or from a conservation measure").

16. Cavanagh, *Responsible Power Marketing in an Increasingly Competitive Era*, 6 Yale Journal on Regulation (1988: forthcoming). Under California's "Electric Revenue Adjustment Mechanism", "[r]evenue differences resulting from the differences between forecast and actual sales are recorded in a balancing account and are periodically recovered from or returned to shareholders", so that changes in sales volumes do not affect earnings. California PUC, D.87-02-030, at 2 (Feb. 11, 1987).

17. Notice of Proposed Rulemaking, Regulations Governing Bidding Programs, Docket No. RM88-5-000, at 70 (March 16, 1988).

18. See *36th Annual Electric Utility Industry Forecast*, Electrical World, Sept. 1985, at 58 (utilities spent more than $500 billion [1985 dollars] between 1974 and 1984 to build new power plants and transmission lines).

19. Cavanagh, *Least-Cost Planning Imperatives for Electric Utilities and Their Regulators*, 10 Harvard Environmental Law Review 299, 318 (1986) (citing sources). See also U.S. Department of Energy, Energy Security: A Report to the President of the United States 107 (March 1987) ("Customers typically look for short payback periods — 6 months to 2 years — for energy conserving investments. Yet many such investments will produce energy savings for years, as in the case of an efficient furnace with a useful life of 20 years."); Northwest Power Planning Council, 2 1986 Northwest Conservation and Electric Power Plan, at 4-6 to 4-10 (review of discount rates applied by consumers to conservation investments).

20. See Alliance to Save Energy, Industrial Decision-Making Interviews: Findings and Recommendations 20 (January 1987: Prepared for Michigan Electricity Options Study) (large industrial customers require conservation investments to repay their costs in two to three years; "[u]nder tight conditions projects may be funded only if they have a payback of one year or less"); Energy Branch, Califor-

nia Public Utilities Commission, 1984 Energy Conservation Program Summary 6 (May 1985) (Utilities' "energy auditors have found that their [commercial and indu5trial sector] customers are reluctant to invest in hardware conservation measures unless the energy savings produce a 100% return within less than two years, and in many cases within six months"); Cavanagh, note 5 above, at 318 n. 57 (citing sources).

21. Commissioner Stalon acknowledges as much in his letter, note 2 above, at 3; see also B. Reddy, *Least-Cost Planning for Electric Utilities*, at 32-33 (National Economic Research Associates: December-1987).

22. See, *e.g.*, L. Ruff, The Basic Economics of Utility Least-Cost Planning and Demand-Side Management 58 (Northeast Utilities: October 1987) (characterizing industries' stringent payback requirements as "a rule-of-thumb method for capturing other constraints, costs and risks"); Cavanagh, note 5 above, at 319 ("[d]ecisions about end use efficiencies often are made by developers and landlords who will not be paying the ensuing utility bills"). For their part, utilities are generally allowed a fixed rate of return on "prudent" investment regardless of its nature; as noted in text, that rate of return falls well below consumers' implicit discount rates for conservation.

23. The calculation appears in Testimony of Ralph Cavanagh before the Montana Public Service Commission, Docket No. 86.12.76 (Feb. 25, 1987), at Schedule 5. The assumed customer discount rate is 65% real, in line with empirical findings reported in notes 19-20 above. This discount rate effectively requires recovery of the conservation's costs in less than two years. If rates are 8 cents per kilowatt-hour, twenty-year savings with life-cycle costs of even 1 cent per kilowatt-hour will not pass muster, because their payback period exceeds the specified interval.

24. See note 20 above.

25. B. Reddy, note 21 above, at Appendix, p. 7.

26. I am indebted for this insight to Thomas Foley of the Northwest Power Planning Council.

27. See, *e.g.*, Bonneville Power Administration, Employment Effects of Electric Energy Conservation 2 (April 1984) ("The literature generally concludes that expenditures on conservation generate more regional employment oppor-

tunities than expenditures of the same size on power plant construction and operation).

28. See California Public Utilities Commission, Evaluation & Compliance Division, 1986 Energy Conservation Program Summary 13-14 & 19-20; 1985 Energy Conservation Program Summary 10 & 13; 1984 Energy Conservation Program Summary 2 & 6. Utilities offered loans and rebates to defray part of the cost of insulating homes; low income customers received efficiency measures at no charge. Commercial customers could obtain rebates for "installing hardware which improved end-use efficiency in lighting, [heating, ventilation, air conditioning], electric motor and refrigeration applications." 1986 Summary at 19. The totals reported in text exclude part of a group of 213,000 residential customers that received incentives to improve appliance efficiencies but did not participate in insulation programs. See 1986 Summary at 15; 1985 Summary at 10; 1984 Summary at 3.

29. See Stalon letter, note 2 above, at 3.

30. In addition, as FERC itself has noted, energy conservation is among "the primary objectives of PURPA." See NOPR, note 17 above, at 4.

31. *Id.* at 40.

CHAPTER 12: SHOULD CONSERVATION PROPOSALS BE INCLUDED IN COMPETITIVE BIDDING PROGRAMS?*

Paul L. Joskow
Massachusetts Institute of Technology

INTRODUCTION

Mr. Chairman, and members of the Subcommittee, it is a pleasure to appear before you today to testify on the merits of the proposal that the Federal Energy Regulatory Commission (FERC) include demand-side options as potential "supply sources in the model "all-source" competitive supply procurement system that it has developed for consideration and voluntary implementation by state regulatory agencies.[1]

On December 11, 1987, I wrote a letter to the Chairman suggesting that there are serious conceptual and practical problems with the proposal. Following that letter he was kind enough to invite me to meet with him and his staff to discuss the issues that I raised in more detail. Since our meeting I have given considerable additional thought to the proposal and have discussed my reservations about it with many other people. I am sorry to report that I continue to believe that integrating demand-side and supply-side options into a single competitive "resource" procurement system does not represent sound public policy. There are both fundamental conceptual and practical problems associated with the proposal.

My analysis leads me to conclude that the broad implementation of this proposal is likely to lead to several undesirable outcomes. In particular, it could result in higher electricity rates, inequitable (i.e., discriminatory) electricity rates, windfall profits for some conservation suppliers, and incentives for inefficient conservation investments. It could also result in a failure to encourage the adoption of the most efficient instruments and delivery systems for encouraging cost-effective demand-side investments that would not otherwise be undertaken voluntarily by consumers. Furthermore,

---

Testimony before the Subcommittee on Energy and Power, House Committee on Energy and Commerce, March 31, 1988.

it would unnecessarily complicate and discourage state experimentation with competitive supply procurement systems, which have the potential to reduce the cost of supplying electricity to consumers. Finally, this approach improperly places the bulk of the burden of electricity conservation on electric utilities and fails to address properly potentially superior alternative institutional arrangements for increasing the efficiency with which electricity is used.

I am not here to argue that there is no role for utilities in encouraging conservation and, more generally, demand-side activities. There are many useful ways in which electric utilities can help consumers to take better advantage of these opportunities. The primary point of my testimony is simply that this proposal, and the conceptual framework from which it is derived, is the wrong way to identify and implement fair and efficient electricity conservation programs. I will present an alternative set of principles to guide the development of electricity conservation programs that is fairer and more efficient than the integrated demand/supply bidding proposal.

PUBLIC POLICY OBJECTIVES

Before proceeding to elaborate on these conclusions I think that it is useful to begin by identifying the objectives that we are trying to achieve with the regulatory policies that we are discussing here today. There is an unfortunate tendency in these discussions to focus on alternative means and to lose sight of the ends that we are trying to achieve.

I believe that as a *society* our primary objectives for the electricity sector should be to maximize the welfare or satisfaction of electricity consumers and to do so in a way that is equitable. We can do this by (a) adopting public policies that encourage electric utilities to *supply* electricity as economically and reliably as possible given technological and contractual opportunities, input prices, and environmental constraints (the supply side of the equation); and (b) adopting public policies that encourage *consumers* to *utilize* electricity efficiently given the costs of electricity and the costs of the alternative ways consumers can transform electricity into useful services that they value (the demand side of the equation). These dual objectives lead to what economists generally refer to as economic efficiency: using society's scarce resources to maximize the well being of our citizens. In addition, I believe that we have an obligation to choose public policies that are fair to electricity consumers and taxpayers. In particular, we should try to avoid cross-subsidization and undue discrimination in electricity rates.[2]

I think that all of us share these very basic objectives. We differ primarily on what the best means are for achieving these ends. Ultimately, the test of competing public policies must be based on how well these policies do in achieving these objectives.

CONCEPTUAL FOUNDATIONS OF THE BIDDING PROPOSAL: CENTRALIZED UTILITY PLANNING AND DECISIONMAKING

To understand the origin of the integrated demand/supply bidding proposal, it is important to understand the novel conceptualization of sound electric utility planning and resource acquisition policies from which it emerges. Most of the analysis in my testimony relies upon a familiar model of decentralized decisionmaking by electricity suppliers, consumers, and suppliers of electricity using appliances, equipment and buildings, who are linked together by regulated prices in an electricity market. It is this model that forms the conceptual foundation for both Title I and Title II of the Public Utility Regulatory Policies Act of 1978 (PURPA).

The integrated demand/supply bidding proposal has evolved from a different conceptual framework. It is derived from a novel model of centralized utility planning and decisionmaking. This approach eschews the traditional economic model of decisionmaking in decentralized markets that carefully distinguishes firm supply decisions from consumer demand decisions, with electricity prices providing the critical linkage between the supply and demand sides of the market. In its place, we are asked to substitute a model in which utility supply decisions and individual consumer electricity utilization decisions are collapsed into a single schedule of equivalent 'supply resources' that we are to assume are at the disposal of the utility.

This conceptual framework is used to support a specific, and I believe inefficient and inequitable, rule of thumb that lies at the heart of the proposal that we are discussing here today. The rule of thumb is that *the utility* should be willing to pay consumers or their agents a fee equal to the marginal cost of additional electricity supplies in return for using less electricity.[3] Thus, if utilities are obligated to pay marginal or avoided cost to cogenerators for additional "megawatts," then they should equally be obligated to pay marginal or avoided cost to consumers or their agents for "negawatts" resulting from consumer conservation actions. The integrated demand/supply bidding proposal is primarily a mechanism to implement this rule.

Most of my testimony is devoted to demonstrating that the rule of thumb that *utilities* should pay marginal cost for negawatts is both inefficient and inequitable. Including demand-side programs in competitive supply-procurement systems simply compounds these problems. Ultimately, the failure of these proposals rests on fundamental problems with the model of centralized utility planning and decisionmaking from which they are derived.

At the very least, I hope that everyone will recognize that the centralized utility planning and decisionmaking model on which this proposal is based represents a very unusual way to think about the allocation of resources in a decentralized market economy such as ours. Oil companies do not have "negagallon" programs, and they do not view consumer opportunities to drive more fuel efficient cars as "supply sources" allowing them to produce less oil. General Motors doesn't pay people to use mass transit (a "negacar" program) or view increasing the use of mass transit as a "supply source" allowing it to produce fewer cars. My neighborhood supermarket doesn't have a "negafood" program that pays me to eat less and doesn't see my going on a diet as a "supply source." The local telephone company does not have a "negacall" program that pays me to talk less on the phone and does not view less talking on the phone as a "supply resource" making it possible to install fewer telephone switches.

More fuel efficient cars, more mass transit, and perhaps even my going on a diet and talking less on the phone may all be very worthwhile public policy goals. But our views on whether they are and, if they are, how best to achieve them does not flow naturally from the kind of centralized planning and decisionmaking framework that we are being asked to

238   COMPETITION IN ELECTRICITY

apply to electric utilities. Indeed, if I suggested that this framework be applied in these other contexts most people would laugh. In light of the fact that this is a rather unusual perspective for analyzing markets for goods and services, and that the costs of the programs that this framework suggests utilities pursue are ultimately recovered from consumers in higher electricity rates, I suggest that one should be at least a little bit skeptical about using it as a sound basis for public policy.

The standard answer that I get when I point out how alien this conceptual framework is to the traditional analysis of supply, demand, prices and the role of markets generally in our economy is that electricity is different. In particular, that because electric utilities have legal monopolies, electricity must be viewed from an entirely different perspective from other goods and services. It is argued that the legal monopoly status of electric utilities requires that we give them broad responsibilities for controlling how consumers transform electricity into electricity services.

The monopoly status of utilities as suppliers of electricity does obviously create differences with unregulated markets. And it is the legal monopoly position of utilities as *suppliers of electricity* that leads to regulatory control and scrutiny of the costs a utility incurs in supplying electricity, the mix of electricity products that it offers, and the level and structure of electricity prices.

The utility's legal monopoly *does not*, however, extend to the use of electricity or the provision of equipment and information affecting electricity conservation. *Consumers* create electricity services, not the utility. They do so by purchasing a critical input supplied by the utility (electricity) and purchasing other inputs from the many competing suppliers of electricity-using appliances and equipment, to transform electricity into lighting, cooling, heating, and other services. A utility is no more in the "electricity services" business than is GE or Sears. The utility has no monopoly over "electricity services" or "the demand side," and there is no reason to give it one. Indeed, in most jurisdictions, electric utilities are legally prohibited from supplying the range of appliances, equipment, and related services that would make it possible for them to be full participants in the "electricity services" business.[4]

The utility's status as a regulated monopoly supplier of electricity at retail therefore provides absolutely no justification for rejecting the traditional model that clearly recognizes the decentralization of supplier decisions and consumer electricity utilization decisions and the role of regulated electricity prices in linking all of these decisionmakers together. Regulation may create some unique problems that in fact support a case for a special role for utilities in demand-side programs, but these situations are conveniently and properly analyzed within the traditional model. It does not require us to invent and rely on a whole new conceptual framework that is unique to electricity. Indeed, the primary guiding principle for regulation of public utilities is to develop regulatory rules that simulate the outcomes that would emerge in a competitive market with decentralized suppliers and consumers.

There is one important difference between a regulated electric utility and an unregulated firm operating in a competitive market that is important but rarely discussed. Because the utility is a regulated monopoly that faces limited retail competition, its regulators have considerable freedom to manipulate rates in order to subsidize some customers and to tax others to pay for such subsidies. "Taxation by regulation" is an outcome that must be of real concern to anyone who wants the regulatory process to yield prices that are equitable. I am increasingly concerned that electric utilities are being chosen as society's instrument for subsidizing conservation not because they are uniquely suited to do so, but because the fact that they are regulated makes it politically expedient to use them as tax and subsidy instruments. It is certainly easier to force a regulated firm to provide subsidies to some customers and pay for them by raising rates to others than it would be to force a competitive firm (like GE or Sears) to do so. Taxation by regulation may also be easier to hide than direct tax and subsidy programs paid for out of general tax revenues. As a result, it is important for us to examine alternative regulatory policies to determine whether they lead to unfairly subsidizing some customers at the expense of others.

THE STANDARD ECONOMIC CASE FOR UTILITY-SPONSORED CONSERVATION PROGRAMS

I will now discuss the standard economic case for utility-sponsored conservation programs. This discussion proceeds within the traditional framework of decentralized decision-makers linked together by regulated electricity prices. I assume that we have a regulated monopoly supplier of electricity. I also assume, as is traditional in the most basic analysis of markets for goods and services in a decentralized economy, that consumers are reasonably well informed and act in their own self-interest. Factors that may lead to imperfections in consumer decisionmaking will be covered later in my testimony.

There are two primary economic rationales for utility-sponsored conservation programs within this framework. First, regulators may have been unable to set the proper prices, leading consumers to act on price signals that do not reflect the true social costs of their decisions. In particular, if prices (on the margin) are *less* than the marginal cost of supplying electricity, consumers will be induced to consume too much electricity; alternatively, they will conserve too little.

Second, the utility may be the most efficient supplier of certain types of demand-side services. This is most likely to be the case for demand-side programs that are necessarily supplied jointly with the provision or pricing of electricity or make use of information to which the utility has favored access as a consequence of its being a monopoly supplier. Conservation programs that require special pricing arrangements or involve load controls that only the utility can provide fall in this category.[5] Programs that can make effective use of the utility's access to customers through customer billing arrangements or meter reading would fall in this category as well. Such programs require utility participation to be implemented efficiently, so we cannot rely on competing suppliers of conservation services to supply them. It also would seem that such programs are poorly adapted to a competitive bidding system, because the utility has inherent advantages in supplying them. These are the kinds of programs that are covered by Title 1 of PURPA. Many of them are best viewed as additional electricity "products." If these products are priced to recover the marginal cost of providing them and consumers are willing to purchase them, then they should be offered. Others can be evaluated in the context of the basic principles for good demand-side programs that I will discuss later in my testimony.

Let me focus here on the problems associated with prices that are lower than marginal cost. Figure 12-1 illustrates the problem. The figure contains a conventional aggregate demand function for electricity and two horizontal lines representing prices and marginal cost. In the figure, price is assumed to be less than marginal cost. Exactly why is unimportant for now, but a typical explanation is that regulators use average-cost pricing and that average cost is below marginal cost. Efficient consumer decisionmaking requires that price equal marginal cost. In Figure 12-1 consumers would consume a quantity equal to q_1 if price were equal to marginal cost. However, because consumers face a lower price they consume out to q_2. Inefficient pricing has resulted in excessive consumption equal to $q_2 - q_1$. There is an associated social loss, represented by the shaded triangle. This area reflects the difference between the value consumers place on the excess electricity they are consuming and the social cost of this consumption.[6]

Obviously, the best way to cure this problem is to set electricity prices so that they equal marginal cost. But let us assume that we can't. What can the utility do then to encourage more conservation? One approach that the utility could take would be to offer to pay consumers to consume less. If a consumer is offered a payment or subsidy to consume less, then the rational consumer will decide to accept the offer and consume less if the subsidy *plus* the reduction in his bill resulting from conservation is greater than cost of the conservation investment plus the value of any electricity services foregone. By offering to pay consumers to consume less, the utility raises the *effective* price of electricity by the amount of the subsidy.[7] These payments are properly viewed as an effort to get the prices right (on the margin), not as utility investments in conservation "resources."

This framework also leads to a simple rule of thumb for determining what the size of the subsidy or payment for conservation or "megawatts" should be. The rule is that payments should be made by the utility for "purchased conserva-

242   COMPETITION IN ELECTRICITY

tion" as long as those payments (per unit of electricity saved) are no greater than the *difference* between marginal cost and price.

What is so special about the difference between marginal cost and price? As I have already discussed, the proper price signal is a price (P) equal to marginal cost (MC). I have also indicated that the effective price perceived by a consumer when offered a subsidy is equal to the subsidy *plus* what he saves by consuming less. Thus, with a payment per unit of electricity saved equal to MC - P plus a reduction in the customer's bill of P per unit saved, the effective price (the sum of the two) is equal to marginal cost.[8] This is precisely the result that we want to get the price signals right.

When a rational consumer faces an effective price equal to the marginal cost of supplying electricity, the *consumer* will compare the marginal cost of additional conservation investments with the marginal cost of additional supplies reflected by the price. He will have an incentive to make investments in conservation up to the point where the marginal cost of conservation is equal to the price of electricity, which, by assumption, is equal to the marginal cost of supplying electricity. Supply-side and demand-side options "compete" fairly with one another through decentralized supplier and consumer decisions when prices are set right. What the *utility* pays for conservation is not the issue. Rather what *society* pays for conservation is the issue. In this case, *consumers* (who are part of society) will be willing to pay up to marginal cost for conservation whenever the effective price of electricity is equal to marginal cost. And this is precisely the outcome that we should be seeking to achieve.

If a utility offers to pay a fee equal to marginal cost minus price for conservation, how does the utility recover the costs it incurs when it provides these subsidies? The only way that it can recover these costs is to pass them through in the rates charged to consumers. If we use the marginal cost minus price rule to determine the maximum amount of the subsidy, will electricity rates be higher than they would have been if no payments had been made for purchased conservation? The answer is no. As long as electricity rates are set to recover only the utility's total costs of production, the application of this rule of thumb cannot lead to rates higher than those that would exist if the subsidies were not made.

Rates could even go down under certain circumstances. Thus all consumers, participants nd non-participants, are either better off or no worse off than they were without the subsidy payments as long as the subsidy does, not exceed the difference between marginal cost and price.[9]

There are three important corollaries to this rule of thumb. First, if price is equal to or greater than marginal cost, then no subsidies are justified. Second, if price is equal to or greater than marginal cost *any* subsidy must lead to higher electricity rates and to higher bills for non-participants. Third, subsidies greater than the difference between marginal cost and price are likely to lead to higher electricity rates and to higher bills for non-participants.

BIDDING FOR CONSERVATION WITHIN THE TRADITIONAL ECONOMIC MODEL

I now want to analyze what happens within the traditional economic model if we require utilities to "pay up to marginal cost for all conservation" either through an administrative pricing mechanism or by allowing any "supplier" of conservation to compete with real supply sources in a competitive supply-procurement system.[10] Clearly, this rule is inconsistent with the rule that I have just derived. A rule or bidding process that requires the *utility* to pay up to marginal cost for conservation pays more than a rule that limits payments to the *difference* between marginal cost and price. In this model, payments greater than the *difference* between marginal cost and price will lead to inefficient consumer decisions, higher electricity rates, and higher bills for non-participants than the fair and efficient subsidy rule I have proposed.

First Numerical Example

These outcomes are best illustrated with a numerical example. Exhibit 12-2 develops such an example. The example hypothesizes a utility subject to regulation that sets price equal to the utility's average cost. At the current level of capacity, average cost and price are less than marginal cost. The assumptions about costs, prices, and expected demand at different prices are summarized over Exhibit 12-2.

244   COMPETITION IN ELECTRICITY

At the prevailing price level the utility faces a dilemma. It does not have enough capacity in place to meet demand reliably. The example allows the utility to balance supply and demand in four different ways:

1. It can adopt a "supply only" strategy to balance supply and demand. In this case the utility only adds capacity and does not implement any demand-side programs. Because the cost of new capacity is greater than average cost, prices must rise above the original average cost when additional capacity is added if the utility is to recover all of its costs. Demand and supply are brought into balance through a combination of additional capacity and price increases needed to pay for this capacity.

2. It can adopt a "conservation only" strategy to balance supply and demand. In this case the utility adds no additional capacity, but pays consumers whatever it takes to conserve enough to balance demand with existing capacity. The costs of these payments must also be recovered through utility rates.

3. It can adopt a program that allows conservation to compete with supply-side sources through an integrated supply/demand bidding process. In this case the utility effectively pays up to marginal cost for conservation and makes up any residual supply deficiency by adding capacity. Both the payments for conservation and the payments for additional capacity are recovered through higher rates.

4. It can adopt my preferred rule of thumb discussed in the previous section. It will pay for conservation, but limit the amount it will pay to the *difference* between marginal cost and price.[11] If enough conservation cannot be purchased to balance supply and demand pursuant to this rule, then capacity is added to balance supply and demand. The utility's payments for conservation and the costs of new capacity are recovered through the ratemaking process.

The example allows utility payments for conservation to be determined in two different ways. First, I assume that in each case where the utility pays consumers to consume less, it is able to pay consumers the *minimum* amount that is required to elicit each unit of conservation that is purchased (Exhibit 12-2b). Lower valued uses are paid less than higher valued uses. The various payment rules then become ceilings on what is paid per unit of conservation. This minimizes the expenditures on conservation payments in each case. Second, I assume that the utility must make uniform payments for all conservation whether or not some consumers would be willing to take less (Exhibit 12-2c). This case is most consistent with what would emerge if conservation programs were integrated with supply-side sources in a simple uniform price auction system.

Exhibits 12-2b and 12-2c display the results. The most important lines on the tables are for the "actual price" of electricity and the "consumer welfare." The "actual price" line tells us what consumers must pay for a unit of electricity in each case after all costs are recovered. The "consumer welfare" line provides a measure of how consumers would value the outcomes in each case.

The numerical results are clear. We get the lowest prices and the highest consumer welfare by applying the marginal cost minus price payment rule described earlier. The "pay marginal cost / integrated bidding approach" leads to significantly higher electricity prices and significantly lower consumer welfare. The numerical examples lead to an inescapable conclusion.[12] *Any system that requires the utility to "pay up to marginal cost for each unit of conservation offered" leads to higher prices and lower consumer satisfaction than does the rule that such payments should be limited to the difference between marginal cost and price, At least within the standard economic framework, the demand-side bidding proposal before us would be inefficient, would lead higher electricity rates, and is likely to lead to higher bill for non-participants compared to the alternative that I have suggested,*

Second Numerical Example

Let me provide a simpler, and perhaps more familiar, example to illuminate why these results emerge and also to demonstrate that the integration of demand-side programs into a competitive supply-procurement system *does not* treat supply and demand sources equivalently. Indeed, it discriminates against real supply options.

Let us assume that we are trying to choose between two appliances (assumptions for this example are all summarized

COMPETITION IN ELECTRICITY

in Exhibit 12-3a): a standard appliance that places a load of 1000 kWh per year on the utility and a second appliance that provides equivalent services to the consumer but places a load of only 900 kWh per year on the utility. To make the relationship with supply-side programs clear let me assume that the second appliance is identical to the standard appliance except it has a small cogenerator on top that produces 100 kWh of electricity.[13] This approach seems to be quite consistent with the view that conservation should be viewed as a "Supply source." Thus, both appliances place a gross load of 1000 kWh on the utility, but the second appliance also produces 100 kWh of electricity internally, reducing its net load on the utility to 900 kWh. The second appliance costs more than the first. By assumption, the difference in cost amounts to $0.12 per kWh "supplied" by the second appliance. The price charged by the utility is assumed to be equal to its marginal or avoided cost, which in turn is $0.10 per kWh in the example.

I have purposely set up the example in such a way that it is obvious that we do not want the consumer to choose the second appliance. The only difference between the first appliance and the second appliance is that the second appliance can "produce" 100 kWh for $0.12 per kWh. But this cost is higher than the utility's cost of generating itself, so it would be wasteful to choose it.

If the "supply resources" provided by the standard appliance were treated in a manner equivalent to a real cogeneration supply opportunity, the customer could receive payment for the cogenerated supplies in one of two ways (see Exhibit 12-3b). The customer could choose a net billing arrangement in which he is billed for his *net* load on the utility system after subtracting the contribution of internal generation (1000 kWh load minus 100 kWh "supplied" = 900 kWh in this case). Alternatively, the customer would typically be allowed to choose to enter into a buy/sell arrangement with the utility in which he pays the utility for his *gross* load based on prevailing retail rates and then sells back the power he cogenerates to the utility at the rate the utility pays for purchased cogeneration. If the retail rate and the cogeneration purchase rate are the same, the customer would be indifferent between the two alternatives. If they are both equal to marginal (or avoided) cost, the potential cogenerator will make efficient investment choices.

The rule that requires the *utility* to "pay marginal cost for all conservation" is consistent with neither of these traditional payment arrangements. Applying this rule has the same effect as if we allowed the customer to pay the utility for his *net* consumption (900 kWh in this case—-equivalent to the bill the customer would see after he conserved) *and* to receive a payment equal to the utility's marginal or avoided cost for the 100 kWh that is "supplied" through conservation. Basically, the customer making this conservation investment gets paid twice. He gets paid, through a lower bill, when he conserves. He gets paid again by the utility for the new "supply" that he has provided.

We can see the consequences of paying marginal cost for conservation in this example. Exhibit 12-3c presents the economic calculations that a rational consumer would go through under each of the three payment alternatives, assuming that the retail rate and the price the utility pays for cogeneration or conservation are both equal to the utility's marginal supply cost. The two conventional methods of payment (columns (1) and (2)) make it clear to the customer that choosing the cogeneration or conservation option is not in his interest since it costs more for the customer to "supply" 100 kWh himself than it does to purchase the standard appliance and purchase 1000 kWh from the utility. This is a good outcome because, as the example has been structured, it would be socially inefficient to choose to "supply" anything to the utility by purchasing the second appliance.

Column (3) indicates that this is not the outcome when we use the third payment mechanism. And this payment mechanism is a direct analogy to the "utility pays marginal cost for all conservation" rule. The third payment mechanism makes it economical for the customer to "supply" electricity by choosing the appliance that "uses" less electricity. Because the customer receives the benefit of a lower bill by "conserving" and also receives a direct payment equal to marginal cost for "supplying" what he has conserved, he has a strong incentive to choose the inefficient appliance. The utility ends up paying the customer $0.20 per kWh for electricity that costs the customer $0.12 per kWh to produce. These $0.12 kwhs replace electricity that the utility could have supplied itself for $0.10 per kWh. Non-participant customers must pay for the windfall profits ($0.20 minus $0.12) that the participating customer earns by exploiting this system. Society is worse off because $0.12 electricity has been substituted for $0.10 electricity. This outcome is hardly what I would characterize as a "least-cost" or equitable outcome. Yet it is exactly what happens when the utility pays marginal cost for conservation in this example.

When a utility pays marginal cost for conservation, whether through an administrative payment or bidding system, the consequence is to give the consumer the *wrong* price signals. Putting demand-side programs into a competitive bidding system does not pay a "competitive market price" for conservation. It pays a price that is too high. Rational participant consumers will, at the very least, be paid too much and will have an incentive to overinvest in conservation. Non-participant customers find that their rates and bills go up to pay for the subsidies.

Third Numerical Example

To make the relevant behavioral relationships clear, I offer a third example that should be quite familiar to everyone. This example will also help to motivate my testimony on the consequences of consumer decisionmaking imperfections.

Let us hypothesize that a customer already has in place a reliable refrigerator that consumes 1500 kWh per year (see Exhibit 12-4a). The refrigerator is much less efficient than are new models. Because it has proven itself to be reliable, the customer believes that it will last just as long as a new refrigerator would. The price (and marginal cost) of electricity is $0.10 per kWh, so the 1,500 kWh that this refrigerator uses annually cost the customer $150 (Exhibit 12-4a).

The customer is faced with a choice of keeping his old, reliable refrigerator or replacing it with one of two models, both of which have features identical to those of the existing refrigerator (see Exhibit 12-4a). The first of these hypothetical refrigerator models is a standard, modern unit. This unit would use 1,000 kWh annually with an operating cost of $100. The annual capital charges for this hypothetical refrigerator are $40, for a total annual cost of $140.[14]

The second of these hypothetical refrigerators is a super-efficient model. It would use only 500 kWh annually at an operating cost of $50. However, the purchase price of this hypothetical super-efficient refrigerator is three times that of the standard refrigerator—its annual capital charges are $120. The total annual cost of this hypothetical refrigerator is $170, which is $20 to $30 more than for the other two models.

Given these characteristics, the rational customer of the traditional model should prefer the standard refrigerator over both the old and the super-efficient models. The standard model saves $10 per year over the old model, which in turn saves $20 per year over the super-efficient model.

Comparing the standard model with the old model (see Exhibit 12-4a), we see that the customer can "purchase" 500 kWh annually of conservation at a price of $0.08 per kWh saved (the annual capital charge per kWh saved). Because this cost per kWh of purchased conservation is less than the price that the customer pays for electricity ($0.10), it is privately rational for the customer to invest in this conservation. If the price of electricity equals the marginal cost of supplying electricity, then this privately rational decision is also socially efficient; it is socially efficient to choose the standard model if the cost incurred per kWh saved is less than the marginal cost of providing the electricity that is saved.

If both marginal cost and price equal $0.10, then investing in the superefficient refrigerator is neither socially nor privately rational. This model saves a lot of electricity, but at a sizeable cost. With this model, the cost per kWh saved is $0.12, which is greater than the price of electricity.

Several observations are in order. When price equals marginal cost, the rational customer will make the socially efficient choice among appliance models. The existence of such cost-effective conservation possibilities provides a market opportunity for customers (or others on their behalf) to invest in conservation at socially efficient levels. We expect well-informed customers to make these choices. The existence of conservation opportunities does not imply that subsidies are needed. Furthermore, just because an appliance model saves energy does not mean that it is efficient for society to choose it (e.g., the super-efficient refrigerator in this example). The costs of saving that energy must be balanced against the costs of the electricity that it saved.

What happens if the utility ignores or is ignorant of the fact that the rational consumer would make the right choice without any additional help and decides to implement a "generic" conservation program that pays marginal cost per kWh saved for any and all refrigerator conservation investments that consumers make? Exhibit 12-4b demonstrates how the rational customer behaves if the utility decides to provide a conservation subsidy equal to marginal cost for every kWh by which the customer reduces consumption. (Recall, in this example, price and marginal cost for electricity both equal $0.10 per kWh.)

Notice that with a subsidy the standard refrigerator is still the socially efficient choice; social efficiency depends only on the marginal cost of electricity and the annual capital charge per kWh conserved. It does not depend on the existence or absence of a subsidy.

However, the privately rational choice *does* depend on the subsidy. The standard refrigerator saves 500 kWh annually over the old model, giving it an annual subsidy of $50. This lowers its annual cost for the customer to $90. The super-efficient refrigerator saves 1,000 kWh annually, so it receives an annual subsidy of $100. This lowers its annual cost for the customer to $70. The rational customer would now choose the super-efficient model over the other two, even though it is *not* the socially efficient choice. Furthermore, the utility has shelled out $100 in subsidy payment that were completely unnecessary because the consumer would have properly chosen the standard refrigerator without any financial assistance from the utility. These subsidy payments must be recovered in higher electricity rates. Those customers who do not participate in this windfall are thus made worse off.

For each kWh conserved, the utility pays exactly what it would pay for new capacity (marginal cost), yet this subsidy induces socially inefficient decisions on the part of customers. How can this be? The answer is that *society*, in purchasing conservation, should be willing to pay up to the marginal cost of supplying electricity. In this example, however, society ends up paying $0.12 per kWh conserved, which is *more* than the marginal cost of supplying that electricity would be. The utility pays its marginal cost for each kWh conserved, but the subsidy induces the customer to pay an *additional*

$0.02 per kWh conserved.

Many economists would stop at this point. They would use my three examples to argue that as long as prices are set right, consumers will make socially efficient decisions. Marginal-cost pricing provides an efficient linkage between decentralized supply and demand decisions. Paying consumers a fee equal to marginal cost to conserve is both inefficient and unfair.[15] Indeed, if it were pointed out that with estimated costs like those in the preceding example (Exhibit 12-4) customers were choosing to keep their old refrigerators, many economists would probably assume that the cost and efficiency estimates are wrong. Alternatively, they might argue that if there are significant decisionmaking imperfections that create barriers that lead consumers to fail to make the right choices, these barriers are not unique to electricity, the barriers are not caused by the utility, and the utility should not be assumed to be the institution that is in the best position to fix whatever it is that is broken.

Economists who take this position are typically vilified by conservation advocates for such evil things as looking at the supply side of the meter only, or assuming that consumers make rational decisions on their own behalf, or assuming that consumers respond to price signals. While I believe that it is desirable to confront directly the problems that clearly exist as a consequence of market imperfections and barriers to efficient consumer decisions, the analysis that flows from the traditional model of decentralized decisionmaking with rational consumers is very useful. While there are legitimate concerns about decisionmaking barriers in certain circumstances, many electricity conservation decisions are not characterized by pervasive barriers to rational and efficient decisionmaking. Whenever this is the case, the traditional economic model with rational consumers clearly indicates that the "new learning" on utility planning, decisionmaking and conservation payments is characterized by serious deficiencies.

THE MYSTERIOUS WORLD OF MARKET IMPERFECTIONS AND BARRIERS TO EFFICIENT DECISIONMAKING

Those who rely on the centralized utility planning and decisionmaking model and propose that utilities offer to pay marginal cost for conservation "supplied" by their customers are inclined to reject my preceding analysis as irrelevant. They argue that consumers do not respond to prices "as if" they were rational and well informed as the traditional decentralized decisionmaking model assumes. We are told that there are a host of barriers to efficient consumer decisionmaking that lead consumers to fail to make cost-effective conservation decisions even when electricity prices are set properly. For example, in Exhibit 12-4, consumers might fail to choose the standard refrigerator even when the prices are set properly. As a result, we are told that the decentralized decisionmaking framework -must be rejected and that the utility must step into the breach by engaging in centralized supply/demand planning and by paying consumers marginal cost per unit of saved electricity to get them to consume less.

Advocates of extensive utility involvement in conservation activities rely primarily on two related types of evidence to support the case that significant decisionmaking imperfections exist. First, they rely on engineering/economic calculations that produce estimates of the expected cost per kWh saved for a variety of existing or anticipated conservation opportunities. They then point out that there appear to be many conservation opportunities which have the characteristic that the cost per kWh saved is less than the marginal cost of additional generating capacity yet consumers are not taking advantage of them.

Second, they rely on studies of actual consumer behavior that try to infer the discount rate that consumers implicitly apply when making conservation investments. These studies often find that consumers use what appear to be unreasonably high implicit discount rates. The high discount rates lead consumers to make "incorrect" tradeoffs between conservation investments today and resulting energy savings tomorrow.[16]

There is substantial controversy about the accuracy of the estimated cost per kWh saved associated with different conservation investments that are frequently cited by conservation advocates.[17] This is not the right place to argue about the accuracy of these estimates and I am not an expert on this subject. My limited experience, however, has been that the cost of conserved electricity relied upon by conservation advocates is often significantly underestimated.

The work that has been done on implicit discount rates

leads to results that are characterized by considerable uncertainty as well.[18] Indeed, estimates of implicit consumer discount rates for energy conservation investments vary all over the map.[19] Nevertheless, it is fairly clear that, especially for residential consumers, estimated discount rates are *on average*[20] surprisingly high and represent a source of legitimate concern.

Despite my reservation about the accuracy of the specific calculations that have been generated to support the case for there being pervasive barriers to consumer decisionmaking, viewed in the aggregate, and after adjusting for obvious biases, I believe that the available evidence *does* suggest that there are significant barriers that lead to inefficient consumer decisions in some areas. Unfortunately, we still know relatively little about what the sources of these barriers are or how best to ameliorate them. Furthermore, there are also many consumers, both residential and business, who are not subject to pervasive barriers to efficient decisionmaking.

The likelihood that there are market imperfections that create barriers to efficient decisionmaking does not, however, imply that the model of decentralized supply and demand decisions must be rejected. It simply requires that we incorporate this decisionmaking into that framework. More importantly, the existence of consumer decisionmaking imperfections *does not* logically lead to the conclusion that a "megawatt" program in which the utility pays marginal cost per kWh of conserved electricity is the proper way to cope with them.

Without good information about consumer behavior we have no way to determine how much of a subsidy is required to get consumers to "behave properly." It is likely that the magnitude and form of the subsidy necessary to induce more efficient decisions will vary from end use to end use and from customer to customer. Some customers may make rational investments in conservation without any assistance, while others may not. Providing the same subsidy to all may needlessly subsidize some investments or, even worse from an efficiency standpoint, subsidize inefficient conservation (as in Exhibit 12-4b). The rule that the *utility* should pay the consumer marginal cost per kWh saved is completely arbitrary.

There is also no reason to assume that the best way of

addressing the barriers that lead to the imperfections is to rely on subsidy payments. Are subsidies the most effective means to get consumers to behave properly? Perhaps information and educational programs would be more effective in some cases? Perhaps the answer lies with tighter appliance efficiency standards and better building codes? Would a loan program or a conservation bank ameliorate some of the barriers? The centralized utility decisionmaking model does not help us to answer these questions. It just tells the utility to throw an arbitrary amount of money at the problem.

In light of these observations, I believe that those who propose private or public subsidies should bear the burden of identifying the source and nature of the decisionmaking imperfections. There are several reasons why this is a necessary first step:

- Consumers may in fact voluntarily choose socially efficient conservation actions, in which case subsidies are unnecessary.[21] We, have seen-instances in which subsidies are even undesirable from an efficiency perspective (Exhibit 12-4b). In addition, customers who think that they may receive subsidies in the future may delay conservation investments that are currently rational. Finally, when price is equal to marginal cost, subsidies lead to higher electricity rates and burden nonparticipants. In short, we would like to restrict the subsidies only to situations where they are really needed to induce efficient behavior.
- Only by understanding why consumers do not make efficient decisions on their own can we fashion efficient instruments to correct the identified market imperfections. Throwing money at these problems is not necessarily the best way of ameliorating these imperfections. Education and information, government mandated standards, loans, shared-savings contracts, etc. are all potentially desirable instruments for ameliorating market imperfections in specific circumstances. Nor is the utility necessarily the best institution for ameliorating these imperfections.
- The cost and efficiency estimates on which the benefits of the socially efficient investments are based may simply be wrong. Is so, consumers may be quite rational in not choosing such investments. Providing subsidies to en-

courage consumers to do so would be inefficient, unnecessarily leads to higher electricity bills, and unfairly burdens non-participants with higher bills.

PRINCIPLES FOR GOOD DEMAND-SIDE PROGRAMS ADDRESSING DECISIONMAKING IMPERFECTIONS

The standard economic model that carefully separates supply decisions and consumer electricity utilization decisions, and that recognizes the critical role of prices linking decentralized decisionmakers together. Can be readily applied to situations in which there are consumer decisionmaking imperfections. We do not have to eschew the traditional decentralization of supply and demand or to conceptualize consumer conservation investments as if they were utility supply "resources" to come up with a sensible set of principles to guide utility and society choices regarding conservation programs.

I have used this framework to derive a set of basic principles for good demand-side programs that accommodate both "rational" consumer behavior and consumer behavior that is plagued by decisionmaking imperfections. These rules also take into account the effects of conservation programs on both participants and non-participants. My analysis leads directly to the following set of basic principles that I believe should guide the development of demand-side programs that are consistent with the efficiency and equity objectives that I identified at the beginning of my testimony.

1. Start by getting the prices charged for electricity right. When PURPA was passed nearly ten years ago, it was clearly recognized that the most important thing that a utility can do to stimulate appropriate customer investments in conservation is to set the right prices for electricity. Electricity prices on the margin should come as close as is reasonably possible to marginal cost. This is just as true today as it was ten years ago.[22]
2. Offer a mix of electricity "products" that reflect diverse consumer needs for electricity contracts with different qualities and characteristics.This includes interruptible rates, time-of-use rates, load management services, etc. These products should also be priced at marginal cost.The

importance of stimulating the availability of a diverse product mix is also recognized in Title 1 of PURPA.

3. If prices on the margin are less than marginal costs, incentives equal to the *difference* between marginal cost and price can be made generally available.

4. Additional incentives should be targeted at end uses and customer classes for which significant barriers to efficient decisionmaking have been demonstrated to result in large losses in economic efficiency. Subsidy payments should only be available for appliances, end uses and customer classes where it is clear that there are significant decisionmaking imperfections that lead to significant losses in economic efficiency. Making payments available for "generic" conservation actions will lead to inefficient conservation activity in those areas for which consumers are already making efficient decisions and will unnecessarily burden non-participants.

The reasons for imperfect decisionmaking are likely to vary widely from end use to end use and from consumer group to consumer group, so the appropriate corrective actions are also likely to vary widely. Some decisionmaking imperfections may be corrected with modest payments, novel contracts that change the time pattern of payments, loans, provision of information, etc. Others may require much more substantial payments. Any system that pays the same amount for conservation from different and uses and customer groups is almost certain to be inefficient and inequitable.

5. We should try to find the *minimum* payment or the most efficient mechanism to overcome market imperfections that lead consumers to make inefficient conservation investments. By keeping the payment as low as is necessary to induce customers to make efficient conservation investments, we minimize the cross-subsidies and the distortions that arise from higher electricity prices. By recognizing that there are a wide range of instruments and delivery institutions other than utility-sponsored negawatt programs that we can draw on as a society, we will search widely for the most effective ways to achieve our objectives. To do so, we need good behavioral information in

order to understand why consumers are not making investments that are in their own self interest and how best to ameliorate the problems that lead to such behavior.

6. *Aggregate societal* payments per unit of electricity saved from conservation investments (customer + utility + government expenditures) should not exceed the marginal costs of supplying a unit of electricity. The maximum utility payment for conservation is therefore equal to marginal cost minus the contribution that the customer would be willing to make voluntarily on his own behalf.[23]

7. When subsidy payments made by the utility lead to higher electricity rates, the benefits of increased efficiency achieved by participants must be balanced against the costs imposed on non-participants as a result of higher electricity rates. There is no magic simple rule of thumb that can be derived to make such a tradeoff. At the very least, a conservation investment induced by a subsidy payment Must result in an increase in aggregate consumer welfare for it to be justified.

8. Efforts should be made to recover costs of conservation programs (over time) from those who benefit from them. The efficiency investments contemplated here have both private gains (reduced bills for customers, reduced marginal prices for electricity services) and societal gains (conservation costs below the marginal cost of supply). This suggests that opportunities exist for "shared-savings" contracts with customers conservation expenditures to be repaid from electricity costs achieved by the customer.[24]

Whatever subsidy payment is made, the utility will have to recover it somehow to keep investors whole. When prices are equal to marginal cost, any subsidy payment implies that electricity rates will have to rise to recover these payments. When price is less than marginal cost, any subsidy payment that is greater than the *difference* between marginal cost and price means that electricity rates will have to rise. Increasing electricity rates in order to recover the costs of a subsidy program will lead to cross-subsidization of participants by nonparticipants and potentially lead to inefficient consumption decisions for non-participants. Shared-savings arrangements avoid these problems since the costs of utility conservation expendi-

COMPETITION IN ELECTRICITY

tures are recovered over time from the customers who benefit from them.

9. We should look for the most effective instruments and delivery institutions to ameliorate decisionmaking imperfections where they exist and should not simply assume that the utility is in the best position to fix the problems. Relying primarily on the utility to encourage conservation by making monetary payments for saved electricity is not likely to be the most efficient means of encouraging conservation in many circumstances. There are many alternative methods for ameliorating the decisionmaking imperfections that lead consumers to underinvest in conservation. In addition to direct subsidy payments, these include appliance and building standards, information and educational programs, state and federal tax incentives, loan programs, etc. A utility is not in the best position to make direct use of these alternative instruments or institutions. It is also far from obvious that taxing non-participant electricity consumers to subsidize conservation is fairer or more efficient than relying, for example, on subsidy programs paid for out of general tax revenues. Furthermore, given how little we know about consumer behavior responses to electricity prices and subsidies when there are decisionmaking barriers, pure subsidy programs that throw money at the problems tend to increase the uncertainty about the savings that will be achieved from conservation and increase the uncertainty about the expected supply/demand balance.

The approach to electricity conservation that I have proposed has an important practical advantage over the integrated supply/demand "utility resource" acquisition model. Once utilities begin to think of conservation as a supply "resource," as they are supposed to do according to this model, they tend to look hard for ways to encourage conservation only when the utility requires additional supplies of electricity. Thus, when a utility has excess capacity, concerns about conservation disappear. Interest in conservation waxes and wanes with the supply/demand balance.

The decentralized decisionmaking framework and the principles that I have derived from it do not necessarily lead to the same result. Conservation initiatives are not justified solely because the utility needs additional "resources". Rather, their justification depends on electricity pricing, product availability, or consumer decisionmaking imperfections If consumers are making inefficient decisions when supplies are tight, they may also be making inefficient decisions when supplies are ample.[25] If there really are pervasive decisionmaking imperfections, they do not come and go with the need for new capacity. Public and private initiatives to encourage conservation may still be desirable even if the utility does not currently need to acquire additional resources to balance supply and demand. Those who have embraced the conservation-as-utility-supply-resource perspective must strain to rationalize continued demand-side efforts when there is excess capacity.[26] The decentralized decisionmaking framework, on the other hand, may provide a sound basis for continuing public or private conservation efforts even when there is excess capacity.

IS THE BIDDING PROPOSAL CONSISTENT WITH THESE PRINCIPLES?

The Chairman has proposed that demand-side and supply-side options should be integrated into a comprehensive "all-source" bidding system that would presumably be open to all "suppliers" of megawatts or negawatts. I have provided numerous examples of how this approach, which forces the utility to pay consumers a conservation subsidy equal to the utility's marginal supply cost, -can lead to undesirable outcomes. To demonstrate how the numerous conceptual problems I have discussed manifest themselves in such a bidding system, I have constructed an example to show how such a bidding system might work.[27] The example incorporates both "rational" consumers and consumers who face barriers to efficient decisionmaking. It also incorporates consideration of decisionmaking barriers that respond well to subsidies and those that do not. In short, this example puts it all together.

A Hypothetical Example of Bidding with Demand and Supply Sources Included

Exhibit 12-5 contains the relevant information for the

COMPETITION IN ELECTRICITY

hypothetical bidding system with both supply-side and demand-side options included. The example hypothesizes a utility that needs 100 MW of capacity (with specific characteristics such as load factor, reliability, time of delivery, diversity, etc.). The price of electricity and the long run marginal cost of electricity supplied by the utility are both equal to $0.065 per kWh. The utility has been ordered to meet its supply requirements through a competitive first price auction mechanism that allows both supply sources and demand sources to compete. All potential suppliers of additional generation and "suppliers" of megawatts are eligible to make bids. The utility then chooses the sources with the lowest bids to meet its 100 MW "supply" requirement.[28]

I have assumed that bidders fall into one of seven categories that I have designated as Sources 1-7 (see Exhibit 12-5a).[29] Source 1 is a conservation option. It has a low cost per kWh saved (see Exhibit 12-5b). However, because the cost of conservation is low relative to the price of electricity, and because consumers act rationally with regard to this source, consumers would choose to adopt this conservation option in a timely fashion *without any subsidy*. Furthermore, the utility's load forecast already implicitly incorporates conservation investments such as these. Of course, if the consumers who would have invested in Source 1 anyway are able to obtain a subsidy payment by participating in the auction, they will be happy to take the money and run. Although these investments would have taken place - without any subsidies, the consumers or entrepreneurs acting on their behalf will be eager to participate in the bidding process. Anything they can obtain will be a pure windfall. They are likely to bid and can bid low and still benefit, so they are thus likely to win.

Source 2 is also a conservation option. This source has a higher cost per kWh saved (see Exhibit 12-5b) than Source 1 but the cost per kWh saved is much lower than the marginal cost of electricity supplied by the utility and the price of electricity. Unlike Source 1, however, consumers who can make this investment will not do so without a subsidy due to undefined decisionmaking imperfections.

Source 3 is also a conservation option. However, the cost per kWh saved is higher than the cost of additional utility supplies. Consumers have no incentive to choose this conservation option and it would be socially inefficient for them to do so. However, if these consumers can get a subsidy that brings their net private cost down below the price of electricity, they will rationally invest in it.

Source 4 is a third-party supply option. We can think of it as cogeneration. The marginal cost of this third-party supply option is less than the marginal cost of conventional utility supplies.

Source 5 is another third-party supply option. It is distinguished from Source 4 only by the fact that it is more costly to supply with this option.

Source 6 is generation provided by the utility. In the example it is assumed to have a marginal cost higher than that of supply Sources 4 and 5.[30]

Finally, Source 7 is a residential conservation option. It has the prospect of saving electricity quite inexpensively, but undefined decisionmaking imperfections lead consumers to fail to make this desirable investment. Indeed, the decisionmaking imperfections are so severe that consumers respond only to very large subsidies. However, with modest changes in building codes these savings would be realized routinely by residential customers. Having the utility throw money at this conservation option is inferior to government actions that do not rely on the utility at all.

Exhibit 12-5b provides the information on the bid characteristics and the results of the hypothetical auction. For each source I have listed the capacity bid, the cost per kWh supplied or saved, the minimum utility subsidy payment needed to induce customers to choose the option, the bid made by each source and the winning bidders. It is important to recognize that in an auction or bidding process such as this, low cost suppliers will not necessarily bid or receive payments equal to their own costs. Rather, they will place bids to achieve a payment as close as possible to that achieved by the last winning bidder's price.[31] As you can see from Exhibit 12-5b, the bidding mechanism leads to the choice of Sources 1-4. Each source gets its bid price.

The Sources Selected Through Bidding Are Inefficient

I will now show that the resulting selections are inefficient and lead to unnecessary cross-subsidies.

In the case of Source 1, the utility has paid consumers $0.05 per kWh to make a conservation investment that the consumers would have made on their own anyway without any subsidy. Indeed, since they would have made it anyway without a subsidy, it is already included implicitly in the utility's load forecast that led to the 100 MW capacity need. Thus, the utility has paid $0.05 per kWh for nothing. Once it becomes obvious that expected demand has not been reduced at all as a result of this "purchase," the utility will just have to go back for additional supplies. All that has been accomplished here is that we have provided consumers (or their agents) who have bid Source 1 with a windfall gain paid for through higher electricity rates.

In the case of Source 2, the subsidy encourages an efficient conservation investment that would not have taken place without a subsidy. However, the utility has paid more than is necessary to induce consumers to adopt it. The excess payments increase electricity rates and electricity bills for non-participants.

Source 3 is chosen despite the fact that it is inefficient. Unless there is something to keep out sources whose *aggregate* cost per kWh of conservation is lower than the utility's marginal cost, these sources can submit bids that could win, and with the subsidy in hand find it rational to invest in an inefficient conservation option.[32] This leads to both social inefficiency and higher rates and bills for nonparticipants.

Source 4 is the only traditional supply source chosen. It comes in at a price below the cost the utility would incur if it generated itself and at a price above the minimum price that would be required to induce this supplier to supply electricity. Since prevailing prices are $0.065 per kWh, while the bid price for this source is $ 0.06, its adoption would lead to a modest *reduction* in rates below what they otherwise would be. All consumers are better off by the inclusion of this option in the utility's supply plan.

A Fairer and More Efficient Approach

Perhaps a better way to evaluate the outcomes that emerge in this hypothetical bidding system is to compare them with the outcomes that would result from applying my basic principles of good demand-side programs to the conservation options and allowing a supply-only bidding system to proceed in tandem. Exhibit 12-5c displays the choices that would have resulted from this alternative to the integrated demand/supply option bidding proposal.

Comparing Exhibit 12-5b and 12-5c, we see that the bidding system (4-2) leads to different choices and different payments than does a true "least-cost" plan (4-3). The differences between the two are quite clear. Consumers would adopt Source 1 without a subsidy, so there is no reason to provide these customers or their conservation entrepreneur agents with a windfall gain that is financed by taxing other customers through higher electricity rates. As a result, since the investment will be made anyway, it does not appear as a demand-side target of opportunity for the utility.

It still makes sense to encourage Source 2 with a subsidy as long as we ignore the impact of any subsidy payments on higher rates for non-participants.[33]

However, the bidding system pays more than is necessary to encourage the investment and, as a result, unduly burdens non-participants with electricity rates that are higher than they need to be to encourage the efficient conservation investment.[34] It should be noted that there is no reason in principle why the utility should be making this subsidy payment. It could just as well come from conservation funds earmarked by the legislature and paid for out of general revenues. It is simply a question of whether the tax required to pay for the subsidies is borne by electricity consumers as higher rates or shared more broadly by society.

Source 3 is dropped from the plan entirely. It was an inefficient investment that also burdened utility customers with higher electricity rates.

Thus, according to this plan we get only 25 MW of efficient conservation savings that we would not have gotten otherwise. We then have 75 MW that must be supplied by supply sources 4, 5 and 6 (i.e., the utility provides a backstop supply of 25 MW) that have been chosen through a supply-source-only bidding process. Electricity rates fall slightly to account for the purchase of Source 4 at less than the equilibrium incremental avoided cost.

Exhibit 12-5d shows the excess payments that would be flowed through as higher rates as a consequence of implementing the bidding system (Exhibit 12-5b) instead of the

COMPETITION IN ELECTRICITY

fairer and more efficient outcome that results from applying my good demand-side principles to conservation options in tandem with a competitive supply-only auction (Exhibit 12-5c). The integrated supply/demand bidding system leads to substantial excess payments that must be recovered through higher electricity rates.

This example also demonstrates both the danger of losing sight of our primary objectives by focusing so much attention on a specific means for achieving them (i.e., bidding) and the fact that there may be superior ways to encourage efficient conservation aside from requiring the utility to throw money at the problem. By keeping our eye on our objectives and recognizing that supply sources and conservation investments simply have very different behavioral characteristics, we would have initially focused on Source 7 and the building code changes required to achieve the associated savings. With modest building code changes we could have reduced load by 100 MW and eliminated the necessity for any more capacity. Source 7 was not even chosen by the bidding mechanism despite the fact that it dominates all of the supply options that submitted bids. The savings achievable through Source 7 require government action, not utility action, to be realized efficiently.

Finally, assuming that the building code changes are adopted, the example demonstrates another flaw in the integrated resource bidding framework. With the 100 MW reduction in load from building code changes the utility doesn't need additional "resources." There would be no bidding for new "resources" at all. However, the decentralized decision-making framework tells us that it still may be desirable to search for low-cost opportunities to induce consumers to make the investments associated with Source 2. Investments in Source 2 would substitute $0.04 per kWh conservation for $0.045 per kWh (short-run marginal cost) electricity production despite the fact that the resulting "resource" is not needed to balance supply and demand.m Although payments for conservation in this case would lead to higher prices, we may decide that the efficiency gains from conservation are worth the costs imposed on non-participants. If conservation options were relegated to an integrated bidding process, after taking account of the benefits of Source 7, this opportunity would be completely ignored because no additional "resources" are required.

It is clear from this example that the integrated resource bidding proposal *does not* represent a straightforward method for creating a simulated competitive market to choose the most cost-effective supply-side and demand-side options. The primary result of integrating demand-side programs into an all-source competitive supply-procurement system is to get the prices relevant for efficient conservation investments *wrong*. Furthermore, it provides decentralized consumer decisionmakers with opportunities to exploit these incorrect prices, leading to inefficiencies and inequities.[35]

SHOULD FERC INCLUDE DEMAND-SIDE PROGRAMS IN ITS MODEL ALLSOURCE BIDDING PROPOSALS?

My analysis leads me to conclude that combining conservation options with supply-side options in an integrated "allsource" bidding system is not good public policy. As a result, I certainly do not think that FERC should include this concept in the model competitive bidding system that it has developed. Indeed, now that I have had an opportunity to think more about this proposal, to the extent that FERC says anything at all about including demand-side options in a competitive supply-procurement systems, I would recommend that it point out all of the problems that may result from doing so.

Even if I have not convinced you that the demand-side bidding proposal is a poor way to foster cost-effective conservation, I hope that I have at least convinced you that it raises a significant number of difficult and complicated issues. FERC has been working on its model competitive bidding system for at least ten months. The Commission has had to confront many difficult problems merely to create a sensible model bidding system that includes supply sources only. Furthermore, there is considerable controversy about whether the proposed model competitive bidding system deals adequately with all of these complications. I see little reason to complicate things further by introducing demand-side bidding into the process at this time. At the very least, FERC's current proposals will give the states the opportunity to make use of competitive supply-procurement systems if they believe that such systems can help to reduce the cost of *elec-*

tricity. This is a worthwhile objective even if we can accomplish nothing further on the demand side. Given the controversy that FERC's proposals have already caused, loading it up with demand-side bidding may very well be fatal to the entire initiative. I believe that this would be a most unfortunate outcome.

As a general matter, it is not at all obvious that FERC is the right agency to get heavily involved in demand-side programs anyway. Conservation decisions are in the end made primarily by retail customers. FERC does not regulate retail rates, it does not approve utility supply plans, it does not issue certificates of convenience and necessity for new capacity, and it does not administer utility conservation programs directly. These are all the responsibility of state regulatory agencies. To the best of my knowledge, the FERC staff has virtually no experience with demand-side programs, while many state commissions already have extensive experience with demand-side programs. Since there is nothing in FERC's proposals that would either require a state to adopt competitive bidding for supply sources or preclude a state from including demand-side programs in a bidding process if it chooses to do so, I suggest that the public will be best served by preserving the separation of state and FERC regulatory responsibility in the conservation area.

CONCLUSION

I am sorry that I have come to such negative conclusions regarding the bidding proposal that is the subject of these hearingm. I tried hard to find some redeeming features of the proposal. Unfortunately, the more I thought about it, the less I liked it. The failure of such an apparently simple mechanism to promote cost-effective conservation simply means that we have to redouble our efforts to identify public policies that can do a better job. I have proposed an alternative, but quite familiar, conceptual framework and a set of principles to guide the choice of good demand-side programs that does not involve integrated supply / demand resource bidding. I think that it can be used to achieve the objectives that we all share.

Thank you for the opportunity to present my views on these important issue

Figure 12-1
Welfare Loss Due To Average-Cost Pricing

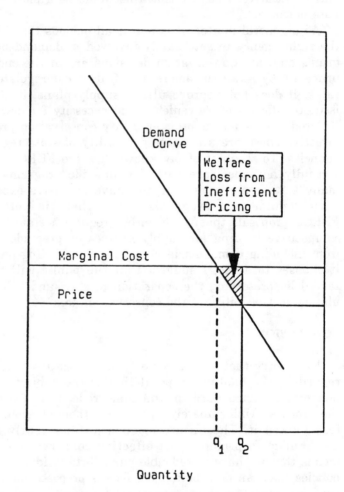

268

Exhibit 12-2a
Alternative Means of Satisfying Demand: Assumptions

Constant Marginal Cost	= $0.0725
Demand Curve is: D(P)	= 300 - 1100*P
Currently Available Capacity	= 100
Average Cost of Current Capacity	= $0.05
Average-Cost Pricing	
Single Customer Class	

Exhibit 12-2b
Alternative Means of Satisfying Demand:
Non-uniform Incentive Payments

Characteristic	Add Capacity	Conserve	Bidding	Add Capacity and Conserve Incentive =MC-P
Actual Price	$0.0628	$0.0932	$0.0772	$0.0625
Demand	230.97	100.00	135.29	220.25
Consumer Welfare	$24,25	$17.73	$21.02	$24.30
Effective Price	NA	$0.1818	$0.1497	$0.0725
Purchased				
Conservation	NA	97.48	79.75	10.96
Capacity Additions	130.97	0.00	35.29	120.25

Exhibit 12-2c
Alternative Means of Satisfying Demand:
Uniform Incentive Payments

Characteristic	Add Capacity	Conserve	Bidding	Add Capacity and Conserve Incentive =MC-P
Actual Price	$0.0628	$0.1087	$0.1069	$0.0628
Demand	230.97	100.00	102.65	220.25
Consumer Welfare	$24,25	$17.73	$18.01	$24.30
Effective Price	NA	$0.1818	$0.1794	$0.0725
Purchased				
Conservation	NA	80.38	79.75	10.72
Capacity Additions	130.97	0.00	2.65	120.25

Exhibit 12-3a
Conservation as Cogeneration: Assumptions

Utility marginal cost and price:	$0.10/kWh
Marginal cost of conservation:	$0.12/kWh
Customer's load without conservation/cogeneration:	1000 kWh
Customer's bill without conservation/cogeneration:	$100
Conservation/cogeneration potential:	100 kWh

Exhibit 12-3b
Conservation as Cogeneration: Payment Methods

Possible Payments for Cogeneration

Customer pays utility for net consumption

OR

Customer pays utility for *gross* consumption and receives payment for cogenerated power

Payment for Conservation through Bidding

Customer pays utility for net consumption

AND

customer receives payment for conserved power

Exhibit 12-3c
Conservation as Cogeneration

	Payment Method		
	Net Billing	*Buy/Sell*	*Negawatt*
Customer's utility bill (with cogeneration):	$90	$100	$90
Customer's revenue from cogeneration:	$0	-$10	-$10
Customer's net bill:	$90	$90	$80
Customer's cost of cogeneration:	$12	$12	$12
Net cost to customer:	$102	$102	$102
Customer's bill without cogeneration:	$100	$100	$100
Customer cogenerates?	No	No	No
Utility's payment/kWh "saved":	NA	NA	$0.20
Increase/(decrease) in social cost of electricity:	$0	$0	$2

COMPETITION IN ELECTRICITY

Exhibit 12-3d
Conservation as Cogeneration Summary

The utility pays $0.20/kWh for cogenerated electricity.

"Cogenerated" electricity actually costs $0.12/kWh.

This $0.12 electricity replaces $0.10 electricity the utility could produce.

Is this a least-cost strategy?

Exhibit 12-4a
Hypothetical Refrigerators: No Subsidy

Refrigerator Type

Annual Category	Old Reliable	Standard	Super Efficient
kWh used	1,500	1,000	500
Operating cost	$150	$100	$50
Capital charge	$0	$40	$120
Total cost	$150	$140	$170
kWh saved	NA	500	1,000
Capital charge/kWh saved	NA	$0.08	$0.12

Price and marginal cost = $0.10/kWh

Exhibit 12-4b
Hypothetical Refrigerators: Subsidy Equals Marginal Cost

Annual Category	Old Reliable	Standard	Super Efficient
kWh used	1,500	1,000	500
Operating cost	$150	$100	$50
Capital charge	$0	$40	$120
Total cost	$150	$140	$170
kWh saved	NA	500	1,000
Capital charge/kWh saved	NA	$0.08	$0.12
Subsidy	$0	$50	$100
Net cost	$150	$90	$70
Net capital charge/kWh saved	NA	($0.02)	$0.02

Price and marginal cost = $0.10/kWh

Exhibit 12-5a
Hypothetical First-price Auction With Supply-side
and Demand-side Options

Additional supplies required:	100MW
Price of electricity:	$0.065 / kWh
Marginal / avoided cost of utility supplies:	$0.065 / kWh
	($0.045 when
	excess capacity)

Source	Characteristics
1	Conservation. Cost per kWh is low, but customers would adopt without any subsidies. Already implicitly reflected in demand forecasts.
2	Conservation. Cost per kWh is relatively low, but customers need a modest subsidy to encourage them to adopt.
3	Conservation. Cost per kWh is very high, but customers will adopt with subsidy that brings net cost below price of electricity.
4	Third-party supply. Cheapest third-party supply available.
5	Third-party supply. Next cheapest third-party supply available
6	Utility supply. Next cheapest supply option.
7	Conservation. Cost per kWh is low, but customers will not adopt without large subsidies. Building code changes could implement this option.

Exhibit 12-5b
Results of Hypothetical First-price Auction

Source	Bid Capacity	Total Cost / kWh	Minimum Payment / kWh	Bid / kWh	Selected?
1	25 MW	$0.02	$0	$0.05	Yes
2	25 MW	$0.04	$0.02	$0.05	Yes
3	25 MW	$0.07	$0.02	$0.06	Yes
4	25 MW	$0.05	$0.05	$0.06	Yes
5	25 MW	$0.06	$0.06	$0.065	No
6	100 MW	$0.065	$0.065	$0.065	No
7	100 MW	$0.03	$0.07	$0.07	No

Exhibit 12-5c
Efficient Supply / demand Plan Without
Building Code Changes

Source	Capacity	Total Cost / kWh	Cost to Customers
2	25 MW	$0.04	$0.02
3	25 MW	$0.05	$0.06
4	25 MW	$0.06	$0.06
5	25 MW	$0.06	$0.06

Exhibit 12-5d
Excess Utility Payments from
Hypothetical First-price Auction

Source	Capacity	Annual Hours	Excess Payments / kWh	Annual Excess
1	25 MW	6,132	$0.05	$7.7 M
2	25 MW	6,132	$0.03	$4.6 M
3	25 MW	6,132	$0.06	$9.2 M

TOTAL = $21.5 M

ENDNOTES

1. Federal Energy Regulatory Commission, Notice of Proposed Rulemaking, *Regulations Government Bidding Programs*, Docket No. RM88-5-000, March 16, 1988.
2. There may of course be conflicts between our efficiency and equity goals.
3. As I shall emphasize in what follows, while "the utility" makes payments for conservation, these payments are costs to the utility that must ultimately be recovered in the electricity prices that consumers are asked to pay.
4. Utilities have been precluded from playing an active role in these other lines of business largely because of real or

imagined concerns about cross-subsidization and unfair competition.

5. In the United Kingdom, for example, residential storage heating technology was developed jointly with a new restricted ff-peak rate that made it economical for consumers to adopt the new storage heating technology.

6. Figures such as this one were used routinely by economists to justify the kinds of electricity pricing reforms that are contained in Title 1 of PURPA. See also Alfred E. Kahn, *The Economics of Regulation*, Volume 1, (New York.- John Wiley, 1970).

7. Assume that the price of electricity is 5 cents per unit of electricity consumed and the subsidy is 3 cents per unit of reduced consumption. If I reduce my consumption by one unit I save 5 cents on my bill *and* get a 3 cent payment from the utility. When I reduce my consumption by one unit I therefore have 8 cents more than I did before. It is the 8 cents that is the effective price associated with consuming more or less electricity.

8. (MC-P) + (P) = MC

9. This result is a matter of simple arithmetic. Price is less than marginal cost by assumption. For each unit of conservation we save MC of cost and lose P in revenue. We limit the maximum subsidy to the difference between the two, so the net impact on revenues is either zero or negative. There is no need for a rate increase to pay for these subsidies. The proper conservation subsidy both encourages efficient consumption decisions and is fair, because non-participants arc not asked to pay any more — and may pay less — to pay for the subsidies.

10. I will continue to assume that customers make rational decisions that are not subject to significant barriers to efficient decisionmaking. Decisionmaking imperfections are considered later in my testimony.

11. At the point where supply and demand are in balance.

12. The superiority of the marginal cost minus price payment rule is quite general.

13. The cogenerator creates no noise and has no waste products, so the appliances offer the same quality of service.

14. These refrigerators are clearly hypothetical since they cost so little.

15. See for example, Larry Ruff, "Utility Least-Cost Plan-

ning: Five Common Fallacies and One Simple Truth.," mimeo, December 1988.

16. This is sometimes simply portrayed as consumers being averse to making longlived "up-front" capital investments. Related sources of evidence are surveys of commercial and industrial consumers that inquire as to the minimum "payback period" that they require to proceed with investments. They often find that the reported payback period is very short, much shorter than the payback period that a utility achieves when it invests in traditional supply sources. This is roughly equivalent to the observation that consumers use high implicit discount rates when they make conservation investment decisions.

17. Yolanda K. Henderson, et al., "Planning for New England's Electricity Requirements," *New England Economic Review*, Jan./Feb. 1988, pp. 3-30.

18. Making the estimates properly requires the application of fairly sophisticated analytical and statistical techniques. Two classic papers on this subject are J. Hausman, "Individual Discount Rates and the Purchase and Utilization of Energy-Using Durables," *Bell Journal of Economics* 1979; and J. Dubin and D. McFadden, "An Econometric Analysis of Residential Electric Appliance Holding and Consumption," *Econometrica*, March 1984. Hausman finds that the average discount rate used in residential air-conditioner choices is 15-24 percent. Dubin and McFadden find an average discount rate used for residential space and water heating of 20.5 percent. These should be compared to "appropriate" discount rates in the 10-15 percent range.

19. The estimates reported vary by an order of magnitude. See "Implicit Discount Rates in Residential Customer Choices," Electric Power Research Institute, February 1988.

20. Both Hausman and Dubin and McFadden find the implicit discount rates used by residential consumers vary inversely with income. The most severe differences between actual discount rates and "appropriate" discount rates is at the lower portions of the income distribution. These results suggest several things. First, conservation programs probably should not be targeted at higher in-

come people. Second, the source of the high implicit discount rates may be capital constraints faced by individuals who do not have high incomes. Third, if capital constraints are the problem, then innovative loan, rental or leasing programs could in principle resolve them without cross-subsidies from non-participants to participants.

21. If a competitive bidding system were available for conservation, such customers would be quite happy to bid and would be in the best position to win. It's a pure windfall for them and a pure loss for non-participants.

22. Progress has been made on this front, but not as much as would be desirable. See Hethie Parmesano, "The Role of Marginal and Avoided Costs in Ratemaking: A Survey," National Economic Research Associates, November 1987.

23. In this regard let me emphasize that comparisons between what utilities spend on traditional supply sources in the aggregate and what they spend on conservation in the aggregate are completely meaningless. Such comparisons are made, for example, in *Power To Spare*, New England Energy Policy Council, July 1987. The relevant comparisons are between expenditures made by utilities on generation with expenditures made by *society* on conservation. Furthermore, it is not aggregate expenditures in either category that are relevant, but comparisons of expenditures on the margin.

24. Wisconsin Power & Light Company recently agreed to pay for energy efficiency improvements at General Motors' plant in Janesville, Wisconsin. The utility's investments are supported by a shared saving arrangement so that it anticipates recovering its investment, including a fair return, and GM retains the residual savings. This approach ensures that the utility's other customers are not being forced to pay for energy efficiency investments at General-Motors. See *Industrial Energy Bulletin*, March 4, 1988, pp. 1-2.

25. Of course since there are differences in marginal cost over the cycle, even the market imperfections framework may lead to different public policies. It all depends on exactly what the relevant market imperfection is.

26. See for example, R. Cavanagh, "Responsible Power Marketing in an Increasingly Competitive Era," mimeo, 1988.

27. There are also numerous practical problems associated with integrating demand side programs into such a bidding system. However, since I believe that this proposal has serious conceptual deficiencies to begin with, I will not dwell on the practical problems.

28. For simplicity, I assume that all of the sources have the same load, time of delivery, and reliability characteristics. In reality they will not, so that some way must be found to adjust for differences in these characteristics across sources so that the bids can be compared on an equivalent basis. This is likely to be very difficult in practice.

29. There may be several bidders in each category.

30. For simplicity, I have not included third-party supply sources that are more expensive than utility supplies. However, this should not be interpreted as suggesting that third-party supplies are always more economical than electricity supplied by a vertically integrated utility.

31. In a second-price auction, all sources would receive the same price, in this case $0.065. The burdens on non-participants and the potential for inefficiencies are greater when demand-side sources are included and a second-price auction mechanism is used.

32. The bidding program adopted by Central Maine Power

tries to guard against the participation of such bidders by requiring that the *total* costs of any conservation programs bid be less than or equal to the utility's avoided cost. This is a clever and desirable constraint on the bidding process. However, it is also likely to be extremely difficult to enforce.

We of course never place this type of constraint on real supply sources. The competitive supply procurement system makes it uneconomical for a supplier to bid if his total cost of supply is greater than the price he will receive from the bidding process. The fact that we must cook up constraints to keep "suppliers" of *conservation* from exploiting the bidding system suggests that supply-side and demand-side options do not naturally fit together in the same competitive supply procurement system.

33. Or alternatively, we conclude that the gains from encouraging the conservation investment outweigh the costs borne by non-participants resulting from the higher electricity rates required to pay for the subsidies.

34. It is conceivable that the efficiency losses from higher prices paid by nonparticipants outweigh the efficiency gains from encouraging Source 2. My suggested approach minimizes the chance that this will be the outcome by minimizing the burden on other customers.

35. I have given some thought to the kinds of restrictions that would have to be placed on conservation "bidders" in such an integrated resource bidding system to guard against these undesirable outcomes. There may be plausible restrictions that can be applied to bidders to minimize the most serious costs of including them in an integrated bidding process. However, this exercise seems to me to miss the point. Our objective should not be to see what we have to do to a competitive supply procurement system to include conservation options in it. Our objective is to develop fair and efficient conservation and supply policies. If demand-side programs don't naturally

fit into a competitive supply procurement system, as they clearly do not, I see no reason why we should be spending so much time looking for ways to fit a square peg into a round hole.

CHAPTER 13: INCLUDING UNBUNDLED DEMAND SIDE OPTIONS IN ELECTRIC UTILITY BIDDING PROGRAMS

Charles Cicchetti
Deputy Director
Energy and Environmental Policy Center
John F. Kennedy School of Government,
Harvard University

William Hogan
Bradshaw Professor of Public Policy
John F. Kennedy School of Government,
Harvard University

INTRODUCTION

The debate over the role of electric utilities in developing demand-side conservation continues, most recently in the context of the FERC's consideration of all-source bidding programs for future electric supply.[1] Many have argued that energy conservation programs should be excluded from all-source bidding systems.[2] We disagree: hence the purpose of this article is to outline an approach which permits an efficient inclusion of demand-side programs in a bidding system. Our suggestion follows the recent trend of unbundling energy alternatives — in this case, separating energy services from kilowatt hours, and customers-as-customers from customers-as-suppliers — in order to provide proper incentives for energy conservation programs and a proper basis for comparison of such programs with supply side options. An unbundled bidding system should satisfy both those who feel there is a great deal of unrealized energy conservation, and those who disagree: it permits their battle for consumers' dollars to be waged on the proverbial level playing feel.

CONSERVATION AND LEAST-COST SUPPLY

Critics of energy conservation programs argue that energy conservation potential is overestimated,[3] the cost are undere-

*Charles Cicchetti, Deputy Director , Energy and Environmental Center, and William Hogan, Bradshaw Professor of Public Policy, Harvard University. The authors would like to express their gratitude to Irwin M. Steltzer, who provided valuable intellectual and policy contributions to our paper. The authors also thank Henry Lee, Carol May, and Mia Watabe. The views expressed are those of the principal authors and do not reflect those of Harvard University or of contributors to the EEPC's research efforts.

stimated,[4] and in any event the attention to energy should focus on market failures.[5] By contrast, proponents of energy conservation identify engineering estimates of substantial potential savings from energy conservation — savings which they allege can be achieved at costs well below those of new sources of supply.[6]

We shall not attempt here, to resolve the debate over the potential magnitude of conservation investments. Indeed, our proposal leaves the decision between consumption and conservation to consumers: they, and not competing experts, would decide on the mix of savings and use. We adopt the framework central to the principles of least-cost planning and attempt to minimize the total cost of meeting customer demands. As usual in least-cost planning, we distinguish explicitly between the demand for energy services, such as customers utilize in the form of heating and lighting, and the demand for kilowatt-hours of electron flow.[7] If the demand for energy services can met at a lower cost through conservation, then we prefer the lower cost alternative. Our definition of total cost includes both the engineering cost of installing more efficient air-conditioners or better insulation, and the cost of inconvenience, organizing contractors, and collecting information in order to identify the most important conservation investments.[8] Hence, conservation investments which have engineering costs slightly below the marginal cost of supply are viewed as more costly if the information and organizational efforts required by the conserver are large enough to outweigh the higher cost of producing and delivering the electrons. It is the total cost — direct and indirect, engineering and inconvenience — that should be minimized.

In defining these costs, we accept in principle the notion that different energy sources will have different externalities. Conservation may reduce environmental effort more than providing additional electricity through alternative sources, and so on. However, for the sake of the present discussion, we assume that these externalities have been captured in the measure of costs associated with both conservation and new sources of supply. To the extent that additional externalities are identified, there is no problem, in principle, in incorporating those in our proposal.

This framework of least-cost planning, or least-cost choice between conservation and supply side alternatives, is not particularly controversial.[9] It recognizes that the goal of an efficient policy is not to conserve electricity independent of cost. In least cost planning, the objective is not to produce a large conservation program in order to comply with regulatory mandates, nor to expand energy demand to increase utility profitability by spreading fixed costs across a wider base of electricity sales. It is, instead, to find the least-cost combination of energy supply and efficiency investments.

DEMAND-SIDE BIDDING ALTERNATIVES

Utilities and regulators have yet to find the best combination of policies to promote least-cost planning. As Moskowitz described, current utility ratemaking practices provide strong incentives for utilities to avoid conservation.[10] Even when there is agreement concerning the economies of utility conservation programs, there are significant differences when it comes to defining a sensible, economically-efficient utility conservation policy.[11] These differences are most obvious when it comes to the matter of demand-side bidding.

There are presently electricity conservation investments that are not being undertaken, even though these investments are cheaper than new generation. The explanations for this fact differ among analysts. Economists argue that since the marginal cost of electricity sometimes exceeds its price (the latter being based on average cost) consumers are not being told the true cost their consumption imposes on society, as a consequence of which they ignore efficient conservation opportunities. They also point to the existence of a number of market imperfections: the lack of a link between price and cost (e.g., renters without individual meters); barriers to the acquisition of information (economies of scale in evaluating conservation investments); and bias as consumer investments against first cost (e.g., capital constraints). Engineers go further: they have a long list of new technologies that have not penetrated the market place (e.g., SL-18 light bulbs), from which they conclude that there is under-investment in conservation and over-investment in new generation facilities.

For whatever reason, then, there appears to be some undetermined under-investment in conservation which presents an opportunity for policy intervention to improve economic efficiency. Amory Lovins concluded in his widely-quoted piece "Saving Gigabucks with Negawatts," that utilities have a role to play in encouraging conservation:

> "...as long as it is cheaper to save electricity than to make it, both utilities and ratepayers can benefit from properly structured utility financial participation in efficiency."[12]

The trick, of course, is to find the "proper structure" for utility programs. And here the causes and extent of under-investment in conservation are crucial. In the most expansive view, Amory Lovins argues that the market imperfections are so large, the new technologies so numerous, and the cost savings so great that utilities have little to fear from offering too much for conservation. Of immediate relevance to the design of bidding programs, he proposed the "elegant concept" of a public auction for "electricity made, displaced, or saved by any means."[13] Under this proposal, demand side alternatives would participate directly in the bidding process. A bidder would offer to install efficient light bulbs for a price. If that bid is lower on a kilowatt-hour basis than the bids to provide other sources of electricity, the conservation bid would win and, after appropriate certification, the bidder would be paid the amount bid, install the light bulbs, and keep the savings on electricity purchases.

This proposal alarms those who see a more modest role for utility-supported conservation investments, such as paying a subsidy equal to or less than the difference between the retail price of electricity and its higher marginal cost. Such a subsidy would be economically efficient, so long as the marginal cost of electricity exceeds the marginal cost of conservation,[14] and would benefit both the utility's customers and its shareholders. More costly conservation investments would decrease economic efficiency.

The economic efficiency conclusions are based on an assumption that no one is prepared to do the more efficient thing and set the price of electricity equal to its marginal cost. Suppose the price of electricity equalled the marginal cost of producing electricity. Customers who receive such a market signal would know that they should conserve when the amount that they save, the price of electricity times the quantity to be saved, is greater than or equal to the incre-

COMPETITION IN ELECTRICITY

mental cost of achieving this level conservation.[15] In such circumstances, paying a subsidy to conserve equal to the utility's marginal cost as proposed by Lovins would obviously be overkill. The conserver would be paid twice for the same decision, once when his/her bill was reduced, and again when receiving a subsidy equal to avoided cost, which in this discussion equals marginal cost and price.

When marginal cost is above the price of electricity, limiting the payment for conservation to the difference between marginal cost and price would promote economic efficiency by avoiding the double payment. And such subsidy would pass the so-called "no-losers" test. But this is less generous than having demand-side alternatives participate directly in the process and receive a payment equal to marginal cost. The idea of restricting the payment to the difference between marginal cost and price, so congenial to economists, has been rejected explicitly by Lovins[16] and by various regulators. This is no mere quibble over form. The disagreement is at the core of the different views of the opportunities of enhancing economic efficiency by including demand- and supply-side alternatives in a bidding system. Cases with representative numbers can yield annual differences in the range of hundreds of millions of dollars, with rate consequences that will capture the attention of all participants.

When it comes to policy recommendations, Joskow is opposed to the use of utility-sponsored bidding systems in which demand-side alternatives compete against traditional generation sources and independent power producers. He stresses the fact that advocates of these programs believe that both demand- and supply-side sources should be able to compete, but that conservation advocates think the winner, including the demand-side option, should be paid the overkill-price, i.e., the avoided (or marginal) cost reflected in the winning bid. Joskow correctly observes that paying the full avoided cost would provide an incentive for efficient competition. And limiting the payment for conservation is likely to be rejected in any final bidding program. Further, Joskow and Ruff[17] are concerned, with some justification, that administratively-determined avoided cost might overlook many alternative, lower cost sources of supply, thereby inflating the payment for conservation.

UNBUNDLING DEMAND-SIDE ALTERNATIVES

It is instructive to examine the basis for more serious observers' objections to including demand-side alternatives in the bidding process. Both Joskow and Ruff see no reason why the utilities should pay customers to use substitute product (conservation). After all, they note, the customer who conserves already benefits from the reduction in his electricity bill, and the utility suffers a revenue loss. As Joskow notes, the butcher does not pay his customers to switch to fish. But Joskow certainly would not object to the butcher adding fishmongering to his line of work, i.e., to selling fish to those customers who eschew meat. So we doubt that Joskow, Ruff or any opponents with an economic efficiency perspective of including demand-side options in bidding schemes would have any fundamental difficulty, (putting aside perhaps conflicts related to market power) with permitting an electric utility or an IPP to provide a customer with demand-side alternatives in return for payments by the same customer. Cicchetti and Curkendall[18] have discussed some of the policies that would allow utilities to simultaneously to sell both conservation and electricity. In their analysis they describe various marketing strategies for public utilities that simultaneously engage for profit both in the electric and energy conservation businesses.

The debate over this issue flows from a superficially plausible but flawed principle that has become ingrained in electricity conservation proposals:

> **"After all, a kilowatt-hour saved is just like an kilowatt-hour generated...so they should be treated alike"**[19]

Well, almost alike. But there is a critical difference. The key is to recognize the bundled services in the sale of electricity or in the purchase of conservation through a Lovins-type auction. The electron flow or the conservation investment is bundled with the energy service. In the case of the sale of electron flow, there is no problem; the utility buys or produces the supply of electron flow and, in turn, the customer pays for the energy service by paying for the electron flow. However, in the case in which the utility pays the customer to make the conservation investment, the situation is

286   COMPETITION IN ELECTRICITY

reverse; the utility buys the "supply" of conservation", but the customer receives the energy service produced by that investment free! The incentive given the customer is wrong. He is paid twice: once by giving him the dollars for the conservation device, again by providing a free service. This misplaced incentive could result in inefficient over-investment in conservation. The effect on other ratepayers is only incidental, despite the fact the effect on non-participants was the focus of early criticism.

As noted above, this distinction between the sale of energy commodities and the sale of energy services is not new. Thoughtful proponents of conservation recognized early that this model would yield the economically correct incentives. Sant[20] proposed energy service companies that would provide heat, cooling, lighting, etc., instead of kilowatt hours of electricity, cubic feet of gas or barrels of oil. Lovins endorses the notion in the preamble to his "Megawatts" article. Whittaker adopted this idea in his suggestion for a regulatory redefinition of the conservation market.[21] Based on this concept, Cicchetti and Curkendall described how a utility might continue to collect money from customers who purchase electricity and energy services. If these customers pay for the services provided, the utility would prefer, unless there was a different regulatory treatment of any mark-ups above cost, the least-cost alternative, whether it was a new generator, a purchase contract or an energy-efficiency-enhancing investment. When an utility markets energy services rather than kWh's, its incentive is to market the least-cost, or more efficient, option.

Another advantage of concentrating on energy services is that such a focus should resolve the debate over how to include demand-side options in the bidding system. Ruff and Joskow oppose the inclusion of such alternatives partly because they fear that regulators will find it difficult to accept the principle of adjusting demand-side bids to avoid the double payment we have described above, with a consequent over-investment in conservation.[22] But the energy service concept should meet their objections: it gives utilities an incentive to "buy," and their customers to use, only such conservation techniques as result in real resource savings — no more, no less.

In short, the energy service concept provides the same

economically-efficient incentives as found in the Joskow and Ruff analyses. And the energy service concept is generally acknowledged as compatible with the framework for least-cost planning.

That leaves a practical objection: for most uses of energy it is so difficult to define and measure the energy service being bought that a market in such services is difficult to establish. Certainly — this criticism continues — energy service is such an amorphous concept that bids to provide it cannot properly be compared with bids to provide "real" kilowatt hours. The objection is met, we think, by the very nature of conservation programs. The programs necessarily include some estimate of the kilowatt hours the customer will save by utilizing a given conservation technique. We see no reason not to accept this estimate as the definition of the energy service currently provided by the utility. The customer should pay for this service as a part of the regular bill for electricity. In the simplest case, the estimated kilowatt-hours would be added to the actual consumption once the conservation bid had been accepted and the investment had been paid for by the utility. The customer would continue to receive the same service he had been getting at the same price paid for other sales of electricity. But that service is now provided by the least-cost mix of supply- and demand-side options. This is the unbundling step.[23] The customer-as-customer would pay the same price for energy service provided as for the electron flow provided. And importantly for the successful implementation of the bidding system, there would be no need to identify this price in advance, thereby simplify implementation. And there would be no need to incorporate an estimate of this price in the bidding process, thereby preserving equal treatment of supply and demand.

The customer-as-supplier would offer the conservation investment in the bidding process to be considered on the same terms as other sources of supply. The winning projects would receive the bid price as determined by the rules of the bidding process without respect to the source of the supply, other things being equal. With the exception that this auction includes only unbundled demand-side alternatives, the auction would be identical to Lovins' proposal. But with the unbundling, the level playing field has been restored, and the incentives for customers and utilities alike conform to

288 COMPETITION IN ELECTRICITY

the incentives for the efficient outcome.

Unbundling energy conservation bids is the most natural application of the energy service proposal. Whittaker's opposition to the use of demand-side bidding stems from his limitation of the application of the energy service concept to conservation from direct utility investments. He makes no provision for payments to the customer-as-supplier. But there is no reason to exclude customers or entrepreneurs from seeking out conservation opportunities and offering them on comparable basis with supply-side alternatives.

Introducing brokers or energy service companies between the utility and the consumer presents no difficulties. They would even be encouraged if there are economies of scale and scope. As long as energy conservation investments are unbundled from the sale of energy services, the incentives are correct: they induce economically efficient behavior by all players. Conservation investments which cost less than the supply-side alternatives can compete on an equal basis and win. But there is no incentive for inefficient conservation investments, as there is in the Lovins proposal.

COMPARING COST EFFECTIVENESS

An example will illustrate the concept further and highlight the key differences between the unbundled auction proposed here and the bundled auction of the Lovins type. Consider an utility with an initial load of 1000 kWhs, a fixed cost allocation of 2 cents per kWh, and an energy cost of 3 cents per kWh. Hence, the average rate (assumed to average equal cost) is 5 cents per kWh. The utility faces an incremental demand for 100 kWh. To meet this demand, the utility is considering buying coal-based power at 7 cents per kWh, i.e., its marginal avoided cost is 7 cents, compared to the average rate of 5 cents.

Initial Load kWh	1000
Incremental kWh	100
Fixed Cost/kWh	2
Variable Cost/kWh	3
Marginal Cost/kWh	7

Buying the coal would raise the total cost and revenue requirement from 5000 to 5700. When spread over the 1100 kWh demand, average rates would be 5700/1100 = 5.18 cents per hour.

Now suppose that there is a conservation investment available at 4 cents per kWh. Clearly, the efficient choice would be to adopt the conservation investment in place of the coal purchase, even if we include the cost of conservation in the revenue requirement. What happens under the alternative bidding proposal?

In the Lovins auction, the consumer offers the conservation investment in competition with the coal purchase. According to Lovins, the bid might be anywhere from 4 cents, the cost of conservation, to 7 cents, the avoided cost. In either case, the conservation proposal would win the bid, the conserver would be paid the price of the bid, and electric load would stay at 1000kWh. The results in terms of (1) generation, (2) sales, (3) fixed cost, (4) variable cost, (5) conservation payments, (6) revenue requirement, (7) average rate, and (8) total resource cost to society appear in the first table in the Appendix. Notice that for the last column, the total resource cost — the measure of economic efficiency — are the same across the range of high to low bids in the Lovins auction. The bid affects only the conservation payment and the resulting average rate.

Now consider the type of auction implied by economists, Joskow and Ruff. Like most economists, and unlike Lovins, they would be surprised that the customer had continued to pay 5 cents when the conservation investment cost only 4 cents. But assume there was a market imperfection that the market imperfection could correct. Here the payment for conservation is limited to the difference between the average rate the consumer will face, namely 5.18 cents, and the avoided cost. This difference, 7 - 5.18 = 1.82 cents per kWh, will be received by the customer offering the conservation. Since the customer will also save the 5.18 cents, the effective price offered to him is the full avoided cost, 5.18 + 1.82 = 7 cents. Since this is greater than the cost of the conservation investment (4 cents), the customer accepts, receives 1.82 cents, saves the 5.18 cents, spends 4 cents on conservation, and ends up 3 cents better off. Again the results are shown on the first table in the Appendix, in the row we have for convenience labeled "Ruff-Joskow". Notice that, consistent with economic efficiency, the total resource cost in column (8) is minimized. The efficiency result in the same as for the Lovins cases, even though there are differences in the various matters normally addressed by regulators, namely conservation payments, rates, and revenue requirements.

Finally, in the unbundled case, which embodies the policy we endorse, the 100 kWh of energy services will be added to the sales (but not generation) whenever the conservation bid is accepted. The customer-as-customer will pay the new average rate for both electricity and energy services. The customer-as-supplier offer the same range of bids as in the Lovins Auction, wins, and receives the same payment. The result again appear as the last two rows in the first table in appendix 1. Once again, the efficient outcome is obtained. Of course, the difference in sales of electricity and energy services leads to different rates.

Apparently all the different approaches lead to the efficient outcome. The differences in rates are, therefore, merely transfer payments, not to be confused with the efficiency test as measured by the total resource cost in column (8). This is the best off all worlds, with only efficient conservation investments being made. But what happens when we change the estimate of the cost of conservation?

The details matter, and we have learned that they are often confusing. Hence we have provided the details in the next several tables of the Appendix, where we consider the case of conservation at the current average electric rate (5 cents), between the average rate and the marginal cost (6 cents), and equal to the marginal cost (7 cents). When the cost of conservation is above the average rate and below the marginal cost, even the economist becomes concerned that there is too little investment in conservation. But apparently the efficiency results are the same for the three types of the bidding processes. There are rate differences, of course, but no efficiency effects in this example.[24]

There is a difference in economic efficiency in the next case, in which conservation cost is 8 cents, 1 cent more than the avoided cost. In this case, the optimal choice is to forego the conservation and purchase the coal power. In the Ruff-Joskow auction, the 1.82 cent subsidy for conservation, added to the 5.28 cent rate saving, is not sufficient to cover the 8 cent conservation cost, so no conservation is ordered, and coal is purchased. In the unbundled bidding, conservation is offered at 8 cents, and loses. The coal purchase wins the bid. Again we have efficient outcome. But in the Lovins case, the result is different. The customer offers the conservation at the below-cost figure of 7 cents, wins the bid, receives the 7 cents, saves the 5.18 cents on the purchase of electricity, spends 8 cents on the conservation investment, and ends up 7 + 5.18 - 8 = 4.18 cents better off. But the economy is worse off, spending 5800 in total resources as compared to the least-cost option 5700. The Lovins method produces an inefficient outcome.[25]

In the most egregious case, shown in the final table in the Appendix, the cost of conservation increases to 12 cents. Even here the customer in the Lovins auction bids 7 cents and sees an incentive of 7 + 5.18 - 12 = .18 cents to make the inefficient investment. Offering the free energy service as apart of the bundle with conservation leads to an inefficient outcome.

Both what we have called for convenience the Ruff-Joskow bidding proposal and the unbundled bidding proposal suggested here yield the efficient outcome in each case examined. They have the same incentives. The principal advantage of the unbundled bid is the ability to treat the demand-side alternative in the same way as the supply-side proposals. The information necessary for the unbundling comes naturally in the development of the conservation proposal. And unbundling eliminates the need to make adjustments in the bids that depend on the prospective rates of the bidders.

Although the unbundled bidding proposal has one more administrative step than the original Lovins auction, it is feasible and involves no more than using the information that is already generated in preparing the conservation estimates. But it has the significant advantages of both plausibility and consistency with economic efficiency. It allows the utility to do just what everyone wants it to do; to exploit demand side alternatives on the same basis as supply-side options, by providing for the collection of the necessary revenues on the basis of energy services consumed and supplied. Unbundling the bids through a tariff or billing mechanism which recovers the necessary revenues, is essential to success. With unbundled bids, demand side alternatives should be included in the bidding process. Without un-

COMPETITION IN ELECTRICITY

bundling, the perverse incentives such inclusion would produce would be likely to reduce economic efficiency.

CRITIQUES AND IMPLEMENTATION

We cannot, here, develop all the relationships between our proposal and conservation marketing programs, tariff, policy, dynamic efficiency and the relevant discount rates in an unbundled bidding system. But we would like to anticipate and consider a few questions and criticisms.

Paying Something for Nothing

Superficially, unbundling energy conservation sounds like asking the customer to pay for kilowatt-hours not longer needed. If the customer were really paying something for nothing, it would be a hard policy to recommend or explain. But this criticism is deceptive, and the customer is not paying something for nothing. If the conservation proposal is real, then the customer by definition maintaining the energy service. If the customer wishes to be paid for providing the conservation, the customer should pay for the energy service retained

Here a comparison with more familiar supply-side option applicable. Assume a customer of a utility offers to build a new cogeneration facility. The customer plans to retain a third of the electric output for his own use, and offers to sell the remaining kilowatt-hours to the utility. It is clear that the utility should pay for the electricity sold back. But we would not expect the utility to pay for the remaining one-third of the kilowatt hours that the customer retained, even though this self-generation would reduce the need for the utility to supply power in just the same way that energy conservation would reduce the need to supply power. Or, if the utility did pay for all the electricity, it would sell the customer the one third the customer used. Either the customer should pay for the facility, keep the electricity produced, and avoid purchases from the utility; just like when the customer conserves electricity on his own. Or the utility could pay the customer to build the cogeneration facility and sell the customer the electricity produced; just like when the customer wants to sell conservation to the utility. But we would not expect the utility to both pay for the facility *and* allow the customer to keep the electricity produced. This truly would be paying something for nothing!

Unbundled conservation separates the energy service from the conservation investment. It eliminates the double payment — paying something for nothing — that creates the perverse incentive for inefficient conservation investments. The customer pays for the energy service. The utility makes the least-cost choice to provide energy service by producing electricity or by investing in conservation.

Isn't This the Same as Joskow and Ruff?

The answer is yes and no. The yes is due to the fact that we and they agree on the economically efficient outcomes and the attendant prices. However, the no is the stronger aspect of this comparison. It is due to the fact that we have separated, or unbundled, the conservation services sold to the utility from the energy services retained by the customer. The former, which we call demand-side alternatives, command a price in the bidding system equal to the avoided cost established by either supply or demand side competitors. The latter is retained by the customer in the form of energy services, e.g., lighting, cooling, etc., and the customer continues to pay the retail price for an equivalent kWh amount of energy services.

Of course, unbundled demand-side bidding and the Joskow and Ruff policy provide efficient incentives. The customer's expected effective price for conservation is the same under both proposals. From an economist's perspective, therefore, the proposals have much in common. If the expected price incentive was all that mattered, we would agree that unbundled bidding offers nothing new. But from the broader perspective of practical implementation, the proposals have at least three important differences. First, unbundled bidding is on its face consistent with least-cost planning and the energy service concept; the Joskow and Ruff proposals require the customer to perform the analysis to show its equivalence and has been (wrongly) rejected by some regulators as inconsistent with least-cost planning. Second, unbundling, as described above, puts the demand-side and supply-side alternatives on a level playing field; this resolves

COMPETITION IN ELECTRICITY

important political difficulties and still promotes economic efficiency. Third, the Joskow and Ruff proposals require an advance estimate of the prospective rates for each customer providing a conservation bid in order to calculate the subsidy and adjust the bid; unbundled bidding does not need such an estimate and furthermore require no adjustment of the bid. Hence unbundled bidding seems easier to implement and equitable on its face.

If the Joskow and Ruff can be put in effect, then it should achieve the efficient outcome, as should unbundled demand-side bidding. However, Joskow and Ruff recognize that the payment, which they find to be efficient is unlikely to be adopted, hence they recommend against any demand-side bidding. But if the practical alternative is adoption of the inefficient demand-side schemes gaining popularity, then unbundled demand-side bidding is preferred.

Gaming

Some with whom we have started our ideas fear that the scheme we propose is susceptible to at least two types of gaming: non-performance, and bluffing. This criticism applies to all conservation programs, but less so to ours since such cheating would pay only when bids exceed retail prices. The non-performer might bid, for example, to supply high efficiency light bulbs to all restaurants in the utility's service territory, win the bid, and simply install low efficiency bulbs. This non-performance might go undetected — a possibility that doesn't exist in the case in which supply-side entrepreneurs win the bid, for in that instance it is "no electricity, no payment."

As a realistic matter, there are two defenses against such non-performance. One is inspection by the utility, probably using its meter readers or customer representatives. Inspections would soon turn up the non-performing contract violator. Any conservation program must be subject to a possible audit.

A second defense is competition. With an opening bidding system, even non-performers would compete with another for the ill-gotten gains. Sooner or later, prices would come down. It would not be possible to sustain both high bids and a high volume of gaming.

The bluffer presents a slightly different problem. He threatens to refuse to undertake even such conservation as can save him some money — the difference between the price of energy and conservation -- in the hope that the utility will make the conservation investment for him, leaving him with all the savings and none of the cost. Suppose, for example, that a builder threatens to install an inefficient heating system, and then "bids" to provide a more efficient system — he would anyhow have installed. This problem can be addressed by some form of certification — an administrative system for disallowing fraudulent bids or limiting eligible conservation investments. Just as even fully competitive markets require rules — against mislabeling, short-weighing and the like — any bidding system would need some policing. But utilities and regulators have sufficient experience with standards to make this a familiar and manageable problem.

Impacts on Non-Participants

Critics of conservation programs often focus on the effects on different customers. Whenever energy conservation investments reduce demand, the utility must spread its fixed costs of operation over a smaller base of total consumption. Under certain conditions, this can cause an increase in average rates. If the conservation program is implemented by the utility at its own expense, non-participants in the program can see their rates rise without receiving any direct benefit. Total cost to society may be reduced and economic efficiency may be improved, but non-participants may feel that they have lost. This hypothetical possibility has motivated the various "no-loser" constraints on conservation programs.[26] In the case of the Lovins-type auctions, the same results obtain since the payments for conservation go to the customer who also reduces electricity demand. This double payment must be financed by the non-participants. While the effect on the non-participants may not affect overall economic efficiency, it raises equity issues that must be considered in the evaluation of a conservation program.

The unbundled conservation programs inherently protect the non-participants from any increase in rates resulting from the conservation investments. To the extent that there are cost saving overall, the non-participants may enjoy lower rates as a result of the conservation program. And average rates for all customers are the same. The unbundling eliminates the subsidy from non-participants.

The sharing by participants in conservation savings are different under our bidding system from those under the proposal by Whittaker. The latter provides that the savings from the conservation program will be shared by participants and non-participants alike. This means that customers have virtually no incentive to participate: the savings resulting from their individual actions will be spread so widely (over all customers) that very little will accrue to the participants. And if the conservation program fails, the total cost is borne by the participants. The incentives and risks are, to say the least, asymmetrical.

The unbundled bidding proposal, on the other hand, permits the supplier of conservation to enjoy any profit that accrues from a successful bid that is greater than the cost of the conservation investment. Hence, in the bidding program, the customer enjoys a symmetric incentive to participate in the conservation program and to make it successful. The incentive effect is an attractive feature of unbundled bidding.

Conservation Market

The previous schematic description of the unbundled bidding proposal captures its essential features. In principle, the individual factory owner, home owner, or store manager could bid to make conservation investments in his own facility. In practice, however, brokers could emerge to exploit economies of scale in information and provide special skills needed to make conservation investments. Here we would vision a close analogy to the energy service corporation. The energy service broker would identify customers who have particularly attractive conservation alternatives. He would then negotiate with the customer for the right to make conservation investments in the factory, home, or store. As part of this arrangement, the customer would stipulate the amount of kilowatt hours saved and agree to have those kilowatt hours continue to be added to his bill. In exchange, the broker would make a payment to the customer for accepting this billing arrangement and allowing for the conservation investment. The broker would then bid to provide the conservation investment. On the winning bids, the broker would make the conservation investment and notify the utility to add the stipulated energy service kilowatt hours to the customer's bill.

The broker would earn a profit by efficiently installing the conservation options at a cost less than the bid, with enough left to make the negotiated payment to the customer. If no profit can be made, this may be the evidence that the conservation investments are really more expensive than many hoped. But if the conservation opportunities are as abundant and low as Lovins claims, then there is ample opportunity for profit, and the bidding system provides a mechanism for entrepreneurs to compete.

Shared Savings and Program Success

Since we have purposely avoided taking a position on the ultimate scale of potential conservation investments, we cannot predict the magnitude of the demand reduction likely to result from an unbundled bidding program. But we emphasize that the program should not be evaluated by how much or how little conservation investment follows. If conservation is really expensive, because of the indirect costs as well as the direct engineering costs, then the unbundling program will leave little opportunity for profit by customers or they representatives, and only a small amount of conservation would follow. If, on the other hand, conservation is potentially of great economic value, and available on a large scale, then there will be ample opportunity for profit, and we should see a major conservation market develop (some of it in the forms of bids, some from utility sponsored programs, some by individual customers whose awareness of conservation opportunities may be heightened by the availability of bidding mechanism and by utility-sponsored programs). But in any case, the test of our bidding scheme program should not be the magnitude of the demand reductions. Our goal is efficiency, not conservation.

The limited experience with utility managed shared savings programs might be proposed as providing insight into the possible success of the unbundled bidding program. In the shared savings program, the utility identifies the conservation investments and agrees to share the savings with the

COMPETITION IN ELECTRICITY

customer. While these programs have a good deal in common with the unbundled bidding program, they do miss the opportunity for savings created by the possibility of a third party, and of a resultant market. Hence, any success of these shared savings programs would be magnified under the unbundled bidding program, since the unbundled bidding program expands the number of potential participants. And the failure of any previous shared savings program should not be viewed as a predictor of failure of unbundled bidding. Unbundled bidding provides the right incentives, and a mechanism that permits a testing of the real opportunities for energy conservation.

Consumers Won't Bid

If the retail price of electricity is greater than the cost of conservation, the rational consumer would make the conservation investment and save the retail price. The consumer does not need to bid, and the utility is not involved. If the obstacle to conservation is that consumers have not noticed the opportunities, it is quite possible that any utility conservation program, regardless of whether it is a direct marketing effort or bidding scheme, might induce utility consumers themselves to compare the price of electricity and the cost of conservation. This result does not trouble us. It is no different than the consumers that decide either to self-generate kWh's and not participate in a supply-side bid, or to switch to alternative fuels at the margin. These results are consistent with economic efficiency and present no complications for unbundled demand-side bidding.

Compatibility With Other Programs

If economic conservation opportunities do exist, allowing them to be bid in an unbundled process provides a powerful tool to the utility in its efforts to obtain supplies at least-cost. And there is no reason for bidding schemes such as the one we are proposing to exclude other proposals. For example, Moskowitz's suggestion for incentive regulation based on a total cost index is compatible with unbundled demand-side bidding.[27] Or if the utility is interested in making investments through direct programs to achieve conservation investments, there is nothing in the unbundled bidding proposal to preclude it from doing so. Those investments can stand on their merits, on a cost-benefit basis. If they are a good idea, the introduction of the bidding program does not make them less attractive. The bidding program, of course, reduces the information requirements for the utility, simplifies the monitoring problem, and has the attractive benefit of including the demand-side programs on a basis equal to the supply-side programs.

CONCLUSION

If demand-side alternatives are to compete with supply alternatives in a bidding system, then the conservation proposals should be unbundled from the energy services. If that is done, the argument about just how much conservation remains to be captured will be solved — in the marketplace, rather than in academic journals.

APPENDIX

Initial Load kWh	1000
Incremental kWh	100
Fixed Cost/kWh	2
Variable Cost/kWh	3
Coal Cost/kWh	7

Conservation Cost/kWh　　　　　　　　**4 cents**

	(1) Gener. kWh	(2) Sales kWh	(3) Fixed Cost	(4) Var. Cost	(5) Consv. Pmnt.	(6) Rev. Reqt.	(7) Avg Rate	(8) Total Resource Cost
Initial State	1000	1000	2000	3000	0	5000	5.00	5000
Coal Plant	1100	1100	2000	3700	0	5700	5.18	5700
Lovins High	1000	1000	2000	3000	700	5700	5.70	5400
Lovins Low	1000	1000	2000	3000	400	5400	5.40	5400
Ruff-Joskow	1000	1000	2000	3000	182	5182	5.18	5400
Unbundled High	1000	1100	2000	3000	700	5700	5.18	5400
Unbundled Low	1000	1100	2000	3000	400	5400	4.91	5400

Conservation Cost/kWh　　　　　　　　**5 cents**

	(1) Gener. kWh	(2) Sales kWh	(3) Fixed Cost	(4) Var. Cost	(5) Consv. Pmnt.	(6) Rev. Reqt.	(7) Avg Rate	(8) Total Resource Cost
Initial State	1000	1000	2000	3000	0	5000	5.00	5000
Coal Plant	1100	1100	2000	3700	0	5700	5.18	5700
Lovins High	1000	1000	2000	3000	700	5700	5.70	5500
Lovins Low	1000	1000	2000	3000	500	5500	5.50	5500
Ruff-Joskow	1000	1000	2000	3000	182	5182	5.18	5500
Unbundled High	1000	1100	2000	3000	700	5700	5.18	5500
Unbundled Low	1000	1100	2000	3000	500	5500	5.00	5500

Conservation Cost/kWh　　　　　　　　**6 cents**

	(1) Gener. kWh	(2) Sales kWh	(3) Fixed Cost	(4) Var. Cost	(5) Consv. Pmnt.	(6) Rev. Reqt.	(7) Avg Rate	(8) Total Resource Cost
Initial State	1000	1000	2000	3000	0	5000	5.00	5000
Coal Plant	1100	1100	2000	3700	0	5700	5.18	5700
Lovins High	1000	1000	2000	3000	700	5700	5.70	5600
Lovins Low	1000	1000	2000	3000	600	5600	5.60	5600
Ruff-Joskow	1000	1000	2000	3000	182	5182	5.18	5600
Unbundled High	1000	1100	2000	3000	700	5700	5.18	5600
Unbundled Low	1000	1100	2000	3000	600	5600	5.09	5600

Conservation Cost/kWh   7 cents

	(1) Gener. kWh	(2) Sales kWh	(3) Fixed Cost	(4) Var. Cost	(5) Consv. Pmnt.	(6) Rev. Reqt.	(7) Avg Rate	(8) Total Resource Cost
Initial State	1000	1000	2000	3000	0	5000	5.00	5000
Coal Plant	1100	1100	2000	3700	0	5700	5.18	5700
Lovins High	1000	1000	2000	3000	700	5700	5.70	5700
Lovins Low	1000	1000	2000	3000	700	5700	5.70	5700
Ruff-Joskow	1000	1000	2000	3000	182	5182	5.18	5700
Unbundled High	1000	1100	2000	3000	700	5700	5.18	5700
Unbundled Low	1000	1100	2000	3000	700	5700	5.18	5700

Conservation Cost/kWh   8 cents

	(1) Gener. kWh	(2) Sales kWh	(3) Fixed Cost	(4) Var. Cost	(5) Consv. Pmnt.	(6) Rev. Reqt.	(7) Avg Rate	(8) Total Resource Cost
Initial State	1000	1000	2000	3000	0	5000	5.00	5000
Coal Plant	1100	1100	2000	3700	0	5700	5.18	5700
Lovins High	1000	1000	2000	3000	700	5700	5.70	5800
Lovins Low	1000	1000	2000	3000	700	5700	5.70	5800
Ruff-Joskow	1100	1100	2000	3700		5700	5.18	5700
Unbundled High	1100	1100	2000	3700		5700	5.18	5700
Unbundled Low	1100	1100	2000	3700		5700	5.18	5700

Conservation Cost/kWh   12 cents

	(1) Gener. kWh	(2) Sales kWh	(3) Fixed Cost	(4) Var. Cost	(5) Consv. Pmnt.	(6) Rev. Reqt.	(7) Avg Rate	(8) Total Resource Cost
Initial State	1000	1000	2000	3000	0	5000	5.00	5000
Coal Plant	1100	1100	2000	3700	0	5700	5.18	5700
Lovins High	1000	1000	2000	3000	700	5700	5.70	6200
Lovins Low	1000	1000	2000	3000	700	5700	5.70	6200
Ruff-Joskow	1100	1100	2000	3700		5700	5.18	5700
Unbundled High	1100	1100	2000	3700		5700	5.18	5700
Unbundled Low	1100	1100	2000	3700		5700	5.18	5700

ENDNOTES

1. See, Federal Energy Regulatory Commission, Notice of Proposed Rulemaking Re: Regulations Governing Bidding

Programs, Docket No. RM88-5-000, March 16, 1988 and the comments filed in that proceeding

2. M. Curtis Whittaker, "Conservation and Unregulated Utility Profits Redefining the Conservation Market," *Public Utilities Fortnightly*, July 7, 1988; A. Lawrence Colbe, "Analysis of Utility Sponsored Demand Side Programs When Customer Wellbeing is Considered," (Cambridge MA; Putnam, Hayes & Bartlett, Inc., 1988); and Paul L. Joskow, Testimony Before the Subcommittee on Energy and Power, House Committee on Energy and Commerce, March 31, 1988

3. Kenneth W. Costello, "Ten Myths of Energy Conservation," *Public Utilities Fortnightly*, March 19, 1987.

4. Steve J. Pickels and Philip Audet, "Second Generation Programs with an Increasing Utility Initiative, *Public Utilities Fortnightly*, December 24, 1987.

5. See Costello

6. Ralph C. Cavanagh, "Least Cost Planning Imperatives for Electric Utilities and their Regulators," *Harvard Environmental Law Review*, 10 (1986); Amory B. Lovins, "Saving Gigabucks with Negawatts," *Public Utilities Fortnightly*, March 21, 1985, p. 24.

7. The distinction between energy services and energy products is central to much of the analysis of the least cost planning framework. See Lovins, Cavanagh, and Roger W Sant, Dennis W. Bakke, and Roger G Naill, *Creating Abundance: America's Least-Cost Energy Strategy*, New York: McGraw Hill Book Company, 1984, pp. 17-30.

8. See Kelboe

9. We recognize that this framework does not embrace everything. It is not our intention here to address objectives such as spawning an infant conservation industry. Or it may be that even after accounting for all the acknowledged environmental and other cost externalities, proponents still prefer conservation and wish to see it pursued because of other general goals for changing the energy configuration of the society. Since these broader perspectives are not the focal points of the demand-side bidding debate, we do not include such conservation investments as cost effective in our present definition of a least-cost planning framework.

10. David Moscowitz, "Will Least-Cost Planning Work With-

out Significant Regulatory Reform," Presented at the Least-Cost Planning Seminar, National Association of Regulatory Utility Commissioners, Aspen Colorado, April 1988 (revised June 1988).

11. See Charles J. Cicchetti and Suellen M. Curkendall, "Are Energy- Efficient Programs Worth It?," Paper Prepared for the Eight Annual International Association of Energy Economists North American Conference, Massachusetts Institute of Technology, Cambridge, Massachusetts, November 19-21, 1986. See also, Cicchetti and Curkendall, "Conservation Subsidies: The Economist's Perspective," in *Electric Potential*, Vol. 2, No. 3, May-June 1986, pp 3-12

12. Lovins, p. 24.

13. Lovins, p. 25.

14. When the marginal cost of electricity does not equal its price, economic efficiency is reduced. If this source of inefficiency is affected by conservation policy the analysis becomes more complex. The debate over marginal-cost pricing, while important, is separable. Accordingly, we will not complicate the present analysis with such refinements.

15. This conclusion assumes that the customer includes whatever discount rate that permits him/her to relate costs and benefits which are not in the same time period.

16. "I do not, however, accept the "no-losers" ("hardly-any-winners") tests as a sound constraint on utility investments in efficiency, any more than they would accept it as a constraint on supply investments. Such tests limit the price of purchased efficiency to avoided cost minus lost revenue, or to average generation cost, because paying more could increase non-participants' rates. Such restrictions result in grossly suboptimal investment which raises everyone's rates and bills, uniformly and perhaps equitably, but unnecessarily." Lovins, p. 25.

17. Larry E. Ruff, "Least-cost Planning and Demand-Side Management: Six Common Fallacies and one simple truth," *Public Utilities Fortnightly*, April 28, 1988, pp. 19-26. See also Kolbe.

18. See Cicchetti and Curkendall, "Are Energy-Efficiency Programs Worth It?"

19. Lovins, p. 24.

20. Sant et al., 17-30
21. See Whittaker.
22. They object, too, because regulators have rejected what those regulators see as "no-losers" tests as too restrictive for utility-managed conservation programs. Utility conservation might cost less than the utility's operating cost. When this occurs efficient conservation investments made under traditional ratemaking could raise rates to non- participants. However, the utility would have no incentive to adopt inefficient conservation options. In this case, rejection of the "no- losers" test seems appropriate. But when the utility goes further and offers to pay others for whatever conservation they are willing to provide, as in the bidding proposal, there may be excess investment in conservation. It is the transition to the auction or bidding process and the payment to the customer, whose bill is also reduced through conservation, that may crate incentives for inefficient conservation. Nevertheless, the unbundling policy, which we advocate to correct utility-sponsored conservation incentives, incidentally also resolves the "no-losers" test.
23. Whittaker refers to this step as a redefinition of the conservation market.
24. In a more realistic example, of course, the rate differences would lead to efficiency effects. This separate debate over marginal-cost pricing is important, but need not complicate the present analysis of alternative bidding proposals.
25. Lovins assumes that there is so much cheap, unexploited conservation that this would never happen. We are reminded of the one-time claim that nuclear power would be too cheap to meter!
26. For a recent discussion of the problems created by this effect on non- participants, see Moskowitz.
27. See Moskowitz

SECTION E

FERC ELECTRICITY COMPETITION INITIATIVES

CHAPTER 14: OVERVIEW OF THE FERC COMPETITION INITIATIVES*

Martha O. Hesse
Former Chairman, Federal Energy Regulatory Commission*

INTRODUCTION

I'm delighted to be here in such beautiful surroundings and among so much collective expertise in electric utility matters. I know you share my goal of continued reliable and low-cost electric utility service for the nation's consumers. And I share many of your concerns about how this goal is to be met in the coming decades.

As I'm sure you know, the FERC is currently pursuing Electric Regulatory Reform. Last June when I spoke at the EEI convention, I said that one of my top priorities was to make regulation of electric utilities more flexible and market responsive. To this end, my goal was for the Commission to undertake a comprehensive review of its regulatory policies toward the electric utility industry.

I remain convinced that competition, where it can be fostered, is the most useful tool available to regulators to encourage the reliable and efficient operation of this industry. The first phase of the Commission's comprehensive review, which addresses regulatory policies toward QFs and other independent power producers, has resulted in three rulemaking proposals issued for public comment on March 16. I'm sure you're going to be hearing a lot about the specifics of these proposals during the next few months. So instead of describing them, I want to present them briefly in the context of how they could help you solve *your* problems. Then I want to move on to the real focus of my talk today, which is not what we've done, but what we will be doing in Phase II of our electric strategy.

Remarks by Chairman Hesse before the Southeastern Electric Exchange , Boca Raton, FL, March 28, 1988

PHASE I RULEMAKING PROPOSALS
Administratively Determined Avoided Cost

A major benefit of the proposal concerning administrative determination of full avoided costs would be to reduce the likelihood that you will be forced to pay for capacity that you don't need. This should eliminate the future possibility of massive overpayments. I don't think anyone can seriously argue that it's in the public interest for utilities like Houston Lighting & Power, Pacific Gas & Electric and Idaho Power to be forced to pay hundreds of millions of dollars for QF capacity that will be redundant for years to come. A second benefit would be that you will have greater assurance that non-price factors such as dispatchability and reliability will be considered in determining the real value of QF capacity and energy for you and your customers. Third, the process itself would be vastly improved, because states would have to explain in writing how they are taking various factors into account when setting avoided cost rates. It would be a process that you — and the Commission — could feel more confident about, since it would go far to eliminate excesses in setting avoided cost rates.

Bidding

The bidding proposal would likewise bring you a number of benefits. First, competitive procurement of QF power will result in a more accurate determination of avoided cost than administrative approximations. Direct competition among QFs, as well as competition between QFs and other sources, will translate into better projects and lower prices. Second, as more and more states decide to enter the bidding arena, it is important that minimum criteria be established so that these bidding programs don't lead to short-sighted outcomes. I am concerned that absent those criteria, the entire focus may be on price, when non-price factors such as dispatchability, reliability, fuel diversity and the experience of the bidder are equally as important.

I also think it is important, and the proposed rule makes this very clear, that utilities should have the opportunity to bid to satisfy their own capacity needs. Our proposed regulations will ensure that successful bidders are never paid more than the cost to the utility of producing the power itself or

310   COMPETITION IN ELECTRICITY

purchasing power from other wholesale sources. Although the proposed rule does not require direct participation by the purchasing utility, it suggests in the strongest of terms that the full benefits of bidding will not be achieved if the power source most knowledgeable about the needs of the system — the purchasing utility — is not allowed to submit bids. And if you do bid in your own service territory through a subsidiary, that subsidiary would be given the same pricing flexibility that is being proposed for independent power producers.

A third benefit of the bidding proposal would be to reduce the likelihood of debilitating after-the-fact prudence reviews. The proposed rules will require states to certify the purchasing utility's selection of the winning bids. Such certification should minimize the potential for controversy when you propose to pass through the costs of purchased power to your wholesale and retail customers. Thorough state review, coupled with state certification, should also provide utilities that select their own bids with protection from antitrust challenges.

Independent Power Producers

The third proposal, on Independent Power Producers, would give you an opportunity to qualify for relaxed price and streamlined corporate regulation. It should also increase your supply options. But of course, relaxed pricing flexibility is not limited to the IPPs proposal. That leads me to my main topic today — Phase II of the electric strategy that I will recommend to my colleagues.

PHASE II OF THE ELECTRIC STRATEGY

Phase II of the electric strategy will focus on bulk power and transmission pricing. Many of you will remember that these were the central concerns of a previous notice of inquiry. Many of you filed lengthy and thoughtful comments in that proceeding. The time has come for the Commission to decide what future policies will be.

Pricing Flexibility in Competitive Markets

Phase II will have two principal tasks. The first task is to explore the extent to which greater pricing flexibility should be granted to electricity producers that sell in workably competitive markets. The market for wholesale electricity is becoming increasingly competitive. PURPA and the Commission's implementing regulations have exempted QFs from seller price regulation. The NOPR on IPPs proposes to grant considerable pricing flexibility to additional producers.

However, qualifying facilities and independent power producers aren't the only producers that lack market power. *I see no reason why pricing flexibility cannot be extended to other producers who do not require strict regulation.*

One of the difficulties in strictly regulating competitive wholesale sales is that there are many different electricity products with many different dimensions of supply. For example, sales can differ with respect to their degree of firmness or interruptibility, the time of the sale, the physical location of the delivery points, and whether load following service is provided. The cost and value of the product can differ markedly as these dimensions change. Relying more heavily on competitive market forces can permit prices to reflect these cost and value differences more easily than can strict regulation.

We've been told by Kentucky Utilities, by Southern California Edison, and others, that traditional investor owned utilities frequently sell power from rate-based facilities in workably competitive markets. I intend to propose to my fellow Commissioners that we consider granting such sellers the maximum possible pricing flexibility allowable under the law, just as has been proposed for independent power producers. Under such a scheme — as in the case of independent power producers — the sales price could be set flexibly through negotiation subject to a cost-based cap at the purchaser's projected avoided cost. Maybe the Commission can't level the playing field perfectly, but granting greater pricing flexibility to such sellers would be a very important step in the right direction.

Of course, the Commission currently grants a fair amount of pricing flexibility to many coordination sales on a case-by-case basis. However, there are several problems with this approach. The first is that this type of process is cumbersome. It can delay market participants from responding to competitive market forces. Second, the Commission has not codified these policies nor explained them in any document that is generally available to the public. Consequently, many in the public do not fully understand what these policies are. This is a complaint voiced by many utilities. Third, the degree of pricing flexibility currently permitted by the Commission is inadequate. For example, coordination sales are often capped at the seller's average embedded cost, which can be far below what competitive circumstances would require — the purchaser's projected avoided cost.

I believe that the Commission should formulate generic policies regarding what types of pricing flexibility are appropriate and under what circumstances such pricing flexibility should be allowed — and it should clearly articulate these policies to the public. As part of this effort, we must explore what additional types of pricing flexibility are necessary and appropriate. In considering who should be eligible for pricing flexibility, we need to develop simple rules — and underscore simple rules — to identify sellers that lack market power. These rules must strike a balance. While inappropriate use of monopoly power harms the public, so do burdensome administrative procedures that obstruct competitive suppliers from responding to market forces.

Thus, our goal should be to exclude sellers who clearly possess market power from the benefits of upward pricing flexibility above the present cost-based ceilings. But our rules should not be so complex that they bog the process down. We won't be doing anyone much good if we end up developing rules that require a full-blown anti-trust type of market analysis for every single transaction. If our efforts are going to lead to anything useful, we will have to create easily applied rules of thumb to distinguish between sellers that have market power and those that don't.

Right at the beginning, we're going to have to decide a threshold question: should the purpose of these rules-of-thumb be to determine if the entire market is competitive — meaning each and every seller lacks market power — or only that the individual seller making the filing lacks market power over the expected buyer? In the proposed IPPs rule, the Commission chose the latter approach. I think the Commission clearly favors that approach. I hope to explore both approaches in Phase II. I'll be very interested in hearing what you have to say.

We will also have to evaluate whether pricing flexibility is appropriate for all types of transactions. In the NOIs, a sharp distinction was drawn between coordination and requirements service. I am not convinced, at this point, that there remains a distinction between these services. Power contracts now vary tremendously in the length and firmness of the power sale. The problems with pricing power based on average embedded cost are common to *all* power sales. It appears to me that the crucial distinction with regard to the appropriateness of flexible pricing is between customers who have access to alternative suppliers and those who do not. Put in more familiar terms, is the customer captive or non-captive? If the customer is no longer captive because it has access to real alternatives, then I can't see any compelling *policy* reason why the seller shouldn't be given pricing flexibility irrespective of the type of contract involved. If a customer does not have access to alternative suppliers, pricing flexibility would be inappropriate no matter how short and interruptible the power sale is.

Similarly, if there is genuine access to alternative suppliers, I also don't see any public interest justification for imposing an obligation to serve on a seller beyond what is written in the contract. The words "obligation to serve" it don't appear anywhere in the Federal Power Act. In an order dealing with a remand of our CWIP rule issued last year, my fellow Commissioners and I concluded that if buyers have access to alternative suppliers, the utility should not have an obligation to serve beyond what is provided by contract. I think we will again address this issue when the Commission considers an innovative interconnection agreement between the Pacific Gas and Electric Company and the Turlock Irrigation District.

I do want to point out, however, that even if a customer is captive, it does not mean that average embedded cost is the appropriate basis for a regulated rate. It is not. Where competition cannot be fostered, we should regulate to simulate the market. I hope to have the Commission address this issue later this year. But you don't have to wait. We would welcome innovative filings that depart from average embedded cost pricing for sales to captive customers.

Transmission

The second task in Phase II will be to re-examine the Commission's regulation of transmission service. Transmission policy has two dimensions: pricing and access. I will turn to pricing first, for increased access is unlikely to improve efficiency unless transmission prices are set correctly.

Transmission pricing should accomplish three goals:

1. to send accurate price signals to generation suppliers and purchasers;
2. to provide incentives to wheel over existing lines; and
3. to provide incentives to build new capacity whenever needed.

We've been told by the Edison Electric Institute, the National Regulatory Research Institute, and others that our present transmission pricing policies don't meet these goals. I think these organizations are right and we need to make some changes.

Current transmission policy, which bases prices on embedded costs, does not meet these policy goals. Embedded cost prices do not reflect the true costs of providing service, including opportunity costs. Thus, they do not provide accurate price signals to ensure efficiency in bulk power markets. Clearly, a different set of pricing policies needs to be considered. When transmission lines are congested, prices should be set so as to allocate capacity to those trades producing the largest benefits. When spare transmission capacity exists, prices should not artificially discourage use of the transmission facilities.

In addition, current transmission prices typically do not reflect the costs of unintended flows imposed on third parties. The physical transmission path of electricity rarely coincides with the path specified by the contracting parties. Consequently, some electricity inevitably flows over the lines of third parties and imposes costs on them. If transmission prices are to reflect the full cost of providing service, these parties should be compensated for the costs of unintended flows over their lines.

I believe that a new transmission pricing policy should

distinguish between situations where the transmission owner possesses significant market power and where the owner doesn't, just as we have proposed for bulk power markets. Where market power is lacking, we should relax regulation as much as legally possible and allow market-oriented prices. Where significant market power exists, transmission prices should more closely reflect the true costs of providing transmission service, including legitimate opportunity costs and the costs imposed on third parties by unintended flows.

Transmission access is a more difficult issue. I don't need to tell this group how controversial it is. Obviously, there is a distinction between increasing suppliers' access to other utilities and increasing retail wheeling. At this point, I am not sure that retail wheeling has anything to commend it as good policy — and it certainly would be inappropriate until problems with stranded investment and the utilities' retail obligation to serve have been resolved. On the other hand, increasing the number of suppliers and their access to utilities with properly priced transmission service may enhance both competition and efficiency. However, it may not be necessary to mandate supplier access to achieve this result.

Better transmission pricing policies could go a long way toward encouraging utilities to provide greater access voluntarily to other suppliers wanting to reach new wholesale markets. Allowing transmission prices that reflect legitimate opportunity costs — without permitting monopoly pricing — may increase the incentives to wheel and to expand transmission facilities.

The Commission has already begun to take a hard look at transmission access in a number of forums. For example, the Commission, in its recently issued bidding NOPR, is exploring the desirability of allowing the states to impose transmission access conditions on utilities that wish to participate in bidding for their own capacity or in another utility's bidding process. Also, the issue of transmission access has been raised in two recent cases. The first is the Utah Power & Light - Pacific Power & Light merger, which is currently being litigated at the Commission. And the second is the filing I mentioned earlier involving Pacific Gas & Electric and the Turlock Irrigation District.

These cases will allow the Commission to focus on the

specific access issues raised in the limited contexts of these proceedings. This should aid the Commission ultimately in developing the most appropriate generic access policies. However, in light of the complexities raised by the access issue, I do not believe that the Commission should attempt to develop any generic policies on access at this time. Instead, I believe the Commission should proceed with transmission pricing reforms first, while addressing some limited access issues as they are presented to the Commission. This strategy would give the Commission time to observe how effective transmission pricing reforms are increasing voluntary access and also to explore further the various issues surrounding various access policies. After the Commission has had time to learn from these experiences, it could then consider whether it should pursue any new generic access policies. In the meantime, I urge you as utilities to continue to come up with more innovative experiments in which you *voluntarily* provide transmission access to others.

I would hope that the review undertaken in each of the two Phase II tasks would result in Notices of Proposed Rulemaking, and that these NOPRs would be completed for Commission consideration before the end of the year.

In addition to work on these Phase II issues, the Commission staff is beginning some preliminary analysis of incentive regulation. This subject is complex, and I'm not sure if final recommendations will be made this year. Nevertheless, I do believe that it is important for us to begin re-examining how to encourage efficient utility performance. The current process of conducting backward-looking prudence reviews is inadequate, because its focus is on assessing blame for past mistakes rather than encouraging efficient behavior for the future.

Lastly, I would like to mention — in case you haven't heard — that in addition to all of the Phase II work underway, there is one more NOPR in Phase I which is currently being developed and will be issued this year. We call it the PURPA Programmatic NOPR, and it will address issues such as allowable waste fuels, better QF certification procedures, QF ownership, and QF reporting requirements.

CONCLUSION

Let me conclude by observing that these broad generic policies which I've just described are not the only front on which the Commission is moving. These generic analyses are being driven, in large part, by filings which *you* in the industry are making. We will continue to act on these case-by-case issues as they arise — we cannot, and we will not, hold off making decisions until the generic rulemakings are in place. In fact, these specific cases help us refine our thinking and crystallize decision options, ultimately enhancing, we believe, the quality of the rulemaking products.

I'm sure that our Phase II deliberations will benefit from our review of Baltimore Gas & Electric's auctioning of its unused share of the PJM transmission capacity, which we approved last August. We also learned a lot from the Orange and Rockland's IPPs proposal submitted on behalf of some industrial customers from whom the utility will buy back peaking power. That, of course, was approved in January. So don't be shy about proposing innovative and creative solutions to your problems. We welcome such filings, because they provide an opportunity to address your specific needs and may help us to sharpen our thinking in the generic proceedings under way.

We will continue to value your opinion in striving for what I believe to be our mutual goal — providing lower cost, reliable electric power service for the American consumer. We can achieve that goal *only* with continued reliance on your knowledge, and your experience and your help.

CHAPTER 15: OVERSIGHT HEARINGS ON COGENERATION AND THE PUBLIC UTILITY REGULATORY POLICIES ACT OF 1978 (PURPA)*

Charles G. Stalon
Former Commissioner, Federal Energy Regulatory Commission

I am pleased to testify on what I think is an important matter of broad public interest. In view of the fact that Chairman Hesse is, wisely I believe, asking the Commission to start a major review of its regulation of electricity, a review that will have major implications for the industry and for its regulators, these hearings will be useful in elevating the level of public debate. The FERC's own views on the limited range of issues that are the subject of this hearing are still in the formative stage. However, I believe the hearing is timely in providing a public forum on the FERC initiative, and perhaps more important, for clarifying what the Commission is undertaking and the probable timeframe for its actions.

INTRODUCTION

The debate about the appropriate economic structure and best means of control of the electricity system is intensifying. That is a healthy response to many of the current problems of the system. Since reform is a purposeful activity, any reform of the system must be premised upon well defined objectives and an explanation of why the objectives are not being effectively pursued in the present structure with the present control systems. Clarity of discussion also requires that distinctions be drawn between end-state objectives and transition paths. Both are discussed herein but the initial emphasis is on why reform is needed.

The theme of the following remarks is that the current system of regulation is broken, that is, it is failing to induce in the electricity industry desirable and attainable levels of

*Testimony before the Subcommittee on Energy and Power, Committee on Energy and Commerce, U.S. House of Representatives, Washington, D.C., September 10, 1987

economics efficiency. Both the structure and the means of control of the industry probably should be changed. While I am largely persuaded that major changes in the structure of the electricity system are desirable, I am also largely persuaded that time exists for debate, research and consensus building before dramatic and nonreversible actions are taken. Performance deficiencies of the system are defined differently by different parties; such differences reflect both different objectives and different emphasis. Clarity of discussion requires that careful distinctions be made. Some of the deficiencies reflect temporary and possibly transient circumstances. Other deficiencies reflect more persistent forces and possibly reflect institutional and perhaps inevitable results of the system. Obviously, one who proposes fundamental structural reforms for temporary and transient problems carries an unusually heavy burden of proof. The argument proposed herein is that the principal deficiencies of the system are not transient but long-standing and institutionalized or reflective of recent social and economic forces that are likely to be durable.

The fundamental question currently before regulatory and legislative policymakers who accept the primacy of the economic efficiency objective is whether that objective can be better furthered by pursuing workably competitive markets in the generating sector of the industry, by reforming and improving the quality of regulation, or by some combination of the two. Since distribution companies (discos) and most transmission companies (transcos) still exhibit natural monopoly characteristics, and will be regulated for the foreseeable future, the conclusion to be supported is that a combination of improved regulation and competitive generating companies (gencos) are desirable.[1]

The following pages assert that, while it is crucially important to improve the quality of regulation, especially the quality of pricing, the best hope for significant improvement in the economic efficiency of the system lies in increasing competition in the generating sector of the industry.[2] While it cannot be logically ruled out that such competition could occur within the institutions of regulated generation, such an outcome seems unlikely. Consequently, increased competition among generating companies almost certainly requires that nonregulated gencos be encouraged and that the existing industry structure be modified by encouraging some de-

COMPETITION IN ELECTRICITY

integration of the present vertically integrated industry. This objective does not require the absence of vertically integrated firms; it does require the presence of many firms that are not vertically integrated.

The debate should not be seen as whether the nation should seek perfect competition or perfect regulation. The technology of the industry will not support a close approximation to economists' definitions of perfect competition; and the experience of a century demonstrates that regulation falls far short of perfection for many reasons, some of which are discussed below. The social choice is probably between oligopolistic competition that can approximate economic efficiency and a tradition-bound regulatory system that has proven resistant to reform and resistant to economic efficiency objectives. While better evidence is needed before non-reversible choices are made, the current record supports the wisdom of limiting the scope of regulation in the electricity industry and expanding the role of competition.

Vertical de-integration of the industry and deregulation of gencos must not be seen as sufficient conditions for creating workably competitive markets among gencos. Nonregulated gencos selling power to discos either directly or through transcos on long-term, fixed-price contracts could not only re-create the principal failures of the present system, they could intensify those failures. Deregulation of gencos is not an end in itself, it is only a means to a workably competitive market. Moreover, a workably competitive market is not an end it itself, it is only a means to improve economic efficiency. Achieving that objective should claim the attentions and efforts of policymakers.

The three principal failures of the regulatory system that workably competitive gencos could partially correct are pricing failures, management incentive failures and legitimacy failures. Pricing failures are the joint result of regulatory traditions and management incentive failures. The legitimacy failures arise largely as a consequence of the first two. These failures have long existed, but until recent years were noticed and emphasized only by careful observers of the system, primarily participants and academicians. In recent years these failures have been more widely recognized. Below, it will be argued that the wider recognition came about because the monopoly power of the generating sector of electric utilities has diminished for macroeconomic, technological and legal reasons. The technological reasons are probably permanent, and some of the legal and macroeconomic reasons are likely to be so also. Forecasting failures have aggravated the effects of these forces on the industry and have naturally given rise to the argument that problems caused by such forecasting failures[3] account for the significant industry problems. Such transient problems, it has been argued, cannot justify fundamental changes.

As would be expected, the proponents of regulatory objectives that de-emphasize economic efficiency support policy prescriptions different from mine. Such proponents usually emphasize the importance to the nation, or to one or more groups, of objectives that they believe economic efficiency will not produce in desired amounts. Such objectives include "price stability over time", "preferred risk allocation", "unit cost minimization", "subsidized services", and "supra-efficient reliability." Such objectives deserve analysis and evaluation, although it is noteworthy that some of these objectives require that the monopoly power of electric utilities be strengthened. One deduction from these objectives, although not one that all the proponents of the listed objectives systematically draw, is that the preferred policy choice would be to discourage vertical de-integration and to encourage horizontal mergers of existing vertically integrated firms. That option is discussed below and rejected as aggravating current problems rather than ameliorating them.

My testimony accepts economic efficiency as the principal objective of electric utility regulation and argues the case that workably competitive gencos promises to partially correct certain regulatory failures and to create strong incentives for both federal and state regulators to undertake further corrective measures. I concede that much remains to be learned about both desired end-states, or industry structure, and desired transition paths before significant policy decisions can be made. However, my principal conclusion is that workably competitive gencos, if that end-state can be achieved, is the best feasible structure for improved efficiency in the electricity industry.

I will first set forth my views as to the current state of the electricity industry and its regulation, and my fundamental conclusion that regulation, at least at the federal level, is in urgent need of a thorough re-examination and reform. I then briefly set forth my views on the reforms I believe the FERC needs to take in each of the major components of its regulation of electricity. Finally, I offer to the Subcommittee my general reactions and thoughts on some of the issues in what has been described as the "first phase" in a potential reform package, based upon the concepts set forth in Chairman Hesse's June 10 speech to the Edison Electric Institute.

MACROECONOMIC CHANGES THAT HAVE REVEALED FUNDAMENTAL DEFECTS IN THE INHERITED STRUCTURE AND REGULATION OF THE ELECTRICITY INDUSTRY

For decades, the electricity industry prospered and grew under the traditional regulatory model. Under this model, most of the nation's power supply (outside of TVA, the power marketing administrations, and the small but growing contribution to generation of the coops and municipals) was produced by the vertically integrated, investor-owned utilities (IOUs) who were typically granted exclusive franchise territories. The price to the IOU of this grant of monopoly power was the acceptance of a general obligation to serve all retail and some wholesale customers in the service territory, and to accept price and financial regulation at both the state and federal levels. This monopoly system permitted electric utilities to reap the rewards of technological improvements, of economies of scale, and of a general expansion of markets. Most of these benefits were passed along to consumers through lower prices and increasingly reliable service. The existence of several kinds of public power agencies demonstrates, however, that the performance of IOUs did not satisfy all political demands for electricity service.

As the technology of transmission and control improved, the pressure to gain coordination economics beyond the balkanized, sometimes quite small markets created by the franchise monopoly, was at first met by horizontal mergers, and later, after the passage of the Federal Power Act (FPA) and the Public Utility Holding Company Act (PUHCA), in considerable part met by increasing coordination between utility systems. In their most advanced form, these coordination efforts comprised power pool and holding company relationships, which were able to take advantage of many of the potential efficiencies of improved transmission and control technology and, through this, to better utilize existing generation sources and to better plan future generation. In their most advanced form, these regional systems achieved a high level of coordination in not only energy exchanges and generating reserve requirements, but also in capacity planning and construction. It is perhaps not surprising that many in this industry see further mergers and more extensive coordination agreements as the proper path to the future.

Pricing and other market mechanisms have been largely ignored as means of achieving greater economic efficiency with one exception to be emphasized later, bulk power markets furthered by the FERC. Errors in pricing by strong monopolists do not produce obviously damaging results to utilities for the major reason that most customers have no options but to purchase from the monopoly utility. Moreover, gross and obvious pricing errors could be corrected over time by regulatory action, and the inability of most customers to move or to arrange for their own generation in the interim normally sufficed to give regulators time to react. Several developments in recent decades have increased the adverse consequences of pricing errors.

The Changing Macroeconomic Environment

The underlying economic and institutional forces that permitted the system to survive and flourish have eroded over the last decade or so and other new forces have put increasing pressure on the system. Three of the most important forces requiring change are macroeconomic developments that have, by and large, been beyond the control of either the utilities themselves or of their regulators:

(1) *Real interest rates have increased.* The macroeconomic policy of the United States from the 1930s until the late 1960s can fairly be described as a low interest rate and high growth policy. High growth rates and high employment rates were not always achieved but low interest rates generally were. In a private enterprise economy, low interest rates encourage capital intensive methods of production. Under such circumstances it is not surprising that the electricity industry emphasized capital-intensive generating technologies and was willing to build long-gestation projects. It was such pro-

jects that demonstrated significant economies of scale in generation.

Macroeconomic policy changed emphasis in the late 1960s in response to persistent inflationary fears. From that time to this, relatively high interest rates have been a part of U.S. macroeconomic environment. Moody's Aaa corporate bond rates that averaged 2.716 percent in the 1940s, 3.302 percent in the 1950s, and 4.35 percent in the first half of the 1960s, increased to 5.668 percent in the last half of the 1960s, to 8.289 percent in the 1970s and 12.93 percent in the first half of the 1980s. This rate fell to 11.37 and 9.02 percent in 1985 and 1986 respectively.[4] By June of 1987 this rate had risen to 9.32 percent.[5] Furthermore, in the first two decades following World War II there were several Aaa IOUs. Today there are few.

These numbers are persuasive evidence that the real interest rate today is significantly higher than real interest rates in the 20 years following World War II. Such increases in real rates of interest tend to decrease the financial attractiveness and economic efficiencies of capital-intensive technologies. For this reason, and others mentioned below, the attractiveness of long-gestation, capital-intensive generating plants is less today than it was earlier. If one insists upon perpetuating or recreating the generating mix considered optimal three decades ago, he should be required to demonstrate how the optimum can be so similar when real interest rates are so different.

When contemplating the future of the electricity industry, it is useful to remind ourselves that the art of macroeconomic forecasting has not improved noticeably since the early 1970s. The appropriate industry structure and the appropriate control system (whether regulation or market forces) should, therefore, be one that does not depend on accurate long-term forecasts. Consequently, regulators and policymakers should be prepared to continue to live in a high-interest rate society, a low-interest rates society or, more likely, a society in which interest rates fluctuate more dramatically than they did in the 25 years following World War II.

More serious and certainly more permanent are two less obvious and less discussed macroeconomic influences on the electricity industry — the business cycle and international competitiveness.

(2) *The intensification of the business cycle.* Over the last several years the nation has been struggling out of its ninth and most serious recession since World War II, when measured by unemployment rates. Moreover, the last three recessions, those after 1974, have produced trough unemployment rates higher than any of the first six by substantial amounts. In fact, it was not until December 1986, after more than four years of recovery, that the civilian unemployment rate fell to 6.7 percent, the highest rate experienced in the first six recessions following World War II. This pattern of increasingly deep and frequent recessions is an alarming one for any industry. One only has to reel off such "troubled industries" as banking, steel, automobiles, shoes and agriculture, to make the point.

The political system has not been unresponsive to the business cycle. Each President since the 1950s has engaged in dramatic acts of economic experimentation such as wage and price guidelines, wage and price controls, tax credits, tax cuts and increases, high interest rates and high unemployment rates in efforts to reconcile two conflicting sets of objectives — the objectives of full employment and rapid economic growth with the objective of a stable price level. It would be naive of regulators and utility executives to believe that this period of macroeconomic experimentation has ended. One can only expect additional dramatic experiments as the nation confronts its macroeconomic problems; and, given the lack of consensus among political leaders over policy, further rides of the roller coaster of the business cycle are likely as the nation seeks the low unemployment rates and high growth that also produce unwanted inflation; and then seeks stable price levels that also produce unwanted slow growth and high unemployment rates.

Certain distinctive characteristics of the electricity industry make it more vulnerable than most to macroeconomic instability, namely: (1) its extreme capital intensity; (2) its highly leveraged capital structures; and, (3) its long lead times for completing major baseload units, which were, until the 1970s, assumed to be the generation plants that best reaped the economies of scale in generation. Macroeconomic forces have combined with these characteristics of the industry, and other influences such as cost overruns (also partly a

COMPETITION IN ELECTRICITY

result of macroeconomic instability), to make supply planning over the last 15 years a nightmare for those utilities that attempted to plan aggressively to assure a reliable and economically efficient supply of electricity for their customers.

(3) *The growing interdependence of world economies.* One of the more difficult adjustments facing the U.S. economy, its business community and its political leaders, has been to recognize and respond appropriately to the fact that the U.S. economy is no longer so large relative to the international economy that the U.S. can pursue domestic programs and business strategies with little regard for their effect on foreign economies or with little concern about the effects of foreign economic policies on our own economy.

One inevitable consequence of this pattern of world development has been the internationalization of many markets. Hence, an increasing number of product and commodity prices are being set in markets beyond national control. Flowing directly from this consequence is a second one — that the U.S. economy must gain the flexibility to respond efficiently to changes in prices determined in international markets, especially for those products or commodities that are important inputs to the U.S. economy, such as oil.

While seemingly far removed from the relatively balkanized, clearly domestic markets for electric power, these international economic forces have in fact had a major effect on the electricity industry. Firstly, there are two direct effects. One is instability in fossil fuel prices and inability to predict these prices. As has been seen vividly in the natural gas area, when the pricing is slow to respond to market forces and is inhibited from doing so by non-market responsive contracts (designed, perhaps, to create long-term price stability), volatile fuel prices can seriously disrupt supply planning and damage the financial fabric of the regulated industry.

The second effect is that monetary policy has become increasingly internationalized. The result is that our economy, and, of course, the electricity industry which traditionally has been heavily dependent on capital markets, must be prepared to live with increasing volatility in interest rates. Both these trends are critical to electric utilities that now find the prices of both their major inputs, namely fuels and investment funds, determined in volatile international markets.

A third major, but less direct, effect is that while the electric utilities themselves do not have to price to compete in international markets (with the exception of those near the Canadian and Mexican borders), some of their major customers, particularly their large industrial customers, do. Where rising electricity prices are major component in the industrials' cost structures, rising prices have helped to undermine their international competitiveness. Utilities have often put economically inefficient pressures on industrial plants either to switch energy inputs; or to self generate; or, as is often the case where neither of these two options is feasible, to simply close down. Hence, even though the utilities have, until recently, enjoyed an almost exclusive monopoly power in their service territories, pricing has become important to their retaining a significant portion of their customer base because some customers, faced with international competition, have lost the flexibility to pass on large electricity cost increases to their consumers. In the last few years utilities, private and public, have been forced to recognize that their monopoly power does not insulate them from all the effects of faulty pricing. However, they have found the old regulatory structure not well suited to an effective response.

How did the electric utilities respond to the 1982 recession, and how should they have responded if economic efficiency was their principal objective? First, we know that the pricing model embraced by the industry and most of its regulators is often charged with being demand insensitive. That is a good generalization, but, in fact, the more accurate generalization is that it is often demand perverse, when demand falls, or fails to rise as forecasted, *ceteris paribus*, the model calls for price increases.

Consequently, in the 1982 recession, and other recessions as well, the electric utilities did not lower their prices as economic efficiency demands. In pursuit of "just" prices, they raised them to protect their "just and reasonable" earnings. In so doing, they refused to postpone profits and, thereby, perhaps to ease their customers' adjustments to distressful economic circumstances. Instead, they aggravated their customers' adjustment problems, and also aggravated the nation's competitive problems in an increasingly interdependent and competitive world.[6]

Clearly, in a world of OPEC, a world of intense business cycles, a world of increasing international competitiveness, this nation should not tolerate an electricity industry that builds and prices its services with little or no regard for demand conditions. Adjusting to economic forces beyond national control is a necessity in such a world. The electricity industry and its regulators must facilitate such adjustments by creating demand-sensitive prices, and not do as they have done in recent years — increase IOU margins when demand falls and narrow them when demand increases. It will be argued below that this inappropriate pricing is primarily the result of the tradition-bound, cost-plus regulatory pricing model. The failure is in the system, not in any particular group in the industry.

Adjusting to the Changed Macroeconomic Environment

Some of the macroeconomic changes of the last two decades may be reversed soon; others are probably permanent. Interest rate levels, for example, may return to 1950 levels, although I think that is unlikely. Intensified business cycles are, I believe, more permanent features of the economic landscape as is intensified international competitiveness. These permanent changes are partial justification for restructuring the electricity industry. They may not constitute the principal justification for such restructuring, but their existence requires any defender of the status quo or the status quo ante to explain how the system can be changed to accommodate the needs of the new macroeconomic climate. Any argument that says the system can continue to build and price as the industry has in the past must justify the burden that such construction and pricing imposes on IOU customers when customers are adjusting to reduced economic opportunities.

REGULATORY AND INSTITUTIONAL CHANGES AND DEFICIENCIES

There are, of course, those who see the old structure of the industry and the old regulatory system as adequate and question whether competition among gencos is really an alternative. A more detailed look at trends in the electric industry itself over the last decade or so indicates an answer to such questions.

Forces Lengthening Gestation Periods

Not only have real interest rates increased, but gestation periods for most generating plants and transmission lines have also increased. This phenomenon is probably more important than interest rate increases in tilting efficient generation methods away from capital intensive ones. The principal causes of the gestation period increases are regulatory and institutional. Environmental regulation and regulatory decision processes have substantially lengthened decision periods and added to the capital cost of certain generating and transmission technologies. Expanded administrative procedures and sunshine procedures have induced larger and more complex records. In so doing, decision time has been further lengthened.

Forces Subverting the Traditional Pricing Model

(1) *Rising cost of generation.* The real cost of replacement capacity, particularly for those forms of large baseload capacity that for decades were viewed as an important source for a declining cost and more efficient industry, has escalated dramatically. Perhaps the most extreme example is nuclear units that are frequently coming into service at costs ten times those originally projected when planned.[7] The significance of this turnaround in the economics of large nuclear units, once seen as the wave of cheaper electricity, is illustrated by the number of major utilities whose financial status has been jeopardized by lengthening gestation periods on a *single* plant. Moreover, the trend is by no means limited to nuclear power. While there still may be some economies of scale to be gained in the generating units of this industry, it is doubtful that they outweigh the various factors increasing construction costs. The bottom line is a gloomy one — the electricity industry is not likely to be any longer a declining real cost industry.

(2) *Increasing volatility of demand.* The second major problem plaguing the industry in the last decade has been increasingly volatile demands that have made supply planning

COMPETITION IN ELECTRICITY

a nightmare for both utilities and state commissions. Longer gestation periods require longer forecasts. Forecasting failures easily result in massive excess capacity on some systems and, consequently, induced "rate shock" caused by the new plants that are not needed. Erroneous forecasts, falling demand and the regulatory pricing model can easily combine to drive utilities into a "death spiral." With utility prices based upon a cost-plus model and rigid non-market responsive pricing, falling demand induces price increases that further lowers quantity demanded, which in turn induces more price increases, etc.

The pricing problem is illustrated by focusing upon just one component of what typically comprises a utility's "revenue requirement" in the cost-plus model — the way it recovers its capital costs and earnings. Capital cost recovery, has, of courses, become an increasingly important component of recent major rate increases as capital costs have escalated. While regulatory commissions scrutinize a utility's rate of return in excruciating detail, they have until recently almost completely ignored the method by which utilities depreciate assets, i.e., the time pattern by which they recover their capital costs. Under the traditional "straight line" method, the utilities are in fact locked into a rigid and front-end loaded pattern of capital recovery that tends to create prices that respond perversely to the business cycle. In recessions, the pricing model tends to increase margins, and therefore prices, to recover capital costs from the declining demand base. The model, moreover, reduces margins in booms when costs are recovered from a growing demand base. This pattern is exactly the opposite of what is required for efficient pricing.

In an industry as capital intensive and as highly leveraged as electricity, even a percentage or two drop in overall sales revenues can have damaging effects on a company's financial condition. Such drops in demand, in my view, were at least as big a contributor to the serious financial crises of major utilities in the early 1980s as were their increasingly expensive construction programs. It is not surprising, therefore, that both utilities and financiers resist price reductions that would compound such financial problems. Consequently, they support pricing models that are demand-perverse.

Demand-perverse pricing models, such as those inherent in the regulatory system, become unsustainable when competition is introduced in the industry. That, no doubt, is why some would prefer to believe that competition will go away, or that it should be prevented from spreading. An examination of two further trends in the electricity industry over the last decade should dispel such thoughts.

(3) *Growth of the bulk power market.* FERC data demonstrates what one would expect from faulty forecasts; namely, bulk power markets are a growing phenomenon. In the 22 years between 1961 and 1983, inter-utility exchange transactions, (which the FERC calls "coordination" transactions), increased about sevenfold, and related wheeling transactions in that period increased about twelvefold. One utility in the 1985 electricity Notice of Inquiry[8] told the FERC of a sixteenfold increase in its coordination sales over the last ten years. The FERC now regulates close to 30 percent of all the kWh sales regulated in the country; a major part of it coordination sales. Moreover, the variety of coordination transactions filed with the FERC over the last decade has expanded. Utilities now engage not only in short-term exchanges of energy and reliability, but also contract for longer term capacity as well.

One of the major reasons for this increase has been the growing disparities between regions and even between neighboring utilities in both the availability of capacity and the price of power. The combination of disparate fuel prices, increasingly expensive capacity additions and, in particular, demand projections gone awry, has given some utilities surpluses of power while others are short of capacity or have very high marginal costs of producing power. Hence, the incentives to purchase in order to lower energy costs or to avoid capacity additions in an age when forecasting is risky, have grown tremendously. While current surpluses will, of course, dry up over time, there is no assurance in an era of increasing macroeconomic uncertainty that planning will turn out any better in the future and that new surpluses and shortages will not emerge.[9] One important thing to remember about at least two of the macroeconomic forces stressed — the intensification of the business cycle and increasing international interdependence (and the related volatility in fuel prices) — is that they are likely to be permanent phenomena that will continue to plague the industry; and they will continue to induce serious inefficiencies if electricity continues to be priced to end-users and to wholesale customers in its present manner.

Another development of significance to a growing and probably more competitive bulk power market that is the product of the industry's troubled economics of the last decade is that few major utility systems seem to be planning baseload additions under the current regulatory system.[10] Yet even under the most modest scenarios for future load growth, there will have to be substantial generating plant construction to meet increased demand and, of course, to replace aging capacity. On the other hand, some utilities have shown an inclination to build, not only for their own needs but also for export, and they have indicated that they would prefer to do so on an unregulated basis. Others have shown an increasing inclination not to build but to import on a permanent basis.

Moreover, there is the growing phenomena of nonutility generators, both qualifying facilities under PURPA (QFs), and other non-PURPA independent power producers (IPPs), who increasingly look as though they will become major and permanent players in the electricity industry. These phenomena portend a growing permanent bulk power market, independent of the life of current utility surpluses. While this market will be incremental to the utilities' existing generation bases, it is potentially massive. In 1982, the Department of Energy estimated that new capacity needs by the year 2000 might require about a trillion dollars (in 1982 dollars) investment in new capacity. While subsequent events have indicated that figure may be too high, one could cut it in half and still be looking at a massive investment in new capacity in the not too distant future. The current original cost asset base of the entire electric utility industry is about 300 billion dollars. I believe this is probably the single biggest industry in capital terms in the United States. To replace and expand this capital stock, even over a decade or two, is a massive undertaking. The decision as to how it should best be undertaken is therefore a serious one, requiring careful consideration of all influences.

I am not prepared to be dogmatic as to what future supply options will best serve the interests of the nation in the 1990s and the next century. Nor am I anxious to engage in the related rather sterile debates of "big" versus "small" and "large baseload" versus "soft path" that have permeated so much of the dialogue on electricity policy for the last demade. I really do not know which is going to prove to be the best long-term supply option. I would feel safer letting market forces, where we can be assured they will operate efficiently or more efficiently than the current regulatory regimes, and the ingenuity of a competitive private sector, make those decisions. I would prefer not to rely on the demand-perverse pricing models of the past to signal when, where, and how much capacity is needed.

Regulators, because of the traditions and procedural constraints under which they operate, can make so few economic decisions really well that it is unwise for them to regulate where market forces can do the job reasonably well. Moreover, it is the degree to which this industry can become competitive, and do so efficiently, over which regulators will have considerable control. Hence, special attention by regulators to the role of competition in this industry is appropriate. Bulk power markets are already quite competitive, and with the growth of a wider array of suppliers they have the potential of becoming more competitive. Regulators will face many tests in this transformation. While competition is a growing, and I think inevitable, force in this industry, it can certainly be constrained and its development distorted by institutional and regulatory barriers, such as the inability to build transmission where needed, or to price it correctly, or denying suppliers access to it.

(4) *The growth of PURPA power.* The fourth recent trend that has shaken this industry is, of course, the phenomenal growth of power generated or offered by facilities qualifying under section 210 of PURPA (QFs). Most of this has occurred since the Supreme Court in mid-1983 removed the chilling effect of major challenges by utilities to the FERC rules implementing section 210. As Chairman Hesse has summarized in her June 10 speech, the growth of PURPA power in certain states has so exceeded the expectations of the framers of the 1978 statute and of the 1980 FERC rules as to almost mandate review by this Commission of how the scheme has developed and how it is meshing with other parts of federal and state regulation of electricity. What has become increasingly clear since 1984 is that this provision of the 1978 Energy Act that was expected to produce a small off-system

adjunct to the utility's role as a major provider of future electricity supply has so grown as to almost fill the demands for incremental generating capacity in some states.

This development has created a variety of tension points between state and federal regulation, in particular between the increasing interest of state regulators in power supply planning and the mandates of the federal PURPA scheme, most of which is implemented at the state level. For example, the California Energy Commission (CEC), which had originally embraced PURPA as a principal solution for future capacity as late as 1984, began within a year or two of its rapid growth to see aspects of PURPA as causing major problems in the CEC's ability to rationally plan the state's energy supply. One of the principal virtues of the PURPA reform concept set forth in Chairman Hesse's June speech is that it might permit state commissions and planning bodies to develop a rational basis upon which to reconcile their own supply planning prerogatives and those enacted by Congress in PURPA, and to do so on a basis that should ensure both a reliable and efficient mechanism for producing capacity additions.

THE DISAPPOINTING RESULTS OF THE PURPA TITLE I REFORM EFFORT

Contrasting how developments under section 210 of PURPA exceeded expectations with the very modest results achieved in retail pricing reform under Title I of PURPA is, I think, instructive as to how ossified the regulatory system has become. It should be recalled that most of the Congressional attention, and much of the initial post-enactment attention of state commissions and of the Department of Energy's intervention and funding programs, went into Title I. Title I required state commissions to undertake a major review of their retail pricing of electricity and to consider a variety of economics-based pricing principles, such as marginal cost pricing, time-of-use pricing and interruptible rates. After considerable efforts by state commissions and utilities, the results were fairly modest. From my experience in Illinois, I can attest to what a painstaking and excruciatingly difficult task it was to get the regulatory system — both the Commission, the utilities, and the customers — to accept even the basic rudiments of time-of-use pricing; and I was dismayed recently to see one of the major utilities in Illinois proposing to discard a major component of the reform.

If there is any clear message from looking at PURPA as a whole, it is that efforts to improve pricing, even in face of the clear needs to do so, were extremely difficult to achieve and the results were very modest.[11] Yet, a single provision that was seen as opening up an avenue to the electricity markets for a relatively discrete group of technologies, not viewed as being a potentially dominant source of supply, has in some areas already come to dominate the future supply scene. It is not surprising then, that this has caused considerable uncertainty and fear amongst those who still believe the regulatory system can be reformed to meet future needs.

Interim Recapitulations and Conclusions

The analysis up to this point can be summarized and the principal conclusions restated in eleven brief assertions:

1. Increasing social concerns with safety and the environment, combined with the lengthened decision processes of participatory democracy, have lengthened gestation periods of, and therefore the relative costs of, capital intensive generating plants and transmission lines.
2. These changes, some of which cannot be seen as temporary, diminish the significance of the natural monopoly justification for economic regulation of electricity generation.
3. Dissatisfaction with the current system of regulation amongst utility executives and utility financiers is common, perhaps even widespread. Some utility executives are warning that the economically efficient mix of generating plants to expand the system and/or to replace those wearing out will not be constructed by utilities under regulation if regulation remains unchanged.[12]
4. The demand perversity of the institutionalized pricing model aggravates economic adjustment problems of utility customers and utility suppliers in an increasingly competitive world economy that requires, instead, im-

proved adjustment performances.

5. The demand perversity of the institutionalized pricing model encourages alternative gencos to enter the business even when a regulated utility could produce the same output at a lower social cost.

6. Section 210 of PURPA has weakened the monopoly power that formerly permitted regulated utilities to use *discriminatory* prices and discriminatory service terms to discourage alternative gencos and to sustain inefficient prices.

7. The attempt embodied in Title I of PURPA to persuade regulatory agencies to reform the institutionalized pricing model produced only small gains in efficiency.

8. The regulatory reform requested by some utilities, namely greater assurances that, regardless of demand conditions, their capital costs will be recovered and their earnings will be stable, promises to aggravate the demand- perversity of the electricity pricing model.

9. The growth of bulk power markets, even under the limited circumstances allowed and the efficiency-limiting pricing model used by the FERC therein, demonstrates the ability of firms to exploit economies of coordination when the structure and control system permits.

10. One set of conclusions that appears inescapable form the above analysis is that the inherited regulatory system:

    i) is falling far short of inducing efficient performance from the electricity industry;
    ii) is not responding constructively to recent changes in the macroeconomic and legal environment; and
    iii) has proven resistant to efforts to reform its pricing models.

11. Another set of conclusions that appears inescapable from this analysis is that:

    i) The natural monopoly characteristics of generation, which is the principal economic justification for its regulation, have diminished and perhaps disappeared in the last two decades.
    ii) Improved technologies of transmission and control have permitted substantial bulk power markets to develop and in doing so have demonstrated the possibilities of further efficiencies.

The final conclusion to be drawn from this analysis is that the inherited structure of the electricity system and the inherited system of regulation exist by grace of inertia. They lack an intellectual economic defense.

REGULATORY RIGIDITIES AND REFORM POSSIBILITIES

I make these eleven assertions not in any effort to ascribe blame to those who managed the utility systems in the past or those who currently manage them, or to those who designed this system of regulation or who currently regulate under it. It is enough to say that circumstances have passed it by. My criticism is directed only to those who refuse to recognize the current realities and to cling to the past by either believing that the old system is not broken at all or that, if it is, it can be readily fixed.

The realities I have described do not, I want to stress, necessarily lead to a conclusion that the old system must be torn down completely or replaced by something completely new. I have always been skeptical of some of the grandiose and ambitious models for reform of the industry that we saw in the early 1980s, such as the forced vertical de-integration of integrated investor-owned utilities in order to separate out the natural monopoly discos from the potentially competitive gencos. One of the merits of proceeding with the reforms such as those discussed by Chairman Hesse in her June speech is that they do not require tearing down the old system but rather leave intact the existing asset base of the industry and focus on a better way of bringing into existence new increments of supply. This method of reform should serve to keep the utilities financially intact and let ratepayers continue to reap the benefits of their successes of the 1950s and 1960s; however, it would not force them to repeat all the mistakes of the 1970s and 1980s. A more competitive generation market need not preclude utilities from building again, and those with current low cost excess capacity or the ability to build efficiently should be able to compete very effectively. A second valuable benefit of incremental reform movements is that they are easier to reverse if experience proves them inefficient.

Strains and tensions in the Existing System

Before I turn to the policy direction I believe the FERC should take, I want to call attention to two forces currently at play that threaten the old system, and will indeed damage it badly if the FERC, in concert with state commissions, does not move with some facility to reform the regulation of electricity.

(1) *Incentives for uneconomic generation*. Many of the pricing errors described earlier have created incentives for new suppliers to break into previously utility-dominated markets. However, far more threatening to existing utility systems, these errors have also created strong incentives for requirements customers, both at the retail and wholesale level, to escape their existing utility systems and seek new sources of supply. This is, of course, one of principal incentives behind the demands for greater wheeling and transmission access at the retail level.

It should be remembered that it was the industrial consumers, exercising their fuel-switching options, that did so much to break down the old system of natural gas regulation and led inevitably to the Commission's actions in Order No. 436. In the electricity area, the ability of the industrials to go off-system, to "vote with their feet" as some of their representatives put it, is probably more modest than in the natural gas area; it essentially amounts to the option to self-generate. To some extent, too, the incentives for industrials to leave utility systems has been lessened by the increasing willingness of utilities, and their state regulators, to permit various forms of discriminatory pricing to industrials, such as "industrial incentive rates" and discount rates conditioned on industrials' agreeing to postpone or cancel cogeneration developments.

(2) *Federal/state conflicts in the current system*. In a similar vein, I see rapidly escalating tensions in relations between the FERC and state commissions, tensions that are primarily the consequence of economic forces recognized in the FERC's decisions in the *Middle South and American Electric Power* cases.[13] These tensions reflect the concerns that many state commissions have for their own jurisdiction over future supply, and for their ability to protect their ratepayers. These tensions are very much a product of the

current system. There is a conflict between the traditional regulatory prerogatives of state commissions, (including their recently increased interest in power supply planning), and the traditional Federal Power Act mandates to the FERC to encourage greater levels of coordination and nonmarket integration between utility systems. If the current system persists and is not reformed in the relatively near future, there tensions will worsen. I want to stress that I make this statement from the perspective of having seen both sides of the picture — as a state Commissioner in Illinois for seven years and as a FERC Commissioner for over three years; and I do not ascribe to either side of that tension an undue desire to protect turf.

Needed Regulatory Reforms

I support Chairman Hesse's proposal that the FERC move with some facility to deal with the major components of the FERC's regulation of electricity; in my view, they all need attention and reform. I, therefore, generally support her agenda for reform, especially as she has indicated some level of flexibility as to the exact order of priorities and as to timing, on both of which I have some views. First, however, I want to briefly survey[14] the general direction of reform which I believe the FERC needs to take in each of its major areas of regulation.

(1) *Reform of the pricing of coordination services.* The pricing of coordination services was one of the principal focuses of Phase I of the 1985 electricity Notice of Inquiry, and an area in which we received a detailed and instructive record from all parts on the industry. I am gratified that Chairman Hesse has, in recent announcements, recognized the importance of this record upon which a good deal of the staff analysis must rely. I believe the Commission should move with some facility to rationalize the increasingly liberal pricing practices that staff has developed over the years for the coordination markets in situations where arms-length bargaining between independent traders in power exists. Many commenters, including most of the investor-owned utilities, conceded that Commission practice had already created a considerable level of liberalization and that we should at least rationalize and codify this level; perhaps we should ex-

COMPETITION IN ELECTRICITY

tend it further.

I believe the Commission should explore the feasibility of market-based negotiated pricing between actors in the market in any situation where we are able to identify a workably competitive bulk power market. If we are able to create meaningful categorizations of markets in terms of their competitiveness, it is not certain that our old categorization of "coordination" and "requirements" service would continue to make sense. I recognize that developing clear criteria for such a determination will require considerable analysis. I suspect that our staff has advanced that analysis since the 1985 Notice of Inquiry. I also think that we may gain some valuable information on this determination from the Western System Power Pools (WSPP) experiment, although I do not believe that the expected results from that experiment should lure us into complacency or distract us from our own analytical effort, or that its timeframe should slow down our generic effort.

One of the most difficult and controversial issues addressed by many commenters in the 1985 Notice of Inquiry was whether any market can be viewed as "workably competitive" without providing for access to transmission facilities by competing suppliers. Again, the WSPP experiment may yield some useful insights into the degree to which some right of transmission access, accompanied by adequate transmission capacity, is a sine qua non of a workably competitive market. My tentative view is that it is unlikely that workably competitive bulk power markets can be created without supplier access rights.

It may be, however, that some sellers are already exposed to sufficient competition by virtue of interconnections with various buyers as to permit the conclusion that they have no monopoly power in the bulk power market. Further, it is almost certainly true that implementation by states of an "all source" bidding scheme would enhance this possibility. Hence, I think the urgings of the investor-owned utilities that our existing pricing of coordination markets could be liberalized further, even to the point of establishing marketplace pricing in certain areas, is a serious possibility that is well worth exploring. It will permit the Commission to move away from the current, rather awkward hybrid between cost-based and market-oriented pricing concepts that currently characterizes coordination pricing, and I suspect, still imposes some constraints on efficient, freely negotiated arrangements. More market-based coordination pricing should, in turn, enhance the efficiency of bulk power markets.

(2) *Reform of transmission pricing.* One of the most urgent issues facing the Commission is that of rethinking its transmission pricing model so as to improve the efficiency of bulk power markets. There are currently three principal regulatory problems facing regulators of the transmission system, the solutions for which are absolutely critical to more efficient electricity supply and to more efficient bulk power markets:

i.   Determining how to assure that efficient amounts of transmission capacity are built on a timely basis.
ii. Deciding who should build, operate and have access to existing and planned transmission capacity, and on what terms.
iii. Learning how to price transmission service or services for those who are given access to them.

A part of the problem with developing an effective strategy towards a more efficient transmission system is that regulatory authority over these issues is both fragmented and incomplete. State agencies have virtually plenary authority over the "need" certification and siting of transmission facilities in their jurisdictions, and the FERC has virtually plenary authority over transmission pricing. But, as state commissioners have pointed out, however well they might certify and site transmission facilities, they will not be built to meet all needs if FERC's pricing of transmission does not provide appropriate incentives. Similarly, while the FERC can increase the economic incentives to build transmission capacity through appropriate pricing, it has virtually no control over state siting and certification procedures where noneconomic factors, such as risks to health and environment can play a major role.

The report of the National Governors' Association's (NGA) Transmission Task Force in February of this year outlined very well some of the major problems facing the nation if it is to ensure development of adequate transmission capacity.[15]

342   COMPETITION IN ELECTRICITY

The NGA recently approved some useful recommendations for improving state certification and siting procedures, although these recommendations were modest in the most troublesome area — the development of large interstate lines for transmission facilities designed to serve the bulk power markets. If there is one area in which ongoing Congressional attention, designed to encourage states to move ahead with these improvements and to face up to the tough interstate issues, would be productive and important to this country's long term electricity future, this may be it.

Improved transmission pricing will also, of course, provide more appropriate incentives to wheel power on a voluntary basis, although it is doubtful that this would lead to sufficient levels of transmission access to maximize the efficiencies of the bulk power markets. Still an improvement of FERC's pricing of transmission is an important and urgent first step in the required direction. Certainly, without appropriately priced transmission service, it would be difficult to advocate a new regulatory regime that mandated such service, since one could not be sure that he would be enhancing efficiency.

In making a strong case for moving ahead with reform of transmission pricing, I am aware that this is one of the most difficult pricing tasks facing the Commission. Because of the technical nature of alternating current transmission grids, accurate pricing of transmission service seems to be an extremely difficult task. There are major costs, such as unintended power flows on other systems, that are barely accounted for in present pricing structures. Fortunately, not only has there been considerable internal staff analysis of transmission pricing, and some useful comments received in the Notice of Inquiry, but there are some major studies on transmission pricing and the technical impacts of wheeling either recently published or soon to be published by major research organizations.[16] Hence, while I think the task of transmission pricing is formidable, the FERC may soon have more ability to evaluate just how formidable it really is.

(3) *Rethinking of transmission access policies.* Transmission access, of course, is the issue that raises the highest level of emotion for many actors in the industry. It was certainly the most actively debated issue in the 1985 Notice of Inquiry and one upon which various interests were most

deeply divided. I think the level of rational debate will be greatly heightened, and the level of emotion reduced, if a clear distinction is drawn at the outset between what might be described as "supplier access," i.e., some right of access on reasonable terms to utility transmission grids for all suppliers of electricity, and "customer access," i.e., the ability of retail and wholesale requirements customers to gain transmission access to reach suppliers other than their "native" utility. Because "customer" or "retail" access raises questions of bypass that go to the very heart of the state-regulated system, it is an especially sensitive issue. My tentative conclusion is that this seems to be an issue that this Commission does not necessarily have to deal with as it turns its attention to the reform of its regulation of bulk power markets.[17]

A truth that must be recognized, however, is that a workably competitive generating market among gencos can only approximate desired levels of economic efficiency if, at a minimum, all gencos have a right of transmission access to a multiplicity of potential buyers. Failure to provide such access will lead to gencos facing monopsony power which will increase genco risk and, therefore, genco costs. Such failures will also limit regional specialization and encourage plant sitings at multiple utility boundaries to reduce buyer monopsony power rather than at economically efficient sites. Hence, I view a greater level of supplier access than we have at present as critical to the development of efficient bulk power markets.

I should stress, however, that even with respect to supplier access, there are fundamental clarifications needed. For instance, is the "right" to transmission access to be limited to a utility's surplus transmission capacity; or does it impose an obligation to build transmission facilities to meet all demands? Would the first "right" really provide meaningful transmission access? Further, would some notion of a utility obligation to build transmission facilities to meet all demands of a bulk power market be meaningful in the absence of an effective regime for certification and siting of transmission facilities on a timely basis? In short, the serious problems in the different areas of regulation of transmission are closely interrelated.

That is one reason, aside from technical complexity, why

COMPETITION IN ELECTRICITY

supplier transmission access is not an easy issue to address. However, I believe it can and should be addressed soon. I define "soon" as when the FERC has created appropriate pricing systems for coordination transactions and transmission services. At that time the agency should be in a position to better assess what sort of mandatory supplier access regime, if any, is necessary, and whether it could be achieved under existing statutory authority, or whether the help of the Congress will be needed. While awaiting reform of pricing before moving on access seems like a rational strategy and ordering of priorities, I am nevertheless cognizant of, and not complacent about, rejecting for the present the arguments that *we cannot* proceed to reform bulk power pricing without mandatory transmission access for suppliers, and that *we cannot* proceed with an all-source bidding scheme without a similar regime. I am prepared to reconsider my views with additional evidence and analysis.

(4) *Reform of FERC regulation of requirements service.* Requirements service regulation is characterized by a cost-plus approach, in most respects quite similar to retail regulation at the state level, though with some significant differences such as FERC's court-mandated requirement to consider "price squeeze" issues. This area of FERC regulation was the primary subject of Phase II of the 1985-86 Notice of Inquiry, which focused upon some of the fundamental pricing issues, such as the efficacy of marginal cost pricing, the efficacy of current methods of capital cost recovery, and various aspects of what may broadly be called incentive rate regulation and existing barriers to such regulation. These are important issues in which the FERC could provide leadership in the reform of the old regulatory system that still pervades much of state regulation, and I do think they should be expeditiously addressed, but they should not distract us from our broader focus of creating efficient bulk power markets.

To my mind, the truly challenging issues with respect to wholesale requirements service is how, as wholesale requirements customers develop their own generation or seek to acquire supply in more competitive bulk power markets, they may be effectively integrated into those markets without causing inefficiencies on their native utility systems. The portion of wholesale service for these customers that typically requires cost-plus regulation seems to be declining. I believe that a solution, compatible with the needs of all the major actors in this market, that would effectively phase out our cost-plus regulation of this area over time is achievable.[18] That to me would be a better focus for our efforts than the inordinate amount of time the Commission, and contesting parties, spend on wholesale rate increases, often quite small in dollar terms, and on related price squeeze issues. The considerable amount of money and time these same parties appear to expend on bitterly contested antitrust suits might also be eliminated.

THE FERC'S INITIATIVE TO EXPLORE PURPA REFORM

I have elaborated on why I think it is necessary to consider reform of all the major parts of FERC's regulation of electricity. I now want to focus upon those elements of reform discussed in chairman Hesse's June speech and subsequently explored in somewhat more detail by the FERC staff through a series of informal exchanges with consumer groups, with state utility commissioners, and with various groups in the industry.

Principal Merits of "All Source" Bidding

As I said earlier, the basic concepts set forth in Chairman Hesse's June 10 speech are sound. My observations concern how I see the proposal fitting into the changes in the industry I have discussed; into what I see as a growing crisis in its regulation; and, in particular, into the evolution of the industry under section 210 of PURPA. The reform package suggested, and I use the word "suggested" only because there has been no Commission decision to formally endorse any specific proposal, seems to me to have three principal merits.

(1) It will give state PUCs a rational basis for reconciling the potentially conflicting mandates of their own supply planning prerogatives and of section 210 of PURPA.

(2) It will give non-QF independent power producers (IPPs) a clearer avenue to electricity markets in those states or utility systems which adopt "all source" bidding. One practical concern with the existing PURPA section 210 scheme is whether it might, in some respect, start to act as a barrier to non-QF IPPs, who cannot call upon the utility's

346   COMPETITION IN ELECTRICITY

PURPA section 210 obligation to purchase their power. PUCs may create a more efficient electricity supply in the long term if the appropriate bidding system is set up and an appropriate contracting regime is developed to accompany it.

Some have asserted that the IPPs proposal in the PURPA reform package is premature and not strictly necessary at this point. I disagree. First, I think it can make an important contribution to immediate rationalization and increased efficiency of the section 210 scheme. Moreover, consideration by the FERC of the role IPPs can play, both in the PURPA scheme and in the bulk power markets, generally is a matter of more serious and urgent concern than meets the eye. The fact that there are not in existence today a significant number of IPPs does not mean there is no urgency to the issue; indeed, I think it argues more strongly for the reverse. We have witnessed over the last three or four years an explosion of development in a narrow range of technologies under PURPA once an avenue to the market was opened for those technologies. It is very possible that a clear avenue or avenues for independent power producers will produce a similar development of hithertofore unutilized supply options that could produce greater efficiencies than does the present system. Of course, this cannot be guaranteed, but the nation will never find out what the potential is unless it moves to reduce or eliminate the serious regulatory and institutional barriers to the IPP potential.

That the FERC's regulatory policy towards IPPs is in need of investigation is almost axiomatic, because in reality the FERC does not have a defined policy. It was clear from our approval earlier this year of the concept of the Ocean State project, which I supported, that we had not developed a clear rationale for the pricing of power from stand-alone independent generators; nor have we approached some of the difficult issues of affiliate relations with purchasing utilities. It is clear, too, that the FERC is likely to be faced with other proposals that will have an IPPs component in them. Even though the FERC will probably continue to consider most of these on a case-by-case basis in the context of their specific facts, the agency needs to develop generic criteria to guide it. I believe that is best done in the context of a generic proceeding such as a rulemaking. That is essentially the approach that Chairman Hesse seems to be supporting.

(3) A third major advantage of the reform package suggested, closely related to the second, is that it would seem to provide a basis for more closely reconciling what are currently two very different regulatory avenues towards what should be a national bulk power market: (1) PURPA, and, (2) our traditional regulation of coordination transactions under sections 205 and 206 of the Federal Power Act. Moreover, it would clarify and rationalize to a greater degree than before the role of IPPs in each of these avenues.

I think there is perhaps a fourth advantage to the package. It would essentially build upon developments that are already occurring in state implementation of section 210 of PURPA, developments which seem to be pushing the parameters of the regulatory scheme the FERC established in 1980. While some states are probing or have started to implement bidding scheme, others are clearly holding back pending clarification of the status of such schemes under section 210. To me, both developments bespeak the necessity of the FERC addressing the issue of when, and under what conditions, bidding mechanisms are a proper implementation of its section 210 rules by state commissions.

Unresolved Issues in "All Source" Bidding Proposals

There are, of course, a myriad of issues that Chairman Hesse's June speech raised, some of which will have to be addressed by the FERC, and some of which are better left to state commissions in their implementation. Even though I think the reform package suggested in her speech, if adopted, would comprise relatively modest reforms, particularly given their voluntary nature, it raises some complex issues in the design and implementation of bidding schemes and of related contracting regimes. However, while important and appropriate for debate, these are essentially questions of the mechanics or implementation of the scheme. Hence, they should be kept in perspective, especially as many of them will probably have to be made not by the FERC, but by state commissions in the context of the particular circumstances of each state, e.g., the degree to which its public utility commission wishes to play an up-front role in administering and monitoring a bidding scheme. It should be underscored that, under the package, the adoption of a bidding scheme is voluntary and that states would be able to do so on their own timetable.

(1) *Burdens on PUCs.* One principal concern in designing the parameters of a bidding scheme is that, however conceptually appealing, it may not in fact be implementable in many states, e.g., those that do not have adequate resources to effectively monitor bidding schemes. Another is that FERC should not impose conditions so strict that it discourages states already contemplating bidding. A particular focus of mine as to the former concern is whether we can expect states to effectively design bidding systems in which the utility can be both bid evaluator and a potential builder of new generation capacity without unduly favoring its own generation.

However, in view of our probably limited authority to mandate a state's decisions as to the future role of its regulated utilities, I believe our best approach, to both these concerns, is to leave flexibility to state commissions on issues such as this. That should enable states to tailor bidding schemes to their own particular circumstances, a philosophy that the FERC has generally applied in state implementation of section 210 of PURPA to date. However, there are certain minimum requirements of an effective bidding scheme that this Commission will have to impose to guard against abuses and to ensure that the potential efficiency gains of a bidding scheme are not outweighed by a series of built-in inefficiencies. This determination, of exactly what we have to prescribe, will present some difficult questions for the Commission.

(2) *Current knowledge limitations.* I have concerns about the analysis necessary for a quality Commission proposal and how quickly we can move towards a Commission decision. My discussions with staff members have reassured me that a good deal of internal analysis is taking place and that we may see some of this in the near future. I will, as I always have, insist on a quality analysis to the degree it is obtainable within the constraints of this agency. However, this ongoing concern should not be translated into a notion that I want to slow the PURPA reform initiative down. Indeed, I believe a good deal can be achieved within the next year or so, though I do recognize the ability of powerful interest groups to slow the process down, if they so choose. My prin-

cipal concern on the pace of progress is that we give ourselves enough time to ensure that we move our decisions on the basis of high quality analysis, and that we allow those who are interested in giving us constructive input sufficient time to do so.

(3) *Important structural issues.* I do not want to prolong this testimony further by a detailed elaboration of all the issues relating to the bidding and IPPs proposals. Rather, I want only to note a couple of fundamental distinctions and make three observations that I hope will assist the debate and analysis.

    i. When talking about *"all source" bidding*, I think it is critical to make a distinction between the ability of all potential off- system suppliers of electricity (i.e., all sources but the purchasing utility) to participate in the bid; and whether the purchasing utility itself should participate in the bid. The latter is, to my mind, a far more difficult and controversial question because it goes to the heart of the future role regulated utilities will play under the state regulatory system. As a former state commissioner, I have expressed some skepticism about the ability or desire of many state commissions to get into the business of running bidding systems. However, this is probably an issue for state commissions to work for out themselves.

Hence, I think it important that the FERC give states flexibility in this regard. Certainly, we should not preclude states from permitting utilities to play a major role in providing new generation for their systems if states so wish. While I have concerns about self-dealing and the ability of state commissions to police that, that potential problem is already present to some degree in view of the ability of utilities to own 50 percent interests in QFs under section 210 of PURPA. Moreover, there is not evidence of the sorts of self-dealing and favoritism towards utility-owned QFs that might raise serious concerns. Southern California Edison, for instance, which seems to be emerging as one of the major critics of the section 210 scheme, nevertheless has one of the largest QF subsidiaries in the business, Mission Energy. Utilities have been creative in suggesting ways in which utilities may

COMPETITION IN ELECTRICITY

continue to play a major role in future generation without raising the self-dealing or favoritism problems. The existence of numerous options for states on this issue should give some assurance that the FERC is not passing down to state commissions unmanageable decisions as to what role they wish their utilities to play in future power supply.

ii. A second difficult issue that has emerged from the dialogue between the FERC staff and industry interests is the degree to which blocks of capacity might be set aside for various generation sources or suppliers. Again, a distinction is useful. To me, there is a difference between: (1) a set-aside that carves out a certain portion of the utility's future needs for a QF-only or for the "all source" bidding system, and permits the utility to supply the remainder under the traditional cost-plus system, and, (2) a set-aside of a certain block of capacity for special preference for certain technologies, such as wind or solar technologies. The former would insulate potentially major parts of the utility's future supply from the efficiencies of the bidding system and, worse, would have the potential of creating a "QF or QF/IPPs ghetto," as the term has been coined. I do not see how the FERC could permit such set-asides without undermining section 210 of PURPA itself. The latter set-aside might, in the name of research and development, be viewed as less objectionable. However, I am generally opposed to *any* form of set-aside, absent strong justification, and I am certainly opposed to excluding certain sources, such as Canadian power, if "all-source" bidding is adopted. Denying potentially efficient suppliers access to electricity markets obviously cannot be a part of a program designed to improve economic efficiency.

iii. Finally, a major focus of dialogue has been the commonly debated issue of *transmission access* for alternative suppliers. A number of groups and, interestingly, some major utilities have urged that an all-source bidding scheme is only meaningful if coupled with transmission access, and that the FERC really should not move forward with the bidding proposal without considering and doing something about supplier access. On the other hand, we have been urged by major interests, including most state commissions, to examine supplier access in the broader context of our overall reform of bulk power regulation. Moreover, as I elaborated above, there are a number of major pricing reforms that can plausibly be viewed as prerequisites to imposing a broader supplier access regime in the name of enhancing efficiency. For these reasons, I believe we can, and should, move forward with the current proposal without, at this point, considering supplier access a necessary ingredient. In so doing, we should recognize that the markets that will be created by bidding systems are likely to be more balkanized and less efficient that those that would develop if a broader supplier access, accompanied by an adequate transmission system, were available.

There is, however, one discrete improvement in transmission access that I think could be achieved under the present PURPA reform proposal. I believe the FERC could create an option for state commissions implementing bidding systems to condition participation in a bidding scheme upon the aspirant participant's not using its monopoly over transmission facilities to deny access to the bid market to another potential bidder. For instance, if a neighboring utility wished to participate in the bid, it would have to make its *surplus* transmission capacity available to a distant utility that also wished to bid. The major problem with this concept is that it may have to be limited to providing surplus transmission capacity, not an easy thing to identify or monitor, unless the bidding specifications were seeking capacity over a long enough timeframe to permit the construction of new transmission facilities. If it were a sufficiently long-term proposition, there are some creative approaches a state commission could adopt to encourage the construction of needed transmission capacity. It could, for instance, allow the distant utility to own and take the financial risk of the transmission addition and require the intermediary utility only to create the regulatory path for its construction and to operate the facility as part of its integrated grid. These are clearly complex questions which a state commission or certification agency would be in the best position to address.

This limited concept for expanding transmission access to bid markets, if it were adopted by the FERC, would essentially create an additional option for state commissions to broaden the bidding market and ensure fair play between potential bidders. The FERC would, of course, have to take a hard look at its legal authority under PURPA to permit states such an option. I would only note that there are in section 210 of PURPA provisions that deal with discrimination.

I fully recognize that there are other major serious issues to be addressed in the process of formulating reform proposals that countenance more competitive means of achieving future supply, such as the reliability of that supply and the role of subsidies. However, I do not feel it appropriate that I discuss today all such issues, on which considerable dialogue and research is yet to occur.

PRIORITIES FOR REFORM

The debate over whether transmission access has to be an element in a PURPA reform proposal raises the broader question as to the Commission's order of priorities, and whether it is appropriate to proceed first with PURPA reform. Some quite cogent critics have suggested that we should move first to reform our regulation of the bulk power markets and of transmission, as the 1985 Notice of Inquiry suggested we would, and then to tackle PURPA. Some have also suggested that we really cannot reform any parts of our regulation in isolation. Since I was a vigorous supporter of the 1985 Notice of Inquiry and that Inquiry postponed PURPA review, my preferences are clear. The order of priorities, however, is less important than a commitment to proceed. All the parts of electricity regulation are interdependent.

Parts Take Meaning From the Whole

While there are important issues in the electricity industry that need tackling, we are not required to proceed under a sense of crisis. I therefore think it is entirely appropriate to deal with our reform of electricity in smaller, carefully crafted packages, always cognizant of the interrelationships to the larger picture. This, I recognize, is not fully comforting to those affected by our decisions who are well aware of those interrelationships and who are nervous about commenting on reforms on one part of the package when they do not have what they feel are sufficient details on other parts. However, I believe we can proceed down this route with a sufficient level of intellectual integrity to ensure that we are taking account of those relationships, as long as there is a clear understanding that we will address those other parts of the package, such as bulk power pricing and transmission pricing and access, in the near future. I expect this is Chairman Hesse's intention.

A Preferred Sequencing

Furthermore, I believe the Commission should move to review the principal components of our regulation of the increasingly competitive bulk power markets, (coordination pricing, transmission pricing and supplier transmission access), and our pricing of requirements service, as part of a single coordinated review. This is necessary to ensure adequate analysis of the critical interrelationships, even if proposals emanating therefrom are considered on an appropriately staggered basis. This would essentially create a large and challenging "Phase Two" to our electricity initiative. However, it would be one that builds analytically upon a very full and, in some areas, sophisticated record created in the 1985 Notice of Inquiry, supplemented by the 1987 PURPA hearings and a good deal of subsequent analysis by Commission staff, by a variety of other organizations such as EPRI and NRRI, and by leading experts in the field. That would leave to a "Third Phase" a review of "incentive regulation" (a major focus of Phase Two of the Notice of Inquiry). This is an area in which the Chairman has expressed strong interest and which I view as most pertinent to reform of the FERC's cost-plus regulation in the requirements area. While I share this interest, I think reform of the FERC's bulk power regulation and of pricing can justifiably take priority. For one thing, these reforms are important to the whole future drection of the industry. Moreover, a decision on new bulk power structures and a decision on how to price and fit our regulation of requirements service into this structure, should precede decisions on how we might reform specific aspects of the requirements area itself.

I recognize this proposal would entail some reordering of the priorities suggested by Chairman Hesse in her July 9, 1987 testimony before the Senate Committee on Energy and Natural Resources. However, she indicated flexibility in her views as to the order of priorities.

LEGISLATIVE PRIORITIES

In speaking about priorities for reform, I have made no mention of legislative priorities. The Commission, over the past several years, seems to be acting under a general assumption that it should first conduct a thorough inquiry and analysis into all the major areas of its regulation of electricity, and to make such reforms as seem reasonable under its existing legal authority, insofar as it can. I think the general view is that if, in so doing, the Commission encounters serious roadblocks, or if its administrative reforms are not working in certain areas due to insufficient authority, then we should approach the Congress for legislation to correct these problems. In general, I support this approach.

There is, moreover, a general view in Washington that this Congress is unlikely to undertake major energy reform legislation, certainly in electricity. Even if that is true, it should not preclude the FERC from recommending discrete and relatively noncontroversial legislative changes over the next year or so that may greatly assist our effort, if one is made, to effectively reform electricity regulation. The Commission staff has already developed a list of potential "technical amendments" to section 210 of PURPA, or to the definitions in section 201 of the Federal Power Act. Some of these changes may be important to the FERC's rationalizing and modernizing of its certification process. Amongst needed legislative reforms may be greater authority to permit utilities a full ownership role in QF's from which they do not purchase.

The analysis of the "proposed" incremental reform can be summarized in four generalizations:

(1) A strong case exists for the FERC moving incrementally with reform of its regulation of electricity with a view towards encouraging a more competitive generating sector. Accompanying this movement should be an emphasis on changing the pricing model for services that remain regulated.

(2) There is recognized need for incremental reform of the FERC's regulation of bulk power markets.

(3) The package of PURPA reforms, and the associated review of FERC regulation of independent power producers under the Federal Power Act, as described generally by Chairman Hesse in her June speech, is an appropriate step and one that I support, subject to two principal cautions. The first is that, as complexity in implementation of the proposal is revealed, the FERC must provide sufficient time for quality internal analysis and for quality industry input, to permit development of a well-formulated proposal for rulemaking consideration. A second concern is that so much implementation must take place at the state commission level. The "proposals" highlight many difficult decisions that state commissions will have to make about the role of the generating sector. I believe that this Commission should not pass down to the state level such difficult decisions without giving PUCs a set of options and expert analysis on the consequences of alternative choices.

(4) Because I believe that reform of all the major components of our regulation, as well as PURPA, is so important, the Commission should proceed with a review of this regulation at its earliest opportunity. We should not let the PURPA reform initiative be viewed as piecemeal reform that was not coordinated with other elements of reform, especially the reform of the bulk power markets. Accordingly, I expect to press for a coordinated review of the major components of our regulation of bulk power markets and requirements pricing as a "second phase," following immediately on completion of, or some progress on the PURPA reform.

FINAL SUMMARY AND CONCLUSION

The principal conclusion to be drawn from this testimony is that restructuring the electricity industry to rely less on regulation and more on market forces to determine prices and capacity in the generating sector has significant potential for improving both the economic efficiency of the generating sector, and regulatory pricing policies in the transmission and distribution sectors. The principal justification for the conclusion is that for technological, legal, and macroeconomic reasons, the economics of scale in generation that justified economic regulation of the generating sector in the early decades of the industry now seem to be attainable in optimal or near optimal amounts by market energized and market disciplined gencos. These reasons are not transient. Furthermore, the pricing traditions institutionalized in regulatory agencies fall short of inducing desired and attainable levels of economic efficiency. Moreover, these traditions have proven to be resistant to reform. Creating market disciplined gencos offers an opportunity to limit the scope of regulatory pricing, and to create constructive pressures to reform regulated pricing in areas where it will still be applied.

The conclusions of immediate relevance are less sweeping. The FERC must not only formulate end-state objectives, it must also formulate transition paths and procedures for testing the wisdom of transition moves. Some proposed regulatory reforms stand independent of the stated end-state objective and others, while desirable steps towards that objective, also have other justification. In the first category are reforms of the regulatory pricing model, (including the capital recovery model), and investigation of transmission issues. In the second category are bulk power market improvements and the clarification of PURPA section 210 bidding possibilities.

I am convinced that significant restructuring of the electricity industry can improve the economic efficiency of the industry and that the FERC should take the lead in developing alternatives, creating the debates necessary to inform, and creating some consensus about both transition paths and possible end-states. In an industry as complex as the electricity industry, especially one that can exploit important economies of coordination only through a difficult to manage, and difficult to optimally price, transmission grid, it is especially important that the public debate be thorough. It is also important that all parties recognize that certain knowledge is needed that does not now exist.

Having said this, it is also desirable to remind ourselves of the paraphrased warning of Dr. Johnson: "If all consequences must be known before action is taken, nothing will be done."

ENDNOTES

1. "Regulation" here and elsewhere in the paper is a shorthand expression for "economic regulation," which in turn is defined as government control over entry and exit conditions and over prices. Such controls need not be absolute. "Economic regulation" is distinguished from safety and/or environmental regulation, and, further, is to be distinguished from ant trust regulation. The debate at hand is whether to relax or eliminate some or all of the price controls and entry and exit controls in the generating side of the industry. No serious proposals have been made to remove antitrust and/or safety and/or environmental regulations.

2. Most of my criticisms of pricing in this system refer to the cost-plus revenue recovery and pricing model that pervades most state retail regulation. This model also permeates the FERC's regulation of wholesale requirements sales, typically between an integrated utility with full service generating capability and a customer utility that is dependent on a long-term basis on the supplying utility for all or part of its generation needs. I do not view these wholesales requirements relationships as part of what I refer to herein as the bulk power markets, which have typically been regulated at the wholesale level under the FERC's coordination pricing formula.

3. The term "forecasting failure" rather than "forecasting mistake" is used to allow for the possibility that the forecasts were based on the best forecasting technology available, but still failed to generate accurate forecasts. By contrast, a forecasting mistake — and evidence indicated many were made — is a forecast not based on the

best available forecasting technology.

4. Table B-68 "Bond Yields and Interest Rates, 1929-86" *Economic Report of the President*, (U.S. Government Printing Office, Washington, D.C., 1987) p. 324.

5. "Interest Rates and Bond Yields," *Economic Indicators, June 1987*, Prepared for the Joint Economic Committee by the Council of Economic Advisers (U.S. Government Printing Office, Washington, D.C.) p.30.

6. One estimate of the significance of such demand-perverse pricing is included in a speech by Mr. Jerry D. Geist to the annual convention of the Edison Electric Institute in June 1986. The speech, titled "Place Your Bets: Three Paths to the Future," noted that the real price of electricity increased 2.2 cents/Kwh between 1980 and 1984, and 0.6 cent/Kwh, or more than 25 percent of the increases was attributable to "demand downturn."

7. A major element in these cost overruns is, however, attributable to accumulated interest, which has been increased both by planning miscalculations and by higher interest rates.

8. Notice of Inquiry, Regulation of Electricity Sales-For-Resale and Transmission Service, Docket No. RM85-17-000; Phase I, issued May 30, 1985, reported at 31 FERC paragraph 61,228; Phase II, issued June 28, 1985, reported at 31 FERC paragraph 61,376.

9. It is worth noting that the art of macroeconomic forecasting has not noticeably improved since the early 1970s. Consequently, the forecasts currently used in the industry as well as those embodied in this testimony should be viewed skeptically.

10. Trade reports in recent weeks noted a couple of exceptions to this generalization.

11. It is worth noting that the FERC was not required by Title I to review its pricing policies and that it has not to date gone through a thorough reassessment of these policies.

12. The June speech by Mr. Jerry D. Geist cited in footnote 6 is an example.

13. See especially *AEC Service Corp.*, 32 FERC paragraph 61,363 (1985); *Kentucky Power Company*, 36 FERC paragraph 61,227 (1986); *Middle South Service, Inc.*, 31 FERC paragraph 61,305 (1985), reh. denied 32 FERC

paragraph 61,425 (1985), affd. *Mississippi Industries v. FERC*, 808 F.2d 1525 (D.C. Circ. 1987).

14. I suspect that, if the Commission moves into these other areas of potential reform, we will have opportunities to expound our thoughts in greater detail.

15. *Moving Power: Flexibility for the Future.* Report of the National Governors' Association Committee on Energy and Environment Task Force on Electricity Transmission (undated).

16. See, for example, *Some Economic Principles for Pricing Wheeled Power*, by Kelly, Henderson and Nagler, National Regulatory Research Institute (August 1987); *Technical Limitations to Transmission System Operation*, Power Technologies Inc. and Electric Power Research Institute (publication imminent).

17. Any effort to deal with retail access at the federal level may have to be a legislative effort.

18. The Commission received some helpful analysis of this area in Phase I of the 1985 Notice of Inquiry. See, e.g., the comments of National Economic Research Associates, Inc., and of Pacific Gas and Electric Company.

CHAPTER 16: REGULATING INDEPENDENT POWER PRODUCERS: A POLICY ANALYSIS*

The Office of Economic Policy
Federal Energy Regulatory Commission

INTRODUCTION AND SUMMARY

In recent years, an increasing amount of electric power has been generated by companies other than traditional electric utilities. Many of these nontraditional sources are eligible for status as qualifying facilities (QFs) under the Public Utility Regulatory Policies Act (PURPA) of 1978. Most QFs have been exempted from traditional public utility regulation under the Federal Power Act (FPA). However, nontraditional producers other than QFs are subject to FPA regulation.

This paper examines the Commission's current regulatory policies toward one important class of nontraditional producers: independent power producers (IPPs). We define IPPs as producers other than QFs that are unaffiliated with franchised utilities in the IPPs market area and that for other reasons lack significant market power. Unlike traditional utilities, IPPs do not sell power in any franchised service territory where they have an exclusive right to sell power to retail customers. Unlike QF producers, IPPs have no legally mandated right to sell power to a local utility. IPP sales are arranged solely through competitive business arrangements, and IPP prices are thus limited by the offers of competing suppliers (including the option of the customer to supply power to itself). The profitability of an IPP is derived solely from its ability to deliver low cost, reliable power and its willingness to assume investment risks.

In addition to discussing current IPPs policies, the paper explores alternative regulatory options for IPPS. In particular, it examines the potential desirability of relaxing the of Commission's regulation of IPPs in light of the absence significant market power possessed by this class of producers.

---

*This is a Staff paper prepared on October 13, 1987 containing a preliminary analysis of the regulation of independent power producers. It does not necessarily reflect the views of the Commission or any of its members

The paper draws a number of conclusions. The Commission should consider relaxing its Current cost-based rate regulation for IPPs. Traditional regulation of IPPs may be unnecessary to protect the public against the abuse of market power, since IPPs do not possess significant market power. In addition, current regulation discourages the development of IPPs because it distorts price signals and does not provide IPPs with the opportunities for financial rewards commensurate with their risks. The development of IPPs resulting from relaxed regulation could provide a number of important benefits. These benefits include helping to alleviate potential future constraints on the nation's electric generating capacity, reducing the cost of electricity to consumers, demonstrating new technologies, and avoiding wasteful investments made to attain QF status, as well as a number of indirect benefits.

While the Commission should consider relaxing its regulation of all IPPs, certain additional safeguards may be necessary for IPPs owned by traditional utilities. These safeguards may need to be considered to address the special problems that may arise due to utility ownership of IPPs.

Relaxing the regulation of IPPs should not affect the current division of jurisdiction between state regulatory agencies and the Commission. In addition, relaxed IPPs regulation should not interfere with the service obligations of franchised utilities.

The paper discusses these issues in greater detail below. The first section begins by describing the current regulatory environment and the problems that arise from that environment. The second section then explores the advantages that might result from relaxing the regulation of IPPs. The third section discusses the Commission's recent orders involving IPPs. The fourth section describes an alternative set of policies, policies that would relax the regulation of IPPs. The fifth section examines the specific criteria that might be used to determine IPP status, and the sixth section explores some of the implications of these alternative policies. This paper does not discuss the scope of the Commission's legal authority under the Federal Power Act and PURPA to adopt alternative regulatory options for IPPs.

THE CURRENT REGULATORY ENVIRONMENT

An Overview of Present Regulatory Policies

IPPs, like most traditional investor owned utilities selling wholesale electricity,[1] are subject to public utility regulation under the Federal Power Act (FPA). That regulation covers four areas. First, prices charged by companies for services under the Commission's jurisdiction are subject to the commission's approval. Second, companies are subject to extensive reporting requirements on their costs, finances, and operations. Third, disposition of property, issuance of securities, and mergers and acquisitions are subject to the commission's approval. Finally, certain interlocking directorates are prohibited unless authorized by the Commission.

The Commission's rate regulation has set prices based on the seller's costs in two different ways. For requirements service (i.e., long term, firm sales to supply most or all of a customer's power requirements), the commission has generally set rates based on traditional cost of service principles. Requirements rates are thus generally designed to recover the supplier's total embedded costs.[2] For coordination services (i.e., all other services), rates often reflect both the supplier's costs and other factors.[3] Thus, rates for coordination service often differ from the seller's costs, although those costs are generally a factor in determining rates.

The Commission's reporting regulations help to facilitate and enforce its rate and non-rate regulation. Jurisdictional companies are required to file substantial amounts of information on their costs, finances, and operations. This information is used to establish cost-based rates and generally to ensure that the filing companies are complying with the Commission's regulations.

The Commission also must approve a wide variety of transactions by jurisdictional companies regarding disposition of assets, mergers and acquisitions, and purchases and issuances of securities. Interlocking directorates between jurisdictional companies and certain other firms are also prohibited unless otherwise approved by the Commission. These prohibitions allow the Commission to protect consumers against the ability of firms supplying inputs to a utility to use the utility's monopoly position to its own advantage.

The Rationale for Regulation

Historically, all sales in the electric industry have been regulated — not only wholesale sales, but retail sales as well.[4] The fundamental underlying rationale for wholesale and retail regulation has been the same: to protect against the abuse of market power.

In the past, all sectors of the electric industry — generation, transmission, and distribution — have been viewed as natural monopolies. That is, all aspects of the utility business were thought to have declining unit costs due to economies of scale. A natural monopoly is "natural" because a single company will always be able to attain lower costs than several smaller competitors and thus can dominate the market.

The retail and wholesale regulatory environments have differed regarding whether to legally sanction the utility's natural monopoly position. Under retail regulation, the utility's monopoly position has typically been sanctioned by the grant of an exclusive franchise to sell retail electricity in a given service area. Under wholesale regulation, utilities have not been granted an explicit exclusive franchise. In addition, under retail regulation utilities typically have been obligated by statute to serve all retail customers in their service areas. But regardless of whether a utility's monopoly position has been sanctioned through an exclusive franchise, both retail and wholesale rate regulation have been imposed to protect customers from the abuse of the utility's market power. Both retail and wholesale rate regulation have typically been cost-based. That is, rates have been set to provide an opportunity for the utility to recover prudently incurred costs and earn a return sufficient to attract capital.

This arrangement has come to be described as a regulatory compact between the regulator and the utility. The regulator has agreed to set rates that provide An opportunity to recover Costs including a reasonable profit, and (under retail regulation) has granted the utility an exclusive franchise preventing direct competition from other suppliers. In exchange, the utility has accepted regulated rates that prevent excessive profits and (under retail regulation) an obligation to serve all customers.

While the underlying reason for regulation and the regulatory compact is the assumption that all electric companies are natural monopolies, that assumption now appears questionable, at least with regard to electricity generation. In many markets generation may no longer be a natural monopoly. In those markets where suppliers lack market power and are thus forced to behave competitively, the underlying rationale for regulation no longer exists.

A number of recent developments support the proposition that generation may no longer be a natural monopoly. First, scale economies may no longer extend to very large unit sizes. Further, construction costs may no longer be lower for large plants.[5] There it some evidence that average production costs may, in fact, be relatively high for the largest units.[6] While the traditional economies of large scale generation are now uncertain, production costs for small scale generators are declining.[7]

Second, technological advances related to transmission control technology and the development of new conductors that reduce transmission losses have led to an expansion of the transmission network and thus the scope of electricity markets.[8] These developments imply that generation may have lost many of its natural monopoly characteristics. The minimum optimal scale unit is now smaller relative to the size of the market. A number of sellers can thus efficiently supply many markets.

Inefficiencies Created by Regulation

Monopolies present a dilemma for public policy. An unregulated monopolist creates inefficiencies by charging too high a price and producing too little output.[9] The traditional public policy response is to check the exercise of monopoly power through the imposition of cost-of-service regulation. The problem is that such regulation is neither costless nor perfect. In attempting to check the abuses and inefficiencies of an unregulated monopolist, cost of service regulation may introduce another set of inefficiencies. Thus, regulating natural monopolies brings both benefits and problems to the public. But where firms lack significant market power, regulation may impose problems without conferring offsetting benefits. At least four problems are at issue.

First, traditional regulation generally sets prices based on past incurred costs.[10] However, efficient prices reflect expected future costs.[11] As a result, regulated prices may encourage inefficient supply and consumption behavior on the part of market participants.

Second, rates set on the basis of embedded costs appear to be "demand perverse".[12] Traditionally, regulated rates attempt to recover the cost of service regardless of the level of demand. Thus, traditional embedded cost regulation does not reflect the relative scarcity or abundance of power. When demand decreases, regulated rates do not fall to encourage market responsive consumption. Instead, they rise in an attempt to recover fixed costs over fewer sales units. But the higher rates may further discourage consumption as the remaining customers curb their consumption in response to the higher rates. This may drive rates even higher.

Third, by tying prices to the actual historic costs of individual suppliers, traditional regulation may blunt the profit a incentives for utilities to minimize their costs. When costs increase, regulators generally allow prices to increase. As a result, utilities are not penalized through lower profits. Conversely, when costs decrease, regulators generally require prices to decrease. As a result, utilities are not rewarded through higher profits.[13] Since profits may not be significantly affected by cost changes a utility may not feel a strong incentive to hold its costs down.

Fourth, cost-based regulation often does not adequately compensate for risk taking. When risky projects are undertaken and fail, political pressures develop to force the firm to bear the project's costs. Using hindsight, the project may be judged to have been imprudent. But when risky projects succeed, political pressures develop with hindsight to judge the project as not so risky after all. The firm may then be allowed to earn only a modest return commensurate with the newly recognized "low" risk of the project. As a result of the poor risk-reward balance inherent in cost-based regulation, regulated firms are often reluctant to pursue options which, though risky, promise large potential rewards. Firms may thus fail to attempt innovative but risky technologies, and instead pursue projects that have more certain, but higher costs. In some cases, firms may elect not to supply services to a market at all.

In sum, regulating monopolies by traditional cost-of-service methods involves a trade-off between the inefficiencies of unrestrained monopoly and the inefficiencies of regulation. Traditional regulation can serve the public interest only so long as the benefits of checking monopoly power are greater than the inefficiencies accompanying regulation.[14] While the "shocks" of the last fifteen years have magnified these inefficiencies, it is widely recognized that these inefficiencies are an inevitable consequence of using traditional cost-of-service regulation to control natural monopolies.[15] And where regulation is applied to firms lacking significant market power, these inefficiencies may not be offset by corresponding benefits.

Current Industry Problems

The problems associated with regulation discussed in the previous section are not the mere creation of armchair theorizing. The history of the industry over the past 15 years is replete with tangible examples. Because of unpredictable changes in economic conditions and the regulatory system's difficulty in accommodating these conditions, significantly more generation has been constructed than is currently marketable at traditionally regulated rates. Moreover, the cost of that capacity has been significantly higher than originally predicted. The regulatory response to this situation has created at least two major problems.

First, regulatory policies have exacerbated the excess capacity problem. Regulated prices sometimes may have been set too high, attempting to recover too much of the capacity costs in the present while not matching cost recovery with current market conditions. The "rate shock" resulting from these high prices has further dampened demand and increased the gap between demand and capacity.

Second, regulators' decisions to permanently disallow recovery of a large portion of these costs have made many utilities reluctant to invest in new, capital-intensive generation capacity. The reason is that utilities perceive that the potential rewards for such investments are no longer commensurate with the associated risks. As a result, the nation faces at least the possibility of reliability problems or more costly electricity supplies in the future.[16]

The reluctance of utilities to invest in future generating

capacity not only illustrates the limitations inherent in regulating firms with market power; it also indicates potential future problems whose solution should be of concern to policy makers. Removing regulatory barriers to the development IPPs may help ameliorate these problems. We discuss these problems and their implications more fully below.

Recent Events in the Industry

Between 1945 and 1970 electric power producers were able to provide extremely reliable service while reducing the real cost, after adjusting for inflation, of electricity for residential, commercial and industrial customers. This favorable performance record created an atmosphere of general satisfaction with the institutional structure of the industry.[17] However, between 1970 and 1985, average residential electricity prices more than tripled in nominal terms, and increased by 27% after adjusting for general inflation.[18]

Several factors contributed to this alarming change. Prior to 1970, the electric power industry experienced relatively constant demand growth, predictable fuel prices, and a stable business investment climate. These circumstances made it possible for utilities to lower costs by investing in efficient, large scale, capital-intensive generating facilities. More recently, however, utilities have been subjected to periods of rapid inflation, higher real interest rates, unexpectedly low demand growth, unexpected fuel cost volatility and construction delays caused by expanding environmental and safety regulation. Each of these trends has adversely affected the producers of electric power.

During the late 1960s, and immediately following the first oil embargo, Federal and state agencies encouraged utilities to commit enormous amounts of capital to the construction of nuclear generating stations and other baseload facilities that required substantial lead-times.[19] The consensus prediction of both utilities and regulators was that demand for electricity would exhibit the substantial and steady growth needed to justify these investments, which were expected to provide a reliable and low-cost source of electric power.[20]

Severe inflation during the 1970s and early 1980s substantially increased the construction costs of these large nuclear generating plants. Surging interest rates exacerbated this problem by increasing the cost of the capital needed to finance these projects. Finally, power plant completion schedules were doubled and in some cases tripled by more stringent safety and environmental requirements.[21] As a result, nuclear generating stations were often completed at multiples of their initial cost estimates.[22]

Disappointing demand growth magnified the effect of these cost increases on retail customers.[23] The sharply rising retail rates required to cover rising costs were accompanied by large and unanticipated reductions in demand growth, precipitated primarily by conservation measures and a week economy. The rapidly increasing rates for electric power during this period, together with the opportunities provided by PURPA, also prompted some industrial customers to bypass utilities by constructing their own generation facilities, thus exacerbating the effects of the cost increases on the rates charged to residential and Commercial retail customers.

Load growth virtually disappeared in some areas, and many utilities unexpectedly found themselves with excess capacity. Between 1974 and 1984, utilities cancelled 97 nuclear generating stations and 75 coal-fired generating plants planned for operation in the late 1970s and early 1980s.[24] The Department of Energy (DOE) has estimated that the sunk costs for the cancelled nuclear plants amount to $10 billion.[25]

Consumer interest groups responded to this "rate shock" by exerting unprecedented pressure on regulatory bodies to audit the prudence of management decisions to build generating plants, especially where construction of the plants encountered cost overruns or produced excess capacity. Between 1945 and 1975, fewer than a dozen prudence cases were brought.[26] Since 1975, however, over fifty cases have been undertaken by state PUCs.[27] Most of these cases involve prudence challenges to the construction costs of, and excess capacity yielded by, expensive nuclear generating stations.

Between 1980 and 1985, more than $6.5 billion of investment in nuclear power plant capacity was excluded from utility rate bases as a result of state PUC decisions.[28] These rulings significantly reduced the earnings of the affected utilities.[29] Delays in obtaining rate increases to compensate investors for the effects of inflation on debt service costs have also reduced investor returns. Utilities with construction projects in progress have become particularly likely to encounter liquidity constraints and problems attracting capital.[30]

Utilities now question the historical presumption that investment costs will be recouped through the retail rates allowed by state regulators. Moreover, existing rate of return regulation may not allow utilities to offset these increasing downside risks with higher potential profitability. Thus, the willingness of utilities to make proper investment decisions has been significantly compromised.

The difficulties of predicting demand growth, interest rates, fuel costs, the high capital costs of constructing baseload plants, and existing excess capacity, coupled with the regulatory decisions denying cost recovery for plants, or portions thereof, considered to be excess capacity, have prompted many utilities to adopt a very conservative strategy with respect to ownership of new capacity. A recent Los Alamos National Laboratory report found:

> Financial risks have become so great that utilities have been forced to shift their focus from the ratepayers to the shareholders. To defend against uncertainty, utilities are now deferring long-run solutions, such as building new coal nuclear power plants. Little construction is being planned to meet the needs of the mid to late 1990's.[31]

This "capital minimization" strategy has been openly voiced by numerous utility executives when explaining plant cancellations or general capital strategies.[32] Under this deferral strategy, utilities are apparently postponing capacity investment while adopting a "wait-and-see" approach to load growth estimation. By delaying investment decisions almost until projected demand materializes, utilities may be forced to satisfy their imminent capacity needs with less capital-intensive generating plants, which have shorter lead-times for construction but relatively high fuel and operating costs.[33] Thus, the utilities may be sacrificing their opportunity to build more capital-intensive plants, which have longer lead-times to build but are more efficient and economical to operate.

370

Although excess capacity is still commonplace among utilities,[34] there is great deal of uncertainty about the adequacy of the existing and planned electric power supply over the next decade. Forecasts show a wide variance in the timing and extent of future capacity needs. Some forecasters predict that adequate capacity will be available at least through the 1990s,[35] while other studies indicate that additional capacity is needed to prevent capacity constraints and reliability problems early in the next decade.[36]

Implications

The foregoing discussion dramatically illustrates the limitations inherent in regulating traditional utilities having substantial market power, especially during periods of economic uncertainty. It thus also suggests the harm that may result from regulating firms lacking significant market power. Regulated prices have not reflected market conditions and have worsened excess capacity problems. In addition, the perceived poor risk-return balance created by recent regulatory policies has made utilities reluctant to invest in future capacity.

This discussion also highlights the potential value of exploring additional options for meeting future electricity supply. The recent events described above raise concerns about the future reliability and cost of electricity obtained, exclusively from traditional sources of generation.[37] Because of these concerns, the public may benefit from allowing non-traditional suppliers of generation, including IPPs, to meet at least a part of its future needs.

As a policy matter, the commission may want to consider policy alternatives that increase the choices available to the public so that the best options may be selected. Relaxing the regulation of IPPs may be an approach that would remove barriers to the development of IPPs, and thus increase the public's future supply options. The goal of the Commission would not be to choose which option — traditionally regulated generation or IPPs — is the "best" approach for meeting this nation's future electricity needs. Rather, the Commission should assure that its regulatory policies do not foreclose developments which would enhance the ability of utilities to provide consumers with efficient, reliable electricity at reasonable cost.

THE ADVANTAGES OF RELAXING-REGULATORY POLICIES TOWARD IPPS

The preceding section described how cost-based regulation may convey both benefits and costs to the consumers of electricity. The benefits of regulation are derived primarily from the ability of regulators to prevent sellers from exercising market power in situations where competition would not otherwise provide an effective behavioral constraint. The costs include the various types of efficiency loss intrinsic to rate-of-return regulation under conditions of uncertainty and costly monitoring.

By definition, IPPs possess no significant market power. It follows immediately that any costs associated with the regulation of IPPs are not accompanied by offsetting benefits. As discussed below, the current regulatory policies toward IPPs may inhibit potentially efficient and innovative investment in electrical generating capacity. A less restrictive set of policies is thus likely to increase consumer welfare.

The Effect of Regulatory Policy on IPP Investment

There can be little doubt that the Commission's present regulatory policies discourage IPP investment. At a minimum, these policies are often costly, and compliance requires great effort. The information reporting requirements are quite lengthy, and the corporate and financial regulations interject a heavy government hand into the decision-making process of the affected firms.

Further, the Commission's cost-based regulation fails to provide proper economic incentives for investment in IPPs. Existing regulatory requirements, particularly rate-of-return regulation, discourage IPPs investment by appropriating much of the gain associated with innovative and efficient production. Under the current system, the potential for gain is, in many cases, not commensurate with the significant risks that accompany capacity ownership.

The risks that must be assumed by IPPs may often be greater than those faced by franchised utilities. Like utilities, IPPs must cope with the uncertainty of future electricity demand. Unlike utilities, however, IPPs have no exclusive service territories, and thus no *a priori* assured market for their power. In securing sales, IPPs must therefore rely exclusively on their ability to generate power efficiently and to price that power competitively. While cost-based regulation may be appropriate for franchised utilities, it is not appropriate for IPPs, given their lack of market power and the significant risks associated with IPP investment.

IPP investment risk is also high relative to QF investment risk. Unlike QFs, IPPs cannot take advantage of the provisions of PURPA that require utilities to purchase QF output at the utility's avoided cost. Cost-based rate regulation presents a clear impediment to the development of IPP capacity in this competitive market environment.

The Potential Benefits of IPPs Development

The disincentives to develop IPPs created by present regulatory policies have potentially important and harmful consequences, for the development of IPPs could provide a number of benefits to utilities, ratepayers, and to the national economy. Specifically, the increased investment opportunities made possible by a more relaxed regulatory treatment of IPPs could help to alleviate possible future shortages by providing needed capacity. In addition, IPPs investment may reduce the cost of electricity to ratepayers by providing inexpensive capacity, demonstrate new technologies that utility managements might view as too risky (and that lie outside the purview of PURPA), reduce the current incentives to "force fit" inappropriate projects into the QF program, and facilitate the efficient operation of the remaining regulatory apparatus. We discuss these benefits more fully below.

Contributions to Available Capacity

The subject of capacity constraints is controversial; there is little agreement about the timing of incremental capacity requirements. However, this very element of uncertainty is what makes the IPPs option so attractive. IPPs represent a potentially important source of reliable and economical power. Relaxing IPPs regulation would not mandate the construction of IPPs, it would simply streamline the administrative process of rate-making and corporate regulation. Construction of IPPs would be encouraged, but not required. Viewed in this light, more flexible regulation of IPPs would provide another degree of freedom to utility managers who must plan to meet uncertain demands.

In some instances, capacity from IPPs may be available more quickly than other types of capacity additions. One example could be utility-owned capacity that is excess to its own service area's needs and therefore is available for sale to willing buyers outside its service area or its "zone of economic influence." Another example — frequently overlooked in the policy debate —is the existing industrial capacity that does not qualify under the PURPA rules. Many industrial plants have electric generating equipment installed. A portion of this capacity was installed many years ago, before cheap and dependable utility service was available. This old capacity is often maintained for back-up service in the event of a utility outage. Other industrial generating facilities have been installed more recently. The reasons why industrial plants have added their own generating capacity are probably as varied as the types of products produced and the production technologies employed, and, in many cases, industrial producers may have no desire to sell electricity. When industrial producers are willing to sell, however, they should not be deterred by unnecessary regulatory requirements.

Accurate data on non-utility generating capacity are difficult to obtain. A data reporting form (the EIA-759) required of all generators larger than 10 MW was discontinued in 1979. In that year, 380 industrial generating facilities with 17,313 MW of capacity were identified.[38] This total includes many industrial cogeneration facilities, although the amount of this capacity that has obtained QF status is unknown, it is clear that only a fraction of the industrial generating capacity that existed in 1979 has since obtained QF status.[39]

Other studies of industrial cogeneration have turned up existing, pre-PURPA facilities apparently not reported in the EIA database.[40] These facilities may not have been reported because their size was less than the 10 MW threshold used by EIA. Whatever the reason for the reporting disparity, a state by state tally of facilities and electrical capacity reported by various researchers indicates a national total of up to 561 interconnected facilities with a total capacity of 18,296 MW. When the facilities identified as QFs are subtracted, nearly 400 industrial facilities remain as apparent non-QFs. The aggregate capacity of these remaining non-QF facilities ranges from about 13,000 MW to 15,000 MW.[41]

Independent verification of the potentially available non-QF, non-utility electric capacity can be gained from an EEI survey submitted to the Commission in May of 1987.[42] In this survey, EEI member utilities reported 3,000 MW of self-generation by electricity end-users in operation at the end of 1985. The EEI study thus suggests that almost 9,000 MW of the 1979 capacity reported to EIA has either been mothballed or retired.[43] Additionally, the EEI study identified 4,000 MW of cogeneration facilities and nearly 1,000 MW of small power production facilities that either had not sought QF status or whose status was uncertain.

Although these various studies on non-utility capacity do not provide similar estimates of existing IPPs potential, they do unambiguously demonstrate the existence of at least some such capacity. A portion of this capacity (either currently operating or currently idle) may be available to utilities in the event of capacity shortages in the years ahead. Every reasonable effort must be made to insure that regulation does not necessarily prevent exchange between willing utility buyers and these potential industrial sellers.

The potential role of non-industrial back-up generators for the limited purpose of helping to meet peak loads has been informally discussed for many years. For example, a utility anticipating a shortage-of peaking capacity might ask its customers with back-up generating equipment to start their generators during periods of peak demand. Such proposals have never advanced beyond the stage of internal discussions — perhaps in part because power sales into the utility's system would expose the generator's owner to the full weight of regulation under the Federal Power Act. It is only reasonable to explore the possibility of lightening this potential regulatory burden.

Construction Cost Implications

Providing needed capacity in the event of a shortage is the first potential benefit of an IPPs policy; providing capacity at least cost is the second. There appear to be a number of situations in which an IPP might turn out to be the lowest cost supplier of electric power.

Existing IPP facilities are very likely to be low cost suppliers of electricity. The capital cost of these facilities is already sunk. Thus, even if the operating cost of the industrial non-cogenerating power plant is higher than that of a larger utility-owned facility, the total incremental cost (fixed and variable) may compare favorably with a newly constructed central station unit. Similarly, existing back-up generating units (typically internal combustion piston engines) may compare favorably with the installation of new combustion turbine peaking units. Both use the same types of fuel, natural gas and light distillate oils. Both have comparable thermal efficiencies, around 30 percent. But the existing back-up units would require little capital investment beyond interconnection equipment.

When new construction of generating facilities is considered, the case for an IPP being the lowest cost supplier is less straightforward than for existing IPP facilities. However, there is evidence that such outcomes are possible. Data on both construction and operating costs of similar power plants reveal a wide range when comparisons are made among utility companies.[44] Some portion of this cost disparity is likely due to unavoidable factors such as variations in land costs and local environmental factors. However, management expertise and engineering skill are also part of the cost equation. It is hard to escape the conclusion that some utilities are better-able to efficiently build and operate power plants than others. There can be little doubt that some IPPs, like some regulated utilities, would be able to build and operate power plants with particular efficiency. An IPPs policy would encourage, but not require, companies with special expertise to put their skills to work beyond traditional bounds.

Finally, the competitive environment in which IPPs would operate provides particularly strong incentives for IPPs to minimize the construction and operating costs of their facilities. As indicated in Section I, traditional cost-based regulation may, in some cases, blunt the incentives for utilities to attain maximum efficiency. For IPPs, however, efficient operation may be a prerequisite to survival in the marketplace.

376   COMPETITION IN ELECTRICITY

Technological Change

The subject of technological change introduces a third likely benefit of relaxing the regulation of IPPs: the demonstration of innovative technologies. Many new technologies have been pioneered by utility companies and by QFs. However, the experience of the past few years seems to suggest that firms not encumbered by traditional regulation may be best situated to develop high-risk technologies.

The impact on utilities of the nuclear experience and the resulting prudence reviews and cost disallowances is debatable. Nevertheless, few industry analysts would dispute that basic regulatory forces tend to inhibit innovation. If a utility company attempts some novel technique for producing electricity -and the effort ends in failure — the company can expect a prudence investigation and a possible disallowance of investment costs. If the new idea works and, for example, power is produced more efficiently, the cost savings will be passed through to ratepayers. The equation of risk and reward is fundamentally asymmetrical.

The Commission's QF program has demonstrated the efficacy of a more symmetrical risk-reward equation. A QF gets paid only when it produces power. Investment costs are not rate-based; a QF will not recover its investment if the project fails, no matter what the reason. On the other hand, if the project succeeds, no regulatory limit is placed on QF profits.

The QF program has fostered development of many new generating technologies. Fluidized bed combustion was a concept much discussed but seldom attempted until PURPA provided incentives for the use of low-Btu waste fuels. Similarly, geothermal power production (from anything other than a dry steam resource), power production from municipal solid waste, and combined-cycle generation were largely undeveloped prior to PURPA, but are now all firmly established. In the area of renewable energy sources, tax advantages provided much of the early stimulus for project development. Debate over tax policy should not; however, obscure the real advances made over the past decade in producing electricity from wind, water, and sunlight.

Although the QF program has encouraged many technological developments, the record of the past seven years has demonstrated certain limits inherent in PURPA. Not all promising technologies are covered by Section 201. Some fuel-efficient power production processes simply do not fit into either of the allowable categories of cogeneration or small power production. A facility that is fueled primarily with fossil fuels — no matter how efficient — cannot qualify as a small power production facility. Similarly, unless at least two forms of energy are produced sequentially — one of which must be electricity and the other useful thermal energy — the facility does not meet the requirements of a cogeneration facility.

From time to time the Commission has been confronted by the necessity of denying QF status to a technologically innovative proposal, simply because it did not fit into the statutory framework. For example, the Commission has considered and rejected numerous proposals for cogeneration facilities that would employ a novel thermodynamic power cycle.[45] The same technical problem — highly efficient conversion of fossil fuel to electricity with little or no potential for recovery of useful thermal energy characterizes a number of alternative power production technologies.[46] The Commission has approved QF status for such technologies, but the potential for cogeneration applications remains limited. Providing project developers an alternative to the present choice between QF status and fully regulated jurisdictional utility status may help foster development of certain high-efficiency technologies that use fossil fuels.

Removal of the PURPA Bias

The fourth potential benefit of a more flexible IPPs policy stems directly from the choice of QF or utility status presently imposed on project developers. Some project developers apparently would like to simply build a power plant, yet feel compelled to meet the PURPA requirements in order to avoid the web of public utility regulation. The result is often a power plant with a contrived thermal application masquerading as a cogeneration facility.

These facilities have come to be known pejoratively as "PURPA machines".[47] Overall, these projects are economical. The power production process makes money and is thus operated at full capacity. The thermal energy process loses

COMPETITION IN ELECTRICITY

money, however, and is minimized to the extent permitted by the Commission's rules.[48] PURPA machines thus represent less than optimally efficient investments in a contrived thermal application.

Most calls for reform in this area suggest that the Commission raise the minimum standard governing the output of thermal energy. In effect, PURPA machine developers would then be forced to either absorb greater losses on contrived thermal outputs, or get out of the business. But rather than engage in a form of regulatory poker — raising the ante and hoping the inefficient PURPA machine players will fold the Commission has the option of simply recognizing the fact that some developers want to build powerplants and not "true" cogeneration facilities. An IPPs rule-making would establish the regulatory framework for such entrepreneurial powerplants. Not all PURPA machine developers are likely to abandon their greenhouses, but to the extent that any do so, resources would be saved. Further, the regulatory burden imposed on the Commission in evaluating the economics of greenhouses (owned by affiliates of the cogenerator) would be reduced. Society as a whole would benefit.

Uneconomic investments in QF projects also arise in contexts other than the frequently discussed PURPA machine. The fact that regulatory exemptions for waste and renewable resource powered small power production facilities extend only to facilities no larger than 30 megawatts fosters undersizing of such projects. One might reasonably wonder why all solar thermal projects and many waste-fired projects are sized exactly at 30 MW.[49] There is no indication that this is the economically optimum size for such facilities one might also wonder why all waste-fired facilities sized larger than 30 MW are equipped for-steam extraction — frequently for delivery to a nearby greenhouse. Perhaps a more flexible IPPs policy would allow developers to build optimally sized facilities, given the available resource and the current state of the art, rather than building to the limits imposed by PURPA requirements.

Indirect Benefits

In addition to the four possible direct benefits of an IPPs policy discussed above, there are several possible indirect benefits which may be realized. By their very nature, these benefits are somewhat speculative, but they nevertheless deserve attention.

If IPPs projects are proposed, utilities will be afforded a wider range of options for satisfying their capacity needs. Even if an IPP is not the lowest cost producer, it may be the "next best" option available. In such a case, the IPP project would be the cheapest avoidable alternative for the utility the utility's avoided cost. Availability of the IPP project may lower the utility's avoided cost. As a result, utilities may be able to reduce the rate paid to purchase QF power. The benefits of such cost reductions could be passed along to consumers.

In a similar vein, a utility's own construction program may prove to be the preferred supply option. If IPPs offer to build capacity, the proposed IPPs projects could serve as a forward-looking benchmark for the reasonableness of the utility's own program. Such a benchmark could prove helpful in evaluating the utility's management decisions on a prospective rather than retrospective basis.

One final benefit of an IPPs program is a reduction in regulatory costs. Of course, this is not the primary motivation for the policy, but the costs of regulation must be recognized. IPPs are already being proposed. At present, each case is handled individually, without any overriding policy. Such case-by-case decision-making absorbs considerable resources on the part of the FERC but the costs imposed on the IPPs are probably greater. Lengthy regulatory delays and large attorney's fees are costs that could be reduced with a clear policy on how IPPs will be regulated.

Impact on Established Sources of Generating Capacity

Creation of a new category of generation suppliers called IPPs does not imply that the established methods by which utilities obtain generating capacity to meet their customer loads must be displaced. Instead, the existence of IPPs merely creates new alternatives for utilities and state commissions to consider in their efforts to reduce the costs of electricity to consumers, allocate financial risks to those groups which voluntarily choose to bear them, and maintain the reliability of the nation's power supply. Such major sources of new and existing capacity as utility construction, QFs, and bulk power market supplies will continue to be available. Thest sources would not be directly affected by reductions in the regulatory burden imposed on IPPS.

To the extent that IPPs offer reliable capacity at an economical price, alternate suppliers of capacity will have to meet the Competition created by IPPs. Certain non-jurisdictional suppliers already have pricing flexibility to meet such competition, and are subject to limited non-price regulation. Although jurisdictional utilities have some flexibility in their pricing of coordination sales, the pricing of longer duration sales is subject to restrictive cost-based ratemaking.

For most utility systems, however, the primary supply alternative is self-supply through the construction of capacity to be included in rate base. The existence of utility market power over its captive retail customers leads to the conclusion that the reduced regulatory treatment proposed for IPPs is inappropriate at this time for utilities or their affiliates selling in a utility's zone of economic influence. This in no way implies that a state commission can not or should not enter into innovative incentive rate agreements with the utility to capture the benefits that market-based pricing can create. Many utilities will be able to compete effectively with IPPs, QFs and other third-party suppliers in terms of price, quality of supply, and investor risk assumption, if given the opportunity and encouragement to do so by their respective state commissions.

RECENT COMMISSION DECISIONS INVOLVING IPPS

While the commission's regulatory policies are intended for traditional utilities with significant market power, those policies may not be appropriate for IPPs, who lack significant market power. Recently, however, the Commission has in some instances applied a different set of regulatory policies for certain independent power producers on an ad hoc case-by-case basis, beginning with *St. Joe Minerals*[50] and *Cliffs Electric*.[51] Specifically, for a limited group of industrial generators, the Commission has reduced the regulatory burden by waiving certain rules. In order to qualify for such treatment, an industrial generator has had to satisfy a two-part test. First, the facility must be built primarily for non-utility purposes. Second, the facility must be used primarily for non-utility purposes. Resolution of this matter has been handled on a case-by-case basis.

Industrial power producers meeting the test have been granted a waiver from the Commission's accounting rules. Blanket authorization has been granted to issue securities and assume liabilities. Reporting requirements dealing with property dispositions and interlocking directorates have been simplified. But the Commission has had to find the rate for power sales to be just and reasonable, and no guidance on how rates will be evaluated has been provided to IPPs.

The new policies towards IPPs may need to be extended to a broader class of entities if the nation is to benefit completely from the full potential of IPPs power. The eligibility for regulatory relief is based on a two-part test that maybe unduly restrictive. The nation may benefit from reducing regulatory burdens to all independent power producers that lack market power, not merely to industrial power producers for whom generation is incidental to their overall business activities.

In short, the Commission's existing regulatory policies towards IPPs generally are burdensome and ad hoc. Moreover, they do not clearly define the group of firms that should be subject to separate, less burdensome regulatory treatment. The primary economic benefit of regulation is to protect against market power. It follows that the type and extent of the Commission's regulation should be based on the degree of market power. The group of firms that lack market power is likely to be significantly broader than those that meet the Commission's present two-pronged test.

AN ALTERNATIVE POLICY FOR IPPS

As previously discussed, the primary economic benefit of regulation is to protect against the abuse of market power. IPPs do not have significant market power. Strict regulation of IPPs is thus not likely to provide significant public benefits. To the contrary, strict regulation of IPPs may harm the public. It discourages the development of IPPs and thereby denies to the public the possible benefits of additional sources of economic and reliable electricity.

This paper has identified a number of benefits which the development of IPPs could provide. The strict regulatory policies currently applied to IPPs may be discouraging the development of these producers. Reduction or removal of these impediments would allow the development of a competitive generation sector with proper economic incentives to provide the additional capacity needed to sustain the industry's current standard of reliability. In addition, relaxing IPPs regulation could lower electricity costs, encourage the demonstration of new technologies, reduce wasteful investment made merely to attain QF status, and provide a number of indirect benefits.

In light of the harm that may be created by strictly regulating IPPs, the Commission may want to consider changing its regulatory policies toward this group. Described below is a more relaxed set of policies that the Commission might consider pursuing.

Rate Regulation

Given the disparity in market power between IPPs and traditional utilities, subjecting IPPs to full-scale, utility-type regulation (including cost-based pricing), as the Commission currently does, is incongruous. The Commission's cost-based rate regulation is premised on a belief that public utilities possess monopoly power, or at least significant market power, and do not compete for sales. Limiting utility rates to cost-of-service plus a fair rate of return is designed to protect against the abuse of such market power. This form of rate regulation is wholly inappropriate for sales by IPPs, because IPPs have no market power, no guaranteed market for their output, and must price their power competitively in order to make sales. Current cost-based pricing fails to provide the financial inducement necessary to offset the considerable risks assumed by IPPs. Restricting IPPs to what the Commission considers a "fair" rate of return is not likely to generate significant investor interest in IPPs because the potential for gain would be substantially outweighed by those risks.

This policy analysis indicates that rates charged by IPPs in wholesale sales should be freed from traditional embedded cost-of-service regulation, to the extent the Commission has the legal authority to do so. It would appear that all IPPs[52] should be afforded the maximum possible pricing flexibility allowed under the FPA. This might include the option of the Commission accepting any rates voluntarily agreed upon between an IPP and its customers. Voluntarily agreed upon rates might include those equal to the purchaser's avoided cost, those determined through a competitive bidding process, and those determined through private rate negotiation, do long as those rates are consistent with the requirements of the FPA.[53]

Non-rate Regulation

As noted earlier, the Commission's regulation of IPPs extends to three non-rate areas: reporting, asset and security transactions, and intercorporate affiliations.

Reporting Requirements

Part 33 of the Commission's regulations, which implements Sections 203 and 204 of the FPA, requires (among other things) that jurisdictional companies file detailed data on costs and operations. These data must be reported in accordance with the Commission's uniform System of Accounts. This information is used largely to set rates for sellers based on the seller's costs. If the Commission no longer regulates the rates of IPPs based on their costs, then this information would no longer be needed, and the Commission could relax or waive these reporting requirements for IPPs to the extent permitted under the FPA.

Asset and Security Transactions

Section 203 of the FPA and Part 33 of the Commission's regulations also impose a variety of procedural and substantive restrictions upon jurisdictional companies relating to their disposition of facilities, to mergers or consolidations, and to acquisitions of certain securities. Section 204 of the FPA imposes procedural and substantive restrictions on jurisdictional companies relating to their issuance of securities. Part 34 of the commission's regulations implements Section 204. These regulations also impose information reporting requirements relating to these transactions.

These regulations are intended to help the Commission to ensure that the asset and financial transactions of jurisdictional companies do not jeopardize their ability to render adequate service to customers. When the customers of jurisdictional companies lack significant alternative supply sources, regulatory supervision of these transactions may be desirable. Service disruptions by these companies can be particularly costly, since their customers don't have ready alternatives. But since the customers of IPPs have significant supply alternatives, such regulatory supervision would appear to be far less necessary. Moreover, these regulations are onerous and costly, and thus tend to discourage the development of IPPs. For these reasons, consideration should be given to relaxing or waiving the regulations with respect to IPPs to the maximum extent permitted by the FPA.

Intercorporate Affiliations

Section 305 of the FPA and Parts 45 and 46 of the Commission's implementing regulations impose restrictions on the ability of officers and directors of jurisdictional companies to hold interlocking positions as officers or directors of certain other firms. These restrictions are intended to help the Commission ensure that potential suppliers of important inputs to jurisdictional companies do not secure excessive prices or other advantages for these inputs at the expense of electricity consumers. Absent these restrictions, an interlocking director might induce a jurisdictional company to purchase inputs from the director's interlocking company at an inflated price, which could be passed on to the jurisdictional company's customers.

When a company's rates are set based on its own costs and the company sells to captive customers, the company has little incentive to discourage this type of activity. Its profits may not be reduced by incurring higher costs. For such companies, regulatory restrictions on intercorporate affiliations may provide some public benefit.

IPPs do not sell to captive customers; their customers have supply alternatives. Cost increases for IPPs cannot easily be passed on to their customers without risking a significant loss of sales. In addition, unlike firms subject to cost-based price regulation, IPPs would lose profits by increasing their costs if their prices were not regulated based on costs. These factors would create substantial disincentives for IPPs to acquire inputs at inflated costs. Thus, regulatory restrictions on the intercorporate affiliations of IPPs' officers and directors are not likely to provide significant public benefits. Such restrictions are likely to discourage the development of IPPs, however. Thus, consideration should be given to relaxing or waiving the restrictions for IPPs to the maximum extent permitted by the FPA.

Filing Fees

The filing fees and annual charges currently assessed to most utilities discourage the development of IPPs because they impose an additional cost of doing business. The current filing fees applicable to FPA-related filings by traditional utilities would be excessive if applied to IPPs. If the Commission should decide to relax filing requirements for IPPs, the staff would devote considerably fewer hours to review of IPPs' filings than it would devote to utility filings. Annual charges have already been recognized by the Commission as creating a disincentive to investment in QFs, and the reasoning applies equally to IPPs.

SPECIFIC CRITERIA TO DETERMINE IPP STATUS

Earlier in this paper, we provided a broad, conceptual definition of an IPP: a generating entity (other than a QF) that is unaffiliated with the franchised utility in the IPP's market area and that for other reasons lacks significant market power. To implement the reforms described in this paper, we must provide a more specific definition of an IPP. In particular, we must establish more specific criteria to determine when a generating entity lacks significant market power.

When Does a Generating Entity Lack Significant Market Power?

General Principles

Market power is the ability to influence the price that customers in a particular area must pay for a product. An individual seller can exercise market power if it can increase

COMPETITION IN ELECTRICITY

the price for its product without losing sales sufficient to make that price increase unprofitable. A seller with market power is thus a price setter rather than a price taker.

The ability of a firm to exercise market power is limited by the willingness of its customers to reduce consumption in response to a price increase (demand-side substitution) and by the availability of alternative supply sources (supply-side substitution). In order to evaluate the market power characteristics of a particular firm, attention must therefore be directed to the demand and supply options available to consumers in the geographic area where that firm sells its product(s).

Application to the Electric Industry

In general, wholesale purchasers (and potential wholesale purchasers) of electric power have limited opportunities for demand-side substitution. Thus, the market power held by individual sellers is limited primarily by the availability of alternative supply sources.

There are two basic ways in which a customer can limit the market power potential of external suppliers. First, they may acquire a significant amount of internal generation capacity. This allows the customer to retain the option of self-supply for at least a part of its power needs. Second, the customer can interconnect with several different generating companies so that power can be purchased from these companies or other noncontiguous suppliers.

Investor owned utilities (IOUs) frequently own substantial generation capacity and are interconnected with other generating companies. These potential buyers are thus largely insulated from anti-competitive price increases by individual external suppliers. By contrast, small municipal utilities (munis) and rural cooperatives (co-ops) often own little or no generation capacity and are interconnected to only one large IOU. This IOU typically surrounds the wholesale customer and is the sole or principal source of the customer's electricity supply. Thus, there is more general concern that this second class of wholesale customer is vulnerable to the effects of market power than there is with respect to large IOUs.

Specific Criteria to Attain IPP Status

As we noted earlier, since market power is specific to particular geographic areas, some sellers may have market power over customers in some areas but not others. However, this paper is concerned only with those generators, IPPs, that lack significant market power in all of their transactions. This section of the paper seeks to identify the unique characteristics of IPPs that distinguish them from other types of generators.

The purpose of this analysis is to determine a few simple, easily identifiable characteristics of the seller that generally indicate that an entity sells exclusively to customers with significant supply alternatives. In the electric industry, two such characteristics can be identified. Specifically, a generating entity is not likely to possess significant market power over any of its customers if:

1) it is not affiliated with any utility possessing an exclusive territorial franchise in the generating entity's market area; and
2) it does not own or control bottleneck transmission facilities, i.e., facilities that constitute the sole or predominant transmission link connected to any relevant market area. (Control of transmission facilities that do not act as a bottleneck are not likely to confer significant market power on their owner.)

Generating entities meeting these two standards could be generally eligible for IPP status and the regulatory reforms discussed in this paper.

As noted earlier, wholesale electricity customers that lack significant supply alternatives are usually distribution companies that possess two characteristics. First, they own little or no generation capacity. Second, they are interconnected to the transmission network of a single integrated utility. The integrated utility typically supplies most or all of the electricity requirements of the distribution company. The integrated utility also typically possesses an exclusive territorial franchise to serve retail customers in the geographic area surrounding the distribution company and thus owns most or all of the transmission facilities in that surrounding area.

Those transmission facilities act as a bottleneck. Since the integrated utility owns all transmission facilities surrounding the distribution company, the distribution company can reach other large utility suppliers of power only by using transmission facilities of the integrated utility. So long as the distribution company owns little or no generation capacity, the integrated utility is able to prevent the distribution company from acquiring significant supply choices by denying access to the transmission bottleneck. Thus in these instances, ownership of substantial transmission facilities provides the integrated utility with an important source of power.

In most cases, generating entities that are unaffiliated with utilities possessing an exclusive franchise in the entity's market area and that do not control bottleneck transmission facilities are unlikely to possess significant market power over any wholesale customers. Without control over bottleneck transmission facilities, such entities could not deny their customers access to alternative sources of supply.

The wholesale customers of such generating entities would in most cases be integrated utilities, which already own substantial generating capacity and are interconnected with neighboring utilities. Occasionally such generating entities might make wholesale sales to municipal or cooperative distribution companies, which already are interconnected with at least one large supplier of power. In host cases, each of these classes of wholesale customers could turn to sources other than the generating entity to supply most or all of their power requirements.

While entities meeting these standards would not usually possess significant market power over any of their customers, some exceptions may occasionally arise. A single large generating entity meeting these standards could, at least theoretically, possess significant market power over particular wholesale customers, at least for a limited period of time.

Specifically, a generator could develop significant market power if it was the predominant source of electricity supply to a customer and no other interconnected suppliers had significant unused or uncommitted capacity. In this situation, the customer's interconnections with other generators would not provide it with significant supply choices because the alternative generators would have little spare capacity to supply electricity. The customer's plight would not likely persist forever. The alternative suppliers could build additional capacity given sufficient lead time, if the customer expressed a demand for it. In the meantime, however, the customer might be subject to market power by its current supplier.

Even in this case, however, the customer often might be able to protect itself against the seller's short term market power through appropriate contract terms, such as those concerning price and termination notice. So long as the customer had significant supply alternatives at the time it entered into a contract, that customer should be able to obtain-adequate contract protection against the seller's market power during the term of the contract. If one seller did not agree to such terms, the customer could turn to alternative suppliers.

Firms satisfying the aforementioned standards might also derive limited market power through their ability to control market access to other low cost suppliers. Specifically, firms which own transmission facilities that provide the sole source of access to a particular geographic area for at least some producers may be able to limit customer access to other low cost sources of supply. Entities meeting the two standards listed above would not generally posses significant market power over particular customers. But the situation might occasionally arise. To the extent such problems were to arise, the Commission could address these situations on a case-by-case basis when particular affected customers raise complaints. In the absence of complaints by affected customers, any entity meeting the two standards could be classified as an IPP.

Who Might Be Eligible for IPP Status?

The standards for attaining IPP status are framed as characteristics of "entities". We use the term entity broadly to mean either entire firms or parts of firms owning physically distinct generating facilities. By defining the term entity broadly, we can envision at least three distinct types of IPPs: industrial IPPs, stand-alone non-utility IPPs, and utility IPPs. Industrial IPPs are generation facilities owned by industrial concerns. The electricity generated by industrial IPPs will often be used, at least in part, for the internal needs of the industrial owner. To the extent that the facility's capacity exceeds the internal needs of the industrial owner, power can be generated for sale in the wholesale market.

Stand-alone non-utility IPPs are generation facilities owned by non-utilities (i.e., companies without an exclusive territorial franchise) for the sole purpose of generating and selling power in the wholesale market. Very little, if any, of the power generated by these facilities would be consumed internally by its owners.

The final category of IPPs are generation facilities owned by traditional utilities but which sell power outside of the utility's zone of economic influence, i.e., the geographic area where the utility has significant market power.[54] So long as these entities serve only power markets outside the geographic area where the utility possesses significant market power, utility IPPs are not likely to possess market power. The reason is that the utility owner of the IPPs has no ability to control the opportunities of any of its customers to acquire power from alternative market sources.

We have described these three types of IPPs in their pure form, distinguishable by their ownership type. However, joint venture IPPs that combine ownership types may also develop. For example, an industrial firm and another non-utility investor might form a joint venture IPP that provides part of its power for the industrial owner's operations and sells the remainder of its power into the wholesale power market.

Special Concerns Associated with Utility IPPs

Entities that meet the standards for IPP status are not likely to possess significant market power in the traditional sense, regardless of who owns them. That is, no IPP is likely to have the power to force a customer against its will to pay excessive prices for its power. The customer will have sufficient supply alternatives to prevent this undesirable outcome.

However, certain special problems could develop from reducing regulation of utility IPPs. These potential problems arise not from any market power possessed by the IPP, but from the market power possessed by the utility owner in its home service territory. Thus, these potential problems are unique to utility IPPs and would not arise for non-utility IPPs. We turn to these problems below.

Mutually Non-Competitive Purchases

Regulated electric utilities are likely to be the primary purchasers of IPPs power. These utilities are typically the sole suppliers of retail power to distinct geographic areas; their retail customers generally do not have access to alternative suppliers. Because competitive pressures are more limited, the incentives for such utilities to minimize their costs are reduced. Absent effective regulation, utilities may find it profitable in certain instances not to minimize their costs.

One way for a utility to profit from failing to minimize costs is through agreements with other utilities to purchase power reciprocally at inflated prices from affiliated IPPs. Specifically, each of two utilities could build an IPP in the other utility's service territory. Each utility could then agree to purchase electricity generated by the other's IPP at an inflated price, despite the availability of lower cost power from other sources. The inflated cost would be passed on by each purchasing utility to its retail customers by raising its retail prices.

Bilateral agreements may be the easiest for utilities to coordinate and enforce, but multilateral arrangements involving several utilities are also possible. Indeed, multilateral arrangements may be harder for regulators to detect, in part because of the "noise" existing in the lack of direct correspondence between physical flows and accounting transactions. However, coordination problems increase with the number of co-conspirators.

In addressing this potential problem, two points are relevant. First, the ease with which utilities can conspire does not depend on the physical distance between the home service territories of the conspiring utilities. A conspiratorial agreement between a West Coast utility and an East Coast utility is in principle no more difficult to maintain than one involving two adjacent utilities. Second, the willingness of a utility to purchase at supra-competitive prices depends on the difficulty with which the regulator (or other interested parties) can discover this practice. The utility must weigh the anticipated profits from this activity against the likelihood of detection in a prudence review or other forum and the magnitude of the resulting penalty.

Daisy Chains

A similar result could be obtained by creating a series of "paper" transactions or a "daisy chain". Such an arrangement would have the following features. A utility IPP would sell its power to a separate entity at an inflated price. While this purchasing entity would take title to the power, it would not necessarily own any physical assets with which it could take physical possession of the power. Ownership of the power generated by the IPP could change hands a number of times, with each owner making a profit on the transaction. (Hence, the name "daisy chain".) But ultimately, the power would be purchased by the utility owner of the IPP at an inflated price, despite the existence of lower cost alternative sources of power. This inflated price would be recovered in the utility's retail rates.

This type of arrangement requires a number of things. First, the owners of the transmission facilities connecting the IPPs with the utility's service territory must agree to provide transmission service. Second, the parties involved in the daisy chain must agree to pay supra-competitive prices to purchase the power, to other aspects of the arrangement, and to keep the ultimate nature of the transaction secret from regulators. Daisy chain arrangements of this nature carry a legal risk to the participants, since such collusion may be a violation of federal law. Further, states have the authority to refuse to pass through excessive purchased power costs to ratepayers.

Unlike mutually non-competitive purchases, the ability of a utility to successfully arrange a daisy chain is likely to depend on the physical distance between the IPP and the utility's home service territory. As that distance grows larger, the utility must bring more transmission owners into the arrangement for it to succeed. The probability of successful coordination will decline as the number of parties necessary for the agreement increases.

In addition, the willingness of the utility and other parties to participate in a daisy chain arrangement again depends on how easily regulators and other interested parties can detect the practice and impose penalties.

Cost Misallocation and Cross Subsidy

Under the alternative policies described in this paper, a utility owner might have both the incentive and the opportunity to misallocate IPP-related costs to native load service. An incentive to misallocate costs might arise if native load rates continued to be cost-based while IPPs rates were not. If a utility was allowed to recoup IPPs-related costs through native load service rates, the profits earned by the IPP (and thus the utility as a whole) could be increased at the expense of the utility's native load customers.

The opportunity to misallocate would arise to the extent that regulators were not able to separate IPPs-related and native load-related costs. A utility would incur most of the same types of costs to generate electricity from an IPP as it would to generate electricity for its native load in its home service territory. Many of these costs may arise from resources pooled within the firm. Costs associated with raising capital, procuring fuel, and designing and maintaining plant are prominent examples. It may be difficult for regulators to determine the portion of these costs that properly belong to an IPP versus native load service, even though the IPP facility may be a great distance from the utility's home service territory.

If IPP-related costs are misallocated to native load operations, native load rates will be higher than they should be. Consider, for example, a risky IPP whose true cost of debt is higher than that for the utility's less risky native load operations. If regulators don't recognize the higher debt cost of the IPP and instead set native load rates based on the utility's average cost of debt, then native load rates will be too high. Native load customers will, in effect, be bearing a portion of the cost associated with the investment in the IPPs facility. Because a portion of the IPP's cost would be covered by this subsidy, the utility's IPP may inefficiently displace a lower cost source of power in its market area.

The importance of the problem of cross subsidy depends on the magnitude of the pooled resource costs and the ability of regulators to allocate these costs properly. This problem is not unique to the utility IPPs. It potentially arises in every case where a company is diversified into both utility and non-utility lines of business.

394   COMPETITION IN ELECTRICITY

How Should These Concerns Be Addressed?

The previous discussion raises questions about the extent to which regulation of utility IPPs should be relaxed. For reasons outlined earlier, traditional cost of service regulation may be undesirable for all IPPs, including utility IPPs. However, because of the special problems identified in the previous section, the Commission should consider whether it needs to treat utility IPPs differently from non-utility IPPs. We discuss how these special problems might be addressed below.

Mutually Non-competitive Purchases and Daisy Chains

Mutually non-competitive purchasing and daisy chaining raise the same fundamental problem. The utility purchasing power from the IPP voluntarily agrees to pay an inflated price, that is, a price greater than that of available alternatives rejected by the customer. Stated differently, the customer voluntarily agrees to pay the IPP a price greater than its actual avoided cost, the cost it would otherwise incur if it didn't purchase the IPP's power.

This behavior would violate the prudence standards of regulatory commissions. If a regulatory commission discovers that a utility intentionally and imprudently incurred costs (adjusted for non-price factors) greater than necessary, the utility would be prevented from recovering the excessive portion of the costs in its rates. Instead, the excess costs would be borne by the utility's shareholders. This prospect should create at least some disincentive to engage in such practices.

However, we cannot be sure how effective this disincentive by itself may be. To provide added protection to the public, the prices of utility IPPs could be explicitly capped by some measure of the purchaser's incremental cost. A number of pricing mechanisms could satisfy this cap. Examples include prices determined through appropriate competitive bidding procedures and administratively determined avoided-cost rates for purchasing QF power. Other pricing mechanisms might also be appropriate. However, utility IPPs should not be allowed to charge prices determined through voluntary rate negotiation that are not explicitly capped by the purchaser's incremental costs. So long as the prices of utility

IPPs are effectively constrained by the incremental cost cap, the problems associated with artificially priced power purchases are not likely to arise.

Cost Misallocation and Cross Subsidy

If a utility was to subsidize its IPP, the resulting problem would not be that the IPP's price was too high. Rather, the price charged by the utility to its native load customers would be too high, and in certain instances the IPP's price might be too low (when competitive pressure so required). Primarily, this is a problem created by imperfect regulation of the utility's native load rates. However, the problem could be exacerbated by relaxing regulation of IPPs. A utility's incentive to cross subsidize might increase if it were not required to reduce its IPP's prices when it allocated costs away from the IPP.

To effectively address this problem, we need to know more about the potential magnitude of the problem and the ability of state regulators to identify cross subsidy. As mentioned earlier, state regulators face the potential of cross subsidy in every case where a utility is diversified into non-utility lines of business. Obtaining comments from state regulators on their experiences involving utility diversification may shed light on how best to address the potential cross subsidy problem for IPPs.

Non-price Regulation of Utility IPPs

The reforms proposed here are not intended to relax the regulations applicable to utilities in their sales to native load customers, where they have significant market power. Price regulation of utility IPPs can be relaxed without relaxing price regulation of sales by the utility owners to their native load customers. However, two non-price elements of FPA regulation may apply to companies as a whole. It may not be possible to relax these regulations only with respect to the portion of company identified as a utility IPP. Regulations relating to financial transactions under Sections 203 and 204 of the FPA as well as those relating to intercorporate affiliations under Section 305 of the FPA fall into this category. As a result, utility IPPs may not be eligible for relaxed regula-

COMPETITION IN ELECTRICITY

tion of their financial transactions or intercorporate affiliations.

In short, while the public may benefit from relaxing the regulation of utility owned IPPs, utility ownership of IPPs raises special concerns. These concerns may require more careful monitoring of utility IPPs and special consideration separate from non-utility IPPs.

Joint Ventures within a Utility's Service Territory

One of the two standards for IPP status is that the entity be unaffiliated with the local utility in the entity's market area. In implementing this standard, a question arises concerning-the nature of the lack of affiliation. Should the local utility hold no equity ownership of the IPP located in utility's zone of economic influence? Alternatively, could the local utility own a "small" share of the entity without compromising the entity's independence? If so, what should be the limits placed on a utility's ownership of such joint ventures? A number of factors should be considered in addressing these questions.

First, there may be benefits from allowing utilities to own a portion of an IPP located in its zone of economic influence. For example, utilities may have superior access to desirable sites to locate generating facilities within their service territories. Without at least partial utility ownership, IPPs might be unable to locate their facilities at the most cost-effective sites.

In addition, utilities are permitted by regulation to own up to 50 percent of QFs, regardless of the location of the QF facilities. If utility ownership of IPPs were limited to a significantly lower percentage, some potential IPPs might reconfigure their generating facilities to meet QF status in order to be permitted a higher utility ownership percentage. This would be undesirable if the IPP technology is the lower cost alternative.

On the other hand, partial utility ownership of IPPs raises concerns about favoritism. A local utility might have a financial incentive to favor purchases from entities that it partially owned over other entities in which it had no ownership interest.

These are questions of considerable importance, and

further input from the Technical Conference and elsewhere will be needed before any conclusions can be reached.

IMPLICATIONS OF LESSENED FPA REGULATION OF IPPS

Non-utility generation is not a new idea. Generation by QFs in particular is increasingly becoming a fact of life for utilities. To the extent that increased pricing and regulatory flexibility afforded IPPs increased their development, utilities may increase their reliance on independent or third party generation. Some of the implications of independent or third party generation are discussed below.

State v. Federal Jurisdiction Over IPPs

A new federal regulatory policy regarding IPPs need not alter the current division of jurisdiction between state regulatory commissions and the Commission. States could continue to have the exclusive authority to approve or disapprove the siting, construction, and operations of IPP-owned thermal electric generating plants. Under current regulatory schemes effective in most states, an IPP would have to obtain a charter from a state before it would be allowed to engage in business as a "public utility" or an "electric company." It would also be required to obtain a "certificate of public convenience and necessity" from the state before it could construct any generating facility. Any such construction would be subject to state siting and environmental permitting requirements. Furthermore, IPPs would be able to make retail sales only after getting permission from state regulatory authorities. The Commission, of course, has no authority in these matters, and therefore would be unable to exempt IPPs from such state regulatory requirements.

In view of the significant authority that states have over the location, licensing and operations of power plants, there is some question as to whether a Commission policy encouraging development of IPPs would be entirely successful without cooperation from the states in facilitating IPPs' entry into the power supply market. Traditionally, the grant of a charter and a certificate of public convenience and necessity grants a utility a territorial franchise in return for the utility assuming an express or implied obligation to serve customers within the franchised territory. Unless vested with the obligation to make retail sales, however, the regulatory requirements associated with franchised service territories would appear-to be inappropiate for third party independent power producers. To the extent such requirements are applied to IPPs, investment in independent or third party generation is likely to be discouraged. However, as a practical matter, states should be more willing to permit IPPs located in a utility's exclusive service territory to serve wholesale customers (including the local utility) rather than retail customers because encouraging IPPs' may increase utilities' purchasing options, shelter consumers from certain types of risks, reduce production costs and provide needed capacity.

Although the retail rates, siting, construction, and operations of thermal electric generating facilities would be administered exclusively by states, the rates for IPPs' sales to wholesale customers would be governed exclusively by this Commission. Wholesale customers of a purchasing utility would, pursuant to sections 206 and 306 of the FPA, be able to challenge the prudence of the utility's decision to purchase power from a particular IPP, once the utility seeks to pass along the costs of the purchase to its Wholesale customers. Although the Commission has exclusive jurisdiction over the justness and reasonableness of IPPs' rates for wholesale sales to utilities, it may be possible for states as well as retail customers to challenge the prudence of the acquiring utility's purchasing decision where that utility seeks to pass along the costs of the purchase in its retail rate cases.

Consistency With Utilities' Obligation To Serve

The question has been raised as to whether IPPs, particularly in the context of bidding for new capacity, are consistent with utilities' obligation to serve. Nothing in the proposals for IPPs and bidding necessarily alters the utilities' traditional role. Utilities' entrance into contracts with independent or third party generators and IPPs would remain strictly voluntarily. The issue of how to integrate increased reliance on wholesale sources of power with the utilities' traditional service responsibilities is not a new question and is fundamentally a matter appropriate for state and utility resolution. Consistency can be assured by maximizing utilities' discretion as to the choice and terms and conditions of power purchases from IPPs. Such choices would remain subject to challenge and scrutiny in wholesale and retail rate cases.

Admittedly, as is the case now with PURPA power, the utility may be able to satisfy its power needs entirely from wholesale sources and may no longer need to be the primary builder of new capacity. Even in those situations where utilities do not want to build, system integrity and reliability can be protected by retaining the utilities' planning and operational responsibilities. Systems should remain centrally dispatched and utilities should retain their planning responsibilities. As is the case already, any concerns about adequate and reliable service due to an increasing reliance on third party generation could be addressed through pricing, and such measures as performance bonds, dispatchability requirements and the selection criteria.

Utilities could insist on a security interest in the independent or third party producers' power plants. In the event an IPP is economically unable to complete or operate a facility at the contractually defined rate, the utility could exercise the security interest to take the plant over. Absent a security interest, eminent domain authority could be used to accomplish the same result. In situations where an IPP defaults and there is an immediate need for new capacity, the reasonable purchase of replacement power could be passed through to the purchasing utilities' customers. This is generally what occurs today when a utility's source of firm power is lost and replacement power is purchased from other sources.

Furthermore, including IPPs in a bidding system for capacity could serve as an effective means for utilities to focus state regulators on the utilities, service responsibilities. This is particularly true in situations where utilities publicly solicit offers for new capacity. Following the solicitation, the utility could decide what type of new capacity it needs baseload, or peaking capacity. The utility could then critique the quality of the offers it receives. This ability to critique the quality of the offers would provide utilities with an excellent forum to assess exactly how independent or third-party power can be integrated with more traditional sources of supply and to ensure that the utilities' ability to satisfy their service responsibilities is protected.

END NOTES

1. The exceptions are companies not interconnected via the transmission grid with more than one state. These latter companies are located in Texas, Hawaii, and Alaska.
2. *Regulation of Electricity Sales-for-Resale and Transmission Service*, 31 FERC Paragraph 61,376 (1985).
3. Wilbur C. Earley, "FERC Regulation of Bulk Power Coordination Transactions", FERC Staff Working Paper (July 1984).
4. A recent exception relates to certain QFs, which were exempted from wholesale rate regulation after the passage of PURPA in 1978.
5. For a review of the literature on scale economies,, see Paul Joskow and Nancy L. Rose, "The Effects of Technological Change, Experience, and Regulation on the Construction Cost of Coal-Burning Generating Units' *Rand Journal of Economics*, Vol. 16, No. 1 (1985).
6. Some data suggest that larger units suffer lower availability factors. See Paul Joskow and Richard Schmalensee, *Markers for Power: An Analysis of Electric Utility Deregulation*, (Cambridge: MIT (Press, 1983), Table 5-2, p.48. Low plant availability pushes up production costs due to increased maintenance expense and replacement power.
7. EPRI Journal, July/August 1987 and OTA, *Now Electric Power Technologies*, 1985.
8. EPRI Journal, November 1982.
9. Stephen Breyer, *Regulation and Its Reform*, Cambridge: Harvard University Press, 1982, pp. 15-16, F.M. Scherer, *Industrial Market Structure and Economic Performance*, Chicago: Rand McNally College Publishing Company, 1980, pp. 14-20.
10. Prices best promote efficiency when they reflect the seller's marginal costs. Firms with monopoly power create market inefficiencies by charging prices above their marginal costs. Those high prices cause consumers to purchase less of the seller's product than is efficient from society's standpoint. For example, suppose that an electric

company charged prices substantially above its marginal costs. As a result, some households might switch to oil or gas to heat their homes if the prices of oil or gas were sufficiently lower than electricity prices. These consumer decisions would be made by comparing the prices of electricity and alternate fuels. But the most efficient decisions from society's standpoint depend on a comparison of the sellers' marginal costs. The cost to society of providing heat to these consumers would be too high if the marginal cost of oil or gas heat (plus complementary equipment) exceeded that for electricity.

11. See Ralph Turvey and Dennis Anderson, *Electricity Economics*, Baltimore Johns Hopkins University Press, 1977, p. 8; Alfred Kahn, *The Economics of Regulation*, Volume I, New York: John Wiley & Sons, 1970, pp. 65-67; and Richard Schmalensee, *The Control of Natural Monopolies*, Lexington, Massachusetts: Lexington Bocks [sic], 1979, p. 29.

12. The term "demand perverse" was first used to describe this characteristic of traditionally regulated rates by Commissioner Stalon in his testimony before the House Subcommittee on Energy and Power, September 10, 1987, pp. 24-26 and pp. 35-36.

13. Professor Harry Trebing, Director of the Institute of Public Utilities, has observed that "Regulation creates an environment in which incompetence is rewarded and efficiency is penalized because the determination of total revenue requirements on a cost-plus basis assures the company that all expenses will be covered while at the same time eliminating the possibility that any gains from greater productivity can be retained." "Toward An Incentive System of Regulation," 72 Public Utilities Fortnightly 22 (1963). See also, Stephen Breyer, *Regulation and Its Reform*, (Cambridge: Harvard University Press, 1982), p. 47 and Alfred Kahn; *The Economics of Regulation*, Volume II, (New York: John Wiley & Sons, 1970), p. 48.

14. See W. Comanor, "Should Natural Monopolies Be Regulated?" *Stanford Law Review*, February 1970, Volume 22, pp. 510-518 and Richard Schmalensee, "Estimating the Costs and Benefits of Utility Regulation," *Quarterly Review of Economics and Business*, Summer 1974, pp.

51-64.

15. See W. Barmol and A. Binder, *Economics, Principles and Policy*, at 490-503 (1979), and materials cited in nn. 9, 13, and 14, *supra*.

16. See "Electricity's Future in the U.S.," *Energy Security*, report to the President, from U.S. Department of Energy, March, 1987, pp. 130-160.

17. See, Paul L. Joskow, "Inflation and Environmental Concern: Structural Change in the Process of Public Utility Regulation", *Journal of Law and Economics*, Vol XVII, No. 2 (October 1974).

18. Based on retail prices as reported by EIA. Adjusted for inflation using the CPI.

19. See, e.g., Jersey Central Power & Light Co. v. FERC, 810 F.2d 1168, 1171 (D.C. Cir. 1987).

20. Jersey Central Power & Light.... 1171.

21. Robinson, *Optimum Tilting of the "Level Playing Field"*, A.B.A. Public Utility Newsletter at 2 (May 1987). Fossil fuel-fired plants became subject to regulation by the Clean Air Act of 1970, 42 U.S.C. Section 7401 (1982), and its 1977 amendments. In 1971, nuclear plants were found to be subject to the environmental impact statement requirements of the National Environmental Policy Act of 1969, 42 U.S.C. Section 4332 (1982). And between 1976 and 1980, most states and many localities instituted laws governing power plant sites.

22. See, e.g., Mississippi Industries v. FERC, 808 F.2d 1525, 1531 (D.C. Cir. 1987), *remanded on other grounds*, No. 851611 (D.C. Cir. June 24, 1987). See also "Construction Cost overruns in Electric Utilities: Some Trends and Implications," The National Regulatory Research Institute (November 1980) and EIA "An Analysis of Nuclear Power Plant Construction Costs," (March 1986).

23. For the period 1963-1973 the average annual growth rate for electricity demand was approximately seven percent. Since 1974, however, the growth rate of demand has only averaged 2.18 percent. (Edison Electric Institute Statistical Yearbook of The Electric Utility Industry: 1982, Washington, D.C. 1983). For further discussion on the reasons for and effects of this sharp drop in growth see DOE, *The Future of Electric Power in America* (June 1983); CRS, *Gold at the End of the Rainbow?* (December

1984); and "Do Utilities Have Strategic Options? Ask The Customer" John C. Sawhill and Lester P. Silverman, *Public Utilities Fortnightly*, March 31, 1983.

24. Congressional Budget office, Financial Condition of the U.S. Electric utility Industry, at 11-12 (March 1986) (hereinafter cited at *1980 CBO Financial Condition Report*).

25. Id. at 12.

26. Roach & Johnson, Prudence of Construction Expenditures 1-4 and n.1 (April 30, 1981) (unpublished manuscript).

27. Id.

28. Oak Ridge National Laboratory, *Prudence Issues Affecting the U.S. Electric Utility Industry*, (July 1987 - unpublished draft). With the addition of a $951 million disallowance for Vogtle Nuclear Station (see "Energy Daily", October 1, 1987) total disallowances for nuclear plants now exceeds 7 billion. Coal plants have also had disallowances over this same period of $127 million (*Prudence Issues...*).

29. Since late 1983 stock prices for utilities with significant nuclear construction have traded well below prices for utilities without significant nuclear construction (Solomon Brothers, Inc. "Electric Utility Monthly," July 1, 1986, page 5). In addition the trade literature has numerous examples of companies' stock suffering from disallowances (for example "Idaho Power Stock Slumps After PUC Denies Equity Return on Valmy-2 Share," from "Electric Utility Week," July 28, 1986 page 11).

30. See *CBO Financial Condition Report* at 19; also *The Dimming of America*, by Peter Navarro, 1984 at 43; and the comments of Alabama Electric Cooperative, Inc., et. al., on Generic Determination of Rate of Return on Common Equity for Public Utilities, Docket No. RM86-12-000 at 62.

31. *The Future Market for Electric Generating Capacity: A Summary of Findings*, Los Alamos National Laboratory (December 1984) at 2.

32. Examples are quotes from utility executives in The Dimming of America, Peter Navarro at 17-18 and the *Wall Street Journal* of February 26, 1986 (page 1) in which representatives of the San Diego Gas and Electric Company vowed it would never build another plant.

33. Given the risks of excess capacity, utilities may have a bias against construction of new fuel-efficient baseload capacity because "under current regulatory practice, the utilities tend to bear the costs of overcapacity while the ratepayers tend to bear the costs of inefficiency." *1986 CBO Financial Condition Report*, at 48.

34. A rough estimate of capacity requirements can be made by reference to reserve margin. For the nation, reserve margin has been above 30% since the mid-1970s, significantly above the historic 20% rule-of-thumb margin for adequate reserves. DOE, *Electricity's Future in the United States*, DOE/S-0057-H5 at 36 (March 1987).

35. For example, one analyst predicts that excess capacity will continue to exist in the year 2000. See Nogee, *Gambling for Gigabucks: Excess Capacity in the Electric Utility Industry*, Environmental Action Foundation, at 17 (December 1986). And a study by the Congressional Research Service, *A Perspective on Electric Utility Capacity Planning*, (August 1983), suggests that demand management and existing supply alternatives could avoid the need for substantial capacity additions.

36. For example, see DOE, *The Future of Electric Power in America*, (June 1983 at 4-2) which predicts the need for 177 GWs of new capacity by the year 2000 if demand grows only by 2 percent annually; and Joseph-P. Kalt, et al., *A Review of the Adequacy of Electric Power Generating Capacity in the United States*, (June 1986) which predicts potential regional capacity inadequacies as soon as the early 1990s.

37. For example, a study by ICF, Inc. *An Analysis of the Electric Utility Industry in the United States*, (Winter 82/83) predicted that annualized generation costs in the year 2000, if a capital minimization strategy is followed, could be as much as $16 billion higher than those predicted under more economically efficient strategies. And James M. Coynes, et al., *The Impacts of an Electric Generating Capacity Shortage*, from Papers and Proceedings of the Eighth Annual North American Conference - "The Changing World Energy Economy" predicts electricity prices that are 25 percent higher under an investment avoidance scenario than under more traditional approaches to capacity additions.

38. Stanley, Warren R.; Analysis of Existing Industrial Cogeneration Capacity; TRW Energy and Environmental Division; McLean, VA; August 30, 1982. The amount that is pre-PURPA (which may have appeared on the EIA-759) is not available.
39. As of January 1987, a total of 126 existing, pre-PURPA facilities had filed as QFs. These QFs yielded 3,390 MW. An additional 40 QFs made filings indicating a mix of new and existing capacity. The total capacity of these 40 QFs is 1,761 MW.
40. General Energy Associates, *Industrial Cogeneration Potential (1980-2001); Targeting Opportunities at the Plant Site*, May 1983 and EEI Report, *Cogeneration and Small Power Production: Facilities and Rates*, February 1980.
41. A precise estimate is not available owing to the uncertain pre-PURPA capacity of the "mixed" new and existing QF category.
42. Docket No. RM87-12-000.
43. id at p.4 Exhibit 13.
44. Paul L. Joskow and Richard Schmalensee, "The Performance of Coal-burning Electrical Generating Units in the United States: 1960-1980," MIT Department of Economics Working Paper, No. 379 (July, 1985).
45. The system appeared (at least potentially) to be highly efficient. But the proposed cycle's high efficiency caused heat to be rejected at a much lower temperature than conventional power cycles. So low was the temperature of the proposed thermal energy output, the Commission could not find it to be useful, as is required by the rules. *Energy Cogen Corp.*, Docket Nos. QF83-108-000, et al. 25 FERC Paragraph 61,316 (1984); *Turbo Gas and Electric, Ltd.*, Docket Nos. QF84-73-000, et al., 30 FERC Paragraph 61,123 (1985).
46. Stirling engines, for example, can produce electricity efficiently, but reject heat at relatively low temperatures in the engine water jacket. Fuel cells produce a similar mix of power and thermal outputs. Yet another technology for which QF status has proven problematical is the use of turbo-expanders to produce electricity at the pressure reduction stations of natural gas pipelines. The energy requirements and energy flows of such applications are not easily characterized as either cogeneration or small
COMPETITION IN ELECTRICITY

cogeneration or small power production. For a more detailed discussion of these and other technologies see G. Samuels and J.T. Meader, *MIUS Technology Evaluation: Prime Movers*, Oak Ridge National Laboratory (April, 1974).

47. A common example of a PURPA machine is a combined-cycle power station with a garden house tacked on the back. Extraction steam, and in some cases condenser discharge water, is used to heat the greenhouse. Such projects stand out because of their large unbalance between electrical and thermal outputs. Extraction of steam is kept to a minimum in order to produce the most electricity possible. The fraction of energy developed as thermal output usually hovers closely above the minimum required by the rules. Most of the reject heat is simply thrown away. If the greenhouse were truly a money maker, it would use all such heat available.

48. For all qualifying cogeneration facilities, the commission is required to find the existence of a useful thermal energy output. Under present practice, a thermal output is considered useful if an unaffiliated buyer is willing to purchase it at some non-zero price. If, for example, a PURPA machine cogenerator purchases natural gas for $2.50 per MMBtu and sells low-pressure steam to an unaffiliated greenhouse operator for $0.25 per MMBtu, the test would be passed. Indeed the energy *is* useful to the greenhouse operator, but the overall transaction may well not be useful to society as a whole.

The greenhouse operator might not be willing to pay a market-derived price for his energy ($2.50). He operates only because of the FERC's requirements for some sort of thermal energy output provided him with a subsidized, below-market price. The cogenerator would prefer to make electricity (which can be sold at a profit) than to sell steam at a loss, but he tolerates the loss because regulation seems to require it as the price of gaining access to wholesale power markets.

49. A quick review of *The Qualifying Facilities Report*, FERC-0118 (January 1987) provides evidence of these sizing decisions.

50. St. Joe Minerals Corporation, Docket No. EL82-19-000, is-

sued December-23, 1983 (21 FERC 61,323), *modified on rehearing* (22 FERC 61,211).

51. Cliffs Electric Service Company And Upper Peninsula Generating Company, *et al.*, Docket Nos. EL83-19-001, et al., issued September 17, 1985 (32 FERC Paragraph 61,372).

52. One possible exception to this and subsequent possible policy changes is described in Part V.C, below.

53. This paper does not address what is the maximum pricing flexibility allowed under the FPA or what minimum legal requirements must be met for rates to comport with the FPA.

54. The zone of economic influence would obviously include the utility's service territory, where it possessed an exclusive retail franchise. In certain cases, the zone might also include an immediately adjacent area, if the utility in question controlled most or all of the transmission facilities interconnected with the adjacent area and the utility serving the adjacent area owned little or no generation capacity.

CHAPTER 17: STATEMENT ON FERC INITIATIVES*

Larry Hobart
Executive Director, American Public Power Association

APPA has been asked to comment on proposals before the Federal Energy Regulatory Commission to (a) clarify certain requirements of the Public Utility Regulatory Policies Act of 1978, (b) provide guidelines for the use of competitive bidding systems to acquire non-utility power under PURPA, and (c) create a new category of independent power producers (IPPs) which would be subject to reduced regulation under the Federal Power Act.

Dealing with "Qualifying Facilities"

Section 210 of PURPA requires that self-regulated utilities, including systems regulated by city councils and elected or appointed boards, implement FERC rules for purchase of electric energy from qualifying cogeneration and small power production facilities at rates which are "just and reasonable to the electric consumers of the electric utility and in the public interest" and not discriminatory against qualifying facilities. The price level of the purchase is at the "incremental cost of alternative electric energy," i.e. the cost of electric energy a utility would generate or purchase from another source.

The statute definitely does not demand purchases when none are required to meet utility *needs*, and clearly contemplates adjustment in price levels to match *realistic alternatives* in particular time periods.

"Need" is measured by requirements which can be affected by cost-effective energy conservation and load management, as well as by production and purchase of power. "Least cost" analysis of the spectrum of opportunities — end-use control, third party generation, and utility power plants — dictates that "qualifying facilities" compete along with all other alternatives to create an adequate, reliable supply of needed

---

Submitted to Senate Energy and Natural Resources Committee, February 2, 1988

electricity at reasonable price with proper protection of the environment.

A key to the choice is consumer benefits. APPA has endorsed the approach of "least cost" planning in which utilities compare a spread of demand and supply side possibilities in the context of long-term plan, present governing bodies with a showing that documents the selections as cost-effective for consumers, and implement the approved program subject to rolling readjustments. The results may be a mix of projects ranging through such activities as rebates for energy efficient appliances, support for waste-to-energy facilities, and joint construction of scrubbed coal-fired generating plants.

PURPA projects are potentially part of the mix. It seems reasonable that they compete along with other electricity conservation and production measures to meet the standards which consumers ask utilities to meet. Whether it is administrative determination of "avoided cost", "competitive bidding", or some other equitable and effective selection process, the point is to permit picking the efficient solution.

Experience by the states and local self-regulated consumer-owned electric utilities indicated that it is possible to apply this approach now, without changes in FERC rules.

Regulation of IPPs

FERC is required to insure that rates charged by jurisdictional utilities are just and reasonable, and that they do not result in undue preference, advantage, prejudice, or discrimination.

Public power systems are affected by the Commission's implementation of this responsibility in several ways:

- About 900 local publicly owned electric utilities buy all or part of their bulk power supply from private power companies whose charges are regulated by the Commission. Appendix A is a list of these systems.
- A number of public power systems participate in power pools whose terms and conditions are subject to approval by the FERC.
- Availability and prices of transmission and coordination services for municipal electric utilities can be determined by Commission action.

With respect to wholesale power purchases, public power systems receive the protections of Section 205 and 206 of the Federal Power Act which deal with filed rates of jurisdictional utilities. Under these provisions, FERC has regulated for many years utilities which look like what are currently described as independent power producers — entities which possess no "significant" market power, have no "captive" customers, do not serve a retail franchise, and control no "essential" transmission. These existing IPPs would include the "Yankee" nuclear plants; energy producers such as Electric Energy, Inc., and. Ohio Valley Electric Corporation; and Cliffs Electric and Safe Harbor Water Power. While the Commission may use waivers, abbreviated filings, formula rate-setting, and reservations of rights to deal with special situations which it may distinguish, it has preserved its ability to collect data pertinent to FERC responsibilities, to review transfers of property, to deal with conflicts of interest, to secure cost-of-service data, and to test rate changes.

For instance, the Commission in February, 1987 stated its view that Ocean State Power, a newly-formed IPP, owns jurisdictional facilities; must make any filings required by the Federal Power Act and Commission regulations, including provision of cost-of-service data; and is subject to rate review under Section 205.

FERC also cannot abandon its statutory responsibilities to determine that rates charged by investor-owned electric utilities subject to its jurisdiction are not adversely affected by IPP purchases. The Commission asserted last year that it will entertain, and has the right to raise itself, prudence challenges in wholesale rate cases which involve the question of whether an IPP transaction satisfies a system's needs at the lowest cost.

This point is of particular importance where utility self-dealing is involved, as is the case with Ocean State. Prior to the construction of the first unit, Ocean State intends to reorganize the partnership to include affiliates of the following companies at the indicated percentages: TransCanada Pipelines Limited (40%), Eastern Utilities Associates (25%), New England Electric System (20%), Newport Electric Corporation (4.9%), and private investors (10.1%).

As of the end of 1987, about 35 private power companies

had formed cogeneration subsidiaries. Of this number, 29 had reportedly made equity commitments, and investments were estimated at $2.35 billion for shares in projects totaling 4,835 MW. A number of these subsidiaries supply power to their parent companies or other utilities. Depending on how they are structured, these projects may be qualifying facilities entitled to "avoided cost" payments from their parent companies. In any case less than arms-length relationships result, to the possible detriment of rigorous supply bargaining. FERC has documented exactly this kind of problem in connection with utility-owned fuel suppliers.

In recent years, a number of private power companies have also sought to reorganize their utilities so as to move regulation of bulk power facilities — power plants and transmission — from the state to the federal level, where it is assumed rate review will be more kind and FERC-approved wholesale changes (representing roughly three-quarters of the cost of delivered power) can be flowed through to consumers without state scrutiny. These efforts to create separate generation, transmission, and distribution firms have been rebuffed by a number of state commission, primarily on the grounds that consumer protection would suffer. However, establishment of a new regulatory category of IPPs as proposed by FERC could be a way out for the IOUs: use of subsidiaries to sell to themselves and others at prices which would be subject to minimal "relaxed" rate regulation at FERC.

Ability of FERC to measure actual and alternative cost-of-service and to adjust rates to meet this test, is the only practical protection which many wholesale customers have in seeking to insure that rates they are charged are just, reasonable, and nondiscriminatory. Under existing law, this means that two points of consumer protection are available: Commission scrutiny of IPPs and/or IOUs. The public interest would not be served by "relaxing" this regulation. Prior regulatory experience does not suggest that existing practices are not working effectively.

It is important to recognize that IPPs are not a new or unique development requiring special treatment; that they can — and do — sell in the marketplace now; that there is no special reason to secure them in perpetuity; that the technologies they employ are technologies also available to electric utilities; and that a utility must screen individual proposals based on standards of cost, size, dependability and dispatchability, location relative to load centers, progress in securing permits, and other pertinent economic and engineering factors.

In a real sense, independent power producers are turnkey projects where the builder keeps the key — a surrogate for utility construction. If they can do a better job of keeping construction costs and operating expenses down, running the plant more efficiently, meeting environmental standards with greater ease — they should be the project of choice. They offer another option — an opportunity to open up the bulk power supply market in a different way.

But we do not need to abandon basic regulatory protections to secure these advantages.

We should also learn something from PURPA experience. While there is no doubt that our 10-year learning curve has shown that small power producers and cogeneration make significant economic and electrical contributions, they have also resulted in some extra expenses, planning difficulties, enhanced reliance on natural gas, and certain environmental conflicts.

The lesson would seem to be: don't enshrine any particular power source with special protection but force them to compete and allow utilities to make the decision subject to public review.

Transmission on Required Consideration

Much of FERC discussion of IPPs is bottomed on a belief that "workable competitive" markets for power currently exist. However, the discussion of change deliberately delegates to a subordinate level one of the basic instruments essential to secure competition: transmission. And when Commission members do discuss transmission, there is a tendency to focus on charges as the secret to effectuating a solution to any access difficulties, a suggestion that exaggerates the cost of transmission in utility accounting and utilizes the wrong wing of economics for the analysis — price theory instead of industrial organization.

Here are some facts about transmission:

- Transmission lines link to load centers 10,475 utility generating units with 656,118 mw of operable capacity, EIA reported last year.
- Transmission capital costs and operating expenses are *not* the major element of electric utility charges.

For major private power companies, the Energy Information administration reported in 1987 that, total generation plant accounted for $173.9 billion, total distribution plant for $83.5 billion, and transmission plant for $42.8 billion.

Similarly, EIA statistics show total generation expenses were $62.8 billion, total distribution expenses were $4.6 billion, and total transmission expenses were $1.5.billion. Expressed in terms of percent of total operation and maintenance expenses, the breakdown was generation, 78.4%; distribution, 5.7%; and transmission, 1.8%. When looked at as a percent of operating revenues, the EIA number were 46.4% for generation, 3.4% for distribution, and 1.1% for transmission.

- A sample of 203 transmission service agreements taken from the 1065 on file with FERC in 1984 shows that postage stamp rates for firm wheeling vary by more than 700% when based on capacity charges and in excess of 4,000% when bottomed on kilowatt-hour prices, that contracts for non-firm kilowatt-hour wheeling differ by as much as 3,400%, and that line loss adjustment factors have a range which is 400% apart from top to bottom.

Because a large number of these arrangements are bilateral agreements, not general tariffs, it is frequently possible to structure the opportunities for wheeling by setting the charges for individual utilities. If the price is set sufficiently high, it can make uneconomic a power supply deal which would otherwise be beneficial to a utility which could be considered a competitor. Thus, "flexible pricing" can be employed as a tool to promote or protect monopolization in the bulk power supply market.

- About 80% of the nation's 612,000 miles of transmission lines are owned by some 200 private power companies out of the country's 3,400 utilities of all ownership.

Ownership of transmission allows monopolization of markets. Here's an example:

On July 2, 1987, the Board of Directors of the Sacramento, California, Municipal Utility District (SMUD) directed its staff to solicit bids for 200 to 400 MW of firm dispatchable energy to be delivered to the District's transmission system at a price of 42 mills or less. SMUD received 49 responses. Among there were these:

- Pacific Gas & Electric Company 400 mw @ 48 to 62 mills/kwh
- Bonneville Power administration 1,350 mw @ 30 mills/kwh
- Southern California Edison 400 mw @ 40 mills/kwh

Both the BPA and SCE transactions depended on PG&E transmitting the power to SMUD. However, PG&E wassimultaneously seeking to buyout SMUD and/or to sell SMUD power at wholesale itself. While a physical path exists for the movement of the power, PG&E declined to agree to carry out the transmission service — even though it would be compensated for performing the wheeling function. The result of this anti-competitive action could be the denial to SMUD consumers of sources of power at lower cost than that available from PG&E.

SMUD is not the only California publicly-owned electric system which his experienced anti-competitive moves by PG&E. The Northern California Power Agency, a joint action agency representing the interests of a group of municipal electric utilities in Northern California, has experienced treatment designed to limit its economic viability. As reported to the California state legislature last fall by NCPA general manager Mike McDonald, "the examples of PG&E withholding transmission service are numerous and widespread."

California is not, of course, the only state where anti-competitive transmission policies of private power companies work to thwart economic transactions sought by publicly owned electric utilities. The case of Geneva, Illinois, provides a Midwest example where FERC solved the problem.

Geneva has a municipal electric system, and bought power

at wholesale from Commonwealth Edison Company. Under terms of a settlement, Geneva and Edison's other full requirements customers may obtain transmission and/or partial requirements service upon one year's notice. Geneva gave notice so that it would secure transmission in order to buy bulk power from a cheaper supplier. Edison filed a rate for transmission service which was designed to make the transaction uneconomic, including a charge for unrequested stand-by service. FERC ordered Edison to file a transmission rate based on Edison's average embedded costs of its transmission system, and to drop the stand-by charge. The Commission pointed out that:

> "By the terms of the agreement, Edison was to enable any of its wholesale customers to pursue alternative power supply options under reasonable parameters. Implicit in such an arrangement must be an agreement that transmission service will be priced reasonably relative to existing service being provided by the utility."

FERC noted that Edison proposed a rate which was approximately four times the price that had been quoted to Geneva during its evaluation of suppliers — "a rate that will effectively preclude the supply switch negotiated by Geneva." Concluded the FERC:

> "Despite the obvious objective of the parties settlement to make available viable supply alternatives for the affected customers, the pleadings make clear that the arrangements negotiated by Geneva will necessarily be foreclosed if the proposed rate is placed in effect. Whatever ultimate findings the Commission might make with regard to the merit of Edison's pricing structure or, conversely, its anti-competitive effects, we know at this point that the filing will immediately subject Geneva to an observable prejudice or disadvantage in the power supply market, that will not be remedied through later refunds. Based on all the circumstances, including the support proffered by Edison to date, it simply has not satisfied its bur-

COMPETITION IN ELECTRICITY

den of proving that its rate proposal is just, reasonable, and otherwise lawful."

What does this kind of opportunity mean to local, publicly-owned electric utilities?

In Wisconsin, a joint action agency supplies the bulk power supply needs of 27 municipal electric utilities. Within a nearly 1,000-mile radius, the agency contracts with 10 different generating utilities in five different states for power and transmission services. The results of this competitive bulk power supply market are savings of $2-3 million per year on a revenue base of about $75 million. The agency's largest "supplier/competitor" lowered its on-peak energy rates from 43.3 mills to 29 mills per kilowatt-hour while also reducing its off-peak energy rates and maintain a steady demand charge — results in direct response to competition in the field of bulk power supply. Here's how the agency's manager, Dave Penn, described the situation to a British correspondent:

"In their efforts to compete this last year, all four of our state's investor-owned utilities implemented unheard of wholesale rate deceases that ranged from 3-11% after being negotiated. Moreover, the state's regulatory commissioners have acknowledged publicly that all of the state's ratepayers have benefited because of this new pencil sharpening and cost consciousness that we helped induce, not just the ratepayers in my member's jurisdictions."

"The advantages of this competitive process are obvious and large. Consumers get cost savings and lower rates. The utilities become more cost conscious and efficient. Transactions between areas of excess and deficit power yield short run savings as well as better long run planning to eliminate this problem in the future. No losses of reliability have been, or would have to be, sacrificed to gain these competition benefits."

"In the U.S. much of the competition of process that I describe is a function of the current excess capacity situation. When supplies become tight again, absent any institutional change, the companies that own the transmission network will exercise that 'natural monopoly' control. They will raise supply prices, restrict entry, and tie access to transmission to other bulk power sales from their own company. They can do this in our country because the private utilities are vertically integrated, owning generation and transmission and distribution, and because no regulatory authority has been given the ability to require wheeling or common carriage. Many of us in the industry are trying to get our policymakers to address this issue now, rather than wait until a crisis or abuses leaves them no alternative."

With respect to transmission, the impression left by FERC is that if prices are set at the proper level, a utility will automatically do what is in the public interest. But the fact of the matter is that maximization of monopoly power and profits may dictate utility decisions which do not match the "reasonable man" ideas of FERC.

FERC has failed to use fully the power it has — application of the antitrust laws, limited authority to order wheeling, actions against predatory pricing, dissemination of information on industry policies and practices, a request for expanded authority form Congress where it is necessary to get the job done.

Terms and conditions for transmission access are key issues for the electric utility industry and the general public. They are important because:

- In normal operations of utilities, transmission is a basic ingredient in making the utility system work well through economic dispatch, diversity exchanges, emergency backup, coordination serviced, shared reserves, and other techniques, which help get the most out of an interconnected system.
- Surplus generating capacity is unevenly distributed throughout the country. To make good use of surpluses, willing buyers and sellers must have ready access to each

other so that: the most efficient units can be operated at their optimum dispatchable levels.

- A relatively few large, vertically integrated electric utilities dominate transmission. Ownership of transmission facilities can create classic "bottleneck" monopoly power over an essential part of utility operations, and block efforts to improve bulk power supply.
- Public concerns about environmental and aesthetic damage limit the number of allowable transmission facilities and encourage multiple use of rights-of-way. Duplication of facilities is also discouraged for economic reasons.
- In the case of new generating plants, major electric generating stations are located where there is a confluence of the necessary elements — a large land area, economic access to a fuel supply, a plentiful amount of water, an adequate transportation system, a place to dispose of surplus heat, and an absence of unacceptable aesthetic insults. There are not many places like that left. To share the sites, transmission access is essential.
- Only with equitable opportunity for utility use of transmission facilities can there be assurance of workable competitive bulk power markets.

Changes in the Utility Industry

In evaluating the questions of qualifying facilities, independent power producers, and transmission, it is important to understand what is happening in the electric utility industry and what is not. Consider these facts:

- Commentators who support "non-utility" power production would have us believe that the era of central station electric service, with large generating units owned and operated by utilities, has ended. However, three public power systems last year brought on line 1,775,000 kw of coal-fired capacity and an additional 1,350,000 kw will be available shortly in second units at these sites, which are also capable of expansion to add even more units. The total operating or under-construction capacity represents nearly 5% of all local public power installed capacity.

The three plants have exemplary records on capital costs

and construction deadlines, offer long-term competitive sources of bulk power supply for a large number of public power systems, use a plentiful fuel with reasonable price stability, demonstrate that environmental problems can be effectively solved, reveal that economies of scale in generation have not disappeared, and show that multiple-utility partnerships are effective devices to share risk and spread benefits.

These facts do not mean that cogeneration and small power production are not significant sources of supplemental supply. They are — and will be. But it is important to keep things in perspective.

- A study by the Washington, D.C. consulting firm Hagler, Bailly & Company recently identified 4,600 cogeneration (production of both electricity and steam or hot water for commercial purposes) and small power projects (80 mw or smaller, fueled by biomass, waste, renewable or geothermal resources). They include more than 2,800 projects with 24,300 mw in operation, and 28,232 mw under construction or active planning. Hagler, Bailly identified about 11,000 mw as either indefinitely postponed or cancelled. The firm predicted total on-line capacity as high as 44,306 mw in 1995.
- Cogeneration projects account for 75% of the total active capacity. Although we hear a great deal about the use of renewable fuels for power production, the Hagler, Bailly study noted that the majority of cogeneration projects (57%) are fired by natural gas with coal fueling an additional 27%. Other fuels such as oil, propane, biomass and wood fired systems accounted for the remainder. Combined-cycle systems and boiler/steam turbine facilities each accounted for 35% of the cogeneration.

Among small power projects, hydroelectric facilities accounted for the largest single block of capacity (2,900 mw) with waste and geothermal steam supplying another major segment 2,000 mw). An interesting fact is that 20,200 mw of the total active capacity — 38.5% of the total tabulated by the firm — is located in either California or Texas. Another arresting statistic is that about 26% (13,600 mw)

COMPETITION IN ELECTRICITY

of the active capacity is owned by the chemicals industry.

What do all these numbers suggest?

Cogeneration and small power production can continue to play a role in future power supply, but the overall impact appears to be highly state-and industry-specific, and the total amount of capacity predicted for the U.S. is a small part of all existing utility resources (647,000 mw) or those expected to be in place in 1996 (716,000 mw).

Much of the capacity discovered by Bailly, is gas-fired and its economic viability will be affected by possible price escalation for this fuel.

All of the approaches described in the study involve conventional technologies that have been employed by electric utilities and industrial establishments for many decades, the embellishment in the case of cogeneration being the use of waste heat as a thermal resource — a practice which has waxed and waned over the years depending on the comparative prices of electricity and fuels matched to the manufacturing or space conditioning needs of a user.

- Discussion of technical approaches leads to a third questionable formulation that is circulated currently — the suggestion that technological change makes necessary radical restructuring of the electric utility industry. FERC Chairman Martha Hesse told Congress recently that "new technologies" and "technological advancements" are compelling rapid and dramatic change in the electric utility industry. The claim does not match the evidence.

What *does* change is the choice of technologies. The fact of the matter is that flawed application of an existing technology is really what causes all the talk.

A major reason for current political debate of restructuring is the very large cost of some nuclear power plants and the lack of load for them to serve. The terrible financial tabs for these "troubled" facilities has caused state regulatory commissions to question the judgement of utilities which continued to build them and has driven "competitive customers" (as opposed to captive "core customers" who don't have alternatives) to seek better solutions. The result has been prudency disallowances" (where a private power company is not permitted to put all or part of a plant in rate base and earn a return on it), and actions by large users to self-generate, co-generate, seek incentive rates, "shop" for electricity from another source, close a plant, or move to a new service area.

The turnaround in declining costs experienced by the electric utility industry that began in the last 1960s was caused by a number of factors: the topping-off of economies of scale, the wild upward curve for fuel prices, spiraling inflation and interest rates, and more stringent regulatory review.

Recently, however, the costs for fuel, construction, and money have fallen, and plans for construction have slowed in an era of excess capacity. The last of the "troubled" nuclear power plants are working their way through the system toward completion or cancellation, and a minority of individual utilities are affected. Real costs of electricity have leveled off and even declined.

• The economics of the electric utility industry have changed because of growing efficiency in end-use due to consumer reaction to power prices.

A National Association of Homebuilders' poll found that more than 68% of existing home owners said that energy efficiency would be their most important consideration if choosing a new home. Seventy percent of new homebuyers rated the quality of insulation and energy efficiency as very important factors in their decision to buy.

Builders have responded to these views of home purchasers by building more energy-efficient houses.

Home-appliance manufacturers contribute strongly. The Association of Home Appliance Manufacturers reported huge percentage increases in the energy efficiency of major household machines.

Comparing 1984 to 1972, the appliance makers found new refrigerators used 34% less energy, new freezers 45% less, new dishwashers 36%, new clothes washers 34%.

Development of power electronic controls permits use of variable speed motors which, together with energy management schemes and lighting improvements, are increasing the energy efficiency of commercial and industrial establishments.

What do all these facts suggest? *They point us in these directions:*

1. The objectives of reform in the electric utility industry should be to improve the lot of consumers by holding power prices down and by aiding the wise use of electricity. Utilities must offer customers a cost-effective menu of energy services designed to meet their specialized needs. Electrical efficiency will be essential to beat the competition.
2. The public today seeks both economic growth and environmental protection. A utility task is to reconcile — trough planning technology — these sometimes conflicting goals. Our cities and towns look for a "sustainable economy" — one which preserves the quality of life and simultaneously plugs unnecessary leaks of energy dollars outside the community.
3. Demand-side answers to energy needs — for example, conservation and load management — must be balanced against supply-side solutions such as coal-fired generating facilities and cogeneration plans, to arrive at a "least cost" answer. But to make the comparison work, cost effectiveness tests must be applied to both sides of the equation. The energy field today is facing a flood of supply — an oil glut, a gas bubble, a coal oversupply, and an electricity excess. Power systems must deal with the entrepreneurial instincts and merchandising mechanisms of a buyers' market, and that fact represents significant pressure to hold costs down. Electricity today competes with fossil fuels, self-generation, and efficient energy management and devices for sales in a mature energy market. Improv-

ing efficiency and keeping costs down is an economic imperative for utilities.

4. Achieving these goals does not require radical change. We do not need to destroy the industry to save it. What is needed is a continuation of progressive planning and access policies initiated in the 1960s but sidetracked by the energy trauma of the 1970s. These policies recognize that the public favors pluralism — the opportunity for choice on what kind of utility serves it at retail; pricing policies based on cost; and continued recognition of an obligation to serve.

5. Working off capacity surpluses will be painful, possibly crippling and even life-threatening to some utilities. However, for most utilities the crisis never materialized or has now passed. To help match surplus sellers with potential buyers, steps should be taken to open transmission access.

6. For the longer range future, when new generation is required to supplement optimum load management and energy conservation and to substitute for retired plants, regional planning must be employed. Planning is necessary to insure that the foreseeable needs of all utilities are taken into account in initiating new generation and transmission facilities which meet least-cost standards and in properly protecting the environment and public health and safety. Planning is required to permit the public to understand power proposals, and to secure a "sign off" which will permit utility implementation.

7. Utilities should assume leadership in carrying out these tasks. But history makes it clear that these tasks will not be addressed equitably in the absence of effective and enforceable government guidelines. Monopolistic control of essential facilities, anti-competitive acquisition policies, and predatory pricing are problems which require public are resolution. Plant sites and transmission rights-of-way cannot be obtained without governmental approval, the necessary authority must be formulated and exercised by Congress, state legislators, regulatory commissions and the courts.

8. The United States does not face an electrical emergency as far as generation is concerned. While national numbers can mask individual utility and regional problems, the fact is that there are large amounts of surplus capacity,

and reserve margins remain high and efficiency in end-use application continues to increase.

The current hiatus in need is the time to prepare for the future. The electric utility industry is part of the social and physical infrastructure of the national economy, just like our roads, bridges, and waterworks. It is what makes American work. It must be maintained and improved a goal which demands public planning.

CHAPTER 18: TESTIMONY AT FERC TECHNICAL CONFERENCE*

James L. Plummer
President, QED Research

My involvement in the subject of electricity competition began in 1981. In July of 1983, I contributed an article entitled "A Different Approach to Electricity Deregulation" to *Public Utilities Fortnightly* which attempted to anticipate some of the steps in increased electricity competition that are now occurring. In 1983 I edited and contributed to a book entitled *Electric Power Strategic Issues*, which drew together some of the early thinking on the possible paths that competition and deregulation might take in the electricity industry. In August 1986, my colleagues and I at QED wrote an article for *Public Utilities Fortnightly* called "Industrial Electricity Ratemaking: A New Ballgame." This article identified the fast movement towards electricity self-generation (bypass) in the industrial sector, and the implications for the level and structure of industrial electricity rates.

I have structured my testimony around the five topic areas and thirteen questions that were posed by the FERC staff in the September announcement of this technical conference.

TOPIC AREA NO. 1: THE NEED FOR NEW POLICIES TOWARD IPPS

Question #1.

What role should independent or third party generation play in meeting our nation's future energy needs? Should utilities be afforded the opportunity to purchase from third party or independent power producers under rates set through competitive bidding or rate negotiations in workably competitive markets when such sources are less costly than other alternatives available to utilities?

Presented before Federal Energy Regulatory Commission Technical Conference on Independent Power Producers, October 23,1987.

Answer #1.

Independent or third party generation can play a very important role in satisfying future electricity needs. In addition, the competitive process, if it is broad enough and not overly constrained by political considerations, can bring enormous efficiency improvements to the operations of the electricity industry as a whole.

As an important aside, I think the term "Independent Power Producers" (IPPs) can be misleading. There may be new players in the game, in the form of Catalyst or other entrepreneurs who build or acquire merchant plants. However, for the most part, the bulk of IPPs will be industrial firms who decide to self generate, and want the additional options of selling to the local regulated utility or other industrial customers. This is already occurring on a grand scale. California utilities has estimated that industrial bypass could take away over 20% of their loads over a ten year period. There will be increasing pressure on PUCs and legislatures to broaden the interconnection and wheeling rights of these industrial firms that are today labeled "self-generators," but will be in the vanguard of tomorrow's "merchant plants" or "IPPs." These industrial electricity producers also have an inherent economic advantage, because they are servicing a thermal load at the point of generation. This makes them less vulnerable to future increases in natural gas prices. The industrial electricity producer who is not dependent on either the political vagaries of QF status or the current low level of natural gas prices is the kind of potential "low cost producer" who the regulated utilities must fear the most in the competitive world to come. He is typically not a new player. He became "independent" of his local utility and PUC after suffering through decades of interclass rate discrimination. He is usually a hardened and cynical old player in the electricity game.

The FERC proposals are one variation of the "top down" type of deregulation that attempts to view a rough institutional future that is better than the current institutional structure. As commendable as this effort is, we should keep in mind that there is a "bottom up" form of increased competition and deregulations already being fought out daily in the trenches of industrial bypass. In industrial bypass regulation, there is no grand vision, only incremental victories and defeats for all parties. If FERC is successful in its reform efforts, then the two forms of deregulation will meet and overlap, and may be compatible in some ways and incompatible in others.

Question #2.

Can third party or independent power production be integrated into the wholesale power market in a fashion consistent with utilities' obligations to provide their customers with adequate, reasonably priced and reliable service?

Answer #2.

Yes. The regulated utility gives up its monopoly status in generation. In return, the regulated utility and its unregulated subsidiaries should be assured of the right to compete on a equal footing with the other players in the competition among generating suppliers. It would be fundamentally unfair to deny the regulated utility the opportunity to compete just because it happens to own downstream transmission and distribution assets, and rate-based generating plants. There are ample federal and state authorities to deal with any abuses or conflicts of interest that may arise. Also, it would be foolish to throw away the decades of learning and technical expertise possessed by the regulated utilities. Just as the IPPs and the QFs can provide "yardstick" competitive reference points for the regulated utilities, so also can the technical prowess of the regulated utilities provide a high standard for the IPPs and the QFs to live up to. There is no reason for reliability to suffer, because regulated utilities and their PUCs can insist that reserve margins be maintained and that reliability standards be built into the competitive contracts (and perhaps also incorporated as non-price factors in bidding). As with other contracts, there can be penalties for bad performance and rewards for good performance. In California, a substantial amount of QF capacity has been interconnected with the utility grid without significant operational problems.

Question #3.

Do current Commission regulatory policies create barriers to the development of independent power producers? If so, which policies operate to constrain IPPs? What classes of IPPs are constrained?

Answer #3.

Yes. Currently, an industrial firm must make a hard choice if it decides to become a self generator rather than a QF. It may be avoiding a lot of unwelcome regulatory burdens, but it is also giving up the option of selling even a portion of the electricity output to regulated utilities. There should be a continuum of possibilities open to self generators, rather than a harsh "either/or" decision. Also the current 50% ownership limitation on regulated utilities operates as an inhibition that could limit competition in the future.

Question #4.

What problems currently exist that could be alleviated by reducing the Commission's regulation of IPPs? Would greater development of IPPs provide benefits that are not already being provided in sale-leaseback arrangements?

Answer #4.

An IPP that is a "price taker" should not have to endure the costs, delays, and inflexibilities involved in conventional FERC regulation. These factors are a serious inhibition to the development of new IPP capacity. The regulatory changes that are being contemplated by FERC could open up dozens of innovative approaches to financing and contracting for IPP power. By contrast, sale-leaseback arrangements are just one narrow project financing alternative, whose applications cannot achieve very many of the efficiency benefits of the competitive processes under consideration.

Question #5.

Does the Public Utility Holding Company Act (PUCHA)

COMPETITION IN ELECTRICITY

impede the development of IPPs? If so, how?

Answer #5.

Many IPPs could fall under the Act's definition of a public utility. Thus, if any other entity owned more than 10% of one of these IPPs, then that entity would become a holding company under PUCHA, with all the attendant joys of a stern SEC guardian. That is enough to scare anyone. This is a relic that ought to be eliminated

TOPIC AREA NO.2 IDENTIFYING AND REGULATING PRODUCERS LACKING MARKET POWER

Question #6.

Are there any public policy objectives served by traditional embedded cost regulation of the price of power sold by producers who do not have significant market power? Are any other purposes by the Commission imposing on such producers an obligation to provide service beyond the terms of their contracts? Are any purposes served by regulating the corporate and financial structure and activities of such producers?

Answer #6.

The FERC can retain some latent authority and capability for regulating all these matters, but still choose to not exercise that authority unless there is widespread nonperformance on IPP contracts.

Question #7.

Can certain power producers be identified generically as not having significant market power, and thus classified as IPPs? What specific criteria should be used to identify these producers?

Answer #7.

It is possible to do that, using the techniques that have

been refined in the literature and legal case histories in the antitrust field. However, I think it is better to focus on the competitive process in which IPP participates rather than the absolute characteristics of each IPP. An IPP that would have a pro-competitive effect in one market might have an anti-competitive effect in another market.

The experience so far strongly indicates that the unregulated subsidiaries of regulated utilities do act independently. I think that these unregulated subsidiaries should be given the benefit of a presumption of independence unless and until there is evidence presented to the contrary in the regulatory process. Thus, it is the market power and economic characteristics of the subsidiary that are important rather than the market power and economic characteristics of the regulated utility. The materials from the FERC staff that refers to "zones of economic influence" seem to make the opposite presumption, and I think that kind of logic could wind up having an anti-competitive impact.

TOPIC AREA NO. 3: RATE REGULATION OF IPPS

Question #8.

Which of the following pricing mechanisms should be used for regulating the rates of IPPs in order to promote economic efficiency in the electric industry?

a) rates set at or below avoided cost determined administratively
b) rates set through a bidding mechanism
c) rates set through private negotiation
d) rates set through other pricing mechanisms

Answer #8.

Any or all of these mechanisms could work in the context of the institutions of a given state. I would be inclined to give state PUCs great latitude over the type of competitive process to use, but more guidance as to what parties could be included or excluded from the chosen competitive process, and what size blocks of power should be included in the competition. (See response to Question #9 below.)

432   COMPETITION IN ELECTRICITY

Question #9.

What would be the appropriate role, if any, for IPPs in a competitive bidding system that the states might adopt under PURPA?

Answer #9.

Of all the issues being addressed in this technical conference, this is the one on which I have the strongest conviction. I do not think that a competitive process that includes QFs and is done with the blessing and/or encouragement of FERC should be a "token competition" or a "set aside competition." Such processes might lessen some of the current problems of avoided cost pricing, but they could create many more problems, and they could become cosmetic symbols of competition that had little real meaning or impact on economic efficiency. If different states could set up different scopes of competition, each could indulge its own prejudices about "preferred" and "not preferred" technologies, whether to admit out-of-state bidders or not, whether to admit bids from foreign entities, and whether to protect its local monopolies or expose them to the winds of full competition. It would be a mess, and there would be serious instances of anti-competitive impacts that emanated directly from the exclusionary decisions of particular PUCs.

As appealing as it is to talk about "states rights" and the states as laboratories for social experimentation, I think this would be dangerous and explosive form of experimentation. It could easily set back other progress toward deregulation and increased competition in the electricity industry. Many states with limited PUC staff capabilities might take the deceptively attractive route of a "limited competition" first, with vague plans for broadening it later. Then, the limited competition would fail because of insufficient players, and kill the possibility of having a broader (and more successful) competition.

Specifically, I think state level competition that excludes IPPs is worse than no competition at all. The IPPs will become important quantitatively, and they should not be denied the opportunity to compete merely because they chose, perhaps for entirely separate reasons, not to elect QF status.

In my view, FERC should prescribe in its regulation that, if a state chooses to use a competitive bidding mechanism, that it should be an "all source" bidding system. By that I mean that it should apply to all increments of new capacity, and that it should include all bulk power market options (including supplies from neighboring utilities, and foreign utilities), potential capacity additions by the regulated utility, QF's, all technologies, and IPPs (including the unregulated subsidiaries of the regulated utility of any other utilities). The greatest protection from abuse comes from including as many actual and potential competitors as possible. That is far preferable to the prospect of PUCs trying to define criteria for delineating "good competitors" and "bad competitors." I never met a competitor I didn't like (except in consulting). I cringe when I think of FERC or PUCs trying to define "zones of economic influence."

An "all source" competition supervised by a PUC is no different *in concept* from the prudency reviews of fuel procurement and bulk power purchases that PUCs now do on a routine basis. It is different in terms of the depth and detail of analysis and PUC staff capability required. Forcing PUCs to either staff up to "do it right" with an all source competition or not using bidding competition at all would protect against the more flaky and political forms of experimentation. Some might question whether expansion of PUC staffs is consistent with the overall spirit of deregulation. In this instance, it is quite consistent.

Question #10.

If the states were to allow the IPPs to directly participate in a competitive bidding process, what flexibility should be afforded to the purchasing utilities and state public utility commissions to determine the role of non-price factors in the bidding evaluation process?

Answer #10.

Wide flexibility should be given to the PUCs and regulated utilities in this area. It is not a serious impediment to implementation of a competitive system. (see answer to

434   COMPETITION IN ELECTRICITY

Question #2 above.)

Question #11.

How can concerns about the reliability, dispatchability, and performance of IPPs be adequately addressed?

Answer #11.

They can be addressed at the PUC level and the company level. These are not serious impediments to the implementation of a competitive system. (See answer to Question #2 above.)

TOPIC AREA #4: UTILITY OWNERSHIP OF IPPS

Question #12.

Under what circumstances, if any, should generating facilities be eligible for IPP status if they are owned by utilities possessing a monopoly franchise to serve retail customers?

a) Should a utility-owned facility be eligible for IPP status only if it is located outside the utility's zone of economic influence? If so, what factors are relevant to identify a utility's zone of economic influence?
b) Should utility-owned generating facilities be eligible for IPP status if they are located in the utility's service territory but their power is sold in markets beyond the utility's zone of economic influence?
c) If utility-owned generating facilities are eligible for IPP status, what steps should FERC take to protect against potential abuses (e.g. self-dealing, daisy chaining, reciprocal dealing, cost misallocation, etc.)?
d) Should a joint venture be eligible for IPP status if the local utility is a part owner of the venture? If so, what limits should be placed on the venture or the utility owning a portion of the venture?

Answer #12.

My view is that the best competitve process is one that strives to maximize the number of players. The exact mechanism that could be used to deal with abuses is a detail that can and should be deferred until the stage of implementing regulations.

TOPIC AREA #5: FERC/STATE ISSUES

Question #13.

What are the policy ramifications for the division of jurisdiction between FERC and state commissions?

Answer #13.

The implementation of these kinds of competitive systems may require that FERC move more quickly than it has to date on resolving issues of wheeling access and discrimination in wheeling pricing. It is possible for FERC to use its existing authorities to assure that a bidder in a state level competition could effectively presume the availability of non-discriminatory wheeling, or at least that one bidder could not use its ownership of transmission facilities as a weapon against another bidder. Some PUCs have coveted the turf of QF wheeling. There is no logical reason for them to resent FERC actions which guarantee the availability of *wholesale* wheeling to the participants in bidding competitions. This is a reasonable division of regulatory jurisdiction that would help the PUCs carry out their roles, and also push FERC more quickly down the road of resolving key transmission access and pricing issues. There is a growing risk that regulatory inertia will delay adding sufficient transmission capacity to accommodate any form of increased competition. The highest priority should be given, at the state and federal level, to clarifying the nature of the obligations to serve and the *obligations to build* in the transmission stage of the industry.

SECTION F

WHEELING ACCESS
AND PRICING

CHAPTER 19: FOR COMPETITION'S SAKE - TRANSMISSION ACCESS FIRST

David W. Penn* and Rodney Stevenson**

Many electric industry participants, including the Federal Energy Regulatory Commission (FERC), have got the regulatory agenda mixed up. They have taken too literally the biblical injunction that the last shall be made first, and the first, last.

In this article we will discuss why the FERC has got things backwards; the necessary but not sufficient role transmission access must play in any schemes to extend reliance on socially beneficial competition; and how the FERC should go about expanding the vision and authorities it has with respect to transmission.

Our goal is to use an institutional economics approach to help reorient the ongoing debates concerning the restructuring of both the bulk power supply industry and its regulation. It is already past the time when we need to step back and look at this broader social picture, rather than limiting ourselves to an out of sequence, piecemeal regulatory approach that is constrained by what certain people think we can, as opposed to should, do.

Chemists and construction workers alike understand that the order of activities is crucial. To mix reagents in the wrong order is to risk a serious accident. And to attempt to pour the upper floors of a building before the foundation is firmly set invites disaster. Likewise with movements towards

---

*David W. Penn is General Manager of Wisconsin Public Power, Inc. System, a joint agency supplying wholesale electricity to its 27 municipal utility members. Prior to that, Mr. Penn was Chief Economist of the Office of Competition in the U.S. Department of Energy. Mr. Penn holds a B.S. degree in economics from Washington University in St. Louis, and an M.A. degree in economics from the University of Wisconsin.

**Rodney Stevenson is Associate Professor of Business at the University of Wisconsin - Madison, where he is also director of the Public Utility Institute. Professor Stevenson formerly was a staff member of the Federal Power Commission. He holds a Ph.D in economics from Michigan State University.

promoting competition in the electric utility industry: placing the cart in front of the horse doesn't get the job done.

Competition has moved to center stage in the debate over appropriate public policy for the electric utility industry. Utilities want to substitute market forces for regulatory authority. Customers and state regulators want more supply options. Federal regulators want to emulate the deregulation movement that transformed other regulated industries.

Led by the FERC and various utility advocates, significant players have argued that the way to achieve effective electric utility competition is to reduce regulatory control over supply pricing and remove restrictions on non-regulated generation. But relaxing regulation is not the same as promoting competition, especially if steps are taken out of order. By asking the wrong question first, the FERC is opening the door to a staircase lacking the necessary bottom stairs. If the regulators want to promote socially beneficial competition, they should first focus on the question of how to achieve open and non-discriminatory transmission access.

INSTITUTIONAL SETTING OF THE INDUSTRY

In terms of size and importance, the electric utility industry has few peers. Annual electricity sales are approaching $200 billion, and yearly investments of 30 to 45 billion dollars in new plant and equipment make the electric utilities America's most capital intensive industry. During the industry's history its financial commitments have often driven regulatory policy toward trading off consumer well-being for investor protection and return.[1]

Not as well known is the fact that the industry is organizationally diverse. There are over 3,400 electric utilities serving more than 100 million customers. Most of the industry is concentrated in 213 (mostly large) privately owned companies that are vertically integrated into all three main functions of the industry-generation, transmission, and distribution. The privates serve approximately 75% of the electric load, and own about 80% of both the generation and transmission facilities. In contrast, there are 2,203 (mostly small) publicly owned electric utilities serving 13% of the load. Over half of the publicly owned utilities provide only retail distribution service. In addition, there are nearly 1,000 consumer-owned, rural electric cooperatives that account for the rest of the industry.[2]

Prior to the 1970s, the electric utility industry was seen as a collection of regulated natural monopolies unencumbered by antitrust concerns. Load growth was promoted, since it brought the opportunity to realize scale economies and cost reductions due to the adoption of new technologies such as nuclear power. The industry was regarded as being safe, low cost, profitable, and predictable.

Perceptions changed in the 1970s. Economies of scale for power generation were exhausted. The energy crisis, inflation, tighter capital markets, environmental constraints, and massive construction cost overruns led to rapidly rising utility prices. As customers turned (rather unpredictably) to greater reliance on conservation and self-generation, load growth fell out of step with new plant construction. By the time most of the large plant construction projects came to a halt, over 30 states had substantial excess generating capacity. Currently the national generation reserve margin is around 35% and will not drop below 25% before 1995.[3]

During the 1970s there was a growing realization that the "natural monopoly" utilities were not immune from competition and from the antitrust laws. In a series of cases the courts demonstrated that the antitrust laws applied to regulated utilities. Amendments to the Atomic Energy Act led to the implementation of Nuclear Regulatory Commission (NRC) license conditions promoting greater competitive interplay in the industry[4]. The Public Utility Regulatory Policies Act (PURPA) encouraged decentralized efforts towards energy independence and stimulated the growth of competitive self-generation[5]. As a consequence, pressures for access to competitive opportunities have grown dramatically.

Federal regulation has not been on the forefront of effective movements towards electric utility competition. The courts have often had to order the FERC and its predecessor, the Federal Power Commission (FPC), to pay attention to the competitive impacts of its decisions[6]. More recently the FERC has sought to consider some of these questions through its 1985 Notice of Inquiry, inviting parties to comment on various sales for resale, and coordination and transmission service and pricing issues.[7]

Without issuing a formal report on the NOI, the FERC

then appeared to move toward a strategy of market driven prices. In a piecemeal manner, the FERC has approved a number of tariffs that give utilities the authority to provide various coordination services on the basis of negotiated rates[8]. During 1988 the FERC published four Notices of Proposed Rulemaking (NOPRs) on avoided cost calculations, competitive bidding, and independent power producers[9]. Chairman Hesse has promised two more, related proposals on coordination sales and transmission pricing that, together with the current NOPRs, would clearly alter the FERC's traditional "just and reasonable" standard for pricing by embracing market enforced, value based pricing.[10]

Conspicuously absent from the FERC NOPRs is direct attention to the issue of fair and open transmission access. As we discuss below, failure to address first the issue of access will undermine regulatory goals of transaction efficiency and equity, as utilities controlling transmission bottlenecks exercise their market power with the help of the FERC market orientation rules.

The inequality in ownership control of transmission access is so great and so fundamental that it cannot be overcome with any scheme of pricing incentives or indirect policies dealing with generation supply alternatives.[11]

WHY TRANSMISSION ACCESS MUST COME FIRST

The importance of assuring open and nondiscriminatory access to essential facilities should be apparent. Consider the consequences of giving Allied Van Lines the right to set up toll booths on the highways and "negotiate" fees for highway access with other movers. Or consider giving Northwest Airlines effective control over the airspace and terminal gates, or allowing NBC to allocate broadcast frequencies, or putting Merrill Lynch in charge of all of the seats on the stock exchanges. While Allied, Northwest, NBC, and Merrill Lynch would no doubt welcome such arrangements, the effect of control over essential facilities being exercised by one of a number of competitors in an existing market vests inordinate market power in the hands of the controlling entity and severely undermines (if it does not kill outright) the competitive process itself. Consequently, before effective competition can thrive in the electric utility industry, or in any geographic market position thereof, fair transmission access must be assured.

All power purchasers depend upon the transmission system of the larger utilities for power deliveries. Within each control area, the transmission function is both a natural monopoly and an essential facility. Most of the smaller utilities exist like islands in the service control areas of the large, vertically integrated companies. The smaller utilities have little hope of constructing their own transmission system. Anti-duplication laws and environmental concerns tend to limit new transmission building to additions to the existing systems or existing transmission corridors. Thus, most of the smaller utilities are captive wholesale customers, prisoners in a sense, of a large privately owned supplier that is also a competitive rival for retail load.

Without assuring open and nondiscriminatory transmission access, relaxation of regulatory constraints over supply pricing will make things worse. It will provide transmission owners the opportunity to capitalize on their substantial market power. The removal of regulatory pricing barriers will raise the market value of existing transmission facilities to their owners.

The integrated, dominant firm would be able to "negotiate" higher prices for supply sales and coordination services. It would be able to raise prices unfairly and inefficiently with buy-sell brokering arrangements for wheeled power or leveraging of its transmission advantage into false competitive advantage for its own generation sales. Thus, the owner of transmission facilities will either continue to monopolize use of the transmission system or price access in such a manner as to extract the long run monopoly rent associated with transmission access. This is what has happened with the Turlock and Modesto arrangements with Pacific Gas & Electric Company, as described below.[12]

The risk of relaxing regulatory pricing barriers to the exercise of market power is highly related to private activity, for-profit ownership. However, it also derives from strategic position, regardless of ownership type. It is not surprising to learn that one of the most heated battles over transmission access today involves Pacific Gas and Electric; the twist is that PGandE, the object of many such complaints, is here the complainant, and the alleged monopolist is a governmental agency, the Bonneville Power Administration.

Transmission access problems are being compounded by many corporate reorganization changes that are taking place in the industry. Mergers extend the reach of transmission owners' market power. Merger activity appears to be on the rise, with the recent merger or merger proposals of: Cleveland Electric Illumination and Toledo Edison into Centerior Energy; Pacific Power and Light and Utah Power and Light; Southern Company and Savannah Electric and Power; Tucson Electric Power or Southern California Edison and San Diego Gas and Electric; the Utilicorp acquisitions; and the recent interest expressed by Central Maine Power and Central Vermont Public Service in Public Service Company of New Hampshire. One prominent spokesman for an investment banking house has rashly and self-servingly predicted that mergers will reduce the number of investor owned electric utilities from 200 or so to 50 in five years.[13]

Holding company formation and diversification activities are creating other competitive problems, in the form of conflicts of interest. Many private utilities are turning to the holding company structure to organize their activities. Within this structure generation and transmission, cogeneration, and "independent power" activities may be transferred into separate subsidiaries. These changes are intended to enhance the overall corporate profitability of sales and of the holding company itself, but they are likely to reduce further a transmission owner's desire to share access to the transmission system with non-affiliate competitors.[14]

These corporate reorganizations portend a shift in industry ethos. The public service orientation of many utilities towards providing high quality service at the lowest possible rates is being replaced with a desire to expand investment vehicles to further enhance the power and financial welfare of the utilities and their managers and shareholders.

Profit maximization is becoming the end, rather than being the means to the end of customer service. The emphasis is on financial rather than engineering options, and the backgrounds of the new succession of industry managers reflects this phenomenon.

The FERC is hastening the process by pursuing relaxation of controls over pricing, without first addressing the question of transmission access.

TWO TOPICAL APPROACHES TO TRANSMISSION POLICY

There are many ways to skin a cat (though few meet with its approval). In pursuing the question of how to attain fair and open transmission access, many alternative approaches should be considered. In this section we contrast two possible alternatives: (1) "voluntary access," including its most recent variant reflected in the Turlock and Modesto agreements; and (2) a priority ordering scheme, as set forth in the California Public Utilities Commission (CPUC) gas transportation rules[15]. We discuss these alternatives, not because they hold out particular promise to be satisfactory, but because they are the subject of current attention and are being offered vigorously by various proponents as transmission access solutions.

Voluntary Access: Turlock and Modesto

Under voluntary access the owner of transmission facilities decides whether or not to grant transmission access. Though the FERC would oversee the terms of service, the decision to grant access lies with the owner.

Not surprisingly, this is the preferred approach of virtually all utility transmission owners. Like a toll road gate keeper, they control an essential facility that is a bottleneck to competitors' transactions and can be used to extract above normal profits and enhance market power. And it does not matter by what currently popularized title the above normal profits are known. Be it "opportunity cost," "marginal cost," "flexible," or "value based" pricing, it is all the same. The consumer and society pay more than is necessary to have a given amount of electric service provided efficiently.

Those who own transmission facilities argue that voluntary access is working well, and point to the dramatic increases in coordination and transmission transactions over the last decade. However, the vast share of the increased transactions are interchanges among utility transmission owners, and not power transmission for non-owner utilities.

For those seeking transmission access, the voluntary system is not working satisfactorily. Other than the rare case in which a utility in financial distress seeks help in return for sharing access, and the cases where wheeling provisions are required by virtue of the NRC nuclear power plant licensing process, very few requests for firm transmission access are granted to transmission "have nots." An untold number of requests are never made because of the likelihood of failure due to the lack of a favorable environment for transmission access.

Even when access is provided, contract terms requiring additional payments — for questionable claims for additional "services," transactions, or parties -- erode the value of transmission service.

High prices for transmission service are often used to avoid the loss of generation sales. Commonwealth Edison, for example, attempted to evade its transmission commitment to the City of Geneva, Illinois by filing very high transmission rates in the name of marginal cost pricing. As another example, a total of 38 responses to Sacramento Municipal Utility District's request for power supply proposals were wholly dependent on PGandE granting reasonable transmission access.

The widespread turmoil over transmission issues is a clear indicator that voluntary access is insufficient.

Recently the FERC has approved two similar, but not identical, negotiated arrangements for transmission and other services between Pacific Gas and Electric and the Turlock and Modesto Irrigation Districts in California.

Under the Turlock and Modesto agreements PGandE will provide specified contract transmission service for twenty years for these two partial requirements customers so that they can buy firm power from other power suppliers. In return, PGandE is released from obligations to serve Turlock and Modesto at embedded cost based rates, beyond negotiated contractual limitations.

PGandE may use flexible, value based prices for coordination and transmission transactions, and it may substitute "binding arbitration" in place of the FERC to resolve all disputed matters other than price. In its decision approving the Modesto agreement, the Commission went out of its way to tell PGandE that, should Modesto return to the PGandE fold, PGandE could price its wholesale firm service at value of service or "market rate" levels.

Other wholesale customers lacking transmission options might view the Turlock and Modesto to transmission arrangements as an incremental improvement over their current situation. Turlock and Modesto sought the best deal that they could get, given their lack of bargaining power under existing market and regulatory conditions. However, Turlock and Modesto have to be concerned about the negative provisions they had to agree to in order to obtain this transmission access. Those terms clearly demonstrate PGandE's market power, which derives from its control of transmission access.

The Turlock and Modesto agreements were the result of a "market oriented" negotiation process rather that the traditional process of filing and contesting before FERC. The agreements that Turlock and Modesto were able to negotiate with PGandE (including a significant provision allowing PGandE to terminate the contract if the Commission altered it) were presented to the FERC as final products which the FERC approved with only minor modifications.

Though the Commission has been careful to state that these decisions were based on a "narrow set of circumstances" and "established no precedent," the Chairman and other FERC representatives have publicized these "innovative" approaches and encouraged similar submissions.

Other FERC commissioners seem to have some qualms about the decisions, however. Commissioner Trabandt stated that "we defer too much to the parties here, especially since one of them has absolute and undeniable market power over the other." With regard to the FERC's approval of the arbitration provision, Trabandt concludes that "we have allowed the parties to remove the Commission jurisdiction over such important matters as controversies over the agreement's wheeling provisions and access questions."[16]

Commissioner Stalon added his view that it appears "Turlock and Modesto gave up more than they had to 'to get something they badly want'."[17]

CPUC Priority Ordering

The priority ordering system of the California Public Utility Commission is somewhat different from the voluntary approaches discussed above, and involves a much larger and more active regulatory role. Under the umbrella of FERC Orders 436 and 500 that encouraged open access gas transportation, the CPUC has unbundled gas utility company services for large customers. These customers are divided into core and non-core groups.

Core customers are those who remain completely dependent on the supplying utility for all service. Non-core customers are allowed to choose from among purchasing long or short term gas supplies from the utility and using the "transmission" (or transportation) system to ship in gas from outside supply sources.

Transmission costs are allocated according to an embedded cost methodology, with a relatively larger portion of plant costs flowing to the core customers. Priority levels of service are established for each customer group. Core customers have a higher priority level than non-core customers, and within the non-core group those who pay more are afforded a relatively higher priority level for service. All non-core transmission contrasts are also available for public inspection, and the utility bears the burden of demonstrating that its service provisions are not unduly discriminatory.

The CPUC model could be applied to the electric industry. It would encourage overall industry efficiency. Further, it has many positive features for wholesale and industrial customers. Wholesale services could be unbundled so customers could choose their level of service and the effects of beneficial competitive pressures could be felt. Costs could be allocated on a reasonable and non-discriminatory basis without creating windfall monopoly rents for transmission owners.

Of course, differences between the electric and natural gas industries would need to be addressed in applying the CPUC model to electric transmission. Electric operations require centralized, system-wide dispatch that affords the possibility of many partners, but only one decision-making center in each major control area. The technology of electric operations does not permit the types of storage options available in gas supply. Also, the gas industry tends to have separate ownership at the production, transportation, and distribution levels, whereas the major part of the electric industry is comprised of vertically integrated companies.

The California PUC model is not without its risks. As with the Turlock and Modesto arrangements, the development of the service contracts and priority charges could be severely one sided, given the market power of the dominant utility. Active, careful, and continual regulation would be necessary.

REGULATION WITH A SOCIAL VISION

We believe regulation is not a necessary evil, but an opportunity to exercise socially enhancing leadership[18]. Regulation is also quite necessary, in that the electric industry is central to the well being of our modern society and is rife with the potential for abuse on monopoly power. Deregulation's retreat from pricing and other adjudicatory responsibilities must be replaced with a broader social vision founded on serving the public interest. Leadership, industry information, and transmission access are needed.

Neither regulation nor competition are "natural acts." Both are discretionary activities whose outcomes are dependent upon social objectives, motivation, institutional setting and execution. To truly promote public well-being, regulation must go beyond the narrow "night watchman role" prescribed to government by classical liberal political philosophy and neoclassical economics. Promoting the public interest means more than just trading the interests of one group off against another.

Rather than simply serving as "traffic cop" for disputant parties, regulation should actively pursue the betterment of public well-being. Regulators should set the public agenda to focus on issues central to equity, efficiency, and the development of socially enhancing values, and create the institutional environment wherein socially beneficial competitive interplay can unfold.

The FERC does not show leadership by retreating from the exercise of regulatory authority. As we have discussed above, reducing regulatory controls over price in an environment of unequal transmission access will only promote the accrual of monopoly rents and not the realization of beneficial competition.

Rather than continuing down its current path, the FERC should demonstrate its social leadership capacity by taking the lead in establishing a transmission policy for the U.S. electric utility industry that promotes fair and open access. The FERC's leadership can be demonstrated both by careful study of transmission problems and opportunities, and by the publication of basic information on transmission arrangements, as well as by using its authority to extend transmission access.

Periodically the Federal Power Commission has conducted industry wide surveys to assess industry needs and regulatory options. The 1964 and 1970 National Power Surveys were such undertakings[19]. In the words of the FPC, the studies were "broadly representative of all segments of the electric power industry and of groups in government, the electric utility industry and the public concerned with environment," and were "intended to serve as a general long-range guide rather than a directive or firm plan."[20] The two National Power Surveys are widely credited with helping to expand industry coordination and pooling, with attendant benefits to ratepaying consumers.

Today's FERC should reactivate its National Power Survey process. It should be conducting ongoing, periodic surveys at five to ten year intervals that provide current information on the industry, as well as benchmarks for comparisons. In particular, the FERC should use a reactivated National Power Survey to map out the steps which need to be taken to achieve fuller transmission system integration and access. It has already been almost two decades since the last Survey was published. The importance of the issues now facing the FERC mandate such an effort.

The FERC should also publish such basic information as its file material on prices and terms of coordination and transmission service transaction. The material should be published on a regular and timely basis in an indexed format complete with filed information on contrasts, letter a-greements, and rate tariff sheets.

Information is essential. One of the primary responsibilities of the early federal regulatory agencies (ICC, FTC, FPC, FCC, SEC, and others) was the gathering and publishing of descriptive information about the regulated industry and its competitors. This information allowed regulators and affected parties alike to evaluate the nature and extent of industry problems so that appropriate regulatory policies could be crafted. This is even more necessary today.

While studies and information are valuable, they are not enough. The FERC should pursue a more expansive exercise of its authority and capacity to implement transmission access. Traditionally the FERC has been very reticent to exercise its existing powers. The FERC has long maintained that it does not have legislative authority to mandate wheeling.

A recent example is the Commission's exceedingly conservative interpretations of Sections 211 and 212 of the Federal Power Act found in Southeastern Power Administration v. Kentucky Utilities Co[21]. In that case, FERC decided that it could not order wheeling unless it "would reasonably preserve existing competitive relationships." In order words, the FERC would not pursue wheeling unless the existing imbalance in market power was maintained.

FERC Commissioner Charles Stalon has recognized that there is need to "rethink" that interpretation.[22]

The FERC is not without the capacity to increase transmission access substantially. In the natural gas area, through its orders 436 and 500, the FERC demonstrated its creativity in finding ways to get pipelines to provide transmission access to those seeking gas transportation service. In a similar manner, the FERC should demonstrate regulatory leadership by the imposition of fair transmission access conditions on utility mergers, hydroelectric licenses, interconnection and pooling agreements, and even in wholesale rate cases. By such actions, the Commission would be exercising its court mandated responsibility to promote the fair competition which is the intent of the country's antitrust framework.

If the FERC feels it lacks the necessary authority to mandate the access needed for efficiency and fairness, it should work aggressively with the Congress to obtain new legislation. The FERC is quite capable of showing the need for new legislation, drafting language alternatives, and seeing its passage into law. With such a program of activity, the FERC can demonstrate positive regulatory direction and provide a degree of predictability and orderliness that is essential to necessary planning by industry participants. In the absence of such action, the Agency's procompetitive initiatives are illogical and incomplete.

REGULATION AND COMPETITION: COMPLEMENTARY, NOT CONFLICTING

Fair transmission access is important to but not sufficient

for the promotion and maintenance of socially beneficial competition. Even with transmission access, beneficial competition may require maintaining regulatory control over supply prices.

When the nation developed its antitrust framework, it was not attempting to enshrine the blood thirsty, no-holds-barred competition of the jungle. Competition based on the aggressive desire to annihilate one's rival in order to capture customers is socially debilitating, through its inevitable promotion of unethical behavior and maintained attitudes of distrust and non-cooperation.

Socially beneficial competition is that which exists when customers face an array of alternatives provided by organizations whose prime interest is service to the customer. Good service allows sustained profits. Such organizations would seek to be of service to customers through continual efforts to progress technologically and to be attentive to customers' needs — not through efforts to confuse customers or to employ marketplace tricks to undercut the competitors.

From the days of common law constraints on regulators, forestallers and engrossers[22] to the current restrictions on insider trading, society through its government has sought to promote socially beneficial competition by limiting the non-socially beneficial options. Maintaining controls over prices and avoiding turning to "market based" or "market negotiated" prices permits competitive activity to be more beneficially channelled into customer service and technological progress.

As a counter example, when the FERC permitted "flexible" tariffs for coordination services, it unwittingly encouraged various utilities to withhold scheduling and cost information and duplicate other utilities; however, there does not appear to be any improvement in the dispatching of economically efficient generation units.

Competition can play a useful role in the electric industry. The current regulatory administration proposes to choose competition over regulation. But this is a false choice. Given the current configuration of the industry, regulation is essential for competition.

1. See R. Rudolph & s. Ridley, Power Struggle: The Hundred Year War Over Electricity (1986), especially Chapters 2 and 8 for their description of the interrelationships between the electricity and financial industries.

2. The statistics in the preceding two paragraphs are taken from *Energy Information Administration, U.S. Department of Energy, Financial Statistics of Selected Electric Utilities*, published annually; Electrical World, Statistical Reports, published annually; L. Hobart, Electric Utility Reform: "Putting the Customer First", Forum for Applied Research and Public Policy, Winter, 8-18 (1986); and American Public Power Association, Comments on FERC Docket Nos. RM88-4 and 5, Attachment A (July 1988).

3. See, e.g., sources cited in Note 2. Sufficient reserve margins are generally held to be in the range of 15-20%.

4. By virtue of a 1970 amendment to the Atomic Energy Act, Section 105(c) of that Act requires a determination of whether activities under the license would tend to create or maintain a situation inconsistent with the antitrust laws. 84 Stat. 1472, 1473, codified at 42 U.S.C. 2135.

5. Pub. L. No. 95-617, 92 Stat. 3117 (1978) codified at Title 16 and other sections, U.S.C. Between 1985 and 1987, self generation doubled to 40,000 megawatts. Cogeneration has risen from less than 10,000 megawatts in 1980 to 24,000 megawatts in 1987. See *Edison Electric Institute, Capacity and Generation, Non Utility Sources of Energy* (1987); and *Hagler, Bailly, and Co., Profile of Cogeneration and Small Power Generation Markets* (1988) (distributed by Utility Data Institute, Washington, D.C.).

6. See, e.g., Guld State Utilities Co. v. Federal Power Commission, 411 U.S. 747 (1973), reh'g denied 412 u.s. 944 (1973); Conway Corporation v. Federal Power Commission, 510 F. 2d 1264 (D.C. Cir. 1975), aff'd 426 U.S. 271 (1975); Kansas City Power & Light Co. v. Federal Power Commission, 554 F. 2d 1178 (D.C. Cir. 1978); Farmers Union Central Exchange v. Federal Energy Regulatory Commission, 734 F. 2d 1486, 1500- 11 (1984).

7. FERC Docket No. RM85-17-000, phase I and II.
8. Perhaps the most conspicuous of these is the Western Systems Power Pool Experiment, FERC Docket No. ER87-97-001.
9. FERC Docket Nos. RM88-000-4,5,6, and 17. See *The Electricity Journal*, "A Dialogue on the FERC Rulemakings", July 1988 at 20; "What FERC Heard: Few Supporters, Many Opponents", August-September 1988, at 43.
10. M. Hesse, Remarks to Southeastern Electric Exchange (Mar. 28, 1988).
11. There is wide recognition that substantial institutional obstacles to moving electric energy efficiently exist, apart from any technical barriers. See, e.g., *National Governors' Association*, "Moving Power: flexibility for the future" (1987); *National Regulatory Research Inst.*, "Non-Technical Impediments to Power Transfer" (1987); *Wharton Econometrics*, "Power Wheeling in North America" (1988); and *U.S. General Accounting Office*, "Electric Power Transmission: Federal Role in System Use and Regulation" (1988).
12. Docket Nos. ER88-219 (Turlock) and ER88-302 (Modesto).
13. Shearson Lehman Hutton, Electric Utilities: "The Case for Consolidation" (1988).
14. For a thorough discussion of the risks some holding company endeavors may pose to the public interest, see Hempling, Corporate Restructuring and Consumer Risk, *The Electricity Journal*, July 1988 at 41-46.
15. CPUC Decisions Nos. 86-12-009 and 86-12-010 (December 1986) and CPUC Decision 87-12-039 (December 1987), and OII No. 87-03-036.
16. 42 FERC paragraph 61,406 at pages 62,200-62,202 (1988)
17. Electric Utility Week, July 4, 1988, at 2.
18. G. Edgar, J.R. Malko, R. Stevenson, "Equity, Social Values, and Public Utility Regulation", in *Alternatives To Traditional Regulation: Options for Reform* (H.Trebing, ed.) (1988).
19. Federal Power Commission, National Power Survey (1964); *The 1970 National Power Survey* (1971).
20. *The 1970 National Power Survey*, Vol. I (1971) at I-iii.
21. FERC paragraph 61,127 (1984).
22. Remarks of Commissioner C. Stalon before Electricity Transmission Conference of National Association of Reg-

ulatory Utility Commissioners, June 2, 1988.

23. "Regrating" means the practice of buying goods to sell again at a higher price without having made any addition to their value. "Forestalling" means going to the place of production to outwit fellow-dealers by purchasing goods before they come into the market. "Engrossing" means buying up the whole supply of a good, or cornering the market. See. E.P. Cheyney, *An Introduction to Industrial and Social History of England (1919)*.

CHAPTER 20: ALTERNATIVE SCENARIOS FOR INCREASING COMPETITION IN THE ELECTRIC POWER INDUSTRY

Peter D. Blair
Program Manager, Office of Technology Assessment, Congress of the United States

INTRODUCTION

There have been many proposals for revamping the electric power industry through competition, deregulation, and restructuring, but few have been sufficiently detailed, particularly in the area of transmission systems operations, to support the kind of analysis required for this assessment[1]. It was necessary to explore how possible regulatory futures of the electric power industry might evolve before examining the technical feasibility of expanded competition. OTA defined five alternative economic and regulatory scenarios to capture a reasonable range of industry futures and to form the basis of our technical analysis. The major features of the scenarios are summarized in table 20-1.

The scenarios range from scenario 1, which makes modest changes in the regulatory procedures for approving new plant construction with no legislative expansion of transmission access, to scenario 5, which would separate the industry into generation, transmission, and distribution sectors and impose common carrier obligations on transmission companies. Four of the scenarios would expand access to transmission services; two scenarios would allow retail customers to seek wheeling orders. The scenarios pose very different implications for the future direction of the electric power industry and its technical and institutional infrastructure. The scenarios derive important elements from some recent proposals for regulatory reform and structural change in the electric power industry, but are not identical with any one of them.[2]

In discussing scenario implementation, OTA generalizes about how electric utilities would be affected and how State regulation might be adapted. The typical utility structure under the scenarios is the vertically integrated investor-owned utility. This model, while applicable to utilities owning over 70 percent of the our generating capacity, does not cover all of the diverse combinations of utility structure, ownership, and State regulation characteristic of the Nation's electric power industry. For many aspects of the scenarios, the ownership structure of the utility is less important than whether the utility controls and operates generating, transmission, and distribution facilities. OTA believes that these generalizations are sufficiently representative of most of the utilities and State regulatory schemes to allow us to draw supportable conclusions about the overall impacts of the scenarios.

The scenarios do not exclude public power agencies or consumer cooperatives from full partici-pation in the competitive generation sector. Although scenarios 4 and 5 involve significant disintegration and restructuring of the electric power industry, they do not include provisions for "privatizing" Federal and other publicly owned power systems. A detailed consideration of the legal, economic, and political implications of such proposals is beyond the scope of this report.

Table 20-1 Summary of Alternative Scenarios

Scenario 1: Strengthening the Regulatory Bargain

- Industry consists of a mix of vertically integrated utilities, IOUs, public power, cooperatives, Federal power authorities, QFs, and IPPs.
- Existing regulatory structure with State preapproval of new generating projects and periodic prudence reviews during planning and construction.
- Negotiated transmission access arrangements.
- Traditional system coordination and control by integrated utilities or control centers.
- Prices set by regulatory proceedings and cost of service. Transmission prices and wholesale rates set by FERC (including approval of negotiated IPP power purchases). State oversight of retail rates and PURPA Implementation.
- Federal and public power agencies and cooperatives affected only to the extent State law provides.

Scenario 2: Expanding Transmission Access and Competition in the Existing Regulated Utility Structure

- Industry consists of existing mix of entities.
- Existing regulatory structure with wider QF eligibility under PURPA including full utility ownership/control of QFs (may require amendment of PURPA).
- New Federal wheeling authority under a public interest standard for wholesale and retail transmission access (requires amendment of the Federal Power Act).
- Traditional system coordination and control by integrated utilities or control centers with contracts for unbundled services.
- Prices set by regulatory proceedings and cost of service. Transmission prices and wholesale rates set by FERC (including approval of negotiated IPP power purchases). State oversight of retail rates and PURPA implementation.
- Federal and public power agencies and cooperatives affected only to the extent State law provides.

Scenario 3: Competition for New Bulk Power Supplies

- Existing mix of generating entities expanded by IPPs and unregulated utility generation subsidiaries.
- Existing regulatory structure with market-based rates for new competitive generation. Utilities use all source procurement for new bulk power needs. Contracts awarded to lowest cost supplier with consideration for nonprice factors.
- Transmission access provided by utilities as a bidding condition, or by privately negotiated arrangements, or under new Federal public interest wheeling authority (no retail wheeling).
- Traditional system coordination and control by integrated utilities or control centers. Unbundled bulk power dispatch, control and transmission servioes provided through contracts.
- Retail and transmission prices set by regulatory proceedings. Wholesale power prices set through competitive procurement except for cost base plants built by utility as last resort supplier. State and Federal regulators oversee terms and conditions of wholesale sales.
- Federal and public power agencies, and cooperatives can participate in competitive generating sector to extent provided by Federal and State law and policy.

Scenario 4: Competition for All Bulk Power Supplies

• Industry structure: Ownership of competitive generating sector segregated from transmission and distribution sectors.
• New Federal and State regulatory systems. Price and entry regulation of generation sector replaced with competitive market. Continued regulation of transmission and distribution utilities and retail sales.
• Revised Federal wholesale wheeling authority. Transmission utility to plan for and provide nondiscriminatory access for bulk power supplies.
• Most traditional utility system planning and coordination taken over by transmission and disribution entities. Competitive generators plan and build generation. Transmission operator assumes responsibility for bulk power system control and operation. Distribution utility retains retail obligation to serve. Unbundled bulk power dispatch, control, and transmission services provided through contracts.
• Bulk power prices set by market through bidding, negotiation. Transmission and retail prices are set by regulatory proceedings. Some State and Federal oversight of competitiveness of generation markets and prudence of bulk power contracts.
• Federal and public power agencies, cooperatives can participate in competitive generating sector to extent provided by Federal and State law and policy.

Scenario 5: Common Carrier Transmission Services in a Disaggregated Industry Structure

• Ownership and control of existing integrated utility industry is disaggregated into separate generation, transmission and distribution segments.
• New Federal and State regulatory system. Price and entry regulation of generation replaced with competitive markets. Distribution utilities' services and retail prices remain regulated. Transmission prices and activities are strictly regulated.
• Transmission sector operates as a common carrier providing nondiscriminatory access to all wholesale and retail customers. Reasonable conditions on reserving transmission services may be imposed.

- Bulk system planning and coordination is split among generation, transmission and distribution entities. Generators identify, plan, and build new generation in response to market signals. Transmission utility assumes responsibility for reliability of bulk system operation. Responsibility for estimating demand and securing adequate power supplies rests with distribution utilities. Unbundled bulk power dispatch, control and transmission services provided through contracts.
- Federal and public power agencies, cooperatives can participate in competitive generating sector to the extent provided by Federal and State law and policy.

SCENARIO 1: REAFFIRMING THE REGULATORY COMPACT

Under the traditional "regulatory contract," a public utility is guaranteed the opportunity to recover all prudent investment committed to public use and to earn a competitive rate of return on its investment. In exchange, the utility assumes the legal obligation to provide adequate and reliable service at reasonable rates to all customers located in its exclusive franchise territory. Scenario 1 reflects the view that only modest changes in existing arrangements and institutions governing the industry are needed to assure continued adequate and reliable electric power supplies. This scenario differs from the status quo by the adoption of measures to reaffirm the regulatory compact between utilities and regulatory authorities (on behalf of utility customers) through:

1. changes to State ratemaking policies to reduce the investment risk for new construction and to allow utilities to attract needed capital;
2. the modification of rules under the Public Utility Regulatory Policies Act of 1978 (PURPA) to address perceived imbalances in the implementation of avoided cost pricing for quali- fying facility (QF) payments;[3] and
3. the adoption of measures to encourage greater access to transmission services for bulk power transfers and the construction of additional transmission capacity.

Proponents believe that a major benefit of regulatory reform for utilities would be the enhanced expectation that over the long term they will be able to recover their prudent capital investment and earn a competitive return for their shareholders. At the same time, customers would be assured of adequate, reliable power supplies at reasonable rates. Some analysts speculate that reduced regulatory risks might eventually lead to savings for consumers from a lowering of capital costs of new utility construction.[4] Some proponents of this scenario argue that more drastic reforms of utility regulation are unnecessary because the problems of the 1970s and 1980s were the result of an unfortunate and unique convergence of events and trends that are unlikely to be repeated, and that the regulatory system and domestic utility industry have largely adjusted to changed conditions. Furthermore, the flexibility with which electric utilities and the regulatory system have responded to recent financial difficulties and competitive pressures attests to the soundness of current institutions.

Transmission access and wheeling arrangements would be negotiated between the participants on a voluntary basis. The Federal Energy Regulatory Commission (FERC) would retain its authority over transmission rates and interstate and wholesale power sales. States would exercise jurisdiction over resource planning, expansion, retail rates, and distribution. Public power agencies and cooperatives would continue to be regulated as now, subject to varying degrees of oversight by Federal and State authorities. These changes may give requirements customers greater input and oversight of power supply decisions by wholesale utilities.

Utilities would remain the primary providers of electric power under scenario 1. Cogenerators, self-generators, and independent power producers (IPPs) would continue to exert competitive pressures on utilities, but, except for PURPA qualifying facilities, alternative generating sources would not be given any special status or preference under State or Federal regulation.

Background

Much of the current interest in increasing competition in generation can be attributed to the problems encountered by the electric power industry over the past 15 years in dealing with declining growth rates, excess capacity, rising fuel costs, and steeply escalating construction costs (especially for nuclear plants).[5] Billions of dollars in new, large-baseload generating plants were cancelled or deferred.[6] Rising utility costs and sharp rate hikes in the 1970s reversed the postwar trend of steadily declining electricity prices and prompted close regulatory scrutiny of utility performance and rate requests. Eventually regulators disallowed recovery of large amounts of imprudent utility investment in both cancelled and completed plants.[7] The specter of disallowances through "after-the-fact" prudence reviews contributed to a growing perception among many in the utility industry and the investment community that the long-standing regulatory compact had been seriously impaired. Many utilities felt that they were no longer assured an opportunity to recover their capital investment and earn a fair return on investment in exchange for their obligation to serve. In comparison with other industries, many utility stocks posted lower returns to investors during the early 1980s.

Spending on new plant construction has dropped sharply in recent years. The most obvious causes are the completion of large construction projects begun in the 1970s and slow growth in electricity use. Some, however, see this drop as evidence that the industry as a whole has become substantially more risk averse and has adopted a capital minimization strategy in response to increased uncertainty over regulatory decisions and greater unpredictability in future demand growth. Some energy analysts view this hiatus in new plant construction with alarm because they fear additional baseload capacity may be needed as early as the mid-to-late 1990s if electricity demand growth increases significantly.[8]

PURPA has increased the amount of non-utility generation and cogeneration and spurred investment in and commercialization of alterative energy technologies. The competitive pressures created by the growth of PURPA cogeneration have forced many utilities to engage in aggressive cost-cutting to lower rates to avoid the loss of industrial customers. At the same time, PURPA has further compounded the uncertainties facing utilities. As implemented in some States, PURPA also has required some utilities and their ratepayers to pay for unneeded energy or QF capacity under long-term fixed-price contracts at avoided cost prices that are higher than the utilities' current marginal costs of generating electricity. Moreover, many critics of PURPA argue that it has disproportionally favored greater reliance on oil and natural gas as fuels.

Undoubtedly, some of the impacts of PURPA reflect the initial difficulties and uncertainties in implementing a complex regulatory scheme. Other problems, however, are caused by the current surplus of generating capacity and lower fuel prices — circumstances that arguably are different from those envisioned when PURPA was enacted in 1978 in an era of rising fuel costs, projected high electricity demand growth, and fears of future energy shortages. Already, many States have initiated changes in their PURPA implementation programs to address these changed circumstances and reduce avoided costs while at the same time preserving PURPA's incentives for alternative generators.

From the perspective of some utilities, PURPA contributed to the further impairment of the tradi-tional utility bargain because, while it left utilities with the obligation to assure adequate, reliable electricity service, it diminished their control over the sources and costs of generation.

Time, lower fuel prices, and lower inflation rates have abated many of the financial threats to the electric utilities.[9] There remain, however, some problems of uncertainty and delay attributed to both the regulatory process and prudence reviews of generating plant construction costs. There is some agreement among regulators and utilities that targeted regulatory reforms would help avoid the conflicts of recent years and restore a balance to the regulatory bargain by assuring the industry of recovery of future prudent investments in new facilities, if needed, while offering similar assurances to consumers and regulators that new capacity costs will be kept under control.

Implementation

The primary responsibility for implementing scenario 1 would rest with State governments. Few changes to Federal law and regulation would be necessary. The major Federal statutory and regulatory structure governing the electric power industry today would remain essentially unaltered. In particular, PURPA, the Federal Power Act, and the Public Utility Holding Company Act (PUHCA) would be untouched and existing statutory standards would not be loosened or expanded substantially by administrative or judicial interpretations. Scenario 1 would not, however, preclude certain relatively selective, but possibly significant, changes in existing administrative rules governing industry structure and operations. For example, FERC might make minor changes or clarifications in rules governing utility avoided costs for purchases from qualifying facilities under PURPA. FERC might impose more stringent technology or efficiency standards on QFs to discourage the proliferation of "PURPA machines." Similarly, FERC could continue its efforts to encourage greater amounts of voluntary wheeling by utilities and to provide additional incentives for expanded intersystem bulk power transactions. Examples include the Western Systems Power Pool Experiment and approvals of more flexible transmission pricing schemes in individual cases.

Transmission access and wheeling rates for wholesale and retail customers under this scenario would depend on voluntary agreements negotiated with the utilities controlling transmission facilities. FERC would oversee wheeling rates.

Federal authority to issue wheeling orders under the Federal Power Act and PURPA would remain limited. The Nuclear Regulatory Commission could order wheeling as part of licensing of new nuclear plants, however, it is unlikely that any new orders will be issued. FERC jurisdiction would largely be limited to setting wheeling rates and approving various proposals and experiments among utilities. Some States would continue to assert authority to require intrastate wheeling as a condition of State initiatives.[10] Antitrust considerations could provide some source of mandatory wheeling as part of a court order or settlement, but such wheeling orders are expected to be rare.

The current statutory split between Federal and State jurisdiction over regulation of electric utilities would remain largely undisturbed. With the existing trend toward greater use of bulk power sales, however, it is conceivable that a greater share of power costs might shift from State to Federal regulatory jurisdiction. Modified State regulatory procedures for review and approval of new plant construction would offer stronger assurances to utilities of recovery of investment than the current system. These changes would likely require State legislation and would probably include a more direct and active role by utility commissions (and the public) in the planning and oversight of new generation sources and transmission facilities.[11] Some observers believe, however, that many States would not significantly alter their existing regulatory procedures because they have already adopted similar reforms in response to the problems of slow growth rates, inflation, cost-overruns, soaring fuel prices, and excess capacity that stressed utilities during the 1970s and early 1980s.

Rolling Prudence Reviews. One regulatory reform that addresses the utilities capital attraction problem is a preapproval process for construction of new generating and transmission facilities coupled with periodic prudence reviews.[12] These determinations would be in addition to State least-cost planning requirements. Regulators and utilities would agree in advance as to the need, type, cost, and rate implications of major new projects. These hearings would allow participation by consumers. Following initial approval, projects would be subject to regularly scheduled prudence reviews from inception to completion. Utilities would be assured recovery of all expenses incurred up to the most recent prudence determination, except of course for losses due to reckless, improper, or negligent actions of the utility. This process has been characterized as a "rolling prudence review" in contrast to the post-construction prudence reviews now common under many State regulatory programs.[13] Preapproval is not equivalent to adoption of a rate scheme that allows recovery for Construction Work in Progress (CWIP) in the rate base before the plant actually is in use. Under the rolling prudence concept, a new plant would become recoverable as part of the rate base only after it began operating and was determined to be "used and useful."

If the circumstances underlying an initial approval of new capacity changed, periodic regulatory reviews could allow projects to be canceled or modified midcourse, but the utility would still be entitled to recover in the rate base the value of its prudent investment to date plus a reasonable return over any recovery period.[14] If the utility chose to continue construction, it would receive no guarantees from that point on that the remaining costs would be allowed into the rate base. When and if the facility began operation, the public utility commission would decide whether the expenditures

COMPETITION IN ELECTRICITY

were prudent. Some utility executives argue that such a regulatory program would "fairly balance the risk to consumers and investors alike and give assurance of adequate and reliable supply of electric power in the future,"[15] In effect, the traditional regulatory bargain would be restored and strengthened, but it would be more comparable to an explicit contract between the utility and the regulatory commission on behalf of the customers.

Institution of a rolling prudence review for new construction projects would reduce the utility's management control over major investment decisions. In some States, however, there is already an extensive degree of regulatory involvement in all aspects of utility investment decisionmaking and, to some degree, this scenario would simply constitute a formal recognition of a regulatory system that already exists, except perhaps for the guarantees accorded to the utility.

A system of rolling prudence reviews is consistent with other current trends in regulatory treatment of utility resource expansion planning and construction. Other regulatory initiatives have been proposed or adopted in recent years to restore the utility's expectation that it will recover its prudent investments or to enhance its cash flow to fund construction. Examples include automatic fuel adjustment clauses, incentive rates, performance bonuses and penalties, advance caps on construction reimbursement, and inclusion of the value of CWIP in the ratebase.[16]

Regulatory reforms aimed at reducing or shifting risk in constructing new large baseload plants may not, however, actually result in the immediate construction of any such plants. Other considerations such as the extent of existing reserve capacity, increased uncertainty in future demand growth, and greater volatility in fuel prices may lead utilities to conclude it is more prudent and cost-effective to build smaller increments of new generation and to buy power from other sources for the foreseeable future."[17]

Under scenario 1 many ongoing State regulatory initiatives could be expected to continue. State commissions would likely continue their efforts to encourage utilities to expand their bulk power procurement practices to include consideration of QFs, other utilities, and independent power suppliers.[18] Under the more standard State PURPA programs, the commissions might review previously established avoided cost rates. In some cases, lower fuel costs and existing capacity surpluses could yield lower avoided cost rates. These changes could lead some higher-cost PURPA pvojects to drop out. In other cases, reviews may lead to increases in existing low avoided cost rates encouraging QF development. The basic PURPA incentive structure would still remain. Utilities would still be obligated to purchase power generated by QFs at avoided cost rates. QFs would retain the protection of existing long-term capacity contracts at avoided cost pricing with host utilities.

States could continue to encourage greater coordination of utility planning and operations through centralized dispatch, power pools, and brokerage arrangements. The States would also continue their efforts to promote workable regional power supply planning arrangements and new means of developing needed interregional transmission capacity. Preapproval will eventually require most State regulatory agencies to increase their expertise in system planning and load forecasting.

Industry Structure. Under scenario 1 the electric power industry would consist of the current mix of investor-owned utilities, public power agencies, cooperatives, Federal power authorities, self-generators, small power producers, QFs, and IPPs. As now, vertically integrated, investor-owned utilities will dominate the generation, transmission, and retail distribution segments of the power industry. Recent trends toward limited industry restructuring through mergers, acquisitions, and internal reorganizations can be expected to continue within the constraints imposed by existing law.

The trend toward greater bulk power competition would continue as power suppliers, sellers, buyers, and State regulatory commissions cope with pressures from prices and technology. In some States or regions a de facto competitive market in bulk power supplies will continue to evolve if FERC maintains its "hands off" approach to reviewing these interutility transfers. Utilities will continue to increase bulk power transfers.

The role of IPPs, and especially utility-affiliated IPPs, remains unsettled because, unlike QFs, they would not be exempt from coverage by the Federal Power Act or PUHCA. Without PURPA purchase requirements, IPPs would have to compete on the underlying economics of their projects.

Non-QF cogenerators and IPPs could continue to contract for the sale and transmission of power to utilities and other purchasers, however, provided suitable arrangements can be negotiated.

System Operations and Planning

Scenario 1 would have little or no impact on system operations and closely resembles the status quo. Table 20-2 summarizes the system operating requirements under the scenarios. Responsibility for maintaining day-today system reliability and coordination of generation and transmission resources would rest with the local utility or centralized control center (under a coordination or power pool agreement).[19] Interutility agreements and operating practices, as well as FERC regional protocols, would continue to govern cooperative activities among utilities. Operational responsibilities and technical standards for non-utility or third-party power suppliers would be based on contract terms with the local utility. As under existing law, State regulators would have the authority to rule on the reasonableness of utility technical specifications in cases of disputes between utilities and third-party generators.[20]

The local utility or regional control center would determine the order of dispatch, maintenance scheduling, and unit loading of utility owned or leased units. For QFs and IPP units, dispatch and scheduling would depend on contract terms with the local utility. Dispatchable third-party generators would likely be treated the same as utility sources if they demonstrate adequate reliability and availability and if unit dispatch is technically feasible. Non-dispatchable third-party generators would not be subject to utility control, except as needed to preserve the stability and reliability of the system. Under this scenario, it is likely that IPPs will be dispatchable under contracts, because their options to sell power to other customers is limited. Emergency curtailments of backup service for third-party generators would be allocated according to State regulated curtailment policies.

Under scenario 1 local utilities would have the responsibility for planning and developing overall generation, transmission, and distribution requirements for the system based on their projections of future electricity supply and demand. These planning efforts most likely would be coordinated with other regional utilities and overseen by State regulatory agencies as part of the preapproval process for new plants. Regulated utilities would retain the obligation to provide adequate and reliable service for current and future needs under this and other scenarios.

In preparing generating capacity expansion plans, utilities will consider various options for securing power supplies, including potential QF sources, and bulk power purchases from other utilities and IPPs, as well as conservation and load management strategies.[21] State authorities would generally approve utilities' generation expansion plans through the certification and preapproval process. QFs, IPPs, and self-generators would plan and build capacity based on their own perceptions of need and profitability. As eligibility requirements are tightened and avoided cost prices are lowered, sponsors might tend to abandon some of the more expensive QF projects currently planned. It is unlikely that any IPP project would go forward without a firm contract with a utility for its power output. Third-party power producers will likely be more successful in areas with low reserve generating capacity margins than in those areas with substantial amounts of existing utility generating reserves or low production costs.

Local and regional utilities would plan and develop transmission system additions subject to regulatory approval. The pressures for increased access to transmission services to accommodate bulk power sales can be expected to continue. State and Federal initiatives toward more flexible transmission pricing may encourage some additional upgrading and expansion of transmission systems. The potential for delays and controversy attendant with proposals for the siting and construction of new transmission lines can be expected to continue. Planning and building distribution system additions would remain the responsibility of the local utility with regulatory approval.

Table 20-2
Alternative Scenarios: Summary of System Operations, Planning, and Development

Scenario 1: Strengthening the Regulatory Bargain

- System Operation: Utility control center. Control of nonutility generation set by contract.
- Generation: Utility obligation to plan, build and purchase. QFs market under PURPA. IPPs negotiate contracts.
- Transmission: Utility responsibility.
- Distribution: Local utility responsibility.

Scenario 2: Expanding Transmission Access and Competition in the Existing Regulated Industry Structure

- System Operation: Similar to Scenario 1 with greater reliance on contractual provisions for nonutility generation control and wheeling.
- Generation: Similar to Scenario 1 with expanded QF and IPP participation.
- Transmission: Same as Scenario 1, but states may require utilities to plan and build adequate transmission capacity for regional needs including retail wheeling.
- Distribution: Same as Scenario 1.

Scenario 3: Competition for New Bulk Power Supplies

- System Operation: Same as Scenario 2.
- Generation: Utility obligation to plan and secure adequate new supplies through competitive means.
- Transmission: Same as Scenario 2, but no retail wheeling obligation.
- Distribution: Same as Scenario 1.

Scenario 4: Competition for All Bulk Power Supplies

- System Operation: Transmission utility assumes bulk system control. Operational responsibilities of generators and distribution utilities set by contracts with customers and transmission utilities.

- Generation: Generators plan and build in response to perceived market needs and solicitations by transmission / distribution utilities.
- Transmission utility obligation to plan and build adequate capacity for instate / regional wholesale needs.
- Local retail utility obligation to plan and contract for adequate supplies. Utility may participate in load management and conservation. Transmission utility may provide brokering services.

Scenario 5: Common Carrier Transmission Services in a Disaggregated Industry Structure

- System Operation: Same as Scenario 4.
- Generation: Generators plan and build in response to perceived market needs and solicitations by local distribution utilities and transmission companies as brokers.
- Transmission: Transmission utility obligation to plan and build adequate capacity for foreseeable needs as common carrier for regional wholesale and retail customers.
- Distribution: Same as Scenario 4.

SCENARIO 2: EXPANDING TRANSMISSION ACCESS AND COMPETITION WITHIN THE EXISTING INSTITUTIONAL STRUCTURE

Scenario 2 would preserve most of the electric power industry's existing structure and regulatory framework, but would expand competition in the generation sector more than scenario 1 or the status quo. Scenario 2 would increase the number of potential bulk power sellers by modifying some of the size, technology, fuel, and ownership limitations for QFs under PURPA. This could largely be accomplished by changes in regulations, but eliminating all restrictions on utility ownership would likely require legislation.[22] At the same time, the ranks of prospective buyers would be enlarged by amending the transmission access provisions of the Federal Power Act to authorize FERC to issue transmission access orders under a broad public interest standard.[23] These legislative changes would increase opportunities for both wholesale and retail wheeling. Utilities and large industrial retail customers could purchase electricity "off system" from traditional and nontraditional power suppliers and have it delivered to them over a more open transmission system.

The principal mechanism for achieving increased competition in scenario 2 is the provision for both wholesale and retail wheeling. If efforts to negotiate voluntary wheeling arrangements failed, any utility (including QFs and IPPs) or a very large retail customer would have legal standing to seek a wheeling order from FERC.[24] There would be a rebuttable assumption that the capacity to wheel exists. The utility denying the wheeling services would bear the burden of proving either a lack of available capacity or that accommodating a proposed wheeling transaction would result in a degradation of service.[25] The utility would be entitled to a reasonable compensation for its transmission services.

In addition to new wheeling authority, Federal and State administrative policies intended to encourage greater competition in bulk power sales within the existing institutional structure and increased access to transmission services would be continued and expanded.

Background

Many industry analysts have argued that the regulated electric power industry would be more economically efficient if more competition were allowed in certain segments of the industry.[26] Among the benefits of competition they cite are: better use of generation and transmission resources, a more flexible and secure power supply, increased efficiencies in utility operations, and lower prices to consumers over the long-term. In addition, utility ratepayers would have less exposure to the risks of construction cost overruns and poor plant performance as these risks would be shifted more explicitly to the shareholders of nonutility generators. A further benefit of allowing limited competition and more wheeling would be a growth in the information and experience available to assist policymakers in evaluating the technical and institutional feasibility of proposals for broader competition and economic deregulation of electric power.

Proponents note that changes in generation and transmission technologies have diminished some of the so-called natural monopoly characteristics of the electric power industry allowing workable competition to exist as a supplement to regulation. Smaller generating units are now in many cases cost competitive with large baseload plants and have shorter lead-times. Increased interconnections and higher voltage transmission lines have made regional coordination of utility operations more feasible. With these developments, some analysts see the subregional, insulated, vertically integrated utility as fast becoming an outmoded and economically inefficient entity. In their view, an industry structure dominated by such entities: inhibits cost-savings that could be achieved with greater coordination and bulk power trades between interconnected systems; makes cooperative agreements and power pooling arrangements difficult to establish; provides unequal access to the benefits of coordination and power pools among buyers and sellers; and allows the owners of transmission lines to exercise monopoly power over their sections of the interconnected systems.[27]

The entrance of small power producers and cogenerators into the generation market under the aegis of PURPA has yielded some benefits, but it also has imposed additional operating uncertainties and costs on electric utilities.[28] Expanding the PURPA model is one mechanism for introducing limited competition into the regulated generating sector. A major advantage of this approach is that smaller increments of increased competition can yield efficiency gains and resolve uncertainties without radically altering present institutional arrangements and risking a costly mistake.[29] At the same time, changes in the criteria for QFs would reduce what some view as inherent market distortions created by PURPA's limitation to small power producers and nonutility firms.

Federal authority to issue wheeling orders rests primarily on three sources:

1. antitrust law (as a remedy for anti-competitive or monopolistic behavior),
2. the licensing power under the Atomic Energy Act, and
3. sections 211 and 212 of the Federal Power Act, as amended by PURPA.[30]

Wheeling orders under antitrust law are rare, and even if a plaintiff is successful, it may take years to work out acceptable arrangements. Wheeling conditions imposed on licensees of nuclear power plants by the Nuclear Regulatory Commission (NRC) and its predecessor, the Atomic Energy Commission have been a major source for guaranteeing transmission access for requirements customers. With no new nuclear power plants on order, additional NRC wheeling orders as part of licensing conditions will be rare. It is possible that NRC might modify some existing licensing obligations, however.[31] Section 211 wheeling orders have been effectively precluded by the heavy burden of proof placed on applicants and the restrictive findings that must be made before an order can be issued. For example, among other things, section 211 requires a finding that existing competitive relationships, such as existing power sales arrangements, not be disturbed.[32] Other difficulties with existing FERC wheeling authority include: the fact that each wheeling application is considered separately; uncertainty over whether QFs and IPPs are included under the broad definition of a utility as any entity that generates power for sale; prohibition on retail wheeling; and Federal court decisions and FERC informal opinions that the 1978 PURPA wheeling provisions narrowed whatever inherent authority may have existed under the Federal Power Act to order wheeling to promote competition.[33]

A fourth possible source of wheeling authority is FERC's ability to "condition" its approval of some desired action on the petitioner's acceptance of certain specified requirements. This conditional authority is inherent in FERC's regulatory and policy responsibilities under the Federal Power Act and other laws.[34]

Implementation

Scenario 2 would be implemented through combined Federal and State efforts. Federal legislation would be required to amend PURPA, the Federal Power Act, and PUHCA. State legislation or regulatory action would be needed to implement the changes in Federal PURPA rules.

Changes in PURPA Requirements. Selected changes in the PURPA eligibility standards for qualifying cogenerators and small power producers would increase the ranks of potential competitors in bulk power markets.[35] PURPA vests with

FERC the responsibility for establishing technical requirements for qualifying facility status, and most of these initiatives could be accomplished through changes in FERC regulations. Modifications have been suggested to the standards on the unit size, technologies, fuel types, and utility equity participation.

Size: FERC rules limit small power producers to no more than 80 MW for PURPA eligibility. There is a statutory limit of 30 MW for exemption from State and Federal utility regulation (including regulation under PUHCA). Under scenario 2, the size cap for small power producers would be raised, for example, to 165 MW as proposed by a former FERC chairman.[36] There are no size or fuel limits on cogenerators, because they are not primarily in the business of generating and selling electricity.

Utility Equity Participation: Legislation would probably be required to allow full equity participation in QFs by utilities and would be controversial.[37] FERC rules interpreting PURPA have allowed utility equity participation of less than 50 percent. Many utility subsidiaries are active in building QF plants, but they must do so as part of a joint venture with another nonutility firm. Under this scenario, unregulated utility subsidiaries would be able to build and own generating units outside their own service territories and sell power at PURPA avoided cost rates. FERC has solicited comments on how they might amend the existing equity ownership rules to expand utility participation in QFs.[38]

Fuel: Qualifying small power producers are limited to those that produce electricity through use of biomass, waste materials, geothermal energy, or renewable resources such as wind, solar, and hydro-electric resources. They may use oil, natural gas, or coal for up to 25 percent of their total energy input.

Technology: FERC rules require that to qualify, energy use by a cogenerator must be sequential and must meet minimum efficiency standards in thermal output. Sequential use means that the rejected heat from a power production or heating process is used in another power production or heating process. This cascading use of energy in sequential processes gives rise to the energy conserving characteristics of cogeneration.[39] Some new technologies, such as extraction turbines, do not use sequential steam to generate large amounts of power. Modifications to the technology requirements might allow additional facilities to qualify.

Operating and Efficiency Standards: FERC regulations impose different efficiency and operating standards on QF units depending on the type of fuel used. New cogeneration facilities using natural gas or oil must satisfy minimum efficiency levels intended to ensure efficiency superior to conventional utility facilities.[40] No such restrictions are imposed on waste plants or coal plants.

Easing of the above PURPA standards for QF eligibility would increase both the number and diversity of participants in bulk power markets and, combined with increased access to transmission service, would broaden the range of purchase options available to utilities and large retail customers. For those customers either unable or unwilling to assume the risks of purchasing power off system, the local utility would maintain a service obligation to either construct or acquire needed capacity to serve their power supply needs.

Revised PURPA eligibility standards could bring some IPP projects under the QF purchase obligations of utilities. At the same time, with greater variety and more competition among alternative sources, the purchasing utility's avoided costs might be driven down, thus lowering required QF payments. IPP and QF projects could use their access to the transmission system to contract with more distant utilities offering more attractive avoided cost payments. IPPs not meeting QF status requirements would still be able to seek mandatory transmission access to move their power.

Transmission Access and Wheeling — Scenario 2 involves two distinct kinds of wheeling to promote greater competition:

1. wholesale wheeling — providing transmission services to utilities and nonutility generators for sale of power for resale (mostly involving sales to utilities); and
2. retail wheeling — transmitting power from other generators (utilities, QFs, IPPs) to ultimate customers which would also allow "self-service" wheeling among facilities owned by a QF or a self-generator.

Expanded transmission access under scenario 2 would increase the market access of both potential buyers and sellers of electric power and lessen the dominance of the utilities controlling the transmission grids.

Scenario 2 would amend the Federal Power Act to change the definition of those eligible to seek wheeling orders and modify the process through which FERC can order wheeling.[41] The restrictive findings required by existing law, which effectively preclude issuance of wheeling orders in most cases, would be replaced by a more flexible "public interest standard." If efforts to negotiate voluntary wheeling arrangements failed, any utility (including QFs and IPPs) or large retail customer would have legal standing to seek a wheeling order from FERC. There would be a rebuttable assumption that the capacity to wheel exists and any utility denying wheeling services would bear the burden of proof of showing that there is either a lack of capacity or a degradation of service that would result from the proposed wheeling transaction. The wheeling utility would be entitled to a reasonable compensation for its transmission services.

In deciding whether to grant a requested wheeling order, FERC could consider all relevant issues including potential impacts on utilities, captive customers, and system reliability. Thus, it is possible that, if a wheeling order allowing an industrial customer to purchase off-system[42] would impose a substantial economic hardship on the utility's remaining customers, FERC could deny the request for transmission access under a public interest standard. (The customer, of course, would always retain the option of self-generation, which would still leave the utility with the same problem of recovering its investment from a smaller pool of ratepayers.) Providing retail customers with access to transmission would provide them with a bargaining tool in seeking to negotiate rate concessions from their retail supplier.

The principal constraints on a customer purchasing off-system under scenario 2 would be the availability of transmission capacity, and any specific contractual provisions with the existing utility supplier on minimum take and termination notice conditions. Arrangements for backup or standby power supplies would have to be negotiated with the host utility, perhaps with review by appropriate regulatory authorities.[43] In some cases the customer would have to negotiate contracts for provision of unbundled control area services provided by the local utility.

Industrial customers going off-system for their power needs would have to negotiate some stand-by or maintenance service arrangement with their native utilities if they were to expect any sort of service obligation. They may also have to negotiate some provisions for later reconnection to local utility service if State regulations do not already provide for this. The contracts between large retail customers and alternative suppliers would likely be more detailed and complex than their previous agreements with a host utility. Many of the services that had been supplied as part of traditional electric power service would now have to be contracted for specifically. Contracts that involve wheeling agreements with third parties will also require more stringent delineations of technical and operating specifications and responsibilities.

Scenario 2 also would encourage the development of new initiatives to provide greater economic incentives to utilities to wheel voluntarily. FERC could, for example, establish affirmative guidelines for the approval of transmission agreements that might encourage wheeling, such as allowing more flexible pricing of transmission services, requiring compensation of other affected parties (such as other utilities experiencing unintended flows or parallel path problems), permitting auctioning of transmission services, establishing strict timetables for negotiating transmission agreements, and expediting their own review of transmission rates and agreements.[44] FERC might also cooperate in providing guidance and technical assistance to State regulators in pricing and contracting procedures for unbundled transmission and control services.

State Initiatives. Because States have the primary responsibility for implementing PURPA under guidelines established by FERC, the States would have to revise their rules and procedures to accommodate the expanded eligibility for QF status. States would have the lead role in implementing changes that permit large retail customers to purchase off system in intrastate transactions. Federal law would not preempt any State laws that characterize an IPP, self-generator, or QF engaged in retail sales as a public utility subject to regulation. States might require instate utilities to wheel power from other instate utilities and nonutility generators to large retail customers.

It is possible that the existing balance between State and Federal regulation could be maintained somewhat if Federal legislation expressly allowed delegation to the States of the authority to implement intrastate retail wheeling under FERC guidelines. State involvement might also be the most politically effective means of implementing retail wheeling because of the substantial equity and fairness considerations involved in weighing the interests of large customers in wheeling power against both the economic impacts on the local utility and the interests of other customers. Placing the decisionmaking responsibility in State hands would move the process closer to the parties that potentially would be most affected by the order.

System Operations and Planning

System reliability and coordination remains the responsibility of the local control center as in scenario 1. Operating requirements for QFs and IPPs would be specified in contracts. System operations would likely be affected more than in scenario 1 as there would be a need to accommodate a greater diversity of generating sources and delivery points.

Dispatch, maintenance, and unit loading operations and procedures would be similar to scenario 1, except that loading and dispatch of transmission accessors not subject to direct utility control would be determined by contracts among the generator, its customers, and the wheeling utility. The wheeling utility would have to adjust its operations to counter any increased uncertainty created by having nondispatchable generators on the system. (Of course, the wheeling utility could impose reasonable technical conditions and charges on the nondispatchable generators and their customers to provide this service.)

Emergency curtailments of service would be allocated according to State-regulated curtailment policies and contracts (same as in scenario 1). For outages of nonutility wheeled power, curtailment and backup power would be based on standby service contracts with the local utility.

Planning and developing generating capacity would be very similar to scenario 1. Under revised PURPA standards, a broader range of facilities would be eligible for QF status, and State law might require utilities to consider QFs as po-

COMPETITION IN ELECTRICITY

tential components of their capacity expansion plans. It is likely that much more QF and IPP capacity would be built under scenario 2 than under scenario 1. As the amount of nonutility generation grows, States or regional utility groups may wish to provide for direct participation by nonutility generators in the planning process.

Planning for transmission additions would be similar to scenario 1 except that State regulators may require utilities to include provisions for adequate transmission capacity for wheeling services in system planning. There is a possibility that some nonutility entities might build private transmission lines, but they would have no eminent domain authority and an uncertain regulatory status. FERC might order a utility to upgrade or expand its transmission facilities to implement a public interest wheeling order. States might also require utilities to expand transmission capacity to accommodate competitive sources.

Distribution additions would be the responsibility of the local utility (same as in scenario 1).

Conservation and load management plans would be developed by the local utility with oversight by State authorities. State regulators may require utilities to include consideration of saving; from conservation and load management strategies as part of their least-cost planning efforts as in scenario 1.

SCENARIO 3: COMPETITION FOR NEW BULK POWER SUPPLIES

Scenario 3 would create an institutional and regulatory structure to support all source competi-tion for new electricity supplies. Bulk power prices would be established through reliance on competitive market forces rather than cost-based regulation. The overall structure of regulated utilities would be maintained, but limited competition for new capacity needs would be introduced in the generation sector. The present electric power industry structure would be expanded by the entry of IPPs and unregulated utility subsidiaries, divisions, and/or spinoffs created to build and operate new generating facilities and to sell power in competitive markets. The numbers of competing buyers and sellers of electricity would greatly increase, as would the number of entities seeking access to the transmission grid.[45]

Under scenario 3, once a need for new power supplies has been certified by the appropriate regulatory authorities, an electric utility would solicit offers for new power supplies from other utilities, nonutility generators, QFs, and its own unregulated generating subsidiaries.[46] Conservation and load management strategies might also be included as competitive options in some State programs.[47] With appropriate safeguards to limit problems of self-dealing and conflict of interest, the unregulated utility subsidiaries could bid for new capacity within their own service territories.[48] Contracts for new electricity supplies would be awarded based on consideration of both price and nonprice factors (e.g., dispatchability, fuel and technology preferences, location, and relative environmental impacts).

Three mechanisms would exist for securing transmission services: 1) voluntary transmission arrangements with wheeling utilities for utilities and retail customers; 2) transmission access preconditions imposed on utility participants in bidding for competitively awarded bulk power contracts; and 3) public interest transmission orders issued by FERC which would be available only to utilities and wholesale power suppliers.

Scenario 3 would effectively create a two-tiered bulk power supply system: new power supplies under a minimally regulated, "workably competitive" market;[49] and existing generation under the current State-Federal scheme of regulated entry and pricing. Existing generating facilities, and transmission and distribution systems would remain regulated. Gradually, however, as old generation plants are replaced, the system would move toward an unregulated market in electric power generation and supply.

Background

Scenario 3 is loosely based on recent suggestions for allowing competition for new electricity sources. These proposals include those of FERC Chairman Martha Hesse,[50] the Keystone Electricity Working Group,[51] and three notices of proposed rulemaking (NOPRs) issued by FERC in March 1988.[52] Scenario 3 is not identical with any of the proposals, however.

Chairman Hesse initially proposed the use of competitive bidding as an alternative to administra-tive determinations to set QF avoided cost capacity payments under PURPA. According to Chairman Hesse, modifications of existing PURPA rules to allow States to implement all-source competitive bidding on an optional basis and to use these results to establish avoided cost rates would also "fit PURPA into an overall electric strategy which will move us toward a more economically efficient industry."[53]

As a further initiative to expand competition, she suggested, some of the regulatory requirements on IPPs could be reduced for any IPP that is not a QF and that sells electric power in areas where it has no service franchises and otherwise lacks significant market power.[54] Eligible IPPs would receive the maximum pricing flexibility under the Federal Power Act's "just and reasonable" standard and would be relieved of certain reporting and accounting obligations because of their lack of market power. Chairman Hesse deferred discussion of transmission access and pricing issues for future FERC action.

The Keystone Group considered, but did not adopt, a draft proposal opening a utility's future bulk power needs to competition among all potential suppliers with the economic and technical capability to develop needed generating capacity. The proposal suggested that existing regulatory and statutory constraints in PURPA and PUHCA on utility ownership of new power supply projects eligible to participate in this new competitive market would be relaxed or eliminated. The existing PURPA administratively determined avoided cost pricing scheme would be replaced; competitive bidding would allow the prices to be paid by distribution utilities for new generation to be set in the marketplace. If independent generators were unable to meet a utility's need for new generating capacity, the utility would function as a "backstop" or a supplier of last resort for whatever remaining need there was for new power supplies. The utility's cost of providing such last-resort capacity would also set an upper limit on what might be paid to independent power suppliers.

Under the Keystone approach, all independent third-party suppliers would have guaranteed access to transmission service on reasonable terms (subject to availability). The draft did not provide much detail on how the access guarantees would work. Transmission access would not be available for retail customers.

In March 1988 FERC formally advanced Chairman Hesse's suggestions for greater reliance on "workably competitive markets" by issuing NOPRs that would:

1. impose additional procedural requirements for determination of avoided costs by State regulators and unregulated utilities,
2. specify acceptable forms of competitive bidding for new power supplies that could be used by States or unregulated utilities in setting avoided costs under PURPA, and
3. establish IPPs as a new category of power suppliers without market power that would be exempted from many of FERC's reporting and regulatory requirements otherwise imposed on electric utilities.

The NOPRs invited comment on two changes involving transmission. The avoided cost NOPR asked whether QFs should be allowed to construct and own transmission lines and interconnection facilities to transport their own power to purchasing utilities without losing their QF exemption from Federal and State regulation as a public utility. FERC also requested comments on how to deal with situations where a QF wishes to provide wheeling services for others over its transmission lines.[55] The competitive bidding NOPR asked for comments on imposing "wheeling in" and "wheeling out" conditions on utilities participating in bidding programs.[56]

OTA's scenario 3, like the previous proposals, would open up competition for new bulk power supplies. Unlike the Hesse proposals and the FERC NOPRs, the use of competitive procurement methods would not be optional. Scenario 3 also does not require creation of special regulatory exemptions for IPPs. Scenario 3 would condition participation in competitive bidding on agreements to provide transmission access to other bidders — somewhat similar to the wheeling mechanisms described by FERC. Unlike the other proposals however, Scenario 3 would include mandatory transmission access for wholesale bulk power sales under a public interest standard similar to that in Scenario 2 and would clearly require congressional action.[57]

Implementation

Conceivably, scenario 3 could be partiably accomplished through administrative actions by FERC. New rules could require States and utilities to use competitive procedures for establishing avoided cost prices for qualifying facilities under PURPA, although this may require a strained interpretation of PURPA and the Federal Power Act. (FERC proposed making competitive bidding optional for State PURPA implementation.) FERC might also formally accept market-based pricing for bulk power sales under its jurisdiction in regions where it found at least a presumption of a workably competitive market. Some observers have concluded that FERC has effectively deregulated many bulk power sales by accepting negotiated arrangements without much inquiry.

Under scenario 3, legislation would be required to expand FERC authority to order wheeling for wholesale transactions among utilities and to assure transmission access for new bulk power contracts. Changes would probably be needed in PUHCA to allow utility subsidiaries and other companies to compete as unregulated entities without coming under the more restrictive provisions of that act.

Many States would require legislation to authorize reliance on market-based mechanisms to set rices for new power sources. Legislation may be needed to vest adequate authority in public utility commissions to oversee and enforce competitive solicitations for new power supplies. A number of States including Connecticut, Massachusetts, Maine, New York, and Virginia, have already sanctioned competitive solicitations as a means of obtaining alternative electricity supplies at the lowest competitive costs. These competitive bidding processes do not, however, necessarily reflect an explicit State policy shift in favor of creating a fully competitive generating sector to replace traditional utility price regulation. Utilities can still build and receive cost of service treatment for new capacity in these States.

Regulators would become more extensively involved in approving determinations of need and in resolving disputes over contract awards under this scenario. The analytical capabilities of State commissions may need to be enhanced and expanded with additional funding and staff. It is presumed that under State competitive bidding programs, considerations of competitiveness and prudence would be addressed before the contracts were approved. Competitively established wholesale power prices would then be passed through to retail customers of the distribution utilities with only limited opportunity for change by State regulators.[58] In some instances regulators may reassert some control over bulk power costs by reexamining the prudence of contract rates and conditions in the context of retail ratesetting and other proceedings. State regulators might disallow full recovery of the purchased power costs if the utility's actions in selecting or negotiating the contract were found to be imprudent (e.g., if cheaper power were available elsewhere). The extent of State agency jurisdiction to review the retail impacts of wholesale contracts has been cast into doubt by a recent U.S. Supreme Court decision.

The ability of State regulators to examine the prudence of wholesale supply contracts in setting retail rates and approving supply plans was assumed in the development of this scenario. This assumption of effective State review of competitive contracts has been undercut by the U.S. Supreme Court's decision in Mississippi Power & Light Co. v. Mississippi ex. rel. Moore, Attorney General of Mississippi involving the dispute over the Grand Gulf nuclear plant.[59] The Court held that FERC authority over wholesale sales preempted any State commission inquiry into the prudence of the management decisions concerning the underlying power supply contract between Mississippi Power & Light, a subsidiary of Middle South Utilities, a public utility holding company, and another of the holding company's subsidiaries. Because of this preemption, the States were required to pass through the wholesale rates to their customers; all prudence issues would have to be raised by States and consumers in hearings before FERC. If extended beyond the facts of the Grand Gulf case, the Court's decision could require Federal legislation to implement scenario 3 in a form that assured effective State oversight of a utility's competitive supply arrangements.[60] Alternatively, new procedures and authority and expanded resources would be needed at FERC to provide an equivalent Federal role.

In scenario 3, State and Federal authorities would no longer directly control entrance into the generation sector (through certification of capacity need), nor would they set

486

wholesale prices for power from new generating facilities. Instead, a system of competitive-bidding or negotiated contracts would establish competitive market-based rates. These competitively established bulk power prices would then be passed through to retail customers of the distribution utilities. This approach may require a preliminary finding that a workably competitive situation exists for new power transactions and continuing market oversight by State and or Federal regulators. Most probably, regulators would be more extensively involved in approving a utility's assessment of capacity needs and in resolving disputes over contract awards.

Prices for "old" power supplies would remain under existing cost-based regulation. New competitive power supply prices could reflect levels of service and other non-price factors. Prices for transmission services would continue to be regulated by FERC. Greater reliance on transmission services may increase pressure for transmission pricing based on actual measured cost of service with allowances for non-price factors.[61] Alternatively, there will also be pressure from transmission owners and others to allow more flexible and value-based transmission pricing.

Under scenario 3, QFs and IPPs would be able to compete to sell wholesale power to utilities. They would not have access to the transmission system to sell power directly to retail purchasers, however, except to the extent that utilities controlling the grid voluntarily agreed to provide wheeling services.

Systems Operations and Planning

System reliability and coordination would be maintained as in scenarios 1 and 2 with primary responsibility resting with the local utility and/or control center. Operational requirements for nonutility generators (e.g., QFs and IPPs) would be based on contract terms with the local utility (or wheeling utilities). More formalized agreements would be needed to replace many of the current informal operating arrangements of integrated utilities and power pools as electric power supply functions are increasingly "unbundled."

Dispatch, maintenance, and unit loading schedules for the system would largely be handled by the local utility or control center. Specific dispatch and scheduling responsibilities of nonutility generators and transmission accessors would be negotiated by contracts among the generators, power purchasers, and wheeling utilities as in scenario 2.

Emergency curtaibments of generation and transmission services would be dealt with as in scenario 2.

Planning and developing generating capacity additions would primarily be the responsibility of the local utility as in scenario 2. Because the States would require utilities to use a competitive selection process (including consideration of non-price factors) for new power supplies, State regulators would be more heavily involved in overseeing utility demand forecasts and determinations of capacity needs. Independent generators would be free to make their own plans for new construction based in part upon the utilities' needs and in part on their own expectations of profit.

Transmission additions would be planned and built by the public utility transmission company or division with review and approval by regulatory authorities. State rules may require utilities to plan for adequate capacity for instate wheeling of new power supplies and to consider regional transmission needs. As in scenario 2, FERC may order a utility to expand its transmission capacity to provide mandatory wheeling services.

Planning and building additions to the distribution system would remain the responsibility of the local utility.

Conservation and load management planning and implementation would be the responsibility of local utilities as in scenarios 1 and 2. State authorities may require consideration of potential contributions of conservation and load management strategies as part of utilities' least-cost planning and in approving retail rates. State regulators might also allow demand side options to compete directly in the bidding process for capacity additions.[62]

SCENARIO 4: ALL SOURCE COMPETITION FOR ALL BULK POWER SUPPLIES WITH GENERATION SEGREGATED FROM TRANSMISSION AND DISTRIBUTION SERVICES

Scenario 4 would restructure the U.S. electric power industry and its regulatory institutions and create a competitive, unregulated generating sector and a structurally separate regulated transmission and distribution sector. Integrated utilities would be required to segregate generation activities, both institutionally and operationally, from transmission and distribution to limit the potential for self-dealing and cross-subsidization. Owners of existing and new generation sources would compete to sell power to regulated transmission and distribution companies. Some transmission companies could also act as power brokers or wholesalers providing bulk power supply planning, purchasing, and delivery services to distribution utilities. Purchasing utilities would be assured access to transmission services for their bulk power needs (capacity permitting).

The scenario would entail substantial rewriting of Federal and State laws governing utility regulation with greater emphasis on authority for overseeing the competitiveness of bulk power markets and regulating transmission services and power brokers. Modifications of the public utility ownership restrictions in the Federal Power Act, PURPA, and PUHCA would allow broader participation in generation markets. State regulatory schemes would also have to be overhauled to accommodate this scenario. The scenario could shift the primary locus of utility regulation from States to the Federal Government, but implementing legislation could maintain a balance by giving greater wholesale authority to State regulators. States would regulate the prices, operations, and quality of service of retail distribution companies. Transmission capacity, services, and rates would be subject to mixed Federal and State regulation.

Background

Scenario 4 is derived from proposals that would structurally disaggregate the electric power industry to allow the generating sector to become both more dependent on the discipline of competitive market forces and free from many of the pricing and entry restraints of the existing regulatory system.[63] Under scenario 4, the organizational structure of the electric power industry would begin to resemble that of the natural gas industry where production, interstate transmission, and local distribution are generally under separate ownership (although there are numerous cases of "upstream" and "downstream" integration).

Scenario 4 would open all power supply contracts to competition, unlike Scenario 3, which is limited to new bulk power sources. Because Scenario 4 would be applied industry wide, it would probably involve a transition period of many years to allow a gradual phase-out of rate-of-return regulation, orderly restructuring and divestiture of assets, and renegotiation of existing arrangements.[64]

Radical industry restructuring has some precedent in the recent experience in breaking up AT&T and deregulating much of the telephone industry. On a much smaller scale, several utilities have sought to revamp their internal structures to set up holding companies, split power system functions into separate subsidiaries, and create unregulated competitive generating subsidiaries.[65] But, there is no precedent for radical restructuring and deregulation of an industry similar to electric power that is characterized by long-term investment, heavy fixed costs, an obligation to serve, and which is in a period of excess capacity. The restructuring under scenario 4 raises major questions of public policy and equitable treatment of stockholders and ratepayers in allocating any increased value for existing assets.

As one benefit of removing most price and entry restrictions from the generating sector and replacing them with open competition, "there would be strong, direct incentives for efficiency in construction, and new units would be built by companies that could offer capacity at the lowest life cycle costs."[66] The principal risk would be threats to the reliability and stability of the overall integrated systems arising from lack of or reduced coordination among competing entities. Proponents believe there would also be substantial efficiency gains in the use of all available generating units to meet regional electricity demands. In their view, these efficiency gains would not likely be achieved under the existing structure because of the disincentives to increased bulk power transfers among utility control areas, difficulties in forming power pools, and transmission capacity constraints.

Implementation

Scenario 4 would require substantial changes in both Federal and State laws governing the electric power industry. The Federal Power Act's jurisdictional and procedural requirements would be substantially revised to reflect the new institutional structures with greater emphasis on creating effective mechanisms for overseeing the competitiveness of bulk power markets and regulating transmission services and power brokers. PURPA and PUHCA would also require amendment to remove statutory barriers to full participation in the competitive generating sector. This would allow utilities' generating companies to compete outside of their regional territories without coming under the full financial and operational restrictions imposed on regulated utility holding companies. Continuation of PURPA's purchase and sale obligations for alternative energy sources might also require reexamination to determine if they still were effective and/or appropriate under a changed industry structure.

The transmission and distribution segments of the industry would continue to be regulated heavily while generation would be subject only to competitive market forces, regulatory oversight, and antitrust laws. Price and entry regulation for the generation sector would be replaced with competitive markets. Generators would still be subject to environmental, siting, financial, and antitrust requirements imposed by other State and Federal laws under scenario 4 and all others. The States would regulate the prices, operations, and quality of service of retail distribution companies. State regulators would review the power purchase contracts of distribution utilities, but the effectiveness of State programs would be hindered without some mechanism to review the adequacy of competitive market transactions. Transmission capacity, services, and rates would be subject to mixed Federal and State regulation. Under this scenario there is the potential for increased Federal regulation and oversight of bulk power supplies and what were formerly intrasystem transmission arrangements. Implementing legislation could, however, provide for a more balanced Federal-State division of regulatory authority to give States greater control over intrastate activities.

Vertical integration of the electric power industry would be reduced by the separation of utility generating segments from transmission and distribution segments.[67] This could be accomplished by creating new subsidiaries or divisions, or by spinning off a new company and then "selling" the required physical plant and other assets to the new entity.[68] Segregated utility generators, QFs, and IPPs could compete to provide power supplies to transmission-distribution and local distribution companies. Age, performance, and fuels of existing units will affect the competitive strengths of the new generating companies. These competitive differences could eventually lead to a consolidation of the industry.[69]

Under scenario 4 local distribution companies would be primarily responsible for securing adequate power supplies from competing suppliers through contract solicitations and negotiations. Regulated transmission companies would own and operate the transmission facilities and be responsible for planning and building networks with adequate capacity to serve buyers and sellers in a competitive market. Transmission companies would function as regional controllers and dispatchers of generation and provide wheeling services for utilities under regulated rate schedules. They could also act as power brokers or as wholesalers linking independent generators and local distribution utilities.

Generators and distribution companies could seek transmission orders from FERC based on a public interest standard similar to that in scenarios 2 and 3. Unlike scenario 2 there would be no mandatory wheeling for retail customers. It is expected, however, that many generators and transmission companies would sell directly to large retail customers under arrangements for bypass or standby payments to local distribution companies.

Distribution companies under scenario 4 would retain an obligation to serve, that is, to plan for and secure adequate electricity supplies for the needs of their franchise customers. But with little or no generating resources of their own, they would be highly dependent on the willingness of independent suppliers to construct needed capacity and the availability of adequate transmission capacity to move the power. Competing generating companies would be under no legal obligation to build new capacity, but would commit to do so if and when the market price was sufficient to assure them an attractive return. Thus, in the generating sector market price signals would displace the utility's traditional service obligation as the principal mechanism for assuring the availability of adequate and reliable power supplies. The experiences of the numerous independent distribution companies that currently obtain their electricity supplies and transmission services from larger integrated utilities could provide helpful precedents.

Transmission under scenario 4 would begin to assume some of the characteristics of a common carrier, but the transmission entity would retain some discretion over who was eligible to obtain service and would not be required to provide wheeling to retail customers. The transmission company could not impose unreasonable or discriminatory conditions on transmission access. It could, for example, specify minimum operating standards to preserve system reliability and require advance notice and financial commitments to reserve firm transmission capacity.

Independent generating companies and local distribution entities would be linked by these newly created transmission entities, which would serve as regional controllers and dispatchers of generating capacity. In addition to this primary role, transmission utilities could also serve as regional power brokers which would make the market for, and be party to, contracts negotiated between independent generating companies and distribution entities. Transmission companies might also assist in the creation of secondary futures markets as a means of hedging against the added uncertainty associated with a vertically segregated industry.

Under scenario 4, transmission access would be achieved primarily through voluntary negotiations; however, the separate transmission entities would have an obligation to provide adequate transmission capacity to support the industry's new competitive structure. FERC would also have the authority to order wheeling for customer utilities on a public interest standard if satisfactory voluntary arrangements could not be reached through negotiation. With FERC's endorsement, States might require nondiscriminatory access to transmission services as a precondition for allowing existing regulated generation, transmission, and distribution companies to participate in the new competitive system. Transmission access for retail customers would be kept on a voluntary basis.

Systems Operations and Planning

System reliability and coordination would be the responsibility of the regulated transmission company or transmission-distribution company. The transmission company would take over many of the day-to-day functions of system coordination that are now the responsibility of local utilities and control centers. Operational responsibilities of power suppliers and local distribution companies would be specified in contracts with State and Federal oversight.

Dispatch, unit loading, and maintenance schedules would be administered by the transmission utility under various contracts between power suppliers and: 1) regulated transmission companies, 2) regulated distribution companies, and/or 3) retail customers. Dispatchable generators would be controlled by the transmission company and compensated for their services according to contract terms.

Emergency curtailments for retail customers served by local distribution companies would be allocated according to State-regulated curtailment policies. For other customers, curtailments would be specified in contracts with the transmission and generation suppliers. Curtailment of transmission services will be based on contractual terms, State and Federal regulation, and system reliability considerations.

Generating Capacity Additions: Future electric supply requirements would be determined by the local distribution company through its planning processes with State oversight. Competition for supply contracts would be open to all generating sources, as in scenario 3. Independent generators would plan and build new plants based on utilities' indications of need and their own strategic plans and profit expectations. Transmission utilities could also contract for generating capacity to aid in preserving system reliability and to allow them to serve as power brokers subject to State and Federal regulation.

Transmission Additions: The regulated transmission or transmission-distribution companies would have the obligation to provide transmission capacity necessary to support wheeling needs for instate utilities. (This assumes of course that wheeling is economical and that wheeling customers are willing to pay for the additional capacity needs.) States could require transmission capacity planning to include consideration and coordination of regional transmission system needs.

Distribution additions would be the responsibility of the locally regulated distribution utility, with oversight by State authorities-same as in scenario 3.

Conservation and load management programs would be provided by local distribution companies, possibly in conjunction with transmission companies. State regulators could require consideration of potential contributions from load management and conservation strategies as part of the distribution utility's least-cost planning processes in this and other scenarios.

SCENARIO 5: COMMON CARRIER TRANSMISSION SERVICES IN A DISAGGREGATED, MARKET-ORIENTED, ELECTRIC POWER INDUSTRY

Scenario 5 would break up the vertically integrated electric power industry by divesting generation, transmission and retail distribution segments into separate entities. All customers (both wholesale and retail) would have the option of purchasing power from any willing supplier with the assurance that such power could be delivered under reasonable terms and conditions. Distribution and transmission services would remain tightly regulated, but entry and bulk power pricing in the electric generation segment would primarily be left to market forces.

The competitive generation segment would include formerly regulated utility generation opera-tions, QFs, and IPPs (although such distinctions among power producers would no longer be relevant). Unlike scenario 4, ownership of generating companies would be completely severed from ownership of transmission and distribution companies. The regulated transmission companies would explicitly be required to provide transmission services as a common carrier (i.e., nondiscriminatory service based on approved wheeling tariffs to all parties requesting service) and to provide adequate transmission capacity. Wheeling to retail customers would be available, although as a practical matter it would likely be limited to very large industrial consumers. Federal and State policies might encourage greater aggregation in transmission services to create coordinated large regional transmission systems either through mergers and acquisitions or through operational agreements among neighboring systems.

Background

Scenario 5 includes many of the key elements of the preceding scenarios including vertical disintegration of industry structure, market-based pricing of generation, and transmission access. Under scenario 5, any generator could sell to any buyer, any buyer could purchase from any seller, and the transmission company would have to wheel the power. Proponents of this radical restructuring of the industry cite a number of technological and public policy reasons for adopting this approach.[70] Chief among them are: the decline of the natural monopoly characteristics of the generating sector; the excess generating capacity in many regions; and the presumably higher social and economic costs to society of "imperfect regulation" compared with "imperfect competition."

The key to having a vigorously competitive and economically efficient electric power industry lies in the evolution of new institutions and arrangements.[71] This is unlikely to be accomplished merely by allowing distribution utilities and others to shop around for the best bulk power deal without first establishing the necessary competitive market environment. Among the changes in industry regulation, operations and structure that would lead to achievement of this scenario are:

- encouraging the regionalization of utility regulation and operations by expanding the use of centralized dispatch of generating capacity within States or regions;
- creating power brokerage and auction markets;
- realigning Federal and State regulatory authority to allow States clear authority in intrastate bulk power and wheeling markets;
- creating federally approved interstate regulatory compacts for governance of central dispatch, auction, and brokerage systems; and
- assuring open and fair access to transmission systems either through mandatory wheeling or through creation of new regional transmission entities.

Implementation

Scenario 5 would require rewriting of existing State and Federal laws and regulations governing electric power generation, transmission, and distribution. Although "deregulated," the competitive generating sector would need continuing oversight to assure the existence of workably competitive markets. In addition, new contractual arrangements and industry practices would have to evolve to assure effective operations under a new disintegrated, market-based industry structure, and to preserve reliability and stability of interconnected electric power systems.

Regulators would approve the transmission company's wheeling tariffs for both utility and nonutility generators. FERC (or perhaps a regional authority) would have the power to issue wheeling orders to facilitate bulk power transfers if satisfactory arrangements could not be made with the transmission company. Wheeling rates would be designed to include adequate signals to assure construction of new transmission facilities. The transmission utility also would have an obligation to plan for and build adequate and reliable transmission capacity to serve regional needs and to accommodate interregional transfers. Wheeling customers could contract for different levels of service (e.g., firm, interruptible).

Bulk power prices would be set through competitive markets and passed through to ratepayers. Power purchases by distribution companies and retail rates would be regulated by State authorities. Retail rates and the need for and prudence of bulk power purchases by distribution companies would be regulated as now by State authorities. Rates charged by transmission companies acting as power brokers and reselling to distribution companies would also be subject to regulatory oversight to assure that there was no cross-subsidization of operations or anticompetitive practices.

This scenario would involve the mobilization and transfer of billions of dollars in utility assets to newly established entities. Because of the complexity of the transactions, it is likely that many years would be required to complete an orderly transition.[72] The essential step in achieving this scenario would be the establishment of a separate and functional common carrier transmission entity. This could be accomplished simply by spinning off the transmission assets and operations of a vertically integrated utility to a new private entity. It could also be accomplished through legislation to create federally chartered and publicly held regional transmission (and dispatch) corporations to acquire all transmission lines and facilities within a designated region.

Systems Operations and Planning

System reliability and coordination would be maintained by the separate, regulated transmission company. The operational responsibilities of power suppliers and local distribution companies would be specified in contracts with the transmission company.

Dispatch, unit loading, and maintenance schedules would be determined by the transmission company in negotiation with generators and governed by contracts as in scenario 4.

Emergency curtailments of electric power and transmission services would be allocated according to contractual arrangements and/or State regulations.

Generating capacity additions would be planned and built by independent generating companies based on their strategic plans, profit expectations, and transmission and distribution utilities' indications of need. Distribution and transmission companies jointly or separately) would project future demand and determine the desired mix of generating resources to meet those needs before soliciting contract bids from power suppliers.

Transmission additions would be planned and built by the transmission utility which would have an obligation to provide adequate and reliable transmission capacity necessary to supply the wheeling needs of anticipated customers. Regulatory authorities may require consideration and coordination of regional transmission capacity needs in planning.

Distribution additions would be planned and built by the local distribution utility as in scenario 4.

Conservation and load management strategies would be developed by local distribution companies in cooperation with transmission companies and regulatory authorities.

ENDNOTES

1. For background information contrasting past proposals for electric power industry reform see: Paul L. Joskow and Richard Schmalensee, *Markets for Power: An Analysis of Electrical Utility Deregulation* (Cambridge,

MA: The MIT Press, 1983); Theodore Barry & Associates, "A Study of Aggregation Alternatives in the U.S. Electric Utility Industry," December 1982, prepared for the U.S. Department Energy, Director, Policy Planning and Analysis, Division of Electric Utility Policy (available through National Technical Information Service), DOE/RG/10295-1; U.S. Department of Energy, Office of Policy Planning and Analysis, "Deregulation of Electric Power: A Framework for Analysis, A Draft Discussion Paper, Phase I Report," September 1982 (DOE/NBB-0021), prepared by the Massachusetts Institute of Technology, under contract number Ex-76-A-012295 (available through National Technical Information Service); and Edison Electric Institute, Economics Division, "Alternative Models of Electric Power Deregulation," May 1982 (prepared by NPS Energy Management, Inc.).

2. For example, scenario 2 transmission access procedures are based in part on recommendations of the Electricity Consumers Resource Council, and scenario 3 includes elements of competitive bidding proposals by FERC Chairman Martha Hesse and the Keystone Electricity Forum, among others.

3. In some cases these changes would lower avoided cost rates, but in others it is conceivable that unrealistically low avoided cost rates would be increased.

4. Public utility commissions might lower the authorized rate of return for utilities because of the reduced regulatory risk, but some analysts question whether preapprovals would actually lead to a reduction in the risk component of capital costs as reflected in market rates. See National Regulatory Research Institute, *Commission Preapproval of Utility Investments* (Columbus, OH: National Regulatory Research Institute, 1981, reissued 1987), hereafter referred to as "Preapprovals."

5. Another reason for the interest in expanding competition is the political preference among some economists and policymakers in favor of market-based institutions and against regulated monopolies. Less reliance on regulation and greater reliance on increased competition in power supplies are seen as mechanisms for attaining the goal of economic efficiency.

6. U.S. Congress, Congressional Budget Office, Financial

Condition of the U.S. Electric Utility Industry (Washington, DC: U.S. Government Printing Office, March 1986).

7. Under many State regulatory statutes, a utility investment in a new plant must be prudent and used and useful (put into service) before it can be placed in the rate base and costs recovered from ratepayers. Prudence reviews are regulatory examinations of the appropriateness of utility demand projections, construction practices, and management decisions and are a precondition for adding a new facility to the ratebase. The reviews are typically conducted after the plant is completed. Prudence reviews have led regulators to disallow all or part of investments in large coal and nuclear plants because of mismanagement and uncontrolled costs and, in some cases, because the completed plant proved to be excess capacity when projected demand growth did not materialize. Some industry analysts contend that prudence reviews have shifted the risks from ratepayers to shareholders and utilities and made it more difficult for utilities to commit capital for construction. Others contend that utilities and shareholders always bore these risks, but that they had historically been minimal until the highly inflationary and turbulent 1970s.

8. For example, see: J. Steven Herod and Jeffrey Skeer, "A Look at National and Regional Electric Supply Needs," paper presented at the 12th Energy Technology Conference and Exposition, March 1985; U.S. Department of Energy, Deputy Assistant Secretary for Energy Emergencies, Staff Report, "Electric Power Supply and Demand for the Contiguous United States, 1997 - 1996," DOE/E-0011 (Springfield, VA: National Technical Information Service, February 1988); Peter Navarro, *The Dimming of America: The Real Costs of Electric Utility Regulatory Failure* (Cambridge, MA: Ballinger Publishing Co., 1985).

9. Many utilities have regained their healthy financial status and are projected to have favorable cash flows in the late 1980s - 1990s. See ch. 2 of *Electric Power Wheeling and Dealing: Technological Considerations for Increased Competition,* Congress of the United States, Office of Technology Assessment, OTA-E-409 (Washington, DC: U.S. Government Printing Office, May, 1989)

10. The success of these efforts is open to doubt. Texas requires utilities to wheel QF power to other utilities. Texas may escape challenge because its transmission grid is physically isolated from other interconnected systems and thus arguably cannot be said to affect interstate transmission flows. Other States are potentially subject to FERC challenges to their authority. New York and Massachusetts require wheeling as a condition of participation in their bidding programs. Florida's attempts to require intrastate wheeling, including self-service wheeling, have repeatedly been challenged by FERC and by several Florida utilities, arguing that Federal law preempts State control over rates, and the terms and conditions of wheeling transactions. 2Florida Power & Light, Petition for Declaratory Order from FERC, EL87-19-000, filed Mar. 11, 1987.

11. State regulatory authorities in Massachusetts have adopted a preapproval process for new capacity. Massachusetts Department of Public Utilities "Pricing and Rate-making Treatment To Be Afforded New Electric Generating Facilities Which Are Not Qualifying Facilities," D.P.U. 86-36-C, May 12, 1988.

12. See "Presentation of Richard E. Disbrow at a Seminar for Virginia's Legislative Leadership and Energy Committee Members, Aug. 10, 1987" for a discussion of this approach. This strategy is also based in part on the remarks of Richard E. Disbrow at the OTA Workshop on Alternative Scenarios for Increasing Competition in the Electric Power Industry, Sept. 28, 1987; and on NRRI, "Preapprovals," supra note 4.

13. The prime attractions of a rolling prudence scheme are that it reduces some of the risk in utility capital investments, while the expanded role in planning, approval, and scheduled project reviews offers equivalent protections and controls for regulators and consumers.

14. Many State regulatory authorities have historically allowed utilities to recover the full costs of canceled plants plus a reasonable return on investment. Some States may, however, be restricted by State authorizing legislation that limits recovery to capital plant expenditures that are both prudent and used and useful, therefore requiring a facility to actually be in operation before any

recovery can be placed in the ratebase. See NRRI, "Preapprovals," supra note 4.

15. Disbrow. supra note 12.

16. See Joseph P. Kalt, Henry Lee, and Herman B. Leonard, "Re-Establishing the Regulatory Bargain in the Electric Utility Industry," Discussion Paper Series (E-87-02), Energy and Environmental Policy Center, John F. Kennedy School of Government, Harvard University, Cambridge, MA, March 1987; Leland L. Johnson, *Incentives To Improve Electric Utility Performance: Opportunities and Problems* (Santa Monica, CA: Rand Corp., March 1985); and NRRI, "Preapprovals," supra note 4.

17. This utility investment preference was previously noted by OTA, U.S. Congress, Office of Technology Assessment, New Electric Power Technologies: Problems and Prospects for the 1990s, OTA-E-246 (Washington, DC: U.S. Government Printing Office, July 1985), ch. 3.

18. This approach is different from scenario 3 which would require the use of competitive procurement procedures for all new bulk power supplies.

19. There are about 150 utility control centers in the United States. Some centers over see the operations of individual utilities, others govern the operations of participating utilities over a region established through coordination agreements or power pools. See chs. 4 and 5 of *Electric Power Wheeling and Dealing: Technological Considerations for Increasing Competition*, Congress of the United States, Office of Technology Assessment, OTA-E-409, (Washington DC, U.S. Government Printing Office, May, 1989) for more on control area responsibilities.

20. Under PURPA, utilities are required to interconnect with small power producers and QFs, and cannot impose unreasonable technical requirements to discourage access.

21. Over half of the States either require utilities to engage in least-cost planning for future electricity needs or are developing such requirements. David Berry, "Least-cost Planning and Utility Regulation," Public Utilities Fortnightly, Mar. 17, 1988, pp. 9-15.

22. PURPA provides that a qualifying facility must be "owned by a person not primarily engaged in the generation or sale of electric power (other than electric power solely from cogeneration and small power production

facilities)." 16 U.S.C. 796(17)(C) and (18)(B). FERC has solicited public comment on several potential changes to its rules on utility equity ownership of QFs. U.S. Federal Energy Regulatory Commission, Notice of Proposed Rulemaking on Regulations Governing the Public Utility Regulatory Policies Act of 1978, Docket No. RM88-17-000, July 19, 1988, pp. 32-57.

23. For examples of this approach, see *Electricity's Future: A Special Report by the Electricity Consumers Resource Council*, July 1987. See also, the proposed "Electric Utility Transmission Reform Act of 1985" introduced by Rep. Peter H. Kostmayer in the 99th Congress, H.R. 2231. The bill would have amended secs. 211 and 212 of the Federal Power Act to provide that FERC could issue an order requiring an electric utility to provide transmission services for another electric utility whenever it was found necessary or appropriate in order to: 1) conserve energy, 2) promote the efficient use of facilities and resources, 3) increase competition in the bulk power supply market, or 4) otherwise serve the public interest. The order could be granted on the application of any State commission, or public utility, or by FERC acting on its own motion following notice to affected utilities and an opportunity for a hearing. FERC could order a utility to expand transmission facilities to provide the needed transmission services, but the wheeling party would pay the capital and operating costs involved. The bill used a broad definition of a public utility as "any person, State agency, or Federal agency that sells electric energy" for its new wheeling authority, but otherwise would not expand FERC jurisdiction over these entities. H.R. 2231 expressly banned orders to deliver power to "ultimate" or retail customers. OTA's scenario 2 would extend eligibility for wheeling services to "qualified" power purchasers to allow very large retail customers to obtain wheeling. FERC or the States would establish standards for determining which retail customers would qualify for wheeling.

24. The issue of what constitutes a very large retail customer would be left to the States. It is assumed that States would limit access to facilities that require 20 to 50 MW or more. For example, a pulp and paper mill might qual-

ify at 20 MW in some States, but in others, facilities might require at least 200 MW (e.g., the power requirements of a large aluminum reduction plant).

25. In deciding whether to grant a requested wheeling order, FERC could consider all relevant issues including the potential impacts on utilities, captive customers, and system reliability. Thus, it is possible that, if granting a wheeling order to an industrial customer to purchase off system would impose a substantial economic hardship on the utility's remaining customers, FERC could deny the request for transmission access under its "public interest" standard.

26. See ELCON, *Electricity's Future,* supra note 23; William A. Brownell, "Electric Utility Deregulation: Analyzing the Prospects for Competitive Generation," Annual Review of Energy 1984, pp. 229 - 262; and F. Paul Bland, "Problems of Price and Transportation: Two Proposals To Encourage Competition From Alternative Energy Sources," 10 Harvard Environmental Law Review 345 (1986).

27. William A. Brownell, "Electric Utility Deregulation: Analyzing the Prospects for Competitive Generation," Annual Review of Energy 1984, pp. 229 - 262.

28. Id., pp. 254 - 255.

29. Id., p. 253.

30. 16 U.S.C. 824j and 824k. See discussion in *Electric Power Wheeling and Dealing: Technical Considerations for Increasing Competition,* supra note 19.

31. Ohio Edison has asked NRC to revise the wheeling obligations included in the license for its Perry Nuclear plant. The license requires Ohio Edison to wheel cheaper coal-fired power from southern Ohio to 21 municipal distributors in northeast Ohio. Ohio Edison has argued that the wheeling requirements should be dropped because the municipals no longer want to purchase the more expensive Perry nuclear power. "Metzenbaum Public Power Fight Ohio Edison Wheeling Request to NRC," Energy Daily, Apr. 4. 1988. pp. 1 - 2. Wheeling issues could also be raised before NRC in reviews of license assignments in mergers and acquisitions.

32. 16 U.S.C. 824j(c)(i). See analysis of Federal wheeling authority in Alvin Kaufman, Carl Behrens, Donald Dul-

chinos, Larry B. Parker, and Robert D. Poling, *Wheeling in the Electric Utility Industry*, Report No. 87-289 ENR (Washington, DC: Congressional Research Service, Feb. 12, 1987).
33. See Kaufman et al., id. Similar conclusions were reached in Harvey L. Reiter, "Competition and Access to the Bottleneck: The Scope of Contract Carrier Regulation Under the Federal Power and Natural Gas Acts," 18 Land and Water Law Review 1-80, 1983; National Regulatory Research Institute, Non-Technical Impediments to Power Transfers (Columbus, OH: National Regulatory Research Institute, September 1987); and Bland, supra note 26.
34. The "wheeling in" and "wheeling out" proposals in the notices of proposed rulemaking would be based on FERC's conditional authority. See note 57 infra. See also the discussion of FERC's authority in ch. 2. *Electric Power Wheeling and Dealing: Technological Considerations for Increasing Competition*, supra note 19.
35. FERC regulations define a small power producer as a facility that produces less than 80 MW of electric power at the same site through use of biomass; waste materials; geothermal energy; or renewable resources such as wind, solar and hydroelectric resources (up to 25 percent of total energy input to QF may be oil, natural gas, or coal). 18 CFR 292.204(1988). FERC defines a cogeneration facility as "equipment used to produce electric energy and forms of useful thermal energy (such as heat or steam) used for industrial, commercial, heating, or cooling purposes, through the sequential use of energy." 18 CFR 292.202(c) (1988). To be a qualified facility, the small power production facility or cogeneration facility cannot be owned by a person or entity "primarily engaged in the generation or sale of electric power" (other than the power produced from the qualifying facility). 18 CFR 292.206 (1988).
36. See Hearings Before the House Subcommittee on Energy Conservation & Power on H.R. 2992 and H.R. 2876 (198 1). H.R. 2876 would have increased QF size cap from 80 to 165 MW and eliminated 30 MW limit exemptions from Federal and State utility regulation. Legislation in the Senate was introduced in 1982 (S. 1885) and hearings

were held. Hearings on S. 1885 before the Senate Committee on Energy and Natural Resources, Apr. 19, 1982. The rationale for this size limit is that it would allow larger QF plants but would be less than some larger utility or IPP planned modular power plants. Legislation in 1981 would have lifted overall size limits to 165 MW.

37. H.R. 2876 would also have eliminated the utility ownership restriction from the definition of qualifying cogenerators and small power producers. Lifting the utility ownership cap was strongly opposed by State regulators and QF developers. See Hearings on H.R. 2992 and H.R. 2876, supra note 36.

38. See Notice of Proposed Rulemaking on Regulations Governing the Public Utility Regulatory Policies Act of 1978, Docket No. RM88-17-000, July 29, 1988.

39. The requirement of sequential use of energy was added by FERC in its technical definition of cogeneration and is not found in PURPA. The sequential use requirement was viewed as critical even though not statutory. See discussion in Pfeffer, Lindsay & Associates, Inc., "Emerging Policy Issues in PURPA Implementation: An Examination of Policy Issues Related to Federal and State Efforts to Encourage Development of Cogeneration and Small Power Production Under Title II of PURPA", March 1986, prepared for the U.S. Department of Energy, Office of Coal & Electricity Policy, ch. 11.

40. Under the Power Plant and Industrial Fuel Use Act of 1978, utilities were largely precluded from building new plants burning oil or natural gas without a special exemption, because these were believed at the time to be scarce fuels. In 1987 Congress repealed the act's fuel restrictions for new utility baseload plants.

41. See the ELCON proposal and Kostmayer bill, supra note 23. The Federal Power Act defines an electric utility as any entity that generates electric power for resale - some have questioned whether that definition brings QFs and IPPs within the class of parties with standing to seek mandatory transmission orders under existing law. The proposals would also extend standing to FERC, State agencies, Federal power agencies, and large power consumers/purchasers.

42. "Off system" refers to purchases from a power supplier

other than the native or host utility currently serving the industrial customer.

43. Some States already require utilities to provide backup services at nondiscriminatory rates.

44. Recent examples of these initiatives include the Western States Power Pool experiment, FERC authorization for Baltimore Gas & Electric to auction off its unneeded capacity on the PJM power pool, and approval of a flexible transmission pricing arrangement between Pacific Gas & Electric and the Turlock Irrigation District, see "PG&E Offers 'New Approach' To Pricing Transmission Services," The Energy Daily, Apr. 5, 1988, p. 1.

45. Although the numbers of competing suppliers and potential customers are likely to increase as a result of changes in this scenario, it is not at all clear whether the number of generators that win competitive supply contracts will increase significantly. It is conceivable that traditional utilities and large independent power producers would win many of the solicitations and that the need to integrate many new entrants into the bulk power network would be much less than if a larger number of small entities won contracts to supply an equivalent quantity of bulk power. We have assumed for purposes of this analysis that competitive solicitations will yield a larger and more diverse mix of generation than under traditional regulation because that result would pose the greatest challenges for bulk power system operation and control.

46. As used here, competitive "bidding" includes not only a structured auction with sealed or firm bids, but also less structured competitive negotiations where participating vendors might be selected based on an initial solicitation of proposals, such as, for example, the process used by Virginia Power Co. in seeking alternative power supplies described in ch. 5, supra note 19.

47. Among the mechanisms for including these demand side alternatives are: 1) to require utilities to consider demand side options as part of a least-cost planning before reaching a determination of now supply needs, 2) to allow demand side options to compete directly with supply options in the competitive solicitation, and 3) to hold a separate solicitation for a desired increment of demand

side options.

48. If a utility chose not to participate directly in the bidding, it might compete indirectly by setting a benchmark based on its own estimate of the costs of building the plant itself and recovering the costs under the base as the supplier of last resort.

49. As yet, FERC has not offered a clear and objective definition of what would constitute a "workably competitive market" under the Federal Power Act. Development of appropriate findings or guidelines for determining whether a workably competitive market existed would be left to FERC under scenario 3 and would be a prerequisite for implementation. A more detailed definition of the term is not needed for purposes of OTA's technical analysis, however.

50. See, for example, "Talking Points for the Chairman," The Edison Electric Institute, Cincinnati, OH, June 10, 1987; and "Remarks by FERC Chairman Martha 0. Hesse," Energy Daily's Annual Utility Conference, Washington, DC, Nov. 6, 1987.

51. The Keystone Energy Forum is an informal discussion group with members from industry, government, academia, trade associations, and public interest groups. The working group meets periodically on subjects of current interest. The draft proposal ("Keystone Electricity Draft," 1/27/88) was prepared to merge concepts brought out in discussions of the electricity working group of the Keystone Energy Futures Project. Although the group discussions are largely off the record, reports about the draft appeared in the trade press. The electricity working group never reached a consensus on final conclusions or recommendations on transmission access issues. They are currently considering issues related to transmission pricing.

52. U.S. Department of Energy, Federal Energy Regulatory Commission, Notice of proposed Rulemaking on Regulations Governing Bidding Programs (18 CFR Parts 35 and 293), Docket No. RM88-5-000, Mar. 16, 1988, very brief summary published at 53 Fed. Reg. 9324, Mar. 22, 1988; Notice of Proposed Rulemaking on Regulations Governing Independent Power Producers (18 CFR Parts 38 and 382), Docket No. RM88-4-000, Mar. 16,1988, very brief

summary published at 53 Fed. Reg. 9327, Mar. 22,1988; and Notice of proposed Rulemaking on Administrative Determination of full Avoided Costs, Sales of Power to Qualifying Facilities, and Interconnection Facilities (18 CFR Part 292), Docket No. RM88-6-000, Mar. 16, 1988, very brief summary published at 53 Fed. Reg. 9331, Mar. 22,1988.

53. Hesse, supra note 51, p. 3. One of the basic overall principles cited in support of her proposal was "The degree of regulation should reflect the degree of market power. Workably competitive markets should be allowed to operate with as little regulatory interference as possible." Id., at p. 4.

54. The rationale for special treatment for this class of IPPs is presented in a FERC document. "Summary of Current Staff Proposal on PURPA-Related Issues," Sept. 11, 1987, pp. 16 - 19.

55. Docket No. RM88-6-000, supra note 53, pp. 85-95.

56. Docket No. RM88-5-000, supra note 53, pp. 87-91. "Wheeling in" would require a utility wishing to bid on the capacity needs of another utility to agree to provide firm transmission services to the purchasing utility for successful bidders that are located within the bidding utilities service territory or that can reach one of its interconnection points. "Wheeling out" would require a utility wishing to bid to supply its own capacity needs to provide firm transmission services to the border of its service area to unsuccessful bidders that wished to sell to another wholesale purchaser. Both forms of wheeling would be subject to "reliability and economic dispatch considerations".

57. Some critics of the FERC competitive bidding and IPP NOPRs have argued that these actions also should be placed before Congress either because FERC lacks the explicit authority to require them and/or because they raise such significant national policy issues that they are more appropriate for legislative action. FERC Commissioner Charles A. Trabandt is one of the most vocal proponents of the latter view.

58. Under existing law, FERC has jurisdiction over the prices for most wholesale power sales. PURPA exempted purchases of QF power from FERC price regulation. States

have jurisdiction over utilities resource planning and construction and retail rates. States are generally required to pass through purchased power costs at FERC approved prices under the "filed rate doctrine." Without a change in PURPA or the Federal Power Act, FERC would have to approve contract prices for purchases from utilities and IPPs under a State competitive procurement program. See discussions in ch. 2, supra note 19.

59. No.86-1970, June 24, 1988.

60. Questions about the prudence of utility decisions in awarding bulk power contracts could arise later if a utility overestimated future demand and was left with a take or pay contract for unneeded electric power. The central issue would not be the contract price, but whether the utility's initial decision to purchase additional supplies was prudent and whether the full costs should be passed through to ratepayers. Another possible subsequent retail rate issue might arise over a utility's prudence in signing a contract with price escalation clauses that resulted in actual contract prices that exceeded those on which the initial bid was awarded.

61. Transmission prices are now commonly set in several ways, postage stamp rates, split the difference in savings rate, and others. See National Regulatory Research Institute, Some Principles for Pricing Wheeled Power (Columbus, OH: August 1987). Edison Electric Institute, Rate Regulation Department, Terms and Conditions of Existing Transmission Service Agreements, 04-85-05, 1985.

62. Regulators in Maine have allowed demand-side management options to compete to provide needed decrements of power capacity. In bidding conducted by Central Maine Power for 100 MW of capacity, 13 of 37 total bids were for demand-side management projects, however these projects represented only 35.6 MW out of more than 1,145 MW offered. On a price basis, the demand side projects averaged 75 percent of the utility's avoided costs, while the supply side offers averaged 97 percent of avoided costs. Issues Review and Tracking, Aug. 4, 1988, p. 1.

63. See for example, Richard J. Pierce, Jr.. "A Proposal to Deregulate the Market for Bulk Power," 72 Virginia Law Rev. 1183 (1986); Aspen Institute, "Electric Utilities:

Structure and Regulation." Energy Policy Forum, 1986;
and William W. Berry, "The Case for Competition in the
Electric Utility Industry," 110 Public Utilities
Fortnightly 13 (1982).

64. At least one proponent of a similar approach argues that
mandatory divestiture, and reorganization of the industry
by courts and legislatures would not be needed because
competitive pressures would force firms to restructure
voluntarily through spinoffs, mergers, and acquisitions
eventually producing the desired efficient industry structure. This process could, however, take as long as 20 or
30 years. Pierce, supra note 64, p. 1214.

65. For example, Public Service Company of New Mexico
proposed a significant corporate restructuring that would
form a holding company, split most generation and
transmission assets into a separate competitive subsidiary, and sell power under long-term contracts to a
distribution subsidiary and its wholesale customers. The
company dropped its proposal in mid-1988 because of the
criticisms raised by some State agencies and the City of
Albuquerque, its largest wholesale customer.

66. William W. Berry, "The Implications of Deregulation for
Electric Utilities, " Comment for the Reason Foundation
Conference on Deregulating Public Utilities, 1987.

67. Under scenarios 4 and 5, the physical division of integrated utility facilities among the newly disaggregated
entities would probably not reflect a clearcut allocation
of generation, transmission, and distribution facilities. It
is likely that at least a portion of the transmission
facilities associated with individual generating stations
might be retained by the generating subsidiary.
Generators might have to construct their own transmission facilities to move power to the point of delivery to
the transmission or distribution companies. Similarly,
transmission and distribution utilities would be able to
retain or acquire small scattered generating units that
provide essential system support or backup services.

68. This financial restructuring and redistribution of assets
will be a complex and controversial aspect of this
scenario for utilities, shareholders, regulators, and
ratepayers alike. If not handled with caution, the transactions could result in a sizable transfer of wealth and

assets from the regulated sectors to the unregulated generators. There could be a tremendous incentive for owners of low cost older plants to move them as quickly as possible into the unregulated market so as to capture a greater profit than would be allowed under regulated historic embedded cost pricing. This could leave a utility's high cost plants in the regulated sector.

69. See, for example, Joskow and Schmalensee, supra note 1, pp. 212-213.

70. See for example, Philip R. O'Connor, Robert G. Bussa, and Wayne P. Olson, "Competition, Financial Innovation, and Diversity in the Electric Power Industry," Public Utilities Fortnightly, Feb. 20, 1986, pp. 17-21; Philip R. O'Connor, "The Transition to Competition in the Electric Power Industry," Illinois Commerce Commission (presented at the American Power Conference, Chicago, IL, Apr. 22, 1985); and Matthew Cohen, Essay: "Efficiency and Competition in the Electric Power Industry," 88 Yale Law Journal 1511-1549, June 1979.

71. See Joskow and Schmalensee, supra note 1, at pp. 104-105, for their "scenario 4" which adopts a similar approach. See also Edison Electric Institute, "Deregulation Issues and Concepts," 1981. The industry structure of scenario 5 resembles that proposed for the utility industry in the United Kingdom after privatization. See ch. 2 box 2-B, supra note 19. The U.S. industry and regulation structure are far more complex than the present government-run British system, so that direct comparisons with the U.K. proposal are of limited value.

72. A detailed transition plan for achieving this sort of industry has been outlined conceptually by Phillip O'Connor, former Chairman of the Illinois Commerce Commission. O'Connor's 10-step process would gradually transform the industry into a vertically disintegrated structure with market-based pricing of generation evolving in conjunction with regulated transmission and distribution entities. O'Connor, supra note 71.

CHAPTER 21: MANDATORY ACCESS: IS IT IN THE NATION'S BEST INTEREST

By Douglas C. Bauer and Bruce S. Edelston*

Electric utilities, like other regulated industries, are very rapidly being drawn into the deregulation debate. The debate is not about routes and fares (as in the airline industry) or about prices of new energy sources (as in the natural gas industry). Rather, it is about access to and use of the utility's transmission network. The closest parallel is probably found in telephone deregulation, where local access networks have been opened up for use by competing long distance carriers. In the electric utility industry, however, the proposal is reversed — the long distance system, here the transmission system, is to be opened up for use by competing electricity generators and possibly end users as well.

Proposals have been advanced to require electric utilities to wheel power not only for other utilities (which is already a fairly common practice) but also for non-utility sellers and purchasers of power.[1] Some proposals would require a Federal Energy Regulatory Commission order to require wheeling services; others would make transmission service available to all those desiring service, at standard rates and without discrimination.

An unusual coalition of interests has developed in support of mandatory transmission access and use. This coalition consists of state regulators (who want to take further advantage of short-term differences in costs between utilities), many federal regulators (who believe mandatory access will lead to improved "market" forces), wholesale and large retail customers (who want to "shop" for lowest cost power sources), and cogenerators and small power producers (who wish to sell their power to the utility with the highest "avoided cost" prices). Reflecting these interests, Representative Matsui (D-CA) introduced legislation (H.R. 5608) in 1984 to amend

*Douglas Bauer is Senior Vice President for Economics and Finance and Bruce Edelston is Manager of Economic Programs for Edison Electric Institute.

the Federal Power Act with regard to its wheeling provisions.

The Historical Debate

In 1935, Congress first sought to address the highly complex issue of competition versus coordination in bulk power supply. Congress carefully weighed the position of two groups: those who argued in favor of imposing "common carrier" obligations on transmission owners as a means of expanding competitive opportunities; versus, those who expressed concerns that such competition would be "destructive" and result in higher costs and less reliable service. The final decision, reflected in the legislative history of Part II of the Federal Power Act, was to restrict the newly created Federal Power Commission's control over the ordering of system interconnections and wheeling. This decision to deny the FPC freedom to mandate third-party transmission services demonstrated a significant reliance on voluntary coordination among the individual utilities to achieve desired levels of economy and efficiency.

Since passage of the Federal Power Act of 1935, there have been numerous efforts to provide the FPC, now the Federal Energy Regulatory Commission (FERC), with additional mandatory wheeling authority. Most recently, in 1978, Congress was presented with a broad range of proposals to open up transmission systems. After considerable debate, Congress made only limited changes in the scope of the Commission's wheeling authority. These changes, reflected in the Public Utilities Regulatory Policies Act of 1978, grant FERC authority to compel wheeling after making several findings, the most significant of which requires that the wheeling order "would reasonably preserve existing competitive relationships" among the utilities affected by the order. In other words, Congress reaffirmed its opposition to introducing potentially destructive competition to the utility markets.

Concurrent with the on-going Congressional debate, numerous court decisions have affected utility wheeling obligations. The most important of these was the Otter Tail Power case (Otter Tail Power Company v. United States, 1973), in which the courts held that mandatory wheeling

COMPETITION IN ELECTRICITY

may be required as a remedy to demonstrated antitrust violations. However, the courts have consistently held that there is no comprehensive utility wheeling obligation under current statutes. The real extent of utility obligations to wheel pursuant to the antitrust laws is currently not entirely clear and will probably be decided on a case-by-case basis.

The final area of law that relates to utility wheeling obligations is the requirements of the antitrust provisions of the Atomic Energy Act of 1954. A number of utilities have been subjected to varying degrees of wheeling obligations under Nuclear Regulatory Commission (NRC) licensing conditions since the early 1970s. These conditions frequently extend to all of a utility's transmission facilities and not just to those lines directly related to the plant being licensed. Thus, the NRC's authority with respect to mandatory wheeling is fairly significant.

Current Arguments

The recent growing interest in wheeling can be traced to a number of factors:

- In an era of rising electricity prices, larger utility customers perceive an opportunity to reduce short-term energy costs through "off system" purchases. In this way, power is purchased from remote suppliers at a reduced rate while the customer enjoys the benefit of retaining the local utility's service obligations to ensure that power requirements are met.
- The possibility of greater intersystem power transfers offers a welcomed alternative to the escalation costs, regulatory uncertainties, and severe financial risks involved in constructing new generating facilities. It is believed that enhancement of the currently extensive transfers would enable utilities to defer new capacity additions.
- Long lead times for new plant construction, together with declining load growth, have contributed to substantial levels of "surplus" generating capacity with low marginal costs in some regions. Many argue that this temporary surplus could be used to a greater extent to "displace" higher cost generation elsewhere.
- Current trends in deregulation have led to analogies bet-

ween contract carriage in the gas pipeline industry and electric power transmission, with a focus on the potential for industrial "competition." In fact, FERC already has initiated an experiment to examine opportunities for competition in selected segments of the bulk power market.

Finally, the Public Utility Regulatory Policies Act of 1978 offers substantial economic incentives for the development of non-utility-owned cogeneration and designated small power "qualifying facilities." As a result, qualifying facilities desire to sell their power to that utility within economic transmission distance that offers the highest "avoided cost" purchase price (i.e., the cost otherwise incurred by the utility to supply an equivalent amount of power). The common denominator uniting these interest is the desire to foster competition in bulk power (and sometimes retail) markets, resulting, proponents of mandatory wheeling say, in a lower cost, more efficient electric power supply system.

The proponents fall into two main factions. One faction advocates placing electric utilities under a sort of common carrier obligation. The utility would be compelled to provide transmission services under uniform and nondiscriminatory terms and conditions to virtually any party requesting them. The utility's options to refuse such requests — whether or not it views them as contrary to the economic interests of its own customers — or to impose advance reservation and notification requirements on the availability of transmission service would be restricted. As a consequence of these imposed conditions, many utilities would be forced to expand transmission capacity to accommodate all requests for service.

A second faction wishes to expand FERC's existing authority to order a utility to provide third-party transmission services. This proposal differs from the "common carrier" obligation in that a FERC order, perhaps with some conditions, would still be necessary prior to mandating a specific wheeling service.

The Investor-Owned Industry's Response

Recognizing the growing interest in mandatory transmission access, the Edison Electric Institute formed a Transmission Access Task Force in 1983 to assess emerging proposals and to provide a forum for exchange of views and information among companies. An industry position, which calls for retention of the current system of voluntary power exchange and wheeling, evolved from the work of the Task Force. That position is based on four major premises:

1. The present basically voluntary system for transmission access has worked well, providing reliability and economy to retail and wholesale customers.
2. New proposals for mandatory transmission access or utilization could impinge upon the safety and reliability of the electric power supply system.
3. New proposals for mandatory transmission access could lead to rate increases for residential and smaller commercial and industrial customers unable to "shop" for lower cost sources of power.
4. New proposals for mandatory transmission access are contrary to the utility's fundamental obligation to serve its customers and will make efficient utility system planning and resource development difficult, if not impossible.

In addition, an aggrieved utility has the right now to seek a mandatory wheeling order from FERC, under suitable economic and reliability conditions.

The Present Voluntary System

An examination of the limited data available concerning wheeling services suggests that investor-owned utilities routinely provide a broad range and increasing level of services on a voluntary basis. Over 118 billion kWh of energy was wheeled by investor-owned utilities in 1981, and amounted to approximately 7.2 percent of the total energy delivered to ultimate customers. This is a sizable figure in light of the fact that wheeled energy accounted for a mere 4.3 percent of the total energy delivered to ultimate customers only a decade ago. In other words, the amount of energy wheeled increased by nearly 141 percent in that ten-year interval while ultimate sales only increased by 42 percent.

Moreover, additional wheeling routinely occurs within

formal power pools and among the member companies of holding company systems. For a variety of reasons, these transactions generally are not reported in industry wheeling statistics. Neither is the substantial amount of energy wheeled between non-contiguous systems in two-party purchase and sale ("displacement") transactions. Clearly, the present voluntary system for transmission access and utilization has worked exceedingly well in terms of both the magnitude and diversity of services offered. (See Tables 21-1 and 21-2).

Potential Impacts on Supply Reliability

Transmission systems are complex electrical networks connecting generating sources and load centers. The flow of electricity from generation to load is determined by the electrical characteristics of the network, and it cannot be controlled or directed from point to point over specific contractual paths. With few exceptions (such as the Pacific Northwest Intertie), wheeling was not a major consideration in the design and planning of today's high voltage transmission network, and current transmission systems are designed to link generators and loads under conditions of multi-directional power flow.

To reduce the need for generating reserves and to maintain reliability under emergency conditions, utilities often have interconnected their transmission systems. These "reliability" interconnections also have allowed utilities to exchange economic power when an interconnected utility has had lower cost power available. Many such economy transfers currently are taking place as a result of the increasing fuel/cost disparity between utility systems. Because of lower-than-anticipated load growth over the past few years, the utility industry has had capacity available to accommodate these inter-utility and interregional economy transfers — a temporary situation at best. Additional transfers would, in many cases, require a strengthening of the transmission system. Efforts in this area, as a rule, have been delayed by local regulatory and licensing problems based on land use, environmental, health, and safety concerns.

Table 21-1
Transmission Delivered by Investor-Owned
Electric Utilities, 1961 - 1981

Year	Transmission Delivered (Thousand mWh)
1981	118,641
1976	70,686
1971	49,928
1966	21,736
1961	10,379

Table 21-2
Summary of the Types and Numbers
of Wheeling Service Agreements on File at the
Federal Energy Regulatory Commission

Agreement Type	Firm Wheeling	Non-firm Wheeling	Firm & Non-firm Wheeling	Total
Transmission Service	453	117	29	659
Transmission Tariff	7	7	2	16
Power Pool Interconnection	5	2	8	15
Coordination Interconnection	104	98	22	224
Coordination/Transmission	16	4	1	21
Facilities	4	4	-	5
Partial Requirements	28	12	1	41
Partial Requirements/ Transmission	43	5	-	48
Full Requirements	11	1	1	13
Full Requirements/ Transmission	17	-	-	7
Full & Partial Requirements	1	1	-	2
Other	3	1	-	4
Total	692	309	64	1,065

Another important feature of transmission systems is their regional diversity, which reflects the substantially different needs and circumstances prevailing among the nation's utilities. Transmission service arrangements must be negotiated individually relative to these circumstances to assure system reliability. Reliable operation requires advance knowledge of how the system will be used, and only minute-by-minute control over a transmission system will ensure that defined limits are not exceeded. For these reasons, "unconstrained" wheeling in which control over access and use are taken away from the system operator directly opposes the functions for which these systems were designed.

Furthermore, reliable operation does not hinge solely on individual utilities, but on coordinated and responsible efforts by all parties in an interconnected system. Through careful power scheduling and continuous monitoring by hundreds of control centers within the network, service continuity is maintained. This requires voluntary compliance with established principles of interconnected operation on the part of all utilities. Without this special orchestration of activities, system operation could become chaotic, and the industry's superb record of reliability could be threatened.

Potential for Rate Increases

It has been the consensus of government policy throughout the electric industry's modern history that the lowest cost and most reliable level of service is provided by a single regulated supplier obligated to serve all customers within a "territorial franchise" (or defined market area.) For this reason, the laws of most states discourage or preclude competition for either wholesale or retail customers. Based on the cyclical pattern of new plants coming into service and the expiration of fuel supply contrasts, at times a given utility likely will have higher production costs than neighboring utilities for a while. Without the stability of exclusive service areas and reasonable protection against "pirating" of existing customers, there would be uncontrolled customer "rate shopping" to take advantage of such short-term rate differentials.

Adverse rate impacts would result if large customers were allowed to shop around and purchase power off-system. In such a situation, the fixed costs of capacity — planned and installed to serve their loads as well as those of the utility's other customers — would be borne by the utility's remaining customers, generally residential and smaller commercial and industrial users. The resulting higher rates would encourage greater numbers of remaining industrial and commercial customers to seek lower cost off-system purchases. Fixed costs then would be reallocated to those "captive" customers left on the system who were unable to contract for alternative supplies. These fewer customers would be required to pay inordinately higher rates for service in what could be a continuous upward spiral.

A utility might also be required to maintain sufficient reserve capacity to serve its former customers' future needs should they desire to return to their original supplier. This is a real possibility if the short-term rate advantages which initially prompted the off-system purchase dissolve or if the customer's off-system supplier has to interrupt service. Additionally, the transmission capacity used by customers purchasing off-system may reduce the utility's own ability to purchase and distribute lower cost power, thereby further increasing rates to its customers.

Without a defined and reasonably predictable geographic market for the output of its power — or a substantially higher rate-of-return on investment — no electric supplier would continue to incur the considerable financial risk of building new generating facilities in an uncertain market characterized by competition among multiple suppliers. The adequacy and efficiency of service will be jeopardized if competition creates disincentives to invest in the most economically scaled plant or to engage in voluntary intersystem coordination. Proposals advocating increased competition through mandatory wheeling do not address adequately the direct trade-offs among competition, efficiency, service obligation, and the resulting shifts in the burdens of costs among customers.[2]

The Fundamental Obligation to Serve

In return for being grated a monopoly franchise territory, a utility assumes an obligation to serve all customers desiring service, at reasonable rates, and without undue discrimination. These responsibilities — together with the capital intensive nature of new power supply facilities and the associated long lead times — dictate the need to impose a corresponding obligation on customers to purchase the output of facilities build on their behalf or to compensate the utility for those costs if they purchase "off system." (Barring this proposition, a reduction in the service level must reasonably be expected.)

Without this purchase "obligation," there would be far greater uncertainty in forecasting and planning adequate generation and transmission capacity — factors which would affect both the quality and costs of electric service. The large capital investments necessary to provide electric service could not be undertaken if, in addition to all the risks now present, there would be no assurance of a customer base to use electricity from new power facilities.

If both retail and wholesale customers were allowed to leave the system and return at will, then careful consideration would have to be given to amending the utility's "obligation to serve" requirements. Without such consideration, utilities might plan for too much capacity (with the result of increased costs to ratepayers) or insufficient capacity (with deleterious effects on reliability). Cost increases also could occur if the utility is required to provide back-up power or transmission capability to the off-system purchaser, or if the utility has an obligation to serve such customers when their source for off-system purchases is no longer available.

Conclusions

Based on the evidence of extensive and diverse wheeling services already provided voluntarily under terms and conditions approved by regulatory authorities, it appears that the real debate is not over utilities' refusals to provide transmission services but rather the unwillingness of some groups to accept the reasonable limitations that have been placed on transmission access and utilization. These limitations protect the legitimate interests of the wheeling utility and its customers. Although the concept of enhanced competition in certain segments of the bulk power market is theoretically attractive, the fundamental economic and engineering attributes of the electric power system, coupled with the entrenched utility service obligations, make it unlikely that greater competition in either retail or full-requirements wholesale markets, as envisioned in recent proposals to broaden transmission accessibility, would benefit the American public.

This is not to suggest that there are no opportunities for increasing economic efficiencies in the electric power supply system. Attention should be focused on some of the positive opportunities afforded by regional differences in power availability and costs. In particular, where transmission bottlenecks prevent the economic transfer of power, it should be an important public policy objective to foster an environment in which new transmission lines can be constructed. Initiatives such as the Southwest Bulk Power Market Experiment, where FERC is examining the effects of deregulating certain types of bulk power transactions, are important as well.

However, mandatory transmission access, beyond that provided for in current law, will primarily result in a mere shifting of cost burdens between electricity users. To achieve real efficiency gains, we must focus attention on the long-term constraints to increasing the level of economic exchanges and wheeling services. Among the constraints that should be examined are transmission bottlenecks and their relief, the design of rates for transmission service that provide proper incentives, and institutional and regulatory barriers that may inhibit efficient voluntary transmission service arrangements between utilities.

ENDNOTES

1. Wheeling is defined here as transmission services provided by a utility on a pre-arranged basis to deliver either (a) power generated outside its own system to the system of another utility or end user, or (b) power generated within its service area by a non-utility to another utility.
2. One of the most hotly contested controversies of the AT&T divesture has been the need to shift some costs to residential users to prevent large business customers from bypassing the local networks, which would leave residential customers with even higher cost increases.

CHAPTER 22: THE PRIVATE POWER PRODUCER PERSPECTIVE ON WHEELING ISSUES*

George M. Knapp, Nixon, Hargrove, Devens & Doyle

The issue of transmission access for purposes of wheeling is multi-faceted, presenting numerous legal and technical issues. The area is hotly contested, with the utilities who control the transmission lines facing off against qualifying facilities (QFs), independent power producers (IPPs), industrials, and often other utilities who wish to gain access to those lines.

I will not attempt to fit together all the pieces of the wheeling puzzle within the scope of this speech. Rather I hope to leave you with an overview of the wheeling issue and some of the more recent developments shaping the perspective of private power producers.

Common sense would *seem* to dictate that when a willing seller of electricity and a willing buyer are stalled in their effort to transfer electricity because an intervening utility declines to wheel the power, the FERC would be the logical entity from which to seek relief. However, although the FERC has broad jurisdiction over interstate transmission rates and conditions of service, it has very little authority to order that wheeling occur.

Noteworthy is the fact that with respect to QFs, PURPA did not address the issue of wheeling to non-local utilities or end-users. PURPA requires utilities to offer to connect with QFs and to buy their power at avoided cost. Furthermore this obligation is not limited to local utilities. However, no mechanism was set in place to facilitate the transfer of QF capacity to a non-adjacent third party.

It might be helpful to step back for a moment and examine briefly the hurdles that have to be overcome in order to obtain a compulsory wheeling order from the FERC. When drafting the Federal Power Act (FPA) in 1935, Congress considered including common carrier language making it a duty of every public utility to transmit energy for any

Presented at the Symposium on Electricity Competition, California Energy Commission, June 30, 1988.

person upon reasonable request. Additionally, it would have empowered the Commission to order wheeling if it found such action to be necessary or desirable in the public interest. These provisions were eliminated prior to enactment, thus preserving the voluntary wheeling actions of utilities within very broad "undue discrimination" parameters.

PURPA added Sections 211 and 212 to the FPA. These sections give the FERC the authority to order the wheeling of power under certain specified conditions. In practice, however, the limitations placed on the FERC's authority render it virtually incapable of ordering wheeling.

First, only certain entities are permitted to seek a wheeling order. In particular, "any electric utility, geothermal power producer or federal power marketing agency" may apply. Electric utility is defined as any person or state agency that sells electricity. Conspicuously missing from the list of possible applicants are qualifying cogenerators and qualifying small power producers other than geothermal QFs. In contrast, QFs are specifically included in the list of possible applicants for interconnection under Section 210 of PURPA. This distinction represents strong evidence of congressional intent that QFs not be included under the generic definition of electric utility for purposes of wheeling. In practice, FERC has adopted an even narrower interpretation of the statute.

However, a very different conclusion might be expected to attach in the case of the new class of IPPs that the FERC is clearly endeavoring to encourage. By definition, an IPP is a generating utility, other than a QF, that is unaffiliated with a franchised utility in the area in which the IPP is selling power, and for additional reasons lacks significant market power. Although FERC is willing to waive many aspects of its regulation over such entities, it recognizes that IPPs are indeed "public utilities" subject to its FPA jurisdiction. Accordingly, it appears clear that an IPP would fall under the generic PURPA definition of an electric utility, thereby establishing the right of an IPP to petition the FERC for a wheeling order.

Although this arguably creates a significant competitive edge for IPPs over QFs, this apparent benefit may only play out in theory, and not in practice. At best, the advantage may be negligible due to the other major obstacles which must be overcome prior to FERC's issuance of a wheeling order. FERC must make a number of specific factual findings, the most significant of which is that the wheeling order, if issued, "would reasonably preserve *existing* competitive relationships." In the SEPA v. Kentucky Utilities order (1984), FERC construed this provision to require it to remain competitively neutral, i.e., to prevent utility load loss. In other words, it will not issue a wheeling order if to do so will improve or detract from the competitive status quo. Given such circumscribed authority, only a handful of applications for wheeling orders have been filed with FERC, and none have been granted.

In sum, Sections 211 and 212 of PURPA allow certain entities to apply for wheeling orders. However, these sections do not allow industrial consumers or QFs to apply and do not authorize the FERC to act on its own motion. Thus in order for a QF or industrial to obtain a wheeling order, a purchasing utility would have to apply to FERC on behalf of the QF — such a situation is very unlikely. Furthermore, even if a wheeling order is requested, Sections 211 and 212 so severely restrict the FERC, that this option is not truly a viable one.

It is important to note that the increasing cry for open access to utility transmission systems is not only being heard from QFs and other producers but from many wholesale and retail customers of traditional utilities who have become more alert to the advantage of shopping around for better electricity rates. QFs are looking to expand the market for their electricity by seeking out power supply contracts with industrial customers. However, this sought-after expansion may be forestalled by utilities who decline to provide the wheeling service necessary to transmit the power to the industrial customer.

The retail wheeling of QF or other producers' power is a major issue with most utilities. A utility which has increased its generating load to service a large industrial customer will not readily "turn over" the customer to another supplier, and throw in wheeling services as a sign of its approval.

Because the FERC's authority to order wheeling is for all practical purposes ineffectual, the industrial customer and/or the QF may turn to the state public service commission in an attempt to obtain a wheeling order. Several state public service commissions have asserted that they have the authority to require a utility to wheel power. However, given the historical way in which the FERC has interpreted its jurisdiction, such an assertion is, at best, questionable.

In Consolidated Edison Company of New York, the FERC held that the transmission of energy within a single state is subject to FERC jurisdiction if made on an interconnected interstate transmission grid. Because all electric utilities in the 48 contiguous states, except those in Texas, are interconnected with other utilities that are part of an interstate grid, nearly all transmission of electricity comes under the FERC's jurisdiction.

The issue of whether FERC's authority over transmission in interstate commerce preempts the authority of state public utility commissions to require wheeling was raised indirectly in connection with two declaratory orders issued by the FERC in response to petitions by the Florida Power and Light Company. In an order issued in 1984, the FERC concluded that the *rates* for wheeling of power by QFs are exclusively subject to its jurisdiction where the transmission occurs in interstate commerce. More recently, in 1987, the FERC issued a declaratory order asserting exclusive jurisdiction over the *terms* and *conditions* of contracts for wheeling power in interstate commerce. In this latter order, the FERC held that a wheeling transaction would be in interstate commerce when the transmission system is interconnected and capable of transmitting power across a state boundary, even though the contracting parties and the contract pathway of the transaction are all in one state.

In the Florida Power and Light orders, the FERC declined to directly address the issue of whether a state commission has the authority to require a electric utility to wheel the energy of a QF in its service territory as a condition to some other relief, such as a bidding order. However, in the Notice of Proposed Rulemaking on Competitive Bidding, the FERC noted that it has to impose conditions to accomplish statutory objectives. But, on the state level, a strong argument can be made that if the state ordered wheeling involving a utility that was interconnected in an interstate grid (which would be the case in all states except Texas, Alaska, and Hawaii), then the transaction would be in interstate commerce and subject to FERC jurisdiction. Under the Supremacy Clause, the FERC would then preempt the state regulation of transmission service, including state authority to order wheeling.

At this stage of the game the only thing that is clear is that the FERC has exclusive jurisdiction over rates, terms and conditions of all wheeling contracts. It might still be possible for a state to require wheeling without specifying the rates, terms or conditions of the wheeling. Because a state's authority to mandate wheeling as a condition has never been squarely addressed by the FERC such authority is tentative at best, and it would not be wise for a developer to place great stock in being able to obtain such an order.

A battle currently being waged in the wheeling arena is over the necessity of mandatory wheeling in the context of effective all-source competitive bidding. All-source bidding has been proposed as an alternative way of establishing avoided cost, and is one of the subjects of the FERC's recently issued NOPRs. The debate focuses on whether utilities' voluntary participation in a bidding system should be conditioned upon their agreement to provide nondiscriminatory open access to transmission services. The theory is that there cannot be a true competitive market if one entity controls the transmission bottleneck.

The FERC, while not marrying the enactment of an all-source competitive bidding program to the provision of transmission services, does recognize that under certain circumstances it would not be inappropriate to do such. To this effect the FERC recognizes a compromise position, upon which it is requesting comments.

The "compromise", known as the wheeling-in/wheeling-out plan, would work in the following manner: if a utility wished to submit a bid to satisfy another utility's capacity needs, it must provide firm transmission service to the purchasing utility for any successful bidder within its service area; conversely, if a utility bids to meet its own capacity, it must then wheel power to neighboring utilities for any unsuccessful bidders that want to sell to another wholesale purchaser.

Due to the inability to overcome the obstacles that have been presented to prevent transmission access, some producers have begun to construct or purchase transmission lines to move power either in or out of the service area of their local utility. In the context of QFs, the potential has existed that ownership of transmission lines could result in the unavailability of regulatory exemptions for the transmission lines.

Section 201 of PURPA defines cogeneration and small power production facilities as facilities which *produce* electric power. Strict interpretation of this section would prevent the classification of transmission lines as part of a producing facility. Thus, ownership of such lines could render a QF a public utility subject to the FPA and the Public Utility Holding Company Act (PUHCA). On a case-by-case basis, the FERC has moved towards a more liberal interpretation. In recent requests by Clarion Power Company and Oxbow for recertification as QFs, the questions presented were whether ownership of a transmission line would cause loss of exempt status. The FERC ruled that the transmission line, if used solely for the purposes of transmitting power from the QF to the purchasing electric utility and transmission of maintenance and backup power from the utility to the QF, would be treated as part of the QF. The FERC emphasized, however, that approval was limited to a situation in which the sole purpose of the transmission line was the transmission of power to and from the owning QF. Any other use of the line could result in a finding of FPA jurisdiction.

In the recently issued NOPRs, the FERC exhibits a willingness to expand its previous rulings in this area, generically allowing QFs to own transmission lines. The Commission proposes to amend its regulations by permitting QFs to construct and own transmission lines, provided that such transmission lines are used to transmit power to and from the QF and the utility. While the basic proposal is in line with *Clarion* and *Oxbow*, the Commission goes even further by inviting comments on the need for, and suggested methods of, regulating QFs who wish to own transmission lines to be used to wheel power for third parties. More specifically, the Commission is investigating options for permitting QFs who own transmission lines to be free to wheel power for others without being subject to FPA or PUCHA regulation. A stumbling block could be the extent to which the Commission should or could find that transmission lines used to wheel power for third parties are part of a QF's facilities used to "produce power". Such a finding would be necessary in order to rely upon PURPA as the basis for allowing a facility to maintain its exempt status.

In *Clarion*, the transmission line was considered an *integral* and *necessary* part of the QF because the purchasing utility declined to construct, own, or operate a transmission line necessary to interconnect with the QF. The FERC justified its holding by stating that a literal interpretation of the statute would defeat PURPA's intent of providing a market for QF power. By using a little fancy footwork the FERC may be able once again to sidestep a strict reading of Section 201 of PURPA. A literal interpretation of the statute would frustrate at least two objectives of PURPA, namely, to provide for the efficient use of facilities and resources by electric utilities, and to encourage cogeneration and small power production facilities.

Coming full circle on this subject, it is possible that the FERC could establish a benchmark for QF third party transmission. For instance, a QF could be allowed to wheel power if the user of the QF's lines had sufficient alternatives available to it, thus negating the QF's market power. In this context, the FERC would have to establish guidelines for what constitutes "sufficient alternatives."

Wheeling issues are part of a complex and evolving body of law affecting an increasingly competitive industry. These issues should be confronted up front when a developer begins to consider market alternatives. Although the issues seem insurmountable, there may be creative ways to approach transmission access.

CHAPTER 23: WHEELING ISSUES: AN IOU PERSPECTIVE*

John L. Jurewitz
Manager of Regulatory Policy and Coordination, Southern
California Edison

Transmission access and pricing is one of the hottest issues facing the utility industry today. The issue has been
raised in the current FERC NOPRs, and Chairman Hesse
has promised still another NOPR later this year to address
the issue. Yet, the topic is not new. It has been debated by
Congress several times and each time Congress has endorsed
voluntary access. I will describe several dimensions of this
complex issue from a utility's perspective.

The American consumer has come to expect and depend
on a reliable and reasonably priced supply of electricity.
These expectations are the result of the highly successful development and performance of the electric utility industry
during the past century. For the most part, this has been
achieved through a system of franchised utilities charged
with an obligation to serve all customers in a specified service territory. As these regional utilities developed, they chose
to become increasingly interconnected. They began using
their interconnected transmission system for economy power
exchanges and emergency support, but always with appropriate physical and contractual provisions to protect the integrity of their individual systems. Without such protection, increased interconnection and exchange would have reduced
system reliability and increased customer costs.

The transmission access debate is caught in a tangled web
of physical, institutional, and policy issues. I'd like to address
each of these dimensions of the problem.

Technical Considerations

Let me begin with the technical dimensions. I cannot
claim to be an engineer, but technical issues cannot be ignored. A basic knowledge of the physics of electrical net-

----
*Presented at the Symposium on Electricity Competition, California Energy
Commission, June 1988*

works is essential to understanding the access issue. The laws of physics cannot be repealed, no matter how hard we may sometimes try. The job before us is to make the institutions fit the technical reality, not vice versa.

Electrical utilities must instantaneously match their generation to customer demands. Failure to maintain this balance causes an unacceptable change in electrical frequency. This reduces the quality of electrical service and can easily damage customer equipment and appliances, as well as generating units. While individual utilities have franchise responsibility for the integrity and reliability of their own systems, all the systems in the Western States are interconnected and under normal conditions operate as one large machine. Such integrated operation is beneficial for all. It enables utilities to achieve greater reliability at lower cost by sharing reserves, exchanging power on an economy basis, and, most importantly, providing each other emergency support. The transmission system is the backbone that holds this machine together and permits these exchanges. To meet these challenges, the system must meet certain critical design criteria. It must enable electricity to be supplied on demand while maintaining constant frequency and voltage, and reliably withstanding likely adverse events.

To achieve maximum social benefits, the transmission system is operated as a single continuously connected network. It is not like a pipeline, highway, or telephone network. These are "switched" networks in which products can be routed. For instance, the telephone system is the ultimate in a switched network. Each telephone can be connected to any other telephone over a unique path. The system takes several seconds to select a path and gives you a busy signal when it is overloaded.

In contrast, the electric system is not a "switched" network. Electricity cannot be directed from one point to another over a specific path. Instead, electricity flows within a network according to strict physical laws. It travels over all available paths between generators and customer loads, dividing itself in accordance with electrical characteristics, called "impedances." If a transmission line is taken out of service, the power originally flowing on that line is instantaneously distributed to all remaining transmission paths. If a customer turns on a light switch, the utility must respond instantaneously. No waiting. No busy signal. If adequate transmission is not available, the system will fail to function reliably.

To assure reliability, transmission systems must be planned and operated with adequate reserve margins. If a transmission line is knocked out of service by a storm or other event, the remaining lines must be capable of carrying the displaced power flow. If they cannot, the result could be cascading outages and widespread power interruptions.

Electricity interchanges among utilities must be "scheduled." This is accomplished through a system of "control areas." A control area is a portion of a power system bordered by metering facilities. Within these boundaries, there is sufficient controlled generation to regulate power flows into or out of the area in accordance with agreed-upon scheduled flows. Power is transferred between control areas when the importing control area reduces generation and the exporting area increases generation simultaneously. Thus, because the network cannot be switched, control is accomplished primarily by manipulating generation at the various supply points. The essential elements of reliable power scheduling are monitoring and control.

If two control areas want to exchange power but are not directly interconnected, one or more intermediate control areas may be needed to "wheel" the power between them. The wheeling utility may have to adjust its own generation internally and must constantly monitor the amount of power flowing over its lines to assure that safe operating limits are not exceeded.

A troublesome aspect of exchanging power within an interconnected network is that all transactions become mutually interdependent. These interdependencies arise from two sources. First, power flows do not follow the paths assumed in contracts. Instead, power divides itself among all parallel paths between seller and buyer. The industry calls this the "loop flow" problem. Second, electrical losses increase with the square of the current. Consequently, marginal losses can far exceed average losses. As one more transaction is added to the network, all other generators must be run harder to achieve the same net power deliveries.

Economists refer to such interdependencies as "externalities." They are a potentially serious cause of failure to achieve efficient resource allocation, primarily because they distort incentives. Buyers and sellers may perceive individual benefits from transactions which, in reality, are far out-weighed by detrimental impacts on third parties. But, the consequences are more severe than under typical congestion. When roads are crowded, you simply cannot get anywhere — but the road itself is not damaged. In contrast, an overloaded electrical network can damage network hardware as well as inadequately protected generators and customer equipment.

Institutional and Policy Considerations

Let me turn now from this broad-brush treatment of tech-nical considerations to a quick overview of some troublesome institutional dimensions of the access problem. First, utilities have made tremendous investments in long-lived capital to meet their franchise obligations to serve all customers within their service territories. Under existing utility regulation, regulators have assured utilities a reasonable opportunity to recover prudent investments through the rates paid, over the long-term, by the customers whom the investments were in-curred to serve. In a very real sense, utility regulation has substituted for the role that long-term contracts play in the non-utility sector. Thus, any policy change which would sud-denly allow franchise customers to "shop" the transmission grid raises serious equity issues, both for the utilities them-selves and for the utilities' remaining customers who may not have the ability to shop around.

A second troublesome institutional consideration is the fragmentation of jurisdiction over transmission issues. In short, the federal government controls pricing and access, while the states regulate siting and the ultimate disposition of most transmission revenues. The FERC has very limited authority to order wheeling and has asserted very broad jurisdiction over transmission pricing. State authority over transmission access and pricing is at best uncertain and at worst non-existent. Unfortunately, with a few recent notable exceptions, the FERC has followed antiquated formulas for transmission pricing based on embedded costs. Such pricing has impeded voluntary wheeling transactions. The FERC has also followed a troublesome practice of interfering with ter-mination provisions in contracts. This has increased market uncertainties and discouraged voluntary exchanges.

Although the FERC controls transmission pricing, for the most part state regulators determine whether transmission profits flow to stockholders or utility customers. As illustrated by the recent regulatory treatment afforded San Diego's Southwest Power Link, state regulatory treatment of cost recovery for transmission lines can have a substantial impact on the riskiness of such investments and seriously affect a utility's willingness to build new transmission.

Clearly, there are other impediments to new transmission. Environmental concerns over aesthetics and yet unsubstantiated fears of health effects are two such barriers. States have traditionally sited transmission interconnections based largely on reliability considerations. It remains to be seen whether appropriate incentives can be created to encourage the siting of new transmission lines based largely on economy transactions.

Finally, let me turn to the institutional problem of federal preference power. This institution presents a clear impediment to increased voluntary wheeling. A utility's transmission lines have been constructed pursuant to its franchise obligation to serve all its customers. When a utility purchases power from a federal power marketing authority, such as BPA, it passes along the benefits of such a transaction proportionally to all its requirements customers, retail customers and municipal utilities alike. If utilities were suddenly required to wheel preference power to municipal utilities, municipal customers would move to the head of the line. Only after their needs were satisfied would any benefits flow to a utility's other customers. Such an arbitrary and unfair redistribution of wealth cannot be justified.

Some Intermediate Observations

Let me pause here to make several observations.

- First, the essential requirement to preserving a reliable power system is constant monitoring and control. No network has been designed to accommodate all combinations of adverse events — nor would it be economical to do so. Therefore, control area operators must have the ability to curtail any schedule when necessary to maintain loadings

within safe limits.
- Second, imposing wide-open common carrier status on electrical transmission would stretch systems beyond their design limits. Existing transmission networks have been planned on the basis of serving the anticipated loads of utility customers and satisfying voluntary contractual coordination agreements with other utilities. Networks must maintain adequate transmission reserve margins. These reserve margins cannot be used for third-party wheeling without jeopardizing reliable service to all customers.
- Third, it is essential to distinguish between "economic" wheeling and "uneconomic" wheeling. Economic wheeling improves the allocation of resources. Uneconomic wheeling merely redistributes income. A great deal of the political demand for third-party wheeling is demand for uneconomic wheeling. This results from regulatory pricing distortions and federal preference power. As FERC Commissioner Stalon has observed, this isn't wheeling power — it's "wheeling money." Indeed, generation patterns may remain completely unchanged.
- Fourth, wheeling power to retail and other requirements customers raises several fundamental policy concerns. Retail wheeling within a control area is not electrical wheeling at all. It is simply bookkeeping. Allowing such wheeling is in direct conflict with the traditional utility structure based on the obligation to serve. A utility's remaining customers would be left to bear the costs of capital projects originally constructed to benefit the departing wheeling customer. Furthermore, retail wheeling would aggravate the uneconomic bypass problem by encouraging development of unneeded new power generation based on the economics of retail rates rather than system marginal costs.
- As a final observation, the reliability of the interconnected electrical network today depends in no small part on cooperation among regionally franchised utilities. Surely, competition exists among these utilities, but it is a constrained competitive environment of voluntary transactions. Each utility sees more benefit in continued interconnected operation than in isolating its system. Mandatory wheeling could encourage rivalry among utilities such that most cooperation would disappear. This would result in substantial

efficiency losses, and perhaps eventual withdrawal of some utilities from the interconnected system.

Issues to Be Resolved

Clearly, there are many issues raised in considering transmission policies. I'd like to turn to several of these next.

- First is the issue of voluntarism versus compulsion. Congress has considered the issue of *mandatory* wheeling on several occasions and has consistently concluded that the public interest is better served by voluntary wheeling. By endorsing voluntarism, Congress has assured that only economic wheeling transactions are likely to take place — transactions resulting in benefits for all parties. Voluntarism also clearly leaves accountability for system reliability squarely with the utility — the entity best able to assure it.
- A second issue is availability of excess transmission capacity. If access is mandated, then this issue become politicized. Highly technical and contentious proceedings are inevitable. Ultimate accountability for system reliability will be spread dangerously thin by this process.
- A third issue is transmission pricing. The FERC's transmission pricing practices must be revised. Embedded-cost pricing of transmission does not provide efficient incentives to wheel over existing lines, nor efficient incentives to build new capacity. Furthermore, pricing distortions elsewhere in bulk power markets will also have to be reformed if improved transmission pricing is to work. Allowing flexible market-based pricing of transmission, or regulated transmission rates which account for all legitimate opportunity costs, will increase utility incentives to wheel and to expand transmission.
- Fourth, it must be realized that wheeling is a complex service which involves much more than simply passive use of transmission lines. For instance, a utility may suffer increased system losses or have to reconfigure its generation when it provides wheeling services. Furthermore, if the customer receiving the power is located within the utility's control area, the utility will have to provide load following, local voltage support, reactive power, and possibly other

services. The cost of providing these services must be reflected in efficient transmission prices.

- Fifth, transmission access raises serious questions about priority of transmission use. How should rights to limited transmission capacity be allocated? Should the utility have priority to use the facilities to benefit all its customers? Should a utility's customers be given priority over other third parties? How much of the available capacity should be used for long-term economy transactions? For short-term economy transactions? For emergency and system reliability purposes? Who will decide?
- A sixth issue involves providing efficient incentives for additional transmission investment. If transmission access is to be increased, investment in more transmission facilities will be necessary. Even assuming that the FERC reforms its pricing to permit the recovery of all legitimate opportunity costs, several additional issues remain. Should transmission be built to accommodate all requests for access? Who will bear the risks of these investments? How will this risk be secured?
- A seventh issue is transmission planning. In order to plan a transmission system, utilities must forecast the likely location of future loads and resources. Mandatory access could bring a large number of additional players to the transmission grid. This could impair future electric system planning by creating uncertainties regarding the size and location of future loads and resources.
- Finally, there is the issue of service obligation. Permitting a utility's requirements customers to make off-system purchases raises fundamental public policy issues. In addition to allowing certain customers to avoid paying for past utility investments made on their behalf, such off-system purchases introduce greater risks into a utility's long-term planning. It would place an unreasonable burden on the utility and its remaining customers for the utility to retain an obligation to serve the full requirements of customers making off-system purchases. But is it really possible to enforce a utility's right not to serve such a returning customer when the customer can easily change its name, or place tremendous political pressure on the utility?

Goals and Principles

So far, I've raised a lot of issues without offering many solutions. The problems are complex and I don't have all the answers. In lieu of specific solutions, I can offer certain general principles I believe are useful in searching for those solutions.

- Transmission policies must, above all else, maintain the integrity and reliability of the electrical system.
- Transmission policies should encourage transactions with true economic benefits, not transactions which merely redistribute wealth among customers by "wheeling money."
- Transmission policies should preserve the benefits of the existing electrical system for the franchise utility customers that it was originally constructed and dedicated to serve.
- Transmission policies should assure that existing contractual obligations and commitments are safeguarded.
- Transmission policies should provide efficient incentives for utilities to expand transmission facilities when the benefits exceed costs.
- Transmission policies should assure that the risks of transmission investments are borne by the beneficiaries of the investment.

Some Final Observations and Recommendations

In conclusion, let me make some final observations and recommendations. Existing transmission access policies are working well. The country today enjoys a reliable and efficient electric system based on voluntary exchanges among utilities. There is no evidence of widespread inefficiencies in today's bulk power markets.

Mandatory access to transmission is not needed and is a course fraught with potential pitfalls. There are many interrelated technical, institutional, and economic problems with mandatory access. Furthermore, the potential gains are small compared to the potential losses. At best, a small amount of increased efficiency might be squeezed out of bulk power markets as a result of increased access. On the other hand, we could face potentially large redistributions of wealth, higher transactions costs, loss of economies associated with interutility cooperation, and diminished system reliability.

Rather than beginning with the access issue, the policy debate should focus first on pricing. Improved transmission pricing policies could go a long way toward solving many, if not most, of the perceived access problems, while maintaining the cornerstone of voluntary interutility transactions. At a minimum, efficient transmission prices must reflect a utility's legitimate opportunity costs. Furthermore, experiments in more flexible pricing methods should be encouraged. The Western States Power Pool is a good example. In the future, such flexible pricing may reduce regulatory expenses and provide efficient incentives to wheel and to expand transmission facilities on a voluntary basis.

CHAPTER 24: ASSESSING THE EFFECTS OF BULK POWER RATE REGULATION: RESULTS FROM A MARKET EXPERIMENT*

Jan Paul Acton and Stanley M. Besen
The Rand Corporation

INTRODUCTION

The supply of electricity, at both retail and wholesale levels, has long been subject to detailed state and federal regulation in the USA. However, much has changed since this regulatory structure was established, and the benefits of regulation are increasingly being brought into question. In particular, electric utility systems are now highly interconnected, leading some to believe that wholesale trade among utilities should be substantially deregulated with the determination of wholesale prices being left to competitive market forces. Several observers have called for reduced regulation of electricity generation, sometimes accompanied by mandatory vertical separation of the generation, transmission and distribution functions.[1] This paper reports results from the first year of a market experiment authorized by the Federal Energy Regulatory Commission (FERC) to assess the effects of relaxed federal regulation of bulk power transactions. In the experiment, FERC authorized a number of utilities to exchange electricity under substantially modified regulation. Using detailed load, cost and transaction data provided by the participating utilities, this paper analyses the effects of changing regulation of bulk power transactions.

----
*This paper is based on a report to the Federal Energy Commission (Acton and Besen, 1985). Preparation of the present paper was supported in part by a grant from the National Science Foundation (SES-8320010). Neither FERC nor NSF necessarily agrees with the opinions expressed. We would like to acknowledge the comments and assistance of many individuals throughout the course of the research, including S. Cardell W. Early, S. Holmes, D. Hughes, L. Johnson, H. Quirmbach, W. Rogers, M. Rosenzweig, B. Tenenbaum and B. Zycher as well as representatives of the six utilities participating in the experiment. T. Hayashi and J. Vernon provided valuable research assistance. This article appeared in Applied Economics, 1987, Volume 19, pages 663-685.

Electricity supply is usefully separated into wholesale and retail provision. Wholesale electricity is provided by utilities that offer bulk power to other utility systems for resale to final customers.[2] Some utilities rely for all or most of their needs on supplies from wholesalers. In addition, there is a substantial, and growing, volume of trade between utilities that have significant amounts of generating capability (FERC, 1983). The objective of this trade is to reduce the cost of serving the combined loads of the trading partners. The prices at which wholesale trade occurs are generally regulated by FERC.

Electricity is supplied at retail both by wholesalers, who also sell directly to final consumers, and by a large number of utilities with little or no generating capacity of their own. Rates for retail sales are regulated by state utility commissions or local government entities.

Weiss (1975) first raised the possibility that wholesale supply could be provided by generators on a competitive, i.e. unregulated, basis to local distributors without generation capacity of their own. Bohn et al. (1984) analyzed the institutions needed to permit numerous generators to compete for the patronage of local distributors. Schmalensee and Golub (1984) have analyzed the extent to which unregulated wholesale electricity markets could be expected to exhibit competitive behavior.

The Weiss and Schmalensee and Golub studies used data on utility costs and generating and transmission capacity to assess the likely extent of competitive behavior if wholesale rates were deregulated. The present study continues this line of analysis by examining actual behavior during a wholesale market experiment in which price regulation is essentially eliminated.[3] An important reason for conducting this experiment was that FERC determined that actual experience and quantitative documentation of the effects of modified regulation were needed to form the basis for any permanent change.[4]

The experiment, which began in January 1984, and involved six utilities in the Southwestern United States, was intended to assess how present FERC regulation of bulk power exchanges affects the efficiency with which electricity is generated and traded. Efficiency is increased by trade that reduces the total cost of meeting a given load.[5] FERC also

COMPETITION IN ELECTRICITY

wished to determine whether, under modified regulation, bulk power markets will behave sufficiently competitively that relaxed regulation will not permit either buyers or sellers to exercise market power.[6]

COORDINATION TRANSACTIONS AND FEDERAL REGULATION

Electric utilities engage in two broad types of wholesale transactions: coordination transactions and requirements transactions. The FERC experiment involved only coordination transactions.

Coordination transactions are made between utilities that typically have sufficient generation and transmission capacity to supply all or part of their own loads except under emergency conditions.[7] These transactions allow utilities to realize reliability gains or cost savings that would not be attainable if they attempted to meet their native loads solely from their own generation resources. Transaction periods for coordination transactions are well-defined and the service generally receives lower priority, and thus lower reliability, than the service provided to the seller's native load or requirements customers. While prices for coordination sales are typically negotiated, FERC requires, with few exceptions, that the prices be cost-based. The rates for most coordination service are based on incremental costs.

Partial and full requirements service involves a long-term commitment by a selling utility to meet part or all of the buying utility's load. Typically, privately owned utilities supply such energy under long-term contract to municipalities or cooperative associations, and once these contracts are in place, they often assume the character of an almost permanent obligation to serve on the part of the supplying utility. Utilities usually regard requirements customers as part of their native load, and the prices for requirements service are generally based on system-wide average costs.

The FERC experiment does not involve any changes in FERC's regulation of requirements sales. Furthermore, since FERC's jurisdiction applies only to privately owned utilities, the regulatory treatments do not directly affect publicly owned utilities and cooperative associations.[8] These utilities may be affected indirectly, however, if modified regulation does affect the markets in which they participate.

Basically, present FERC regulation of wholesale rates attempts to establish prices that yield an allowed rate of return on the rate base of the selling utility. One element that is employed in determining rates is a utility's estimate of its profits from coordination sales. FERC will approve rates if, at the anticipated level of coordination sales, the utility will earn its allowed return. Once rates are approved, however, there is no ex post "truing up", so that a utility may earn more or less than its allowed rate of return if profits from coordination sales are greater or smaller than those that were estimated.

Figure 24-1

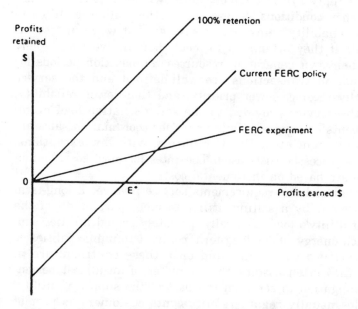

Under this rate-setting procedure, utilities, in effect, pay a lump sum "tax" equal to estimated profits from coordination sales and retain 100% of actual profits at the margin. Figure 24-1 illustrates this arrangement with the line labelled "Current FERC policy". The line shows retained profits as a function of actual profits, where E is estimated profits. The line "100% retention" shows retained profits if FERC made no attempt to take profits from coordination transactions into account in approving rates. Its slope is the same as under present regulation, but its abscissa is zero rather than E. The line labelled "FERC experiment" reflects 25% retention of all profits as authorized in the FERC experiment (discussed in more detail in the next section). Utilities that are subject to this experimental treatment need not estimate their profits from coordination sales, but they must "flow through" to their customers three-quarters of their actual profits. Note that profits retained under the experimental treatment may be greater or smaller than under current policy since the experimental treatment involves no "tax" on estimated profits but a lower rate of retention of actual profits at the margin.

THE FERC BULK POWER MARKET EXPERIMENT

Advantages of an experiment

FERC decided that a field experiment, or demonstration, was needed to inform its policy deliberations. This reflected a balancing of considerations of cost, length, complexity and credibility of results of a "real world" experiment against those of a simulation or a laboratory-based study. A simulation study might be conducted with fairly sophisticated computer models that take account of utility costs and generation and transmission capacity. Its advantages include its ability to examine a wide variety of regulatory treatments and to measure the full potential gains from adopting these treatments. Its disadvantages include the fact that it may not reflect the actual behavior of utilities and their personnel in a real-world setting. In any event, although simulation studies can be helpful in identifying areas of potential gains, they often do not provide justification for major changes in regulation.

A laboratory experiment can analyze the behavior of a small number of individuals, perhaps drawn from the personnel of electric utilities, who are subjected to a series of alternative treatments in a market setting. The advantage of such an experiment is that a much greater set of treatments can be examined much more rapidly and at less cost than if actual exchanges of energy must take place among utilities. However, although laboratory experiments have been used to test a variety of alternative incentives and organizational forms of markets, they may face significant problems of transferability of their findings to the real world of electric utility operation and coordination with other utilities.[9]

Field experiments, or demonstrations, with actual trades among utilities hold the promise of greater credibility than simulations or laboratory experiments, but they do so at a cost. First, they require a more limited experimental design. For example, in general at any given time, only one set of treatments may be applied to all utilities, and only a few sets of treatments can be analyzed during the entire experiment. Second, the costs of data collection and analysis are far greater than those of laboratory experiments or simulations since statistical analysis is required to control for factors that can be set deliberately by the experimenter in a laboratory or in a simulation. Finally, participating utilities must be willing to accept some changes in their routine operations.[10]

There is no universally correct decision regarding the choice among field experiments, simulations and laboratory experiments. The choice in a particular situation will depend upon the policy question under examination and the costs and effectiveness of the various alternatives. However, field experiments are likely to be helpful both in developing a more precise understanding of what modifications of regulation might be appropriate, and in providing information about the likely outcome of such modifications.[11]

The experiment

In the FERC bulk market power experiment, four treatments were approved: 1) explicit flexibility in setting the prices at which bulk power exchanges occur; 2) modification of the regulatory treatment of the revenues from those exchanges; 3) provision of meaningful access to the transmission system; and 4) provision of information about bulk power trades to participating utilities. Treatments 1, 3 and 4, began on the first day of the experiment for all utilities. Treatment 2 only came into effect for a utility when new rates were approved. As a consequence, its effective date varied among participants. The basic dimensions of these treatments are as follows.[12]

First, the experiment permits greater flexibility in setting prices for coordination sales than does present regulation.

The purpose of this modification is to determine the effects on the volume of trade and efficiency of supply if regulation of pricing were relaxed. It also permits an analysis of the extent to which wholesale markets behave competitively when there are few, if any, regulatory constraints on prices.

Under present FERC regulation, coordination transactions are usually priced either at (a) the seller's incremental cost plus an "adder" to allow the recovery of unquantifiable or difficult-to-quantify variable costs; or (b) at a price midway between the incremental costs of the buying and selling utilities, so-called "split-the-savings" pricing. By contrast, prices on experimental transactions between participating utilities can be set anywhere between a widely separated lower and upper bound. The lower bound is one-half the seller's incremental costs and the upper bound is twice the seller's fully allocated costs. A "zone of reasonableness" based on averages of these values for the participating utilities was established before the beginning of the experiment. As a result, any price between 9.54 and 93.4 mills/kwh is permitted for experimental transactions. Given this wide zone, prices in the experiment are effectively unregulated. Second, the experiment explicitly permits selling utilities to retain a specified fraction (25%) of the profits from wholesale exchanges for their shareholders. This is intended to serve as an inducement to utilities to increase the volume of trade if such increases are feasible. However, as noted above, current FERC regulation actually permits sellers to retain, at the margin, 100% of the profits from coordination transactions. Although the experimental treatment may result in larger retained profits under some circumstances, it is unclear whether it actually increases the incentive to trade. There is no added inducement for utilities making purchases.

Third, the experiment requires that the transmission network be sufficiently available to participants in the experiment that there is open access to all potential trading partners. This means that participating utilities must have at least one contract path to each potential trading partner and that those utilities that operate the transmission network do not systematically frustrate trades in order to exploit their market position. This contrasts with present regulation under which utilities generally have no obligation to provide "wheeling" services even where they have the physical capacity to do so.[13]

Fourth, to promote the efficient functioning of the market, the experiment requires that price and quantity information about bulk power trades be made available to all participating utilities. This involves the provision of monthly summary statistics of aggregate trades to each participant.

It should be observed here that these treatments are not of equal importance. In particular, not all of the participating utilities took advantage of the revenue treatment at the outset of the experiment and some participants had not done so even by the end of the first year.[14] Moreover, it appears that the pre-experimental tariffs provided participants with satisfactory access to the transmission grid. Potentially the most significant treatment was that participating utilities had substantial freedom in setting prices for transactions covered by the experiment.

Trade in two commodities is subject to experimental treatment. One of these commodities is economy energy, which is traded on an hour-to-hour basis and can be interrupted at the discretion of the seller. Economy transactions can take place for up to 30 days. The other commodity is block energy, which involves trades that extend over periods of at least one month.

Characteristics of the participating utilities

Six utilities in Arizona, New Mexico and West Texas decided to participate in the FERC experiment. The experiment does not include utilities in California, Nevada or Utah, although Southwest utilities presently exchange significant amounts of energy with these utilities. The participating utilities include three with relatively large amounts of generation capacity: Arizona Public Service (APS), (3,426 MW peak capacity in 1984); Salt River Project (SRP), (3,226 MW); and Southwest Public Service (SPS), (3,706 MW); two utilities with moderate amounts of capacity: El Paso Electric (EPE), (990 MW); and Public Service Company of New Mexico (PNM), (1,337 MW); and a relatively small generator, Farmington Electric (COF), (67 MW). These utilities also vary considerably in the dollar value of their revenues, from a low of $30 million per year (COF) to over $800 million (APS). The six participating utility systems serve approxi-

COMPETITION IN ELECTRICITY

mately 80 percent of the final demand in Arizona, 75 percent in New Mexico, and 5 percent in Texas.

The utilities vary widely in the fuels used, and therefore in the marginal costs generally experienced. Some generate virtually all of their energy from coal-fired units, some primarily from gas-fired units, and some from a mixture of fossil-fired and hydroelectric resources.

In recent years, the six utilities collectively sold over 6 million MWh of bulk power and purchased over 4 million MWh annually in coordination transactions, with substantial net coordination sales outside the region.[15] The participants range from Public Service of New Mexico, which is preponderantly a seller and makes few purchases, to El Paso Electric, which is primarily a buyer.

The participating utilities represent a diverse pattern of ownership and operation. There are four investor-owned companies and two publicly owned companies, Salt River Project and Farmington Electric. Since the two publicly owned systems are not regulated by FERC or the state utility commissions, they are affected by the experiment only to the extent that it affects the behavior of their trading partners or their access to the transmission network.

It should be emphasized that state regulation applies to a much greater fraction of total utility revenue than does federal regulation. FERC regulation applies to as little as 2 percent of the total revenue (for APS) and to as much as 35 percent (for PNM). Moreover, part of the revenues subject to FERC regulation are for partial or full requirements sales to other utility systems, and are not affected by the experiment. The sales that may be affected by the experiment accounted for less than 1 percent of total revenues for three of the participating utilities, and at most for 10 percent of the revenue for one utility system.

Specific limits of this experiment

Four features of the FERC Southwest experiment should be noted before considering the empirical findings. First, the four experimental treatments were employed simultaneously, so that it is impossible to "unbundle" them to determine their separate contributions. Therefore, any conclusions about the effect of regulatory change apply to the entire set of treatments.

Second, utility participation was voluntary, and some utilities chose not to participate, leading to a possible selectivity bias if only those who expected to gain joined the experiment. However, the majority of non-participants were relatively small, publicly owned utilities not subject to FERC regulation, so the loss may not be severe. The most notable exception is Tucson Electric Power Company, which participated through most of the preliminary design meetings, but elected not to join the experiment.

Third, the study is limited to utilities in a three-state area, and major utility systems in California, Utah, Nevada and other states that trade significant amounts of electricity with utilities in Arizona and New Mexico were not invited to participate in the experiment. This limitation may be the most significant one in the experimental design.

Finally, although the experiment was authorized for both 1984 and 1985, FERC has not supported analysis of data for the second year. The results reported in this paper may thus be sensitive to the omission of data from 1985, especially because SPS was not connected to the other participants until October 1984.

EFFICIENCY ANALYSIS

Overview of the approach

To evaluate the effects of the experimental treatments on the performance of the bulk power market in the Southwest, it is necessary to determine how the market would have performed if the experiment had not occurred. This section describes the general approach taken to the problem of specifying the counterfactual situation to provide a benchmark against which behavior during the experiment is to be compared.

In a competitive and frictionless bulk power market in which utilities exploit all trades that reduce the cost of meeting their combined load, the marginal cost of generating electricity would, with some qualifications, be the same for all utilities.[16] The reduction in costs is an efficiency gain and results from differences in marginal cost among the utilities. Such a hypothetical bulk power market provides the ben-

COMPETITION IN ELECTRICITY

chmark for the present analysis of the FERC experiment.

Using marginal cost and load data supplied by each participating utility, statistical cost functions were estimated that relate system marginal cost to load and a number of other factors for all participants.[17] The statistical approach attempts to explain the system marginal cost of each participating utility, rather than attempting to take into account the marginal cost of each generating unit, stochastic outages of generation and transmission equipment and stochastic changes in the spatial distribution of demand within a system.[18] An approach based on these latter factors can yield more finely tuned marginal cost estimates, but at a much higher computational cost. However, it may be a less reliable indicator of anticipated marginal cost — the marginal cost the utility's system dispatcher may have been expecting at the time generation or trading decisions were made — than the present statistical approach.

Because the statistical cost functions are estimated over a series of hourly observations, they effectively "average" over times of normal operating conditions and those when there are unit outages, derating of generating units, and unit start-up considerations. A system dispatcher usually takes account of these factors in scheduling coordination transactions, so the estimates of both potential and actual efficiency gains contain some error by failing to adjust for these factors. In general, it appears that the calculations will tend to understate both potential and actual efficiency gains.[19]

The algorithm for calculating potential and actual efficiency gains

To separate the effects of the experimental treatments from other factors, the concept of exogenous demand is introduced. Exogenous demand is defined as native demand (i.e. retail sales to the utility's customers), plus net sales to non-participating utilities, plus net firm sales to participating utilities. That is, it is the non-discretionary sales obligations of each participating utility. The rationale for distinguishing between discretionary and non-discretionary sales is that exogenous demand must be met regardless of opportunities for trade in the bulk power market. In the case of native demand and firm sales to other utilities, each utility has an obligation to serve that must be met except under highly unusual circumstances. In the case of sales to non-participants, it is reasoned that, for participants in the Southwest experiment, these sales are generally to California utilities and are sufficiently attractive that the participants would try to make them regardless of whether they make sales to participating utilities. In other words, it is assumed that transactions with non-participants are inframarginal, and that non-firm transactions with participants take place at the margin. Thus, it follows that only these non-firm transactions may be affected by the change in experimental incentives and market conditions.

In brief, the efficiency analysis for the base case under non-experimental and experimental conditions consists of six steps:

1. Calculate the cost of meeting exogenous demand without discretionary transactions among participants.
2. Calculate the cost of meeting exogenous demand with full (frictionless) trading.
3. Calculate the potential gains to trade, defined as the results of step 1 minus the results of step 2.
4. Calculate the actual gains to trade using data on actual transactions.
5. Compare the actual gains to trade with the predicted gains from step 3.
6. Compare the relationship between actual and potential gains under non-experimental and experimental conditions.

It should be noted that both the actual and potential gains to trade are obtained using the statistical marginal cost functions and are affected by the accuracy with which these functions are estimated.[20] Since the actual and potential gains are measured from the same cost functions, errors in the estimates will be reflected in both variables.

These six steps, for an example involving two utilities, A and B, facing exogenous demands Q_A and Q_B, and having marginal cost functions MC_A and MC_B, are shown in Figure 24-2. Because utility A's marginal cost at its exogenous demand, MC_A, is less than utility B's marginal cost at its exogenous demand, MC_B, the total cost of meeting their combined load falls if utility A increases its generation and

COMPETITION IN ELECTRICITY

Figure 24-2

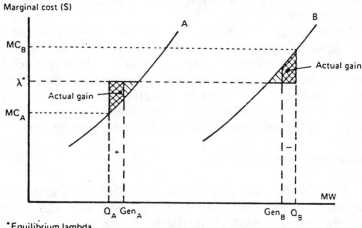

*Equilibrium lambda

utility B decreases its generation by the same amount. If there are no limits to transmission between the two utilities, total costs continue to fall as utility A increases its generation, and utility B decreases its generation, to the point at which marginal cost is the same for the two systems. The resulting value of marginal cost is designated "equilibrium lambda". This is the price that would prevail in the hypothetical competitive market.

The gain in efficiency from trade, the net costs saved, is given by the difference between the reduced costs to the buying utility and the increased costs to the selling utility. In Figure 24-2, the reduced cost to utility B is the area under its marginal cost curve between GenB, and QB and the increased cost to utility A is the corresponding area under its marginal cost curve. The net saving of is shown by the sum of the shaded areas. If the marginal cost curves are continuous, the efficiency gains can be stated mathematically as

$$\text{Gain} = \int_{Gen_B}^{Q_B} f_A(x)dx - \int_{Q_A}^{Gen_A} f_B(x)dx$$

where f_i is the marginal cost for utility i, Q_i is the exogenous demand for utility i, and Gen_i is the generation level of utility i after trades take place.[21]

Actual gains to trade will be less than or equal to potential, depending upon whether the utilities trade to the point at which their marginal costs are equal.[22] If only some of these trades are made, actual gains are smaller than potential, as shown in Figure 24-2. Potential gains may vary because of shifts in utility marginal cost functions and / or changes in the exogenous demands faced by each utility.

Two alternative cases

The efficiency analysis consists of calculations under two alternative cases that differ chiefly in their estimates of the potential gains to trade.[23] In the base case (Case 1) neither stochastic generating unit outages nor transmission bottlenecks and outages are taken into account. The result is that the base case involves calculated potential and actual gains under ideal conditions. In Case 2, these outages and bottlenecks are taken into account. Since the calculations cannot account fully for these market frictions, and transaction costs are not taken explicitly into account, it will be expected that the fraction of potential gains actually realized will always fall short of 100 percent. The cases are as follows:

1. Base case (Case 1): Full frictionless trading among participating utilities is assumed in calculating potential gains to trade. Actual gains are compared with the potential amount.
2. Generation / transmission constrained case (Case 2): Generation and transmission constraints are taken into account in calculating potential gains to trade.[24] Actual gains are compared with this constrained potential amount.

Empirical findings

The findings are based on data from 1983, the base year, and 1984, the first year of the FERC experiment. In late September 1984, Southwest Public Service (SPS) became

COMPETITION IN ELECTRICITY

connected to other participating utilities over a 200 MW transmission line that significantly altered the trading possibilities for participants. Since there are no comparable pre-experimental observations with this intertie in place, it is misleading to attribute changes in the fourth quarter of 1984 completely to the experiment. Findings with and without SPS are presented where appropriate. The analysis is confined to one each of the five weekdays each month, selected at random, and to the hours 8 a.m. to 10 p.m.[25]

Measuring the effect of the experiment on efficiency

Two types of measures of the effect of the experiment on the extent to which participating utilities exploit potential efficiency gains are employed. The first is simply to calculate, for the two cases, the change in the ratio of actual to potential gains between 1983 and 1984. These calculations implicitly assume that the relationship between actual and potential gains is proportional. Using these measures, it can be determined whether the proportion of potential welfare gains that is exploited by the participating utilities changed significantly during the experiment.[26]

The second type of measure involves estimating a statistical relationship between actual and potential welfare gains that is not required to be strictly proportional. Using this measure, it can be determined whether the experiment affected the intercept, the slope, or both the intercept and slope, of the relationship between actual and potential welfare gains.

The base case

The base case is an ideal against which the other — more realistic — case can be compared. The utilities cannot be expected to achieve 100 percent of potential gains in either case, but Case 1 is less representative of the real-world circumstances faced by utilities.

Technique 1: average proportion of potential gain realized. The results of the analysis of base case can be summarized as follows: actual efficiency gains, in dollar terms, increased between 1983 and 1984. At the same time, however, the potential gains to trade also increased. Because potential gains increased between 1983 and 1984, all of the increase in actual gains cannot be attributed solely to the experiment. In fact, the average hourly value of the percentage of potential efficiency gains actually achieved is roughly the same in 1984 as in 1983, although there are significant fluctuations in different seasons of the year.

Table 24-3 compares average hourly values of the actual gain as a percentage of the potential gain in the two years on a seasonal basis. In winter and summer the percentage increased by statistically significant amount and in the spring and autumn it decreased by a statistically significant amount between 1983 and 1984.[27] For the year as a whole, the percentage declined slightly, but the difference is not statistically significant.

Table 24-3.

Case 1: Actual and Potential Gains to Trade in Experimental Coordination Transactions with no Constraints

	Na	1983 Actual Gains	1983 Potential Gains	1983 Actual / Potential	1984 Actual Gains	1984 Potential Gains	1984 Actual / Potential
Jan - Mar	225	$668,680	$1,642,852	41%	$1,142,387	$2,504,923	46% *
Apr - May	150	$758,381	$2,144,338	35%	$714,878	$2,700,324	26% *
Jun - Sept	300	$695,974	$2,599,034	27%	$799,086	$2,699,644	30% *
Oct - Dec	225						
Excluding SPS		$834,322	$2,199,728	38%	$438,077	$1,988,822	22% *
Including SPS		NA	NA	NA	$758,309	$2,548,268	30% *
Annual	900						
Excluding SPS		$734,139	$2,184,379	34%	$780,624	$2,473,372	32% *
Including SPS		NA	NA	NA	$860,682	$2,613,233	33%

Dollar figures are average monthly amounts.
NA = not applicable.
*Indicates difference between 1983 and 1984 value is statistically significant at 0.05.
a number of observations each year.

COMPETITION IN ELECTRICITY

Technique 2: regression analysis. Another way to analyze the effect of the experiment statistically is to estimate an equation of the form

Actual gains = a + b(experimental year)+ c(potential gains)
+ d(potential x experimental year) + e(seasonal variables)

where actual and potential gains are measured in dollars per hour and the unit of observation is one hour. Other variables take the value one in the experimental year, or the value one for a particular season, and zero otherwise.[28]The results for 1983 and 1984 are shown in Table 24-4, which also gives the results for Case 2. These regression results are for data that include trades with SPS. Note that in Case 1, the coefficient of potential gains is highly statistically significant. The coefficient on the variable, experimental year, is positive and indicates an upward shift during the experiment of $543 per hour. Offsetting this effect, the interaction between potential gains and the experimental year variable is negative; that is, although the curve shifts upward, its slope flattens by 8 percentage points as a function of potential gains. In the experimental year, actual gains per hour are $114 lower at the mean value of potential gains in 1984 ($8,016).

Table 24-4
Regression Analysis of Actual Gains to Trade in Experimental Coordination Transactions (with SPS)

Case	Constant	Experimental Year	Potential Welfare Gain	Potential X Experimental Year	Winter	Spring	Summer	R^2	N
Base	-291.17 (2.20)	543.06 (2.94)	0.3822 (21.46)	-0.0820 (3.40)	681.48 (9.27)	-220.65 (2.74)	-453.44 (6.64)	0.33	1800
Generation & Transmission Constraint	623.42 (8.78)	-501.05 (5.59)	0.4242 (30.28)	0.1171 (5.92)	111.02 (1.96)	22.99 (0.38)	109.33 (2.14)	0.61	1800

t-ratios in parentheses
N = number of observations

Case 2: analysis taking account of generation and transmission constraints

Technique 1: average proportion of potential gains realized. The results of the base case do not take into account constraints in the transmission network or the unavailability of generating units. Table 24-5 presents the results of the analysis when curtailed baseload marketable resources and transmission constraints are taken into account. Potential gains to trade fall significantly when these constraints are introduced. As a result, the average hourly value of the ratio of actual to potential gains rises notably from 34 to 61 percent for 1983 and from 33 to 58 percent for 1984. When the year-to-year effects were considered, it was found that taking these constraints into account also led to the conclusion that the average hourly value of the percentage of potential gains obtained fell in three seasons under the experimental market conditions when compared with the pre-experimental period. For the year as a whole, the decline was from 61 to 58 percent when trades with SPS are included in the analysis. Each of these changes is statistically significant.

Table 24-5

Case 2: Actual and Potential Gains to Trade where Generation/Transmission Constraints are Considered

	Na	1983 Actual Gains	1983 Potential Gains	1983 Actual / Potential	1984 Actual Gains	1984 Potential Gains	1984 Actual Potential
Jan - Mar	225	$668,680	$973,616	69%	$1,142,387	$1,989,202	57% *
Apr - May	150	$758,381	$1,254,258	60%	$714,878	$1,261,396	57% *
Jun - Sept	300	$695,974	$1,154,319	60%	$799,086	$1,268,807	63% *
Oct - Dec	225						
Excluding SPS		$834,322	$1,430,670	58%	$438,077	$1,045,887	42% *
Including SPS		NA	NA	NA	$758,309	$1,364,782	56% *
Annual	900						
Excluding SPS		$734,139	$1,194,887	61%	$780,624	$1,391,941	56% *
Including SPS		NA	NA	NA	$860,682	$1,471,664	58% *

Dollar figures are average monthly amounts.
NA = not applicable.
* Indicates difference between 1983 and 1984 value is statistically significant at 0.05.
a Number of observations each year.

Technique 2: regression analysis. The regression analysis of Case 2 in Table 24-4 indicates that 42 percent of increased potential gains were realized in the non-experimental year and 54 percent were realized in the experimental year. At the same time, the constant of the regression fell from $623 to $118 in the experimental year. The combined effect of these two changes is that actual gains are calculated to be $28 higher in 1984 than in 1983 at the mean value of 1984 potential gains, $4,515. At the 1984 mean plus one standard deviation ($6,644), the predicted actual gain is $277 higher in 1984 than in 1983.

Figure 24-6

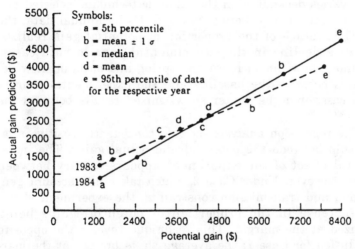

Figure 24-6 illustrates these findings with the actual range of data for 1983 and 1984 (plotted from the 5th percentile to the 95th percentile of potential gains to trade in both years). Essentially, the curve rotates about the mean value in 1984, so that actual gains in 1984 exceed those in 1983 for any value of potential above the mean (about $4,500). Each of these effects is highly statistically significant and the overall goodness of fit is reflected in the high value of R^2.

The limitation of the first of these measures, the percentage of potential gains that is realized, can also be easily

seen with the assistance of this figure. The average proportion of potential welfare gain realized is found by connecting
a line from the origin to the point containing mean values of
potential and actual welfare gains. Although both potential
and actual means are higher in 1984 than in 1983, the average proportion falls in 1984. This occurs despite the fact that
the 1984 relationship between the entire set of actual and
potential values in 1984 becomes steeper. By looking only at
mean values, the average proportion fails to detect this increased response to potential gains found by the regression
approach.

Conclusion of efficiency analysis

The efficiency analysis presents a decidedly mixed picture
that varies depending on the analytic technique selected and
the case and period being analyzed. Using annual data, the
hourly average of the proportion of potential gain realized
shows a decline in the experimental year in both cases.
Summer shows an increase and spring and autumn show decreases between the baseline and the experimental year in
both cases, but the winter shows mixed results between the
cases.[29]

The regression analysis shows a consistently positive relationship between the potential and actual gains. The incremental effect of the experiment appears to vary between
cases, however. Under Case 2, which takes into account generation and transmission constraints, the experiment shows
an increase in the proportion of potential gains being
realized at the margin. This technique reveals the opposite
conclusion for Case 1: the average shifts up, but at the margin a smaller proportion of potential gains is realized.

These findings, which should be regarded as suggestive,
could benefit from further refinement of the empirical
techniques employed and from the analysis of data from the
second year of the experiment. During much of 1984, several
considerations may have contributed to modest or unrepre-
sentative response to experimental conditions, including:

• The fact that behavior may reflect start up and learning.
• The fact that none of the utilities elected to take the experimental revenue treatment before June 1984, and one

privately owned utility had not done so by the end of 1984.
• The fact that one utility effectively participated in the experiment only from October 1984 onward.

The added number of observations available in the 1985 data, as well as their possibly more representative nature, might help in refining the measured effect of the experimental treatments on the realized gains to trade. However, FERC has not authorized analysis of data from the second year, so that the results reported here may be the only ones available.

AN ANALYSIS OF COMPETITION IN THE SOUTHWEST BULK POWER MARKET EXPERIMENT

One of the major economic objectives of FERC regulation of bulk power market transactions is to limit or prevent the exercise of market power by utilities.[31] This section describes the analysis of the extent to which prices in the Southwest market deviated from those that would be expected to prevail under perfect competition in both the baseline period, 1983, and in 1984, when participating utilities were permitted substantial freedom in setting prices. The extent to which market "competitiveness" changed as a result of the bulk power market experiment is also examined.

Market structure and potential competition in the Southwest bulk power market

The experimental bulk power market is clearly not structurally competitive. Indeed, by almost any standard, the market is highly concentrated on both the demand and supply sides. The Herfindahl index for buyers, the sum of the squares of the market shares for each participating utility, is 7,855 for 1984 and 8,517 for 1984, based on the physical volume of purchases. For sellers, the figures are 7,525 and 4,496.[32] These figures are large even when compared with the smallest possible indices for markets with five or six participants, 2,000 and 1,666, respectively.

Although there is substantial measured concentration in the experimental Southwest bulk power market, the actual market prices need not differ significantly from those we predict would have been observed if no utility had exercised market power. This could be so for one, or all, of three reasons.

First, the fact that there is substantial concentration on both sides of the market, i.e. among both buyers and sellers, means that the structure of the market may be characterized as bilateral monopoly, or more accurately, bilateral oligopoly. Where a small number of buyers face a small number of sellers in a market, price determination may involve a bargaining process instead of the impersonal setting of prices that occurs where a market is perfectly competitive. However, if the bargaining strength of buyers and sellers is fairly well balanced, the result may be a price close to the competitive price, although the process of price determination is quite different.

A second possibility is that the experimental market is actually embedded in, and part of, a larger market that includes utilities in the Southwest that chose not to participate in the experiment as well as utilities in other areas that were not invited to participate. In assessing market structure, it is appropriate to expand the definition of a market to include all buyers and sellers who compete with, and therefore constrain the market power of, any group of buyers or sellers. To define a market to exclude these competitive alternatives runs the risk of characterizing it as more concentrated, and less competitive, than it really is.

On this interpretation, the actual market is far less concentrated than measures indicate, and the market power of both buyers and sellers is effectively constrained by the availability of other trading partners. Here, any attempt on the part of utilities within the Southwest market experiment to raise prices above, or lower prices below, the competitive price will induce firms in the experimental market to shift their purchases, or sales, to non-participating utilities. These include other utilities in the Southwest as well as those in other areas, including California.[33]

A third possibility is that although the market is quite concentrated, in that a small number of buyers and sellers make most of the transactions, if existing sellers (buyers) were to attempt to raise (lower) price, enough additional sales (purchases) would be made by other participating utilities to prevent prices from changing very much. Even a monopsonistic seller will be unable to raise prices very much

564   COMPETITION IN ELECTRICITY

above its marginal cost if there are other potential sellers that can produce a substantial amount of additional output at a marginal cost that is not much greater. Similarly, a monopsonistic buyer may be unable to lower prices greatly if other buyers will attempt to purchase large additional quantities as prices are reduced. On this interpretation, market concentration is a misleading measure of market power because it does not account for the selling and purchasing capacities of potential sellers and buyers.

Measuring market competitiveness

To determine the effect of giving utilities substantial pricing freedom, the algorithm used to estimate the potential gains to trade among participating utilities was employed to estimate the price in a hypothetical competitive market with the same demand and cost characteristics as the experimental Southwest market, equilibrium lambda. If no buyer or seller attempts to exercise market power, and if there are no other barriers to efficient trade, this is the price that would prevail.[34]

The competitive price is estimated for both Case 1, the base case with no constraints, and Case 2, where there are generation and transmission constraints, and deviations between the observed market price and the competitive price divided by the market price are calculated to create the Lerner index of monopoly power.[35] The indices are calculated for each hour and are averaged over each year, and for each of four seasons in each year.[36] Mean indices for both 1983 and 1984 and for four seasons in each year are presented in Table 24-7. Differences between the mean indices from year to year are also shown. A value of the Lerner index that significantly exceeds zero indicates that the observed market price exceeds the hypothetical competitive price. A value below zero indicates that the price is below the hypothetical competitive price.

Several things should be noted about the results in Table 24-7. First, in Case 1, where generation and transmission constraints are not imposed, in 1983 the mean Lerner index is significantly different from zero only in the summer; it is not different from zero in the other three seasons nor for the year as a whole. In 1984, the mean index is statistically different from zero in each season and for the year as a whole. In Case 2, where generation and transmission constraints are imposed, the mean Lerner index is significantly different from zero in each season of both years and for both years as a whole.

Table 24-7.
Mean Lerner Indices for the Southwest Bulk Power Market Including Trades with SPS

	N	1983	1984	Difference
Case 1: No Constraints				
Jan - Mar	15	0.037 (0.031)	0.093 (0.028)	-0.0556
Apr - May	10	0.049 (0.026)	0.255 (0.029)	-0.2065*
Jun - Sept	20	-0.133 (0.025)	-0.104 (0.039)	-0.0326
Oct - Dec	15	0.033 (0.017)	0.202 (0.022)	-0.1689*
Year	60	-0.019 (0.016)	0.083 (0.024)	0.1014
Case 2: Generation				
Generation / Transmission Constraints				
Jan - Mar	15	-0.386 (0.038)	-0.198 (0.024)	-0.1881*
Apr - May	10	-0.340 (0.045)	-0.215 (0.032)	-0.1287*
Jun - Sept	20	-0.464 (0.029)	-0.276 (0.032)	-0.1896*
Oct - Dec	15	-0.395 (0.032)	-0.230 (0.029)	-0.1646*
Year	60	-0.406 (0.018)	-0.234 (0.015)	-0.1722*

NA = not applicable
* Indicates difference between 1983 and 1984 value is statistically significant at 0.05.

Second, in three out of four seasons under Case 1, on average observed prices exceed competitive prices, while in every season under Case 2, on average prices fall short of competitive prices. Since actual market prices are the same in both calculations, these results indicate that estimated competition prices are generally lower in Case 1 than in Case 2.

Third, and most important, are the comparisons between the mean Lerner indices in 1983 and their counterparts in 1984. In Case 1, there are significant differences between the mean Lerner indices for the second and fourth seasons and for the entire year. In both the second and fourth seasons, the indices are positive and rose significantly in 1984. For the year as a whole, the mean Lerner index which was negative, but not significantly different from zero, in 1983 became positive and significantly different from zero in 1984. In Case 2, which may be regarded as more realistic because it takes into account generation and transmission constraints, the

COMPETITION IN ELECTRICITY

mean Lerner indices were significantly closer to zero in 1984 than in 1983 in all of the comparisons. Using these comparisons, one would conclude that market competitiveness had increased between the two years.

What appears to have happened is that market prices, which were above estimated competitive prices in Case 1 in 1983, rose even further above them in 1984. This suggests that the market was becoming more monopolized. By contrast, market prices were below estimated competitive prices in Case 2 in 1983 and rose toward competitive prices in 1984. This suggests that the market became less monopsonized. In Case 1 the price movement suggested a less competitive market and in Case 2 a more competitive one.

Conclusion of competitiveness analysis

If there are many trading utilities on both sides of a market, none of which had substantial market shares, the likelihood that market power could be exercised is quite small.[37] The number of utilities that would have to agree to fix prices, and the likelihood that there would be cheating on any price-fixing agreement, are both so large that no cartel could be sustained. In such cases, the structure of the market generally guarantees a competitive outcome.

The Southwest bulk power market clearly is far from being structurally competitive. With large measured concentration on both sides of the market, it is more appropriately characterized as bilateral monopoly or oligopoly. As a result, one is forced to examine the actual behavior of prices in the market to determine whether it performs competitively. The general finding from the examination of Case 1 is that, on average, observed market prices did not differ significantly from the hypothetical competitive prices in the Southwest bulk power market in 1983 but were significantly greater than the hypothetical competitive prices in 1984. In Case 2, observed prices were generally significantly below competitive prices.

The most striking finding in relation to the bulk power market experiment, however, is that, in the more realistic of the two cases, Case 2, measured market competitiveness actually appears to have increased between the baseline and experimental periods. Indeed, since the test of these differences is conservative, it implies that the market did not become less competitive after the participating utilities had been granted substantial freedom in setting prices, and indeed may have become significantly more competitive.

CONCLUSION

The first year results from the FERC bulk power market experiment yield a decidedly mixed picture, with the statistical findings about the effects of modified regulation on market efficiency and competitiveness being sensitive to the period of time analyzed and the analytic technique being employed. Nonetheless, there is no strong evidence of a large effect of the regulatory treatments in the experiment. Indeed, since this experiment involved only six utilities, an unregulated market encompassing a larger number of utilities is likely to function at least as well as did the experimental Southwest market.

More generally, the methodology developed to analyze the FERC experiment should prove useful in evaluating other experiments of this type. However, caution is advised in that where the regulatory treatments are small relative to other factors that determine market efficiency and competitiveness, it will always be extremely difficult to estimate the effect of the experimental treatments. In these circumstances, additional data or more elaborate statistical models are likely to provide only limited improvement in statistical precision, and important uncertainties are likely to remain. At this stage, perhaps the most persuasive evidence will come from general utility experience if FERC chooses to adopt these regulatory changes on a permanent basis.

REFERENCES

Acton, J.P. and Besen, S.M. (1985) Regulation, Efficiency and Competition in the Exchange of Electricity: First- Year Results from the FERC Bulk Power Market Experiment, R-3301-DOE, The Rand Corporation, Santa Monica, California.
Bohn, R.E., Caramanis, M.C. and Schweppe, F.C. (1984) Optimal pricing in electrical networks over space and time, The Rand Journal of Economics,15,360-77.

Cohen, M. (1979) Efficiency and competition in the electric power industry, Yale Law Journal 88, 1511-49.

Dansby, R.E. and Willig, R.D. (1979) Industry performance gradient indexes, American Economic Review, 69, 249-61.

Dowlatabadi, H. and Evans, N. (1986) Electricity trade in the UK: economic prospects and future uncertainty, Energy Policy, 14, 35-44.

Earley, W.C. (1982) FERC regulation of bulk power coordination transactions, staff working paper, Federal Energy Regulatory Commission, Office of Regulatory Analysis.

Edison Electric Institute (1981) Deregulation of Electric Utilities: A Survey of Major Concepts and Issues, Economics Division, Washington, DC.

Edison Electric Institute (1982) Preliminary Assessment of Proposals for Deregulation of Intersystem Power Transactions, Economics Division, Washington, DC.

Federal Energy Regulatory Commission (1983) Public Service of New Mexico et al., Opinion and Order Finding Experimental Rate to Be Just and Reasonable and Accepting Rate for Filing, Docket No. ER 84-155-000, issued 30 December.

Federal Energy Regulatory Commission (1985a) Regulation of Electricity Sales-for Resale and Transmission Service, Notice of Inquiry, 18 CFR, Part 35, Docket No. RM 85-17-000 (Phase I), issued 30 May.

Federal Energy Regulatory Commission (1985b) Regulation of Electricity Sales for-Resale and Transmission Service, Notice of Inquiry, 18 CFR, Parts 35 and 290, Docket No. RM 85-17-M (Phase II), issued 28 June.

Fels, N.W. and Heap, D.N. (1983) Compulsory wheeling of electric power to industrial customers, Fordham Law Review, 52, 219-33.

Hahn, R.W. (1985) An experimental examination of spot markets for electricity, Draft paper, School of Public Affairs, Carnegie-Mellon University, 5 August.

Hughes, D. (1981) Innovative government policies for the electric utilities industry, speech given at the Third International Conference on Energy Use Management, Berlin, 29 October.

Hughes, D. (1982) Address before the Twenty-First Annual Iowa State Regulatory Conference, Iowa State University, 19 May.

Keeler, T.E. (1981) The revolution in airline regulation, in Case Studies in Regulation: Revolution and Reform (Ed.) L. W. Weiss and M. W. Klass, Little, Brown, Boston.

Lerner, A.P. (1934) The concept of monopoly and the measurement of monopoly power, Review of Economic Studies, 1, 157-75.

Mitre Corporation (1983) Proceedings of the Mitre-EEI Conference on Electric Power Deregulation, 16-17 November, 1982, Washington, DC.

Pace, J.D. and Landon, J.H. (1982) Introducing competition into the electric utility industry: an economic appraisal Energy Law Journal, 1, 1-34.

Penn, D.W., Delaney, J.B. and Honeycutt, T.C. (1975) Coordination, Competition and Regulation in the Electric Utility Industry, US Nuclear Regulatory Commission, Washington, DC.

Plott, C.R. (1982) Industrial organization theory and experimental economics, Journal of Economic Literature, 20, 1485-527.

Scherer, F.M. (1980) Industrial Marker Structure and Economic Performance, 2nd ed., Rand-McNally, Chicago.

Schmalensee, R. and Golub, B.W. (1984) Estimating effective concentration in deregulated wholesale electricity markets, Rand Journal of Economics, 15, 12-26.

United States Department of Justice (1984) Merger Guide Lines of Department of Justice-1984, Fed. Reg. 49, 26824, Washington, DC.

Weiss,L.W. (1975) Antitrust in the electric power industry, in Promoting Competition in Regulated Markets, (Ed.) A. Phillips, Brookings Institution, Washington, DC.

ENDNOTES

1. For discussion of these proposals see Penn et al (1975), Cohen (1979), Edison Electric Institute (1981; 1982), Pace and Landon (1982) and Mitre Corporation (1983).

2. In the USA, privately owned utilities own about 78% of the generation capacity and supply directly about 76% of final demand. Over 3000 municipal and cooperative systems own about 22% of the generation capacity and supply about 24% of final demand. See Edison Electric Institute (1982).

3. FERC Commissioner David Hughes (1981) first called for such an experiment and articulated some general design principles in Hughes (1982). In December 1983, FERC (1983) authorized a two-year experiment. We assisted FERC and the participating utilities in the design of the experiment and in evaluating its effects.

4. FERC (1983, p.4). Recently, the Commission opened a series of inquiries to determine if several aspects of its regulation of bulk electricity sales and transmission rates should be changed; see FERC (1985a; 1985b).

5. Throughout this paper, the term efficiency refers to the cost to society of meeting a given electricity load. Whether the loads being met are efficient is not considered.

6. Competition in these experimental markets is important because its presence may contribute to the goal of economic efficiency. However, because factors in addition to the exercise of market power may reduce efficiency, separate analyses of efficiency and competition have been undertaken.

7. For a detailed discussion of coordination transactions and FERC regulation of them see Earley (1982). Broadly speaking, there are four types of coordination transaction: (1) emergency service, which provides energy for capacity deficiencies in those situations that could not be prevented given proper management or planning, and is provided only for a period of time necessary for the buyer to reestablish its own service, usually within 24 to 72 hours; (2) short-term service, in which power is provided on a conditionally interruptible basis for a period of less

than one year to a utility lacking sufficient power during scheduled maintenance, needing capacity for an extended outage, or for economic reasons; (3) economy energy, which is unconditionally interruptible energy supplied when a seller's incremental cost is less than a buyer's decremental cost; and (4) firm service that is backed by reserves of the seller, which is usually interruptible only under force majeure events.

8. Two of the participants in the Southwest experiment do not fall under FERC jurisdiction.

9. See Plott (1982) for a review of the literature on laboratory-based market analysis. See Hahn (1985) for discussion of a recent laboratory experiment involving hourly economy trades among electric utilities where the subjects were employees of rural utility systems.

10. Beyond these general limitations, the specific FERC experiment in the Southwest has some specific limitations that are summarized at the end of the section.

11. It is widely believed that the 'natural' experiments provided in unregulated intrastate airline markets in California and Texas were instrumental in promoting deregulation of fares and entry in the US airline industry. See Keeler (1981, pp. 61-2).

12. Greater detail can be found in Acton and Besen (1985) or FERC (1983).

13. See Fels and Heap (1983) for a detailed discussion of the regulation of wheeling.

14. The effects on retained profits may explain the slow pace at which utilities elected this treatment. The first utility to adopt the experimental revenue treatment did so halfway through the first experimental year, the second utility did so after 9 months, and the third after 12 months. One privately owned utility, and two publicly owned utilities were never under the experimental revenue treatment during 1984.

15. This is true even if trades with other utilities in Arizona and New Mexico are included.

16. The qualifications include limits on transmission capacity and costs of search.

17. In order to protect the confidential, proprietary nature of the data supplied by the participating utilities, the actual values of individual cost functions are not reported, al-

though a more-detailed description of the relationships is found in Acton and Besen (1985).

18. Where appropriate, variations in marginal cost by year and/or season are taken into account in the cost functions. These presumably capture changes in fuel costs as well as outages due to planned maintenance.

19. The reason for this bias is the following: unexpected outages and increases in demand make the actual marginal cost greater than it would be under normal conditions. Sellers will be less likely to sell when marginal costs are above normal and more likely to sell when they are below normal (for a given load). Therefore, their gains will tend systematically to be higher when trading. Conversely, buyers will be more likely to purchase when marginal costs are above normal which will again lead to actual gains being larger than those calculated from average circumstances.

20. The marginal costs reported by participants for individual trades are not used in calculating actual pins, in large part because these reported figures often depend on the order in which the utilities make their trades.

21. It is also a condition of equilibrium that $f_A(\text{gen}_A) = f_B(\text{gen}_B)$ and that $\text{Gen}_A - Q_A = -[\text{Gen}_B - Q_B]$, net of transmission losses.

22. The concept potential pins to trade is equivalent to the concept net trading benefit in Dowlatabadi and Evans' (1986) simulation of the pins to trade between Scotland and England and Wales. In that study, however, it is assumed that all of the potential gains can be realized.

23. Other cases are reported in Acton and Besen (1985).

24. This case is based on two types of data provided by the participating utilities. First, the generation constraint is based on an hourly value of curtailed baseload marketable resources supplied by five of the utilities. This value is intended to reflect the additional amount of energy that a utility could supply using available and operating generation capacity, for which no willing buyer had been identified. Changes in this value reflect the interplay of supply and demand conditions at both buying and selling utilities, including scheduled or unexpected outages of equipment. Second, for one of the utilities, there are estimates of the transmission capacity available for import-

ing energy at any hour. This utility is located at the edge of the network connecting participating and non-participating utilities in the Southwest. Unlike other participating utilities, whose transmission capacity is affected by both installed capacity and flows throughout the system, this utility is effectively constrained to particular limits in its capacity to transmit purchased energy.

25. Holidays are also excluded. By limiting the analysis to these days and hours, the late-night periods when utilities may be constrained by minimum operating conditions on generating units are avoided. Monthly totals are calculated for the hours 8 a.m. to 10 p.m., Monday to Friday. Each month has a standardized value of 21.73 workdays (5/7 x 365/12).

26. In the analysis the sum of potential and actual gains in a given hour is always compared and the performance of individual utilities is not examined.

27. Tests of significance for the difference in the ratio of actual pins to potential gains present an issue in error propagation because the numerator and denominator of the ratio may be correlated. The tests of statistical significance for changes in this ratio are based on the following formula for estimating the variance of a ratio:

$$\text{var}(A/P) = \text{var}(A)/[\text{avg}(P)]^2 + \text{var}(P)[\text{avg}(A)]^2/[\text{avg}(P)]^4$$
$$- 2\text{cov}(A,P)[\text{avg}(A)]/[\text{avg}(P)]^3$$

where A = actual, P = potential, avg = average hourly value, var = variance and cov = covariance.

28. The specification reported in Table 2 is the most useful one in our judgement, although simpler models were also tested that eliminated either the shift variable for experimental year or the change in slope that is provided by the interaction of experimental year and potential gains to trade.

29. Recall that not all of the year-to-year changes are statistically significant.

30. Beyond these three factors, the absence of utility participants from California, Utah and Nevada may contribute to the modest observed response. Their absence from the experiment continued in the second year.

574   COMPETITION IN ELECTRICITY

Another factor may be that the effects of the experimental treatments are so small that they are difficult to separate from other factors that affect the volume of trade.

31. The other major objective is to permit utility rate payers to share in the pins from these transactions.
32. The US Department of Justice (1984) defines a market as highly concentrated if the Herfindahl index is 1800 or greater. Because the identities of utilities as buyers or sellers can shift over time, the indices reported in the text were obtained not by averaging hourly Herfindahl indices but by summing the squared market shares calculated for an entire year. The strengths and weaknesses of the Herfindahl index and other measures of market concentration are discussed in Scherer (1980). For a sophisticated analysis of the conditions under which particular measures of market concentration should be employed, see Dansby and Willig (1979).
33. We recognize that this interpretation is not entirely consistent with the approach taken to estimate the competitive price. In our algorithm, it is assumed that prices in the experimental Southwest market are determined solely through the interaction of participating utilities in the Southwest Transactions involving non-participants are treated as intramarginal.
34. Note that the failure of firms to exercise market power is sufficient, but not necessary, for the competitive price to prevail.
35. The Lerner index is usually calculated using the deviation between price and marginal cost. See Lerner (1934). In the present context, the competitive price is the marginal cost of all utilities in a competitive equilibrium. Schmalensee and Golub (1984) use a similar measure of competitiveness in which comparisons are made using competitive quantities.

On an hour-by-hour basis, Lerner indices are trade-weighted averages computed as follows:

$$L_h = \frac{\sum\limits_{i=1}^{n_h} [mwh_{ih}(p_{ih} - \lambda_h{}^*) / p_{ih}]}{\sum\limits_{i=1}^{n_h} [mwh_{ih}]}$$

where h   denotes hour h,

       i   denotes trade i in hour h,

      nh   denotes the number of trades in hour h,

     mwh_{ih} denotes megawatt hours traded in trade i in hour h,

     p_{ih} denotes price of trade i in hour h, and

     λ_h denotes hypothetical competitive price in hour h,

Performing tests of statistical significance on changes in the ratio of the general form (x - y) / x presents a more difficult problem in error propagation than the one considered in the efficiency analysis. Correlations between hourly observations, as well as correlations between the numerator and denominator, prevent simple statistical tests of changes in mean values. Rogers suggested an approximation that yields 'conservative' tests of statistical significance. Since the Lerner indices in Table 6 are mean daily averages of the hourly Lerner indices, the problem of hour-to-hour correlation is reduced. The daily averages were employed in calculating standard errors of the ratio of interest. This yields conservative tests of significance, i.e. the standard errors presented may be larger than the true standard errors. Thus, an insignificant difference in Table 6 may in fact be significant.

36. These are the same hours as those used in the efficiency calculations. Where transactions in any hour occur at different prices, a weighted average is taken using quantities as weights.

37. This ignores market power that might be held by utilities that control access to the transmission grid.

SECTION G

ISSUES OF INDUSTRY STRUCTURE

CHAPTER 25: AND THEN THERE WERE 50

Edward Tirello
Senior Vice President, Shearson-Lehman Brothers

There are five trends in the electric utility industry on collision courses: increasing cash flow, competition, diversification, deregulation, and — the logical extension of all this — amalgamation.

There are 150 major, investor-owned electric companies today. In five years there will be 50.

The 50 that survive will be quite happy about it, but the other 100 will take exception to what I'm going to say. However, I'm going to cite to you why I don't think they have any choice.

Cash Flow

For the past 10 or 15 years, stopping basically in 1984, electric utilities were primarily construction finance companies. And except for 10 or so companies currently finishing up big projects, everyone else has pretty much stopped building big power plants. They have become totally different companies. They have become big net cash generators.

Another outcome of this change is utility sensitivity to interest rates. In their base business, utilities are not as interest rate sensitive as they once were and the reason is relatively simple. Without a monster construction program there is no big financing program. Since they are not borrowing money the rate is not that important. What they are doing with these low rates is refunding high coupon debt with low coupon debt. This obviously lowers their embedded costs.

Inflation is coming down. The commissions are lowering the return on equity. Does that mean reduced cash flow and the end of the industry's hopes for the future?

That's not really so. The premise is correct but the conclusion is not.

When the commissions were authorizing 16% returns, the industry was earning only 10%, and much of that was not in the form of cash.

Now commissions are authorizing lower returns — between 13 and 14 percent — but companies are earning those returns and earning them in cash. There's a great difference — 16 percent but little cash compared to 13 or 14 percent and a lot of cash. And that's what we're interested in. The new tax act knocked off the investment tax credit and some other things that were great when utilities were building. But even though they're not building, depreciation stays relatively the same. That helps cash flow.

Something happened in regulation recently, which I think is going to change the way utilities operate.

In New York, which is relatively hostile to utilities, the commission did something which I think is going to happen across the country over time. They said to Consolidated Edison that, even though the authorized return on equity is 15.9 percent, over the next three years the base return will be 12.9 percent. If the company earns more it can keep 50 percent for the shareholder and 50 percent will be refunded to the ratepayer.

Now there is a stronger motivation to cut costs. Savings are not all given back to the ratepayer. This trend is going to change the industry radically.

Another area to think about is technology, because it has a strong effect on competition. We don't see the industry building the large, 500 MW coal-fired boiler with a scrubber. It's a great piece of equipment, very reliable. The only problem is, it takes 10 years to build when you get all the regulatory stuff in, new superconductivity technology, to build new, long distance transmission lines. I see utilities allying themselves with railroads, building new power lines down the railroad right of way, going from the Midwest to, for example, Virginia, and hooking into the grid and sending the power north or south. I didn't make that up. A utility manager explained that to me. The more progressive companies are already in this.

A Utility's Five Competitors

We see every utility as having five competitors. I didn't think they had any a few years ago, but they have five now.

The first one is obviously the utility's industrial customer. He can choose to produce his own power or not.

The second one is the cogenerator.

The third one is the alternative energy producer.

The fourth competitor is what I see Central Vermont Public Service putting together and I think every company is going to have this. It is the equivalent of the telephone reseller. I call it the marketing subsidiary of the company.

This subsidiary is going to buy power from the parent, from alternative energy producers, from industrial customers, from cogenerators, and from anyone else in the area who's making power, then repackage it and re-sell it in the marketplace.

Sometimes the subsidiary will be in competition with the parent, but they figure that somebody is going to come in and skim the cream off the market as these cogenerators and the alternative energy producers have already done. They feel that they might as well get that cream.

The fifth competitor is the utility's neighbor. We see this coming and, believe me, utility neighbors and customers are working on it.

Buying into Cogeneration

This cogeneration business is an undercapitalized industry. We hold a seminar on it every year, so we meet all the new participants and every year it seems like half of them are gone.

Over time, we see half of each one of these companies, whoever the survivors are, being owned by the electric companies. They're only allowed to own half according to the law.

The reason is relatively simple. Electric utilities have the deep pockets. They have the money and they really have the expertise. These other people, in most cases, are promoters.

The more intelligent cogenerators have been approaching electric utility companies and asking them if they would sell them their old, depreciated power plants, so they can do exactly what Northern Sates Power is doing. Some utilities are foolishly going to sell them, and the smart companies are going to keep them and do the same thing. I know of one cogenerator who is out there making bids on as many as he can.

Industry Consolidation

The companies with the strongest transmission ties and the lowest cost generation are going to basically swoop in and steal the large industrial and commercial customers away from their weaker neighbors, forcing the consolidation of the industry.

Most utility executives claim there are absolutely and positively no benefits to consolidation. They say they're in a pool, they're economically dispatched, so there are absolutely and positively no savings. And finally, they say the regulators will never allow this to occur.

I want to know the name of that regulator, because I've spoken to them and I haven't run into one yet who's said he's opposed to it.

There is a tremendous amount of money to be saved as a result of consolidation. Labor, for example, offers some big potential savings.

One of the most labor-efficient utilities is Tucson Electric. Eight years ago, they had 1,400 employees. Now they have 1,000 employees and twice as many customers. That's efficiency.

At the other end of the spectrum are high-cost companies that fear somebody will come in, fire 10 percent of the employees, and pay for the company with the savings produced. There's a wide spectrum of companies there.

The benefit from consolidation that makes the most sense to me is the economic dispatch and maintenance of power plants. When a utility's generation units are on line, they are economically dispatched. However, when they are off line, they're not. When a plant is taken down for maintenance, it may not be the optimal time to have taken it down. Had it been part of a larger, coordinated system, the company might have been able to make substantially more money at that moment in time selling power from that unit into the grid.

Let me give you an example. Texas Utilities owns three companies that are supposed to have been fully coordinated for the past 20 years. They decided to merge the three companies to make one. They discovered that they saved 50 million dollars a year forever by having one computer and one maintenance program instead of three computers and three maintenance programs.

They also discovered they saved $50 million a year forever by combining all development programs. We think there's a third $50 million dollars a year just by putting the three companies together.

The next one I'd like to mention is Centerior Energy, the recent merger of Toledo Edison and Cleveland Electric Illuminating. They said for the next fifteen years, they'll save somewhere between $75 and $125 million a year.

The 1988 saving will be $90 million. They say that $50 million are in construction deferrals. That's nice, but I'm not interested in that. The $40 million is actual savings resulting from putting things together and merging some of the operations — without laying people off. The point is, that's a forever situation -- they'll have another big savings in 1989, another one in 1990.

The biggest bucks to be saved from consolidation lies in nuclear plant operations. A company with one nuclear plant has almost as much cost as one with seven, for example. Look at Duke Power Co., which has seven nuclear units and a neighboring utility with one. You can't tell me that you can't do better running a single system with eight nuclear units versus two separate systems. Duke's engineers will explain to you exactly how that's done.

CHAPTER 26: BLINDED BY THE LIGHT: RESTRUCTURING PUBLIC UTILITIES FOR THE PROMISE OF A COMPETITIVE ENERGY FUTURE*

Mary B. Bushnell
Chairman, Illinois Commerce Commission

NEW DIRECTIONS FOR THE ELECTRIC AND GAS INDUSTRIES

Regulation seems at times to be a dark and endless tunnel. Today, even the tunnel's principal architects, the regulated industries, find its path a menacing one. Many now see a light at the end of the tunnel in the form of competition. They are joined by certain academicians, financial analysts, and even many regulators who envision a bright, competitive energy future that leaves regulation's darkness far behind. It is a future that also entails fundamental restructuring of this nation's energy utilities.

It is possible for us to be blinded by the light of competition. Restructuring our nation's energy service markets for the promise of competition is not a task to be undertaken lightly, let alone blindly. As uncomfortable and unpopular as it may be, it will be well worth our while to reflect upon both the forces of change and the perils of change as we make our way toward a more competitive energy future.

THE FORCES OF CHANGE

We are all intimately familiar with the history of the utility industries and their regulation. As recent as the 1950s and 1960s the industries prospered and their prosperity, at least on the electric side, was evident in the commitment of massive resources to the construction of new generating plants.

In the 1970s, dramatic inflation and cost escalations signalled the end of the golden era of construction. Regulators

*Presented at the conference, "Electricity's Future: Is Competition the Light at the End of the Regulatory Tunnel? Annual ELCON Conference, Washington D.C., October 8-9, 1987. The views expressed in this paper are those of the author and do not necessarily represent the views of the Illinois Commerce Commission or its individual members.

began sending signals to the energy utilities as well. We put the rubber stamp away and began taking a long hard look at utility finances and rate structures. As regulation and regulators became less dependable, in the customary sense, utilities had to face harsh economic realities and an increasingly hostile public.

It is no wonder that to many the time for change is now. Several potential industry trends may signal that restructuring is already underway. One is the trend toward consolidation, evident in the increase in the number of mergers and acquisitions. One Shearson Lehman Brothers analyst reports that their motto is to reduce the number of the nation's electric utilities from 150 to 50 in five years.

With mergers, acquisitions, and even the creation of holding companies and subsidiaries, a utility remains vertically integrated and in control of total operations from production to distribution. Another potential trend today is vertical disaggregation, whereby utility operations are broken up. The New Mexico Public Service Company plan is the most dramatic attempt at this strategy.

Still another apparent trend in the electric industry is the continued expansion of cogeneration and independent power production. Coupled with the possibility of wheeling, these power sources will also have an impact on the structure of the industry and the nature of competition within it.

It remains to be seen whether these potential trends will become actual trends. And with consolidation and disaggregation happeningsimultaneously no one can be certain about what structure the energy industries will actually have or what benefits it will have over the existing structure after the so called "shakeout".

There may be some very good reasons for restructuring the energy service markets, for encouraging a more competitive environment, and for lessening the regulatory burdens on energy providers.

However, I find many of the reasons that have been advanced to date for restructuring the energy industries to be less than compelling, particularly from a public interest perspective.

The "Failure" of Regulation

One of the key reasons for the restructuring movement is the purported failure of regulation. Not only have regulatory mechanisms failed to replicate competition and competitive outcomes, but it is said that regulators themselves, particularly at the state level, have failed to protect and promote the utility industries as they did in the early history of regulation.

Many public utility commissions have become highly proactive. In Illinois, the General Assembly established a more aggressive regulatory philosophy through the 1985 Public Utilities Act and the state Supreme Court has reinforced our statutory mandate to closely scrutinize factors affecting utility rates.

In general, prudence reviews, management audits, "used and useful" tests, and other areas of expanded regulatory oversight are viewed as punitive and are also having a chilling effect on the utility industries. In fact, much of what regulators are demanding is exactly what competition should bring about: a product of value at a reasonable price.

In most cases, today's regulators are not trying to punish the utilities. They are merely imposing performance standards that any truly competitive firm should be able to meet. If a company is prepared to meet the performance standards of a competitive marketplace, why can it not meet the performance standards of regulators?

Expansion into wholesale power will allow some utilities (or major parts of them) to get out from under state regulation and deal only with the more friendly Federal Energy Regulatory Commission. At least some utilities also seem to prefer the risks and uncertainty of restructuring / competition to the continued risks and uncertainty of regulation and the unpredictable behavior of regulators.

The "Failure" of Deregulation

Another reason for the restructuring movement is the limited success of the deregulation movement — at least from a political standpoint.

Interestingly, even with the possible failure of regulation, the deregulation movement has not achieved much momentum so far. If anything, experience at the federal level with the telecommunications and transportation industries has caused even some of the nation's foremost champions of deregulation to pause.

The deregulation movement has "failed" in part because it is a myth that deregulation results in automatic competition. Competition depends on a competitive market structure, not on the removal of regulatory controls. As long as economic power is concentrated, the potential for monopoly abuse will persist.

But it is also a myth that restructuring will result in competition. One form of restructuring is simply to disaggregate the utility industries into the three key sectors — production, transmission, and distribution. Economic power can still be concentrated within each sector. To economists, the idea of breaking up monopoly industries is hardly new. It may be a first step toward deregulation, but restructuring alone does not constitute deregulation. Nor, as I have stated earlier, does it result in competition. Restructuring no more results in competition than shuffling a deck of cards guarantees a winning hand.

Because of the current skepticism about deregulation, restructuring is probably a more politically expedient strategy and a more realistic strategy than attempting full-blown deregulation. And, according to its proponents, restructuring can still accomplish lesser regulation and greater competition.

The Promotion of Bypass

Still another reason for restructuring comes from energy customers. After years of paying rate levels that exceed costs, large users of electricity and natural gas are demanding lower prices — and they have the economic clout to be heard, in part because they can take advantage of available fuel options.

Large users threaten to bypass the regulated distribution company and take their business elsewhere or generate their own power. Certain considerations, such as the possibility of wheeling and the certainty of cogeneration, make bypass more feasible and more economical.

Restructuring may promote bypass by expanding the wholesale market for power and allowing large users to make purchases directly from energy producers, but bypass

COMPETITION IN ELECTRICITY

will occur in any event if it is economic bypass.

In the course of restructuring, regulatory review will shift from the states to the FERC. Industrial customers will not have to contend with rate structures determined by state commissions that allocate revenue requirements across customer groups. They will be able to negotiate directly with producers and tailor contracts to their individual needs.

For these reasons, industrial customers are emerging as strong proponents of restructuring in some service territories. Of course, the customer who remains captive of the distribution company may pay the price of other users' bypass.

The Wall Street Connection

A final but critical reason behind restructuring that I will address is the profit motive. I strongly suspect that Wall Street (or the financial community in general) actually sees dollar signs at the end of the regulatory tunnel.

When the construction cycle was in full swing, electric utility stock and bond sales flourished. Once large users of external funds, these firms have become cash generators looking for new ways to channel the cash flow. Many utilities also enjoy a cushion of capacity that will see them through at least the next decade. Financial analysts fear that regulation threatens utility profits that were once a sure thing. They also use not-so-subtle ways to intimidate regulators. Commissions, like the utilities they regulate, can be "downgraded" and accused of contributing to a "deteriorating regulatory climate."

Absent the ambitious construction programs of the past and in the face of unfriendly regulators, Wall Street has begun to seek new ways for utilities to make money and to ensure that it has a "piece of the action."

From the Wall Street perspective, restructuring is simply a way to divert retained earnings, avoid rate increases, and shield the rate of return from regulatory scrutiny. The profit motive has become one of the driving forces behind the restructuring of the energy service markets. (I cannot help but think that someone is trying to milk the cow twice).

THE PERILS OF CHANGE

Some of the potential costs of restructuring can already be identified. This is not to say that restructuring cannot or should not occur. It is merely to point out that without thoughtful consideration, we may be giving up more than we bargained for. In addition to putting certain fundamental regulatory principles at risk, there is also the risk of being wrong.

Reliability

Regulation provides certain assurances about the reliability of public utility services. Restructuring may change all that.

The average guy on the street wants reliable service at a reasonable price. In other words, there is a value to that service as well as a cost. Regulation makes it at least possible to balance these factors and seek optimum prices. We have learned from the telephone industry that there is a societal value to having someone to call at the end of the line. There must also be value to providing that same person with reliable energy services.

Restructuring and competition make no promises about service reliability. Performance standards in the energy business may actually multiply. Market forces will tug at the unregulated side of the industry while regulation will continue to impose high standards of performance on the other side. The push and pull may not be conducive to overall performance by individual firms and reliability may suffer as a consequence.

Finally, restructured firms will also require special management skills that utilities have evidenced they do not necessarily have. As they invest, diversify, and restructure, utilities become more risky. Of course, there is no "guaranteed" return for the unregulated business venture. Interestingly, less reliability may adversely affect both shareholder satisfaction and ratepayer satisfaction. Perhaps Wall Street should think twice about restructuring after all.

Equity

Restructuring and competition also have implications for equity because of certain geographic and demographic realities. It is likely that competition will be most vigorous and viable in diversely populated metropolitan areas. Large energy users located there stand to benefit.

The equity risk is the potential development of a two-class society when it comes to utility services, with the "center" class benefitting from scale economies and competition while the "peripheral" class lags behind in both technological and economic terms.

The hardest hit will be the residential customer located in the periphery. Not only will he be unable to take advantage of competition, he will bear the burden of costs no longer covered by those who are able to bypass the local energy distribution system. We all know from experience how well that will go over.

The greatest uncertainty will be for the commercial energy user. Despite the vital and growing importance of the service sector to the nation's economy, commercial entrepreneurs are treated, for the most part, like residential consumers. They too cannot afford to bypass the local energy provider and reap the rewards of competition.

This sort of uneven development will serve only to accentuate the disparities that already exist between urban and rural customers and between large and small energy users.

The loss of equity assurances is not healthy for the utility industries or for the nation. It is not in the public interest. We should not trade equity for competition, but use competition to promote equity and other public policy goals. I would welcome any suggestions or comments on how to accomplish this goal.

The Obligation to Serve

Another significant risk in the restructuring movement is releasing public utilities from their obligation to serve. It is an obligation whose enforcement in reality falls to regulators who usually have a statutory mandate to assure that utilities meet their service obligations.

Technological and economic realities favor the continued regulation of the distribution and probably the transmission sectors of the electric and gas industries. As long as they hold exclusive franchises, distributors can take advantage of scale economies and avoid duplication.

And as long as exclusive franchises are granted, regulation must protect customers from monopoly abuse. Service obligation is really a two-way street. Customers continue to be obligated to buy from a monopoly provider, which in turn is obligated to provide the service reliably.

Some large utility customers would like to be released from their obligation to buy from the local utility monopoly, which would violate the scheme of exclusive franchise. If released, these customers can no longer claim a service obligation from the local utility and all the benefits that go along with it. Customers who leave the system must be made to pay a premium should they choose to return — perhaps a re-entry fee.

The problem is not really the obligation to buy or to serve, but the price implications when only the distribution sector must meet that obligation and only for certain customers. State regulators, for example, have little control over wholesale power rates approved by the FERC. These costs are normally passed on to retail customers.

Our only chance to control these costs will be to scrutinize each power purchase made by the distributor and assess its overall prudence. But unless there is a truly competitive market out there, we will have few opportunities to disallow recovery of an entire purchase because the distributor could have gotten a better deal elsewhere.

Once again, small users will pay dearly for the privilege of being captive customers who are obligated to buy from the utility which is obligated to serve them. There is no easy way out for these customers.

The Risk of Being Wrong

In any attempt at change, the greatest risk is the risk of being wrong. Being wrong can also be very costly.

First, there are limits to the practical application of economic theory. Mergers and acquisitions, for example, may signal a full-blown consolidation movement in the electric industry. Consolidation, of course, tends to concentrate economic power, which in turn may actually lead to regulatory reform. This is clearly not consistent with the expectation that restructuring will lead to deregulation.

Second, federal regulators and legislators have had little

time to react to the restructuring movement. The evolution of competition at the production level depends largely on federal policy, particularly with regard to wheeling. Also, the FERC must cope with the regulation of an expanded wholesale power market. Despite the impression that FERC regulation is less hostile than state regulation, the federal response to changes in the industry is not entirely predictable, especially with changing administrations.

Third, state regulators will have a lot to say about the restructuring movement before it is entirely accomplished. They need to see thoughtful and comprehensive proposals by utilities that include a genuine vision for the future. Regulators will need to be convinced that it will be beneficial. In the end, we may determine that restructuring is in the public interest but this determination will depend on a finding of both short and long-term benefits for ratepayers as well as shareholders.

Public utility commissions will also look very carefully at who will pay for restructuring and its consequences. This will place an added burden on already overburdened commission staffs. Someone will have to pay for this additional oversight, and it should not be captive ratepayers. Fee schedules will have to be devised to foot the bill.

Finally, restructuring may not live up to expectations. It may not lead to the desired goals of efficiency, competition, and deregulation. It may also not be as profitable as Wall Street and utilities hope it will. Restructuring in the electric industry is an entirely unproven approach. If the movement fails, if utilities simply become riskier, and if investors lose interest, ratepayers may be left holding the bag. Ratepayers have paid for the past mistakes of the same utility managers who now want to direct a restructured industry. They should not face that possibility again if restructuring fails.

Summary

In sum, I find some of the reasons for restructuring — the failure of regulation, the failure of deregulation, the promotion of bypass, and the Wall Street connection — to be less than compelling. I also find that path to restructuring and competition to be somewhat perilous. Long-standing regulatory principles, such as reliability, equity, and the obligation to serve, may be at serious risk. Moreover, we must also consider the risk of being wrong.

CONCLUSION

I have rather pessimistically addressed, for the most part, the wrong reasons for restructuring energy utilities and the perils that go along with restructuring. This is not to say that there may not be some very right reasons for restructuring. But the advocates of restructuring have elevated form over substance.

I want to be convinced that restructuring will balance the interests of shareholders and ratepayers; that it will have significant benefits for customers of all classes; that it will play a part in a least-cost energy future; and that it will help energy providers meet high standards of performance while keeping prices competitive. In Illinois, restructuring must be consistent with the legal mandate for public utility regulation to be effective and comprehensive and to promote the goals of efficiency, environmental quality, reliability, and equity.

Simply put, regulators must be able to find restructuring to be *in the public interest.*

Some of the zealots of competition will argue that for a regulator to worry about the perils of change and the future of regulation is purely a self-interested response to the threat of unemployment. But the preservation of regulation is not merely a matter of survival for regulators; it is a matter of the survival of certain fundamental principles embodied in regulation.

Perhaps we can only hope that the "light at the end of the regulatory tunnel" is not the afterglow of regulatory principles sacrificed on the brightly lit pyre of competition.

Restructuring is an experiment in economics and public policy. It is experimentation with the public interest as well, which is why we must be so cautious. In the mean time, what we really need is enlightened regulation. Too much is at stake for us — either the industry or regulators — to go blindly into the future.

James Plummer*
QED Research, Inc.

The Electric Power Research Institute (EPRI) was created
in 1973. Before that time, individual utilities carried out low
level R&D, and joint research ventures were awkwardly and
slowly implemented through industry committees. Influential
members of Congress, particularly Senator Warren Magnu-
son, were pressuring for creation of a federal agency to carry
out electricity R&D. EPRI was partly the electricity industry's response to that threat. EPRI has been an enormous
success. It is taken as a given in this chapter that R&D is
desirable and that nobody would want to return to a pre-
EPRI condition of R&D in the electricity industry. The purpose of this chapter is raise issues regarding whether the
movement toward a competitive structure in the electric utility industry may imply modifications of the current EPRI
system.

FEATURES OF THE CURRENT EPRI SYSTEM

A hybrid organizational form

EPRI is a non-profit corporation that has both similarities
and differences with the following types of organizations:

> a. **Research consortiums**. Private companies often
> form research consortiums that go beyond just
> "joint ventures" or "cooperative research" in the
> sense that more than just a handful of companies
> are involved, the research portfolio includes many
> diverse technologies, and the institution is con-
> sidered to have permanent rather than temporary
> status. Examples are Microelectronics Computer
> Corporation (MCC) in the computer industry and

---

*The author was Director of the Energy Analysis Departtment at EPRI,
1979-1982, and has since been President of QED Research, in Palo Alto,
California*

Sematech in the semiconductor industry. However, unlike EPRI members, the members of these consortiums maintain very active in-house R&D programs, and their contributions to the consortium are small relative to their in-house efforts. Also, the consortiums do most of their actual research in-house, whereas EPRI contracts out almost all of the research.

b. **Other regulator-approved research organizations.** The Gas Research Institute must seek approval of its budget level from the Federal Energy Regulatory Commission (FERC), and then the contributions are embodied in the rates that FERC approves for natural gas pipelines. GRI allocates its money among research efforts in a very similar manner as EPRI, through a structure of committees that have representation from throughout the gas industry. Bellcore is a research organization that contains the parts of the pre-divestiture Bell Labs that the regional Bell operating companies (RBOCs) still wished to maintain as common research efforts. However, since the RBOCs are now engaged in intense competition among themselves and with other competitors, only a relative small research effort has remained in Bellcore.

c. **National laboratories and Federal Contract Research Centers (FCRCs).** In some ways, EPRI resembles some of the national labs and FCRCs. It receives some of its funding of individual projects from federal agencies. Many of its staff have come from the national labs or other parts of the federal government, and its contracting procedures resemble federal contracting procedures. In terms of its occasional involvement in public policy issues, EPRI sometimes takes on the appearance of public policy "think tanks" such as the Rand Corporation. However, EPRI has its own industry sources of funding, and thus does not depend on federal support.

COMPETITION IN ELECTRICITY

d. **Trade associations.** EPRI serves three electric industry trade association, who are represented on its board—the Edison Electric Institute, the American Public Power Association, and the National Rural Electric Cooperative Association. EPRI does not get involved in lobbying efforts or public policy issues that pit one of these associations against another. However, on those issues where there is consensus among the trade associations, and they want EPRI's involvement to help the overall industry, EPRI sometimes becomes a willing or unwilling participant in public policy debates.

Contributions and membership

EPRI's member utilities account for about 60% of the kilowatt hours sold in the United States. Of EPRI's contributions in 1988, 86.3% came from investor-owned utilities, 7.6% came from nonfederal government agencies (mainly municipal utilities), 2.8% came from federal agencies, and 3.3% came from electric cooperatives. The contributions to EPRI from each member utility are based upon a formula that is a function of kilowatt hours **delivered to ultimate customers and** revenue **collected from ultimate customers.**[1] It is important from the perspective of electricity competition that EPRI's contributions formula is based on final retail sales, because it means that EPRI will suffer little if any loss of revenue even if all new generating capacity were built by non-regulated entities. Consistent with the form of the EPRI contributions formula, it is the operating electricity distribution companies that are formally EPRI members. If that operating company is owned by a holding company, the holding company is not formally an EPRI member. If that holding company also owns a non-regulated small power subsidiary, the non-regulated subsidiary is not an EPRI member and should not receive the benefits of EPRI membership. At the present time, this distinction is not being recognized or enforced by EPRI or its operating company members. It is only a matter of time before independent small power producers or regulators complain. More on this issue later in this chapter.

The parameters of the EPRI contributions formula have not changed since 1986. The parameters of the contributions formula are determined by the EPRI Board of Directors. There is no formal review by the three trade associations, although there may be informal consultations. There is no review by the National Association of Regulatory Utility Commissioners (NARUC). Once an individual utility learns from EPRI what its dollar contribution must be, that amount of money is included as an expense in the regular rate case review with each state regulatory commission. Although it varies a lot from utility to utility, the EPRI contribution typically makes up about .25% to .35% of a typical electricity rate. Thus, it does not get too much attention in most rate case hearings. There have been questions raised by regulatory commissions about whether the composition of EPRI spending matches the needs of ratepayers of a particular utility.

Part of the EPRI contributions system is a "hold back provision" that allows EPRI members to keep up to 20% of their dollars they owe EPRI under the contributions formulas if the money is used for "local R&D." Virtually all EPRI members hold back the entire 20%. There is no audit or review to determine whether the 20% is really spent on R&D.

In 1988, EPRI collected $341 million from members, had $3 million in other income, and $3 in separate funding of projects, for total revenue of about $347 million. EPRI's total expenses were about $362 million.

The results of EPRI research are owned by EPRI. Members in good standing are allowed use of those results without charge. Those who are not members in good standing of EPRI have to license the technologies. EPRI has made the terms of licensing more expensive in recent years to encourage more utilities to become EPRI members, and to generate revenue for EPRI.

Some large utilities (e.g. American Electric Power) and many smaller utilities have never been EPRI members. Many utilities that have been EPRI members have stopped paying all or part of their contribution at one time or another because of financial difficulties. For example, the Pennsylvania regulators required Pennsylvania utilities to devote part of what would otherwise have been EPRI contributions to the cleanup expenses at Three Mile Island.

These kinds of incidents were tolerated without much penalty until the mid-1980s when EPRI adopted a tougher stance and required members to be fully paid up in order to have the privileges of EPRI membership. Those utilities that have returned to EPRI membership have not been required to make up past shortfalls in order to become full members in good standing.

Much more serious than temporary shortfalls by individual members, in recent years there has been an accelerating pattern of utility dropouts from EPRI membership. The larger utilities (excluding coops and small municipal utilities) that have dropped out of EPRI in the past few years are as follows:

1985: United Illuminating

1986: Central and South West
Dayton Power & Light
Detroit Edison
Gulf States Utilities
Louisiana Power & Light
Mississippi Power & Light
New Orleans Public Service
Utah Power & Light

1987: Consumers Power
Public Service of New Hampshire

1988: Portland General Electric
Public Service of New Mexico

1989: Sacramento Municipal Utility District
Southern California Edison

There were many motivations involved in each of these decisions. Some of these utilities and/or their regulators were advocates of "unbundling" part of EPRI contributions, which will be discussed later in this chapter.

The loss of Southern California Edison (Socal) was particularly important because of its size (its $15.3 million EPRI contribution was 4.5% of EPRI contributions), and also because Socal has been one of the most progressive utilities in the country in terms of its own R&D effort and its other activities in the areas of demand side management and renewable resource supply technologies. Socal's reasons for dropping out of EPRI were that it had an internal R&D budget that was underfunded and devoted 70-80% to customer end use projects, whereas EPRI's budget allocates only about 10-12% to customer end use research. Also, Socal was one of the main advocates of "unbundling" EPRI contributions.

A bundled portfolio

EPRI's Annual Reports and R&D plans show the following allocation of contract research funds:

	1988	1989-91 Plan
Customer systems	9.2%	12.2%
Environment	26.6%	27.8%
Generation	46.8%	40.8%
Delivery	13.0%	14.0%
Planning	4.5%	5.3%

Table 27-1 shows how the 1989-91 R&D Program Plan is broken down among Strategic Program Elements.

Table 27-1

Composition of EPRI 1989-91 Program Plan by Strategic Program Elements

CUSTOMER SYSTEMS

Customer Support Planning and Technologies	4.6%
Residential and Commercial Technologies	2.5%
Industrial and Transportation Technologies	5.1%

ENVIRONMENT

Environmental and Health Assessment	12.5%
Safety and Environmental Control Technology	15.2%

GENERATION

Fossil Power Plants	10.7%
Nuclear Power Plants	10.9%
Advanced Fossil Power Plants	12.3%
Advanced Nuclear Power Plants	1.8%
Renewable Resource Power Plants	3.0%
Energy Storage	2.1%

DELIVERY

Transmission and Distribution	8.1%
Advanced Delivery Systems	5.9%

PLANNING

Planning Methods	1.4%
Exploratory Research	3.9%

One has to be careful using EPRI's program labels. For example, "Environment" includes "Safety and Environmental Control Technology," which in turn includes the programs for Light Water Reactor Safety, Nuclear Seismic Risk, Radioactive Waste Management, and Occupational Radiation Control. So, if one asks "What percent of EPRI's budget is nuclear?" the answer might or might not include these programs that, by themselves make up 7.5% of EPRI's budget. The overall answer to the nuclear percentage question is that about 21% of the EPRI budget is nuclear related.

Under the current EPRI system, a contributing utility has no choice as to how its dollars are spent. For example, even if a given utility has no nuclear plants and never intends to build any, it must contribute pro rata to the nuclear R&D efforts the same as other utilities.

"UNBUNDLING" AND OTHER CURRENT CONTROVERSIES

Proposals for partial or full "unbundling" of EPRI contributions have been around for a long time.

In the mid-1980s, EPRI commissioned a consultant study to suggest possibilities for the consideration of EPRI management. That study suggested that the funding of EPRI activities be divided into three parts:

1. **The core program.** This would include most of the activities in EPRI's environmental programs, much of the exploratory research program, and other elements of EPRI considered to be essential to the "common good" of all electric utilities. Depending on how the boundaries of a core program are defined, it would probably amount to about 20-30% of the current EPRI budget. The contribution to the core program would be mandatory for all EPRI members, and the composition of spending within the core program would not be controlled by individual contributors.

2. **The "cafeteria choice" or "unbundled" program.** Individual EPRI members would have no choice over their total contributions to these programs, but they would control how their dollars were spent within these programs. So, for example, a utility could decide to spend none of its money on nuclear programs.

3. **The "venture capital" or "proprietary" programs.** An individual utility would not have to contribute at all to any of these programs. However, the utilities that do contribute to these programs would own the technologies in proportion to their contributions to them. EPRI members who did not contribute to a particular program would have no easier access to the technology results of the research than a non-member.

The third "tier" of "venture capital" contributions has not yet been seriously considered, but the "second tier" of "unbundled" or "cafeteria" contributions has been seriously studied. The EPRI Planning and Evaluation Division was charged in 1987 with estimating how utilities might choose to use their unbundled dollars if they had the choice. In 1988, EPRI conducted a survey of the Chief Executive Officers of EPRI member utilities. EPRI asked CEOs how they would allocate dollars among twelve categories of R&D if they were given a chance to reallocate 25% of their utility's annual contribution. The results of that survey have not been made public, but the 1988 EPRI Annual Report states:

> "Their top choices for more funding included end-use technology, the area of power transmission and distribution, exploratory research, and environmental and health assessment—at the expense of some generation research. Actual budget allocations recently approved by our Board generally reflect this shifting emphasis."

The issue is whether this "pretend unbundling" via surveys of CEOs will be enough to satisfy those EPRI members and regulators that would prefer a real unbundling. Southern California Edison is known to have argued for unbundling much more than 25% of contributions.

Demand side v. supply side R&D

To many utilities and many regulators, a primary meaning of "competition," "deregulation," and "market driven" utilities relates to the interface between utilities and their customers. "Demand side management (DSM)" has blossomed from nothing in the early 1980s to be an area of focus in the late 1980s and early 1990s.

Especially with regulated utilities not building much new capacity of their own, attention has shifted to the customer side of the meter. EPRI has substantially increased the absolute dollars spent on demand side R&D, but 10-12% of the EPRI budget is not enough to satisfy many EPRI members and many regulators. EPRI management believes that most demand side research programs are inherently less expensive than supply side research programs, and so it is possible to get to the same marginal net benefit level in demand side programs without spending as much money. The problem is compounded in a political sense by the fact that there is enormous variation among utilities and regulatory commissions in the amount of emphasis put on demand side research programs.

As will be discussed later in this chapter, the disputes over the relative emphasis to be given demand side research in the EPRI budget has the potential for creating some serious institutional problems for EPRI.

Small power R&D

For the next five or ten years at least, much of the generating capacity coming on line in the United States will not be large scale baseload generating plants built by regulated utilities. For many reasons outside the scope of this chapter, much of the new generating capacity will consist of smaller scale (less than 100 megawatts) units, many owned by QFs, self-generators, or IPPs. This presents some problems for EPRI. Most of its research is directed toward the technologies now on line rather than the technologies that will be coming on line in the foreseeable future.

Since EPRI contributions are based on retail sales of electricity, EPRI in a sense gets credit in contributions for kilowatt hours that are generated by plants (QFs, self-generators, and IPPs) that are not owned by EPRI members. It is inevitable that the new players will raise the issue of whether they should have access to EPRI technologies. What will EPRI do when the first merchant wholesale supplier demands either membership in EPRI or access to EPRI technology based on the fact that his kilowatt hours are contributing to EPRI downstream? When *The Energy Daily* (January 28, 1988) asked EPRI President Richard Balzhiser this question, he was "...not sure how EPRI will accommodate in its membership ranks the independent power producers whose interests are far different from those of the utilities."

Some EPRI operating company members are owned holding companies that also own unregulated small power subsidiaries that own QFs or IPPs. Even though these unregulated subsidiaries are not entitled to the benefits of EPRI membership, they are now enjoying those benefits for free. This creates an unfairness when these "affiliate subsidiaries" compete against non-affiliated independent QFs, self-generators, and IPPs.

EPRI's research portfolio is so large and diverse that it does include technologies that are used by small power producers. An example is fluidized bed combustion in coal-fired cogeneration plants. However, because gas-fired technologies are so dominantly used by independent power producers, and

COMPETITION IN ELECTRICITY

EPRI has not emphasized those technologies, the degree of overlap between EPRI technologies and those used by independent power producers is probably still small. Many of the gas-fired technologies used by small power producers were funded by private vendors such as General Electric, or by other research institutes such as the Gas Research Institute. The small degree of overlap between EPRI technologies and the technologies typically used by independent power producers will become more evident as state bidding systems grow in volume and as bypass competition increases from industrial, commercial, and agricultural firms. EPRI will argue that it is working on the long-term supply technologies that will be used in the 21st century. However, if the 1990s are the decade of small power technologies, EPRI may be perceived to be on the sidelines.

Renewable Resource Technologies

Regulators have sometimes complained about the low proportion of the EPRI budget that is spent on renewable resource technologies such as solar, wind, hydro, and biomass. These complaints are not as frequent or as vocal as they were five or ten years ago. Even though EPRI has only devoted a small amount of funds to these technologies, these funds have produced some notable successes. Examples are the EPRI solar research projects in the areas of high-efficiency concentrator cells, red-spectrum-absorbing silicon alloys, and multijunction thin-film cells.

BEYOND UNBUNDLING—POTENTIAL COMPETITORS TO EPRI

It is probable inevitable that EPRI management will sooner or later have to accept some form of unbundling of EPRI contributions. Too many utilities have already voted with their feet, and too many of the more progressive utilities are restive under the bundled portfolio system.

In the coming world of competition in the electric utility industry, it is pertinent to ask whether there are other structural changes in electricity R&D that might bring more of the benefits of competition to the R&D portion of the industry.

CHAPTER TWENTY SEVEN   605

The internal R&D programs of individual utilities

Southern California Edision and some of the other utilities that have dropped out of EPRI are one that are known for having substantial in-house R&D programs. Thus, they may have felt that there was a direct competition between their own programs and their contributions to EPRI. The 20% "hold back" provision as it now operates does not really accomodate the needs of those utilities that do a lot of research, because even a utility that does zero internal R&D gets the full 20% credit. It would be useful to know how the R&D programs of individual utilities have grown in recent years, and what the pattern of that growth has been by type of utility and the subject areas of the R&D. It would also be useful to know more about the amount of cooperative R&D among utilities and with other R&D institutions.

X-inefficiencies and EPRI

The term "X-inefficiencies" was invented by economist Harvey Leibenstein.[2] It refers to the problems of weak motivation and resource misallocations *internal* to firms that are not subjected to enough *external* competition. As monopolies go, EPRI is probably more benign than most, but it could definitely benefit from having some more external competitors.

In the early days of EPRI, then-President Chauncey Starr was fond of saying that he did not want EPRI to become a place where people came to spend a whole career. In the 1989-91 EPRI Program Plan, it is stated that the typical EPRI Project Manager has been at EPRI for eight years. The typical Program Manager has been there 10-12 years, and the typical Department Direcor or Division Director even longer. The vision that Chauncey Starr had of a constant renewal of intellectual talent at EPRI has given way to relatively fixed group of people with relatively fixed positions on technology issues. This problem will become worse over time.

If EPRI had to "sell" its positions and ideas to its members, in competition with other research institutions, then there might be more rapid adaptation by EPRI management to the rapid changes occurring in the electric utility industry. Unbundling of EPRI contributions would certainly help.

It is useful to at least pose the question of whether EPRI would also benefit from having more external competition. If EPRI could use some external competitors, from where might those competitors come?

Proliferation of new state-sponsored R&D institutions

Several states have created R&D organizations.

The New York Energy Research and Development Authority has been in existence almost as long as EPRI and has an annual budget of about $13 million, it is funded by a tax on New York utilities. The budget is controlled by the state legislature.

In the early 1980s, North Carolina created the Alternative Energy Corporation, which has carried out a successful program of research on renewable technologies and energy conservation technologies.

California created the California Energy Commission in the mid-1970s, which has as one of its functions an R&D program on alternative supply technologies and energy conservation technologies. More recently, the California Public Utilities Commission has stimulated California electric utilities to create the California Institute for an Energy Efficient Economy (CIEEE). It will have an initial budget of about $5 million and be mainly devoted to new innovative end use technologies. The initial staffing comes from individuals previous with or on loan from the Lawrence Berkeley Laboratory. The CPUC did not take the funding for CIEEE out of the funds that go for the EPRI contributions, but rather added those funds on top of the EPRI contributions.

More recently, regulators and utilities in Wisconsin have created the Wisconsin Center for Demand Side Research. It is a non-profit joint effort of the Wisconsin Public Service Commission, the gas and electric utilities, and the University of Wisconsin. The contributions to it are on top of EPRI contributions. The regulatory staff describes its function as doing research on demand side technologies that are more focused on Wisconsin needs than the more generic EPRI programs on demand side technologies.

Evolution of separate joint ventures and User Groups into EPRI competitors

As EPRI has developed new technologies, both EPRI and its members have recognized that the users of those technologies are subsets of utilities that have common interests in the applications of those technologies. EPRI tries to get those subsets of utilities to fund the applications work outside the EPRI budget. The current User Groups are:

Boiling Water Reactor Owners Group
Steam Generator Owners Group Program
Seismicity Program
Hydrogen Control Program
Nuclear Fuel Industry Research Program
Utility Acid Rain Precipitation Study Program
Nuclear Construction Issues Group Program
Below Regulatory Concern Program

This list does not include all the smaller User Groups for less important technologies or software packages.

Each of these groups has its own history and motivations. The line between R&D efforts, that EPRI wishes to fund, and "applications efforts," that EPRI does not wish to fund, is never very clear. In the real world, the funding for these User Groups comes from utilities after they have tried and failed to arm wrestle EPRI into funding particular activities. EPRI sometimes lends its Project Managers to help reduce the costs of running these User Groups.

Naturally, the utilities that have an intense interest in these User Groups often feel that they get more out of their funding of a particular User Group than they get from their EPRI contributions. This creates a tension between EPRI and the utilities that are part of the User Groups.

The National Regulatory Research Institute

EPRI carries out programs of research in non-hardware areas such as forecasting methodologies and planning software, although such research has diminished and been hidden in less controversial programs in recent years. To the

COMPETITION IN ELECTRICITY

limited extent that EPRI still does non-hardware research, it competes with the National Regulatory Research Institute (NRRI), which is the research arm of the National Association of Regulatory Utility Commissioners (NARUC). The activities of NRRI are funded by contributions from the regulatory commissions of the states. There are both "bundled" contributions that go to fund the NRRI general budget and "unbundled" contributions that particular states make to studies in which they have a special interest.

Relations between EPRI and NRRI have been relatively cool. Although EPRI has on rare occasion joint ventured some small studies with NRRI, there has been relatively little collaboration. No individual utilities have contributed funding to NRRI studies.

The national laboratories

The national laboratories have collaborated with EPRI on numerous research programs. Sometimes the collaboration is initiated by the U.S. Department of Energy, the parent federal agency that has nominal jurisdiction over the national labs. Although the national labs are under some federal restrictions regarding competing with private sector activities, individual utilities have sometimes funded some of the activities of the national labs on a "cooperative research" basis.

Regulator-induced spinoffs from EPRI

If regulators were collectively dissatisfied with EPRI, one could envisage a regulator induced split-up of EPRI along either functional lines or geographical lines. This would be analogous to the court-imposed regional splitup of the AT&T system, or the statutory geographical breakup of utility holding companies in the 1930s, or the earlier court-imposed geographical splitup of Standard Oil. In those forced spinoffs, the previously combined units quickly became competitors.

In the early days of EPRI, there was considerable sentiment for splitting EPRI into regional research centers, each with a different functional mission that would be matched to the need of the utilities in that region. That idea has not been heard much in recent years. However, there continues to be heavy resistence to paying the very high costs involved in keeping a high level technical staff in Palo Alto, one of the highest cost of living areas in the country.

There is no sign that regulators consider any of the problems of EPRI to be so serious as to warrant a forced spinoff approach.

A GRADUALIST APPROACH WITHIN THE CONTEXT OF THE PRESENT EPRI SYSTEM

Four reform measures

Radical surgery is not needed to bring EPRI closer to the competitive structure that the electric utility industry is moving toward. It is possible to preserve the level of R&D funding embodied in the present EPRI system, but also bring the benefits of competition to the R&D portion of the industry. This could be done by adopting four reform measures, all of which are well within the spirit and letter of the EPRI system:

1. Gradually unbundle most of EPRI contributions. The unbundled percentage could start with the 25% level specified in EPRI's 1988 survey of utility CEOs and progressively increase up to a maximum unbundled percentage of about 65-70%. The remaining contributions would be the still-bundled "core program" of truly environmental programs plus some exploratory research.
2. Gradually increase the "hold back percentage" and qualify under it contributions by utilities to competing research entities. The current "hold back percentage" of 20%, which is taken by all utilities and never audited is a sham. There should be an audit to see where that "money" goes. Other research institutions should be eligible for part of that money if individual utilities wish to use it for non-EPRI and non-internal research. It is difficult to say how high the hold back percentage ought to go over time, because it depends on whether other research institutions, new and old, responded to this opening up of the system with research projects that utilities found attractive.
3. Clarify that non-regulated small power "affiliated subsidiaries" are not EPRI members and not eligible for EPRI benefits. This is the only interpretation that is consistent

610   COMPETITION IN ELECTRICITY

with the form of the EPRI contributions formula, and the only way of maintaining basic fairness in the competition between the "affiliated" small power producers and the independent small power producers.

4. Staff EPRI more with people on temporary loan from utilities and regulatory commissions. EPRI has become a "career service," with all the implications of vested bureaucratic interests. Enforcing Chauncey Starr's original concept that EPRI not be staffed with a career service would provide for more flexibility and interchange of ideas between EPRI and the constituencies that it serves.

These changes could preserve the best of the current EPRI system, while improving upon it substantially.

Long-run v. short-run focus

One counterargument to opening EPRI up to competition is the contention that it would lead to a short-term focus by researchers. A corollary to this argument is that research managers and researchers themselves need to be insulated somewhat from the demands of the businesses they serve. In a recent article, Peter Drucker rejects that argument and states "...the successful innovations in both pharmaceuticals and computers—and in other fields—are now being turned out by cross-functional teams with people from marketing, manufacturing and finance participating in research work from the beginning." Drucker goes on to argue that R&D efforts should be forced to "sell" their products just like anyone else:

"Increasingly, therefore, the research lab may become a free-standing business, doing research work on contract for a multitude of industrial clients. Each client would then need a "technology manager" rather than a "research director" —someone who can develop business objectives based on the potential technology, and technology strategies based on business and market objectives, and who then defines and buys the technical work needed to produce business results."[3]

The four reform measures described above need not result in the sinking of all basic research or all long-term research at EPRI. Some of it would remain in the still-bundled core program. Other pieces would be funded by EPRI members with particular long-term needs.

ENDNOTES

1. The exact formula is 22.6 cents per megawatt hour delivered to ultimate electricity users plus .0929 per dollar of revenue collected from ultimate electricity users.
2. Harvey Leibenstein, "Competition and X-Efficiency," *Journal of Political Economy*, May 1973, p. 766.
3. Peter F. Drucker, "Best R&D Is Business Driven," *Wall Street Journal*, February 10, 1988, editorial page.